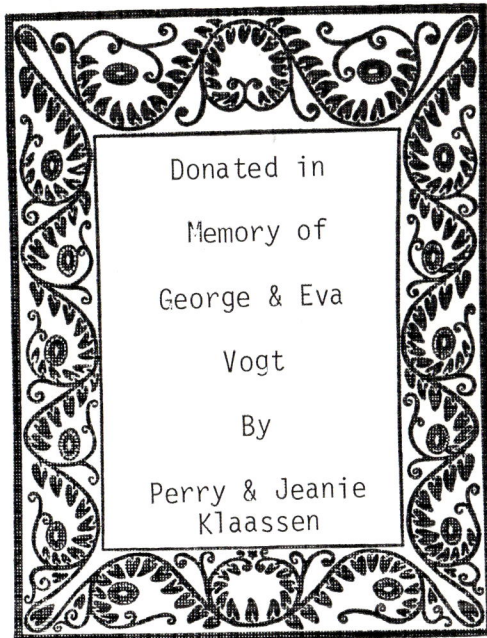

Donated in

Memory of

George & Eva

Vogt

By

Perry & Jeanie
Klaassen

UNDERSTANDING EDUCATIONAL RESEARCH: AN INQUIRY APPROACH

UNDERSTANDING EDUCATIONAL RESEARCH: AN INQUIRY APPROACH

Charles D. Hopkins
Indiana State University

Charles E. Merrill Publishing Company
A Bell & Howell Company
Columbus Toronto London Sydney

Published by Charles E. Merrill Publishing Company
A Bell & Howell Company
Columbus, Ohio 43216

This book was set in Times Roman and Helvetica
Production Editor: Martha Morss
Cover Design Coordination: Will Chenoweth
Cover Photo: Larry Hamill

Library of Congress Catalog Card Number: 79-90706
International Standard Book Number: 0-675-0-8162-9

Printed in the United States of America

3 4 5 6 7 8 9 10   85 84 83 82 81

CONTENTS

PREFACE

Understanding Educational Research is a book designed for use in an introductory course in research. The emphasis throughout is upon understanding the research *process* — from formulating the research question to communicating the results of that inquiry. It is my hope that the structure of the book will allow students to grasp the process as a whole as well as each specific step in that process.

Some of the material contained in this work was originally published in *Educational Research: A Structure for Inquiry* (Merrill, 1976). The changes made for this edition have been so extensive, however, that it is essentially a new book. This edition is intentionally directed more toward the teacher who will encounter research in educational journals, teachers' magazines, and the like. The five articles which appear in the sample studies section of the book are used to point out specific steps in the research process. Focusing on these examples throughout the book will help sharpen students' critical skills in analyzing research processes and products. In addition to these sample studies, I've included a unique chapter entitled "Looking at the Complete Study" which analyzes a recent journal article in its entirety. What prompted me to write this chapter was the feeling that most research courses do not synthesize all of the elements of the research process into a unified presentation. Both the sample studies and the chapter synthesizing research are intended to involve students in analyzing research processes and products, making this text extremely useful for "consumers" of research. At the same time, it contains all of the information students need to become good "producers" of research (see, for instance, the chapters "Drawing Conclusions" and "Writing Research Reports"). The Check Your Understanding sections, located within the chapters, extend students' understanding by asking them to apply the principles of research to their own work. Where appropriate, additional activities have been included at the end of the chapter; instructors can assign these projects to further increase their students' knowledge of research.

Throughout, the book uses APA style consistently for citations, entries in reference lists, and bibliographies. Since APA is becoming the accepted style of educational journals, this book itself can serve as a model for that style.

This edition also introduces a new approach to covering statistics, an approach which actually combines two approaches. First, since many instructors prefer to minimize computation, the most important computations have been placed in a programmed appendix. Second, to promote understanding of important statistical concepts, statistical ideas have been discussed in the chapters concerned with the three types of research (chapters 9, 10 and 11). Naturally, it is difficult to avoid statistics when discussing experimental designs and even some descriptive methodologies, so statistical concepts have been treated in the text as necessary.

To bring the book up to date with recent changes in the field, there is a new chapter on the computer. This chapter also covers the use of hand calculators for statistical computation.

Even with all of these changes, however, my original purpose in writing an educational research book remains the same. I hope students will gain an appreciation of the research process as well as learn how to conduct research studies. Too many books present the specifics without giving the student an opportunity to put them all together. Mark Twain reportedly said of his wife's swearing, "She knows all the words but can't quite get the tune," — I hope this book goes beyond words, or mere description, and helps students to *get the tune* of research — to understand what it means and how it furthers education. This book, I hope, reflects the structure of that inquiry process— research—and can help students "put it all together."

Few of the ideas or procedures named here are solely mine. The ideas spring from an endless list of students, colleagues, teachers and others who have caused me to consider research in so many different ways. My particular thanks go to the various reviewers for their specific suggestions. Readers of various drafts of the manuscript were: James Algina, University of Florida; Richard L. Antes, Indiana State University; Wayne Cleveland, Central Missouri State University; William Everndon, East Tennessee State University; Thomas Gans, University of Wisconsin, Oshkosh; Gordon Ruscoe, University of Louisville; Robert Schissel, University of Wisconsin, Whitewater; Patricia Simun, California State University, Los Angeles; Benjamin F. Smith, Morgan State University; and John Towner, Western Washington University. While I could not incorporate all of their comments, the manuscript was markedly improved thanks to their help.

I am grateful to the Literary Executor of the late Sir Ronald A. Fisher, F.R.S., and to Longman Group Ltd., London, for permission to reprint Table III from their book *Statistical Tables for Biological, Agricultural and Medical Research* (6th edition, 1974).

C.D.H.

PROLOGUE

There are two major aspects of a formal study of research. The first of these is learning how to *conduct* research. This aspect is primarily concerned with procedures of research and ways of conceptualizing the research process. The second major aspect is knowing how to use the results of the many research studies. This aspect is primarily concerned with using or "consuming" the conclusions drawn from studies.

This book addresses both of these equally important parts of research. The contents of the book seek to build a structure of inquiry for the research process. This emphasis has a dual rationale. First, no book on research can provide its readers with specific information about every possible occurrence in the day-to-day progress of research. Second, an understanding of the basic framework is an efficient way to learn the inner workings of the total process. Reading about a series of isolated experiences without a unifying strand contributes little insight into either of the two phases of the research process.

The emphasis upon structure in this book should bring both the consumer and the practitioner aspects into balance. You will not find the answer to all of your questions about research in this book—no book can provide all these answers. My intent is to reveal to you the framework of the research process so that you can utilize it as a producer and/or consumer of research. References to other sources you may need in these roles are included throughout the book. Explanatory sections on four important aids to educational inquiry —the library, the proposal, the computer, and the research report—will help you expand your knowledge using these tools of inquiry.

I hope that your study of this book inspires yet a third aspect of research. Research can be an interesting, fascinating study in itself, and the aesthetic rewards associated with careful study of formal inquiry procedures add an interesting third dimension.

C.D.H.

The following people have made major contributions in the preparation of this book.

Copy reader and friend: Margie Hopkins

Administrative editor and prodder: Marianne Taflinger

Copy editor and prober: Susan Glick

PART ONE

RESEARCH AS INQUIRY

Individuals often have differing notions about the nature of research when they first study educational research. To clarify this book's approach, Part I defines research activities as a part of the process of structured inquiry. It also describes how educators use that structure to investigate questions about education.

Inquiry, in a broad sense, is not new to any reader of this book, since it is a part of the learning process from birth. What may be new here is the idea of a structure for inquiry consisting of procedures that have little likeness to trial and error or other informal approaches for providing answers to questions that arise in day-to-day activities.

Part I offers a common meaning for the word "research," delineating what research is and what research is *not*. This very broad definition of research in all areas then becomes a base for developing the following sections dealing specifically with educational research.

This part also focuses on observation of phenomena as the major element in all scientific investigation of problems found at all levels of problem-solving strategies. Finally, the last chapter in this part presents an aid to inquiry—the library. The library is both a way to communicate answers which researchers find for their questions and a storehouse of knowledge which can help someone seeking new answers to new or old questions.

CHAPTER ONE

INQUIRY STRATEGIES

Like most men I hold certain cherished beliefs which I think valid because they follow logically from known and obvious facts.

—Carl L. Becker

Humans are questioning beings. It is this very process of investigating questions—called **inquiry** *—that has resulted in humanity's privileged place in the world. Ignoring the disputes over creation and evolution, our uniqueness is based, to a large extent, on our ability to ask questions. Apparently, unlike any other animal life, humans are able to ask questions, find answers, and communicate and store knowledge which has been created. Each generation is thus able to build on previously gained knowledge without starting anew with each succeeding generation.

The questions of the earliest people arose from the mysteries of the physical world and dealt primarily with phenomena of physical nature. Evidence of these unwritten—often only implied—questions survives in ancient myths, where questions about nature are tied to mythological explanations in stories and songs passed from generation to generation. Most definitions of "myth" agree that myths are stories used to explain and answer questions about deity, the origin of the universe, the current order of things, matters, and events. Myths are often obvious attempts to give reasons for the mysteries of natural phenomena by personifying forces of nature.

Within each culture, a unique set of stories evolves. Investigations of the patterns in myths, folk tales, and legends make interesting studies in literature. Every developing culture has an accumulation of stories which collectively represent the popular answers to that culture's early questions. Since early humans were all directly affected by nature, the first questions were understandably centered around that which was the closest to common

---

*The first time a word which is denoted in the glossary is used in the text, it will appear in **boldface** type. As indicated here, the use of the word **inquiry** is described in the glossary.

experience. For example, myths from the Native Americans, early Scandinavians, and early Greeks may focus on different characteristics of a subject and vary in level of sophistication, but common to them all is the theme of explanation. This is testimony to early people's development of the question. The Greek story of *Phaethon,* the Norse tale of *Balder and the Mistletoe,* and the Native American tales *Determination of Night and Day* and *Determination of the Seasons* (Thompson, 1929, pp. 38–40) are examples of how different cultures explained the phenomena associated with nature through "weather myths." The type of weather familiar to each people is also reflected in the stories and ideas of deity. In fact, the concepts of gods were in large part a reflection of the climate in which the culture developed. The cold, often harsh climate of the north, for example, produced the harsh gods Odin and Thor. Myths from other cultures are equally determined by the weather.

Parallel to the study of literature to reveal early questions is the study of the evolution of music. As do common stories, popular songs offer answers to implied questions in the minds of a people. The question a song states or implies may reflect a personal dilemma or one which encompasses the total society of the singer. The study of folklore has used knowledge of such societal concerns to explain many of the early question songs which have evolved as folk songs over the centuries.

The developmental level of a question can also be determined from its answers in whatever form. The early myths reflect questions about nature. Legends and hero stories that appeared later reflect questions about more sophisticated aspects of human relations and expose the development of the human mind. The Greek myths contrast with most other cultures' stories in that they deal more with the cosmic forces of nature, human traits, and human emotions.

There is little, if any, evidence to indicate an early effort to unify folklore into a workable body of knowledge. Later attempts were made to seek out strands which did provide some continuity in the total scheme, to provide a base for further questioning and speculation. For example, as the Greeks developed a more complex philosophy based on existing knowledge, their questions became more and more complex. Present-day inquiry continues to ask more and more complex and unifying questions. Nevertheless, gathering knowledge in bits and pieces with no unifying feature in the process continues today. Boas (1959) finds major deficiencies associated with this uncontrolled proliferation:

I am presupposing therefore that no one learns anything unless he puts a question to experience and that knowledge is a series of questions and answers. . . . We do not add one by one new atomic truths to our accumulated store of truths. There is always the possibility that the whole edifice which we have erected on the foundation of the past may topple like a heap of jack straws at any moment. Hasty generalizations, neglect of negative instances, fallacies in inference, wrong identifications, all are symptoms of the weakness of our knowledge. And I confess to being incapable of explaining this if knowledge is a complex of elementary sense-data. (pp. 4–5)

Inquiry Capability

Throughout the centuries, information was gathered by inquiry through observation and personal experience. Trial and error was the inquiry process most often used. Even today the trial-and-error approach is used to answer many questions which arise. Most of a child's early learning comes through that mode of inquiry, and the mode also serves to answer many practical problems for all ages. However, trial and error does not provide the information necessary to answer all questions.

The early utilization of trial and error allowed development of concepts useful for practical everyday affairs. This knowledge was then used to establish a common-sense approach to inquiry. Gradually better methods have been developed. Inquiry strategies may today be conceptualized as being in a state of evolution. Current methods do provide more answers than earlier strategies, but there still is much to be discovered about how to conduct inquiry.

Common Sense

Trial-and-error answers—including answers which seem to be self-evident—lead to common-sense solutions. It is not clear how a person uses common sense to arrive at tentative answers, since the process is not structured beyond the use of intuition to generate a personally acceptable explanation. Also common sense does not generate the same answer to the same question for everyone using that approach. For the last reason alone common-sense answers lack validity for making general and reliable decisions.

The use of common-sense answers did lead to further refinements in inquiry, however. When questions were answered, knowledge was created. As people gained knowledge of the world, they became aware of the orderliness within the universe and found that some common-sense answers allowed predictions to be made with reasonable degrees of accuracy. **Prediction** remains today one of the major functions of science. Nevertheless, when common sense alone is used to answer questions, as the questions become more sophisticated, less accuracy is found in the resulting predictions. The process lacks necessary structure.

A major defect in attacking questions through common sense alone is that the varying human element of subjectivity is involved in the process. The observer may consciously or unconsciously select evidence to support what he or she already believes, may generalize from insufficient data, or may knowingly or unknowingly ignore important contributing factors. Personal feelings, opinions, biases, and prejudices can strongly influence what the observer observes and the conclusions made from those observations. To overcome these shortcomings in the common-sense approach, people have developed more sophisticated procedures of inquiry to structure the observer's thoughts systematically during the search for explanations.

Deduction

The first systematic approach to inquiry utilized the **syllogism** as a model of thinking. Syllogistic reasoning is a form of deductive reasoning which moves from a **generalization** to a specific case. The syllogism is made up of a **major** premise based on a proposition considered to be self-evident or previously established fact, a minor premise which is a particular case attached inescapably to the major premise, and a logically deduced conclusion. The following syllogism is a common example:

Major premise: All men are mortal.
Minor premise: Professor Williams is a man.
Conclusion: Professor Williams is mortal.

This example is consistent within itself but the viability of the conclusion rests on the truthfulness of the major premise. In fact, the ultimate usefulness of any syllogism depends on the generalization used as the **major** premise. If the basic generalization, the major premise, is false, then **the** conclusion may be false, as the following example illustrates.

Major premise: All animals with black fur are cats.
Minor premise: This animal has black fur.
Conclusion: This animal is a cat.

This syllogism is consistent within itself. Nevertheless, because the **major** premise is not true, certain conclusions could result in an error, as, for example, if the animal mentioned in the minor premise were a dog **with** black fur.

Since the conclusion of a syllogism rests on generalizations or **facts** which are currently accepted or on what is dictated by an authority such as the state or church, the foundation for such reasoning could be established by authority and dogma little related to observation and experience. The syllogism has often been misused in this way. Since it consequently could **not** establish truth and add to what was known, the syllogistic model of **thinking** could not serve as an enduring strategy of inquiry.

Induction

The process of moving from a set of specific observations to a generalization is known as the "inductive process of reasoning." Early people undoubtedly gathered information from many cases to form common-sense answers, **but it** was many years after the introduction of the syllogism that a more **formal** system of inductive reasoning was used in the inquiry process. Early **people** made observations and found that, over the years, certain causes seemed **to** be related to observed effects. For example, a wind shift from the north **to** the south seemed to be related to a particular change in the weather, or **good** fishing seemed predictable from certain weather conditions. Today **our** **hypotheses** are still formed from such inductive procedures.

Inductive reasoning structures inquiry into two stages. First is **the** collection of information through many specific observations. Then **the** process moves from these specifics to a generalization. The major limitation of the collection stage is that an observer can rarely observe every case. The selection of what is observed may be biased, knowingly or unknowingly, so that the generalization developed has little, if any, credibility. Use of the formal induction process precludes forming a generalization before collecting data and then selecting facts to support that generalization without considering other information. Inductive reasoning in its purest form is merely a way of gathering data. It lacks direction. Unless a person knows what to look for in a mass of data, it is doubtful that any generalization will be found.

The deficiencies of both deduction and induction left inquiry with the question: How can subjectivity be built into some inquiry method and still not prejudice the result? Today there seems to be agreement that those who seek answers must have direction, that to be productive they must look for something. Since the human element has consequently not been completely removed, total objectivity has not been reached. This apparent impasse brings us to the next stage of evolution in the inquiry process—a combining of two strategies which apparently overcomes the ineffectiveness of one method and places some control on factors which need restraint in the other method.

Problem Solving

A combination of the inductive and deductive processes is used to answer many present-day questions. This procedure relies on the inductive method to generate a hypothesis and the deductive method to test that hypothesis. Refinement of inquiry techniques has brought us a long way from early attempts to investigate important questions and solve important problems.

A technique that combined the inductive and deductive methods was produced and utilized in formal studies of observed variations in natural events. These studies were prompted by the need to make inferences about causes underlying the variations. Certainly the effects of the variations could be observed, but the question of how to establish the causes remained. The search of science thus became the search for cause-and-effect relationships. New inquiry strategies are still evolving for formally structuring inference in order to facilitate the scientific search for causes to observed effects.

We are still in the midst of an evolution to sophisticate techniques of investigation. Knowledge that has been created through research procedures must be organized into a dynamic functional body of knowledge covering the operation of general laws, rather than being limited to a static state characterized by banks of knowledge holding facts in isolation as unrelated bits and pieces with no mechanism for tying them together. Future improvement in inquiry procedures will undoubtedly move us far beyond our present level of knowledge and capacity to generate that knowledge. The purpose of this book is to move a little further along in the evolution of the inquiry process.

The Research Hypothesis. The gradual replacement of the major premise used in the deductive method by a **research hypothesis** structured inquiry is a new technique commonly referred to as **problem solving**. As early as 1910,

John Dewey in *How We Think* presented five stages for the act of problem solving in his analysis of reflective thinking:

> Upon examination, each instance (of reflective thinking) reveals, more or less clearly, five logically distinct steps: (i) a felt difficulty; (ii) its location and definition; (iii) suggestion of possible solution; (iv) development by reasoning of the bearings of the suggestion; (v) further observation and experiment leading to its acceptance or rejection; that is, the conclusion of belief or disbelief. (p. 72)

By minimizing the deficiencies of both the deductive and inductive reasoning approaches, this system of answering questions provides checks and balances for inquiry strategy. Problem-solving strategies start with induction to the point of establishing a conjectured solution (the hypothesis) and then move to deductive tactics to test the tenability of the hypothesis in a specific case. Hypotheses can be revised and tested empirically with new subjects, situations, or events, and new **data.** By combining heavily supported hypotheses, scientists develop **theory** and eventually establish natural laws.

The output of the process is knowledge, new information about relationships between or among elements studied. Central to this process is the human mind. In 1959, the philosopher George Boas offered this view of the human mind as a problem solver:

> It has been traditional in philosophy to consider the human mind as a sort of mirror reflecting a world which is alien to its nature. . . . Whatever it is, it [the world] is always objects seen, observed, contemplated, enjoyed, apprehended, intuited, as if knowledge were a simple dyadic relation between two terms, the knower and the known. At times, as in the so-called empirical tradition, the known is the starting point of knowledge; at times as in Platonism and mysticism, it is the terminus. The purpose of these lectures is to suggest, if not to prove, that it is more fruitful to consider the human mind as a questioner, a doubter, a solver of problems, and that *knowledge is always the answer to some problem.* (Italics added.) (p. 1)

All present knowledge is the result of literally billions of questions that needed answers and problems that required solutions. Many times— probably most of the time—the search for an answer generates more questions. This phenomenon requires that some kind of **structure** be used to direct people as they investigate questions. This need for structure has given rise to a **scientific approach** to solving problems, an approach intended to be more efficient than trial and error. Such an approach is a **model** to structure the attack on new questions and old questions which have not yet been answered satisfactorily, as will be discussed in a later section. The combination of the inductive and deductive processes has produced just such a modern scientific approach to problem solving. An integral part of this scientific approach is the hypothesis, as mentioned earlier. The hypothesis is an outcome of thought processes about the problem being considered. The input that produces the hypothesis is all of the information that is logically connected to the problem. The hypothesis, the output of the process, is a generalization that amounts to conjecture about the problem's solution. In a formal representation of this process, the problem is usually reduced to a direct question, while the hypothesis is a tentatively presented answer for that question.

The level of credibility of a hypothesis will depend on the input available to the person stating the hypothesis. Hypotheses range from near-blind guesses to quite well-developed statements that approach the credibility level of a theory. Dewey said, "There is a distinction between hypotheses generated in that seclusion from observable fact which renders them fantasies, and hypotheses that are projections of the possibilities of facts already in existence and capable of report" (1929, p. 78). A hypothesis is generated from gathered information and is developed to provide a guess that can be tested deductively. The hypothesis in problem solving can best be viewed as the proposed answer to that question asked by the inquirer.

Testing the Hypothesis. Some hypotheses can be tested directly. The direct test for a hypothesis is most often found in questions from the physical sciences where matters are largely straightforward and most subject to full intellectual control. For example, if a commuter bus that is scheduled to arrive at 7:45 A.M. does not come at the expected time, several hypotheses could be offered as reasons why it missed the scheduled time, the implied question being, Why did the commuter bus fail to arrive at 7:45 A.M.? Possible hypotheses (proposed answers) include:

1. The scheduled time has been changed.
2. The bus has been delayed but will come later.
3. The bus has had mechanical trouble and will not come at all.
4. The bus drivers are on strike.

Each of the above hypotheses (others might be proposed) could be tested *directly* by seeking out information that is generally available. Not all questions in the physical sciences are so straightforward. Nevertheless, the subjects of study in the physical sciences are easier to define and the necessary data are, by their nature, more open for public view than the personal—often hidden—data collected from human subjects in the human sciences.

Most questions examined in the natural sciences are testable by *direct* methods. Although it is true that the natural sciences deal to a large degree with public **facts**, this statement is not to be interpreted as meaning that all questions in this area are easily answered. Knowledge based on public facts is, in general, accepted as the most reliable knowledge and consequently is the most trustworthy.

A question about a physical property is likely to end up with the same answer over a large number of independent **observations.** Even if hypotheses differ, the answer should surface much the same for all observers. For example, several hypotheses were proposed as possible reasons why the commuter bus did not arrive at the expected time, but the final answer should be clearly definable from public facts. Chemical questions can also be answered in a direct way. To the untrained eye two similar pieces of substances—sample A, a diamond, and sample B, a piece of glass—might look the same. If someone guessed sample A to be glass while someone else guessed sample A to be the diamond, a physical test to determine the true composition would produce the same answer under repeated observations. Similarly, if the light does not come on when a controlling switch is thrown, one of several different hypotheses could be developed to be tested. Again, each of these could be tested directly. Hypotheses that can be tested directly are those that can be investigated by the use of public facts—that information open to interpretation without deduction and on which general agreement can be obtained through many independent observations.

Some hypotheses can not be tested directly. Questions generated in the human sciences are primarily answered by facts not equally available to all observers. Personal data about attitudes, fears, emotions, achievement, aptitudes, and other equally important traits are located deep within the individual. They cannot be observed directly. Furthermore, one observer's interpretation may not be in agreement with those of other observers, and the information derived is more open to revision as a result of additional probing by investigation. Medical diagnosis, identification of learning disabilities, and determination of the subject's locus of control are all elusive, because observation is likely to vary among observers. An example of this variability among observers might occur with teachers making a decision about the level of creativity of a student named Debbie. The English teacher may rate Debbie very high, given her writing ability, while the art teacher finds he must rate her much lower in her use of creativity when producing art objects in the ceramics class. This disparity may result because creativity can exist in different forms or because each teacher looks for different behavior as a sign of creativity.

General agreement may be difficult to obtain from independent observations. When several art teachers rate Debbie's creativity in art, there is likely to be some variability among the teachers' observations. Hypotheses that must be tested indirectly are those that can be investigated only by use of personal facts—that information which is difficult to obtain and open to individual interpretation.

☐ CHECK YOUR UNDERSTANDING

For the following situations, decide whether the person used induction or deduction (I or D) and whether he or she used direct or indirect testing (D or I).

1. Professor Antes wanted to find out if blonde men really do have more fun. He observed four blondes and ten men with other colors of hair at a fraternity picnic. From his data, he concluded that blondes do have more fun.   Induction (I) or deduction (D)   Direct (D) or Indirect (I)
2. Two junior high school students decided that some numbers rolled with two dice should come up more than other numbers. They rolled two dice

1000 times and counted the number of 12's that appeared. They concluded that 12 should appear about one time out of 40.   I or D   D or I

3. The campus union board members wanted to have a free movie and give each student attending a chocolate or vanilla ice cream cone. Since they had not done this before, they did not know how much ice cream of each flavor to buy. They sent a questionnaire to a selected sample of 300 students asking each to indicate whether he or she would attend and to choose a preferred ice cream flavor. From the returns, they concluded that 600 would attend and that 350 would prefer vanilla and 250 chocolate.   I or D   D or I

4. Through the years, meteorologists observed that tornados generally move from the southwest to northeast. How did they arrive at this viewpoint?   I or D   D or I

5. Professor Higgins read that students are more interested in elementary mathematics if the classroom has supplementary materials for the students to use voluntarily. She located some classrooms that seemed to be much alike except that some classes had extra materials and some did not. She asked each student to rate his or her interest in mathematics on a scale of 1 to 5. From this she concluded that the interest was higher for those who had extra materials available.   I or D   D or I

Answers

1. Deduction—Direct (D—D)   He worked from a generalization to see if it was true in a specific situation. Data were collected from the direct actions of the men.
2. Induction—Direct (I—D)   They collected data from many cases and formed a generalization. The data were collected directly from the readings of the dice.
3. Induction—Indirect (I—I)   They could not use a general rule so they collected a set of data on specific cases to form a generalization. They did this indirectly by getting personal information about each student in the sample.
4. Induction—Direct (I—D)   The generalization was formed from many separate cases. The data came directly from the actions of the weather.
5. Deduction—Indirect (D—I)   She tested a generalization in a limited population to see if it held in a specific case. Since she did not observe for differences beyond asking for personal feelings, the testing was done indirectly. If she had tested this by recording actions that are assumed to reflect interest, then the method would have been direct.

Problem solving can be structured for both direct and indirect testing through the scientific approach to inquiry. Problem solving is to be considered a way of structuring an attack on a question that utilizes the *inductive* approach to generate a hypothesis. The *deductive* approach is then used to test the hypothesis by providing support for or evidence against the hypothesis. The hypothesis is the integral part of the problem-solving process that bridges the gap between a generalization obtained inductively and the deductive approach to testing that generalization. A widely used model for organizing procedures for problem solving—the scientific approach—is described in the next section.

Scientific Approach

The primary goals of science are to understand, explain, and through understanding alleviate important problems that perplex human beings and to explain the workings of the universe. Throughout the years, the strategies of inquiry have become more complex to overcome the limitations imposed by simpler strategies, the kinds of answers generated and the inadequacies of explanations proposed. The dynamics of science allow for inadequacies by building into inquiry a component which allows continuous revision of explanations. Given more information, what was inadequate may become more adequate. Theories become more complex. More adequate basic concepts allow better understanding of the universe and laws which govern it.

Science generates answers which are tentative. As human thinking is recorded and new knowledge is generated, beliefs become more accurate. New evidence causes older theories to be discarded, expanded, or revised to encompass all available information. This dynamic approach to explanation and theory formulation allows for correction of misinterpretation.

Science also presents a tentative approach to inquiry. Behavior of a subatomic particle or a human organism can only be predicted within a statement which includes a probability of occurrence. Consequently, science does not expect to make absolute predictions about probabilistic events. It is true that basic to the universe are laws which systematically govern behavior, and science seeks these laws. Although this order is assumed, it is likely that the absolute truth to most questions will remain, to some extent, unknown. Given this uncertainty, statements of science must be made including reference to the probability of behavior. The reachable goal of science is to make that probability as high as possible through structured inquiry about the rules and laws of nature.

The Scientific Method

There is no paucity of material about the scientific method. Books and professional publications from the physical and human sciences devote pages and pages to the scientific method. Wide reading in these materials reveals one conclusion very clearly: there is not one method of science which is applied throughout inquiry. There is no one technique that can be isolated as "the scientific method" to be used in the same way in all disciplines.

Another conclusion this reading will foster is that all writers are discussing the same thing—a *structured approach* to solving problems. Only in this consensus does the scientific method exist. It becomes, then, that general model which is used in different ways as a structure of inquiry for solving different types of scientific problems. The five stages in problem solving from Dewey's analysis of reflective thinking have been widely used as a model in delineating the steps in the scientific method (1910, p. 72). By 1933, the five aspects of reflective thought mentioned earlier in Dewey's writings had developed into (1) suggestion, (2) intellectualization, (3) the guiding idea (hypothesis), (4) reasoning (in the narrower sense), and (5) testing the hypothesis by action (pp. 107–115).

As different writers explain what they mean by "the scientific method," the discussion centers around those steps in a process that organize progression of inquiry from the development of a problem to its solution. These steps may vary in number from three to more than 10, depending on how the process is viewed. If one scientific method exists, it is the general set of rules, accepted by scholars, that is used to explain phenomena through systematic pursuit of knowledge. Different disciplines use this structure in different ways relying on the nature of a study's subject matter to direct a specific scientific approach.

The following abstract about a study details how the investigation of a very specific phenomenon of nature was conducted using a scientific approach to study a complex occurrence of nature.

Berrit, Georges R. *(Océan de l'O.R.S.T.O.M., Paris).* **Les eaux froides côtières du Gabon à l'Angola sont-elles dues à un upwelling d'Ekman?** [Are the upwellings of the tropical African coasts correlated with the winds?] *Cahiers O.R.S.T.O.M., Paris, Ser. Océanographie,* 14(4): 273–278, **1976.** Refs. English and French summaries. DN-HO, CU-S.

Doubt exists concerning the Ekman theory of the seasonal intertropical upwellings off the African coasts; winds are weak and fluctuate from one season to the other. Ingham (1970) demonstrates that cold waters off Mauritania and Senegal are linked with trade winds, but the problem is different off the Ivory Coast (Ingham, 1970). The correlation between wind and temperature in the southern part of the eastern tropical Atlantic, between Cape Lopez and Cape Fria, is investigated. On the basis of historical data of winds (Steigner and Ingham, 1971) and temperatures (Mazieka, 1968), the authors drew curves of seasonal variations in the Marsden squares along the coast (3341, 3343, 3701, and 3703). Winds, parallel to the coast, S, SE, or SW, were taken into account. Figures show seasonal variations of strong winds (› 10 knots) and winds favorable to upwelling, and a curve gives the percent of calm. For the Marsden square 3703 (south of Mossamedes), good agreement was found between strong winds and low temperatures off Mauritania. Regarding the other squares, upwelling coincided with a maximum of calm and a minimum of strong and total winds in a favorable direction. It was concluded that no Ekman upwelling occurs in this area, at the scale of a few hundreds of miles. Consequently, interannual motor variability was not found in local winds, but phenomena of larger scales, in other regions, were investigated. The upwelling may be dynamic, caused by undercurrents arriving at the surface. The variability of temperatures at the seasonal scale was linked with the variability of undercurrents that were influenced by the oceanic scale. *Subject Headings:* **Upwelling theories; Wind effects on oceanic upwelling; Tropical Atlantic.**—*Auth.* *

---

* Reprinted from *Meteorological and Geoastrophysical Abstracts,* January 1978, 29(1), p. 181.

This abstract illustrates how the general model of scientific investigation was used to pursue an answer to a specific question about a natural phenomenon. As in most cases of structured inquiry, only tentative answers have been proposed, but added knowledge allows a better understanding of the phenomenon. As will be seen later, the study of educational problems also has this characteristic of tentativeness for research findings in education.

A Scientific Approach

Although the scientific approach cannot be isolated as a set of procedures to be applied to all problems, certain elements are common to scientific inquiry. For an inquiry to qualify as a scientific investigation, certain procedures are acceptable while others are unacceptable. The art of good inquiry rests in being able to use acceptable procedures. Seven steps that form the structure of inquiry for this book can be helpful in organizing problem-solving strategies:

1. A felt difficulty
2. Problem identification
3. Information
4. Hypothesis
5. Observation
6. Conclusion
7. Replication

Although listing and numbering these steps according to a sequence implies a rigid order of inquiry, the actual process is rarely applied in that exact order. This is not meant as a prescription for the process. As the inquiry process unfolds, the scientist will be working at several points at a time moving up and down this general list throughout the inquiry process. Such flexibility is important because it allows diversified attacks to establish truths which a lockstep approach would restrict.

Let us now turn our attention to each of these parts in isolation.

A felt difficulty. The scientific approach to the process of inquiry is set in motion by a doubt, barrier, obstacle, or experience that causes bewilderment. The way to an end or goal may be blocked. An unexpected or unexplained event may perplex. The resistance of a felt difficulty can be recognized when trial and error and common sense do not provide viable answers or when other scientific attacks have been little better in clarifying a particular area.

Problem identification. This phase brings the difficulty under study so that the problem is clearly recognized. The felt difficulty has been narrowed down by this stage so that the range of the study can be brought into focus for the investigator and others interested in the same area. At this point, the problem is usually phrased in the form of a question. The answer to that question becomes the goal for the output of the study. Once the problem is sharply delineated, the direction of the investigation becomes clearer and ways of proceeding can be selected. The question can be referred to when making important decisions within the study. If a proposed technique or focus helps to clarify an answer, then it is probably an acceptable procedure for the study. If not, it is not likely to be rewarding.

Information. The first search for an answer should be made within present knowledge. The most efficient way to answer a question is to find that someone else has investigated the same problem area and supplied you with an answer you consider valid. The decision to accept an answer depends on your confidence in the investigation. If an answer is found that is satisfactory to the investigator, this is of course the terminal phase of the inquiry process. Even if an answer is not likely to be found in present knowledge, reading about closely related topics builds background for further study of the problem. If an answer does not exist in present knowledge, closely related information may provide a basis for hypothesis development. The more knowledgeable someone is about related problems and the broad area of concern, the better she or he will be able to attack the new problem.

Hypothesis. When the answer is not found in present knowledge, the most logically developed proposed answer is stated as a hypothesis. The hypothesis is stated in a declarative sentence. It then serves as an explanation to be tested by vigorous investigation. The hypothesis is formed inductively as a generalization. It serves as a major premise to be tested deductively by empirical means.

The hypothesis provides a very important element of the scientific approach by giving something for collected data and **results** to support or not support. Without the guidelines of the problem and the direction of the hypothesis, data collection would rarely be highly profitable in adding knowledge.

Observation. In this stage of inquiry, a well-developed design is produced to collect, organize, and analyze data pertinent to the question under study. The results should be organized in the best way to reach a decision about the tenability of the research hypothesis.

"Observation" is used in the broadest sense here and includes more than simply perceiving through the human senses. In addition to naturalistic observation, devices to extend the human senses and formal **measurement** are considered to be observation. **Correlational studies** which establish relationships and experimental studies which seek to establish cause-and-effect relationships are in the broadest sense also extensions of perception and incorporate observation of many kinds in procedures. "Science" has been defined by some writers as simply observation. This focus certainly calls attention to this part of the scientific approach, even though that definition hardly carries the true spirit of scientific investigation. Since observation is so important to research, a complete chapter is devoted to it in Part I as a part of the orientation to inquiry.

Conclusion. The results gleaned from the collected data are used as bases for the **conclusions** of the study. The researcher interprets the meaning of the results as it relates to the problem under study. This phase of inquiry (1) may verify and support the hypothesis and in turn any theory that it is linked to, (2) may cause the researcher to reject the hypothesis as untenable, or (3) may bring about a modification of the hypothesis to be tested with new data.

The conclusions of the study become new knowledge or further answers to knowledge being tested for its tenability. Except for further testing in the final step, this completes the structure for securing answers to questions generated by problems.

Replication. The hypothesis should be retested using new data gathered from new subjects using the same **design.** Such retesting is called "replication." Retesting a hypothesis under different conditions of time, location, and/or other factors will strengthen the value of the original results if the same outcome is observed. If a different outcome is found, it may indicate that (1) there has been a previous wrong decision, (2) the hypothesis does not hold under different conditions, or (3) the hypothesis is now invalid. Pooling the results of many studies will provide data that are more trustworthy. If the same study is conducted 50 different times with different subjects and the same outcome is found for 47 of those times, it is likely that the supported outcome would be difficult to debate. The tendency to let one study stand alone as testimony frequently causes the replication phase to be overlooked.

A scientific approach depends on clear identification of a problem to make it work. Without the problem and its carefully structured solution, there is no science. The use of a hypothesis allows the researcher to develop a clear idea of a possible answer to a certain question and permits the researcher to place part of the problem-solving activities outside the mind. This element of objectivity is the power of the scientific approach and why it is so widely used in inquiry today to answer questions and to add information to the body of knowledge.

Educational Research and the Scientific Approach

Using the scientific approach to study educational problems is not necessarily evidence that education is a true science nor that the teaching/learning process is a science. However, the study of educational problems can be approached scientifically. Researchers of educational problems are directed by clearly accepted **paradigms** for methods of inquiry into questions in education, even though the human sciences lack paradigms for the substance of their inquiry. The accepted methods of inquiry lend coherence to researchers' efforts. Paradigms on the substance of inquiry in human sciences will come only when our ability to explain and predict behavior has increased greatly. In *The Structure of Scientific Revolutions*, Thomas Kuhn referred to parallels of scientific development within nature. Education must also seek to parallel as closely as possible the processes of natural science. A science becomes mature by continuing with the thesis "that the price of significant scientific advance is a commitment that runs the risk of being wrong" (Kuhn,

1970, p. 101). The relative immaturity of the human sciences as sciences compared to the natural sciences often leads the educational researcher into areas where theory about education is, at best, confusing, sometimes conflicting, and occasionally totally lacking. Kuhn's discussion of the paradigm as a unifying feature for members of a scientific community explains how research workers in education may attack problems in education using accepted methods of the scientific approach for problems in this area.

The seven steps listed in the previous sections form a structured (scientific) approach to problem solving. For convenience of study and to give direction to problem solving in education, we may categorize the problems to be encountered in education into three broad classes:

1. **Research**
2. **Development**
3. **Evaluation**

The next section explains these classifications to clarify how they are different as well as how they are alike. The differences should help to distinguish those educationally oriented questions that can be attacked by research strategies.

Problems in Education

Within the broad field of education, the nature of problems and their associated questions vary widely. Confusion in dialogue often arises because clearly delineating divisions have not been established between strategies of inquiry. A major step toward ordering this confused state is found in the article "Toward a Taxonomy of Empirically-based Problem-Solving Strategies" (Gephart, 1973) that evolved from a series of symposia including professors of educational research held in the fall of 1972. A **taxonomy** was developed "to sort out the confusions about complex relationships among the empirically-based processes of evaluation, development, and research by suggesting a taxonomy of empirical methods" (Gephart, 1973, p. 39). The taxonomy associates the "need to know" with research procedures— procedures that have as their major purpose the creation of generally applicable knowledge. The taxonomy associates the "need to choose" with evaluative procedures whose major purpose is providing "information which rationally weights each of the alternatives in a specific decision situation" (Gephart, 1973, p. 39). It in turn associates the "need to do" with development procedures whose major purpose is producing "the tools and procedures needed in operations" (Gephart, 1973, p. 39).

The taxonomy in Figure 1–1 shows the relationships among problem-solving strategies and at the same time points up their differences (Gephart, 1973, p. 40). It is helpful to study levels I and II carefully to check the orientation of the three processes and to reflect on how problem-solving activities in business, industry, government, physical sciences, biological

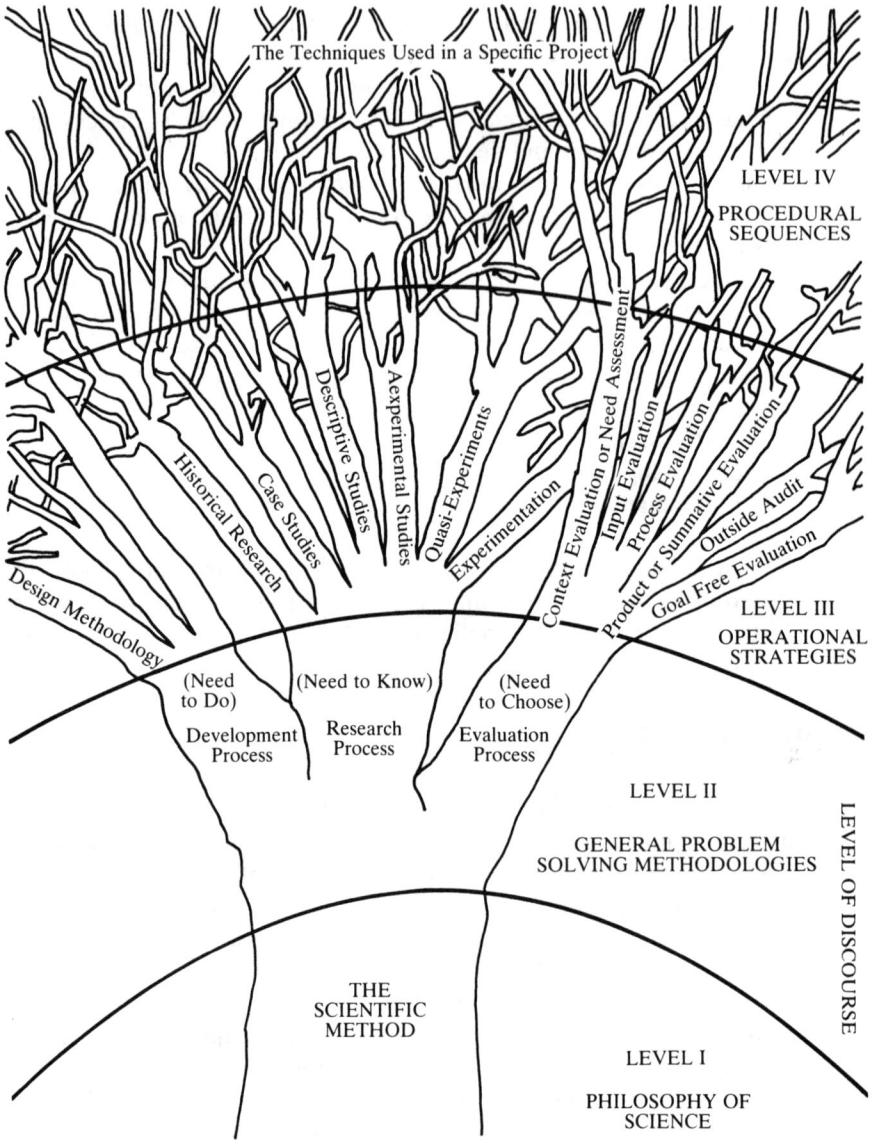

The Techniques Used in a Specific Project

LEVEL IV
PROCEDURAL SEQUENCES

Design Methodology
Historical Research
Case Studies
Descriptive Studies
Aexperimental Studies
Quasi-Experiments
Experimentation
Context Evaluation or Need Assessment
Input Evaluation
Process Evaluation
Product or Summative Evaluation
Outside Audit
Goal Free Evaluation

LEVEL III
OPERATIONAL STRATEGIES

(Need to Do)   (Need to Know)   (Need to Choose)

Development Process   Research Process   Evaluation Process

LEVEL II

GENERAL PROBLEM SOLVING METHODOLOGIES

LEVEL OF DISCOURSE

THE SCIENTIFIC METHOD

LEVEL I

PHILOSOPHY OF SCIENCE

Note. From *Similarities and Differences in the Research and Evaluation Processes* by William J. Gephart, Robert B. Ingle, & Gary Saretsky (Bloomington, In.: Phi Delta Kappa, 1973). Copyright 1973 by Phi Delta Kappa. Reprinted by permission.

FIGURE 1–1   Taxonomy of Problem-Solving Strategies

sciences, social sciences, behavioral sciences, and education differ. The first level is the foundation used by all three strategies based on a philosophy of science—the scientific method. The second level is designed to organize problem-solving activities rooted in the scientific approach into more scientific problem areas and associated strategies.

All fields utilize many strategies for problem solving. Some are research procedures, that are in level II of Figure 1-1 channeled into the center branch in the taxonomy tree. Some of these procedures are associated with evaluation, shown on the right branch of the tree. Others are procedures of development, shown at Level II channeled into the branch to the left.

Continuing into the operational strategies (Level III in the taxonomy tree), specific procedures associated with each general methodology appear in the taxonomy. At this point more specific means for arriving at solutions appear. Procedural sequences (Level IV) are specific to a particular question and reflect the techniques of observation used to collect information for the study.

The use of research and development centers and divisions in the certain fields—such as industry and government—underlines the separation of procedures for problem solving. In industry, for example, the difference between research activities and development activities is clearly defined, although the two work hand-in-hand to accomplish a goal for the sponsoring company. The same is true of evaluative procedures in industry: there is a clear-cut division in terms of activities and roles. The divisions may be housed together, but distinct differences exist within the organizational structure.

☐ CHECK YOUR UNDERSTANDING

The Gephart taxonomy is helpful in identifying and selecting the proper problem-solving strategy for problems (questions) that arise. For each of the following situations, identify which strategy—research (R), evaluation (E), or development (D)—would be utilized in inquiry.

1. The Gold Bluffs School District has arranged a series of inservice meetings for interested middle-school teachers. The purpose of the meetings is to produce a sequence of topics of mathematics and new approaches to the three-year, middle-school mathematics program to prepare students for the new high school program.   (R E D)
2. A researcher needs a test to measure a specific human trait but can not locate an acceptable standardized or previously constructed device. She proceeds to construct a device which is considered satisfactory.   (R E D)
3. A company that makes lawn mowers has been collecting information about the several aspects of building lawn-cutting devices. This information is forwarded to the company engineers who use that data to construct a new innovative lawn-cutting device for owners of small city lots. What strategy do the engineers use?   (R E D)
4. Through the years, a teacher has observed what she considers to be an association between ability to perform certain basic physical functions and the development of reading skills. She wants to pursue an answer to this by a strategy of inquiry. Which one would she use?   (R E D)

5. A classroom teacher has introduced a modified instructional unit to teach about U.S. colonial history. He wants to determine the effectiveness of the change in program on this class of students. (R E D)
6. A teacher has been concerned about the effect of noise level while students study on their understanding of concepts to be developed from that study. What mode of inquiry would he use? (R E D)

Answers

1. (D) Production of curriculum and instructional sequencing is a development (need to do) strategy. The creation of the new middle school program to dovetail with the new high school program falls in that inquiry strategy.
2. (D) Creation of tests and instructional materials are doing activities. Although the test is built to serve the research study, the test construction is a development (need to do) strategy.
3. (D) Creation of lawn mowers is like building tests and educational materials. Research may have been used to create some of the data, but the actual designing and building is a development (need to do) strategy.
4. (R) This item is based on a question whose answer would be widely generalizable as new knowledge about how students learn to read and what contributes to that learning. Investigation for causes of observed effects usually requires the research (need to know) strategy.
5. (E) Judgments about effectiveness of new and innovative practices must be made within the context of evaluation (need to choose). Decisions about further changes are made in light of the outcomes as judged by the evaluation strategy.
6. (R) Another widely generalizable answer is expected from this question. Cause-and-effect relationships are identified by well-conducted studies based in the research (need to know) strategy.

Summary

This chapter offered a brief review of human inquiry methods as a background for understanding present methods of attacking problems through a structure of inquiry. The historical development of problem-solving techniques culminated with the hypothesis serving as a bridge between the inductive method, which provides generalizations, and the deductive method, which moves from a generalization to specifics.

The chapter also discussed the scientific approach as a problem-solving technique. The process was broken down into seven steps to facilitate a study of the parts and their relationships: (1) a felt difficulty, (2) problem identification, (3) information, (4) hypothesis, (5) observation, (6) conclusions, and (7) retesting of the hypothesis by replication.

The "Taxonomy of Empirically-based Problem-Solving Strategies" became a vehicle for clarifying the general problem-solving strategies of evaluation, development, and research which are widely used in inquiry. Clarification of the role of each strategy gives a clearer picture of research activities in education and will help overcome difficulties which exist because of a tendency to lump many techniques which are not research activities under one title, "research."

The focus of the rest of the book will be on investigations that structure inquiry about educational problems using research techniques. No judgment about the relative value of the different strategies has been made nor is any intended. Each must be viewed as important in its own right, since each particular strategy solves problems of a specific type.

In later chapters, we will examine more thoroughly the three major research methodologies. The first covers questions based in the past, hence the name **historical research.** The second covers questions rooted in the ongoing events—**descriptive research.** Finally **experimental research,** the third methodology, covers questions based on a need to control by **manipulation** of certain conditions in a laboratory-like situation in order to study the effects of the different conditions.

References

Becker, C. L. *The heavenly city of the eighteenth century philosophers.* New Haven: Yale University Press, 1932.

Boas, G. *The inquiring mind.* LaSalle, Ill.: Open Court Publishing, 1959.

Dewey, J. *How we think.* Boston: D.C. Heath, 1910.

Dewey, J. *The quest for certainty.* New York: Minton, Balch, & Co., 1929.

Dewey, J. *How we think.* Boston: D.C. Heath, 1933.

Gephart, W. J. Toward a taxonomy of empirically-based problem-solving strategies. In W. J. Gephart, B. Ingle, & G. Saretsky, *Similarities and differences in research and evaluation processes.* Bloomington, In.: Phi Delta Kappa, 1973. The content of this article evolved out of three 1972 sessions of the National Symposium for Professors of Educational Research. Credit for these ideas must be shared with Robert B. Ingle, Gary Saretsky, and the many participants of NSPER 1972.

Kuhn, T. S. *The structure of scientific revolutions* (2nd ed., vol. 2, no. 2). Chicago: University of Chicago Press, 1970.

Thompson, S. *Tales of the American Indian.* Cambridge: Harvard University Press, 1929.

CHAPTER TWO

RESEARCH STRATEGIES

There is nothing more powerful than unfettered scientific thought.

—Vladimir Vernadsky

The term "research" carries a prestigious ring in contemporary society. Since the term has such status, it is little wonder that many matters which are not strictly research oriented are called research. There are also many very legitimate kinds of research, and this variation adds to confusion about what constitutes proper research procedures. Although there may be other definitions of research that are valid, this chapter develops one way of viewing the question for the sake of consistency. In this view, the major identifying feature of research as used in a contemporary sense is that it structures the production of answers to previously unanswered questions, and thus generates new knowledge which can be widely applied within educational settings.

What Research Is Not

One approach to explaining a concept is to discuss what that term does not mean. To delimit the borders of this discussion of research, it must be emphasized that research is not evaluation (the need to choose) nor is it development (the need to do). Communication of recorded knowledge is likewise not research. Research does not consist of going to the library or other source of present knowledge to find the answer to a question that someone has formulated. To read widely about a subject and write a review of the writing or to search and find an answer which has already been established must not be considered research, although the teaching-learning process may find this to be effective pedagogical procedure. Best (1977) says:

Teachers frequently assign a so-called "research project" that involves writing a paper dealing with the life of a prominent person. The students are expected to read a number of encyclopedias, books, or periodical references and synthesize the information in a written report. This is not research, for the data are not new. Merely reorganizing or restating what is already known and what has already been written is not research, valuable as it might be as a learning experience. It adds nothing to what is known. (p. 9)

Helmstadter (1970) says that "once a problem has been solved and recorded, the transmission of the information to others is a matter of communication and teaching, not research" (p. 4). The concept of research does not include use of present knowledge to add to an individual's knowledge. This does not mean that teachers should no longer assign "research papers" through which students use existing knowledge to add to their own understanding. Rather it emphasizes that such activity simply does not fit the definition of research as it is used for contemporary problem-solving procedures, the sense in which the term will be used in this book.

This definition does not preclude historical research as a way to synthesize what is known and to produce new knowledge using data from the past. The key term in this distinction is *new*. Also, use of present knowledge and knowledge about the past to answer new questions can be considered scientific research, assuming acceptable procedures are used. Using knowledge in this way has many pitfalls, but someone skilled in the methodology can function as a researcher when better methods are precluded by circumstances.

What Research Is

Inquiry procedures which are associated with the need to know are classified by the Gephart (1973) taxonomy as research strategies. When the problem requires that the answer be a principle which can be applied generally, the problem-solving strategy will be research.

Definition

Throughout the years, the definition of "research" has been closely related to the concept of a diligent and systematic investigation designed to revise and discover knowledge. Although books have been written about research without a definition being stated, the implied meanings fit with the preceding concept.

The Gephart (1973) taxonomy associates the "need to know" with research procedures that have as their major purpose *the creation of generally applicable knowledge*. There is agreement among definitions of research that research procedures are problem-solving methodologies designed to add to present knowledge.

Three definitions from recent writings reflect the contemporary meaning of the term.

McGrath (1970) says:

> Research is a process (tool) which has utility only to the extent that the class of inquiry employed as the research activity vehicle is capable of adding knowledge, of stimulating progress and of helping society and man relate more efficiently and effectively to the problems that society and man perpetuate and create. (p. 20)

Helmstadter (1970) notes:

> In summary then, an operationally useful (though not rationally perfect) definition of research can be given: Research is the activity of solving problems which leads to new knowledge using methods of inquiry which are currently accepted as adequate by scholars in the field. (p. 5)

Kerlinger (1973) reluctantly "attempts" a definition:

> Scientific research is systematic, controlled, empirical, and critical investigation of hypothetical propositions about the presumed relations among natural phenomena. (p. 11)

The following synthesis of current views of research will provide the definition of research used in this book:

> *Research is structured inquiry that (1) utilizes acceptable scientific methodology to solve problems and (2) creates new generally applicable knowledge.*

What Researchers Do

The activities of researchers can be classified by categories of purpose: (1) to familiarize, (2) to classify, (3) to establish relationships, and (4) to show causality.

Familiarization. Naturalistic observation and early exploration of a problem area may prompt a researcher to begin collecting information about existing knowledge to give further insight into the problem. At a more primitive stage in the growth of science, this level of inquiry served as the total purpose of exploration and produced the final answers. Today, however, hypotheses rather than answers are more likely to be the output of this activity. At this level researchers must allow for flexibility and be open to discovery from many directions. They should consider all possible contributing factors to familiarize themselves with a topic of possible study.

Classification. Description involves sorting out a collection of people or objects and developing categories to organize the data. Observing a particular attribute across a population or seeing different examples of a phenomenon may reveal ways of grouping or separating certain elements according to observed similarities and differences. Some sort of classification system evolves in this process of describing. A blue ball is more like a blue bat than a red ball is like a blue bat. A yellow ball is like a yellow banana if color is being considered. A yellow ball and a yellow banana are not grouped together if the observer is focusing on the phenomenon of how well each object rolls down an inclined ramp. An example of a classification system which organizes problem solving along one dimension is the taxonomy presented in Chapter 1. Classification is important to research as a way of describing. More importantly, it is a part of some more encompassing strategy of problem-solving.

Establish Relationships. An investigation should go beyond familiarization and classification and seek out relationships among phenomena. If two or more events or circumstances are related, they go together. They may happen at the same time or they may vary or change in some consistent way. They may vary directly—that is, change in the same direction. For example, within a human population height and weight are said to vary directly, because in general the taller someone is, the heavier he or she is. This generalization holds for the population in general, but it does not necessarily hold for each specific case when all possible pairs of individuals are compared. An example of an inverse relationship has been established between administration of polio vaccine and the occurrence of poliomyelitis. The occurrence of the disease lessens with increased use of the vaccine. When relationships become established, the power of prediction grows, assuming that there is indeed a connecting factor or cause-and-effect relationship involved in the observed changes.

Show Causality. In addition to the first three purposes listed for research activity, the researcher also seeks to explain the cause of an observed effect. To give a complete explanation about why a phenomenon exists, a cause must be established. To accomplish this purpose requires the highest level of the art of researching. Cause-and-effect relationships are bases upon which theories and natural laws may be established about phenomena.

The preceding discussion of activities and purposes does not address the issue of research methodology. The three methodologies—historical, descriptive, and experimental research—use these activities in different ways and for different reasons. Nevertheless, all methodologies involve familiarizing oneself with the area, classifying data, establishing relationships, and showing causality. The desire to explain and predict is common to all methods of research.

Research Characteristics

The special use of the scientific approach in research strategy structures the procedures into a systematic logical sequence. This sequence is clear in the following list of research characteristics.

1. Research activity focuses on the solution of problems. Research is an outgrowth of the age-old human desire to explain the universe as completely as possible through inquiry.
2. Research is conducted only after all other sources of answers have been exhaustively examined. There is no need to engage in research if the proposed question has been answered to the satisfaction of the asker and is currently available in present knowledge.
3. The research process is directed to problems based on a need to know. The research role does *not* include problems found in **formative** or **summative evaluation** or problems centering on the development of tools, programs, and procedures.
4. Research processes study presumed relations between natural phenomena. Studies are designed to (1) establish relationships and/or (2) study observed relationships for the cause-effect direction between or among **variables.**
5. Research is used to test hypotheses, the more important of which are tied to general theories. The hypothesis is used to bridge the gap between the generalizations proposed by inductive investigation and the testing of the generalization by the deductive process.
6. Research findings add to knowledge by providing new knowledge. Communicating existing knowledge is not a research activity.
7. Research is an orderly investigation that provides outcomes that withstand criticism of people knowledgeable in the area of study. Findings should be above legitimate attack by knowledgeable colleagues. Furthermore, all procedures should be reported in detail so that the findings can be subject to others' reactions as a check against conscious or unconscious human error committed by the investigator. All aspects of research activities connected to the inquiry must be open to scrutiny by experts.
8. Research can be conceived of as a chain of reasoning starting at problem formulation progressing through investigation to findings. The total process—from problem isolation to the addition of new knowledge—is logically structured inquiry into some well-defined problem.

The abstract on page 28 is an example of a research study in which new data were collected about a specific question which confronts teachers of primary grades.

ABSTRACT 1523*

EC 10 1523   ED N.A.
Publ. Date Fal 77   6p.
DeStafano, Michael A. and Others
Teachers' Views of the Treatability of Children's School Adjustment Problems.
Journal of Special Education: VII N3 P275–280 Fal 1977

Descriptors: Emotionally Disturbed;*Student Adjustment;* Adjustment Problems;* Teacher Attitudes;* Mental Health;* Role Perception;* Primary Education;

Compared were the views of 134 primary grade teachers and mental health personnel concerning the treatability and prognosis of primary grade children's school adjustment problems. Primary grade teachers rated each of nine hypothetical referrals, depicting three predominant types of school adjustment problems (acting out, shy-anxious, learning), on four dimensions: appropriateness of referring the child to the school's mental health services, ease or difficulty for a mental health person to work with such a child, how much a mental health person would enjoy working with the child, and a treatment-prognosis estimate. Shy-anxious children generally received the most positive ratings. Teacher judgments were compared to prior, similar judgments made by mental health personnel. The latter gave significantly high appropriateness ratings, indicated that the children would be significantly less difficult and more enjoyable to work with and judged prognosis to be more favorable. Teachers, however, saw mental health services as more appropriate for children with learning problems than did mental health workers. (Author/DB)

☐ CHECK YOUR UNDERSTANDING

Abstracts of longer articles or reports are used to inform a reader quickly about what to expect in the detailed materials. By reading an abstract, the reader should be able to identify the strategy used if the material deals with inquiry of a specific problem. What statements in the preceding abstract suggest that this is a study based in the research process?

Answers

1. A comparison was made of views of two different groups.
2. Procedures were research oriented.
3. Results seem to be generalizable beyond the subjects studied.
4. The results are not written to be limited to any specific group of primary teachers.

Educational Research

Many of the problems that arise in education are problems to be solved by evaluation or development procedures and, as such, cannot be considered answerable through research strategies. Answers to the questions of research contribute to construction of generally applicable theories, which serve as a base for decisions about practical matters. A wide range of educational questions has the nature of a need to know, and they require a strategy of research to arrive at answers. **Educational research** can thus be defined in the following way:

> *Educational research is scientific inquiry about an educational question that provides an answer which contributes toward increasing the body of generalizable knowledge about educational concerns.*

Since the field of education is broadly based in many contributing disciplines, educational research may contribute generalizable knowledge to closely related areas. The educational practitioner can also be expected to use knowledge from those same areas to make practical applications of theory to school situations. For these reasons, educational research is not as clearly delimited as the above definition might imply. To help in educational decision making, the professional educator often goes to sociology, psychology, anthropology, and other areas that study human action and behavior in society.

An Early Use of Educational Research

A pioneer in educational research, J.M. Rice, gave impetus to further study of educational practices by using scientific methods in an early research study devoted to the investigation of the way spelling was presented in the classroom (1897a). He wanted to find out what teachers accomplished in different classroom situations and determine what the more successful teachers were able to attain. The results of the study showed that students learned no more in a 40- or 50-minute period than in a period of 10 or 15 minutes. Rice concluded that since the compensation for spelling time is not appreciable past a minimum, the waste of time should be eliminated.

In a follow-up article the same year, Rice (1897b) discussed professional criticisms of his research and also presented favorable reaction to his scientific approach. Of particular interest is a letter received from a Dr. Eucken, Professor of Philosophy at the University of Jena. In his letter, Eucken indicated that his independent research in the same area—investigating conservation of pupils' time—had resulted in the findings similar to Rice's. A small class of primary pupils met requirements of excellence with only five to eight hours of instruction per week. Eucken concluded that instruction, particularly in the lower grades, should be simplified. He opined that pupils spend far too much time in the classroom for the amount of learning accomplished (pp. 412–413). The results of these early studies opened other areas to investigation of teaching practices. Professional communication allows research workers to augment or interpret their results with information from other researchers.

Use of Inquiry in Education

Criticism of the Rice study from colleagues continued at the time, although more and more educators began to see some value in scientific procedures. At a meeting of superintendents in the spring of 1897, Rice asked, "How can we tell at the end of eight years whether the children who have had 40 minutes of spelling instruction are better spellers than those who had only 10?" No one attempted to answer the question, but some replied that "the question could never be answered" or that Rice was wasting time by asking silly questions. The meeting closed with most classing it "a failure" (Rice, 1913, pp. 17–18).

Nevertheless Rice's early studies encouraged investigation of practices in other subject areas. By no means was the scientific approach widely accepted for education by the scholars of the early 20th century. Acceptance of scientific studies in education were firmly rejected by many educators at all levels. By 1902, Rice had this to say about the use of the scientific approach to educational problems:

> In view of the circumstances that during its long period of existence pedagogy has established no facts, that side by side with it, in other fields, facts have multiplied and developed into sciences, it is perfectly legitimate to ask whether pedagogy will admit of purely scientific treatment, whether it is possible for use to accumulate such facts as will lead to the discovery of certain fundamental pedagogical laws and certain methods and processes upon which all educators must agree. (1913, p. 2)

At the same time, Rice developed two propositions:

> It may be that the nature of the child mind is so elusive, and the influence of natural endowments, heredity, and environment so varied, that all definite observation is rendered impossible, or it may be that we have not applied proper methods of observation. (1913, p. 3)

Paraphrasing Rice, the two propositions become:

1. The nature of a child's mind negates any scientific study through direct observation.
2. Proper methods of observation have not been applied to educational problems.

The best statement about present opinion in education would be that probably each of the two propositions has some degree of validity. Personal facts are more difficult to obtain and interpret than public facts, making educational studies difficult to carry out. Also, research methods used to study problems are at best in need of increased sophistication.

One of the basic premises used in early attacks on scientific studies was that education was an art and could not be approached in a scientific way. Many still view it as more of an art than a science. The difference between education as an *art* and education as a *science* can be explained in this way:

The science of education deals with the facts and principles that build an organized body of knowledge about educational concerns.

The art of education deals with the practical applications of that knowledge to the educational scene.

Those problems that deal with building an organized body of knowledge about educational concerns through the scientific structure of inquiry are unquestionably research questions. Educational research is scientific in that knowledge about general truths and about the operation of general laws has been obtained and tested through a scientific approach to solving problems.

Educators do not consider this created knowledge final in any sense. Rather, given more and better information, they hold this knowledge to further testing and recognize that it is subject to change. Most of the knowledge is incorporated in theories at various stages of sophistication. To go beyond that, it must be said that all fields of study have found it difficult to establish natural laws—those immutable principles held to be derived from nature. The universe is certainly structured on a framework of natural laws, but as yet most of these have escaped human recognition or understanding. Few, if any, natural laws have been drawn from the body of knowledge about educational concerns. However, through scientific investigation, the gulf of ignorance can be narrowed, and some difference in the educational process is perceptible as a result of research activities.

Does Research Make a Difference?

The contribution of research to the process of education is widely debated by professional educators and other interested persons. Many of the negative comments have been directed toward the inability of research to give immediate answers that have permanent applicability.

In answer to the question of how research can influence practice, three propositions have been defended (Kerlinger, 1977, p. 5). First, there is little direct connection between research and educational practice. Second, relevant bodies of research aimed at theoretical understanding of psychological, sociological, and other behavioral scientific phenomena may have a beneficial influence through indirect effects on educational practice. A corollary is that basic research is more important than applied research in its potential effect on education. Third, two major obstacles to research influencing educational practice in the long run are the pragmatic-practical notion that research should pay off and that it should be relevant to contemporary social and educational problems.

Research can study relations but its stated purpose is not making decisions or taking action. Research makes a difference when knowledge that has been gained by research is used at a more concrete and specific level. Understanding the purpose of research as a science should help those who criticize research to direct their criticism where it can be more effective.

It is in the nature of science that answers produced are not always right. An integral part of the scientific approach is the correction factor that permits science to correct itself when it is wrong. The test of differences in the school setting brought about by educational research lies in the practices it produces and how they change over a five- or ten-year period (Page, 1975, p. 5). The fact that practices change should not be used as evidence against the scientific approach to educational problems. Rather this flexibility should be seen as part of the strength of the theory-development process through which change is influenced within the school setting.

The nature of human characteristics studied by educational researchers present many difficulties that are not encountered by researchers in the physical sciences. Progress can only be made through persistent, patient, and purposeful probing. Evidence that research does have an impact on practice is the gradual changes in common beliefs over time as a function of the new knowledge created by research studies. Changes in the educational scene (political actions excepted) are for the most part the product of research. The changes made in the past should give encouragement to present-day educational researchers as they attack problems scientifically.

Although it is difficult to establish cause-and-effect relationships between specific research and educational change, some examples can be cited where there would be general agreement that certain changes have been made as a result of a research study or series of related studies. For example, the research of Piaget has had impact on theories of learning and the way that instruction is organized, especially for young children. Many years passed between the time of researching and the perceived changes, primarily because little weight was given to Piaget's conclusions based on the small samples used for data collection. However, studies conducted on larger numbers of subjects, for the most part, have supported Piaget's conclusions. The understanding of the development of the immature mind as revealed by his research gave direction for curriculum developers, especially in the area of sequencing and timing the introduction of new concepts. This research caused educators—especially in mathematics and science—to consider how a child actually thinks as they organize instruction.

It is more difficult to find evidence of educational change influenced by a single study, because change in education often comes about when educators combine the conclusions of studies to direct decisions. To identify the effects of a study, a period of time must pass to allow implementation by practitioners. The effects of an early study can be documented by current expert opinion (Suppes, 1979). In 1917, Thorndike reported the results of a study about how students learn to read. The impact of that study on the way reading was taught is documented by Russell (1961) and Singer (1978). The Thorndike study resulted in "a change in the definition and subsequent teaching of reading from a process of just sounding out words to getting meaning from the printed page through reasoning or problem solving processes" (Singer, 1978, p. 58).

Other influential studies about reading are pointed out in these sources and other areas of educational research have produced equally influential studies, but most studies do not influence such clearly identifiable changes.

Applying the Scientific Method to Educational Problems

The educational problems that can be pursued scientifically are those that are *testable*. The assumption that underlies this immediate limitation is that there are some educational problems that transcend experience: they are by their nature **metaphysical** and as such are not amenable to **empirical testing.** Questions that depend on value judgments or beliefs are also untestable. Statements like the following are not testable through research methodology:

Sex education should be a part of the primary-grades curriculum.
Boys should take a course in homemaking before graduation from secondary school.
One year of military training between the ages of 18 and 21 would build character for adult life.

Questions generated from these statements—Should sex education be a part of the primary-grades curriculum? Should boys take a course in homemaking before graduation from secondary school? and Should one year of military training between the ages of 18 and 21 be required to build character in boys and girls for adult life?—are not likely to produce generally accepted answers among all individuals nor answers based on objectively obtained information. Consequently, the scientist does not deal with these kinds of issues, since any result will remain indeterminate. The scientist is aware that questions like these must be dealt with, but his or her concerns are with questions and hypotheses that allow for the availability of objectively obtained data for observation and testing. Other kinds of questions can be approached through a structure of problem solving and are discussed in the remainder of the chapter.

The taxonomy in Figure 1–1 was developed to aid in the discussion of roles of those working to solve educational problems through problem-solving techniques. Like all models that attempt to abstract reality, it has some shortcomings. The sharp divisions made in the taxonomy are often less clear in reality because of the more complex nature of the real-world settings. As the developers of the taxonomy state:

This presentation recognizes that in a real life problem situation there may be a need to know, to choose, and to do merged. The recognition of the taxonomy is not an expectation that we can make every problem situation a "pure" application of research. The taxonomy should help us merge the research, development, and evaluative processes as we seek to solve real and complex problems. (Gephart, 1973, p. 43)

Any strategy used in problem-solving can be associated with one of the three strategies, but a person working with one problem may wish to use more than one of the strategies. The strategies are different enough that the different roles are discernible in the activities of the person working to solve the problem. The discussion of the three strategies in the following sections will help those engaged in problem solving to communicate as clearly as possible.

Evaluation and Development

Evaluative procedures are in the branch of the taxonomy tree in Figure 1–1 that deals with problems based on a need to choose. Evaluative procedures, although not research oriented, are those techniques associated with the gathering of information for judging alternatives when making decisions. Education uses evaluation in many ways, but the area most directly related to teaching-learning activities is determining the extent of student learning. Other forms of evaluation are problem appraisal, accountability, and determination of the effectiveness of teaching, teachers, and administrators.

Evaluation as assessing effectiveness is the area described in this view from a comprehensive handbook on student evaluation:

> The intent of this book is to present a broader view of evaluation and its place in education. We are primarily concerned with its use to improve teaching and learning. Briefly, our view encompasses:
>
> 1. Evaluation as a method of acquiring and processing the evidence needed to improve the student's learning and the teaching.
> 2. Evaluation as including a great variety of evidence beyond the usual final paper and pencil examination.
> 3. Evaluation as an aid in classifying the significant goals and objectives of education and as a process for determining the extent to which students are developing in these desired ways.
> 4. Evaluation as a system of quality control in which it may be determined at each step in the teaching-learning process whether the process is effective or not, and if not, what changes must be made to ensure its effectiveness before it is too late.
> 5. Finally, evaluation as a tool in education practice for ascertaining whether alternative procedures are equally effective or not in achieving a set of educational ends. (Bloom, Hastings, & Madaus, 1971, pp. 7–8)

Educational evaluation helps to further valid decisions about a wide array of school problems. The evaluator gathers information and uses it to make judgments about school-related events and to present alternatives to the decision makers in specific educational settings.

The many directions of educational evaluation make a statement of the precise role of the evaluator difficult. Borich says that attempts to define the evaluator's role have been no more successful than definitions about the role and qualifications for corporation presidents (1974, p. 30). Basic to an understanding of evaluative strategies is the recognition of evaluation as a feedback mechanism that is essential if school people are to learn from their experiences.

Developmental procedures focus on problems based on a need to do. These include developing instruction, curriculum, and materials associated with the ongoing in-class parts of the process of education. Developing theories of instruction, creating tests and other materials, as well as formulating broad and local curriculum changes are also part of these more general classifications of scientific activity.

One technique of curriculum development, **action research,** uses a model of great interest to several disciplines. It is a well-structured model consisting of continuous feedback channeled to attack specific problems in one particular school setting. Since the intent of the activity is not to produce generalizable knowledge and the orientation is to only one setting, this type of procedure is a tool of the curriculum specialist, *not* the researcher. Within the total model of action research is a part that utilizes research strategies, however. Specific subparts of the major question can be directed as questions to be answered by research when present knowledge is inadequate.

Many of the problems of curriculum change are of a complex nature, and could merge the three areas of evaluation, development, and research. Usually the change is prompted by some specific disturbing situation, but thorough investigation of the particular problem area requires viewing it in the context of the total school scene. In order to study the specific situation, a comprehensive diagnosis and study must be made. The major task is one of curriculum change, which is classed as development. Nevertheless, each stage of development will use evaluation information of all types to defend and give feedback to the development work. Furthermore, research techniques may be needed to study effectiveness in objective terms.

Although action research and curriculum change fall outside the sphere of evaluation and research, curriculum developers may need to call on these areas for their particular contributions—for example, in developing instructional tools. Development of instructional tools refers to activities devoted to production of appropriate textbooks, films, manuals, software for computer-aided instruction, and other devices to be used in the learning setting. Successful development of a product requires a wide knowledge of educational theory and the utilization of evaluative information as a feedback about the product's effectiveness.

Research

The third problem-solving strategy in the Gephart taxonomy is associated with the need to know. The remainder of this book will discuss at length research in education as it relates to the addition of knowledge about the educational process. Metaphysical questions, questions based on values, questions of evaluation, and development questions lie outside the parameters set for educational research. It is true, however, that the same person may work in two or more of these areas at different times in different projects or perhaps within the same study. The researcher may find that a particular type of test is needed to gather data. If no suitable **standardized test** is available, the next step may be to develop the needed test. When working on such a development task, the researcher's role changes to that of a *developer*. Thus, different roles are associated with each strategy. The distinctions between roles are helpful when communicating with colleagues about professional activities.

Because of the wide range of research problems in education, no one formula can be an infallible guide for the educational researcher. The seven-step model provided for the scientific method can serve, however, as a general model to be adapted for solution of a particular problem and its unique set of circumstances. It should *not* be viewed as a "do-it-yourself kit," but rather as a way to structure a logical approach for isolating an answer to a researchable problem.

Although there is a general sequence of research steps, it is misleading to use them in staircase-like progression. The structure of research inquiry requires that several research steps be considered at once so that the total of the procedures presents a logical sequence. A researcher may skip ahead to a later step to consider a decision at an early point in light of its effects elsewhere in the process. In most cases there will be a natural order that is unique to the problem under study, but the steps are never independent of each other.

There can be little direction in research without a clear and concise presentation of the problem under study. When the researcher has reduced the problem to a well-prepared question, he or she has isolated the most important element in making the scientific method function for the educational setting. If the question meets the criteria for a research study, then the researcher can direct the rest of the procedures to answering the question. Ultimately, the answer to this question is the product of the research study.

The interdependent nature of the parts of a research procedure precludes working in one area in isolation from all of the others. Maybe this is the reason why people engaged in research often make statements like "I am confused; I need to talk to someone about this" or ask "What do I do next?" When a research worker makes comments such as these, she or he may be experiencing the same feelings and frustrations that a long-time researcher was suffering when he said that research is *organized confusion*.

The confusion may be explained by recognizing that it is the nature of research to deal with the unknown. Consequently, frustrations with the process are not reserved for the newly initiated. At least one rewarding moment exists for every study—that moment when it all fits together as a *structure of inquiry*. This most likely occurs when the engineering provides a vehicle for answering the question and, in turn, adds to present knowledge.

For this book, the strategy of research is presented as three methodologies: historical research, descriptive research, and experimental research. These terms are not entirely satisfactory for delineating subtle differences nor for pointing up common components and similarities. These are commonly used names but are by no means the only way to classify research activities.

Historical Research. Common to all definitions of history is the concept of the past. Attacks on questions about past events constitute historical research. Historians write history—narratives of events which have already happened. However, history is more than a static reporting of happenings and becomes a dynamic and integrating force which describes past developments. When a researcher asks an educational question about the past, historical research methodology is appropriate for seeking out the answer.

Historical research methodology focuses on determining the accuracy of statements which have been made or can be made about past events. Critical reading of any material might be considered informal application of historical methodology. Since any educational study has a basis in the past, each study is to some degree an historical study. An understanding of the scientific approach to educational history supports not only historical research but also descriptive and experimental studies.

Descriptive Research. Common to all definitions of description is the concept of explanation. Attacks on questions which can or must focus on the study of variation that already exists in nature constitute descriptive research. **Correlators** (correlationists) observe the natural ongoing events of the world. Description is, nonetheless, more than a static reporting of collected data. It also involves analysis of the data to allow for derivation of a conclusion. When a researcher asks an educational question about present conditions and experimental control is precluded, descriptive research methodology is appropriate for seeking out the answer.

Descriptive research methodology focuses on identification of relationships—especially causal relationships—without the benefit of laboratory-like conditions. Each of the human sciences is restricted in its research practices by the nature of the subject of study, the human being. Medical research can only study disease as it occurs naturally. The effects of administering a prescription as a possible cure are confounded by factors which must be left uncontrolled for ethical or moral reasons. Although physical harm may be the most obvious limiting factor, subjects must also be protected from psychological impairment. Their rights to privacy must be respected. These restrictions direct the study of many educational questions toward descriptive research.

Experimental Research. Common to all definitions of "experiment" is the concept of control. Attacks on questions which allow for strict control of contributing variables constitute experimental research. **Experimenters** (experimentalists) observe events which they have created—happenings which would not have taken place had the experiment not been conducted. Experimentation is the most sophisticated method for deriving answers to questions, because of the confidence associated with conclusions from studies in which procedures are controlled for the **confounding effects** of variation from extraneous variables. When a researcher asks an educational question about present conditions and control can be gained, experimental research methodology is appropriate for seeking out the answer.

Experimental research methodology focuses on setting up conditions which allow for direct statements about causes of observed effects. As previously mentioned, the needed control may or may not be obtainable within the cultural and ethical standards which guide the researcher nor within the nature of the question. If control procedures can be included in observation, then the researcher can organize the study of the educational question within the framework of experimental research.

The three methodologies must be carried out within the restrictions imposed by the scientific approach. Procedures are limited to those considered acceptable by academicians in research and in the basic branch of study. From early days, human beings have been aware that order is associated with nature. The structure of inquiry into educational problems is based on the premise that the order can be better established by use of the scientific approach than by intuition supported by unsystematic observation.

□ CHECK YOUR UNDERSTANDING

Most research studies can be identified as using either the historical, descriptive, or experimental methodology as an operational strategy for research. For each of the following research questions, identify which methodology would most likely be used to structure the inquiry process.

1. How does melodic presentation of subject matter affect the length of attention span for learning in preschool children?
2. How are teachers' expectations of tall children reflected in those students' achievement?
3. What effect does the quality of student handwriting have on a teacher's evaluation of essay responses to items on a secondary home economics test?
4. What effect did the editorial policy of the Silver Bluffs *Register* have on education in the state of West Dakota between 1970 and 1980?
5. What changes in mathematics instruction in 1980 as compared to 1965 can be attributed to the thrust of "modern math" for those years?
6. Which is more effective in development of motor skills—part or whole learning?
7. How are the two characteristics—college grade point average and on-the-job counseling effectiveness—related?

Answers

1. Experimental. The implied relationship seems to be one that would allow the differences on the variable of supposed causes (melodic presentation) to be easily provided by researcher manipulation. The effects variable (attention span) can be measured and a cause-effect relationship investigated by an experimental research design.
2. Descriptive. Since the variable of height of children cannot be directly manipulated, the researcher can not introduce the needed control for an experimental study. Ex post facto research (see Chapters 10 and 11) which assigns members to groups by selecting individuals of different heights at the same age allows some element of the control needed for

an experiment. Factors not controlled for add questions about conclusions for an ex post facto study.

3. Descriptive. The effects of differences in handwriting quality may be difficult to establish. Nevertheless, a relationship may be established by comparing the overall relationship or by comparing two groups which differ according to handwriting quality. The first is probably best established by a correlation and the second by ex post facto techniques.

4. Historical

5. Historical. In both questions 4 and 5, the data needed for a decision will be found in material from the past. Also note that all studies have this basis. To some extent researchers must direct some activity for all studies toward finding a historical basis.

6. Experimental. The *researcher* has the opportunity to manipulate differences in the variable of cause—type of learning—and to observe effects on motor skills.

7. Descriptive. A question asked about a relationship when the researcher is without the means to establish possible cause-effect direction will be descriptive in nature. If a relationship is established, possible cause-effect direction can be hypothesized for a new study using new data in a new experimental design.

Summary

Research has been associated with the need to know. The activities of researchers—familiarization, classification, establishment of relationships, and search for causes—reflect that basic need. Research, rather than evaluation and development strategies, is used in education when the problem is based on a need to know. This chapter defines "research" using a synthesis of recent writings about the research process:

> *Research* is structured inquiry that (1) utilizes acceptable scientific methodology to solve problems and (2) creates new generally applicable knowledge.

Educational research is the application of research methods to educational problems and is defined as:

> *Educational research* is scientific inquiry about an educational question that provides an answer which contributes to increase the body of generalizable knowledge about educational concerns.

The focus of educational research must be those questions that are testable, those problems which can be approached scientifically. Problems that are basically metaphysical or those which imply answers that are at best value judgments are not amenable to scientific inquiry.

The three methodologies of research—historical, descriptive, and experimental—outline the strategy of research. The attack on problems is structured with scientific principles of investigation to overcome difficulties of unsystematic observation. A well-developed question generated by the problem is the most important element in a scientific approach. Educational research has been presented in this book and elsewhere as being somewhat confusing and at times frustrating, but as a process which also has its rewarding moments. One such reward comes when the researcher sees a study fit together as a *structure of inquiry*. Another is seeing changes in educational practices come about as a result of the development of educational theory.

References

Best, J. W. *Research in education.* Englewood Cliffs, N.J.: Prentice-Hall, 1977.

Bloom, B. S., Hastings, J. T., & Madaus, G. F. *Handbook on formative and summative evaluation of student learning.* New York: McGraw-Hill, 1971.

Borich, G. D. (Ed.) *Evaluating educational programs and products.* Englewood Cliffs, N.J.: Educational Technology Publications, 1974.

Gephart, W. J. Toward a taxonomy of empirically-based problem-solving strategies. In W. J. Gephart, R. B. Ingle, & G. Saretsky, *Similarities and differences in the research and evaluation processes.* Bloomington, In.: Phi Delta Kappa, 1973.

Helmstadter, G. C. *Research concepts in human behavior.* New York: Appleton-Century-Crofts, 1970.

Kerlinger, F. N. *Foundations of behavioral research.* (2nd ed.). New York: Holt, Rinehart, & Winston, 1973.

Kerlinger, F. N. The influence of research on education practice. *Educational Researcher,* September 1977, *6,* 5–12.

McGrath, J. H. *Research methods and designs for education.* Scranton, Pa.: International Textbook Co., 1970.

Page, E. B. Accentuate the negative. *Educational Researcher,* April 1975, *4,* 5.

Rice, J. M. The futility of the spelling grind. *Forum,* April 1897, *23,* 163–172. (a)

Rice, J. M. The futility of the spelling grind, Part 2. *Forum,* June 1897, *23,* 409–419. (b)

Rice, J. M. *Scientific management in education.* New York: Hinds, Noble, & Eldredge, 1913.

Russell, D. H. Reading research that makes a difference. *Elementary English,* January 1961, *38,* 74–78.

Singer, H. Research in reading that should make a difference in classroom instruction. In S. J. Samuels (Ed.), *What research has to say about reading instruction.* Newark, Del.: International Reading Association, 1978.

Suppes, P. (Ed.). *The impact of research on education: Some case studies.* Washington: National Academy on Education, 1979.

Thorndike, E. L. Reading as reasoning: A study of mistakes in paragraph reading. *Journal of Educational Psychology,* June 1917, *8,* 323–332.

Vernadsky, V. quoted in Y. Shishima, Vladimir Vernadsky and the modern theory of the biosphere. In A. A. Mkrtchian (Ed.), *Soviet Life,* June 1974, p. 38.

CHAPTER THREE

OBSERVATION

Without a constant and alert exercise of the senses, not even plays and games can go on; in any form of work, materials, obstacles, appliances, failures, and successes must be intently watched.

—John Dewey

"Keep your eye on the ball." Why is this an often repeated phrase directed to the beginning tennis player? Is it so that the player will hit the ball in the precise center of the racket face? Probably not, since the well-constructed racket will return the ball well from a large portion of the surface area of its strings. Why does the batting coach for a baseball team admonish players in the same way? Certainly it is important that the bat come in contact with the ball within limits. However, even with some error associated with the way the ball hits the bat, the swing can result in a hit.

The phrase "Keep your eye on the ball" can usually be interpreted as "Focus carefully on what you are doing" or "Concentrate." The coaches are saying "If you are to succeed in the task at hand, you must give undivided attention to what you are doing." The player must avoid letting a series of thought processes get in the way of the one important swing of the racket or bat. Many coaches will tell a player to let the subconscious take over the task and not to focus on all of the small tasks involved, keeping rather a general "mind set" on the overall task at hand.

The art of researching is much different from playing tennis or baseball, but the meaning behind "Keep your eye on the ball" is just as important to the task of research as it is to the encounter on the tennis court or ball field. The researcher must learn to develop internal conditions that allow a focus on the task from that moment of observation when the problem is met to the drawing of conclusions, which also involves observation. Skills in observation must be developed to direct all aspects of the research strategy.

Science has been defined as observation. Although the true spirit of science may be lost in such a simplified definition, many of the ongoing activities of science consist of observation. Observation in science is more than an unstructured look at some phenomenon. To promote the orientation to research as a structure of inquiry, this chapter deals with the heart of science: systematic procedures for collecting information to aid in the search for answers.

Nature of Observation

Observation is a natural part of any interaction process involving humans. The interaction may be between two people, among several people, or between one or more persons and the environment. This discussion of observation will deal with aspects of observation that relate directly to the research process.

Research observation generates facts that will be used to investigate the tenability of the researchers' hypothesis. Any fact which is used to form results and base conclusions comes from an observational procedure. That fact is called an "observation." To be useful to the researcher, observation must be structured according to acceptable data-collecting procedures. The fact may be generated by structured direct observation, administration of an educational or psychological test, or one of a host of other observational procedures.

Since researchers deal with many types of questions and the gamut of variables, the procedures of observation vary widely. The kind of data needed largely directs the choice of how to proceed with observation. For our purposes, observational procedures can be studied under two major divisions: **direct observation** and **measurement.** Direct observation is structured by use of **checklists, scorecards, rating scales, anecdotal records, mechanical devices,** and **unobtrusive** arrangements. Measurement is structured by use of rating scales, mechanical instruments, and educational/psychological tests. Some data from direct observation can be considered **measures** of some property, so the two divisions do overlap. This overlap will be explored in the section on measurement later in this chapter.

Unsystematic observation of phenomena will rarely reveal relevant data. To be meaningful for a research study, observations must be collected or created with purposeful direction. Generally acceptable procedures must be used in data collection, and a frame of reference is essential to establish a system for interpretation of the results into conclusions.

The researcher does not accept the proposition "To see is to believe." Experience with sense data makes the researcher less than fully confident about data collected by the senses. Human frailties, experience with **optical illusions,** and natural distortion lead to this distrust of sense data. This attitude prompts researchers to take steps to improve data by objectifying observation through extension of the natural senses in all possible ways.

If observations are to be meaningful for research studies, they must have acceptable levels of **reliability** and **validity.** The usefulness of the observations for testing a hypothesis and forming research conclusions depends first on how consistent the observation procedures are in generating data, and second on how well the procedures do what they ought to do.

Reliability is the consistency of observations yielded over repeated recordings for either one subject or a set of subjects (Hopkins & Antes, 1978, p. 79). An observational technique is reliable if it consistently gives the same result (observation) every time for any given phenomenon or set of phenomena.

Validity is the degree to which an observation accurately describes or quantifies the attribute being observed (Hopkins & Antes, 1978, p. 79). How well an observational technique does what it is supposed to do includes both consistency (reliability) of whatever it does and the added dimension of indeed doing what it is used to do. The observations (scores) generated by a history achievement test must measure only achievement in history. Including measures of general knowledge or knowledge in other subjects reduces the usefulness (validity) of the scores for decisions about history.

An observational technique may be high in reliability but low in validity. For example, a weighing device could consistently weigh a 10-kilogram object at 12 kilograms. The scale would be considered reliable but not valid. Another weighing device might generate weights ranging from 7 to 14 kilograms on repeated weighings. The second scale would be neither reliable nor valid. For a weighing device to do what it is used to do, it must weigh the 10-kilogram object at 10 kilograms each time.

All procedures of observation must be constantly checked for reliability and validity. A large portion of the rest of this book discusses ways to generate data which have high validity for the study in which they will be used. The rest of this chapter is directly related to how observational procedures can be made more valid.

Everyone has some skill in observation—skill used to interpret the environment through the senses. The researcher must push beyond the simple task of unstructured direct observation into more complex observation requiring more than mere sense reaction. The following section, based on four psychological factors associated with techniques of observation, directs the researcher to aspects of observation which are basic to all steps of the scientific approach but especially crucial in collecting data.

Psychological Factors of Observation

Observation in laboratories or in clinical settings is highly structured. Prearranged conditions can control many factors which have in the past reduced the quality of data and thus resulted in either questionable or incorrect answers. Although laboratories and clinics do generate certain types of data well, the conditions for reproducing many phenomena are artificial and a question remains about the generalizability of findings to the real-world setting.

Much of the activity associated with answering educational questions must take place in the real world. Although a large amount of the educational researcher's time is spent abstracting, planning, and theorizing in the university academic setting, he or she must at some time move into the real world to test the theories with objectively obtained information. Much of the success of research rests in the researcher's ability to collect data which are relevant to the study.

A scientist uses the term "observation" somewhat differently from the way it is usually used. Any data about subjects that are used as bases for drawing conclusions are called observations, but procedures of observation do not necessarily incorporate techniques of observation by human beings. A reading on the Brain Wave Analyser, developed by Dr. J. P. Ertl, is a scientific observation, although the only direct observing done by the investigator consists of recording readings from the dial. Data gathered from a tape recorder, videotape camera, or other machine that records on a magnetic tape are observations. Educational and psychological tests provide data that are observations. Direct observation by human beings also generates such data. Valid conclusions depend on objective data such as that available from a machine, so it is important for the human observer to develop skills in obtaining reliable facts.

Observation and its interpretation include four psychological factors that must be considered: *attention, sensation, perception,* and *conception* (Van Dalen, 1973, p. 37). Since observation is basic to science, these factors permeate those actions of the researcher mentioned earlier: familiarization, classification, establishment of relationships, and identification of causes.

Attention

Attention is a condition of readiness requiring a selective narrowness of receptivity. Successful observation demands that the many stimuli constantly assailing the senses be carefully screened, since the mind is not capable of attending to all of them. The skill that the tennis coach sought to develop in the student when she said "Keep your eye on the ball" is the selection process that here is called "attention." The researcher must become proficient in selecting from all received stimuli only the specific ones that are relevant to the task at hand.

Learning to concentrate is an important part of observation. The research observer must focus on that portion of all stimuli which pertains to the problem and tune out or ignore the portions that do not relate to the problem. However, the concentration of attention on a specific area of concern must not cause the researcher to miss pertinent data. He or she must be sure the selective attentiveness includes a way to pick up all important **information**—including data that do not support, as well as data that do support, the hypothesis. Any other pertinent data should also be included in observation. The attention should be so objective that the data are complete and not **biased,** knowingly or unknowingly, by the researcher.

Sensation

Our awareness of the world comes through the senses. Sense organs can distinguish sounds, smells, sights, tastes, and other physical feelings.

Sensation is the stimulation of the sense organs which allows us to experience an event. Changes in the environment are communicated to us through the senses. The researcher uses human senses to provide an awareness of that part of the world's phenomena which pertains to a specific question.

Sense organs are limited in their capacity to provide all of the information a person needs. Many times the senses must be augmented by using instruments like eyeglasses and hearing aids. Even with these helps, many sounds and sights are not picked up because they are outside the limits of human capabilities. Such limitations restrict the range of stimuli that can be used in data interpretation. Other instruments may be needed in research to help pick up stimuli and thus extend the range of observation. Microscopes, telescopes, scales, thermometers, and educational/psychological tests are examples of tools used to supplement human senses and extend awareness of stimuli not otherwise apparent.

A researcher must give thought to the quality of the signals and use techniques that provide clear and undistorted impressions on the senses. Any instruments used must be of the highest sophistication available. In the case of data-gathering **test instruments,** the researcher should consider producing specific instruments for the study.

A special problem arises when human behavior is studied directly: the observation procedure itself may introduce a new factor not present in a more normal situation. When observing human subjects, the researcher must take steps to remain as inconspicuous as possible. Visibility of the observer and/or observational tools must not change conditions of the subjects nor affect the situation appreciably.

Perception

Observation is more than paying attention to a circumstance and picking up the stimuli. What has been picked up must be interpreted. Anything that is viewed must be linked to the past through experience. Sensations are *perceived* in light of past experiences. A sound is merely a noise until the person who hears the sound identifies and categorizes the sensations by comparing it to like sounds from the past. This process of interpretation is *perception.* Since meanings are the products of individual minds, different interpretations may come from different persons, although the sensations or physical stimuli being received are the same in each case. A sound that comes from a distance on a clear summer evening may sound like a train to one person, a truck to another, and a plane to another, although they all receive the same waves of sound.

A person's perception of received stimuli is reflected also in the interpretation of what are called "optical illusions." An optical illusion is a figure that appears to change as a person perceives it, while in reality the configuration of the figure does not change. Of course, the change in the figure is the result of a change in the interpretation or perception of it by the viewer. A classic example is the "face or vase" illusion shown in Figure 3–1, where a figure changes appearances from face to vase and back to face. Although the researcher is not likely to have this same problem with observed stimuli, the example does point up the importance of interpretations based on the researcher's perception. What something *appears* to be may be quite different from what it *really* is, but to the beholder it is what she or he sees in it.

FIGURE 3–1   Face/vase Illusion

Optical illusions can be psychological as well as visual. Rooms have been built in psychology laboratories in which all the objects appear to be the wrong size. However, an awareness of this distortion may depend on a background of experiences and on knowing that an adult is larger than a child, regardless of how near or far away the child is standing.

Another difficulty in perception is that the sensations received may not be interpretable in the received form. The light rays coming to the eye from a pencil partially submerged in water will show the pencil to be bent. The eyes are accurately picking up the stimuli, because refraction caused by water does bend light rays. The question of whether the pencil is actually bent or straight requires viewers to perceive this scene in terms of what they know about pencils and what they know about viewing objects under water. An early research study required subjects to study light refraction and then measured how the learning affected subjects' ability to shoot at targets under water.

The data and/or information collected in research are at least as difficult to work with as the previously mentioned physical sensations received by the five senses. Developing procedures to provide valid interpretation for research studies in the form of conclusions requires integration of the sensations into interpretable form. Perception of data about human behavior and/or information of all types requires a high level of observational skill.

Conception

When past experience does not give the information necessary for interpreting received signals, the mind must turn to something else. When a person must create an answer through some intellectual process other than recalling past experience, he or she is working at the level of *conception*. When a person hears a noise on a summer evening that she has never heard before, she may interpret it in this way: "I have never heard a noise like that before, but it sounds more like a truck than anything else I can think of." With this intellectualization, she has bypassed the limitation of experience and has developed an imaginary concept to explain the unknown. The conceptualization permitted visualization of what could not be perceived directly from experience. Conception moves beyond perception by building imaginative concepts.

Scientists have developed many **constructs** (or conceptualizations) to explain human behavior. Creativity, hostility, and motivation are three such terms which have been used to explain how someone has conceptualized certain human actions. In these cases, to create a construct certain events which can be directly observed are connected with assumed internal states or processes which remain hidden.

Hypothesis development generally takes place at the level of conception. Most problems and resulting questions in education occur because of a lack of knowledge about a situation. Explanation is proposed through a carefully constructed conceptual scheme, and the researcher tests it for tenability using objectively obtained information from a real-world setting.

Observation in Educational Research

The educational researcher uses observation to identify problem areas. Observation also helps in acquiring a background of knowledge pertaining to the problem for developing a hypothesis. The researcher also uses observation to gather data for testing the hypothesis and develops conclusions only after observing the results of the data collection. Each of these tasks utilizes observation in a different way. The first use of observation may be at the level of looking and seeing while studying an obstacle in education. At this level *attention* and *sensation* help establish the problem and its limits. *Perception* comes into play during organization of present knowledge and interpretation of data gathering and treatment results. *Conception* is the process involved when the researcher must go beyond present knowledge to develop hypotheses and theories.

The researcher cannot depend on the everyday observation that serves most of us very well and cannot be satisfied with uncontrolled observation. The process of merely looking at phenomena does not provide the reliable data needed for valid inferences. The observer must put observed events in a frame of reference and describe events in interpretable categories. For educational studies based in human behavior, two methods of observing the behavior are (1) observing people in a natural setting or a devised setting and (2) questioning subjects directly about their behavior.

Observation and Hypotheses

The art of conceptualization is a special area of observation that requires the researcher to depend heavily (almost exclusively) on his or her own ability to integrate informal observations about relationships to formulate hypotheses that make statements about cause and effect. If a hypothesis is too broad to be tested as formulated, observation can deduce testable hypotheses from within it. Since this is the level of abstraction from outside past experience, hypotheses may be difficult to develop.

Difficulty in formulating hypotheses about human behavior is magnified by the many variables contributing to any behavior. Early studies were univariate as are many current research studies. In univariate studies, the *if-then* statements involve only one variable for the *if* clause (the antecedent) and one variable for the *then* clause (or "consequent"). Most problems are actually multivariate, however, and thus require combining a set of hypotheses into a more encompassing theory. Nearly all hypotheses are connected to some broader theory.

In most cases, separating the variables for study is a somewhat artificial strategy and must be accounted for in the conceptualization of the hypotheses, the interpretation of conclusions drawn from studies, and ultimately in the theories developed. More advanced studies involve multivariate relationships that allow a higher level of conceptualization for the research and, in turn, require more sophistication of both formal and informal observational techniques.

Special Problems in Human Inquiry

The perplexing uncertainties in educational inquiry result from two conditions mentioned in this chapter. First, the four psychological factors of observation limit the researcher. Second, the many interacting variables which contribute to human behavior are difficult to study as a whole. Furthermore, the isolation of certain variables for study must be interpreted at some time in the context of the total phenomenon. Those who conduct educational research should be aware of imperfections, as Jacobo A. Varela was when he said this about social technology:

> Sometimes there are failures because of erroneous diagnosis, incorrect design, or faulty application. And sometimes we meet problems that we cannot even attempt to solve—because we lack the ingenuity to devise a solution or because the principles we have taken from psychological research cannot handle the problem. (1978, p. 90)

Observation of Human Behavior

Some observation can be done directly. You may know that there is a bird in the birdbath because your vantage point allows you to see the bird. Even with direct observation, careful attention must be given to details so that clear interpretations can be made. Can you clearly distinguish that the activity of splashing and bathing is being created by a bird and not by some other small animal that decided the water looked inviting?

Observation of human subjects to record their behavior is not as direct nor as simple. The data which the researcher needs is, to a large extent, deep within individuals, and not open for direct viewing. Attention must be given to sorting out pertinent actions of an individual or group from those actions which have no bearing on the question being studied. The techniques presented later in this chapter are intended to overcome the limitations of human observational powers and to control for confounding of the data by extraneous factors.

Inferences from Observation

The data collected by observation especially for a specific study must be interpreted to test the tenability of the associated research hypothesis. Do these data for this specific case support the generalization that was developed through inductive reasoning? The researcher must make inferences about what the data indicate. Stated as conclusions, these inferences are the output of the research process. The researcher develops the methodology for a study as a unique set of procedures which allows him or her to make correct inferences from the data with a high level of probability.

Prediction of Future Behavior

To a large extent, science is directed toward prediction. Scientists must ask what do we know that will allow correct prediction of future behavior? How well this can be done rests on two factors: first, how successfully observation has generated facts for the study and how well they were interpreted; and second, how well the new knowledge was synthesized with what was already known about related aspects of the theory.

The person who wishes to use the conclusions of research must consider them in the context of local conditions. Under varying conditions, the results of research studies may imply different actions. The special problems associated with educational inquiry do not allow predictions to be applied to widely differing sets of conditions. For this reason, prediction of human behavior is likely to be less clear-cut than what most would desire. The consumer of research will need to be prepared to make the synthesis of knowledge for special sets of conditions and different sets of students. For example, educators predict that students should be ready to undertake learning to read in the first grade. This prediction holds in general, but physical and psychological development, cultural backgrounds, and similar influences cause some students to be ready to learn to read much earlier and others to be delayed a year or more in their reading readiness.

Objectivity in Observation

Maintaining objectivity in observation is an ideal in research that is sometimes difficult to achieve. Researchers may be called upon to conceptualize circumstances they do not fully understand and may then be required to form perceptions of what the collected data reveal to them. Their interpretation may be hampered by poorly generated data or by insufficient data and may then result in erroneous hypotheses or invalid conclusions.

Attempts to interpret sensations are also frequently made more difficult by a number of intervening human characteristics. Many obstructions to objective observation are associated with one or a combination of the following human characteristics:

1. *Personal interest.* A strong personal commitment may cause the observer to see what he or she wants to see.
2. *Early decision.* A time limit on observation may not provide time for all the needed information to be collected.
3. *Anticipation.* A mental set about what is expected may result in a faulty inference.
4. *Personal knowledge.* If a person knows little about an area, he or she may draw on knowledge from another area to explain sensations erroneously.
5. *Emotions, prejudices, values, physical condition, and other personal constructs.* Faulty inference can be influenced by these human characteristics subconsciously and may be difficult to identify.

Most of the above difficulties arise from the fact that observers are human beings working within the constraints of a human system. Mark Twain has been credited with saying that the worst thing that can be said about someone is that the person has human characteristics. Since researchers are human beings, they must take steps to overcome these built-in difficulties.

The most effective approach to increasing validity is to build as much objectivity into research procedures associated with observation as possible. Certain research procedures can help to reduce errors in perception and conception and thus increase the degree of validity. A researcher should develop a wide background of knowledge in the problem area. Anyone works better in a situation where she or he has much knowledge, so the researcher builds knowledge to a high level. Studying other views that are different from their own helps some researchers. Some investigators even try to support a view opposite their own through gathering of appropriate information. In formulating background, hypotheses, and methodology, writing with words that have common meanings makes clear how a researcher is using words. Giving definitions for words or concepts that are less well-known is also important. To limit the influence of personal biases, a careful researcher writes about specific acts, rather than about judgments or interpretations of the acts.

Once the data are gathered, the good researcher examines them with a questioning mind. Rather than accepting any data at face value, he or she develops techniques, invents or constructs new instruments, and uses available tools to provide the most clear signals to interpret the data. A system of recording data is also important. Since any delay in recording data may contribute to inaccuracies, a system of prompt, precise data recording must be developed to provide a means of quick and accurate recording of the facts and to produce a permanent record. Finally, the researcher should use quantification of data whenever possible. Numbers are more exact in reporting and help to avoid ambiguity associated with vague statements about size, quantity, and so forth.

All aspects of the researcher's observation can be improved by building objectivity into research procedures. Building a structure or frame of reference for the observer(s) is a crucial part of this study development. It is not enough to view a situation and report general observations in a narrative report. Methods for educational observation require guided actions of individual observers in the presence of sensations. Some reasonable technique for translating the received stimuli into interpretable observations or data is necessary for transmitting the behaviors into interpretable results. The following sections use the preceding discussion of objectivity to provide ways to structure observation and generate meaningful data.

Direct Observation

When data are gathered directly so that there are no intervening elements between the observer and the observed, the researcher has chosen the method called "direct observation." Since the process is conducted without any intervening persons, conditions, or devices, a record of what actually happened is available for problem clarification, formulation of results, and drawing conclusions. The formal and most structured direct observation is used in collecting the data for testing the researcher's hypothesis. Direct observation can be carried out in nearly all aspects of data collection and proves to be quite versatile. Nevertheless, there are some practical difficulties with collecting information in this way, so that the researcher must consider the following advantages and limitations of direct observation.

Advantages

Given a well-planned structure and trained observers, direct observation has the following advantages:

1. It can be useful in collecting data about nonreaders, young children, people with mental handicaps, and laboratory animals.
2. Interaction between the observer and a subject can be initiated and carried on.
3. The procedure can identify levels of skill development.
4. It allows actions to speak for themselves.
5. It provides a record for future comparison.
6. It avoids rationalization and artificial presentation.
7. It does not require a special laboratory setting.

These advantages are implicit in the nature of direct observation: it allows action to speak for itself, is versatile, and can be carried out at almost any time.

Limitations

Despite the advantages to direct observation, the researcher must recognize its limitations in collecting data. Direct observation is time-consuming, and its cost in money, as well as time, is usually considerable. From the standpoint of procedures, the use of supplementary devices may alter natural, ongoing events. Finally, the procedures may reflect observer biases. The procedural limitations can be reduced to some extent; however, the cost factor will be difficult to control. Carefully planned use of devices can reduce external influences to a minimum, while thorough training of observers should control for any bias input from observers.

Techniques of Direct Observation

All research procedures include direct observation at some time in the process. The extent of this observation may only be to gather background material or inspect the results of a study. At other times the major data-gathering techniques may be based on procedures of direct observation. Direct observation is especially valuable when studying very young children, other nonreaders, laboratory animals, or processes; but it is not limited to these uses. Direct observation should be included more frequently in research activities, but it is many times forgotten when planning such activities. This section describes unobtrusive observation, checklists, rating scales, scorecards, and ranking as tools for collecting data in direct observation.

The most important part of developing techniques of direct observation is training the observer. Training for the particular task involved in each study should be thorough enough that observations by different observers are consistent. Such preparation should include actual observation by the observers so that they can become accustomed to the mechanics of the procedure. This practice will also help the researcher gauge how well between-observer differences have been eliminated. The following are general suggestions for preparing observers for a particular study:

1. Observers should be included in the planning of the data-gathering procedure.
2. Observers should know the purpose of the study; but if a comparison of subjects or groups of subjects is involved, they should not know which subjects are in each of the different groups.
3. Observers should have the opportunity to test the techniques in practice before making observations for the study.
4. Cultural differences between the observer and the observed should be investigated for any possible effect on the validity of the data being collected.
5. Effects of the observer on the observed situation should be investigated. The natural conditions of the setting should not be appreciably altered.

In planning the observational structure of each study, researchers create from particular techniques or combinations of techniques a unique design for the study. The techniques presented in the following five sections cover some traditional observational methods for educational research that have withstood the test of time. A researcher may need to use one or some of these or may need to develop some other unique approach for providing valid data. Carefully considered procedures will let the researcher see in the design what will be the result of techniques used in the study. This is the best assurance that the question under study will receive an appropriate answer.

Checklists. The behavioral observer needs a well-devised instrument to record observations. A tally sheet in the form of a checklist (see Table 3–1) facilitates this recording by avoiding the need to write a narrative description of observations. A checklist has two major advantages in observation: it is a time-efficient method of recording, and the data are objective. Time is sharply limited when the observer must record ongoing events that do not lend themselves to special time-out periods for data recording. Checklists provide a way for the recorder to keep up with events.

In addition to being time-efficient, the checklist limits the amount of judgment the observer must exercise while performing the observation. The list assures that the observer will give attention to those facts important to the study while avoiding unimportant aspects and forces him or her to leave judgments until later when there is more time for consideration.

TABLE 3–1   Checklist for the Return of Service in Tennis

Directions: Below are definable aspects that are important to successful return of serve. Check each one for each service return for one set. Determine the percentage of attainment for the set.

Number of returns	1 2 3 4 5 6 7 8 9 10 11 12 13 14 15 16 17 18 19 20 21 22 23 24 25 26 27 28 29 30 31 32 33 34 35 36 37 38 39 40 41 42	%
Back straight	~~LHT~~ ~~LHT~~ ~~LHT~~ ~~LHT~~	100
Knees bent	~~LHT~~ ~~LHT~~ //	60
Watch ball come off server's racket	~~LHT~~ ~~LHT~~ ~~LHT~~	75
Correct backswing	~~LHT~~ ~~LHT~~ ////	70
Get the ball while it's rising	/	5
Contact the ball before it gets to you	~~LHT~~ ///	40
Stroke fluidly through the stroke	~~LHT~~ /	30
Racket head above the wrist	~~LHT~~ ~~LHT~~ ~~LHT~~ /	80
Recover position for next return	////	20

Checklists which are customarily used in judging musical performance and gymnastic competition furnish those judges with a record for evaluation. Thus they avoid an evaluation after the fact with only memory to rely on. Many products are also evaluated through a structure provided by a checklist. Researchers use them for the facility that they provide and also for their ability to provide well-organized objective data for interpretation.

When building a checklist, researchers should make sure that the specific points to be observed are listed. Descriptions of the points should be complete but not lengthy. These points should be listed in the order in which they are expected to occur. The observer's reaction should be reduced to a simple response—such as a tally or a check. Also, the checklist should include enough space for compiling the data. In addition, observation by checklist requires that a frame of reference be established and a recording scheme be developed. One subject should be observed at a time, and a checklist should be made for each subject.

The checklist allows the observer to notice subparts of the phenomenon during the ongoing action and later review the behavior for the interrelatedness of the separate parts. Researchers find that, given care and skill in preparation, a checklist can facilitate observation by generating objective and well-organized data.

Rating Scales. Rating scales, an extension of the checklist technique, allow an observer or subject to record the intensity or degree of impressions. Rating scales are used to eliminate reflection by memory of what happened, to provide a structure for recording that does not interfere with what is being observed, and to generate a detailed record of behavior.

A researcher constructs a scale for some factor by arranging certain categories in a linear fashion showing varying amounts or intensities. Informal scales are used in everyday conversation—witness, "Rate that performance on a scale of one to ten" or "Check that hamburger on a scale of one to ten." Research studies use the rating scale as an aid to observation in much the same way, although the procedure is more structured and the data gathered are more objective.

Many important variables in the teaching-learning process—such as motivation, interests, attitudes, and self-concept—can be quantified by assessing their degree or intensity, while they may not lend themselves to closer degrees of measurement. If some sort of order can be established to quantify amounts of a variable, a researcher can construct a rating scale to differentiate varying degrees of the variable. A rating scale could be devised, for example, to record the observer's perceptions of the degree of cloudiness in the sky. Such a rating scale would include categories that vary from a completely clear sky to a completely cloudy sky. A "cloudy sky scale" might look like this:

```
        1         2         3         4         5         6
        |---------|---------|---------|---------|---------|
     Clear                                          Completely
   (no clouds)                                       overcast
```

The scale units for the cloudy sky scale have been rather arbitrarily set here at six. There is no established rule about the number of units to use in a rating scale, but observation of the variable may give some direction to the appropriate number of categories. Too few points on the scale result in only a crude measure with little meaning. Too many points make discrimination by the observer too difficult. Three points on the scale to measure cloudiness might look like this:

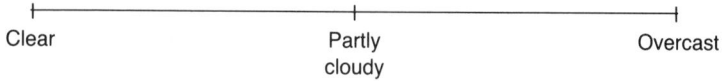

Clear	Partly cloudy	Overcast

The points in this scale have been named rather than numbered. This technique is used in rating scales where statements describe varying degrees of the variable being observed. Three points on the above scale are probably of little use in recording sky conditions for scientific study, although the scale may be quite useful in predicting weather conditions.

A scale with many points may or may not be of help to the observer. It is questionable whether the fine divisions in the following 50-point scale would provide more usable data about sky conditions than the 6-point scale.

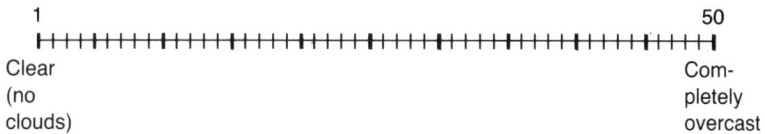

1   50

Clear   Com-
(no   pletely
clouds)   overcast

For observations of human behavior, a statement that describes specifically a point in relation to other points will in general increase the reliability of observations. Studies of the numerical power of words used to describe observations indicate the importance of choosing the correct descriptors. Relationships of adjectives—such as *disgusting, inferior, ordinary, pleasant,* and *admirable*—have been studied as to favorableness and the effect on the favorableness when the words are modified by a particular adverb—such as *decidedly* (Cliff, 1972).

Researchers should use descriptions for points on a scale to help objectify scaling techniques. An example of a rating scale for judging a particular behavior might look like this:

Admirable	Charming	Good	Bad	Disgusting	Contemptible

If the researcher has reason to believe that the distance between all adjacent pairs of points is equal, or nearly so, then for statistical treatment he or she could assign numbers to the points. The numbers may or may not appear on the original scale.

1	2	3	4	5	6
Admirable	Charming	Good	Bad	Disgusting	Contemptible

The following are some guidelines for developing scales:

1. Do not have too many or too few points on the scale. Too few result in a crude measure. Too many points make discriminations difficult, and the procedure becomes time-consuming for the observer.
2. Use an even number of points on the scale. This forces the observer off the center of the scale, that happy medium that everyone wants to hit. The completely neutral response (which is rarely a true response) can be avoided by using a rating scale with an even number of points.
3. Allow reactions at only the listed points. If the observer marks between points, the interpreter is forced to make an arbitrary interpretation. Even if the observer is also the interpreter, reflection will be difficult.
4. Select meaningful descriptors for the categories. Careful selection of adjectives and modifying adverbs gives direction to the observer. Cliff (1972) discusses this selection process in more detail.

In addition, one subject should be observed at a time on all of the points to be considered, and a separate rating scale sheet should be used for each subject. When a rating scale is being used as a part of a self-reporting device, the subjects (respondees) must understand explicitly how to use the scale and record reactions.

An adaptation of the rating scale, the **product scale,** may be used to judge completed work (products) according to varying degrees of merit. Using this technique, completed work by each subject is compared to models of varying quality to assign to it a particular rating in the scale. For example, a researcher might collect samples of students' handwriting and select six examples which range along the continuum of handwriting quality. These models would be selected to represent a scale which had nearly equal intervals between adjacent points. Each student in a study could then have a handwriting sample compared to the product scale. The six possible ratings might be very poor, poor, low average, high average, very good, excellent. Each product would then be given one of the ratings. If equal intervals are assumed, then mathematical treatment would be appropriate for analyzing the data. When the global aspect of a complex product is being observed, a product scale may be the best tool to use. Observation of a complex phenomenon may best be structured through use of a rating scale.

Scorecards. Researchers might also use a numerical device called a "scorecard" to structure observation of a complex entity. This device is a further extension of the principle of structuring used in the checklist and the rating scale. Though rarely used for observing human behavior, the scorecard is frequently used to evaluate school buildings, communities, textbooks, and school programs. Scorecards have also been designed to categorize socioeconomic status of individuals, families, and groups.

In designing a scorecard, each important contributing factor is listed on the scorecard, and a predetermined number of points is assigned for each one in relationship to its importance among the others listed. The total

4C. *Intramural Athletic Program*		
General Standards	Points Possible	Points Scored
Adult supervision is provided for the program	3	
Detailed management and leadership are supplied by pupils	3	
Competition is among teams of pupils classified by age, height and weight	3	
Pupils are used as umpires, referees, judges, and scorers	3	
Intramural activities are not held during the daily instructional period	3	
Round-robin and ladder tournaments are held in intramural play	3	
Activities Used in Competition		
Bat Ball	3	
End Ball	3	
Long Ball	3	
One Old Cat	3	
Pin Soccer	3	
Softball	3	
Prisoner's Ball	3	
Soccer Dodgeball	3	
Triangle Ball	3	
Basketball Throw	3	
Captain Ball	3	
Circle Soccer	3	
Corner Kickball	3	
Handball	3	
Feather Ball	3	
Rotation Soccer	3	
Shinney	3	
Square Soccer	3	
....	3	
....	3	
....	3	
Total Points Allowed	60	
Scorecard Summary Sheet		
Division IV—Program (Activities)	Points Possible	Points Scored
A—Activity Emphasis (Instructional Period)	58	
B—Activities Taught (Instructional Period)	342	
C—Intramural Athletic Program	60	
D—Achievement Tests in Individual Athletic Events	40	
Total	500	
Total Scores	Points Possible	Points Scored
Division I—Instructional Staff	500	
Division II—Facilities	500	
Division III—Program (Organization)	500	
Division IV—Program (Activities)	500	
Total for Scorecard	2000	
Divide Score by 2	1000	
Percentage Score for School (Divide by 10)	100	

Note. From *A Scorecard for Use in Evaluating Physical Education Programs in Elementary Schools* by N. P. Neilson and G. W. Arnett (Salt Lake City: University of Utah Press, 1955).

FIGURE 3–2 Section of a Scorecard for Evaluating an Elementary School Physical Education Program

points marked on the scorecard are intended to be an indication of the overall evaluation.

A major problem arises when the validity of the data collected on such measures is investigated. Since the observation rests primarily on *reported* information, the value here is questionable. Other questions arise about the use of scorecards when important intangibles make contributions to the entity, but are not recognized on the scorecard. Despite these drawbacks, scorecards can help structure observation for some research studies and are very useful in gathering particular kinds of data.

A scorecard for physical education programs in elementary schools (Neilson & Arnett, 1955, p. 53) provides a model that can be adapted to other special uses for research purposes, since the general procedures are the same regardless of the purposes involved. Any use of a scorecard would seek to get a total picture of some complex entity.

The Neilson-Arnett scorecard lists four major divisions: instructional staff, facilities, program (organization), and program (activities). Each of these divisions has from 4 to 7 subcategories, giving 23 aspects, each having a subscore. The final page of the scorecard and the subdivision of Division IV called the "Intramural Athletic Program" are shown in Figure 3–2. The total for subdivision 4C is recorded in the summary sheet for the division, and the total Division IV total is recorded in the master scorecard. The total for the 4 divisions is the total for the master scorecard. The master scorecard also offers a percentage score for the school's physical education program.

Rankings. Observation may require comparing those subjects being studied to each other, rather than to some absolute scale. An ordering by ranks provides an opportunity for the researcher to give serial numbers to the elements being studied (Hopkins, 1974, pp. 5–7). A rank order assigns a position number for each number in a distribution of values, so that all of the values greater than any one value are on one side and all smaller values are on the other side. All values that are the same are assigned the same number. One example of a **ranking** might occur when a judge is asked to evaluate a set of paintings by assigning a one (1) to the painting that she judges to be the best, a two (2) for the next best, and so on. For five paintings—AB, AC, AD, AE, and AF—she might judge them as shown in the accompanying table.

Paintings	Ranks
AD	1
AE	2
AB	3
AF	4
AC	5

Each position indicates the judge's ranking of the art object in relation to all of the others without assignment of definite quantities to the attributes being judged.

Ranking allows the researcher to differentiate within groups when observation takes place within a limited range of a continuum. It also permits handling quantitatively data that cannot be more exactly discriminated. Assigning ranks for a variable under study may assist the observer in building objectivity into a stubborn situation where more refined techniques cannot be used.

Unobtrusive Observation. Plans for observation must take into account the effects of the observer or observation device on the data collected. Are the data collected the same as data which would be generated in a purely natural situation? If the intrusion of the observation technique or device seems a deficiency in the study, the researcher should investigate to see if there is some way to collect the data from a natural situation in such a way that the person being observed is unaware that observation is taking place. Viewing through a one-way glass is one example of unobtrusive observation (Webb, Campbell, Schwartz, & Sechrest, 1966). Viewing through a one-way glass is also a way to invade someone's privacy. When using such unobtrusive observation, the researcher and assistants must always consider the moral, ethical, and legal implications of their actions. Observational devices must not go too far in intruding on the privacy of subjects. This factor is probably most obvious when using unobtrusive measures, but possible physical and psychological damage must be considered and avoided in all observational procedures and devices.

Unobtrusive observation is commonly used in assessing interest where some form of bias might otherwise intrude to distort responses from subjects. For example, a study of students' interest in mathematics might use one of several ways to determine student interest. An interest test (inventory) might be administered. The students might be asked the question Do you like to study mathematics? Under either approach, the student would know that certain responses would be preferred. Consequently, their responses could provide invalid data. When the desired answer is probably apparent to the subjects being questioned, the responses may be biased in that direction. Another biased trend might be based on a counter response, if for example some students answered the opposite way from what they perceived was the desirable response. Such a trend might be explained among students as a backlash against a person whom they see as an authority figure.

Rather than administering an interest test or asking a direct question, the researcher might choose to observe actions which indicate interest in mathematics, the unobtrusive approach. The number of entries in mathematics at the science fair might be an indication of overall interest in mathematics. The manner in which the student approaches computational practice or extra reading in topics might similarly indicate interest. Use of a math corner in the library or in an elementary classroom could measure interest.

Other applications of the unobtrusive approach to observing interest are placing sensors in the floor of art museums or noting the wear of floor covering to measure interest in particular pieces of art or collections. The number of books on a topic checked out of the library could give an indication of the degree of interest in a particular topic. Any unobtrusive approach should establish a direct relationship between the measure and the characteristic being assessed, however, to make conclusions valid. For example, the apparent surge of interest in a particular topic of study may increase the number of books checked out in that area, but the interest might have been temporarily created by a movie or television program that appeared at about the same time.

Sampling Observation

Since a researcher rarely has a complete set of data available for forming results, some decisions must be made about how to select the data for analysis. Samples of the data must be collected to stand as a representation of total data. Three sampling plans used with direct observation are event sampling, trait sampling, and time sampling. The answer to the question, Can the behavior best be recorded and interpreted on the basis of division by units of behavior or units of time? will be influenced by the particular research problem being considered. Creative ideas about using checklists, ratings, scorecards, mechanical devices, and tests for each of these sampling methods can be found in published research or may be developed especially for the particular research study.

Event sampling uses occurrences of behavior in individuals or in interactions between and among individuals in the setting being observed. Examples of individual behavior include temper tantrums, teacher questions, student questions, errors in a tennis match, and acts of creativity. Examples of interactions are quarrels, voluntary in-class debates, and incidents of submission and domination. An advantage to event sampling is that natural settings provide a closeness to reality and continuity to an integral occurrence not possible in time sampling.

Trait sampling is much like event sampling except that specific behaviors are reported rather than whole events. The observer may be looking for aggression within subjects and would thus note occurrences of aggressive behavior according to a schedule. Four types of incidents to be observed in this example could be "Bites or kicks," "Hits or shoves," "Calls others dirty names," "Teases gently."

Time sampling selects different points in time for recording observations. The observer might, for example, record on a checklist what is happening every 15 seconds over a predetermined time span. The sampling might occur at 10-minute intervals for certain time periods throughout a day, week, or other appropriate time block. Time blocks should be chosen at random over a long enough time period to assure a **representative sample.** There are many ways to set up selection of samples. Decisions about the length and frequency of the blocks will be influenced by the particular study and the type of data required.

Behavior observation systems from past studies can give direction to the researcher using direct observation, but new and creative approaches for current studies will provide the most valid data and may contribute new methodology for observation techniques. Those working in this area are encouraged to try new methods of direct observation which will permit the educational researcher to function better in the important areas of human interrelations in the classroom and other group interaction. Data-gathering instruments and schedules that organize observation work and provide data which can be treated with some form of systematic analysis must be created for these complex situations.

Research activities for considering a question and producing a subsequent answer cause the researcher to be engaged in observations of many kinds. The educational researcher dealing with human behavior will need to rely heavily on direct observation to provide valid answers for research. The value of the outcomes (conclusions) rests largely on the degree of quantification provided through observation.

☐ CHECK YOUR UNDERSTANDING

Since a researcher can not record everything that happens, she or he must decide what sampling procedure to use for data collection by direct observation. Which sampling techniques—Event (E), Trait (TR), or Time (TI)—would be most appropriate for each of the following situations?

1. What proportion of the time does a student turn in class assignments?
2. Determine the degree of aggressive behavior in individual subjects of a study.
3. Make a study of classroom interactions—pupil-to-pupil, pupil-to-teacher, and teacher-to-student or teacher-to-students.
4. Determine the number of times a preschool child falls asleep during rest periods during a four-week observation period.
5. What proportion of the allotted study time did individual subjects of a study actually devote to study?
6. Determine the number of books that a student checked out of the library.
7. Assess the exhibition of creative acts outside of music and art classes.

Answers

1. [E] This is something that does or does not happen, and it is not tied directly to a trait. Thus the observer should look for events.
2. [TR] If direct observation were used here, exhibition of a construct would be related to examples of specific behavior.
3. [TI] Since the length of time an interaction takes place is important, this direct observation would likely be recorded by time or proportions of time. Interaction analysis schedules (for example, Flanders, 1970) are usually based on establishing interaction by segments of classroom instructional time.
4. [E] Same as number 1.
5. [TI] The researcher must develop some technique to measure the time on the study and the time off the study.
6. [E] Same as numbers 1 and 4.
7. [TR] Same as number 2.

Supplementing Direct Observation

Many of the techniques used with direct observation are too time-consuming to use with large numbers of subjects. In some cases, psychological factors may limit the validity of data collected through direct observation. To overcome these deficiencies of direct observation, certain extensions can supplement direct observation and augment the list of tools available to the researcher.

In general, direct observation may be supplemented in two ways: special devices and testing. Certain devices extend the human senses in areas where the senses alone fail to provide data with the desired degree of validity. These are in most cases mechanical devices—such as movie cameras, videotape recorders, and sound recorders—that provide permanent records of events for careful study. These devices also include machines to extend the senses—such as microscopes, telescopes, and listening devices. Tests are also used to gather data as instruments of measurement for cases in which physical measuring devices, such as rulers, yardsticks, weighing scales, and odometers, are not appropriate. These tests are used primarily to measure constructs associated with achievement, aptitudes, and personal-social growth.

Both mechanical devices and tests are observational procedures which can generate facts for study.

Mechanical Instrumentation

Movie cameras, videotape recorders, sound tape recorders, counters, timers, and hundreds of other mechanical devices are available to aid in observation. Some provide a record that can be studied intensely and repeatedly by teams of observers. Instruments that record mechanically are not affected by human biases, emotions, or selective and capricious memories. Of course, the human element still enters into interpretation, but it should contribute only minimally if readings are carefully checked through viewing by other observers. Other devices extend the human senses and supply observations not possible within the human limits. Instrumentation serves three major purposes in observation. It provides a purely objective record of what happened as the events occurred. Each record is, of course, limited to the scope of the recording device. A movie camera does not give a complete view of a classroom, so the record is limited to what appears on the film. A tape recorder picks up only sounds within its range. Instrumentation further provides a way to gather sensations not available through the human senses. This contribution is limited by the level of sophistication of the devices. Some are very refined, but others remain relatively crude. Finally, instrumentation provides a way to quantify many variables under study. The noise level of a situation can be recorded in decibel units; the speed of electrical impulses within and between parts of the brain can be measured; and other characteristics can be quantified reliably and objectively by instruments.

A major limitation of mechanical devices is that these instruments are more easily used in the laboratory than in natural settings. Furthermore, the use of any instrument should be carefully checked to see if it introduces any change into the natural environment under study. Any alteration of the setting may change the measure of what is being studied. A researcher may expect a television camera to provide useful information for a study but find upon its introduction to a classroom that the camera significantly changes the environment and interacts with the setting so much that it cannot record the usual or natural interactions which take place when it is not a part of the scene.

During the planning stage of a study, the researcher should find out about mechanical devices available for use in the study, investigate carefully how they could contribute to the study's needs, and then use them for their value in the refinement of observations. Since the researcher wants to remove personal influences external to the natural setting as much as possible, mechanical instruments can make a large contribution to a research study.

Tests

A large portion of psychological and educational data consists of observations made by testing devices used as measuring instruments. When possible, the sophistication provided by well-developed and validated tests should be utilized for research studies. Tests also serve as **operational definitions** of that which is being measured. Researchers should consider three questions when developing or selecting tests for research studies:

> **What should be measured?**
> **How can it best be measured?**
> **How do I know that I am measuring what I intended to measure?**

Through the tasks on a test, a direct relationship should be established between the characteristic and its definition.

The major role of educational tests is to measure in the **cognitive domain.** Psychological tests are designed to measure other aspects of human behavior. The next section on measurement deals directly with educational and psychological tests.

Other Techniques

Less used techniques for aiding in educational observation will be discussed as tools for specific uses in the chapters on research methodology—historical, descriptive, or experimental. Several techniques are **questionnaire, interview, attitudinal scale, opinionnaire, self report,** and **sociogram.**

☐ CHECK YOUR UNDERSTANDING

After looking up the denotations in the glossary for "other techniques," which of those listed would seem to be most useful for each situation that follows.

Keep in mind that more than one may be used effectively. Be prepared to defend your choice.

1. The president of a large educational association wants to collect demographic data about the membership.
2. The resident hall director asks you, the 10th floor assistant, to find out how many of the 30 present residents will graduate next May and if they plan to move to graduate housing.
3. A researcher wants to establish the social structures of a class before and after a unit on self-awareness.
4. A researcher wants to determine the student interest levels about current world events before and after a unit on reading newspapers.
5. A social scientist is studying the feelings of different ethnic groups toward refugees from a war-torn country migrating to your country.

Answers

1. Questionnaire
2. Interview—possibly a questionnaire
3. Sociogram—possibly a self report
4. Self report
5. Attitudinal scale or opinionnaire

Measurement

What is measurement? It is the process of measuring. Simple enough? Lyle Jones would say no, not really. Jones reports that the word "measure" has 40 different meanings and may refer to any of the following uses: the process of, the result of, the instrument for, and the units used in measuring (Jones, 1971, p. 335). Agreement on one meaning of "measurement" appears unlikely given this complexity, especially upon considering the many purposes measurement serves.

The major purpose of all measurement is to perform observation to provide information about specifically indicated characteristics of objects, organisms, or events, where that information will be numerical representations of the attribute being studied. The outcome of measurement for research is a set of observations to be used as data. Measurement **quantifies** with an accuracy not available from the human senses alone and extends observational procedures beyond direct observation.

The subject of measurement is not the objects themselves, but some property of the objects. A "room" itself is not measurable, but its variables of length, width, height, and volume can be measured. These characteristics can be expressed in **quantitative data.** Human subjects are *not* measurable, but they too can be measured on such characteristics as height, physics achievement, motivation, creativity, or any other trait that can be isolated. Since the characteristics of most concern in education are not quantifiable by simple mechanical devices such as rules, scales, and odometers, special problems are associated with educational measurement. The rest of this chapter introduces those measurement principles most directly related to educational research and presents selected topics of practical use.

A Definition

Since the words "measure" and "measurement" are used in so many ways, we will use this working definition:

> *Measurement is a process of assigning by rule a numerical description to the observation of some attribute of an object, person, or event.*

The remainder of this chapter investigates the *process* of measurement as used by the educational researcher, as a means of observation.

The process of measurement is basically the same for the many sciences—physical and human—but the techniques used to assign the numerical descriptors and the precision with which they can be assigned vary considerably. All measurement is made according to rules. The rules for measuring characteristics of physical objects—such as boards, desks, and doghouses—are much better than rules associated with such attributes as motivation, creativity, and biology achievement. Kerlinger says:

> Measurement is a game we play with objects and numerals. Games have rules. It is, of course, important for other reasons that the rules be "good" rules, but whether the rules are "good" or "bad," the procedure is still measurement. (1973, p. 427)

To understand attempts to quantify traits like intelligence, creativity, and motivation as measurement requires the understanding that assigning a number constitutes measurement. Any property that can be isolated can be measured. The property may be complex and the rules for dealing with it may not be "good" at this time, but the scientist continues to refine the rules. He or she may be encouraged by the thought that if something exists, it must be measurable through assignment of a numerical description.

It is possible to satisfy our definition of measurement with poor procedures. Poor procedures develop from lack of knowledge about setting up an **isomorphic** relationship between the structure of measurement (the rules) and some numerical structure which includes the same rules. For example, if a researcher collects a set of data and wants to find an arithmetical average (mean), she or he first must be sure that the data are amenable to the two processes of addition and division. If the data are the carefully measured heights of 25 first-grade children, the average would be meaningful, since the rules are isomorphic to the structure of arithmetic. If the data were hair color of the same 25 students and the researcher assigned numbers of 1 for brown, 2 for blonde, 3 for black, and 4 for red, the data could not be averaged. The rules of assignment would not, in this case, be isomorphic to the structure of the arithmetic processes. The arithmetic for averaging one blonde at 2 and one redhead at 4 can be performed, producing $(2 + 4) \div 2 = 3$. The problem then becomes interpreting the resulting 3. It has no real-world meaning, because our measurement rules do not permit the arithmetical operations of addition and division needed for a meaningful interpretation of the 3. The kinds of data which are collected and the rules used to collect them dictate what kinds of interpretive procedures can be used. Since a large part of data for research is generated from measurement, this topic must be well understood both by those who use the results of studies and those who conduct them.

The idea of distinct levels of measurement is important for the educational researcher when he or she must treat collected data. The operations that can be performed on a given set of scores depend on the rules used in the numerical assignment. The next section discusses four distinct levels of measurement and their relation to the research process (Gardner, 1975).

Four Levels of Measurement

The levels of measurement may be presented in hierarchical order. We will begin here with the lowest level. The factor which limits manipulation of data characteristic of a particular level is—as mentioned before—the rules used in numerical assignment. These rules are determined by either the nature of the variable or our lack of ability to develop appropriate rules.

Nominal Scales. Measurement at its lowest level involves numerical assignment simply to classify characteristics into broad categories. In the earlier hair color example, the classes brown, blonde, black, and red, described numerically, could have been described just as easily with some set of symbols other than numbers—alphabetical symbols, for example. In fact the symbols—brown, blonde, black, and red—would serve as well as any numerical expression for the categories, except for the convenience of recording. Any set of symbols used to categorize an attribute into distinct classes constitutes a *nominal scale*.

Since other symbols besides numbers can be used to classify nominal variables, some experts in measurement exclude as measurement the process of assigning numerals for identifying categories of classification where the numerals *cannot* be treated mathematically. If this procedure were excluded from measurement, it would prevent many educational procedures for quantification from being called measurement.

There are two rules for nominal measurement: (1) all the numbers of a **level** of a particular attribute are assigned the same numeral and (2) no two levels are assigned the same numeral. The classes must be **exhaustive** and **mutually exclusive.** The numeral used to identify the class is assigned arbitrarily and the numerals cannot be treated mathematically. Nevertheless, since the elements assigned to each class can be counted and compared mathematically, it seems for our purposes that procedures for nominal scaling are legitimately considered measurement (Kerlinger, 1973). The only relationship that can be found among categories and given attention is that of equivalence or the lack of equivalence. After the subclasses have been counted, a statement can be made about the frequency count in each class. Statements about the class with the highest frequency of occurrence, the class with the lowest frequency, and classes that have the same frequencies are also possible. Comparison by percentage or ratios of totals can then also take place.

Statements about results of nominal scaling can only be statements regarding same classes or different classes. In a running race, the finishers can be compared as finishing in the same time (tied) or different times. If the results were reported with only information about ties and differences, the reported data would be at the lowest—or nominal—level. Reported in this way, the operations that can be performed on the data about running ability are limited by the rules of assignment, not by the nature of the attribute itself. The importance of using the "best" rules for assignment of numbers is pointed up by the race example which used a "poor" rule.

Some variables are amenable only to the nominal measurement scale. Examples include sex, race, eye color, and hair color, where criteria can be set up only for broad categories with no order as to relative number values for numerals used for assignment. However, the members of each category can be counted and comparisons made among frequencies for the categories.

Ordinal Scales. The next higher scale of measurement adds rank ordering to the rules of assignment. **Ranking** is possible whenever the classes, in addition to being different, are in some relation such that *a* is greater than *b* and *b* is greater than *c* through all of the classes. The result is an *ordinal scale.*

The basic difference between a nominal and ordinal scale is that, in addition to the relation of equivalence, the relation of *greater than* has been incorporated in the rules of assignment for the numerical descriptor. The numbers assigned as ranks are quantitatively relative in regard to the trait being measured, but they do *not* indicate quantity in absolute terms nor are the intervals between the numbers necessarily equal.

For example, if a running race is assumed to measure race-running ability, then in addition to categorizing only same or different in regard to the trait, a ranking will permit statements about how the runners compare relatively. The runner finishing first has greater race-running ability (at least for the one race) than all other runners, the second finisher has more than all others except the one who finished first, and so forth. Statements about the relation *less than* can also be made in rank ordering. The rule for assigning numbers to ranks utilizes a numerical scale which permits, in addition to statements about the same or different class, a comparison of relative quantity among the numerical description of ranks.

Interval Scales. The next higher scale of measurement is introduced when the rules of assignment involve numerical description such that numerically equal distances on the scale represent equal numerical distances or quantities of the attribute being measured. If the assignment of numbers is made in such a way that the length of the distance between objects can be determined from the scale values, then the measurement is *interval scaling.*

To qualify as an interval scale, equal distances on the measuring scale must represent equal distances on the property being measured. This permits statements about differences *within* the scale. The thermometer is an example of a measuring instrument that measures at this level. A difference of 5 degrees any place on the scale is the same as a difference of 5 degrees at any other place on the scale. If the unit is the degree, then the two 5s represent the same quantity ($15 - 10 = 5$ and $175 - 170 = 5$). If the unit were instead a rank, the difference of 5 ranks would not necessarily represent the same absolute difference. If assignment of a numerical descriptor is characterized by use of a constant unit and an arbitrary zero point, then the measurement is interval scaling.

To continue our example, in addition to ordering the finish of a running race, timers could measure runners' times with a stopwatch. Assume that the first three finishers had the following times: 54 seconds, 56 seconds, and 60 seconds. Statements could be made about intervals between pairs of runners—for example the interval between second (56 sec) and third (60 sec) is two times as long as the interval between first (54 sec) and second (56 sec):

$$(60 - 56) = 2(56 - 54) \text{ or } \frac{60 - 56}{56 - 54} = \frac{4}{2} = 2.$$

Use of an ordinal scale to report the rank order of one, two, three associated with first, second, and third place does not give this information.

The rule for assigning numbers on an interval scale permits statements about distances within the measuring scale. The equal interval on the attribute being measured allows intervals to be added or subtracted. Statements about ratios of differences within the scale can be made. However, a restriction is placed on ratio statements comparing original measurements, because the rule of assignment involves an arbitrary zero point. For example, the temperature of 50 degrees (either Celsius or Fahrenheit) is only twice as much as 25 degrees when the researcher speaks of measurements within the scale. A reading of 50 degrees does *not* represent twice as much heat as a reading of 25 degrees, because the zero on the thermometer does not represent a total absence of heat.

Ratio Scales. The highest level of measurement is obtained when the rules of assignment include an **absolute zero** for the scale. The zero for such a scale represents a total lack of the attribute which is being measured. If assignment of the numerical descriptor includes all of the rules for assignment of the lower scales plus a true zero point, the measurement is on a *ratio scaling*.

Numbers on a ratio scale represent absolute amounts of that attribute being measured. Jimmy, who weighs 86 pounds, is twice as heavy as his brother, who weighs 43 pounds. Compare the measurement of weight with the measurement of temperature. A temperature of 86 degrees does not represent twice as much heat as a temperature of 43 degrees.

Since most educational questions are based on psychological factors rather than physical factors, the educational researcher will only rarely be involved with variables which permit measurement on the ratio scale. From the viewpoint of educational research, the distinction between interval and ratio scaling is not important. It thus becomes convenient to think of three scales rather than four when choosing statistical designs for studies. Table 11–1 shows the characteristics of the four types of scales, defining relations and statistical procedures appropriate for each scale.

Using the Scales. Let's return now to discussion of the running race described earlier. What can be said about the running ability of two brothers, the older being the first-place finisher (54 sec) while the younger brother ran the race in 108 seconds? These statements can be made on the basis of the differences in the times for running the race:

1. The two brothers have different amounts of race-running ability (nominal).
2. The winner of the race had the greater race-running ability (ordinal).
3. The difference $(60 - 54 = 6)$ between first and third place is only one-ninth of the difference $(104 - 54 = 54)$ between the two brothers (interval).

Can it be said that the winner at 54 seconds has twice the race-running ability of the brother who ran the race in 108 seconds? Obviously the answer is *no* because there is no absolute zero for the variable being measured—race-running ability. Therefore the data are not ratio scaled. Since the elapsed time *is* measured on the ratio scale, it can be said that the younger brother took twice as long to run the race as his brother did, but the rules of assignment of the numerical descriptors do not allow statements of race-running ability at the ratio level of measurement. The higher the level of scaling, the more information the data contain; therefore, the researcher should develop measurement procedures which generate data at the highest possible level.

Characteristics of Measuring Instruments

Although the educational researcher deals with objects and persons, he or she does not measure objects and persons. In general, the concerns of measurement are with properties or traits of objects and persons. Are we thus to assume that the researcher measures properties and traits? In most cases the answer is no, since the attributes being considered do not allow the type of direct measurement possible when a carpenter measures a board with a steel rule. Studying the trait of creativity, or measuring the trait of creativity, allows neither direct observation nor direct measurement. Physical characteristics are, in general, open to direct measurement, while personal characteristics must be measured indirectly.

Since the properties of human subjects which are of interest to educators are not visible, the educational researcher will usually be looking for effects that indicate or give clues about the trait being studied. There are some analogies to this process in the physical world. Thermometers are used to indicate the effect of temperature differences on a liquid (alcohol or mercury) in a tube. The thermometer does not measure temperature directly, but a scale along the side of the tube indicates differences in temperature *indirectly*. In education, the achievement test for physics is intended to measure achievement in physics *indirectly,* because what a student knows can not be displayed for public inspection. Most measurement in the human sciences has the same characteristics of measuring indirectly as the physics test does. Measurement activities for researchers involve developing the ability to define what is being measured, finding or inventing instruments to measure, and establishing a relationship between that being measured and the measuring instrument.

The following sections discuss the properties of measuring instruments: validity, reliability, and usability. Each property will be considered in relationship to other aspects of the research process.

Validity

The most important property of any measuring instrument is its validity. Validity of a measuring device is the degree to which the device measures what it is supposed to measure. A measuring stick that is marked in feet can be used to measure the dimensions of a table and the measurements will be listed to the nearest foot. Is the device valid? Yes, it measured the characteristics of table width and length. How accurately it measured these characteristics is another question. Could a furniture maker in a distant city use measurements that were given to the nearest foot for width and length to build a table that would fit neatly into a dining room alcove also reported to the nearest foot? She might do this by good luck, but not by good management. The measurement rule useful for the assignment of table measurements is not presented in units of a foot. *A measuring device is valid to the degree of accuracy with which it measures that property to be measured.* The result of a measurement should quantify *what* it is supposed to measure and do it accurately.

In measuring physical characteristics, establishing validity is not a large problem. To convey the size of the table to the furniture maker, the unit of measure could be made as small as necessary by calibrating the measuring stick into smaller equal parts. The directness of physical measurement also contributes to establishing a high degree of validity in measurements for physical properties. In contrast, many of the properties that the educational researcher deals with allow only indirect measurement and questionable definition of the traits. Questionable definitions mean that the validity of the measurements is also questionable. It thus becomes necessary to state validity in terms of *degrees* of validity.

The degree of validity for each measuring instrument (mechanical or test) used in research must be determined and reported. The researcher should establish (1) general validity, (2) the specific type of validity, and (3) the appropriateness for using the instrument in the present study. Validity for mechanical instruments is relatively easy to establish, while test validation is more difficult. For a thorough discussion and bibliography on validity, see Cronbach (1971).

Reliability

The ability of a measuring device to do whatever it does consistently is known as reliability. For a measuring device to have high reliability, it must do whatever it does in the same manner all of the time. The definition of reliability makes no reference to a device being able to do what it does properly. Reliability requires only that it perform its function with consistency. A school dismissal bell that is set to ring at 3:00 P.M. each day but instead rings at 2:50 P.M. each day has a high degree of reliability. Is this a valid instrument? No! To be valid, the bell must do consistently what it is used for—that is, it must ring each day at 3:00 P.M. To ring consistently at 2:50 P.M. is enough to establish reliability, but validity has one more attribute to be considered—that of doing what it is being used for.

The degree of reliability is always less than perfect, since all measurement contains some amount of variability. Variability associated with measurement is referred to as **error.** The school bell that rings at 2:50 P.M. each day does not ring at exactly the same time, since the triggering mechanism is affected by factors of temperature, humidity, and such chance errors or factors of the mechanism itself that cause it to vary the time that it rings. The error is likely to be small, since mechanisms set to ring bells tend to perform much the same each time. As the amount of error associated with measurement increases, the reliability of the measuring instrument is lessened, and in turn our confidence in the measurements is correspondingly lessened. The measurement lacks reliability to the degree that error is associated with assignment of the quantification.

Exact measurement of continuous variables does not exist, because any recording by units involves the concept of a reported value representing a range or interval on the measuring scale, thereby building some error into the measurement. Most variables of educational concerns are continuous, although the most important element of the educational process—the human being—is a discrete variable. When quantifying a human population, only positive whole numbers can be used. Most traits, however—like motivation, history achievement, or scholastic aptitude—can take any values on scales used for measurement at the choice of the person who decides the rules for measurement. Even measurement of variables by assignment to categories includes nearness when the variable is continuous. Not all eyes that are assigned to the class of "blue" are exactly the same shade, and some in that class may be very close to another assignment.

Additional error is involved in reading dials and marks on measuring devices. The readings on the dials and scales of measuring devices will vary, depending on the person reading them and the different relative positions of the readers. Differences in interpretation of scoring responses on tests contribute to variability in those scores. As previously mentioned, instruments used to measure are themselves a source of variation through imperfections within themselves. Chance errors further reduce the reliability and in turn the validity of measurement. Sources of chance errors include:

1. Imperfections in the measuring instrument itself
2. Interpretations—reading or scoring—of the instrument information
3. Inconsistency in the subjects being measured

The chance error referred to here is not to be confused with a mistake. Error in measurement has more to do with variation. The more variation associated with the quantification, the less the reliability or the more the unreliability. "The degree of reliability of a set of measurements is a very important consideration, both in the practical day-to-day use of tests and in empirical research (Stanley, 1971, p. 356).

Prediction is a part of all scientific work. If a researcher is to make predictions, the data used as a basis for the predictions must be generated by reliable measurement procedures. Reliable conclusions are based on reliable data. Low **correlation coefficients** in studies of association (**correlation**) can be the result of data that are not reliable.

Reliability is one factor contributing to the degree of validity for measuring instruments. A test is not able to do what it should do (validity) without doing it with consistency. The relationship between validity and reliability is best stated formally in this way:

Reliability is a necessary but not sufficient condition for validity.

Of course, a test may do what it does with high reliability but may still not be doing what it should. Reliability for a test instrument is usually established by a statistical procedure using correlation or **internal consistency** methods. Several sections of Stanley's (1971) discussion of reliability are devoted to what he calls "logical and empirical aspects" of determining reliability. The following are mentioned in his discussion as sources of variation that affect test reliability:

I. Lasting and general characteristics of the individual
II. Lasting but specific characteristics of the individual
III. Temporary but general characteristics of the individual
IV. Temporary and specific characteristics of the individual
V. Systematic or chance factors affecting the administration of the test or the appraisal of test performance
VI. Variance not otherwise accounted for (chance) (p. 364)

These topics are especially important in influencing how the researcher views measurement within the study and in affecting the eventual research conclusions. Building high reliability into measurement procedures contributes to increasing the validity of the measurements and, in turn, the accuracy of the conclusions. The researcher must keep in mind that establishing reliability for measurement is necessary but that establishing validity, which includes the condition of reliability, is more important.

Usability

The **usability** of a measuring device refers to its practicality for a particular situation. Major concerns for the researcher are administration, collection of data, interpretation of data, and cost of time and money. Each of these must be considered in light of the others. A movie camera might provide an excellent way to observe a situation, but to be assured that the introduction of the camera is having no effect on the interaction may take special attention. The cost of concealing the camera and related logistics may be too expensive for the budget and/or may not be practical for the natural setting. In most cases, if the use of mechanical devices is feasible, cleared for use by the administration, and not too expensive, they should be used. The data are easily obtained using such devices and in general are also easy to interpret.

Special problems arise with the use of educational/psychological tests. An individually administered test might provide the best data in a particular study, but the length of time involved in gathering data with few testers used for test administration might affect the validity of the data. An individually administered test might also be too expensive for the research budget.

In administration, factors to be considered are recording of responses, the time required and the number of sessions needed, and standardized instructions for both those administering and subjects taking the test. If the test will be used in different places with different groups, the conditions of the setting must be as similar as possible to make valid comparisons. Scoring procedures should be sophisticated to provide data which can be meaningfully organized and treated for results. For research purposes, **raw scores** are usually used, but **standard scores** provided by standardized tests may be used if they are appropriate for treatment procedures. With a large number of subjects, machine-scoring services for standardized tests or hand-scoring procedures using scoring masks can save time. Either of these methods can also be used to score data efficiently, organize the data for treatment, and report results for interpretation.

Proper administrative procedures are important to the reliability and validity of the measurement. It is unfortunate that many otherwise excellently planned research studies are rendered invalid or have their validity reduced because of data obtained through casual approaches to using measuring devices and/or scoring. Scoring problems are created mainly when responses must be judged subjectively by the scorer. Reliability and in turn validity of measurement are enhanced by carefully administered measuring devices and attention to detail in all scoring procedures. Both later chapters and educational measurement books will help the researcher establish appropriate procedures for particular problem areas.

Other Characteristics

Other characteristics of measuring devices are important in varying degrees depending on how the researcher will be using the scores. Ebel (1972, pp. 359–382) lists 10 important characteristics for classroom tests that researchers can also consider as important to other measurement procedures for research. They are *relevance, balance, efficiency, objectivity, specificity, difficulty, discrimination, reliability, fairness,* and *speededness.* Each is important in its own right and should be considered to the degree that it relates to the measurement being used for the study, regardless of whether the measuring instrument is a test or some other measuring device. Ebel's list of 10 characteristics for a classroom test is especially important for a study that requires that a special test be developed. Selecting a test from among standardized tests is discussed in the next section.

Choosing a Test

Although not all data for educational research are generated by tests, the paper-and-pencil test is widely used for educational measurement. The researcher who decides that testing is the best way to obtain the necessary data must decide between an existing test or a test to be developed especially for the particular study. Much time and effort are required to constuct a high-quality test. Considerable skill is also required to accomplish the task. For these reasons, researchers in general look to existing instruments first. Instruments developed for other research studies may be appropriate for similar studies, and much time can be saved if an *appropriate* testing instrument has already been created. The emphasis must be on appropriateness because what might be an excellent measuring device (test) in one situation may not be so in what appears to be a similar setting. Two references for prepared tests are *The Mental Measurements Yearbook* series (Buros, 1978) and *Tests in Microfiche* (Educational Testing Service, 1975 to date). Information about most standardized tests is available in the yearbooks, and *Tests in Microfiche* (TIM) lists and gives copies of tests which have been used in research studies but have not been published as standardized tests.

Thousands of tests have been written which cover very broad areas of achievement (test batteries) through the continuum to very specific areas (for example, marital communication). Tests and scales in TIM are most likely to cover aspects outside the classroom scene and deal primarily with psychological and social aspects of education. The yearbooks include tests from all of the areas, but educational tests comprise a large portion of the entries.

The yearbooks include a list of standardized tests, a list of books about tests and testing, a periodical directory, a test publishers' directory, and indices. The researcher can find the following information about listed tests: test name, author, publisher, appropriate age (or grade levels), date, cost, references for information about its use, and one or more critical reviews of the test, in addition to other pertinent information. In addition to the achievement batteries covering several curricular areas, tests on specific subject matter are listed. Character and personality tests are divided into projective and nonprojective. Intelligence tests are divided into group and individual tests, with a special listing for tests that measure specific areas thought to relate to intelligence. In addition to multiaptitude batteries, areas such as mechanical ability, vocations, and interests are given separate attention. Miscellaneous tests range from "computer programming" to "courtship and marriage."

Selecting a test to be used for research purposes requires searching through all tests available to be sure that the test does measure what is to be measured. Some tests are usually on file in libraries and also available in specimen sets from test publishers. Several tests should be identified that may be appropriate, then compared on their important characteristics. The one that provides the most valid measurement for the particular study should be selected.

Guidelines can aid the researcher in organizing data about several tests to help in making comparisons for selection (see Figure 3–3). The guidelines can, of course, be modified by adding more categories or deleting any that appear in this sample list that are not important to the particular investigation. Sources for the needed information are *The Mental Measurements Yearbook,* the test manual, the test itself, and professional journals, such as *The Journal of Educational Measurement* and *Educational and Psychological Measurement.* An excellent way to tell what a test measures may be to take the test yourself.

TEST INFORMATION FOR

_____

(Name of test, date, and author)

1. Publisher
2. Cost
3. Purpose of the test
4. Grade levels or ages
5. Number of equivalent forms
6. Test content
7. Administration time and directions
8. Validity
9. Reliability
10. Norms provided
11. Test format
12. Scoring procedures available
13. Manual (complete? usable?)
14. Review(s) from Buros, *The Mental Measurements Yearbook*
15. Personal evaluation

FIGURE 3–3 Guidelines for Evaluating a Standardized Test.

If a test can not be located to meet the needs of the study, then developing a special test is better than using an inappropriate test merely to save time. Appendix A gives an overview of test development to guide a research worker who needs to develop or has developed a special test for a study.

Interpreting the Data

Once data are obtained they must be interpreted. Interpretation procedures depend on the type of scale that generated the data. Kerlinger says that the scales in behavioral and educational research are "mostly nominal and ordinal . . . , though the probability is good that many scales and tests used in psychological and educational measurement approximate interval measurement well enough for practical purposes . . ." (1973, p. 438). There is general agreement among researchers and statisticians that most of our data are not interval (as we would like them to be), but there is no general agreement as to what to do about it. In general, Kerlinger's preceding statement is accepted and most researchers use ordinal data as interval data with the assumption of equal intervals in scaling. To follow the rules rigidly would deprive the researcher of many techniques of analysis that have been shown to yield satisfactory results. On the other hand, when ordinal data are used as interval data, misinterpretations may occur. The paradox is not easily resolved, but those who oppose the use of the assumption of equal intervals apparently decrease in number each year (Gardner, 1975).

Nunnally agrees with Kerlinger when he says that those who oppose the use of the assumption of equal intervals "will have to admit that deviations from those assumptions usually have scant effects on the analyses which are performed" (1970, p. 21). He feels that most psychological data except nominal data and data obtained by ranking are meaningfully expressible as interval data. He adds:

> The real issue does not concern whether or not to use the intervals on measurement scales in mathematical analysis—if they are there, why not use them? The issue is one of which calibration of intervals will prove more useful in the long run. Consequently, there is nothing wrong with performing mathematical operations that take seriously the intervals of measurement when investigating intelligence tests, personality tests, and other measurement methods employed in psychology. With the foregoing considerations in mind, it would be foolish of psychologsts not to employ those powerful methods of mathematical and statistical analysis which assume interval scales, *unless the data were originally obtained from ranking methods*. (Italics added.) (1970, p. 21)

The conditions of measurement in education seems to be: when characteristics are described in categories, measurement is *nominal;* when characteristics are described through assignment of ranks or ordered in some way, measurement is *ordinal;* when the scale that assigns the numbers has equal intervals, measurement is *interval;* when equal intervals can be assumed for ordinal data without serious error, the data can be considered as *interval* for statistical treatment; and, of course, any measurement from absolute zero with equal units in the scale is *ratio* measurement. Selecting statistical procedures requires consideration of the condition of measurement and the level of the observations. These procedures are very important to the selection of the statistical design.

☐ CHECK YOUR UNDERSTANDING

The characteristic being observed for a study may direct the researcher to the most useful observational procedure. Taking into consideration the strengths and weaknesses of the several ways to observe, choose the best way to generate valid data for each of the following situations.

1. Measurement of history achievement
2. Interest in the physical sciences
3. Interests to direct students' career choices
4. Student beliefs about peer influence on behavior
5. Measure acuity of vision
6. Student attitude toward substitute teachers
7. Aggression of preschool children in a play situation
8. Past record of hostility in a student

Answers

1. Achievement test, either researcher-made or standardized. The test seems to be the most direct way to measure this characteristic objectively.
2. Unobtrusive observation. Although particular interests can be measured by self-administered devices, the question of how similar the reported data are to true interests is not answered. Probably the best way is to observe ongoing real-world events with no change for the subjects.
3. Standardized interest devices. This is a difficult task to deal with and should not be attempted except by someone who has given this topic long study. Well-accepted standardized devices are available to the researcher.
4. Questionnaire or personal interview. This situation is likely to require much information from the subject. The best way to ask for it is through a self-reporting device.
5. Mechanical device. Measurement of physical characteristics is best accomplished using mechanical instruments because of the high objectivity associated with them.
6. Rating scale. By providing a set of statements which the student rates on a scale, the attitude should be identified assuming the right statements are presented.
7. Checklist. Direct observation with a checklist that indicates occurrences of aggression in observed acts.
8. Anecdotal record. Past records may give indication of hostile tendencies. If not, interviews with parents, teachers, and others may give the needed information.

Summary

Valid conclusions for research studies rest on valid and interpretable information in the form of data. To get data of this kind, the researcher must use various techniques of observation to obtain data which give clear and undistorted signals for analysis procedures. The term "observation" has been used in a very broad sense to encompass all information-gathering techniques including, for example, visual viewing (through the senses), mechanical instruments, and educational/psychological tests. Any bit of data is called an observation.

Four psychological factors of observation are attention, sensation, perception, and conception. Attention is a condition or preparation for readiness to receive selected stimuli. Sensation is the actual receiving of physical impulses. Perception is the interpretation of received stimuli in light of past experience and knowledge. Conception is the creation of an interpretation in the form of a proposed answer through some intellectual process.

Observation of people suffers certain limitations simply because of human nature. The scientific approach to research furnishes procedures designed to reduce human errors associated with perception and conception. These procedures include objectifying observation by supplying background knowledge of the problem area, studying different viewpoints, communicating in clearly understood or defined words, examining data with a questioning mind, recording data in a system, and quantifying data when possible.

Researchers should train personnel specifically for each data-gathering procedure used in a research project, so that the observers become accustomed to the mechanics of gathering techniques. They should be prepared to use one or more of the following to assist in observation: unobtrusive observation, checklists, rating scales, scorecards, mechanical instruments, tests, questionnaires, interviews, attitudinal scales, opinionnaires, self reports, and sociograms.

Problems in getting a representative sample from direct observation can be overcome by carefully planning the observation through event sampling, trait sampling, or time sampling. Event sampling and trait sampling utilize behavior occurrences, while time sampling chooses time units for recording observations.

Measurement is the process of assigning a numerical description to observations according to a rule. In general, educational measurement assigns the number through an indirect approach, looking for indications of a factor's influence rather than measuring the factor directly as might be done in most physical measurement. Four levels of measurement—nominal, ordinal, interval, and ratio—form a kind of hierarchical order based on the rules they use for assigning numerical descriptions. This chapter discussed each as it relates to measurement practices and data manipulation. When choosing appropriate statistical procedures for data treatment, the researcher should consider the scale of measurement. Most data in the behavioral sciences—except those obtained by nominal assignment or by ranking—can be treated as interval data.

The characteristics of validity, reliability, and usability are also important considerations when building or choosing a high-quality measuring device for research purposes. Special attention has been given to test selection at the close of the chapter.

Previously reported research studies provide traditional, unique, and creative approaches to the very important area of observation. Even with these models, however, each new research study requires a structure tailored especially for the question under study. A researcher must be prepared with knowledge about how others have functioned but must also be ready to be creative in his or her own right in order to bring out new observational techniques. Those individuals who devote full time or a portion of their time to research are constantly developing their skills in observation to enhance valid research conclusions. In addition, new and better methods are being developed. As theoretical and practical knowledge grows, researchers will be provided with new tools to attack important problems in education. The educational researcher must keep abreast of the development of these new observational tools and utilize them to refine the state of educational research.

References

Buros, O. K. *The eighth mental measurements yearbook.* Highland Park, N.J.: Gryphon Press, 1978.

Cliff, N. Adverbs multiply adjectives. In J. M. Tanur, F. Mosteller, W. H. Kruskol, R. F. Link, R. S. Pieters, & G. R. Rising (Eds.). *Statistics: A guide to the unknown.* San Francisco: Holden-Day, 1972.

Cronbach, L. J. Test validation. In R. L. Thorndike (Ed.), *Educational measurement.* Washington: American Council on Education, 1971.

Dewey, J. *How we think.* Boston: D. C. Heath, 1910.

Ebel, R. L. *Essentials of educational measurement.* Englewood Cliffs, N.J.: Prentice-Hall, 1972.

Educational Testing Service. *Tests in microfiche.* Princeton, N.J.: Educational Testing Service, 1975 to date.

Flanders, N. A. *Analyzing teaching behavior.* Reading, Mass.: Addison-Wesley, 1970.

Gardner, P. L. Scales and statistics. *Review of Educational Research,* Winter 1975, *45,* 43–57. (A historical and contemporary consensus.)

Hopkins, C. D. *Describing data statistically.* Columbus: Charles E. Merrill Publishing, 1974.

Hopkins, C. D., & Antes, R. L. *Classroom measurement and evaluation.* Itasca, Ill.: F. E. Peacock Publishers, 1978.

Jones, L. V. The nature of measurement. In R. L. Thorndike (Ed.), *Educational measurement.* Washington: American Council on Education, 1971.

Kerlinger, F. N. *Foundations of behavioral research* (2nd ed.). New York: Holt, Rinehart, & Winston, 1973.

Neilson, N. P., & Arnett, G. W. *A scorecard for use in evaluating physical education programs in elementary schools.* Salt Lake City: University of Utah Press, 1955.

Nunnally, J. C., Jr. *Introduction to psychological measurement.* New York: McGraw-Hill, 1970.

Stanley, J. C. Reliability. In R. L. Thorndike (Ed.), *Educational measurement.* Washington: American Council on Education, 1971. (Excellent coverage of reliability and a bibliography.)

Van Dalen, D. B. *Understanding educational research* (3rd ed.). New York: McGraw-Hill, 1973.

Varela, J. A. Solving human problems with human science. *Human Nature,* October 1978, *1* (10), 84–90.

Webb, E. J., Campbell, D., Schwartz, R., & Sechrest, L. *Unobtrusive measures: Nonreactive research in the social sciences.* Chicago: Rand McNally, 1966.

CHAPTER FOUR

AN INQUIRY AID:
THE LIBRARY

A university library is no longer part of an ivory tower world; it is a practical, service institution, accountable for every aspect of its performance.
—James Thompson

The college or university library serves many purposes. It is a convenient place to wait out a sudden rainstorm, a quiet place to study when the residence hall is noisy, a source of information for assignments or readings, and a storehouse of knowledge. Most of what is known can be found in libraries. Every year libraries add thousands of books, monographs, journals, documents, and other materials to their collections. This body of knowledge is useful to the person who seeks ready-made answers to questions that arise. It also provides a sound basis for research studies. The search for information in the library is the major concern of this chapter. Although this search may be time-consuming, it is a necessary part of educational inquiry. Skill in the use of the library helps avoid spending excessively large amounts of time trying to locate all available information about a specific problem, minimizes frustrating fruitless evenings spent blindly searching in the wrong sources, and rewards the student with the desired material and a personal sense of accomplishment. This chapter is designed to help students make trips to the library personally rewarding and productive.

Collection development has always been the primary activity of academic libraries. Recent emphasis on interpreting these collections has resulted in library instructional programs and services which make the resources of academic libraries more accessible to all levels of users. In addition, increased sharing of resources among libraries now greatly expands any single collection. Automation has also entered the library field as an important new research tool—particularly automated computer searches available using selected data bases. Although services vary among libraries, library users can obtain current printed bibliographies suited to their needs for such familiar resources as ERIC, *Psychological Abstracts,* as well as many other collections which have been computerized.

In general, all libraries have the same facilities and offer the same services for students, although each library has a unique organization and regulations vary from one library to another. Most campus libraries have printed guides about layout of the resources, regulations, services, and special facilities. Some libraries conduct tours to explain exactly how they can be used. If a conducted tour is not available, a personal orientation tour will familiarize you with how and where information can be obtained. You will find the following essential to the use of the library for a research search:

1. Location of the card catalog and its organization
2. Location of the stacks. Find if they are open to students. If special permission can be arranged to use closed stacks, it should be obtained.
3. Procedures for checking out a book and tracing a book that is listed but not on the shelf
4. Determining whether **periodicals** are distributed through the stacks. If they are centrally located in a periodicals room, find it.
5. Location of the reference section and its organization
6. Location of special collections, such as indexes, curriculum materials, rare books, reserve books, and microfilms
7. Location of study and listening carrels
8. Information about borrowing books by interlibrary loan
9. Information about computer services including automated searches

This early orientation to the total workings of the library will do much to promote efficient work. For special problems that arise, the professional staff members of the library are anxious to provide their expert skill and knowledge to help in any way that they can. The reference section is an especially important part of the library, since most of the search in the library for research purposes is for material that is unknown to the person looking. This information can be discovered through the use of indexes, abstracts, and other **reference materials** found in the reference section. The information needed for a thorough understanding of a selected research problem, as well as the material for the resulting thesis chapter "Review of Related Literature," will be available through using the tools described in this chapter.

Scientists make progress by starting where others have stopped. Reviewing the literature allows an investigator to compile what others have found. A separate chapter or section in a thesis then formally presents the investigator's synthesis of previous studies about the topic under study. Historical research requires special consideration in formulating this section. Since the data to be used in testing the hypothesis for a historically-based question is from the past, the researcher must decide how to divide related literature from the data to be used in the study. Descriptive and experimental research rely heavily on related literature as a starting point for a study to aid in designing a study and as a reference point for interpreting and discussing new findings.

☐CHECK YOUR UNDERSTANDING

Take a tour of your campus library and be sure to find out all the information and procedures in the list on page 84. If no formal tour is available, seek out the information mentioned in this list from library personnel and printed guides.

Indexing the Library

Most of us learn quite young to use the index to a book when looking for a particular topic or to determine whether the book covers a topic of interest. We consult the index rather than resort to a page-by-page search. The library should be approached in the same way, by using the appropriate indexes. Generally, the main card catalog indexes all material in a library, but other special lists in other card catalogs throughout the library give a second listing in special areas and/or augment and supplement the main card catalog index.

Most large libraries use the Library of Congress classification system. Letters of the alphabet serve as principal headings (see Figure 4–1), with numerals standing for subcategories. For extensive holdings and libraries with individual collections, this system seems superior to the Dewey decimal system still used extensively as a classification system in public libraries and some college and university libraries. All books are coded and placed on the shelves serially according to the code prescribed by the classification system being used. A library guide gives directions within the library's specific organizational layout.

Typically the entries for a card catalogue are on 3″ × 5″ cards and include all or part of the information given in the Library of Congress listing. One card for each piece of material is alphabetized by the first letter of the author's last name. If the material was written by more than one person, a card will be entered for each author (see Figure 4–2). When no author credit is given in the book, the card will be entered alphabetically by the name of the editor, organization, or other relevant party.

Expect to also find a card listed alphabetically by title, disregarding *a, an,* and *the* (see Figure 4–3), and another listed by subject (Figure 4–4) either in the main index or in a separate index contiguous to the main index. The subject card helps to identify material when neither a title nor an author is known and when the researcher is making a survey of publications in a certain subject area. In searching subject indexes, and indexes for periodical literature as well, the key to success is determining the proper topic headings to look for in the index.

Classifications in the Library of Congress System

A		General Works—Polygraphy
B		Philosophy, Religion, Psychology
C		History—Auxiliary Sciences
D		History and Topography
EF		American History
G		Geography, Anthropology
H		Social Sciences
I		vacant
J		Political Science
K		Law
L		Education, General Works
	LA	History of Education
	LB	Theory of Education
	LC	Special forms and applications
	LD	US Universities and Colleges
	LE	American Education (Outside US)
	LF	European Education
	LG	Asia, Africa, Oceania
	LH	School Periodicals
	LI	vacant
	LJ	Fraternities, Societies
	LT	Textbooks
M		Music
N		Fine Arts
O		vacant
P		Language, Literature
Q		Science
R		Medicine
S		Agriculture
T		Technology
U		Military Science
V		Naval Science
W		vacant
X		vacant
Y		vacant
Z		Library Science—Bibliography

FIGURE 4–1   Major Headings for Library of Congress Classifications

A list of topics, or *descriptors,* is often available for periodical indexes and can be used to discover possible subject headings related to the question under study. An item is generally listed only once, so a complete search requires consulting a number of issues of the index for periodical literature. Begin with the most recent issue and work back through older issues. Bibliographies found with published articles give additional sources. However, bibliographies cite only sources prior to the publication of the bibliography and can never bring the search to the present, making search through more current sources still necessary.

LB1028.B755

Broudy, Harry S., comp.
Philosophy of educational research [by]
Harry S. Broudy, Robert H. Ennis [and]
Leonard I. Krimerman. New York, Wiley [1973]
   xvi, 942 p. 23 cm. (Readings in educational research)
   Bibliography: p. 893–921.

   1. Educational research. I. Ennis, Robert Hugh,
1927–joint comp. II. Krimerman, Leonard I., joint comp.
III. Title.

ISBN 0–47110625–9   27J173
370/.72   72   72–002332

FIGURE 4–2 An Author Card

LB1028.B755

   Philosophy of educational research.
Broudy, Harry S., comp.
   Philosophy of educational research [by]
Harry S. Broudy, Robert H. Ennis [and]
Leonard I. Krimerman. New York, Wiley [1973]
   xvi, 942 p. 23 cm. (Readings in
educational research)
   Bibliography: p. 893–921.

   1. Educational research. I. Ennis, Robert
Hugh, 1927–joint comp. II. Krimerman,
Leonard I., joint comp. III. Title.

ISBN 0–47110625–9   27J173
370/.72   72   72–002332

FIGURE 4–3 A Title Card

LB1028.B755

Educational research
Broudy, Harry S., comp.
Philosophy of educational research [by]
Harry S. Broudy, Robert H. Ennis [and]
Leonard I. Krimerman, New York, Wiley [1973]
xvi, 942 p. 23 cm. (Readings in
educational research)
Bibliography: p. 893–921.

1. Educational research. I. Ennis, Robert
Hugh, 1927–joint comp. II. Krimerman,
Leonard I., joint comp. III. Title.

ISBN 0–47110625   27J173
370/.72   72   72–002332

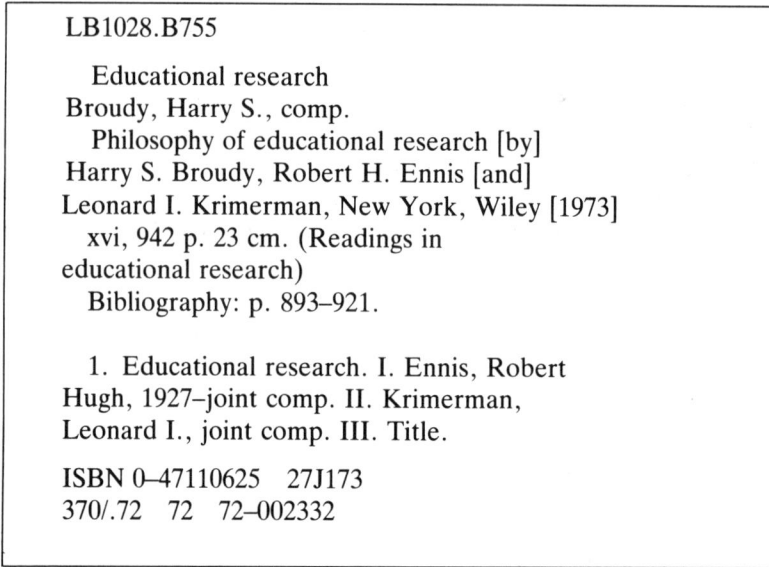

FIGURE 4–4   A Subject Card

If bound periodicals are distributed by classification through the library, an index for these will generally be located with the main index. The periodical index may instead be found along with the collection of current issues. If current issues and bound issues are together in a special collection, expect to find the periodical index in the same place. The entries in the periodical index indicate the names of periodicals and particular issues that the library has in its collection.

To find entries within the journals, the researcher must consult special indexes. One general index to popular magazines and two for professional educational literature are widely used in educational research:

Readers' Guide to Periodical Literature. New York: H.W. Wilson Co., 1900 to date. From 1900 to 1929, the *Guide* covered all periodical literature including educational journals. Since 1929 the *Guide* has listed only popular magazines, but it is still helpful in obtaining information outside educational journals.

Education Index. New York: H. W. Wilson Co., 1929 to date. A cumulative author-and-subject index to the contents of over 200 educational periodicals, plus proceedings and yearbooks on education and most publications of the U.S. government that deal with education. This index replaced entries about education in *Readers' Guide.* For entries about education prior to 1929, see the *Readers' Guide.* From September 1961 to September 1969, the *Education Index* did not include an author index.

Current Index to Journals in Education. New York: CCM Information Service, 1969 to date. A monthly companion to *Resources in Education*, this publication indexes articles in over 300 education journals and articles about educational concerns in other professional journals. In total, nearly 750 periodicals are indexed for articles about education. A main entry section is arranged alphabetically by clearinghouse name and numerically by clearinghouse accession number. An EJ code accession number is also listed. Other information and an annotation are included in each entry. (see Figure 4–5).

Instructions for using each periodical index, a list of the journals it indexes, and a key to abbreviations accompany each issue. A few minutes spent learning how to use a new index will save much time searching blindly through it. The primary use of a periodical index is searching within a subject area. Major subjects are broken down into subcategories—for example, "RESEARCH, Education"—with corresponding subtopics—such as "Aims and Objectives" and "Methodology" (Figure 4–6). Subcategories often change from issue to issue, depending on the articles listed. A search for reports about a specific person's research can be made by author. A title search is appropriate if a title is known but the author's name is not known. The many ways to use indexes become apparent as they are used.

Other indexes that educators find helpful include *Social Sciences Index*, *Humanities Index*, *New York Times Index*, *State Educational Journal Index*, *An Annotated Index of State Education Journals*, *Index to American Doctoral Dissertations*, *Art Index*, *Music Index*, *AIM-ARM Index*, and *Cumulative Book Index*.

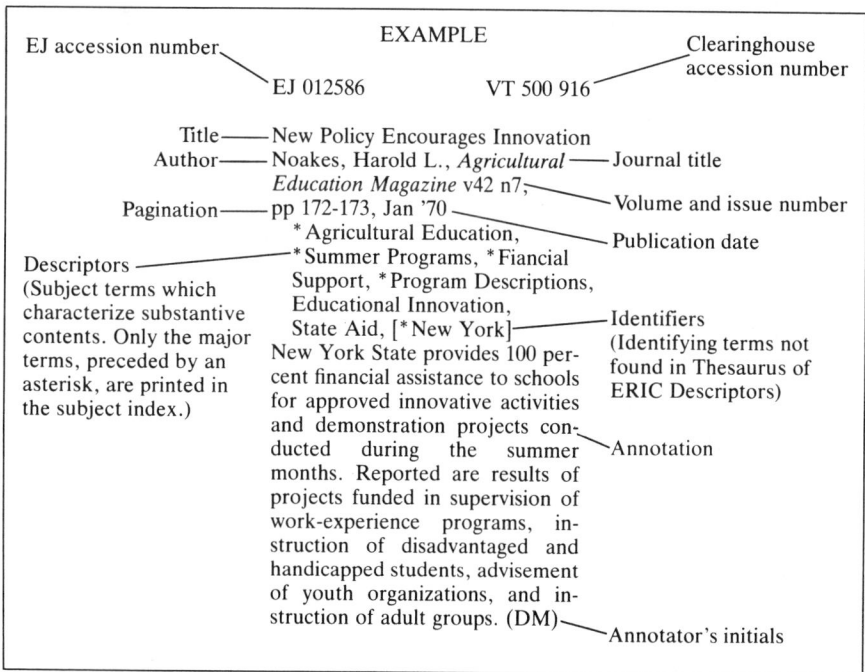

FIGURE 4–5 Entry from *Current Index to Journals in Education*

RENNER, John Wilson, and Lawson, A. E.
Piagetian theory and instruction in physics. bibliog pors Phys Teach 11:165-9 Mr '73
Promoting intellectual development through science teaching. pors Phys Teach 11:273-6 My '73
—and others
Evaluation of the Science curriculum improvement study. bibliog Sch Sci & Math 73:291-318 Ap '73

RENTAL services
Twelve reasons for renting electronic test equipment. R. E. Herzog. il Ind Educ 62:66-7 Mr '73

RENTSCH, George J.
Need for alternative schools within the public school system. por Sch Mgt 17:8-9+ Ap '73

RENZULLI, Joseph S.
Talent potential in minority group students. bibliog Excep Child 39:437-44 Mr '73

REPARATION
Making the victim whole. D. E. J. MacNamara and J. J. Sullivan. bibliog Urban R 6 no3:21-5 '73

REPAIRING
See also subhead Maintenance and repair under subjects, e.g. Audio-visual equipment—Maintenance and repair; School buildings—Maintenance and repair

REPEATED measurements designs. See Experimental design

REPERTORY grid technique. See Research, Educational—Methodology

REPETITION
Repeating questions in prose learning. W. M. Boyd. bibliog J Educ Psychol 64:31-8 F '73
See also
Reviews

REPORT cards
When a computer fills out students' report cards. J. H. Mulski and M. Levy. il Ind Educ 61:57-9 O '72

REPORTERS and reporting
Needed improvements in education news coverage as perceived by media and education gatekeepers. H. K. Jacobson. bibliog J Educ Res 66:274-8 F '73

REPORTS and records

Computer aids
GRADER: an automated gradebook system. N. J. Castellan, jr. il Educ Tech 13:56-60 Ap '73
Improving the education of migrant children. P. F. Hogan. il Am Educ 9:20-4 Ap '73
When a computer fills out students' report cards. J. H. Mulski and M. Levy. il Ind Educ 61:57-9 O '72

Forms
Evaluation of educational media. W. E. Hug. il Improv Col & Univ Teach 21:33-4 Wint '73

REPORTS to parents
Good news notes: painless plan for polishing PR. Nations Sch 91:40 Mr '73
School and home communications. A. L. Casey. Sch & Com 59:35 Ap '73

REPOUSSÉ work
Metal mask. R. Reinke. il Arts & Activities 73:36-7 Mr '73

REPRESSION (psychology)
Research findings on the kibbutz adolescent: a response to Bettelheim. J. Jay and R. C. Birney. Am J Orthopsych 43:347-54 Ap '73

RESEARCH
See also
Religious research

Methodology
Adolescence of political socialization. R. M. Merelman. bibliog Sociol of Educ 45:134-66 Spr '72
Problems in the analysis of patterns of abilities; with reply by G. S. Lesser. D. Feldman. bibliog Child Develop 44:12-20 Mr '73

Colleges and universities
Fictitious conflict between research and education. J. E. Lannutti. Educ Rec 54:83-4 Wint '73
In-service education: the university's role. P. W. Kirby. Educ Lead 30:431-3 F '73
Plea for research subjectivity. E. Scriven and A. Harrison. Improv Col & Univ Teach 21:38-9 Wint '73
Research and publication in the small college: a comparative study of faculty members' perceptions and attitudes. S. A. Clark. bibliog J Educ Res 66:328-33 Mr '73
Teaching-research controversy. J. H. Wilson and R. S. Wilson. Educ Rec 53:321-6 Fall '72; Same cond. Educ Digest 38:56-9 F '73

Graduate schools
Publication by the graduate student: some negative considerations. J. W. Cortada and J. H. Stone Educ Forum 37:179-81 Ja '73

RESEARCH, Educational
Capsulized R&D; Council of educational development and research. C. Reynolds. Am Educ 9:back cover Mr '73

Administration
Surveys for local education agencies: theoretical and practical considerations. F. J. Brieve and A. P. Johnston. Calif J Educ Res 24:79-92 Mr '73
Who does what—when, where and why? Cooperative institutional research program. il Col Mgt 8:40-1 Ap '73

Aims and objectives
In-service education: the university's role. P. W. Kirby. Educ Lead 30:431-3 F '73
Plea for research subjectivity. E. Scriven and A. Harrison. Improv Col & Univ Teach 21:38-9 Wint '73

Bibliography
California educational research association; research papers of the fifty-first conference. Calif J Educ Res 24:93-8 Mr '73

Criticism
How we all failed at performance contracting. E. B. Page. bibliog Phi Delta Kappan 54:115-17 O '72; Reply. J. K. Miller. bibliog 54:394-6 F '73

Evaluation
Good news: research on the nongraded elementary school. B. N. Pavan. bibliog El Sch J 73:333-42 Mr '73
Retrospect and prospect in educational research. W. Taylor. Educ Res 15:3-9 N '72

Implementation
Relationship of educational research to educational technology. A. M. Gallegos and H. F. Rahmlow. bibliog il Educ Tech 13:44-7 Ap '73
Research results for the classroom. E. J. Schneider and M. K. Burton. il Todays Educ 62:44-5 Mr '73

Methodology
Application of repertory grid techniques to the study of choice of university. W. A. Reid and B. J. Holley. bibliog Brit J Educ Psychol 42:52-9 F '72
Classroom behavior of teachers; ed. by N. Flanders and G. Nuthall; symposium. bibliog il Int R Educ 18 no4:427-568 '72
Dependent variable: measurement issues in reading research. J. R. and J. J. Tuinman. Read Res Q 7:413-23 Spr '72
Eta-squared and partial eta-squared in fixed factor ANOVA designs. J. Cohen. Educ & Psychol M 33:107-12 Spr '73
Learner analysis; some process and content concerns. T. M. Schwen. bibliog il AV Comm R 21:44-72 Spr '73
Research-service model for support of handicapped children. M. J. Guralnick. bibliog Excep Child 39:277-82 Ja '73
Technique for minimizing subject-observer looking interactions in field settings. J. A. Grimm and others. bibliog J Exp Child Psychol 14:500-5 D '72
What you see is not necessarily what you get. H. G. Petrie J Educ Res 66:inside cover F '73
Wheel and the table: the relative merits of two alternative instruments for collecting semantic-type data. C. Orpen. Brit J Educ Psychol 42:86-7 F '72
Within-subject variation, measurement error, and selection of a criterion score; with reply by F. M. Henry. R. Hetherington. Res Q (AAHPER) 44:113-18 Mr '73

State and federal aid
Trailblazer in an age of R&D. D. A. Erickson. bibliog Sch R 81:155-74 F '73

Student participation
Involving undergraduates in research. A. Rothstein. JOHPER 44:71-2 Mr '73

Teacher participation
Action research: a valuable professional activity for the teacher. B. G. Rainey. Clearing H 47:371-5 F '73
Undergraduate-graduate research collaboration program. F. V. Scalzi and P. Kovacic. J Chem Educ 50:205-7 Mr '73

Teaching
Research: the preservice missing link. M. B. Marks. J Teach Educ 23:453-6 Wint '72
See also
California educational research association

Great Britain
Retrospect and prospect in educational research. W. Taylor. Educ Res 15:3-9 N '72

FIGURE 4–6 A page from *Education Index*

Abstracts

Publications that briefly summarize research studies enable the scholar to keep up with current research in certain areas without going to original reports. Abstracts report enough about each study to give a clear picture of the problem and the scope of the study. In general, an abstract is complete enough to allow a researcher to decide whether reading the original article would be profitable. Abstracts can be obtained from a variety of sources.

Resources in Education (RIE),* first published in 1966, is a monthly publication of the Educational Resources Information Center (ERIC), a federally funded project that has the charge of identifying and listing those publications of interest to educators. The listing includes résumés of project reports, speeches, and other materials that are difficult to find through other sources. Materials listed in RIE are available to the researchers in either **microfiche** (MF) or hard copy (HC). A few listings are included for materials available only from an outside source, which is given in the listing. Microfiche is a filmed reduction from about 24 to 1 which permits reproduction of nearly 100 pages on a $4'' \times 6''$ card. Machine readers project the material on a small screen for individual viewing.

Costs for microfiche and hard copy are given with an ED code number for the citation (Example: ED 085 666) for access to ERIC materials. Many large libraries keep complete files of ERIC listings on easy-to-read microfiche cards. ERIC has a goal of having a copy of each important document of educational research and research-related materials on file plus other education-oriented materials such as bulletins, speeches, project reports, and much other information not otherwise generally available.

Included in each issue of *Resources in Education* are sections on document résumés, subject index, author index, institution index, new thesaurus terms, lists of other ERIC products, how to order ERIC publications, and how to order ERIC document reproductions. A companion publication, *Thesaurus of ERIC Descriptors,* lists descriptors for searching ERIC materials, descriptor groups, and a rotated descriptor display to aid in choosing likely descriptors.

An integral part of the ERIC operation is a series of clearinghouses scattered around the country, each devoted to a special interest area—for example, urban education. The clearinghouses acquire, review, abstract, and index documents for *Resources in Education.* In addition, they prepare bibliographies and interpretive summaries of ERIC-listed materials on special topics. Current addresses for all clearinghouses appear in each issue of *Resources in Education.*

Computer searches of all material listed in ERIC are available at any of several places that have the listings computerized. ERIC *tapes* and ERIC *tools* are also available for special uses. Special announcements about changes within ERIC appear in each issue of RIE, and current mailing addresses for computer searches and other services are also listed.

---

*Originally *Research in Education* (1966–1974), the title change to *Resources in Education* reflects the broader scope of the documents to be found in ERIC.

Psychological Abstracts gives summaries of studies, books, and articles in all fields of psychology along with many educational articles. Published by the American Psychological Association, each issue is indexed by subject and author. This is a good source for experimental research.

Dissertation Abstracts International: Abstracts of Dissertations Available on Microfilm or as Xerographic Reproductions gives a monthly compilation of doctoral dissertations submitted by United States, Canadian, and European universities. Each issue is arranged by broad topic with subject and author indexes. Complete copies or individual pages may be purchased. This publication continues *Microfilm Abstracts* (vols. 1–11, 1938–1951) and *Dissertation Abstracts* (vols. 12–29, 1952 through June 1969).

Other abstracts of interest to educators include *Exceptional Child Education Resources, Sociological Abstracts, Child Development Abstracts and Bibliography,* and *Mental Retardation Abstracts.*

Reviews of Literature

Some sources give reviews of educational research, usually organized chronologically. Articles listed by subject topics organize and integrate the research performed. This is usually the best place to get an early grasp of what has been reported, up to the date of the review's publication.

Encyclopedia of Educational Research is a publication of the American Educational Research Association, printed in about 10-year intervals (1940, 1950, 1960, and 1969). Long critical essays by specialists which summarize and interpret research within very specific areas of education (for example, Physiology and Psychology of Reading) make up the encyclopedia. The essays point to needed research and excellent comprehensive bibliographies accompany each article. An excellent overview of research in special areas of education makes this a good starting point for a search of the literature.

Review of Educational Research supplements the *Encyclopedia of Educational Research* by reviewing major research findings for more active fields between issues of the *Encyclopedia.* Before June 1970, each issue was devoted to a series of specific articles about a broader field—for example, educational evaluation. Since that date, reviews have been made about specific topics, but there is no general theme running through all the articles of one issue.

Encyclopedias

An encyclopedia is a reference work which contains a collection of articles giving general information about subjects or topics. An encyclopedia should be used as a first source in investigating an unfamiliar subject or as an overview.

The *Encyclopedia of Education* is comprehensive, covering the history, theory, research, and philosophy as well as the structure and fabric of education. *Education Yearbook,* 1972 to date updates the *Encyclopedia of Education.*

Other encyclopedias useful in beginning a search include *Encyclopedia Britannica,* and *Encyclopedia Americana.* Of a more specialized nature are *Encyclopedia of the Social Sciences, International Encyclopedia of Social Sciences, Encyclopedia of Sports,* and *Encyclopedia of Mental Health.* To locate encyclopedias about other very specialized areas, consult the library main card catalogue under the heading, "Encyclopedia."

Guides

For further help in locating materials, the researcher may turn to books called "guides." Although these guides are often used to help a person obtain needed information, many times they include basic information themselves.

Documentation in Education, by A. J. Burke and M. A. Burke, is a discussion of how to do research in education which includes long and useful bibliographic essays on the materials helpful in conducting research.

Sources in Educational Research: A Selected and Annotated Bibliography, by Theodore Manheim, cites and annotates basic titles useful in general educational research and covers the subject-oriented research—for example, comparative education.

Mental Measurements Yearbook, by Oscar K. Buros, gives information regarding forms, manuals, grade levels, publishers, and prices of educational, psychological, and vocational tests, plus reviews of the tests by testing experts. Published at approximately six-year intervals, these yearbooks represent the most thorough coverage of standardized tests available and include complete listings of books about testing, along with annotations.

Handbook of Research on Teaching, edited by Nathaniel L. Gage, contains articles about research on teaching. Special chapters on specific topics give overviews of research in special subject-matter areas. Chapter 5, "Experimental and Quasi-experimental Designs for Research on Teaching," by Donald T. Campbell and Julian C. Stanley, has been printed separately and has become a classic in the history of research design. Chapter 10, "Analysis and Investigation of Teaching Methods," by Norman E. Wallen and Robert M. W. Travers, is a must for all studies of teaching methodology.

Second Handbook of Research on Teaching, edited by Robert M. W. Travers, was prepared to update the first handbook but became a much more comprehensive source. However, coverage of topics does tend to be narrower in scope. Part II, "Methods and Techniques of Research and Development," is composed of chapters devoted to deep coverage of very specific topics of concern to a researcher—for example, "The Use of Direct Observation to Study Teaching" and "The Assessment of Teacher Competence."

Guide to U.S. Government Serials & Periodicals, by John L. Androit, includes an extensive listing of government publications about education.

Government Publications and Their Use, by Laurence F. Schmekebier and Roy B. Eastin, aids in identifying, locating, and using government publications.

References to References

There are some reference works that discuss information sources and how to use them in reference work and others that give comprehensive reviewing service for reference books.

American Reference Books Annual, published each year by Libraries Unlimited, Inc., aims to review all reference books published or distributed in the United States. The section on "Education" is subdivided for easy use by anyone searching literature. Included in some reviews are book reviews that have appeared in periodicals, giving an overview of reviews for the one book. A cumulative index to the first five editions has been compiled by Joseph Sprug. It is titled *Index to American Reference Books Annual 1970–1974: A Cumulative Index to Subjects, Authors, and Titles.*

A Guide to Reference Books (9th edition), edited by Constance M. Winchell, lists by author, subject area, and type of reference work important books in English and other languages. Supplements by Eugene P. Sheehy have augmented the listing of the eighth edition.

A Guide to Reference Material, by A. J. Walford, published in three volumes by the Library Association is international in scope and includes U.S. publications.

Reference Books: How to Select and Use Them, by Saul Galis and Peter Spielberg, lists about 200 basic reference books that are frequently used in the humanities and social sciences and gives a concise summary of the contents of each book.

Introduction to Reference Work (3rd edition), by William A. Katz, in two volumes gives detailed descriptions of reference works and how they are used. Part II of Volume II analyzes how a reference librarian finds answers. The accompanying flow charts diagram the reference process and give direction to organized library searches. These are valuable aids in developing skill in the use of the library.

Dictionaries

Dictionaries are reference sources which help define terms and often point out related terms.

Dictionary of Education, edited by Carter V. Good and prepared under the auspices of Phi Delta Kappa, gives entries for educational terms and terms from closely related disciplines.

Webster's New International Dictionary of the English Language is a general dictionary for use in writing.

Roget's International Thesaurus of Words and Phrases (or the abridged title) lists closely associated words as families. It too is useful during the writing process, helping a writer to choose the word most closely related to a certain idea to be expressed.

A glance at the reference section of a university library will reveal many books not mentioned in the foregoing sections. The brief coverage given here should provide, however, a way into a set a materials that will, in turn, lead to other sources of information. Types of reference works not mentioned here but useful for special problems include almanacs, biographical references, directories, atlases, gazetteers, reports of statistics, bibliographies, and newspapers.

A thorough understanding of how to use sources in locating information is a step toward building background for research problems and finding answers to questions. This working knowledge must be updated by checking for new reference materials listed in *American Reference Books Annual*. Current publications of older references should also be checked periodically for coverage, since they may expand their coverage or drop some coverages included in the past.

In addition to keeping current on the preceding references, the researcher needs to remain informed about bibliographical and information-retrieval systems currently available. Since this approach to locating sources is expanding so rapidly, a detailed description here would be less than useful in a short time. The researcher should seek up-to-date information about systems similar to ERIC and its retrieval systems. Learning how to choose descriptors for computer searches facilitates using these facilities which are expanding explosively at present. An up-to-date listing of the materials listed in retrieval systems is available from the Washington office of Educational Resources Information Center. Skill development in use of the library is a continuing process because of the rapid changes made in storage of information and paths to that knowledge.

Organizing a Library Search

A systematic library search starts with material that gives very broad coverage to topics. As the search continues, the scope of material should become more and more specific. A literature search for an educational question might well be organized according to the following steps, adjusting the reference materials to fit the study and topics to be covered.

Steps in a Search

1. List the variables being studied and broad topics of the study.
2. Look up each variable and topic in the *Encyclopedia of Education*. Update the coverage by consulting the companion publication *Education Yearbook*.
3. Look up each variable and topic in the latest edition of the *Encyclopedia of Educational Research*. Update the coverage from articles in the supplementing journal *Review of Educational Research*.
4. Select descriptors for ERIC materials from the *Thesaurus of ERIC Descriptors*.
5. Do a manual search of RIE and CIJE using the selected descriptors or initiate a computer search through ERIC using the descriptors.
6. Consult *Education Index* using the variables and topics as major subjects.

7. Check *Dissertation Abstracts International* and *Psychological Abstracts*. They are likely to have information for most educationally-oriented studies.
8. The path now becomes very specific as the search goes to articles and such. Bibliographies which accompany journal articles and books are helpful in getting leads to other related materials.
9. Finally, the search must be tailored to the study using special reference materials for special areas and following directions received from success to this point. The depth that will be needed for this specific search will also guide the reading to the desired point of closure.

Integrating the Steps

Among the steps listed for a library search, the first eight entries should be sufficiently rewarding for a student who is searching for information to be examined during a quarter or semester course. A person who is writing a review for a thesis, dissertation, or journal article will find need for further searching using the special services of the library—such as ordering dissertations from microfilm and other materials through interlibrary loan. Reading through guides and reference materials and consulting reference librarians should complete an exhaustive reading about the topic under study.

Efficient use of time spent in the library depends on at least two factors. The person must first know what to search for. Second, he or she must have knowledge of reference materials and skill in their use. Before starting a search, the student should decide how someone else might categorize the information needed. Once the variables for the search have been established in this way, the student can begin reading in these areas to get an overview of the topics. A broad overview provides the context for more specific topics. The *Encyclopedia for Education* and other more specific encyclopedias offer the broad coverage needed at this stage. Entries in these sources may not give information that will actually be used in the final paper's review section, but the time is well spent because early orientation to the area of study is important.

After the broad scope of the study has been assimilated, an overview of the research which has been done can be found in articles from the *Encyclopedia of Educational Research* and the companion publication *Review of Educational Research*. These articles present information in subtopics, usually sequentially so that the articles are chronological. The extensive bibliographies which accompany the articles allow for a broadening or narrowing of the reading. In addition to reports of conclusions from research studies, other related articles may be included by the writer.

To extend reading into specific studies and articles, the student should consult three periodicals. Using a study's variables and major topics as subject topics, the student will find direction from the *Education Index* to articles in over 200 education periodicals. Since articles may be categorized under subjects other than the terms originally chosen by the student, other subjects which could possibly include information for the study's background should be considered and investigated. Two periodicals from ERIC, *Resources in Education* (RIE) and *Current Index to Journals in Education* (CIJE), extend the coverage to educationally oriented articles in over 700 journals and a wealth of other information not generally available through other searches.

The keys to all material in RIE and CIJE are the descriptors found in the *Thesaurus of ERIC Descriptors*. These descriptors serve this set of materials in much the same way as subject topics serve *Education Index*. The rotated descriptor display is the entry point to the *Thesaurus*. By using the variables and broad topics of a particular study, listings of descriptors which contain these terms can be located. These descriptor listings identify categories which will help locate information. After deciding which descriptors in the display seem appropriate for locating material for the study, those descriptors should be found in the descriptors section of the *Thesaurus*. Here additional descriptors are listed which allow the scope to be broadened or narrowed according to subcategories listed for each descriptor.

There is no rule of thumb about how many descriptors should be used in a search. The more descriptors used, the more material will be listed for consideration. If a researcher chooses relatively few descriptors, some material may be missed. Too many descriptors will cause the researcher to spend time on some material not relevant to the study. After the list of likely descriptors is made, the next step is to go to RIE and/or CIJE and look for specific articles and material for the review. See Figure 4–7 for the plan of an ERIC search.

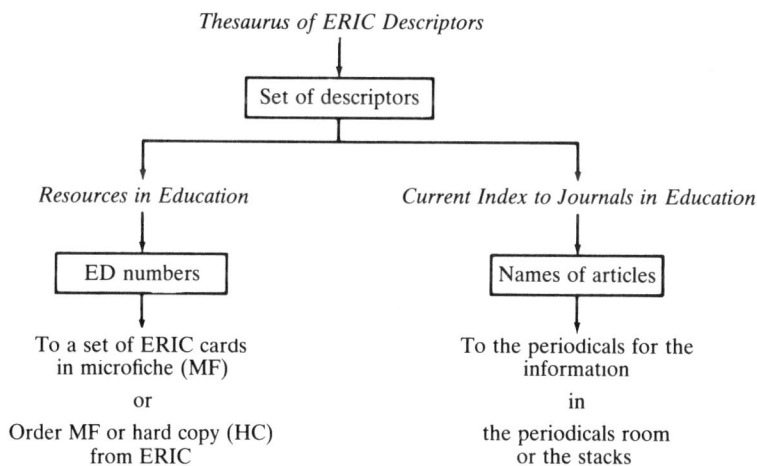

Thesaurus of ERIC Descriptors

Set of descriptors

Resources in Education

ED numbers

To a set of ERIC cards
in microfiche (MF)

or

Order MF or hard copy (HC)
from ERIC

Current Index to Journals in Education

Names of articles

To the periodicals for the
information

in

the periodicals room
or the stacks

FIGURE 4–7 Plan for an ERIC Search

When using RIE, the student first finds materials by title in the Subject Index under the descriptors selected from the *Thesaurus*. Following the title is an article code number preceded by "ED." For example, ED 067 788 identifies the article "Deafness and Mental Retardation." For more complete information about the article, the search can turn to the Documents Résumés section where extensive information including an abstract is provided. If the abstract suggests that the article is pertinent to the review, then the complete article is available in ERIC materials or from the original source.

When using CIJE, the student first finds materials by title in the Subject Index under descriptors selected from the *Thesaurus*. After the title is an EJ number which is then found in the Main Entry Section (see Figure 4–5) where more information is given. If the main entry suggests that the article is pertinent to the review, then the article can be explored in the publishing journal.

Dissertation Abstracts International and *Psychological Abstracts* are helpful in extending the search into possible new areas. Instructions for using these works are in the references themselves. An author index and a subject index are included in biannual issues of *Psychological Abstracts*. A computer retrieval service is provided through many campus libraries.

Direction for further maneuvering becomes difficult at this point, because of the many choices which must be made depending on the particular topics and the nature of the study. Bibliographies which accompany articles, dissertations, and other materials are helpful and may be particularly rewarding. Other reference materials mentioned previously may push the search still further as may use of guides to reference department materials.

☐CHECK YOUR UNDERSTANDING

Using the steps outlined on pages 95–96, at least through step 7, find citations to begin background reading for *one* of these topics:

1. How does an individualized reading program affect the reading ability of a disinterested reader?
2. How does classroom discipline affect creativity in elementary art objects?
3. How does the dropout rate change as a function of an increased intramural sports program at the secondary level?

Organizing the Information

A successful search of the research literature for information about a subject produces much material that must be recorded, organized, and reported. The student or researcher can do much to facilitate the above tasks while still in the library by structuring the recording of the information when it is first written down. What is recorded is dictated by the purpose or need for the information. Since our discussion is directed toward research, this section will discuss gathering background information for research studies. Other purposes will, in most cases, demand similar procedures but may require recording different information.

Using Cards

The first requirement for data recording is something to record on. Information should always be recorded on individual bibliographical cards or separate sheets of paper. Do not try to beat the system by using the backs of envelopes, sheets of wrapping paper, or other odd-shaped pieces of paper. All entries should be on the same size page or card to facilitate arranging them in writing the final report. Different sizes are cumbersome and smaller ones tend to get lost among the larger ones. Since the material will not necessarily be written from in the same order as it has been collected, each article, book, or other entry should be recorded on a separate sheet of paper or note card to facilitate organization for final writing.

Most long-time writers and researchers use cards because of the ease of arranging order and structure into a formally presented review of the literature. The cards allow much more flexibility in arranging material into interpretable form and for developing a narrative report. The size of the card is not crucial, but 4″ × 6″ is usually considered minimum, and 5″ × 8″ is more widely used. If a person writes quite a lot about each source or includes extensive quotations, the larger cards will help the researcher avoid using more than one card for an entry. For long copy and historical study data, 8½″ × 11″ paper may be best for recording narrative reports.

Information for the Card

The information to be recorded on the cards will vary with the nature of the study and the kind of material being read. The following sections direct the recording of data to allow for efficient organization and factual reporting in a review.

Bibliographic Entry. Since each research report includes a bibliography, the necessary information for the entry should be collected while the material is in hand. Second trips for material to complete an entry are not necessary if all the needed information is recorded along with the information from the material. The card should first have a complete bibliographic entry for the item as it would appear in a bibliography. The student should decide (with the help of any regulations that apply to selection) what form the final bibliography will take (APA, Campbell, Turabian, Dugdale, or similar style manual forms) and learn that form. The entry in Figure 4–8 is in APA form (American Psychological Association, 1974). Other styles vary somewhat, but in general they include the same information—for a book: author or publishing agent; complete title; place of publication; publisher; and date of publication. Other information may need to be included for special cases. See the **style manual** you choose in any case. An entry for a periodical is different and usually includes author, complete title, name of magazine or journal, volume number, pages, and date. Entries for other types of materials take special formats, and the manual should be consulted for the information necessary and the form to be used.

In addition to the entry, list the library call numbers somewhere on the card. With computer preparation of cards, call numbers are now being written across the top of cards rather than down the left side (example: LB1028.S39). This code may be included on the card above the bibliographic entry.

The final bibliography is easily assembled by alphabetizing the cards by author and typing directly from the cards. Make sure that all of the information for the entry is on the card before leaving the book or article.

Research Study. Recording information for a research study should include as a minimum the following additional information (see Figure 4–8):

A. Bibliographic entry
B. Purpose of study (include question asked and hypothesis)
C. Research method used (historical, descriptive, or experimental)
D. Kind of data used (test scores, judges' ratings, and so on)
E. Statistic used (chi square, median test, and so on)
F. Results and researcher's conclusions
G. Personal reaction
H. Any other information that the researcher deems important—such as description of the subjects studied

---

A. Anderson, H.E., Jr., & Bashaw, W.L. An experimental study of first grade theme writing. American Educational Research Journal, 1968, 5, 239-247.

B. The purpose of the present study is to examine differences in mode of discourse for first-grade themes. The general hypothesis is that stimulation in a given mode of discourse will improve the quality of compositions in that mode but decrease the quality of themes in another mode.

C. Experimental

D. Ratings of themes by readers

E. Analysis of variance

F. Results of the present study would seem to support Piaget's conjecture in some respects. The D themes required some logical organization of thought but a minimum of abstraction as compared to the writing of

(over)

FIGURE 4–8 Side One of a Bibliographical Subject Note Card (for Sample Study No. 4, page 231)

Other Material. Recording information from other kinds of sources is not as direct as recording about an actual study. The material will be organized differently and includes opinions, ideas, suggestions, and a host of other kinds of statements. Selecting important and significant material from an article based on the writer's opinion or other general writings requires skill that is largely developed by trial and error. The best guide is to record only what will bear directly on the subject under study, plus a summary of additional information found in the article. Those engaged in historical research in the library should use this type of note taking almost exclusively. Carefully selected notes that are complete and understandable provide the basis for answering the question by giving the background information and/ or data to be used in drawing conclusions. Carelessly collected and recorded notes provide little if any support in answering the research question and can cause great inconvenience and frustration.

General Considerations. When recording on the cards in the library, the researcher should set up certain guidelines to establish a firm data base for the study. Decisions about what is related should be clearly defined by specific parameters. As the reading progresses, these limits can be adjusted to narrow the scope or expand the scope. If the limits are set too close, the background data collected will be insufficient to support the study. If the limits are set too wide, on the other hand, the base will encompass more information than needed, resulting in wasted time in reading.

Information can be recorded as quotation, paraphrase, or summary. Regardless of the form, record the page numbers that correspond with the note, because this information will be needed when the note becomes a part of the paper reporting the literature review. Direct quotations are discouraged in final writing, but a direct quotation on a card can be used as such if the meaning is lost in a paraphrase. If you are quoting directly on your note card be sure to mark it with quotation marks for your information about how to handle it in the report.

Some Notes on Note Taking

1. Use cards or separate sheets of paper. Put only one reference on a card or sheet: 4″ × 6″ cards are easy to handle; 5″ × 8″ cards allow for more narrative.
2. Write the bibliographical entry and library call numbers at the top of the note card.
3. Classify cards by subject heading and/or color-coded edges on cards to help in the final organization. The classification may be organized around an outline for final writing.
4. Be sure that each note is written clearly and completely in a way that it will be understood when needed. Do not plan to recopy cards, since this introduces a chance for error. Use a typewriter if possible.
5. Develop skill in paraphrasing so that the original meaning remains, but the note is in your own words. Mark clearly all direct quotations and record the page numbers for each note.
6. Organize a filing system for all notes. Find a secure permanent place and file the notes as soon as they are made. If they must be carried about, an accordion folder with your name and address on it is a convenient way to transport them.
7. For those articles which are particularly important to the review and for material that requires quite long copy, the researcher should

consider photocopying the material rather than using several note cards. One note card with the bibliographical entry and a reference to the copy can be used to record the material.

Research-oriented Journals

There are many publications that report educational research, and a thorough search of their contents can be made through appropriate indexes. However, some journals are more research-oriented than others. At the risk of limiting your search (do not let this replace a more thorough search), the journals in the following list are presented as being research-oriented publications:

American Educational Research Journal
Educational and Psychological Measurement
Educational Researcher
Harvard Educational Review
Journal of Educational Measurement
Journal of Educational Research
Journal of Educational Sociology
Journal of Experimental Education
Journal of Special Education
Measurement and Evaluation in Guidance
Most psychological journals, including:
  Journal of Educational Psychology
  Journal of Experimental Psychology
  Journal of Psychology
  Journal of School Psychology
  Psychological Bulletin
  Psychological Review
Reading Research Quarterly
Research Quarterly
Review of Educational Research
Sociology of Education

Activities

1. Using the steps for a search and note cards prepare a reference list for one of the questions on pages 126–127.
2. Using the steps for a search, prepare a reference list and a set of abstracts for the references for a question from pages 126–127. (Do not forget to use note cards.)
3. Using a question from pages 126–127 in chapter 5 or one of your own, conduct a search of the research literature and prepare a bibliography of 12 entries which relate to the question. Use the steps for a library search to direct the quest, and obtain entries from as many different sources as possible.

This activity can be extended. For example:
   a. Prepare a note card for each entry according to directions given in the chapter.
   b. The bibliography can be extended to include an annotation for each entry.
4. Prepare a "Review of Related Literature" for a question that is agreed on by the student and instructor.
5. Investigate through the library sources of data banks of material related to your area of specialization. Include information about how to do a manual search and/or order a computer search. Keep this as a reference and update the entries every six months for a continuing personal reference.

Summary

The researcher spends time locating answers to important questions. Closely related to answering questions is the storage of the answers. Most information is to be found in libraries, making them an integral part of the research process. Researchers use libraries primarily to gather information about the field being studied, knowing that valid research is based on their knowing as much as they can about closely related topics. Skillful use of the library requires (1) an overall understanding of its organization, (2) knowledge of reference materials—indexes, guides, and so on—to ferret out the needed information and (3) skills in recording the information.

Indexes for the library have been presented to familiarize the student with a way of locating information quickly. In addition to the card catalogue that lists most materials except periodical articles, the *Readers' Guide to Periodical Literature, Education Index,* and *Current Index to Journals in Education* are all used to give complete coverage to educational information. For other areas, more specific indexes are available. Other aids to library search are abstracts, encyclopedias, guides, handbooks, yearbooks, dictionaries, and references to references.

Bibliographical and information-retrieval systems should be consulted to complete the review of the research literature. The Washington, D.C., office of the Educational Resources Information Center lists currently available retrieval systems and their contents.

Information should be recorded on 4″ × 6″ or 5″ × 8″ cards and should include a complete bibliography entry plus pertinent information. For reporting about research, the information should include the purpose of the study, type of research, kind of data, statistics used, results, conclusions, and a reaction statement.

Some suggestions about searching and note taking have been given to aid students in developing skills in recording information about research questions. The selected list of journals that are research-oriented should also be useful as an aid to the search for studies about educational concerns.

References

American Psychological Association. *Publication manual* (2nd ed.). Washington, D.C.: Author, 1974.

Thompson, J. *An introduction to university library administration*. Hamden, Conn.: Archon Books, 1970.

Bibliography: Part One

Allen, G. *Graduate student's guide to theses and dissertations: A practical manual for writing and research*. San Francisco: Jossey-Bass, 1973.

American Psychological Association. *Publication manual* (2nd ed.). Washington, D.C.: Author, 1974.

American Psychological Association, *Standards for educational and psychological tests*. Washington, D.C.: American Psychological Association, 1974.

Barzun, J., & Graff, H.F. *The modern researcher* (3rd ed.). New York: Harcourt, Brace & World, 1977.

Becker, C.L. *The heavenly city of the eighteenth century philosophers*. New Haven: Yale University Press, 1932.

Best, J. W. *Research in education* (3rd ed.). Englewood Cliffs, N.J.: Prentice-Hall, 1977.

Bloom, B.S. (Ed.). *Taxonomy of educational objectives: Cognitive domain*. New York: David McKay, 1956.

Bloom, B.S., Hastings, J.T., & Madaus, G.F. *Handbook on formative and summative evaluation of student learning*. New York: McGraw-Hill, 1971.

Boas, G. *The inquiring mind*. LaSalle, Ill.: Open Court Publishing, 1959.

Borich, G.D. (Ed.). *Evaluating educational programs and products*. Englewood Cliffs, N.J.: Educational Technology Publications, 1974.

Brogan, G.E., & Buck, J.T. *Using libraries effectively*. Belmont, Cal.: Dickersen, 1969.

Buros, O.K. *The eighth mental measurements yearbook*. Highland Park, N.J.: Gryphon Press, 1978.

Campbell, W.G., & Ballou, S.V. *Form and style: Theses, reports, term papers* (5th ed.). Boston: Houghton-Mifflin, 1978.

Cliff, N. Adverbs multiply adjectives. In J.M. Tanur, F. Mosteller, W.H. Kruskal, R.F. Link, R.S. Pieters, G.R. Rising (Eds.), *Statistics: A guide to the unknown*. San Francisco: Holden-Day, 1972.

Computers and the humanities. Flushing, N.Y.: Queens College of the City University of New York, September 1966 to date.

Cronbach, L.J. Test validation. In R. L. Thorndike (Ed.), *Educational measurement*. Washington, D.C.: American Council on Education, 1971.

Dewey, J. *How we think*. Boston: D.C. Heath, 1910.

Dewey, J. *The quest for certainty*. New York: Minton, Balch, 1929.

Dewey, J. *How we think*. Boston: D.C. Heath, 1933.

Ebel, R.L. (Ed.). *Encyclopedia of educational research*. New York: Macmillan, 1969.

Ebel, R.L. *Essentials of educational measurement*. Englewood Cliffs, N.J.: Prentice-Hall, 1972.

Educational Testing Service. *Tests in microfiche*. Princeton, N.J.: Author, 1975 to date.

Englehart, M.D. *Methods of educational research*. Chicago: Rand McNally, 1972.

Flanders, N.A. *Analyzing teaching behavior*. Reading, Mass: Addison-Wesley, 1970.

Gardner, P.L. Scales and statistics. *Review of Educational Research*, 1975, *45*, 43–57.

Gephart, W.J., Ingle, R.B., & Saretsky, G. *Similarities and differences in research and evaluation processes*. Bloomington, In.: Phi Delta Kappa, 1973.

Good, C.V. (Ed.). *Dictionary of education* (3rd ed.). New York: McGraw-Hill, 1973.

Helmstadter, G.C. *Research concepts in human behavior*. New York: Appleton-Century-Crofts, 1970.

Hopkins, C.D. *Describing data statistically*. Columbus, Oh.: Charles E. Merrill, 1974.

Hopkins, C.D., & Antes, R.L. *Classroom measurement and evaluation*. Itasca, Ill.: F. E. Peacock Publishers, 1978.

Hopkins, C.D., & Antes, R.L. *Classroom testing: Construction*. Itasca, Ill.: F.E. Peacock Publishers, 1979.

Jones, L.V. The nature of measurement. In R.L. Thorndike (Ed.), *Educational measurement*. Washington, D.C.: American Council on Education, 1971.

Jones, R.H. *Methods and techniques of educational research*. Danville, Ill.: The Interstate, 1973.

Kerlinger, F.N. *Foundations of behavioral research* (2nd ed.). New York: Holt, Rinehart, & Winston, 1973.

Kerlinger, F.N. The influence of research on education practice. *Educational Researcher*, 1977, *6*, 5–12.

Krothwohl, D.R., Bloom, B.S., & Masia, B.B. *Taxonomy of educational objectives: The affective domain*. New York: David McKay, 1964.

Kuhn, T.S. *The structure of scientific revolutions* (2nd ed., vol. 2, no. 2). Chicago: The University of Chicago Press, 1970.

Lehmann, I.J., & Mehrens, W.A. *Educational research—Readings in focus*. New York: Holt, Rinehart, & Winston, 1971.

Manheim, T. *Sources in educational research: A selected and annotated bibliography*. Detroit: Wayne State University Press, 1969.

McGrath, J.H. *Research methods and designs for education*. Scranton, Pa.: International Textbook Co., 1970.

Mouley, G.J. *Educational research: The art and science of investigation*. Boston: Allyn and Bacon, 1978.

Mouley, G.J. *The science of educational research* (2nd ed.). New York: Van Nostrand Reinhold, 1970.

Neilson, N.P., & Arnett, G.W. *A scorecard for use in evaluating physical education programs in elementary schools.* Salt Lake City: University of Utah Press, 1955.

Nunnally, J.C., Jr. *Introduction to psychological measurement.* New York: McGraw-Hill, 1970.

Page, E.B. Accentuate the negative. *Educational Researcher* 1975, *4,* 5.

Phi Delta Kappa, *Educational evaluation and decision making.* Itasca, Ill.: F. E. Peacock Publishers, 1971.

Rice, J.M. The futility of the spelling grind. *Forum* (April 1897), *23,* 163–72.

Rice, J.M. The futility of the spelling grind, Part II. *Forum* (June 1897), *23,* 409–19.

Rice, J.M. *Scientific management in education.* New York: Hinds, Noble, & Eldredge, 1913.

Russell, D.H. Reading research that makes a difference. *Elementary English* (1961), *38,* 74–78.

Sax, G. *Empirical foundations of educational research.* Englewood Cliffs, N.J.: Prentice-Hall, 1968.

Schwab, J.J. Problems, topics, and issues. In S. Elam (Ed.), *Education and the structure of knowledge.* Chicago: Rand McNally, 1964.

Shishima, Y. Vladimir Vernadsky and the modern theory of the biosphere. In A.A. Mkrtchian (Ed.), *Soviet Life,* June 1974, pp. 38–40.

Singer, H. Research in reading that should make a difference in classroom instruction. In S.J. Samuels (Ed.), *What research has to say about reading instruction.* Newark, Delaware: International Reading Association, 1978, pp. 57–71.

Stanley, J.C. Reliability. In R.L. Thorndike (Ed.), *Educational measurement.* Washington, D.C.: American Council on Education, 1971.

Suppes, P. (Ed.). *The impact of research on education: Some case studies.* Washington: National Academy on Education, 1979.

Thompson, J. *An introduction to university library administration.* Hamden, Conn.: Archon Books, 1970.

Thompson, S. *Tales of the American Indian.* Cambridge, Mass.: Harvard University Press, 1929.

Thorndike, E.L. Reading and reasoning: A study of mistakes in paragraph reading. *Journal of Educational Psychology* 1917, *8,* 323–332.

Thorndike, R.L. (Ed.). *Educational measurement* (2nd ed.). Washington, D.C.: American Council on Education, 1970.

Todd, A. *Finding facts fast.* New York: William Morrow, 1972.

Travers, R.M.W. *An introduction to educational research.* New York: Macmillan, 1978.

Van Dalen, D.B. *Understanding educational research* (3rd ed.). New York: McGraw-Hill, 1973.

Varela, J.A. Solving human problems with human science. *Human Nature* 1978, *1*(10), 90.

Webb, E.J., Campbell, D., Schwartz, R., & Sechrest, L. *Unobtrusive measures: Nonreactive research in the social sciences.* Chicago: Rand McNally, 1966.

PART TWO

THE PROBLEM:
A QUESTION AND ITS ANSWER

Research activities are directed by the investigation of a problem. The heart of any research project lies in the question formulated about this problem. The output of a research project is the answer to the question. Each aspect—problem, question, and answer—is needed as an integral part of the process. This part of the book studies the research process from problem identification through development of a hypothesis and establishment of a way to plan a specific study. These four chapters also address the overall planning of research and offer a general structure for collecting, organizing, and treating data.

Part II is not designed as a do-it-yourself kit. It will only provide general treatment on some topics which are developed in later chapters. The next four chapters use the steps of the scientific method to structure the inquiry into educational questions. Special attention is given to the proposal as a vehicle for organizing systematic inquiry into a research problem. Keep in mind the working definition of educational research as a scientific structure of inquiry into educational questions that provides answers which contribute to generalizable knowledge about educational concerns for those questions.

CHAPTER FIVE

RESEARCH PROBLEMS

Those problems are the ones which, when solved, will extend the precision and scope of fit between existing belief, on the one hand, and observation of nature, on the other.

—Thomas S. Kuhn

Problem-solving strategies have been developed under the assumption that solutions are discoverable through a systematic attack on problems. Technology in all areas is designed to attack problems using existing knowledge. Research activities are designed to create knowledge that does not exist. Nowhere have all problems been solved, and engineering in any area is likely to generate additional problems in the process of solving a particular practical problem. For example, by developing supertankers to transport oil throughout the world, technology has made the dimensions of canals, depths of channels, and loading and unloading facilities in ports inadequate, thus creating more problems. In general, solving a problem does not mean that there is one less problem to solve. Rather the usual condition is that there are more problems, not less.

The solution to one problem may provide only a temporary way of continuing while new attacks are made on the original problem. Students of civil engineering have not been content with a bridge design to serve all situations—they do not look for the one answer to spanning all gorges and rivers. They know that even a basic problem varies given different conditions and that, to solve new problems that arise with a new set of conditions, they must design new kinds of structures by combining known facts about bridge building.

Educators, as well as parents and politicians, express opinions that the education process is either ineffective or inefficient in producing within students whatever they think education should provide. The implication is that the problems associated with education have not been solved. To a great extent, the problems have been solved if "solution" is interpreted to mean that certain answers have been created. The problems have not been solved if "solution" means that the problem no longer exists and a ready-made answer has been filed for reference to each situation. Education is much like other areas where solutions must be synthesized for a specific set of conditions—as, for example, in the bridge building mentioned earlier or in the medical profession, where diagnoses must be made in light of many contributing factors and known or accepted facts.

All of us could become more comfortable with problem solving if it were approached simply as studying problems rather than solving them in such a way that a particular issue had to be settled once and for all time. Certainly solutions are needed, particularly solutions for wide general application. In the final sense what is needed, however, is a body of knowledge that provides a technology which can be used effectively on a wide basis by combining what is known from research in many disciplines to apply to a specific case.

The aim of educational research can best be viewed, then, as the study of educational problems. In the process we would expect to find solutions which will allow educators to develop a technology of education. Nevertheless, if practitioners wait for research to come up with real-world answers, then the process of education will be both inefficient and ineffective. Civil engineers did not wait for the perfect road surface before building an interstate highway system. Educators can not wait for the development of a perfect theory before the doors of the school are opened.

Practical application of what is known about the technology (science) of education allows teachers to provide the best set of learning experiences they can based on known principles. Problems in the classroom have no simple solutions; however, the role of educational research allows solutions to problems within the scope of the scientific approach.

The scientific approach is a problem-solving strategy, and as mentioned in an earlier chapter, the *problem* is what makes the scientific method work. The solving of problems, the central element of scientific inquiry, provides an output of knowledge, but there is general agreement that merely accumulating answers in isolation does little to create a working body of knowledge. The scientific approach to solving educational problems is structured to go beyond the simple addition of facts to known knowledge. It is directed toward developing a body of scientific principles about educational concerns.

In the past, the trend in educational inquiry has been to deal with practical problem questions whose answers could be applied to a specific situation. Methods used for such inquiry are called *applied research* techniques. Other kinds of problems may be of interest to researchers and of importance to education simply because they represent the unknown at this time. Research directed to answering questions of a fundamentally theoretical nature, rather than those of a practical nature, is referred to as *basic research*. Of course, basic research can supply answers to practitioners' questions and/or contribute to the body of scientific principles about educational concerns. Both types of inquiry are to be encouraged for the field of education, because of their potential contributions to the educational process used in our schools and to knowledge in general. Each type of inquiry complements the other. What is applicable in a specific situation may be generalizable to other situations. What is discovered about the unknown can be implemented in specific learning activities in real-world settings.

The Sample Studies section of this book offers reports of how five problems were attacked by different researchers. These studies will be referred to throughout discussion in the rest of the book to illustrate various aspects of research. Although they and the rest of the discussion deal with basic research, it is quite clear that each study was conducted in a real-world setting.

Overviews of Five Studies

The five studies beginning on page 203 have been included to serve as references for specific points made in the discussion of research. Each one is directed to a different type of problem. The discussion will compare these studies to show how research principles can be applied in different contexts. Before continuing with the following sections that refer heavily to the sample studies, the student should read those studies. The following five sections refer to the studies' numbered paragraphs as reference points in the narrative.

Study Number 1

The study "An Analysis of Male and Female Roles in Two Periods of Children's Literature," conducted by Judith Stevinson Hillman, is an example of historical research and how information from the past can be used in a research study. It also reflects the sensitivity of educational researchers to changes in society and culture.

Notice in this study how material from the past is used to investigate a contemporary question. In the initial reading, notice how well the author integrated this study into information from other research (pars. 2–5), the use of hypotheses in historical research (par. 15), the sampling technique used to select materials analyzed (pars. 9, 10), the analysis (pars. 11–14), and the reporting of results (pars. 16–22, and Tables 1–3).

Study Number 2

The study "The Effect of Keyed Response Sequencing of Multiple Choice Items on Performance and Reliability," conducted by John C. Jessell and Walter L. Sullins, is an example of how research can provide basic knowledge to be used by practitioners and people involved in professional testing as they engage in test development. Information from studies like this is specific basic knowledge. In isolation, the conclusions of the study give very little direction about how to build a test. However, one consideration when building a multiple-choice test is how to distribute correct choices among the items so that correct answers are not the result of **test-wiseness** among students. The answer given by Study Number 2 contributes to the general field of testing by giving the test constructor some hard data.

Notice in this study the directness with which the researchers deal with the topic of study, their approach to the problem, and their report of the findings. In the initial reading, focus especially on the purpose (par. 2) and the conclusion (pars. 13, 15, 17).

Study Number 3

The study "A Longitudinal Study of Who Seeks Counseling When," conducted by W. Harry Sharp and Barbara A. Kirk, is an example of basic research to collect data from a natural situation in a real-world setting. Information from a study over an extended period of time (**longitudinal**) allows a practitioner to see changes over time and make behavior comparisons between points in time. The careful attention given to the conduct of the study and to explanations by the researchers not only make the results useful on the campus where the data were gathered but also expand the chances that the results will be applicable in other university settings. The answers contributed by Study Number 3 give counselors an overview of when students are likely to seek counseling and who should be expected at what times.

Notice in this study the thoroughness with which the study is explained. Difficulties with the study over time require careful attention to these details. In the initial reading, focus especially on the abstract of the study (par. 1), the purpose (par. 7), conclusions (pars. 33–36), and cautions on interpretation of results (pars. 37, 38).

Study Number 4

The study "An Experimental Study of First Grade Theme Writing," conducted by Harry E. Anderson, Jr., and W. L. Bashaw, is an example of basic research in a controlled real-world classroom setting. Information from studies conducted in conditions as laboratory-like as possible in a real-world setting permits generalization into many other situations which allow the same conditions. Results under these conditions are also used to blend with other findings to give practitioners direction for guiding learning experiences. The control allows these researchers to establish cause-and-effect relationships and connect the conclusions of this study with general theory. The answers contributed by Study Number 4 give the practitioner information about children's learning and possible use of class time as well as testing a theory of child development put forth by Piaget.

Notice in this study the care taken in setting up the procedures of the study to allow the mode of discourse to be manipulated by the researcher to see related effects in theme quality. In the initial reading, focus especially on the way the authors connect the study to theory (pars. 1, 2, 25, 26), the purpose (par. 3), the hypothesis (par. 3), teacher training (par. 8), conclusions (pars. 23–27), and considerations of possible effects of outside factors (pars. 22, 27, 28).

Study Number 5

The study "The Relationship of Sibling Caretaking and Attentiveness to a Peer Tutor," conducted by Ronald Gallimore, Roland G. Tharp, and Gisela E. Speidel, is an example of correlational research which utilizes structured situations for data collection. There was no direct manipulation of a variable which could be considered **experimental treatment;** however, the researchers assigned students to groups for study according to the amount of sibling caretaking in each family. Results under these conditions allow the researcher to make statements about relationships, but this does not allow statements about cause and effect. The answers contributed by Study Number 5 are probably most valuable as bases for developing hypotheses for further testing. They also extend the study of an earlier research undertaking.

Notice in this study the use of the question to direct the reader to the heart of the study, the careful description of the subjects studied and the measurement procedures used, and the logical synthesis which the writers present to the reader. In the intitial reading, focus especially on the use of the question (par. 2), the connection made to calls for research from practitioners (par. 3), and the section on the rationale for using a particular measurement procedure (pars. 14, 15). Notice also how results are reported from the data (par. 18, 19, 20) and how the authors pull from those data suggestions about how they interpret the data (par. 20, 21). Restrictions on outcomes for the study are presented (par. 22) for the reader's benefit and as an aid to other researchers who may study in this or related areas.

Selecting a Problem

Selecting a research question is a process not easily explained. A long-time researcher probably has a list of possible studies tucked away in a corner of the mind if not in a corner of a desk drawer. A student who is in the mainstream of a research-oriented department or division of a university comes to recognize how the questions seem to appear on their own as ongoing research generates new problem areas. But students who have not reached this awareness may question how to select that one problem to study as an initial effort. The scientific approach commences when an indeterminate situation is encountered. Such a barrier is the first step of the scientific approach. How that barrier is revealed may take many forms.

Sources of Educational Problems

The first awareness of a need for research (the barrier) is most likely to occur in the process of performing professional duties. A person in counseling is not likely to study a question which relates to how the time of day affects the accident rate in a secondary school woodshop. A teacher in the woodshop is likewise unlikely to be investigating the response sequencing of multiple-choice items, even though constructing tests may be necessary for that class. A research worker in education is most likely to be someone in a discipline who has a need to fill the obvious blanks which appear in careful study of that discipline.

The original sources of most research problems in education are those broad areas of the educational process which are most obvious to educators. Major questions such as the following arise as educators carry out their professional roles:

> How can the language arts subjects be taught so that reading retardation is no longer a problem in the secondary school?
>
> What procedures can be implemented to reduce the dropout rate to a minimum?
>
> What type of counseling technique is best to use with elementary school students?

The questions above and others like them evolve from very important areas of concern for educators—how to teach better, interest students, and so on. The answers to questions like these would have a large impact on educational policies, but such broad questions are generally not researchable in that form. The major difficulty that researchers have when confronted with such questions is that the scope of the problem is too great. There are too many variables involved. Educational research can contribute to improving education by providing ways to study significant parts of a large problem and thus make small additions to knowledge about the major problem. However, attacking a major problem through a single study is generally a futile attempt. Each researcher needs to develop a mind set that recognizes the contribution to knowledge made through studying specifics.

The first two questions listed earlier about the language arts and the dropout rate are probably not answerable in a generalization that will be widely applicable. However, each contains many areas that might be investigated. It takes self-discipline for a researcher to avoid attempting to answer such broad questions. There is a tendency for those who are new to research to try to solve problems that are large in scope because these problems are the most visible. The considered choice of a problem is not only important, but it becomes crucial when relevant answers are the desired output of the research process. Most researchable problems may be seen as a part of some larger problem. The answers to questions under study will, in general, be tied to educational theory about the principles relating to that large problem.

The third major question listed earlier about counseling techniques is not one that will produce one answer for all situations. It cannot be tested because not all possibilities can be investigated. By carefully choosing counseling theories for study, the researcher can make statements about particular theories in specific situations. The answers for these particular conditions will provide information for situations having the same conditions. Good counseling practices for students in postsecondary vocational schools may be quite different from good counseling practices for elementary-school students. Similarly, successful counseling practices for elementary schools in one geographic location may be quite different from good counseling practices for elementary schools in another geographic location, because each has a unique set of characteristics. At the same time, however, some practices could conceivably be appropriate for all counselors in all kinds of situations. The underlying need reflected in this question is not to decide what is the universally best practice, but to find how varying practices work given different times and settings. Findings about counseling practices contribute to counseling theory and should be reflected in school settings as counselors improve their techniques.

What has been said about this counseling question holds true for other areas as well. A question that asks what is best should always be rewritten so that it will produce a plausible answer. For example, question 1 below could be improved by modifying it into the researchable question (1a) which follows it.

1. What is the best way to develop understanding and retention of mathematics principles?
1a. Which is more effective in developing understanding and retention of basic mathematics principles—the traditional drill approach or a contemporary mathematics program intended to develop meaning?

Research efforts may be viewed as the pursuit of knowledge by teams. Other researchers might explore other questions about teaching mathematics that also relate to the broad area of question 1:

1b. How should hand calculators be used in the classroom during the period of learning computational skills?
1c. Is this different for elementary, secondary, or college groups? For mathematics majors?

To answer these questions, the effects of using calculators on learning must be determined. The practitioner can then organize learning activities according to the established principles. Derived principles help the teacher who asks questions like:

How should drill be used in classrooms? Is it different for elementary, secondary, and higher education students?

Specific questions which could be asked from just one broad question—even in the limited area of teaching mathematics in the elementary schools—are too numerous to mention. The added dimension of varying conditions with different sets of circumstances expands the number of these potential research problems to limitless proportions. The concept of a team working together may help individual researchers see how studying a very specific problem makes a contribution toward solving a larger problem. Even the individual working alone is probably part of a larger body of individuals and teams working on a number of lesser studies to contribute toward solving a larger problem through pooling their results. Thus the body of knowledge about education accumulates.

Problems Generated From Practice

The direct experiences of educators provide likely sources for much research study. A felt need or obstacle arises very naturally during teachers' day-to-day activities. The tasks of selecting and sequencing pupil activities and other facets of the interrelations between teaching and learning make educators aware of discrete aspects of the teaching-learning process appropriate for research questions. The need for inquiry becomes evident to practitioners when they are required to make a decision on the basis of incomplete information. In fact, the beginning researcher of educational problems will most likely choose problems from personal professional experiences. Although many of these studies deal with immediate problems, the solutions to those problems often contribute to the larger body of generalizable knowledge.

The area of study in these cases is most likely a part of the discipline that the researcher knows well, one in which his or her level of expertise will permit working with a high degree of understanding. A thorough knowledge of the field provides the background needed to identify gaps in knowledge and questions which need further investigation. Professional experience in areas such as the following are sources for generating research problems:

1. Teaching methods in a subject-matter area—science, reading, language arts, mathematics, social studies, foreign language, home economics, business, technical
2. Teaching at various educational levels—nursery school, kindergarten, primary grades, middle school, junior high school, secondary school, higher education
3. Teaching in nonacademic areas—recreation, extracurricular activities, religion
4. Teaching in various learning environments—in nondirective or authoritarian environments; in settings with varying physical aspects, such as temperature or noise
5. Social interactions in the classroom
6. Nongraded elementary schools
7. Programmed instruction or self-study texts
8. Use of classroom time
9. Special education services
10. Teacher expectations of students
11. Teacher attitudes toward change
12. Nutrition and learning
13. Parent education
14. Continuing education or adult education
15. Learning activity packages
16. Educational media—print and nonprint

Of course, it is impossible to give an exhaustive list of areas for which researchable questions may be formulated. Certainly researchable problems may be found in many areas not listed here. The preceding list does offer some direction to students who may, as a course assignment, be required to identify a specific problem for study. Whether he or she is a beginner or not, the researcher should choose to work in an area which is familiar, and should select a problem that holds genuine interest.

A Problem from Practice. An elementary school teacher continually works to develop mathematical concepts for students. One topic which receives considerable attention is that of physical area. Very early in school experiences, teachers present activities that provide opportunities for pupils to form the concept of area and later to develop formulas to compute quickly the areas of two-dimensional figures. The interpretation and understanding of the area for a circle is difficult for many young pupils.

Given this problem in interpretation, a teacher might wonder how practice in estimating areas of rectangles and squares would help students to estimate the areas of circles. This problem could become the basis of a research study with a research question such as:

> What effect does practice in estimating the area of rectangles and squares have on students' test scores on a test that requires estimating the areas of circles?

The results of the study to answer the above problem question may shed light on the question of transfer of learning with implications far beyond the limits of the immediate classroom where the question was researched.

In Study Number 4 (page 231), the implied questions are, How will the stimulation in a given mode of discourse affect the quality of compositions in that mode? and How will the stimulation in a given mode of discourse affect the quality of compositions in another mode? As in the example concerning the area of a circle, answers to these questions are likely to be generalizable beyond the classrooms where Study Number 4 took place.

Answers to the research questions posed in the mathematics and theme-writing examples not only are important basic knowledge about transfer of learning and child development but also are sources of knowledge which can direct plans for student learning. Each problem came from practice but was related to an educational theory which has implications for classroom settings beyond the place where the study was conducted.

Problems Generated in Theory Construction

Another source of research problems is the construction of theory. A theory consists of systematically organized knowledge which uses assumptions and accepted principles to explain a specified set of phenomena. The theory becomes a context to guide observation. Moreover, theories provide frameworks for investigation within which researchers can interpret their observations. Theory construction is an ongoing process directing the researcher in the search for knowledge. A theory is useful in educational settings only if it holds for the specific situation. It should be examined for truthfulness before it is adopted widely and implemented in the schools.

Some sources of educational problems using theory construction for direction are

1. Theories of learning—animal and human
2. Personality theories
3. Sociological theories
4. Theories of instruction
5. Measurement theory
6. Theories of behavior change

This list names types of theories that can suggest where research is needed.

The two areas from which problems can be identified—experience and theory—are not mutually exclusive. Many difficulties that arise in education have roots in both of these areas. The resulting research problems could be identified as problems derived from *both* theory and experience.

A Problem from Theory. In 1963, the Working Conference on Research on Children's Learning met in Cambridge, Massachusetts, for two weeks to study how children learn. The monograph written to report the conference indicates that an earlier meeting had been held in November, 1962, and that the meeting ended with the development of three categories of questions relating to learning (Bruner, 1966). The first focused on attitudinal and affective skills, the second on cognitive skills, and the third on stimulus control. The group disbanded in 1962 with the expressed task of preparing working papers for the 1963 meeting. One such paper presented under the category "attitudinal and affective skills" suggested three possible investigations about how children learn (Kagan, 1966, pp. 34–39). These proposed investigations were considered first from the general area of human learning, then as a category within that broad field, further as a division within that category, and finally as a specific study.

The narrative of the paper developed several hypotheses about how the indicated factors affected student learning based on accepted learning theory. The final section proposed some specific investigations for possible study:

Suggested Investigations

These ideas contain implicit suggestions for several critical investigations. Let us make some of them explicit.

Project 1:
To study the effect of *similarity* between teacher and child on the child's receptivity to learning. In this investigation one would vary sex of teacher and the degree to which the child perceived basic similarities between self and teacher interests, class, and ethnic and racial membership, and then study differential learning in individual or classroom situations.

Project 2:
To study the effect of the sex-role appropriations of the material to be presented on ease of acquisition. One would create maximal and minimal congruence

between the sex of child and content of material to be mastered and contrast the ease of learning.

Project 3:
To study the differential effectiveness of curriculum change on children high and low on initial motivation to master. In this study, one would assign children to groups high or low on initial receptivity based on indexes of their perception of school and intellectual mastery. One-half of each group would be assigned to one of two curriculum treatments with the presumption that the effect of curriculum would be marked for high receptives but negligible for the lows. These are but samples of studies by which one might attempt to assess the importance of initial receptivity (Kagan, 1966, pp. 38–39).

Using this approach, many small studies, generated by considering the major area of how children learn, can tie together the various aspects of learning, strengthening or reconstructing the original theory as the results dictate. The results of many separate studies can accomplish what would be impossible if the large problem were attacked in its entirety within one large question. Interrelated research is especially helpful in building the body of knowledge about education.

Another source of specific problems is the concluding section of most reports about specific educational research projects. Every research study generates more questions, and it is the custom for the investigator reporting the research to list problems related to the problem under study. Look at the final reports of research studies for sections titled *Recommendations for Further Study.* In general, such sections are part of concluding statements.

Problem Clarification

The second step of the scientific approach is to identify the problem. It may seem on the surface just encountering an indeterminate situation would indicate the problem clearly enough. This is not so in most cases. Clarifying what the barrier is involves going beyond identifying that there is one. A high dropout rate in secondary schools across the country may be of great concern (a problem area) to the general public as well as to educators. The high dropout rate is the most visible effect of an underlying problem. Questions for research should, however, be directed at the causes—cultural, school, sociological, or other—which contribute to the obvious effect.

To bring the problem of excessive dropout rate down to reasonable dimensions the broad question, Why do so many students drop out of school? must be reduced to separate researchable questions: What influence does a specific factor have on the dropout (or retention) rate for schools? Why is the dropout rate higher in some schools than in other schools? Some of the factors to be investigated are home life, community support of education, counseling programs, type of curriculum, extracurricular activities, sports—intramural and interschool—teacher morale, and so on. Problem clarification at this level consists primarily of the decision about what aspect of the larger problem will be studied in a specific investigation.

In each of the five sample studies, the purpose of the study was to look at a specific aspect of sexual bias, test development, child development, counseling at the university level, or cultural differences. Either stated or implied in each study was one or more questions which the study intended to answer. Studies 3 (par. 7) and 5 (par. 2) each used a direct question to guide study.

The problem question gives direction to the study. A well-developed problem question will clarify for both the researcher and the interested reader just what the study is designed to do. When planning the methodology of the study, the researcher can be guided by the study's question. If the plans help to answer the question, then they are appropriate research procedures. The answer to the problem question should be the product of the research.

A distinction is made between the purpose of a study and the problem of the study. If the purpose of the study is stated, it should not replace the problem question. The purpose of a study might be to contribute information about how students learn, while the problem might be to determine how the similarity of teacher and pupil affects the child's receptivity to learning. (See Kagan's "Suggested Investigation," in Bruner, *Learning About Learning.)*

Unlike studies 3 and 5, studies 2 (par. 2) and 4 (par. 3) did not use the research questions to direct the reader's attention to what was studied. In each case, the authors did, however, make it clear what was being investigated. Stating the question might have clarified the problem for the reader, but in these cases there is no great difficulty in distinguishing the implied question. Some studies neglect this important point or fail to make the question clear. When the question itself is stated, readers should have no doubt what is being studied.

One successful method of clarifying the purpose and the problem of a study is to state the purpose of the study as an investigation of the problem question, as in the following case:

> The purpose of the study is to investigate one aspect of learning by answering the following question—How does similarity of teacher and pupil affect the child's receptivity to learning?

In Study Number 3, a modification of this principle is used in paragraph 3. Other modifications could be equally effective if the direct question being studied is stated.

The researcher might also find it convenient to add a short paragraph that **delimits** the scope of the study. The question alone does leave much detail unstated. Consequently, a short addendum to the question directed to specific points provides the opportunity to eliminate any ambiguity in the question. A narrative for the above question might indicate *what* teachers and *what* pupils are to be part of the study. The paragraph might read something like this:

> Specifically for this study, teachers and pupils of the first three grades of the elementary school are investigated for discernible relationships of

likeness or difference and how any similarity is reflected in the student's ability or inclination to receive learning through classroom activities.

In Study Number 3, a short paragraph after paragraph 7 discussed what breakdown was made in subjects studied—male-female, class standing, on-campus/off-campus residence, and so on—to give more definitive parameters. Defining terms in such a paragraph also helps clarify the direction of the study. Any term defined for a study limits that study in some way. After the problem has been chosen and carefully stated in researchable form, a search of existing knowledge on the topic should be made to discern an answer to the problem question.

Criteria for Writing Questions

The following criteria are useful in writing questions for research:

1. Is this a research question? Answering this question will help eliminate any questions dealing with evaluation and development. The question may also be rewritten to indicate that a research study is appropriate.
2. Does the problem involve a question about a relationship between two variables?* Considering this question eliminates any research questions that ask only about the status of the situation. For example, What is the dropout rate at Central High School? is not a question for research.
3. Does the presentation of the problem imply that it can be tested empirically? The researcher should be reasonably assured by asking this question that there is some way to obtain objective data about the question under study. If not, there is no reason to continue.
4. Can the question be answered *yes* or *no?* If it can, rewrite it so that it asks the degree, extent of, or effect of some element to avoid a simple yes-or-no response. Most answers to research questions mean more than a simple *yes* or *no.*
5. Can the answer be derived without taking a moral or ethical position? Questions which involve a set of values are not likely to be generalizable and therefore are not within the scope of research questions.
6. Have you used good grammar and correct spelling, while avoiding awkward sentence structure? Problem questions are difficult to construct so that all points are covered and arranged to present the problem clearly with no ambiguity.

---

*Criteria 2 and 3, along with the research question itself, make up the three criteria for problem presentation outlined by Kerlinger (1973, pp. 17–18):
  1. The problem should express a relation between two or more variables.
  2. The problem should be presented clearly and unambiguously in question form.
  3. The problem and its presentation should be such as to *imply* possibilities of empirical testing.

The question to be studied should inquire about the relationship between two variables so that generalizable knowledge will be created in the answer. The **status study** is important and it should be conducted, but conducting it is more of a record-keeping process than it is research. The relationship studied to answer the research question may involve questions based in the past, past to present, present, or an artificially created situation. It is possible to "observe" the past by collecting data which are considered acceptable as facts.

A good research question cannot be answered *yes* or *no*. Answers to good research questions are not dichotomous. Generally, direct questions requiring a yes or no answer can be answered without using the research process. The question, Can the listening skills of second-grade pupils be increased? implies an answer that is already known. Many questions about how to increase these skills and about effective procedures for developing them are still unanswered.

As the criteria mentioned, the question should be one that requires an answer in terms of degree or a way to accomplish already determined goals. A question should generate a generalization which can be supported or not supported by the critical experiment and observations made in the research investigation. The question, Does the method of teaching reading affect the reading achievement of first-grade students? has a rather obvious answer "yes." The basic question that should be asked is, What differences in achievement are brought about by different methods of teaching reading to young children?

□CHECK YOUR UNDERSTANDING

Use the following question and evaluate it as a research question using the six criteria listed in the previous section: Do perceptions of the women's movement differ among college women?

Answer

1. The scope of this question is probably too great to cover within one study. The question is so broad that it would be difficult to decide if and when it has been answered.
2. The question does seem to focus on a relationship between two variables. The question does seem to recognize different perceptions as a function of different persons. However, this varying relationship is probably most readily answered from knowledge about human beings in general—they are different.
3. There would be ways to collect data about this question, but without specific direction, the researcher would most likely find the scope of the question too large.
4. The question asks for a yes-or-no response set, clearly inappropriate to the criterion for a research question.

5. An answer can be found without taking a moral or ethical position.
6. The language used in the question is clear and correct.

Modifying the Question. Defining a specific problem for study can take many paths. When the question asked is too broad to handle, a suggested improvement would be to break the larger question down into smaller parts and look at a specific factor or at selected factors implied in it. A study derived from the practice question on the women's movement might focus on differing perceptions as a function of the student's age. The question might then become, How do college women perceive the women's movement as a function of the differing ages of the students?

Other variables associated with the original question that might be isolated for study include class rank, major subject area, and marital status. These variables and others could be viewed in isolation through separate studies and the information could then be pooled. Given enough support in the way of time and financial help, the careful researcher could conceivably develop an answer to the more general question modified to the following form: How do perceptions of the women's movement differ among college women?

When selecting a problem for study, the researcher is well-advised to write a question that she or he would like answered and then check it against the six criteria. If, given these guidelines, the project seems feasible, the investigator can then turn to gathering as much knowledge as possible about the specific topics by consulting other research.

Help for the Student

For the first-time researcher or student of research, the selection of a problem question to study seems formidable—maybe overwhelming, even with the suggestions made previously. Initial ideas are often quite global and need to be refined. Reading journals and books can be helpful in a search for a question. Theses, dissertations, and other full reports of research are likely to include a section about research needed to extend that investigation or complement it.

Since the first ideas about a problem will in most cases be too broad to study, the student must zero in on a well-confined area to investigate. The prospective researcher may want to seek direction from someone else to help pinpoint a question that is more researchable, but still worthy of study. A colleague, an advisor, a professor, or an expert in the field of study where the problem is based should be able to provide guidance and help in choosing an interesting, reasearchable problem. These advisors should be able to raise questions for consideration when choosing a problem for study. Two such basic questions are, Can the problem be solved by a research strategy? and, Can it be carried to conclusion? (Time, money, available data, and knowledge of the field are important to the latter question.)

The person consulted will have the experience to help decide if the problem is important enough for the answer to add to the body of knowledge about educational concerns. Perhaps more important, she or he may be able to direct the questioner to research already completed on the subject which indicates some general agreement within the profession about the answer. This does not mean that one research study should be used as a reason for not conducting the study. The prospective researcher must decide if and when the evidence research has produced is sufficient and valid enough to accept as factual. By this time, the student should be dealing with significant phenomena related to what is already known about educational concerns.

A List of Problem Questions. A class of students taking the introductory research course had studied how to write questions for research studies. The following list of problem questions was developed by those students for a class assignment. Each question was later developed into a proposal for a research study. The questions are presented here as the students first presented them for review. Most were rewritten later in another form, for clarity and sophistication, before they were usable for the term's research projects. They are included here to indicate the wide range of topics studied and to provide examples of different approaches to selecting problems.

How are teachers' expectations of tall children reflected in those students' achievement?

What are the effects on reading achievement for two ways of grouping—flexible and rigid?

What are the reasons for parents encouraging apathy in their children toward art?

How are those students who need speech correction associated with those same students who also need remedial reading?

Is there a difference in attitude toward change for experienced teachers as compared to less experienced teachers?

How is the ability to speak a foreign language affected by two uses of classtime—pattern drills and informal conversation?

What effect does discipline have on creativity in elementary art?

What is the impact of malnutrition, associated with the child from low socioeconomic background, on the development of that child's reading skills and comprehension?

What is the effect of an individualized reading program on the reading ability of the disinterested reader?

What effect does the number of items on a mathematics test have on the measurement of mathematical skill at junior high level?

What effect does the lactose deficiency have on the achievement of the primary children?

What effect does student handwriting have on a teacher's evaluation of essay responses to items on a secondary home economics test?

What effect does verbal interaction between mother and child have on a child's verbal competence in the initial school years?

Which of the following methods of instruction for fourth year mathematics would be more effective in moving students to desired outcomes—a teacher in the classroom or the teacher on instructional television?

What is the effect of short-term parent education on the behavior of the parent toward the child?

How are the two characteristics—college grade point average and on-the-job counseling effectiveness—related?

How does melodic presentation of subject matter affect the length of attention span for preschool children?

What is the effect on achievement in the basic business class in the time spent when a workbook is used for a wide range of planned activities?

*How does the degree of women's liberation in developing Southern Asian countries compare to the liberation of United States women?

*How can the special needs of graduate students be met by on-campus housing?

*To what degree do influencing factors determine the clothing purchases of teenage students?

*What is the effect of weight lifting on the performance of distance runners?

*What are the differences in the child's growth as determined by different infant feeding formulas?

Selected problem questions gathered from other students' papers that pose questions in other areas of education are:

Which is more effective in developing motor skills—part or whole learning?

How does a prepared learning sheet, given to students before they read the assignment, affect the student's performance in a high school United States history course?

What effect will quiet background music have on the aggressive behavior of emotionally disturbed children?

What effect does IVTC program #732 have on skill development in an automotive program at the post-secondary-school level?

What are the parental attitudes regarding the use of male teachers in early childhood education?

How do coloring books affect the child's visual perception?

These two lists of problem questions show the wide range of problems that confront teachers. These are not presented here as models for writing research questions, but, rather as illustrations of areas of concern.

---

*Some students were not teachers and those students chose topics appropriate to their professional fields.

□CHECK YOUR UNDERSTANDING

Check some or all of the two lists of student questions to see if they meet the six criteria introduced earlier. Look especially for (1) two variables, (2) relationship, (3) empirical testing possibilities, (4) *Yes-No* answer structure, and (5) clarity of the question. Can the question be improved? In most cases, these original questions were refined before they became part of a proposal.

Summary

This chapter discussed the parts of the scientific approach which deal with formulating clearly delimited problems for research. Selecting a topic for study was approached as a process of reducing a broadly based problem into researchable questions. Practical experience and theory construction were suggested as sources of problems for research studies.

The chapter offers six criteria for writing questions. These help organize the definition of a problem into a question to be investigated. The answer to that question then becomes the output of the research study. Problem solution is thus reduced to devising a question and deriving an answer by research.

The final section aids students in research classes. as it helps them select specific problems for study. The list of problem questions included here gives some direction for a newly initiated researcher who may have difficulty identifying a problem to study—one which is significant enough to be interesting but not so large that the complexity would be overwhelming to the first-time researcher or student of research.

References

Bruner, J. (Ed.). *Learning about learning.* Washington: U.S. Government Printing Office, 1966. FS 5.212:12019.

Kagan, J. Motivational and attitudinal factors in receptivity to learning. In Jerome Bruner (Ed.), *Learning about learning.* Washington: U.S. Government Printing Office, 1966.

Kerlinger, F.N. *Foundations of behavioral research.* New York: Holt, Rinehart, & Winston, 1973.

Kuhn, T.S. *The structure of scientific revolutions* (vol. 2, no. 2), (2nd ed.). Chicago: University of Chicago Press, 1970.

CHAPTER SIX

RESEARCH HYPOTHESES

But it is hard to conceive modern science in all its rigorous and disciplined fertility without the guiding power of hypotheses.

—Fred N. Kerlinger

Selecting a problem and reducing it to question form gives the research worker initial direction when searching for the answer. Since creating a question requires substantial background knowledge, the researcher may be able to speculate about a probable answer to the question after this initial stage. It is doubtful that the researcher's confidence in the accuracy of this speculation would be very high immediately following problem clarification. A proposed answer to the question is apt to be something more than a blind guess, maybe more at the level of an educated guess. What the researcher tries to do at this stage is to function at the hypothesis level. A hypothesis is more than an educated guess. The research hypothesis should be the most probable answer to the question after the researcher has considered all present knowledge. It is a tentative statement that will be tested for its tenability.

Hypotheses are stated with varying levels of confidence depending on how much related knowledge is available about the question being proposed. Hypotheses may be stated in different formats, but in general each hypothesis will be a statement about a relationship between two or more variables. Before formalizing a research hypothesis, the research worker should take enough time to collect as much related information about the topics to be studied as possible. To determine what is currently known on a topic, the investigator must read widely in the literature.

Literature Review

The third step in the scientific approach to solving problems is engaging in a search for information about the variables, topics, and related factors of the study. Since most of what is known is reported in professional writing, this search is referred to as a "review of the literature." This search should also include examination of books, interviews, personal correspondence, and any other sources which will bring to bear more information than what is reported in the journals.

Purposes

The search through all sources serves the researcher in two fundamental ways. First, more knowledge acquired about the related topics means a better developed study. Research findings, expert opinion, and tested procedures enable the research worker to build a better attack on the problem. Second, the collected readings provide background for the research hypothesis. Developing a hypothesis based on a wealth of information allows the researcher to connect the problem to related problems and later link the findings of the study to educational theory. The information collected in the literature search also aids in synthesizing an individual study's conclusions with other educational knowledge.

A third use of the collected information is to give background for the reader of the final report of the study. Theses, dissertations, and sometimes **proposals** include a section which reviews background knowledge. Commonly called a "review of literature," "review of related literature," or "review of related research," this essay usually appears as the second chapter of a student's thesis or dissertation, but it may be incorporated within the report in different ways.

The Search

Problem solving begins when an indeterminate situation causes a problem to be developed and attacked. The researcher may be like a person who enters a darkened theater and must stumble around trying to find an empty seat. After a period of time in the dark, vision returns to near normal. Likewise, the researcher hopes to find light in the darkness. A review of the literature begins that revelation by giving an overview of what is known about topics and variables basic to the study. The search methods described in Chapter 4 can be used to direct exploration for relevant information.

Reading the literature aids the research worker by revealing definitions and descriptions of variables in the study along with relationships among those variables and other variables. The researcher also gains insight about work that has been done and ways to extend previous studies. Previous studies can indicate what is important or unimportant. Conclusions derived from previous structured inquiry, as well as reports of experience and opinion, give starting points and direction for new studies.

The review of the literature is conducted by locating, reading, evaluating, and synthesizing reports of research, expert opinion, and all information related to the problem. Before a search is commenced, however, the question for study will have been refined. Therefore, the investigator should have general ideas about what to look for. There is no rule to follow which tells what to read. The parameters for the search should be wide enough to encompass all closely related literature but not so broad that too much time is spent reading literature that is only distantly related.

A common error made by those engaged in their first literature search is to consider only an article or report that encompasses all topics and variables under study. Keeping to these restrictive criteria will produce little background information. Divisions in an outline for the search should be made according to major topics and variables (see Figure 6–1). The resulting review will then include coverage for each individually. A summary for each subject division can be used to synthesize literature on each topic. With background information on each major subject, a broad background of knowledge will provide a solid context for developing the new study and a basis for the research hypothesis.

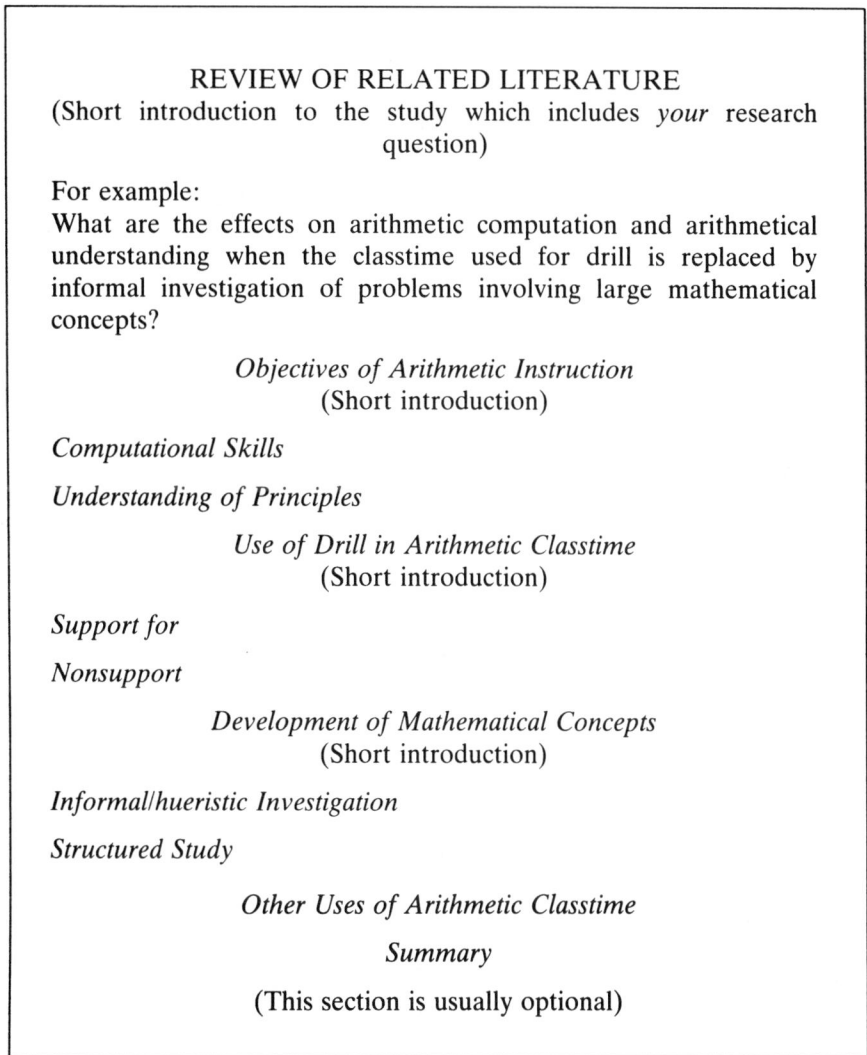

REVIEW OF RELATED LITERATURE
(Short introduction to the study which includes *your* research question)

For example:
What are the effects on arithmetic computation and arithmetical understanding when the classtime used for drill is replaced by informal investigation of problems involving large mathematical concepts?

Objectives of Arithmetic Instruction
(Short introduction)

Computational Skills

Understanding of Principles

Use of Drill in Arithmetic Classtime
(Short introduction)

Support for

Nonsupport

Development of Mathematical Concepts
(Short introduction)

Informal/hueristic Investigation

Structured Study

Other Uses of Arithmetic Classtime

Summary

(This section is usually optional)

FIGURE 6–1   A sample outline for a review of the literature

Review of Related Literature

Presenting the review in a separate chapter or section of the final research report is a format most suited to studies which use descriptive or experimental methods. An integrative study—historical or philosophical—presents special problems in handling background information. There is no clearly defined line in such a study between what information should be considered background and what should be considered facts to be used in the integrative study. However, a section of background allows the researcher to establish for the reader the starting point selected for the study. Since the success of any research rests on the advances made by previous investigations, this aspect of the integrative study is no different from studies in general, but the point of departure for an integrative study may be more difficult to pinpoint. The conclusions for any study can provide a starting point for the next investigation, and a conclusion for one study may become a hypothesis for the next study. This concept is easiest to apply to historical or philosophical studies, but it also holds true for descriptive and experimental studies.

By describing existing research in the "review of related literature" and explaining what is known about the problem, the research worker establishes a familiarity with the main sources of data. For long-time researchers the major contribution of a literature search is to give them insight into the problem and reveal ways to proceed. The writing of the reviews becomes secondary to their primary purpose—understanding. The student may be eager to get to the actual study and hurry through the search to get started on the rest of the process without knowing that a complete search may save much time later.

Although the written review does not include a hypothesis statement, the information gathered from the search is used to develop a research hypothesis. The next section discusses how hypotheses are developed from background knowledge and their relationship to the total research process.

☐CHECK YOUR UNDERSTANDING

1. How does a practicing researcher use information collected in a search of professional literature?
2. Write a short paragraph that summarizes how the search supports the research process.
3. Why is a search of the literature *not* considered research?

Answers

1.(a) The information provides a context for the research question. This background knowledge allows the researcher to function at a high level.
   (b) The researcher synthesizes the information into a research hypothesis—the proposed answer to the question.

2. The search supports the research process by establishing previously discovered knowledge and principles as a starting place for the new study intended to extend or revise what is presently accepted as truth. The information also generates a bridge between what is questioned and what is observed within the study.
3. The search adds nothing in the way of new knowledge. The process is communication of previously discovered knowledge.

The Hypothesis

The basic purpose of scientific investigation is explanation through theory. There does not seem to be a built-in guidance system which steers a researcher through evidence, or a special radar that clearly points up incidents which coincide with a theory or those which refute a theory. As a research worker goes about the business of observing phenomena, how can he or she distinguish between positive evidence and negative evidence? To a large extent, direction comes from hypotheses.

Theory is intended to provide explanation through propositions. A theory is a formulation of apparent relationships and underlying principles of observable phenomena which have been verified to some degree. It lacks the support needed to class it as a natural law. A theory can be applied universally; it does state general rules. However, a theory must fit the facts and be reconstructed when new information discloses a part of the theory that does not hold. Theories are refined as more knowledge is gained; however, a theory can not be tested.

Enter the hypothesis—it can be tested. By use of a hypothesis, a researcher can support, refute, expand, or qualify propositions suggested by theory or conceptualized schema that the researcher has formed from background reading and personal experience. The scientific hypothesis can be tested with empirical data. It represents something which the data/information collected within the framework of the study's methodology must either support or not support. Support for a hypothesis is, in general, support for a part of a more encompassing theory, while nonsupport may cause the theory to be rebuilt in part or in total.

Nature

A hypothesis is created when a researcher can form a connection between what is known and what is unknown and formulate a possible solution to the problem. In other words, the hypothesis conceptualizes what can not be perceived in light of the researcher's present knowledge and allows a tentative solution set. The conceptualization may allow a leap across a gulf of ignorance, or it may fail to explain or give an acceptable answer to the question. For the purpose of discussion a hypothesis is defined as follows:

A hypothesis is an explanation of the relationship between two or more variables expressed as a proposition.

The research hypothesis is a statement about a relationship between the variables under observation in the research study. Speaking informally, the research hypothesis is the researcher's best guess as to the answer to the problem question.

Statement

Hypotheses are created only after considerable reflection on what is known. Most researchers prefer to have blocks of time that can be devoted to organizing and collecting data, considering each part in relation to other parts, and reorganizing the total in light of each contributing part. After performing one of these tasks, the investigator may want to consult colleagues and discuss progress toward an explanation. New viewpoints may be uncovered through such consultation during the evolution of the hypothesis. At some point in time (before observation for the study begins), the researcher must conceptualize the hypothesis for the study. This statement will be referred to when conclusions are drawn later about what the observations imply about the problem. As mentioned before, the hypothesis gives the data/information something to "support" or "not support."

The hypothesis may be stated in different ways, but each hypothesis should

1. Be in the form of an answer to the proposed question
2. Include an expressed relationship
3. Be testable through empirical investigation
4. Be stated clearly using the simplest terms to convey the thought
5. Be consistent with what is known
6. Be linked to a commonly accepted theory

The following are some examples of hypotheses for educational research problems (based on the questions in Chapter 5):

Melodic presentation of subject matter increases the attention span of young children.

Strict discipline reduces students' creativity as reflected in art objects.

Poor handwriting reduces the evaluation of students' papers for an essay test in a secondary home economics test, and good handwriting increases the evaluation.

Quiet background music reduces the aggressive behavior of emotionally disturbed children.

□CHECK YOUR UNDERSTANDING

Although you may not have the background knowledge necessary to develop a defensible hypothesis which is a valid tentative statement for each of the questions from Chapter 5, write a hypothesis for each of the questions which does meet the other criteria for a good hypothesis. If you find that it is difficult to write an acceptable hypothesis, check the problem question. A poorly presented question that does not meet the desired criteria for a researchable problem may be difficult to answer with an acceptable hypothesis statement. Try rewriting the question, keeping the same implied question but checking carefully against the criteria for problem questions. It should now be easier to write the hypothesis. An exception to this approach to writing hypotheses is given in the next section.

Exception. One type of question in the Chapter 5 list does not appear to meet the criterion requiring a direct relationship between variables. In such cases, the hypothesis must be stated differently. An example of this type of question is, What are the reasons for parents encouraging apathy in their children toward art? The hypothesis for this question should be a listing of factors which contribute to apathy. The research hypothesis could be stated:

> There are two reasons why parents encourage apathy toward art in their children: lack of personal appreciation of art and a feeling that school time should be spent in the content subjects.

Using Hypotheses

A hypothesis that meets the listed criteria is a very powerful tool for educational inquiry. It has been said to be "the most powerful tool." This power originates in the several ways that hypotheses serve the research process.

1. The hypothesis states relationships that are empirically testable and can be found to be either probably true or probably false. The researcher uses the hypothesis as a vehicle to connect the collected data to the original question.
2. The hypothesis also gives direction to the study. The researcher uses the hypothesis to unify what is uncovered in a study with what is already known, because an unending accumulation of data without preconceived ideas or anticipation of outcomes would not only be inefficient but fruitless.
3. The hypothesis is evidence that the researcher has a sufficient background of knowledge to propose explanations and thus extend the body of educational knowledge. In this way, the researcher uses the stated hypothesis to show his or her competence to work in the field of study.
4. The hypothesis gives continuity to the study by providing a basis for drawing conclusions. When drawing conclusions, the researcher uses the hypothesis as a reference point, relating the answer given in the collected data with the original question.

In summary, the ultimate contribution of the study depends upon how well the research worker can integrate the problem question, hypothesis, collected information, conclusions, and theory. To a large extent, the importance of the contribution rests on the refinement of a hypothesis and its use in building the structure of the research process. Subsequent hypotheses will extend investigation into the problem to achieve greater depth or explore new areas of inquiry.

Testing Hypotheses

Hypotheses are created to be tested. Any hypothesis remains an **assumption** or conjecture until supportive evidence is collected or until the hypothesis is disconfirmed by negative evidence. As mentioned in Chapter 1, most questions in the natural sciences can be tested by direct deduction from public facts. However, as scientists ask more sophisticated questions, even the natural sciences must rely to some extent on facts which are not directly observable to formulate hypotheses. For example, the planet Pluto was "discovered" before it was directly observed. Certain data indicated that a planet should be there, but no one had sighted or photographed it directly. Phenomena in education must, for the most part, be studied indirectly, so that hypotheses too must be tested indirectly.

The term *assumption* has two meanings in research. The first usage is to recognize the assumption as a hypothesis that has no power of explanation or prediction until it is supported by deduction from observation. The second usage is to state a basic postulate for a particular study. The assumption used as a postulate is accepted by the researcher without thought of proof in the study. Basic assumptions and hypotheses are alike in that they are accepted tentatively. They differ in that the hypothesis will be tested in the study—the assumption will not. For example, a researcher may hypothesize (assume) that rigid discipline in the school setting will reduce student creativity. To test this relationship he or she may administer a paper-and-pencil test to measure the dependent variable, creativity. There is some disagreement among educators whether or not creativity can be measured by a paper-and-pencil test. For purposes of the study, the researcher may thus have to state the following assumption as a postulate for the study: The "Some Name Creativity Test" is a valid measure of student creativity if administered and scored according to the manual's instructions.

Solutions to educational problems are likely to have several basic assumptions which range from axiomatic assumptions that nearly everyone agrees upon but cannot be said to hold for each case to assumptions that are supported to a much lesser degree. Those which have near-universal agreement probably do not need to be listed, but others should be stated to ensure that colleagues know what is being accepted as true for the study.

Just as a study may have more than one assumption underlying it, it may also have more than one hypothesis. The problem might be complex enough to have a major hypothesis that is too broad to be tested in that form. Other testable subhypotheses would then have to be derived from the major hypothesis and tested separately. In such a case, the major hypothesis would not be tested directly, but the design of the study would test each of the subhypotheses. Thus the researcher could draw conclusions about them and then about the major hypothesis. It can be said that the subhypotheses, although each is tested separately, are used to test the major hypothesis. Hypotheses which encompass such a complex set of relations are approaching the level of theory and could possibly be interpreted as theories with adequate support.

Research problems are not directly testable. A problem must be tested indirectly through the problem question and the hypothesis that it generates. The best way to answer the question, How does noise level which exists while students are taking a history test affect their scores? is to use a hypothesis and test it. *Possible* hypotheses include:

1. A high noise level causes a reduction in history test scores, while a low noise level causes history test scores to increase.
2. A high noise level causes history test scores to increase, while a low noise level causes a reduction in history test scores.
3. Different noise levels have no effect on history test scores.

Each of the listed hypotheses is a statement about a proposed relationship between the two variables, noise level and test scores. A research hypothesis may be stated in different ways, but each statement should meet the criteria listed earlier. It is likely that a thorough review of present knowledge about the effects of noise on performance of human beings would tend to support one of the above three hypotheses. Studies of the effects of noise on performance in offices, factories, homes, and other environments including classrooms would give information about what to expect in the history testing session. Of course the researcher must choose only one of the hypotheses to test in a given study.* At this point she or he makes a commitment in the form of an educated guess about the outcome and tests the conjecture (the hypothesis). The researcher now has something to test.

Although there are different ways to test a hypothesis, the strand that is common to all hypothesis testing is the use of collected information and the subsequent interpretation of how the data fit with the hypothesis statement. When later chapters discuss the three major methodologies, it will become clear how the researcher structures a set of procedures for a specific study and tests hypotheses. The key notion to keep in mind is that while variables themselves are not tested, the relations between variables stated as hypotheses are.

The hypothesis must be formed before the data are gathered. To be useful, information must be gathered with a purpose in mind. However, it is not necessary to guess correctly in stating a hypothesis to add knowledge to the bank of information about educational concerns. Scientifically speaking, it makes no difference in the outcome whether the researcher has guessed

---

*The betting windows at race tracks are closed before a race is run. The management finds that this works much better than leaving the windows open for, say, 30 minutes after the completion of the race. Research studies do much the same thing, and people in research tend to view their studies in much the same way. The race, of course, is the gathering of information to be organized for interpretation and reporting of results. After the race is run and results reported, conclusions are drawn objectively.

correctly or incorrectly, since the results should be the same. Of course, if the hypothesis is tied to a theory, positive results for the study will strengthen an already developed theory. A scientific investigation uses ground rules to remove the researcher's emotional biases from the study and provide opportunities for objective decisions. This is one area where those ground rules are important.

The tendency in many researchers to associate failure with a study that does not support its hypothesis is unfortunate. The researcher does not place his or her professional reputation at stake when testing a hypothesis. A well developed and adequately conducted study adds to the body of knowledge, regardless of the results. Only through risking a hypothesis can the investigator tell positive from negative evidence and thus push back the frontier of ignorance. Even negative evidence is negative only in relation to the hypothesis under study. It is not a negative statement about the science of education generally or about the researcher specifically.

Hypotheses in Studies

The hypothesis in Study Number 4 (par. 3) provides an example of how a hypothesis can be used in research. Although this journal article does not present a full-blown review of literature, results of certain key studies are reported to give the reader some background information. The hypothesis statement itself implies that the authors have quite a lot of information to be able to make a statement of relationship at this level. Careful reading of the "Method" section (pars. 5, 6, 7) shows the close relationship between the data produced and the information needed to test the hypothesis. It seems apparent that the researchers used the hypothesis to guide data collection. Furthermore, notice that the "Results" section (pars. 16–21) reports data so that direct reference can be made to the research hypothesis.

The use of the hypothesis as a bridge between the study's findings and the problem and as a link to the conclusions is evident in the "Discussion" section (pars. 23, 24, 25, 26). The reader is left to construct the specifics for "the first hypothesis" (par. 23) and for "the second hypothesis" (par. 24), since although these hypotheses are implied in the general hypothesis (par. 3), they are not spelled out for the reader. To avoid any ambiguity for the reader, a more direct discussion would have included a statement of these implied hypotheses. However, there should not be confusion in the mind of a serious reader in this instance. Since a writer has no control over how readers may interpret what they read, it is best to eliminate any possibility of misinterpretation by making all assumptions and hypotheses explicit.

Studies 2, 3, and 5 do not state their hypotheses. The authors of each article chose to allow the results to speak for themselves. Study Number 3 pointed up in paragraph 5 that little background information existed and used a related field (psychiatry) to give data (par. 6) which might be related to counseling. Paragraph 7 implies that the ultimate problem is understanding the interaction between the characteristics of students and the campus. This study is not designed to investigate that interaction but seems more like a study which will provide certain information that will allow hypotheses about the interaction. Further research which will extend this study is implied in paragraph 7. Hypotheses may thus be used to extend study of the problem into greater depth.

Study Number 2 avoids the use of a research hypothesis, but paragraph 2 implies that the relationship between response arrangement and test performance has not been established with empirical evidence. Discussion in paragraphs 13 and 15 could have been facilitated by the unifying principle of the hypothesis. Paragraph 2 in Study Number 5 implies a hypothesis, but again it is not stated.

Is There Proof Within Research?

Two words that should not be used with hypothesis testing are "prove" and "disprove." It is not the purpose of research to set aside for all time the answer to a problem with a proof, since that is an impossible goal. There must always be room to change a decision given more and/or better information on the problem. Any claim to "proof" based on hypothesis testing must be qualified as being based on present knowledge.

At one time, the *Periodic Table of the Elements* had places for 92 elements. Not all had been identified, but there was general agreement among scientists that there could be only 92 elements. Secondary-school students were sometimes told that it could be proven that there could not be more. The *Table* now contains more than 100 elements, and more will probably be isolated in the future. At that earlier stage of the science, it would have been much better to have said that it is "unlikely" that there could be more than 92 elements, but more might be found given more information on this subject. People can make conclusions only from present knowledge. More knowledge might prove us wrong, but rarely, if ever, would it prove us right.

The terms to be used with hypothesis testing are "support" and "nonsupport," rather than "prove" and "disprove." The results of a study either support the hypothesis or do not support it. If any proof exists within the research process, it is in the nature of convincing evidence. Evidence may compel acceptance of a fact as truth, but it should not force an unyielding commitment by the researcher to his or her decision. The hypothesis that the researcher uses to direct the study, the research hypothesis, is tested with empirical data, and any outcome is tentative and may need to be altered given more information.

The Unhypothesis

A discussion of the hypothesis would be incomplete without referring to a part of research methodology that is often erroneously associated with research hypothesis testing. There is a term, **null hypothesis,** that causes much confusion in the area of research, especially for those who are working in this field for the first time. Although the null hypothesis is more directly related to statistical tests, it is introduced here to clarify that it is not a statement of conjecture and that it is used for a different purpose than the research hypothesis. It exists because present statistical procedures cannot test the research hypothesis directly (a few special cases excepted). In a statistical test for mathematical significance, the tenability of the null hypothesis is what a test of significance tests. Since the term *null hypothesis* is in wide use, the tests of significance discussed later will be presented with a null hypothesis to test. The relationship between the research hypothesis (the researcher's best guess for an answer) and the null hypothesis (the **unhypothesis,** a part of a statistical test which is not a guess) will become clear when statistical methodology fully explains the role of the null hypothesis and its use in testing for mathematically significant differences among groups studied.

This author chooses to call a null hypothesis the *unhypothesis,* because it has nothing to do with what the researcher expects to find as an answer to his question. There is no guessing, no background of information to support it, and no connection with theory. It exists as a part of the statistical treatment for some descriptive studies, but more often as a part of the statistical treatment design of experimental studies.

The statement of a null hypothesis is *not* just a negative statement in terms of treatment effects. For example, given the question, How will melodic presentation of subject matter affect the attention span of young children? the following hypothesis could be developed:

Research hypothesis:
　　Melodic presentation of subject matter will increase the attention span of young children.

Not a null hypothesis:
　　Melodic presentation of subject matter will not increase the attention span of young children.

The null hypothesis is *not* just a statement that makes a positively stated research hypothesis negative. Remember, it is not used at all in the development of the researcher's hypothesis giving expected outcomes of the study (a guess or conjecture). It is used as part of statistically based decision-making procedures. If a statistical test were used for a study of the effects of melodic presentation of subject matter on young children's attention span, the null hypothesis might read:

There is no difference in the mean attention span of third grade pupils when subject matter is presented in a traditional way and when it is presented in melody.

This statement is then used as something for the statistical test of significance to test (see Chapter 11). A study which uses the null hypothesis should also use a research hypothesis, but not all studies that have a research hypothesis will have a null hypothesis.

☐CHECK YOUR UNDERSTANDING

Which of the following are examples of the null hypothesis/unhypothesis and which are research hypotheses?

1. Correct pronunciation of new words is a function of the amount of phonics built into the primary school language arts program.
2. There is no statistically significant difference in student performance on a test of U.S. history for different levels of student reading comprehension.
3. The number of words spelled correctly by students who studied 30 minutes each school day is not significantly different from the number spelled correctly by students who studied 15 minutes each school day.
4. The interest level of disinterested readers is greater if a traditional reading program is replaced by an individualized reading program.

Answers

1. Research hypothesis
2. Null hypothesis
3. Null hypothesis
4. Research hypothesis

Theory Development

Scientific approaches to problem solving go beyond the solving of problems in isolation. Although the solution of a problem generated by a felt need is important for the individual experiencing the need, the two major purposes of all true scientific activities are to *explain* and to *predict* and then, if possible, to control the occurrence of phenomena. The individual project hypothesis, developed from present knowledge and experience, is intended—through testing—to predict as well as explain. Theories developed from scientific activities should form generalizations which can be used to make predictions for future events.

A theory explains and predicts phenomena through established relationships among variables, using the theory's antecedent-consequence (cause-and-effect) knowledge as the basis for prediction. A theory is intended to integrate, organize, and classify the many facts supplied by isolated studies and provide meaning as a contribution to a body of knowledge. Kerlinger sums this in a definition: a theory is

> A set of interrelated constructs (concepts), definitions, and propositions that presents a systematic view of phenomena by specifying relations among variables, with the purpose of explaining and predicting phenomena. (1973, p. 9)

Theory development addresses those results of observation in which the process symbolized by the constructs interacts in such a way that deductions are permitted. Theories are formulated by fitting together the results of observation and study. Theory is not vague conjecture: conjecture—yes, vague—no. The hierarchy of guesses might be expressed in this order: blind guess, educated or rational guess, hypothesis, theory, and law. The hypothesis is developed to be tested; the theory is developed to explain and predict.

Theories are conceived, growing through revision. Some theories get started and must be aborted. Scientists often deal with false starts and theories that need to be revised. The whole process of theory development involves a continual sophistication of the knowledge about interaction of processes to allow deduction for explanation and prediction. The input for theory development comes from the results of the research activities of observation, study, and experimentation. Theories contribute to the development of science through

1. Organizing existing knowledge in particular areas. A theory brings together and gives deeper meaning by connecting the results of individual studies.
2. Explaining adequately for today the results of research studies. The scientist's explanation is never ultimate and must be left open to change given more data.
3. Predicting future phenomena. Although it has not been established as an absolute truth, a theory allows prediction with a high level of accuracy.
4. Controlling the occurrence of phenomena. Difficulty in manipulating variables limits the educator; nevertheless, a goal of science is to allow control through theory.
5. Providing new leads for inquiry. Rather than being terminal, a theory generates further investigation.

One step above theory is law, *natural law*. With adequate confirmation, some theories lead to establishment of a principle that is accepted with little question, thus becoming a natural law. Regularities among phenomena can be explained by laws, and the search of science is the way to express these regularities. A basic scientific premise holds that if the conditions of any given situation could be reproduced in total, the phenomenon would be duplicated. Given different conditions, the phenomenon may or may not occur. Theories provide working tools for researchers who seek to discover conditions leading to a given phenomenon. Enlightenment as to why it does not occur in what appears to be similar conditions establishes regularity in prediction which in turn results in establishment of natural laws.

The ultimate goal of science is discovery of the natural laws. A theory can be viewed as a bridge between the hypothesis and the natural law. Progression toward these laws commences with recognition of a problem. Formulation and testing of a hypothesis related to that problem provide knowledge for developing theories. The well-developed theory that is accepted with little question becomes a law. To keep this status, a law must explain every case that it is intended to explain—no more, no less. Failing to do this, the law must be rebuilt or discarded, depending on its ability to fit with the new evidence. The difference between a theory and a law is sometimes a function of the person viewing the interpretation given to explain phenomena. What might appear to be a natural law to one person may only seem a theory for someone else. Although both persons have the same information, the interpretation may be quite different. However, each discipline has certain generalizations that have withstood the test of time, are widely accepted by experts in the field, and may be considered to be natural laws.

From Problem to Hypothesis

Veteran researchers consider problem clarification and hypothesis development especially difficult for students who are making their first formal study of the research process. This concluding section for Chapter 6 illustrates how a very large problem area is reduced to a specific question, and how a proposed answer (a hypothesis) is developed to be tested with data collected for the study. The problem area we will focus on is the use of classtime. Teachers and other curriculum workers must decide how best to use the time students are in school to foster learning. The continuing need for inquiry into time allocation is a problem that has received much study.

From the early 1900s (Thorndike, 1908) through the 1930s (Brownell, 1935) and the 1960s (Hopkins, 1965), to the present time, researchers have asked the specific time-use question, How can we best use classtime to meet the objectives of elementary school mathematics programs? Developing mathematical computational skills and understanding of mathematical principles must both be considered when designing classroom activities. Early evidence seemed to support the use of drill to meet stated objectives, but later evidence indicated other techniques to be equally or more successful in meeting objectives. Most contemporary elementary mathematics programs divide classtime so that both drill and meaningful activities are used in the classroom program. The overall question generated by the problem of how to present mathematics is, What is the best way to present a program of elementary mathematics? As usual the first question is too large to research as it stands and probably touches on several areas within curriculum development. Within the scope of the very large question are many smaller researchable questions, however.

A more limited focus of the larger problem of how best to present the mathematics program is the use of classtime. A research study might explore two different uses of arithmetic classtime as they relate to the students' achievement in arithmetic computation and understanding of basic arithmetical principles. The following researchable question could evolve from this aspect of the large problem: What are the effects on arithmetic computation and arithmetical understanding when the classtime used for drill is replaced by informal investigations of problems involving large mathematical concepts? This question meets the three criteria set for researchable problems. It deals with a relationship between the variable of "use of classtime" and the criterion variables "computation" and "understanding." It is in the form of a question; and it implies the possibility of empirical testing.

Basically there are two questions being asked. One deals with the effects of two different uses of time on computation and the other deals with the effects on understanding. Two research hypotheses will then be needed to direct the investigation. Three possible research hypotheses can be developed from the question concerning effects on computation:

1. The ability to compute is facilitated by replacing drill with informal investigation of problems.
2. The ability to compute is lessened by replacing drill with informal investigation of problems.
3. The ability to compute is not affected by replacing drill with informal investigation of problems.

Three possible research hypotheses can be developed from the question focusing on effects on understanding:

1. Arithmetical understanding is increased by replacing drill with informal investigation of problems.
2. Arithmetical understanding is lessened by replacing drill with informal investigation of problems.
3. Arithmetical understanding is not affected by replacing drill with informal investigation of problems.

Of course, in an actual study the hypotheses would be stated in more specific terms than those used here to ensure clear and unambiguous statements. The researcher would choose one hypothesis from each set of three to serve as the research hypotheses about treatment effects on the two criterion variables—computation and understanding. Also, in an actual study the terms would be defined so that it is clear to the reader what the researcher means by "drill," and "informal investigation of problems," "computation," and "understanding." The choice of research hypotheses would be determined by available information and/or theory that applies to the particular question. A researcher might choose the following statements of research hypotheses to test, basing the decision on all information available:

1. There is no difference in computational ability between a class of students taught with the drill approach and a class where the time spent for drill is replaced by informal study of problems dealing with large mathematical concepts.
2. The understanding of basic elementary principles is increased for a class where drill has been replaced by informal study of problems dealing with large mathematical concepts.

Other pairs of hypotheses might be chosen if other researchers conducted a study dealing with the same question. Hypothesis selection depends on the researcher's view of present knowledge and theory and personal past experiences.

After the researcher has clearly delimited the problem, presented it unambiguously, and developed the research hypothesis, she or he next turns to the task of answering the question. The next chapter, "Designing the Study," describes the process of structuring research activities into a workable plan to collect observations for study and procedures for testing the research hypothesis.

Summary

This chapter focused on that part of the scientific approach which deals with formulating research hypotheses. Developing a hypothesis from information gathered in a literature search connects the problem with present knowledge and gives an anchor for forming conclusions from collected data. The hypothesis ties the study together in other ways also. The specific use of hypotheses in the sample studies shows how researchers can utilize the hypothesis in educational research.

The concept of absolute proof does not exist in research. It is unrealistic since any belief should be open to alteration or change as a result of new knowledge which is not consistent with the belief. The hypothesis is a conjecture which can be supported to some extent but which has not been tested. It is the statement of a relationship which is to be tested, as opposed to an assumption which is accepted as a postulate for the study but will not be tested within the study. This chapter also discusses the null hypothesis (unhypothesis), a necessary part of some statistical procedures. The student should not confuse the null hypothesis with the researcher's conjectures about outcomes of the test of the research hypothesis.

The chapter ends with an explanation of theory development and the sample development of an indeterminate situation into a problem with the accompanying formulation of research hypotheses. The latter serves as an example of how a researcher might function when working within the scientific approach to problem solving.

The last two chapters have focused on the problem question and the researcher's proposed answer. The next chapter describes setting up general plans to test the hypothesis through data collected for the study.

References

Brownell, W.A. Psychological considerations in the learning and teaching of arithmetic. *The teaching of arithmetic* (10th yearbook). Washington, D.C.: The National Council for Teachers of Mathematics, 1935.

Hopkins, C.D. The emerging elementary mathematics program. *The Teachers College Journal*, January 1965, *36*, 151–152.

Kerlinger, F.N. *Foundations of behavioral research.* New York: Holt, Rinehart, & Winston, 1973.

Thorndike, E.L. The effects of practice in the case of a purely intellectual function. *American Journal of Psychology*, July 1908, *19*, 374–384.

CHAPTER SEVEN

DESIGNING THE STUDY

The fact is that the major effort in the undertaking of research should be devoted to the planning stage.
—Robert M. W. Travers

After a problem has been clarified and reduced to a question and the hypothesis has been developed from related information, the researcher needs to develop procedures and techniques to test that hypothesis. To do this requires a planned strategy designed to select subjects, to observe and/or measure them, and to develop ways to interpret the observations as support or refutation of the previously stated hypothesis. All research studies need a plan or general design to direct inquiry about a problem question. The word *design* has two meanings in research. In experimental research, "design" (**statistical design**) refers to the selection of the proper statistical tools for treating the data. The meaning of "design" used in this chapter is a much more encompassing one referring to the total methodology:

1. Selection of subjects or other sources of **information**
2. Choice of a sample to study
3. A basic framework to:
   a. Gather the information
   b. Organize the results
   c. Interpret the results

The design referred to here, then, is the master plan of inquiry. Within this framework, experimental research can be said to utilize as a part of its overall design a section referred to as statistical design. The use of the term should be clear in context.

The major purposes of the design stage of research are to develop a way to gather data that delivers clear messages and to choose proper techniques for picking up those messages, techniques that allow recognition of ways of interpretation. It may seem strange to refer to a set of numerals as delivering messages, but the researcher gathers the data to tell something about the variables under study. The success of the research depends on being able to establish a plan to acquire clear, concise, and detailed facts and techniques to organize the information and transcribe it into the results of the study.

The contribution of the study rests in the procedures set up as the design. The study must gather the appropriate data from the correct sources in such a way that they will relate to the proposed answer (the hypothesis) and, in turn, to the problem question under study. The plan should be a logical sequence of procedures that will provide interpretable results. The products of the plan are results to be used in developing the conclusions of the study and in connecting these conclusions to present knowledge and implications for modifying present practice.

The type of information gathered determines whether the research study is considered a qualitative study or a quantitative study. The distinction between the two is made on the basis of how they describe observations— whether on a numerical scale (quantitative) or in words (qualitative). The difference rests in being able to assign meaningful numbers (those that can be treated mathematically) in quantitative studies. Any use of numerals for identification or labeling would not be mathematically meaningful and would not constitute a quantification. Quantification comes rather from counting occurrences within categories. The section on rating scales in Chapter 3 discussed this distinction.

A study's adequacy depends, in general, on the ability of its design to provide a way to answer the question in specific terms which are generalizable beyond the sources of the information. The rest of this chapter will expand the view of design introduced here, discussing methods for obtaining appropriate facts for a historical or other qualitative study and those for generating appropriate data for a quantitative study.

Three Stages of Design

Educational research provides the structure for scientific investigation of problems which is designed to establish facts and principles about educational concerns. The structure for the research process is built around three sequential phases. The first set of activities is devoted to planning the attack, the second to implementing the plan, and the third to generating generalization from this study to the field of education.

Planning

The important decisions about a study's procedures are made in the planning stage. To a large extent, they determine the worthiness and validity of the final product of the research process, an answer to the **problem question.** Before the researcher goes farther into the study, a final check should be made about whether the study can be expected to be worthy of the time needed for close examination. The researcher must decide on the question,

Is this a researchable problem? Before this question can be answered, four
other questions deserve consideration:

1. Is the answer already known?
2. Can the solution to the problem be determined from objectively
   obtained data and/or information?
3. Is this a question that can be answered without checking established
   policy or using speculation?
4. Are there any ethical aspects which would preclude carrying out the
   study?

For an area to be researchable, the first and last questions must be answered
"no," the second and third "yes." First, if the answer to the question is
known, the time and money spent on a research project would be wasted.
Second, a scientific approach to the solution of problems assumes that the
information needed can be obtained objectively and organized meaningfully
for interpretation. Third, an independent interpretation of the results is
necessary if a contribution is to be made to present knowledge. Within the
school setting, particular questions are answerable through guidelines and
direction coming from the administrative level. These questions are not open
to research. Speculation is useful for the researcher only as a means of
getting to a hypothesis not as support for one.

Fourth, ethical considerations are important because of the human
subjects involved in most educational research. Inanimate objects can be
studied in almost any way without fear of permanent damage, but studies of
human beings must be carefully checked to see that the subjects under study
are not affected adversely by any procedure or treatment. In order to assure
that the rights of human subjects are protected, the researcher should be
certain that any risk to an individual is outweighed by potential benefits to
that person. Furthermore, the researcher must obtain consent by adequate
and accepted methods.

The possibility of harm to a subject is most obvious as a result of
procedures that may induce a potentially altered physical state or condition.
However, some procedures used in studies of human beings could involve
varying degrees of discomfort, harassment, invasion of privacy, or threat to
the subject's dignity. Not only do moral and ethical restraints bear on this
question of risk, but public school and university guidelines also provide
frameworks within which to work. Federal regulations and laws further
govern procedures for research involving human subjects.

The planning stage also involves selecting a carefully defined (delimited)
area to study, defining terms, listing assumptions, developing the methodology, and identifying possible **limitations** of the study. Planning also means
that the researcher must look ahead to anticipate how data can best be
organized for interpretation and how conclusions will be drawn. Since this
chapter on designing a study must consider the two latter stages of the
research process, brief overviews of these stages follow to emphasize how
planning must be dovetailed with the investigation stage and the generalization stage.

Investigating

After all important decisions have been made and the plan has been deemed valid, the next stage is implementation. Since the procedures have been determined before this stage, the implementation is a routine matter that follows specifically the directions for the overall design. The investigation stage starts with the systematic execution of the design: selecting the subjects, providing the treatment, and/or collecting the data/information for analysis.

All sets of data hold multiple messages. It is the purpose of the investigation stage to distill clear messages from the data and, through appropriate analytic techniques, to extract the messages without distortion. During the planning stage, procedural design should be developed completely to avoid having to make decisions about procedures during the investigation stage. The products of the investigation stage are usually referred to as *results*. Procedures of investigation include some or all of the following data treatments:

1. Ordering and/or tabulation of the gathered data (Hopkins, 1974, pp. 1–27)
2. Descriptive analysis (Hopkins, 1974, pp. 29–81)
3. Correlational analysis (Hopkins, 1974, pp. 83–98)
4. Inferential analysis (Ferguson, 1976, pp. 187–479)
5. Summary of results
6. Analysis of historical data

Each of these procedures will be examined specifically in the chapters on methodology. The investigation stage does not include interpretation of data nor evaluation of findings, but it should include an objective report of the analysis and results of data treatment. Tables that summarize results are usually compiled at this stage. **Qualitative data**—especially data for historical studies—will generally be organized along a characteristic dimension, such as time, geographic region, variables studied, or other appropriate topics. Analysis of qualitative data consists of an objective presentation of the information.

Any contribution a study makes to the general body of educational knowledge grows out of its data. Consequently, the importance of careful presentation of these outcomes cannot be overemphasized. Logical organization and clearly presented summary tables will help determine what contribution the study makes. Without this organization, any contribution might be hidden and not be apparent to anyone, including the researcher who is conducting the study.

The summary should synthesize the results of the study to provide a basis for conclusions. Findings that tend to contradict each other should be pointed up, as well as results that support each other. Findings from one study may also be compared to findings of other studies to help establish a basis for the generalization stage.

Generalizing

Although the investigation stage provides the pulling together of the data into a synthesis, the major reporting of conclusions is left for the generalization stage. The most important aspect to keep in mind in drawing conclusions is to *be sure that the conclusions represent what the data have demonstrated.* Of course, the way to do this is to base the conclusions on the data rather than on what the investigator would like to find.

The report must be scientific, and the investigator must follow the scientific approach to the finish. This means that he or she must view a conclusion which does not support the best guess (the research hypothesis) as equally important to the body of scientific knowledge as an outcome that supports the hypothesis. It usually is as important for scientists to know what is not true as to find an outcome that confirms the research hypothesis.

Unfortunately, there is a cultural—perhaps human—bias that views being right as much better than being wrong. Nevertheless, scientists must be aware of this tendency and make instead straightforward statements of their conclusions about the relationships between the variables under study, which in turn relate the findings to the hypothesis. These conclusions will also relate the findings of this study to the current body of knowledge.

At the generalization stage, the researcher makes statements about the **implications** of the study, discussing them and relating them to present theories, present educational practices, and anything else that seems appropriate. Although the researcher is free to write anything relevant in this section, she or he must take care to back up and support conclusions with the results. The research should also suggest further required research directly or closely related to the problem under study. This gives direction to others interested in the same problem area.

The importance of the generalization stage is self-evident since it is the section that presents the answer to the original problem question and ties it to present knowledge. Undoubtedly this is one of the most important aspects of scientific inquiry. Chapter 13 offers more direct help in drawing conclusions.

Overview of Research Design

The structure of inquiry has been developed through the three major areas—planning, investigating, and generalizing. The researcher enters the planning stage after making a decision to attack some obstacle. This stage serves to clarify the question and to find out if the answer is already a part of present knowledge. If it is not, the researcher develops a theoretical framework and design to provide an answer.

The investigation stage implements the procedures designed to answer the problem question—identifying subjects, making observations, gathering appropriate data, obtaining the results, and synthesizing the results. This activity provides a basis for drawing conclusions.

The generalization stage evaluates the results of the study by drawing conclusions and relating them to present knowledge, stating implications for educational practices, and proposing further research related to the study.

When a final report of the research study is made after implementation and completion, the three stages may be represented in different ways, depending on the type of final report being prepared. Two types are shown in Tables 7–1 and 7–2 detailing how the components of the research process are synthesized into reports.

TABLE 7–1 Thesis or Dissertation Format

Chapter Number	Chapter Title	Structure
1	Presentation of Problem	Planning Stage
2	Review of Related Literature	Planning stage
3	Procedures and Techniques	Planning stage*
4	Analysis of Data	Investigation stage
5	Findings, Conclusions, Implications and Recommendations	Generalization stage

TABLE 7–2 Journal Manuscript

Section	Section Title	Structure
1	Not titled (includes title, author's name, institutional affiliation, an abstract)	Overview
2	Not titled (includes the introduction plus a summary of the related literature)	Planning
3	Method (includes a description of the subjects, apparatus, procedures)	Planning*
4	Results (summarizes the data and interpretive devices and techniques)	Investigation
5	Discussion (includes conclusions, implications, recommendations)	Generalization

Delimiting the Scope

Having developed a clear question and a related hypothesis, the research worker will need to clarify the precise scope of the study. A theory is intended to explain a phenomenon for particular sets of conditions. Since each study is conducted with a unique set of conditions, the conditions for the study should be consistent with a proposition or set of propositions deduced from theory. For example, it might be inferred from the Piagetian

---

*When implemented, the methods, procedures, and techniques are also a part of the investigation stage. Therefore, this section could be said to belong in part to both planning and investigation.

stages of development that each stage of development would be expected to affect learning differently. A study that deals with student learning based on those stages, then, would need to be specific about which stage of development was relevant for the students in the study. To understand the influence of the different developmental stages, a series of studies could be conducted in which all conditions are held the same except for the developmental stage of the subjects being studied. Differences among the outcomes of the individual studies might yield insight into the stage of development as a cause of the differences.

When the study has been **delimited,** the scope of the study should be well in focus for the research worker and others who are knowledgeable about this research. After the researcher has decided what is to be included and what is to be excluded, the hypothesis may need some modification to conform to these delimitations.

The **delimitation** of the study allows the researcher to specify those aspects of the study that cannot be included in the research question. Trying instead to put all of these details in the question may be confusing, since qualifying phrases may cloud the basic question under study. A short paragraph about the specifics of the study written in conjunction with the question allows a clear presentation of the basic question which avoids getting involved with distracting details. Even further clarification results from subsequent definition of the variables and technical terms for the study.

Definitions

While writing the problem question and hypothesis, the researcher becomes aware of what specific terms mean generally and what meaning the words have for the particular study. For consistency within the study and for clear communication with those who will read the study, certain words, methods, and concepts which relate to the study should be carefully defined so that everyone understands just what each means.

Special Definitions

The research worker does not need to define all words that are used to communicate about the study. However, a definition is necessary wherever a term may be interpreted differently by different people. A special definition is often appropriate for one or more of the following:

1. Major variables. All major variables for the study should be defined. Since the study involves a relationship between these variables, understanding these terms is crucial.
2. Practices. A carefully explained definition should overcome any ambiguity about practices. For example, an approach to learning that uses a heuristic form of learning should be explained carefully rather than simply saying that the investigation was conducted to study the discovery approach. Since what might be heuristic to one person might appear quite expository to another or what might seem to be

exposition to one might be classed as heuristic by another, the researcher needs to explain specifically what he or she means by "discovery." Carefully stated procedures help to define practices.

3. Special meanings. If a commonly used word acquires a special meaning in the study, this could create real ambiguity—especially for those who are not directly involved in the study. Special meanings of words should be avoided wherever possible, but if one must be used, the meaning attached to the word in the particular study needs to be made clear.

4. Newly invented terms. If it becomes necessary in the course of the study to produce a new term, it must be specially defined. This may be necessary if more than one term is used to name a particular variable or topic, or if the researcher is dealing with an entirely new idea.

5. Technical terms. Any word that requires special and/or unusual knowledge should be made clear. Words specific to an area would be considered technical terms, because a reader from outside may not know how the word is used within the scope of the area of study.

Various kinds of definitions are appropriate. In general, the definition will be presented as a word definition or as an operational definition. Word definitions are more common. A good source of word definitions for educational studies is

Carter V. Good (Ed.). *Dictionary of Education* (3rd ed.). New York: McGraw-Hill, 1973.

An authoritative source should be consulted whenever possible, at least as a basis for the definition. Modification can be added as needed. Remember when dealing with words that they can mean whatever the user chooses. As Lewis Carroll wrote:

"When I use a word," Humpty Dumpty said, in rather a scornful tone, "it means just what I choose it to mean—neither more nor less." (Gray, 1971, p. 163)

The best course of action is generally to use the word as it is commonly understood by the audience which will be interested in reading about the study—that is, choose the meaning currently used in the discipline unless there is good reason to do otherwise.

Operational Definitions

Word definitions substitute conceptual representations for the expression being defined. One major fault with word definitions is the circular chain of definition: if a person looks up the words used in an explanation, then looks up the words used in the resulting definitions, and continues this follow-up process, eventually the word that was originally defined is used to define another word. A way to overcome this not-so-small vexation in a study is to use what has come to be called an *operational definition*. The operational definition tells, in terms of performance, the outcomes that the word implies.

For example, rather than define the characteristic of "weight" as the "heaviness of the mass of an object," it might be better to define "weight" operationally as "the reading of the dial on a particular appropriate set of scales," giving the name and model number of the weighing device. Assuming that the scales are available to all, there would be no interpretation of words needed. Anyone could read the dial, within degrees of inaccuracies of measurement. A definition that explains how a trait is to be quantified operationally—such as the one for "weight"—is a *measured operational definition*. Most **dependent variables** in a study can be defined by this kind of an operational definition if they are measured for effects from different treatments (levels) on the **independent variable.**

An *experimental operational definition* tells how the researcher manipulates a variable under study. Treatment of the independent variable can often be explained by this kind of operational definition. In behavior modification, a researcher might have tokens to be cashed in for candy or toys. This procedure would provide an experimental operational definition. By telling how subjects will be tested under varying circumstances, the investigator has defined the variable using an experimental operational definition. In each form—measured and experimental—the operational definition describes in terms of actions (operations) and tells how something will be measured or manipulated.

To help distinguish between the two forms of operational definitions, note the differences between the two following definitions:

Measured operational definition—"Popularity" is the number of choices an individual receives from other classmates as indicated by the use of the sociometric device in Appendix A.

Experimental operational definition—Treatment of the independent variable, "counseling technique." For one group of subjects, the interviewer will face the subject and keep eye contact as much as possible and for the second group, the interviewer will turn in the chair and look at the wall and/or the window while conducting the 10-minute meeting.

Many of the terms in education are at best only roughly defined. A term may be so global that it encompasses different ideas for different people, or it may merely mean something different to different people. There are some terms—such as "intelligence"—for which there is common agreement about what it is generally, but disagreement about many of the aspects that must be dealt with when formally defining it. An operational definition explains specifically what a word means to the investigator creating the study.

The researcher must make sure when planning a study that she or he understands the meaning of the terms used and conveys that meaning to others. It is true that the researcher can define a term in any way that he or she desires, but that definition should be defensible.

☐CHECK YOUR UNDERSTANDING

Some of the following definitions are operational definitions. Identify those that are operational definitions and further classify each as either an experimental operational definition (EOD) or a measured operational definition (MOD).

1. Mental ability: the level of mental functioning will be indicated by a score on the *Wechsler Intelligence Scale for Children.*
2. Occupational interest: the occupational orientation of the individual will be determined by *The Strong-Campbell Interest Inventory.*
3. Revengeful: full of spite, especially to exact punishment for a perceived wrong.
4. Reward: a teacher will administer reward by a warm remark and a gentle touch of the shoulder, arm, or hand of the student.
5. Hostility: unfriendliness.
6. Motivation: a subject's degree of motivation will be determined by the score from the weighted checklist exhibited in Appendix A.
7. Discipline: any restriction of student privileges, but not to include any physical punishment.
8. History achievement: a score on the 38-item, multiple-choice test exhibited in the appendix determines the level of achievement over the Colonial period of American history.

Answers

1. MOD. The definition states in actions how the characteristic is to be quantified.
2. MOD. Although not a direct measurement as such, the definition explains in operations how interest is ascertained.
3. This is not an operational definition, merely a statement about what the term means.
4. EOD. Explains by actions how something will be exhibited.
5. This not an operational definition, merely a synonym for the word.
6. MOD. The definition states how something will be quantified.
7. EOD. The definition explains in actions how to identify an action that would be considered an example of that being defined.
8. MOD. The definition states in actions how the characteristic is to be quantified.

Assumptions

For any study, there will be some underlying propositions that are taken for granted. Many must be assumed to be true whether they are clearly demonstrable or not. Although it is not necessary to make an exhaustive list of a study's assumptions, the researcher looks carefully for those important to the study and lists them to help establish the theoretical framework used as a basis for organizing the inquiry procedures. If an assumption is axiomatic, it probably does not need listing. If it is accepted instead as best knowledge or as one alternative for a questioned proposition, it should be listed. Examples of stated assumptions are

> Creativity can be measured by use of a paper-and-pencil test.
> Student behavior is a function of the specific setting in which it takes place
> Frustration is a product of anxiety.

Researchers list assumptions to help provide a setting for the study and to prepare for evaluation of the conclusions of the study. The decision to list or not to list an assumption lies with the investigator. A guide for this decision should be that all assumptions which relate directly to the problem should be listed. These assumptions should be supported by as much evidence as can be collected from the research literature to form a strong base for developing valid conclusions and to clarify under what conditions the conclusions will hold.

Limitations

The last part of this chapter deals with some common elements of research methodology. Chapters 9, 10, and 11 extend that examination into specific considerations for three types of studies. These procedures make up a large portion of a research design.

As each aspect of methodology is considered, the researcher must make decisions in the context of the total set of procedures. These decisions involve choices about how to proceed in the observation. Each alternative may have advantages and limitations. What the researcher hopes to do is make each choice so that, in the overall study, the advantages are maximized and the limitations minimized. For example, if two different methods of teaching are being investigated, the researcher must consider who will do the teaching. If a different teacher is used for each method, differences in the dependent variable measures might result from teacher differences not methods. If the same teacher teaches both methods, differences observed in the dependent variable may result from differences in the teacher's level of preparation. Either of these alternatives has an inherent limitation that must be considered when drawing conclusions. The decision affects the generalizability of the results.

The researcher should consider all possible alternatives and make selections which reduce the number of limitations. For example, an attempt to overcome the problem of how many teachers to use to teach a variety of methods could utilize strengths from each alternative. The methodology could call for using different teachers who are selected by their choice of method and experiential background. Each teacher would then use his or her method of preference and best preparation.

After the methodology is as close to ideal as possible under the circumstances, the researcher must list its limitations. In general, limitations are a function of a lack of **internal validity** or **external validity** which will be discussed later. These limitations will be considered when the researcher draws conclusions about the results. Listing limitations for the reader recognizes that the researcher was aware of them but could not overcome them in the study. Listing the limitations says to the reader "I am aware of these difficulties, but circumstances do not allow them to be overcome without creating greater limitations."

Together the delimitations—the factors which restrict the scope of the study—and limitations—those deficiencies of the methodology—determine the range of generalization which can be made from a study. Identifying the source of the limiting factor categorizes it as either a delimitation or a limitation.

Methodology

A set of information gathered for the study becomes the basis for a conclusion about the answer to the problem question. Methodology—a part of the overall plan—structures the specific procedures about what or who will supply the data, how the data will be obtained, and how they will be analyzed.

Methodology focuses on that part of the scientific method called "observation." Methodologies for the three major types of research are so diverse that each will be dealt with separately in Chapters 9, 10, and 11. However, certain elements of methodology are common to all studies.

Choosing a Methodology

The choice of a basic framework for a study is made in light of the question asked. When an event or events has already occurred, the framework for the plan uses historical research techniques for structure. The important steps include location of remains and records, their criticism both internally and externally, and interpretation of information found to bear on the case in point.

Whenever the researcher sets out to study a situation as it currently exists, the framework of the study is descriptive. Descriptive research, in addition to describing, interprets present conditions. Included with study of conditions is study of relationships, present practices, attitudes, and trends that seem to be developing. Conclusions for descriptive studies are based on results of data analysis which interpret by comparison, contrast, and cause-effect relationship.

When the researcher investigates for cause-and-effect relationships by manipulating one or more variables and studying the effects on one or more other variables, the study is framed in a structure of experimental research. The role of science to explain, control, and predict suggests conditions that permit manipulation of the independent (experimental) variable and allow employment of techniques that eliminate or equalize effects of associated variables.

Contemporary scientific thought judges the **experiment** as the best approach to research, and its use is to be encouraged in educational studies even though laboratory-like conditions are difficult to obtain in most educational settings. The decision to use one strategy rather than the others must be made by taking into consideration the nature of the question and the availability of usable data from appropriate subjects. Since all questions are worthy of study, the educator should attack all problems with the best available methodology and approximate experimental conditions as closely as possible.

Selecting Sources of Information

The problem question gives direction in deciding the type of data needed and the source or sources of information needed, but specific decisions must be made about exactly what **primary sources** and/or **secondary sources** to use in a historical study, or what phenomena or human subjects to observe or measure for a descriptive or experimental study. Since no research outcomes can be based on a set of total information, most empirical research requires sampling. The researcher's first concern in developing methodology is apt to be to answer the question, Where and how can data that relate to the problem be obtained?

For the qualitative study, the data will be found in documents, relics, and/or accounts of firsthand witnesses. For the quantitative study, the data will be created by the study of designated objects or subjects. In either case, a good study obtains all of the information required but no more, since it is inefficient to use the researcher's time and the subjects' time to gather data which do not bear directly on the question being studied.

Qualitative Data

A qualitative study—usually based on a question best answered by a study of the past—may examine closely an institution, a movement, an idea, a person or persons, and their interrelationships. In planning such a historical study, the researcher uses the focus of the clearly delimited problem question to indicate the type of data needed to answer the question under study. The source of information should be made clear by the question asked. If the question asks why an idea about student learning was tried and discarded, the answer will probably be found in written materials. The researcher then identifies specifically what materials would be most likely to have pertinent information. The decision to use particular journals for specific time periods and certain authors most likely to write about the point under study, or other specific sources, is a part of the planning. Searching through written materials requires as much direction as any other method of study. Of course, the decision to look in certain places does not preclude the use of other sources or rule out information found by chance. Structuring the attack should in no way be a limiting factor. A well-planned attack will reward the investigator by the time saved in the search.

A qualitative study that asks a question about the type of materials included in physics textbooks during the years 1930 through 1939 would send the researcher in a specific direction. The source would be the actual textbooks of that period. Some studies utilize combinations of written material, relics, and eyewitness accounts as sources of information. Much of the planning for a historical study lies in making decisions about where to look for the needed information. Conclusions are then made based on the information and presented as the answer to the proposed question. If a hypothesis has been formulated, the conclusions should state whether the data supported or refuted the hypothesis. The chapters on historical research (Chapter 9) and the library (Chapter 4) give more attention to the selection of information and to the use of a hypothesis in qualitative studies.

Sampling Qualitative Data. The plan for a study that uses qualitative data for analysis should include sampling procedures for collecting the information. The problem of sampling is particularly relevant in a situation where the amount of material to be examined is overwhelming. If the material is printed in journals or documents, the investigator must make decisions about which sources to use in order to compile a representative sample without laboring through every scrap of evidence. With modern retrieval methods using data storage and computer disk files, this is not the major problem today that it was in the past. Nevertheless, the researcher needs to decide on specific procedures, including sampling techniques if they are needed.

The analysis of the problem should consider the sampling dimensions to be used. The **sample** might be taken in terms of time intervals, events, writings, issues, or persons. The plan should indicate clearly the way that the material will be sampled and the data required to answer the question. Procedures for selecting a sample which permits generalization are essential also, as will become clear in the next major section on selecting subjects. All parts of the plan must contribute to assuring that the sample is representative of a clearly defined **population,** and that the reader is aware of procedures used for selection.

Quantitative Data

The sources of data for a quantitative study are a product of the study itself, since the data are created through procedures designed for that one particular research study. Although there are research designs of a general nature, each study is unique unto itself. The planning for a quantitative study creates a specific design for answering a specific question. Studies of a quantitative nature use *observational devices* to gather data. Checklists, rating scales, tests, and questionnaires are all examples of data-gathering devices. These are not sources of data but are rather instruments to aid in observing and measuring whatever is being studied. The source of the data is the subjects under study. A class of biology students may be studied through the use of a biology achievement test. The test is not the source of the information, the biology students taking the test are.

The research question dictates the type of data needed in a study and most likely also directs the researcher to possible sources of data. All available sources should be considered, placed in an order of priority, and evaluated for use depending on how well the data relate to the problem under study. A study that seeks to explain conditions as they presently exist (a descriptive study) in general utilizes different types of data than does a study that manipulates conditions (the experimental study). Since in a descriptive study the only manipulation comes in the methods of observation and in the analysis, the researcher is limited to data that are available through normal events. Anything that he or she studies would have happened without the study's observation or measurement. In general, the investigator collects data for descriptive studies through surveys, case studies, documentary analysis, and job analysis. Data for correlational studies, on the other hand, will most likely come from measurement.

Experimental studies use data of a more technical nature, since the study is designed to examine the manipulation of one or more variables by the experimenter. The plan that requires quantitative data must specify the kinds of data needed and the best sources of those data. The chapters on experimental research, descriptive research, and the research proposal each cover the selection of sources as they relate to a particular type of study.

Selecting Subjects

Since education deals primarily with human beings, a large proportion of the studies in this field gather data about characteristics of designated human populations. The study itself is generally directed to a particular population, but the researcher must decide which specific individuals (the sample) within the larger grouping will provide the data. In research, the term *population* means any clearly defined aggregate or set of people or things. The term *sample* means a subaggregate or part of the population. For example, the population could be the members of the American Educational Research Association, and a sample could be a selected part of the membership. A population could be all the letters that Abraham Lincoln wrote while president, and a sample could be those letters which a collector had accumulated. In most educational studies, total populations will be too large to permit a contribution from each member, since studies are limited by available time and financial support. In planning for the study, the researcher must decide what population is being studied and which particular elements (the sample) of that population will provide data for the study. A sample that has the same characteristics as the population as a whole (a representative sample) is very important to generalization. Such a sample permits inferences and generalizations from the sample to be applied to the population as a whole.

When selecting subjects and their use in a research study, the researcher must pay attention to external validity. Population has two aspects which must be considered by the researcher to promote high external validity. Bracht and Glass described these aspects in discussing experiments, but all studies should take these considerations into account, even though the experiment does allow for more control:

Population of Validity
A. Experimentally Accessible Population vs. Target Population: Generalizing from the population of subjects that is available to the experimenter (the accessible population) to the total population of subjects about whom he is interested (the target population) requires a thorough knowledge of the characteristics of both populations. The results of an experiment might apply only for those special sorts of persons from whom the experimental subjects were selected and not for some larger population of persons.
B. Interaction of Personological Variables and Treatment Effects: If the superiority of one experimental treatment over another would be reversed when subjects at a different level of some variable descriptive of persons are exposed to the treatments, there exists an interaction of treatment effects and personological variable. (Bracht & Glass, 1968, p. 438)

Other components of external validity are discussed in the section on experimental methodology.

It may be that because of some limiting factor—such as a small number of subjects geographically convenient or some other administrative difficulty—the researcher will not be able to have a sample that meets all of the characteristics needed to allow generalization from the sample to the target population (or what the researcher perceives to be the target population). All studies should attempt to approach as closely as possible the methods described in the next section, where desirable sampling procedures for providing representativeness are outlined. A representative sample is needed to reduce **sampling error** to a minimum. Sampling error is the difference between a measure of a characteristic in the sample and the population. A sample that has nearly the same characteristics as the population allows generalization from the sample to the population. A few studies will be conducted in which all of the procedures are ideal, and some studies will be conducted in which most all the procedures violate the set of ideal procedures. Most studies will fall somewhere in between.

In the case where a class or group used as a sample represents the total population, sampling is not used, and there is no problem with sampling error.

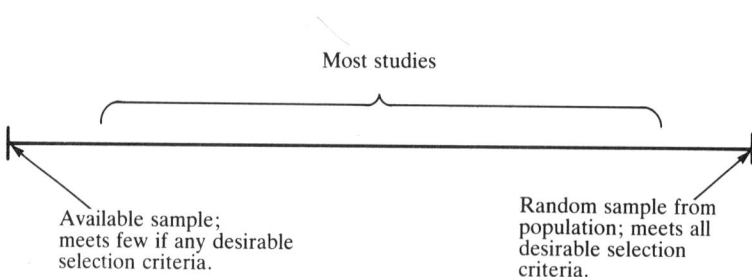

Most studies

Available sample; meets few if any desirable selection criteria.

Random sample from population; meets all desirable selection criteria.

The "available," "incidental," or "grab" sample simply uses intact classes or groups for study. The researcher should avoid this approach whenever possible. If the grab sample is the best sample that can be obtained, it must be used. The use does not make this approach more desirable, nor does it give the confidence that better procedures provide. Nevertheless, all questions deserve examination even if this means using less-than-ideal procedures. The limitations imposed by inferior procedures can reduce the value of the outcomes by reducing external validity.

The Swiss psychologist Jean Piaget studied the development of children's thinking for more than 50 years. Until recent years, little attention was given to his writings because his studies were of individual children or relatively small numbers of children. For a period of about 15 years, he studied mostly his own children. Today studies of large numbers of children are supporting many of the conclusions derived from his small samples. Since about 1960, scholars of American psychology and education have recognized Piaget as one of the major theorists of developmental psychology (Elkind, 1974, p. ix). Much of what Piaget has contributed to education would have been lost if he had restricted his studies to ideal research situations. An example of his procedure follows:

> The second period of Piaget's investigations began when, in 1929, he sought to trace the origins of the child's spontaneous mental growth to the behavior of infants; in this case, his own three children, Jacqueline, Lucienne, and Luarent. Piaget kept very detailed records of their behavior and of their performance on a series of ingenious tasks which he invented and presented to them. The books resulting from these investigations, "The Origins of Intelligence in Children," "Play, Dreams and Imitation in Children," and "The Construction of Reality in the Child," are now generally regarded as classics in the field and have been among the major forces behind the scurry of research activity in the area of infant behavior now current both in America and abroad. (Elkind, 1974, p. 16)

Ferguson acknowledges the need for compromise in the development of experimental procedures when he says:

> In practice, experiments are clearly not always conducted in the way our statistical preconceptions suggest they should be conducted. Experienced experimentalists are frequently aware of this. Much of the art of the experimentalist is concerned with reading conclusions from data which do not satisfy some conditions necessary for rigorous inference. (Ferguson, 1976, p. 133)

What holds for the experimentalist is also true for researchers using results of surveys and other data-gathering devices common in descriptive studies. Nevertheless, the researcher must consider carefully what is open to compromise and what is not. Later chapters devoted to specific types of research will expand on how the researcher can function with less-than-ideal conditions.

Along with the representativeness of a sample, the researcher must also consider sample size. A rule of thumb for beginning researchers is to use as large a sample as possible. This guideline is reasonable, because most questions about sample size involve the differences between a sample's data and the characteristic values of its. population. Determining the optimum sample size involves statistical concepts which go beyond the scope of this book. If a researcher is concerned that a particular sample is too large, a statistics book may lend some insight (Hays, 1963, pp. 204–206, 332–333).

Sampling Techniques

When the scope of a quantitative study—either descriptive or experimental—does not permit gathering information from every subject in the population, planning procedures must include decisions about how the subjects in the sample will be chosen. Studies sampling sources of information (such as books and journals) when complete reading is not possible, studies sampling geographic regions (especially in studies of field populations), and other studies with limited sampling plans also use the following procedures for selecting human subjects in selecting samples for their research.

Sample-selection procedures should not introduce any bias between characteristics of the sample and characteristics of the population. If the elements of the population can be individually identified, a **random sample** can be obtained. To obtain a strictly random sample, the sampling selection procedures must provide equal probability that each element in the population can appear in the sample and also must ensure that each choice of a sample element is independent of all other choices. The researcher must be sure that the procedures for selecting a sample are not a function of any of the subject's characteristics. **Random selection** is a safeguard against that.

What Kind of Sample?

The selection procedures determine whether a sample is random. Some procedures which at first appear to be random are not random. The usual use of the term "random"—meaning haphazard or without order—is not the definition used in sampling for research. Rather than being haphazard, a definite rule for selection controls the procedures to assure equal probability and independence, thus generating a random sample for statistical procedures.

An example that comes close to meeting these rules for randomness but technically falls short is the procedure of drawing names from a hat. Assume that a sample of 60 is to be chosen from a population of 400. The names may be placed in a container so that the folded papers are all the same size and mixed well. Without looking, the researcher draws a first name for the sample, then a second name, and so on. What is the probability that any one of the 400 would be selected on the first choice? (Answer: 1 in 400) What probability is associated with the second choice? (Answer: 1 in 399) Next? (Answer: 1 in 398) The probability for selection is *not* constant, as required; therefore the sample is not random. An attempt to overcome this problem of unequal probabilities would call for replacing each paper into the container before the next paper is drawn, thus keeping the probabilities for selection equal. As it works out, however, if the condition that a paper will not be used if drawn a second time holds, the conditional model has the same probabilities associated with it as the model that does not use replacement (Hodges & Lehmann, 1970, p. 92). Although either procedure for sampling—with or without replacement—falls short of meeting the required criteria, neither would in most cases inject bias to sample characteristics when compared to the population characteristics, unless the population were very small and the sample itself were very small.

If a roster for potential subjects is ordered alphabetically or listed in some systematic arrangement, every *n*th name could be chosen for the sample. Called **systematic sampling** this procedure can be viewed as having no bias, in most cases, although the possibility does exist that the characteristics may not be independent of the ordering. Thus the sample is again not a strictly random sample. Other types of sampling include time, event, trait, and cluster sampling, which are used in special cases.

Random Sample

When each element of a population can be identified, a more acceptable— and the most commonly employed—sampling procedure is using a **table of random numbers.** A table of random numbers consists of several pages of columns containing digits that have been generated in such a way that there is no pattern to their sequence (see Figure 7–1). In other words, in such tables there is the same probability of any digit following any other, and the selection of each was independent of all other choices. Such tables can be found in statistics books or in other similar sources (see Rand Corporation, 1955, & *Table of 105,000 Random Decimal Digits,* 1949).

Using a Table of Random Numbers. Figure 7–1 shows a page from a table of random numbers. To use a table of random numbers, assign consecutive numbers to the elements of the population being studied, perhaps using the alphabetical order of surnames. Start at any point in the random number table and proceed down (or up) the table, using the appropriate number of columns to identify enough tabled numbers to satisfy the chosen sample size. For a sample of 60 out of 400, for example, three columns are needed. The first 60 numbers that appear indicate the elements for the sample and the 60 names associated with those numbers become members of the sample.

Let's use Figure 7–1 to choose a sample of 10 random numbers from a population with 200 elements to illustrate the procedure. Any entry rule that

77513 03820	86864 29901	68414 82774	51908 13980	72893 55507
19502 37174	69979 20288	55210 29773	74287 75251	65344 67415
21818 59313	93278 81757	05686 73156	07082 85046	31853 38452
51474 66499	68107 23621	94049 91345	42836 09191	08007 45449
99559 68331	62535 24170	69777 12830	74819 78142	43860 72834
33713 48007	93584 72869	51926 64721	58303 29822	93174 93972
85274 86893	11303 22970	28834 34137	73515 90400	71148 43643
84133 89640	44035 52166	73852 70091	61222 60561	62327 18423
56732 16234	17395 96131	10123 91622	85496 57560	81604 18880
65138 56806	87648 85261	34313 65861	45875 21069	85644 47277
38001 02176	81719 11711	71602 92937	74219 64049	65584 49698
37402 96397	01304 77586	56271 10086	47324 62605	40030 37438
97125 40348	87083 31417	21815 39250	75237 62047	15501 29578
21826 41134	47143 34072	64638 85902	49139 06441	03856 54552
73135 42742	95719 09035	85794 74296	08789 88156	64691 19202
07638 77929	03061 18072	96207 44156	23821 99538	04713 66994
60528 83441	07954 19814	59175 20695	05533 52139	61212 06455
83596 35655	06958 92983	05128 09719	77433 53783	92301 50498
10850 62746	99599 10507	13499 06319	53075 71839	06410 19362
39820 98952	43622 63147	64421 80814	43800 09351	31024 73167
59580 06478	75569 78800	88835 54486	23768 06156	04111 08408
38508 07341	23793 48763	90822 97022	17719 04207	95954 49953
30692 70668	94688 16127	56196 80091	82067 63400	05462 69200
65443 95659	18238 27437	49632 24041	08337 65676	96299 90836
27267 50264	13192 72294	07477 44606	17985 48911	97341 30358
91307 06991	19072 24210	36699 53728	28825 35793	28976 66252
68434 94688	84473 13622	62126 98408	12843 82590	09815 93146
48908 15877	54745 24591	35700 04754	83824 52692	54130 55160
06913 45197	42672 78601	11883 09528	63011 98901	14974 40344
10455 16019	14210 33712	91342 37821	88325 80851	43667 70883
12883 97343	65027 61184	04285 01392	17974 15077	90712 26769
21778 30976	38807 36961	31649 42096	63281 02023	08816 47449
19523 59515	65122 59659	86283 68258	69572 13798	16435 91529
67245 52670	35583 16563	79246 86686	76463 34222	26655 90802
60584 47377	07500 37992	45134 26529	26760 83637	41326 44344
53853 41377	36066 94850	58838 73859	49364 73331	96240 43642
24637 38736	74384 89342	52623 07992	12369 18601	03742 83873
83080 12451	38992 22815	07759 51777	97377 27585	51972 37867
16444 24334	36151 99073	27493 70939	85130 32552	54846 54759
60790 18157	57178 65762	11161 78576	45819 52979	65130 04860
03991 10461	93716 16894	66083 24653	84609 58232	88618 19161
38555 95554	32886 59780	08355 60860	29735 47762	71299 23853
17546 73704	92052 46215	55121 29281	59076 07936	27954 58909
32643 52861	95819 06831	00911 98936	76355 93779	80863 00514
69572 68777	39510 35905	14060 40619	29549 69616	33564 60780
24122 66591	27699 06496	14845 46672	61958 77100	90899 75754
61196 30231	92962 61773	41839 55382	17267 70943	78038 70267
30532 21704	10274 12202	39685 23309	10061 68829	55986 66485
03788 97599	75867 20717	74416 53166	35208 33374	87539 08823
48228 63379	85783 47619	53152 67433	35663 52972	16818 60311
60365 94653	35075 33949	42614 29297	01918 28316	· 98953 73231
83799 42402	56623 34442	34944 41374	70071 14736	09958 18065
32960 07405	36409 83232	99385 41600	11133 07586	15917 06253
19322 53845	57620 52606	66497 68646	78138 66559	19640 99413
11220 94747	07399 37408	48509 23929	27482 45476	85244 35159
31751 57260	68980 05339	15470 48355	88651 22596	03152 19121
88492 99382	14454 04504	20094 98977	74843 93413	22109 78508
30934 47744	07481 83828	73788 06533	28597 20405	94205 20380
22888 48893	27499 98748	60530 45128	74022 84617	82037 10268
78212 16993	35902 91386	44372 15486	65741 14014	87481 37220

Note. Richard P. Runyon and Audrey Haber, FUNDAMENTALS OF BEHAVIORAL STATISTICS (2nd ed.), ©1971, Addison-Wesley, Reading, Mass. p. 320. Reprinted with permission.

FIGURE 7–1   A Table of Random Numbers

uses 3 digits can be used. The table may be entered at the top, bottom, middle or either side, and columns or rows read in order for selecting sample elements. For this example, the middle 3 digits from the sets of 5 digits are used. The table is entered from the top in the second set from the left side. This sample will be the names associated with the first 10 numbers less than 200. The table entry looks like this:

    77513 03820   86864 29901   68414 82774   51908 13980
           37174
           931

The first number for the sample will be 034, second will be 113, giving the sample numbers of 034, 113, 066, 026, 097, 137, 046, 023, and 170, from the second column, and 130 from the third column. Given a different rule and starting place, a different sample would be chosen. All samples chosen in this way are random—each element of the population has equal probability of inclusion in the sample and the choice of one element for the sample has no bearing on any other choice. The sample is also a random sample of all possible samples of 10 that could be chosen from the 200 population elements.

Stratifying Samples. With random sampling, there is no control on sample characteristics beyond probability and independence. Statistical procedures are dependent on random selection, and they are basically a study of what can happen when samples are drawn at random. A mathematical model which uses a sampling distribution compares what a researcher sees in an experiment with what could be expected when abstracting from the model. A technique that may be used to give added control to sample characteristics when the population can be divided into strata on one or more variables is called **stratified random sampling.** The method of stratifying a random sample allows equal allocation from each population class stratum to the sample and retains randomness through equal probability of selection. The strata are the different levels or categories of a characteristic. For example, the strata for the characteristic of hair color could be black, brown, blonde, and red.

To stratify a human population according to the variable *sex,* the population is divided into two classes based on sex. One half of the cases for the sample are chosen from the class female and the other half from the class male, using random procedures for selection from each class. This selection is represented graphically in Figure 7–2. Selection from identified strata of male and female controls for any bias on the sex variable. Stratification on two variables, sex and past achievement levels, would be developed as Figure 7–3 shows.

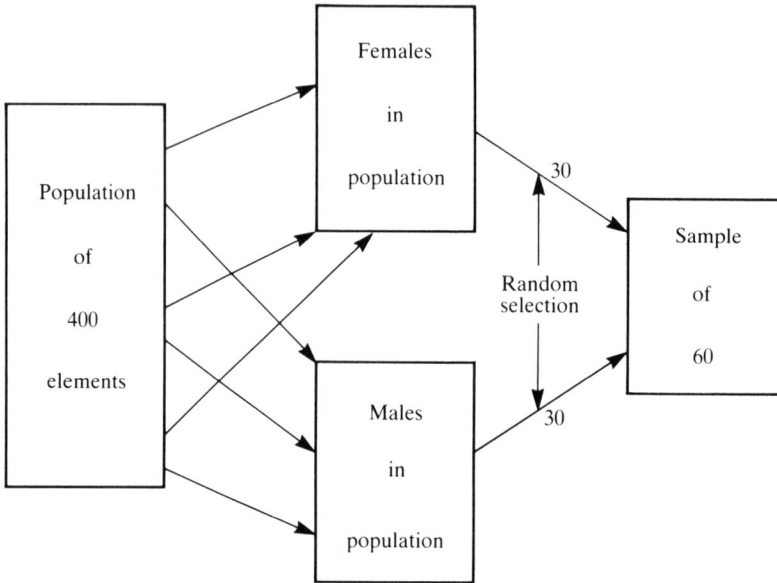

FIGURE 7–2   Selecting a Random Sample of 60 Elements from a Population of 400

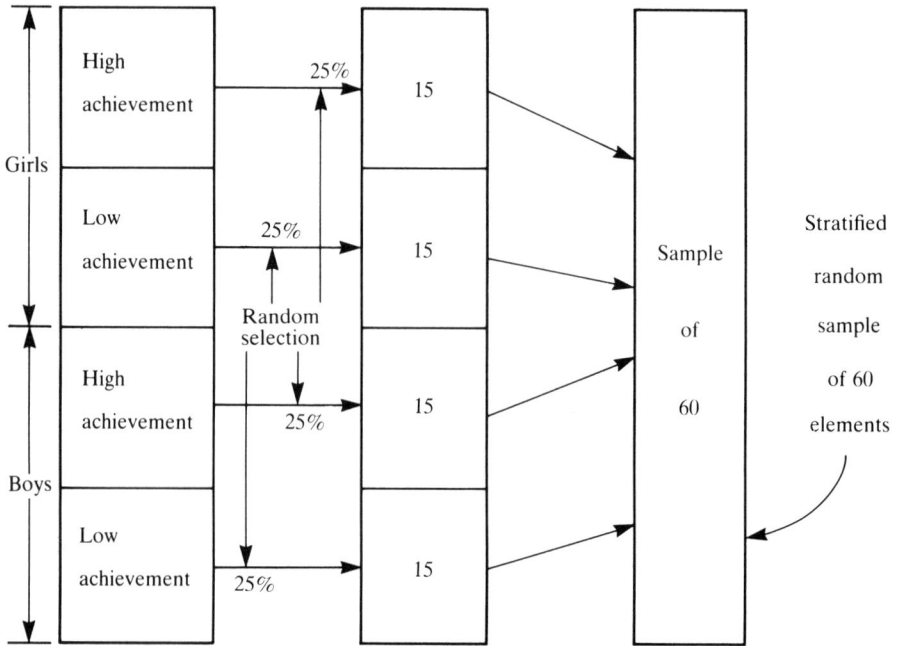

FIGURE 7–3   Stratification of a Sample on the Variables of Sex and Achievement

The procedure for creating a proportionally stratified random sample requires information about proportions within specific populations. The only added feature in this technique is selecting members from a group for the sample in the same proportion that the group represents within the population. Figure 7–4 represents this selection schematically.

The researcher constantly strives to make the sample representative of the population's characteristics. Stratifying a sample gives the researcher control of important variables in order to make the sample more representative of the parent population. Theoretically a population of elements which can be listed could be stratified on all variables. However, in all practicality, this is impossible for a human population. The number of subjects within each cell or group used for selection would be just too small. If they were stratified for all variables, the cells would probably consist of one member each, since no two human beings are exactly alike on all variables. In practice, stratification should be limited to the two or three variables that the researcher feels are most important to control. When deciding about stratification, it becomes most important that the characteristics of the entire population be considered in relation to the problem under study before undertaking the sampling techniques.

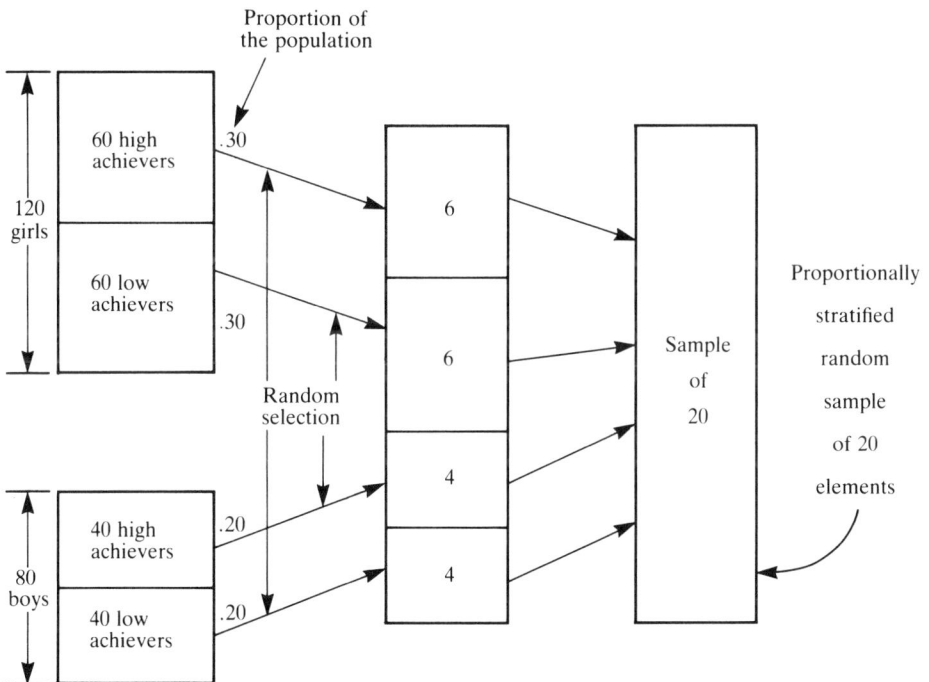

FIGURE 7–4 Proportionally Stratified Random Sample

Selecting a sample that is representative of the population is a difficult task. Many populations are too large to allow the researcher to make the list required for the above techniques. Where possible, procedures that generate a random sample should be used. Unfortunately, the researcher must often use other procedures in practice. Designs constructed without regard to real-world conditions must, in many instances, be altered when it becomes necessary to carry out the study under real-world conditions. When planning the study, the researcher must make decisions with an awareness of how close he or she can expect to find or create conditions that fit the abstract, ideal design. How can the medical researcher of a particular ailment be sure that the subjects with ailments who are admitted to one clinic for study are like others who go to other clinics across town, in another state, or in another country for the same ailment? How can a basketball coach generalize from one player who is seven feet tall to all other human beings who are seven feet tall? How can a researcher of educational practices generalize from Harlan, Kentucky, to Harlem, New York? The next section deals with problems of generalization from samples that do not meet the criterion of equal probability in assignment. *Equiprobability* means that the sample is representative for statistical procedures and further generalization. When equiprobability is not possible, other steps must be taken.

Sampling without Randomness

This section discusses generalizing from samples that are not obtained randomly. Students probably think that this cannot be done, since equiprobability is needed for generalization. Where it is possible, random sampling should certainly be used; however, much research would be impossible if the investigator were restricted to those studies amenable to random sampling. Much of the art of the researching lies in being able to put together a workable plan where actual conditions do not allow all the stated criteria to be met. One condition that is often difficult to meet is that of drawing a sample from a population at random. The task then requires putting together a plan that will be acceptable by colleagues who are considered experts or authorities in research procedures. It is too much to hope (or expect) 100 percent agreement from everyone, since many times a single choice must be made from one of several alternatives. Often, several alternatives will have their proponents—hence the disagreement. A plan should be examined logically, so that each choice and each part can be defended as the best choice within the framework of acceptable research practice. The best rule of thumb follows these guidelines:

1. Consider all alternatives.
2. List the relative strengths and weaknesses of each alternative.
3. Weigh the alternatives carefully.
4. Make the best rational decision on these bases.

Where the choice is not ideal, the researcher should choose that compromise which provides more advantages than any one of the other choices.

Criticism of research in all fields is based on unacceptable practices—where acceptance means what is generally accepted in the field. "Unacceptable" may, in some cases, be in the eye of the beholder, especially when all authorities do not agree about just what is acceptable practice. An attack on research procedures may mean that the reviewer would have made a different choice than the researcher did at one or more places in the design. This attack may, in some instances, be an arbitrary decision based on personal biases. In other cases, it may be based on widely accepted procedures of research. A carefully considered plan of procedures cannot control for arbitrary attacks, but it can do much toward controlling attacks based on accepted practice.

A common criticism is to question the representativeness of a sample, since in most cases random procedures for the study exist at only the abstract level. Sampling procedures should approximate as closely as possible the theoretical assumption of equiprobability. If sampling procedures assure approximately equal probability, then theory based on that concept can be used in sampling for the study. Two examples of approximating equal probability have been mentioned—systematic sampling and drawing names from a container. In each of these methods for obtaining a sample, the list used for the population must be exhaustive. Samples drawn from lists that do not provide a complete record of the elements of the population may cause bias within the sample. A list of registered automobile owners might, in some cases, be considered representative of the total population. It could then be used to draw a sample that would allow generalizing about the total population. However, if the public transportation office of a large city were studying habits of people using the city bus lines, they would find that a list of licensed car owners would not be appropriate for sample selection, since the ownership or nonownership of an automobile is probably not independent of use of city buses. A study examining the characteristics of car owners' use of bus lines could use the list of registered car owners, because the list would include all owners—it is exhaustive. The researcher must make sure that the list used for selecting a sample is, in fact, the appropriate listing of the population under study.

Generalizing Results. The methods just discussed have little relevance if the population elements for a study cannot be listed. A special education teacher may have 4 autistic pupils in an entire school district. An experimentalist may study 50 white rats in a T-maze. A study may assess all kindergarten pupils in a school district on the dimension of creativity exhibited in art objects. How can results of research on any of these groups be considered generalizable? A posteriori investigation of sample characteristics may show that the sample does not differ greatly in important traits from the population. For the autistic children, the characteristics that class them as autistic identify them with others classed the same way and allow them to be representative of other children with like characteristics. The sample of white rats could be compared to other rats on the basis of physical characteristics and possibly on some performance tests.

Other variables of sex, age, aptitudes, socioeconomic background, and the like can be reported for subjects in a study. The conclusions drawn for that study on subjects with certain traits can then be generalized to other subjects with like traits. Carefully reported research lets those reading about the research have a basis for drawing their own generalizations and deriving implications for other subjects.

The kindergarten children may be studied and compared to the population at large with respect to sex, age, mental measurements, socioeconomic background, and other variables that the researcher would consider important for the study of creativity as exhibited in art objects. If the sample shows no bias on important variables, the researcher may consider the sample representative and use it as if it were a random sample. Such use assumes that the conditions closely approximate the results expected from equiprobability sampling. The acceptance of generalizations from the study will rest primarily on how well others agree about how closely this assumption is met.

Reader Generalization. A very useful technique in studies in which random sampling cannot be used lets the reader generalize from information provided in the report of the study. In addition to data used in the study, the investigator can provide demographic information about sample characteristics. For example, by giving the average IQ, a measure of the variation of IQ scores, the socioeconomic breakdown, age range, and other pertinent data, the researcher provides the reader of the research an opportunity to make generalizations to similar groups. The results of a study on subjects with particular characteristics will be generalizable to groups with like characteristics. A difference on only one variable might cause the study's conclusions not to be generalizable to another situation. For example, two sets of sixth-grade students might be very much alike on all variables except geographic location. There is probably enough difference reflected among individuals growing up in a rural midwestern community and individuals growing up in the inner-city schools of a large metropolitan district to preclude generalizing from one to the other, even though all are much alike on variables like age, sex, and IQ.

☐CHECK YOUR UNDERSTANDING

See how the following situations vary and how a researcher would be open to possible criticism for each. Which of the following selection procedures would give a sample that would be considered representative for research purposes? Which would be suspected of possible bias because of selection procedures?

Population	Sample selection procedures	Representative (Yes/No)	Bias (Yes/No)
1. All of the 5,000 students at Zee University	Choose the first 50 students who enter the Business building after 10:00 A.M. on May first.		
2. All of the 5,000 students at Zee University	Choose the first 50 students who enter the bookstore after 10:00 A.M. on May first.		

Population	Sample selection procedures	Representative (Yes/No)	Bias (Yes/No)
3. All of the 5,000 students at Zee University	Choose every 100th name from the registrar's alphabetical student list.		
4. All of the 5,000 students at Zee University	Use a table of random numbers to choose 50 names for the sample.		
5. All students enrolled in courses offered by the English Department	Use those students enrolled in English 479—Literary Criticism.		
6. All sixth-grade students in the United States	Use all sixth-grade students in Terre Haute, Indiana, schools.		
7. All psychology textbooks published between 1930 and 1940	Use all psychology textbooks published in 1935.		

Answers

1. Probably not representative, because the sample would most likely be loaded with business-major students. The bias would be an overrepresentation of business students in the sample when compared to the proportion in the population.
2. Probably a better representation of the several schools than in (1), but there are many selection factors that determine who goes to the bookstore and who does not. The bias could come from several sources. Those living close to the bookstore are more likely to shop there than those who live farther away. Those on tight budgets may not visit the bookstore as often as more affluent students. Try to think of other possible selection factors that might bias the sample.
3. This is systematic sampling and would in most cases not be suspected of creating a biased sample. It is usually an acceptable procedure, although it does not provide equal probability in sample selection. The sample should be representative with no bias.
4. This procedure would provide a representative sample for all statistical procedures, and it should not be a biased sample.
5. Not representative because those enrolled in English 479 are probably more sophisticated English students than all but a small segment of those enrolled in all English classes. The bias is toward English majors being overrepresented in the sample.
6. Students from any one limited geographic area are not likely to be representative of a much larger area because of differences in important

characteristics. There is much room for bias, thus the importance of listing sample characteristics for the reader.

7. Although the chosen data was the middle of the decade, the books of 1935 probably would not be representative of books from the 10-year period because of the amount of change over 10 years. Bias would be toward those topics of most concern in 1935.

Random Assignment

In many research plans, groups are compared to identify differences between the groups after different treatments. To look for differences after treatment, it is necessary to be able to say something about differences before treatment is applied. The best way to accomplish this is to start both groups to be compared at the same level. The selection of two samples from the population at random defines two samples that are considered the same on all variables. If the two are the same when the study starts and the difference at the end is appreciable, the difference can be attributed to different effects.

When the population being studied does not permit random selection of subjects to allow for equal groups, **random assignment** of subjects to groups can be used to equate the groups for statistical tests. When subjects have been chosen for the study and all are to be assigned to treatment groups, random assignment will control for all variables between (for two groups) or among (more than two) groups. For the two-group study, each subject can be assigned a number and—by random procedures—can be assigned to one of the two groups by alternating the assignment according to the sequence of appearance in a table of random numbers. A modification of this procedure will allow assignment to any number of groups under study.

A combination of random sampling and random assignment can be used to select and assign subjects to groups. A selection of subjects can be made randomly, and then those subjects can be assigned to groups randomly.

If a research study involves only two groups and the number of subjects to be assigned is not large, a coin-flip method can be used in the absence of a table of random numbers. The procedure calls for writing the name or identifying number for each subject to be assigned on a separate piece of paper, folding all papers to the same size, placing all papers in a container, and mixing well. A person then draws two papers from the container and places them on a table so that one is to the left and the other is to the right. The researcher must then set a ground rule for a coin flip. (Example: If heads comes up, the one to the left goes to group A; if tails comes up, the one to the right goes into group A. Of course, the remaining one will always go to group B.) The person continues to draw pairs and flip the coin until all subjects have been assigned. Equiprobability in *assignment* is assured by this method. This assignment generates equally sized groups and equates the groups for statistical tests of significance.

Further randomness in assignment can be used when assigning treatment to the two groups. The researcher must devise a rule when assigning the treatment to the two groups. (Example: If heads comes up when the coin is flipped, A will get treatment C, or if tails comes up when flipping the coin, group A will get treatment D. Group B will then be assigned the other treatment.) To assign 30 students to 2 treatment groups when using the coin-flip procedure to assure randomness,

1. Write the names (or numbers) of subjects on like pieces of paper, fold and mix well in a container.
2. Draw two papers with names (or numbers) and place one to the left and one to the right.
3. Devise a rule for a coin flip.
4. Flip the coin and assign each to a group.
5. Continue drawing pairs and assign to groups until papers are exhausted.
6. Flip a coin to assign treatment to a group.

Random *sampling* procedures are used to control for bias externally in comparing sample characteristics to population characteristics. Random *assignment* controls for bias internally so that each subject has an equal probability of appearing in either of the two groups.

☐ CHECK YOUR UNDERSTANDING

Which of the following selection procedures would give samples that would be considered equal for research purposes? Which would be suspected of possible bias because of selection procedures?

Subjects to be assigned	Assignment procedures	Equal Groups (Yes/No)	Bias (Yes/No)
1. 30 white rats to 2 groups	The first 15 caught go to group A, and the last 15 caught go to group B. A coin is flipped to assign treatment to the 2 groups.		
2. 40 students to 2 groups	Each student is assigned a number, and a table of random numbers is used to divide the 40 by alternating assignment to the 2 groups. Group A is then assigned the experimental treatment.		
3. Students in 2 introductory speech classes to 2 groups	The treatment was assigned randomly by flipping a coin, and the 8-o'clock class became the control group and the 11-o'clock group became the class to receive the experimental treatment.		
4. 40 students to 2 groups	Each student is assigned a number and a table of random numbers is used to divide the 40 by alternating assignment to the 2 groups. A coin flip is used to assign the experimental treatment to group A.		

Answers

1. The first 15 were the easiest to catch and may be more passive—that is, less active and/or less aggressive. Bias would be toward whatever variables contributed to their being caught first. The assignment of treatment to groups would introduce no *new* bias.
2. Equality acceptable for statistical procedures. Arbitrary assignment of treatment could violate equal probability, but this is probably not a serious error. Flip a coin to assign treatment for the two groups.
3. The assignment of treatment by a coin flip is acceptable. The bias would result in selection to the two class periods. Time, instructor, meeting place, and type of class organization could contribute bias.
4. Randomness has been used in both assignment to groups and assignment of treatment, therefore representing equal groups and no bias in the sample.

Other Sources of Bias

Bias may appear in some quantitative studies when volunteers respond to a survey for a descriptive study or receive treatment in an experimental study. The fact that some people volunteered and contributed data while other participants did not volunteer introduces bias into any study based on volunteers. In most cases, the bias originates in the self-selection of the subjects. Subjects likely to volunteer may be more outgoing, more gregarious, or more highly motivated than those who did not volunteer, thus providing a nonrepresentative sample.

When a study uses a questionnaire to gather information, the elements of the population chosen to receive the questionnaire may be a representative sample, but the responding individuals—those actually supplying the data—may be a poor representation of the population. A question concerning a controversial issue may trigger responses from those either strongly for or strongly against. For example, one individual strongly against a proposal for an innovative elementary curriculum may, through influence and/or effort, see that others also opposed return the questionnaire and thus weight the sample data. The sample then consists of a disproportionately large number of "against" votes when compared to the number in the total population who are "against." The same may happen if the eager ones are "for" the issue. Ways of coping with these problems are presented in later sections.

Collecting Data

All research studies—whether qualitative or quantitative—need information about the variables under study. The information may come from documents, objects, animals, or human beings. Information in the first form requires organization before it becomes meaningful enough that its hidden messages about questions under study can be interpreted. For quantitative data, this organization might be as simple as listing a set of scores in order of their magnitude. The largest value is listed first and other values arranged so that each succeeding value is larger than all of those falling below. Qualitative data organization is likely to be quite complex and require in-depth study to decide how to arrange this kind of information in the best way.

Qualitative Data

One major function of data processing is organizing qualitative data to facilitate interpretation. The organization of qualitative data may be as complex as providing a structure to interpret large amounts of factual data that cannot be reduced to numbers. Data collection procedures must be chosen and implemented to supply data which are easily organized. The manner of collection can facilitate the organization of the data if the design specifies the appropriate way to organize the data. For example, the researcher can often arrange a survey questionnaire so that computer cards can be keypunched directly from the returned forms. Without preplanning, an intervening step may be required to put the data into interpretable form. The use of bibliography cards to record data from a historical study allows arrangement of material through an ordering of the cards. This many times saves at least one organizational writing of the material. Other equally time-saving procedures can be incorporated if the researcher coordinates data collection procedures with an appropriate organizational scheme set forth in the research design.

Traditionally, the complexities of collecting information from relics, documents, and bibliographical materials have required so much time that many important investigations were either scaled down in scope or not attempted. Many of the questions left untouched by researchers in the past are now open to investigation through the use of computers capable of storing nonnumeric information in disk files. New techniques have turned the previously limited coverage given bibliographic and governmental data into comprehensive coverage, and much of what in the past was left to accidental discovery has now become part of routine investigation.

Researchers have always been cautious about researching questions that might overextend their capacities for handling data. Modern researchers must still be aware of limitations attached to treating data but—at the same time—must be aware that many questions unanswerable in the past are researchable today.

Descriptive research uses observational techniques such as **surveys**—both interview and questionnaire—to gather data. The nature of these data requires different techniques to organize. Some data may be qualitative, while other data are quantitative. The data-gathering techniques for descriptive studies should be developed to provide quantified data amenable to appropriate treatment. Computers have reduced laborious hand calculations to near-instantaneous machine calculation. Furthermore, previously un-answerable questions dealing with such subjects as astronomy and education can be investigated because organization of large quantities of nonnumeric data can be handled routinely. Researchers should not limit a study unnecessarily by assuming that a question remains unanswerable for all time. What was unanswerable yesterday may be treated routinely today.

Quantitative Data

Since numbers provide exactness in reporting, ambiguity associated with statements about size, numbers, and such can be reduced to a minimum. Whenever possible, researchers use quantification of information for this reason. Data collection procedures are best organized to allow efficient quantification. In general, experimental studies generate data in quantified form, and the organization for data treatment is easily accomplished. If procedures require special collection tools—such as a checklist or score-card—the collection instrument should be arranged for organization of the data by quantification.

Designing Collection Techniques

The best rule of thumb for directing the choice of data-gathering techniques is to fit together a plan that calls for the most appropriate kind of data and that supplies them in sufficient quantity to provide results for making valid conclusions.

What data and how much? The necessary data must be gathered and steps taken to avoid gathering unnecessary information. Gathering unneeded data can be expensive in money and in time. The time of researcher and subjects is wasted if information gathered is not used. In experimental studies, the investigator will need to take a careful look to be sure that the required data do not violate any ethical right of the subjects. The data required must in no way demand procedures that would affect subjects negatively.

Where can the data be obtained? In many educational studies, data are gathered from subjects in a school setting. In most cases, permission to conduct the study must be obtained from proper administrative officials. Administrators must know specifically what data are wanted, how they will be used, and how results will be disseminated. For historical studies, documents and school records need to be examined. Written permission should be obtained early in the planning stage to avoid developing a research plan and discovering that, for some reason, the information is not available.

How should the data be collected and recorded? For most experimental studies, collecting and recording data is not a major difficulty. For descrip-tive and historical studies, on the other hand, this may be the major decision of the designing process. Many sources may be opened only through the willingness of particular individuals to open document files or to reveal information—personal or public—that they possess. For a historical study, the availability of primary sources is crucial, since reliance on secondary sources reduces the validity of the study. The data should be recorded in such a way that it will be interpretable in that form.

When should the data be collected? The researcher should make a special effort to avoid collecting data during any time period that would be considered atypical with respect to general conditions. If test scores are being gathered, the time of day, day of week, or place on the school calendar all may cause conditions to vary. Such atypical times as the day before or after a vacation, first or last period of the day, Monday or Friday should be avoided for data gathering. Surveys and other requests for information should be timed to avoid any conditions that would bias the information gathered.

For each study, the appropriate data-collection methods developed contribute to the unique design for that study. Particular data-gathering instruments should be identified or created to elicit the exact data needed to provide an answer to the question. The tools for data-gathering are discussed in the three chapters devoted to historical, descriptive, and experimental research.

Organizing Data

Data must be assembled in some way other than by haphazardly recording bits and pieces to be fitted together at some later time. A very important aspect of any design is the plan for organizing the facts for interpretation. The organization should be directed by the type of information needed for the study and how the data will be analyzed. Careful coordination between data-gathering procedures and data treatment will be governed by these organization procedures. Efficiency can be built into the methodology by recording the original raw data in an easily interpretable form. Such a design can do much to expedite analysis. Certainly qualitative studies using words will need a much different arrangement at this stage than a quantitative study, where the facts are sets of numbers. Quantitative data should be organized for treatment and presented to readers through the use of tables and graphs. For hand calculation or desk calculators, the frequency-distribution data and contingency tables provide tools for organization. If a computer is to be used, the data should be organized through a deck of punched computer cards or in some other form that can be easily transferred to cards. The results should be reported in appropriate tables.

There are no rigid guidelines for organizing qualitative data. The final organization takes place as the report narrative is composed. While gathering nonnumerical data, the investigator will find the following suggestions helpful in organizing the prose into a well-presented, logical sequence for valid interpretation:

1. Use bibliography cards to record the information extracted from sources.

2. Record comparative study information fact-to-fact, and leave interpretation until later.
3. Keep factual the documentary evidence and the information gained from relics to avoid interpretation at recording time.
4. Keep a time line to place the gathered information chronologically.
5. Be objective in deciding the emphasis to be given to gathered information.

When planning for the study, the researcher will want to structure the data organization with an eye to the type of data to be gathered and the interpretation procedures to be employed. Specific techniques for organizing data are discussed in the chapters devoted to the three types of research activities.

Treating Data

To provide interpretable results, the data gathered must be examined carefully. The planning of the research must include a definite direction for data treatment, since much of the success of data analysis rests on the ability of the data-gathering procedures to provide interpretable data and on the choice of appropriate methods for the analysis. The treatment of the data is intended to provide a solid basis and support for the conclusions drawn from the study. Any valid decision about the research hypothesis rests on the researcher's ability to show that the data treatment for the study is appropriate and that the results are adequate for forming valid conclusons.

Historical Studies

Data treatment for a historical study can best be viewed as the evolution of an outline that the researcher develops as the theme of the study takes shape. The plan for a historical study should include a tentative outline based on the types and sources of data being used and the process of validating the data through formal criticism. Developing a working outline encourages thoughtful review of gathered data and should provide a logical sequence for an objectively obtained decision about the proposed question. By the time the material is collected, the arrangement of the data should conform closely with the form of the final report.

The validity of the decision will be enhanced by (1) a mastery of the information, (2) clearly perceived relationships, and (3) conclusions based on objectivity rather than researcher bias. The original outline from the plan and the evolved outline from data treatment should build as much objectivity as possible into what is, at best, more subjective than most would like research studies in education to be.

Educational research using the historical approach is intended to obtain facts (information) with historical authenticity and to derive valid conclusions (interpretation). Tilden expresses well the relationship between the two:

Information, as such, is not Interpretation. Interpretation is revelation based on information. But they are entirely different things. However, all interpretation includes information. (1957, p. 18)

For historical research studies, the treatment of the data is the interpretation given to obtained data.

Descriptive Studies

Descriptive studies requiring documentary analysis use much the same treatment procedures as those used for the typical historical research study: a tentative outline, a working outline developed as the information is being gathered, and a written narrative for basing conclusions. A descriptive study that asks a question about present conditions utilizes data of a different nature. Information from surveys, interviews, checklists, rating scales, and other data-collection devices for gathering data about present conditions can, in most cases, be expressed as descriptive statistics to assist in analyzing the data. Correlational techniques are useful in investigating relationships between variables, and scaling devices provide ways for creating data that the researcher can treat statistically.

For many studies in the behavioral sciences, the data gathered may not meet all of the assumptions required for parametric tests of significance. The data from many descriptive studies are frequencies, ranks, or values, obtained where the assumption of normality of distribution of scores does not apply or cannot be tested. Today nonparametric techniques for hypothesis testing are suited to data of this nature and should be used when the more powerful parametric tests are not appropriate. The names of these tests allude to the reasons for their suitability. They are often called *distribution-free tests,* since they assume nothing about the distribution of the population, or *ranking tests,* suggesting their other advantage: they may be used with scores which are not exact in a numerical sense but which may be ordered in ranks (Siegel, 1956, p. vii).

The investigator should become aware of the techniques available for interpreting data with the above characteristics. Computational simplicity is an advantage, as is their usefulness with small samples. Siegel's (1956) book on nonparametric tests was the first to attempt to gather many nonparametric techniques under one cover. It is still widely used by researchers. The student of research would benefit from familiarity with the ways to treat these kinds of data presented in *Non-Parametric Statistics for the Behavioral Sciences.*

In addition to the descriptive analysis and data analysis, the element of interpreting meaning is a task belonging to the researcher. Conclusions are interpretations that consist of generalizations, formed through reasoning, and judgments by the researcher. Careful coordination of treatment procedures provides a bridge between the gathering of data and the conclusions.

Descriptive studies which require both documentary analysis (utilizing strictly qualitative data) and analysis of present conditions (utilizing quantitative data) use both sorts of data. Types of descriptive studies using both are case studies, community studies, antecedent-consequence studies, trend studies, and studies that compare the present with the past—*comparative studies.*

Experimental Studies

As used in research, the term "experimentation" refers to inquiry activities in which laboratory conditions or near-laboratory conditions allow a variable or variables to be manipulated with strict control over the other remaining variables. Such research investigates the effects on certain clearly identified dependent variables. Since the researcher has strict control of the situation, most of the treatment for data from experimental studies uses statistical techniques providing precise answers to aid in making interpretations and conclusions. The data are quantitative and—if properly gathered—will provide what most researchers feel is the best basis for making decisions. Within the overall research design (the plan), statistical treatment is organized around a statistical design which explains data treatment. Consequently, the plan for an experimental study must identify the appropriate statistical design for analyzing the data. Interpretation of conclusions is the product of experimental studies, and it takes much the same form of generalization as the conclusions for historical and descriptive studies.

Pilot Study. After the design of a study is completed, the researcher may implement a **pilot study** to check on how well the design procedures are articulated and to identify any places where the logistics and mechanical aspects need further attention. A pilot study is a scaled-down version of the full-blown study, using a small number of subjects who will not be used to provide data for the major study. It gives the researcher and any aides who will be participating in the study an opportunity to see how well the plan fits together logistically and a chance to correct any difficulties encountered with procedures or mechanical devices. Sampling techniques need not be a part of the pilot study, since the data will not be analyzed and reported. Although a pilot is used primarily with experimental studies, other methodology can often use a pilot study. For example, a questionnaire might be circulated to a few persons who will not be responding to the final form. Using this preliminary, the researcher can obtain feedback about ambiguous or awkwardly-stated parts of the questionnaire and get reactions to indicate how the questionnaire will be received when delivered for the study.

The Researcher's Role

In the descriptive study and the historical study, it is generally left largely up to the researcher to remove himself or herself from making interpretive decisions at certain places in the process, thus providing more objectivity to the results. Do not interpret this to mean that experimentation in education is 100 percent objective—it still remains much an art. Light gives us a step into this idea when he says:

My colleagues and statistics students sometimes seem a bit startled when I share with them my belief that data analysis is an art as much as it is a science. It must seem to them a bit incongruous that the same fellow who on one day interprets significance levels and suggests specific statistical techniques such as two-stage least squares should on another day question how "scientific" such a process is. (1973, p. 318)

Light discusses the importance of data treatment and sums up his argument with, "A good analyst, who has insightful judgment both in selecting a model and scaling responses for different variables, can draw useful inferences from his research. A poor analyst, of course, cannot" (1973, p. 319). The reader of the research should go beyond the reported results and make a judgment about the particular design. The researcher should go beyond using a model simply because someone else used it in a somewhat similar situation or because it is simple. Contrary to what many believe, even quite sophisticated statistical designs do not in themselves provide ready-made conclusions to research studies. The researcher must check the design for the degree of validity of the total design. The principles to be considered are discussed at length in Chapter 11.

The two specific areas of collection and treatment of data are so closely related that it is difficult to separate them except for formal discussion. The subjects to be studied make up an integral part of the decisions made in the basic plan for the study. In practice, the researcher must consider each facet in its interrelationships with other aspects. A person observing a researcher would find it difficult to sort out design-development activities precisely enough that it would be clear how to classify each activity, because all aspects are being fitted together at the same time.

Sample Abstracts

The following three abstracts represent basic differences that must be taken into consideration when developing designs for research studies. The first abstract gives a brief account of a completed study about a question based in the past. The second abstract reviews a completed study about a question based in the present with no manipulation of variables. The third abstract describes a controlled study where the investigation created conditions for collection of data. This third study approaches classification as an experimental study because the groups were studied in regard to differences on a set of characteristics. The study is not a true experiment where the researcher manipulated a variable within the study itself, but the same basic design is used in this example of ex post facto research. The major difference between this and an experimental study is that the differences in the groups reflect different characteristics (assigned variables) rather than differences in treatment of the independent variable. Experimental and ex post facto research have similar design patterns but are different in substance. Other research studies in education approach the true experiment more closely than the study of assigned variables, but relatively few studies in education are true experiments.

Abstract of Historical Research*

A HISTORICAL STUDY OF THE TEMPLE CITY ———— **Title**
DIFFERENTIATED STAFFING MODEL, 1965 TO 1975   **University**
                                               affiliation
Author ————— HARRIS, Richard Arlen, Ed.D. University of Southern———
California, 1978. Chairman: Professor Murdy———   **Major**
                                                  professor
Date

Purpose. The purpose of this study was to historically study the Temple City Differentiated Model, to objectively assess the goals of the project, and to determine significant educational contributions. The study further attempted to: (1) determine some of the major problems that prevented full implementation of the goals of the project or impeded their utilization, (2) determine the factors leading to the **Implied** model's final demise, (3) synthesize the evidence to assist in **questions** the formation of new programs, and (4) sequentially study the process of change.   **Research**

Procedure. The historical method was used in the study. ———— **method**
Selected Findings. (1) The District Senate was not successful in its endeavor to involve staff in district level decisions. (2) Teaching staff felt that the collegial evaluation procedure was a positive component of the model. (3) Teaching staff were positive about the training that they had received. (4) Individualized instruction was seen to occur much more frequently under modular scheduling. (5) Independent study was an integral part of all of the schedules, but was the greatest source of controversy and problems to building administrators. (6) There were not enough alternatives for students who could not utilize their independent study time or freedom within the classroom. (7) There was no substantial evidence to support the objective

Results 1-14 ———— of improved student cognitive improvement. (8) The Master Teacher concept was never fully implemented due to lack of funds and the inability to agree upon a viable job description. (9) The Senior Teacher Role was fully implemented. (10) Staff and Associate Teacher Roles were unsuccessfully implemented due to the inability to develop a job description that could specifically delineate their roles. (11) There was no indication that role differentiation had significantly improved staff communication, cooperation, and morale. (12) A lack of communication became a problem because administration seemingly did not spend more time with the community. (13) The secondary teachers were more supportive of the program than were the elementary teachers. (14) The additional costs for the model were approximately 10–14%.

Selected Conclusions. (1) The lack of administrative stability was instrumental in preventing full implementation of the model. (2) The loss of key administrators as the "charismatic" change agent is significant in slowing the process of change. (3) In any innovative program, there must be alternatives for students who do not meet the criteria established for the target group. (4) Significant data **Conclusions 1-7** in cognitive improvement by students does not seem to

———

*Reprinted from: *Dissertation Abstracts International*, June 1978, *38A*, pp. 7052-3A.

become apparent in the short period that was studied. (5) The fatigue factor became a significant factor in changing the minds of teachers who supported the program at its outset. (6) Administrators must have time to deal with the support both internally and within the community, but the overriding causes for the eventual demise of the model were financial factors beyond the control of the district staff, staff fatigue brought about by defending the project as well as its added work-day burden, and the support generated by a vocal minority in the district.

Implications — Selected Recommendations. (1) Innovative programs should involve as many people as possible affected by the programs to establish a sense of ownership and improve communications. (2) Some commitment by administrators to stay throughout the program should be established whenever possible to maintain some stability in the innovative program. (3) Administration should establish a line of communication to determine feedback from staff regarding morale and fatigue. (4) There should be a number of alternatives for students who could not function in the innovative program.

(Copies available from Micrographics Department, — **Source of the original work** Doheny Library, USC, Los Angeles, CA 90007.) The dissertation titles and abstracts contained here are published with permission of University Microfilms International, publishers of *Dissertation Abstracts International* (Copyright © 1978 by University Microfilms International), and may not be reproduced without their prior permission.

Abstract of Descriptive Research*

A STUDY OF PHYSICAL EDUCATION INJURIES AMONG HANDICAPPED AND NON-HANDICAPPED — **Title** CHILDREN

Order No. 7808473

Author — KARPER, William Blaine, Ed.D. New York University, — **University affiliation**
Date — 1978. 118pp. Chairman: Professor Raymond Weiss — **Major professor**
Number of pages

Problem

The problem was to determine the extent to which injuries — **Implied question** were sustained by handicapped children in physical education on the elementary level (K–6) and to determine the nature of those injuries. Specifically, the investigator compared injuries (incidence and nature) of handicapped — **Delimitation** children to those sustained by non-handicapped children.

Procedure

Physical education injury data were collected for 342 educable mentally retarded (EMR), 471 neurologically impaired (NI), 286 emotionally disturbed (ED), and 16,777 **Subjects by group** — non-handicapped boys and girls on the elementary school level (K–6). The handicapped children participated in special — **Differences of groups** and mainstreamed physical education, and the non-handicapped children participated in mainstreamed and regular physical eduction. The information was obtained by mail from elementary school physical education teachers in ten school districts in New Jersey using an injury report form and two other small information report forms. Data

---

*Reprinted from: *Dissertation Abstracts International*, June 1978, *38A*, pp. 7210A.

Data collection —————— were collected once per month from the participating teachers for a six month period during the 1976–1977 school year. Chi-square analysis was applied to only male injury —— **Statistical** data, because the amount of female injury data received was **analysis** insufficient for analysis.

Findings

Connection to hypotheses —————— As was hypothesized, the handicapped children in this study sustained a greater incidence of injury than the non-handicapped children. In addition, handicapped and non-handicapped children injured similar body parts. Contrary to what was hypothesized, the handicapped children sustained different types of injuries than non-handicapped children in the initial analysis. However, a second analysis, excluding the non-specific injury category of "bump," showed similar types of injuries sustained by the two groups. All three classificiations of handicapped children sustained similar types of injuries, and injured similar body parts as was expected. Contrary to what was hypothesized, the three handicapped groups sustained different incidences of injury. —— **Results**

Conclusions

Conclusions 1-3 —————— Based upon the findings of this study, it may be concluded that: 1. Handicapped children (EMR, NI, and ED) sustain a greater incidence of injuries than non-handicapped children on the elementary level. 2. There is no evidence that body part injured differs for handicapped (EMR, NI, and ED) and non-handicapped children on the elementary level. Evidence for a relationship between type of injury and being —— **No** handicapped (EMR, NI, and ED) or non-handicapped is **conclusion** conflicting permitting no conclusion to be drawn. 3. EMR, NI, and ED children on the elementary level differ in incidences of injuries. There is no evidence that the three groups differ in type of injury or body part injured.

Abstract of Ex Post Facto Research*

ABSTRACT 1126

Exceptional child accession number —————— EC 10 1126   ED N.A.

Publ. Date Jun 77 ——————   7p.

Authors —————— Briggs, Chari; Elkind, David ——————————————————————— **Date**

Title —————— **Characteristics of Early Readers.** —————————— **Volume and issue numbers**

Journal title —————— *Perceptual and Motor Skills:* V44 N3

P1231-1237 Jun 1977 ——————————————————— **Date**

Pages ——————

Subject terms —————— Descriptors: Early Childhood Education;* Reading Development:* Student Characteristics;* Reading Skills;* Research Projects; Parent Role; Parent Child Relationship;

Thirty-three early (before kindergarten) reading children and 33 matched control children were given a battery of tests and their parents were interviewed about 47 —————————— **Methods**

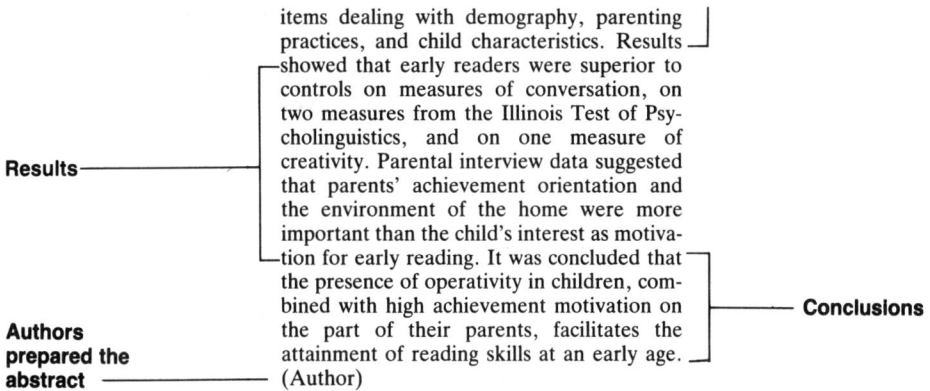

Results ——————————— items dealing with demography, parenting practices, and child characteristics. Results ┐ showed that early readers were superior to controls on measures of conversation, on two measures from the Illinois Test of Psycholinguistics, and on one measure of creativity. Parental interview data suggested that parents' achievement orientation and the environment of the home were more important than the child's interest as motivation for early reading. It was concluded that ┐ the presence of operativity in children, combined with high achievement motivation on   ——— **Conclusions** the part of their parents, facilitates the attainment of reading skills at an early age. ┘

Authors prepared the abstract ————————— (Author)

Summary

After a problem has been isolated and delimited and hypotheses developed from extended reading and experiential background, a specific plan of attack is necessary to answer the research question. Referred to as a "design," the plan structures, through specific procedures, ways of gathering specific data from specific sources of information and ways of interpreting the obtained data.

Sources of data are the attributes of objects, animals, and human beings. The source of the data will, in most cases, determine the type of data gathered. This, in turn, limits and/or directs interpretive procedures. It becomes important that the interpretation be as objective as the situation will permit, but lack of objectivity should not limit what is researched. Inquiry procedures can be developed to answer educational questions of all kinds. Very difficult situations demand that the researcher function as an artist as well as a scientist, keeping in mind that it is

> Far better an appropriate answer to the right question, which is often vague, than an exact answer to the wrong question, which can always be made precise. (Tukey, 1963, pp. 13–14)

The research plan, including methodology, is concerned with the following areas:

1. Procedures associated with identification of sources of information and/or selection of specific elements to supply data
2. Techniques to be used to collect the data
3. Processing (treating) the data
4. Organizing the results in interpretable form
5. Summarizing the results to provide a basis for drawing conclusions

This chapter has discussed the above topics as they relate to research generally and provided a brief overview for each area of historical, descriptive, and experimental research. The topics related to sampling receive more attention here because of their close relationship to both descriptive and experimental research. Other topics introduced here are treated at greater length in the chapters that follow.

From this focus on planning and designing a study, we turn in the next chapter to discussion of the research proposal, a vehicle for organizing a plan of attack for the study.

References

Bracht, G. H., & Glass, G. V. The external validity of experiments. *American Educational Research Journal,* November 1968, *5* (4), 437–474.

Elkind, D. *Children and adolescents. Interpretive essays on Jean Piaget* (2nd ed.). New York: Oxford University Press, 1974.

Ferguson, G. A. *Statistical analysis in psychology and education* (4th ed.). New York: McGraw-Hill, 1976.

Gray, D. J. (Ed.). *Lewis Carroll: Alice in wonderland.* New York: W. W. Norton, 1971.

Hays, W. L. *Statistics for psychologists.* New York: Holt, Rinehart, & Winston, 1963.

Hodges, J. L., & Lehmann, E. L. *Basic concepts of probability and statistics.* San Francisco: Holden-Day, 1970.

Hopkins, C. D. *Describing data statistically.* Columbus, Oh.: Charles E. Merrill, 1974.

Light, R. J. Issues in the analysis of qualitative data. In Robert M. W. Travers (Ed.), *Second handbook of research on teaching.* Chicago: Rand McNally, 1973.

Rand Corporation. *A million random digits with 100,000 normal deviates.* New York: Free Press, 1955.

Siegel, S. *Non-parametric statistics for the behavioral sciences.* New York: McGraw-Hill, 1956.

Table of 105,000 random decimal digits. Washington, D.C.: Interstate Commerce Commission, May, 1949. Statement no. 4914, file no. 261-A-1.

Tilden, F. *Interpreting our heritage.* Chapel Hill: University of North Carolina Press, 1957.

Travers, R. M. W. *An introduction to educational research.* New York: Macmillan, 1968.

Tukey, J. W. The future of data analysis. *The Annals of Mathematical Statistics,* 1963, *33,* 13–14. Quoted in Light, 1973, p. 318.

CHAPTER EIGHT

AN INQUIRY AID: THE RESEARCH PROPOSAL

The process of developing detailed proposals is often an excellent means for people to organize their plans.
—Human Resources Network (Nowlan et al.)

The research proposal offers a unique way to synthesize the many parts of research into a workable attack on a problem. It serves not only to communicate to others about what is planned but also to organize clearly the design topics discussed in Chapter 7.

From time to time funding agencies—both public and private—release calls for proposals for educational research projects. These announcements say in essence, "We have some money to spend on worthwhile research. If you want to use some of it in your quest for knowledge, write a report in the form of a proposal telling us (1) what you are seeking, (2) how you intend to go about finding it, (3) how it is significant to educational theory, (4) how you are qualified, and (5) how much money you will need to see the task to completion." Each call for proposals gives some idea of how the above information is to be submitted and what types of studies the funding agency considers important. In most cases, guidelines for preparing a proposal are available. These guidelines are generally structured so that detailed information will be provided about the five areas listed earlier.

Proposals open communication between funding agencies and researchers. When finally accepted, the proposal is a contract that serves as a two-way insurance policy. The funding agency says, "We are willing to back you financially if you do what you have included in your proposition." The researcher agrees, "If you will finance me, I will carry out the research as proposed." The proposal thus becomes a vehicle for encouraging investigation about educational concerns.

This chapter offers a framework for planning research in proposal form. The proposal represents a synthesis of the entire research process and, as such, serves here to tie together our discussion of the structure of research.

Chapters 9, 10, and 11 use this structure in special ways to examine the three major research methodologies.

In addition to structuring the design of studies for funding agencies, proposals are used for organizing advanced theses and dissertations. A proposal provides a similar structure for a student and a thesis committee as it offers the researcher and the funding agency. Classroom teachers also have a professional commitment to add to their knowledge about education. Whether this contribution is structured through a formal proposal and study or based on experience, the professional literature benefits from a large component of articles from classroom experiences. The researcher who works alone also can use the framework of the proposal to organize the design for a study. The design's unique set of procedures and definitions can be referred to often during the investigation stage and helps give direction when writing the final report. The proposal supports the synthesis of the three stages of research activities—planning, investigation, and generalization. Foresight and careful consideration of procedural details should precede the formal search for an answer, and a prospectus, plan, or design in the form of a proposal is the best way to assure reasonable success in that search.

In general, proposals required of students are the same as proposals provided to funding agencies, with one exception. Most student proposals omit the budget section unless a class instructor chooses to include it as part of an assignment to serve as a simulation of a proposal for funds. The discussion of the educational research proposal in this chapter does not include the development of a budget. Guidelines for funding proposals are usually very specific about how to present the budget. Certainly, the cost of conducting research is not less important for students, given the low level of most student income. So this area does remain a consideration for the student who is planning to conduct a research study for a class or degree assignment and who lacks adequate funds. In this case, the student would be wise to seek out different funding sources and follow the budget guidelines already established.

Proposals are not unique to the field of education. Research and development contracts with funding agencies are also common in the business world. Although proposals for research in education and research in business may be prepared for different purposes, they have much in common. Figure 8–1 is from a publication prepared from a lecture given before the Technical Writers' Institute.

Most of the following discussion about proposals for educational research is geared to producing a proposal like that defined in Figure 8–1. Especially important to this discussion is the last italicized sentence. Researchers should apply those criteria for proposals of all kinds.

The components developed within the framework of this chapter are used, in general, in all educational proposals. The arrangement of these elements may vary from one set of guidelines to another. The procedures for proposal writing presented here are built around a set of instructions that the

---

A PROPOSAL IS AN OFFER TO SELL
—Something
—To someone
—At sometime
—For some price

Figure 9

A. Defining a Proposal

Let us first consider what a proposal really is. As shown in Figure 9, it is an offer to sell a specified something to a specified someone at some specified time for some specified price. In most cases, the something must be specified in extensive detail, even though none of the items to be delivered may exist at the time the proposal is submitted.

The someone may be complicated, too. Frequently, the party who buys the thing, the potential customer, may not be the party to whom the seller must deliver the thing. To the potential customer, the proposal must be credible; he must be persuaded that the seller (or bidder) can and will deliver as specified, and must further be persuaded this particular seller offers the best combination of such factors as low cost, high quality, and cost and performance reliability. *Furthermore, the proposal must be sufficiently clear and free from ambiguity that the party who is to accept delivery understands exactly what he is to get and how it will perform.*

Note. From *Preparing Effective Proposals* (2nd ed.) by Louis L. Ullman (Troy, N.Y.: Technical Writers' Institute, 1971), p. 5. Italics added. Copyright 1971 by Technical Writers' Institute.

FIGURE 8–1 Proposal Preparation

author has used with students of educational research for several years. Student reactions to various forms of this framework have helped refine it to its present level of sophistication. The outline in Figure 8–2 lists those elements that make up a proposal. The four broad topics—background of the problem, presentation of the problem, methodology, and bibliography—are discussed separately. Keep in mind that the proposal provides a structure for the research design and allows the integration of the several parts into a logically conceived strategy.

The Proposal Title

Each proposal should have a title. If possible, the title of the final report can be developed and serve as a title for the proposal. The title should include

Elements of a Research Proposal

I. Background of the Problem
   A. All research is a chain of reasoning. In this section, describe the facts, theories, personal concerns, or actual conditions in practice that have led you to regard this as research worthy of study. Theory, historical development, and present status of the problem deserve consideration, along with a projection of the research into the future listing possible outcomes. The significance and relevance of the study must be demonstrated in this section, and you should indicate the nature of the problem.
   B. Justification for your selection of the problem should be based on one or more of the following:
      1. Gaps in knowledge; need for new knowledge
      2. Need for clarification of conflicting educational practices
      3. Need for hard data to be used in evaluation of alternative practices or policies
      4. Development of new or refined research procedures for scholarly work in the field
   C. Your comprehensive understanding of the field should be reflected by your ability to cite references of significant publications and current journal articles related to the problem. Summarize points of view, significance, and relevance by referring to the chosen problem.

II. Presentation of the Problem
   A. This section should propose a clearly defined problem presented as
      1. A question you propose to answer
      2. A hypothesis (subhypotheses) to test
   B. Delimit your problem by fencing in and isolating it from all other problems in the field. Be aware that not all of the world's ills will (or can) be solved by one study.
   C. Also include in this section:
      1. Definition of terms—this clarifies meanings of important words for the study.
      2. Assumptions—a list establishes the study's theoretical framework.
      3. Limitations—these include any restriction to generalizability of results or other limiting aspects of the study.

FIGURE 8–2   Outline for Developing a Research Proposal

III. Methodology
  A. The methodology should be presented in detail and each step explained specifically, so that another researcher will be able to repeat the study exactly as you intend to carry it out.
  B. Discuss in operational terms the statement of procedures for:
    1. Sampling. Describe selection of subjects, materials to be examined, or where searches are to be made.
      a. The description gives a good clue to generalizability.
      b. The characteristics of the sample provide an operational statement of groups to whom you hope to generalize.
    2. Data treatment. Indicate how you will structure your procedures so that you can gather and process data which will be indicative of whatever effect you want to measure. This section explains a method that
      a. Best fits the problem
      b. Yields the most reliable and valid data
      c. Is manageable, feasible, and economical in both cost and time
  C. The methods by which you propose to process and treat the data should be described in such a fashion that their appropriateness to the problem is clear. Your method of tabulating and organizing the data should be shown and methods of data analysis described. Describe all statistical procedures to be applied to the data.

IV. Bibliography
  A. Include in this bibliography:
    1. The references which led you to select the problem
    2. References which are pertinent to the basic problem of the study
    3. Any material that is closely related to the problem under study
V. Check your proposal as a chain of reasoning.
  A. The proposal should:
    1. Give background for the problem
    2. Present the problem
    3. Tell how you intend to attack the problem by finding the answer to a question implied by the problem
    4. Present a selected bibliography to guide an interested person into the literature

FIGURE 8–2 (Continued)

the variables being studied, the relationship between the variables, and the population being studied.

An appropriate title for a study can easily be adapted from a well-developed research question. This title meets the three criteria: "Effects of Replacing Arithmetic Drill Time with Informal Investigation on Arithmetical Computation of Fifth-grade Students." You may recognize that this title comes from a research question given in Chapter 5: What are the effects on arithmetical computation when classtime used for drill is replaced by informal investigations of problems involving large mathematical concepts?

Background of the Problem

The researcher should develop the section on the problem's background as a context for the research question. This section begins the "chain of reasoning" development for the proposed research and leads the reader into the specific question being investigated. A brief historical development should work into a discussion of present status and then project the possible outcomes into the future. Occasionally a full-blown review of literature is requested but this aspect is usually left for the final report. The state of knowledge in the problem area should be reflected in citations and summaries of significant publications and journal articles.

A part of the background section should be devoted to indicating the specific importance of the study for education and—if justification is important—a case should be built for conducting the study. Whether a study is significant to the field of education depends on the contribution of possible conclusions to the existing body of knowledge about the process of education. The development of the theoretical framework of the study may be sufficient to show this importance, but further educational significance may lie in one or several of the following areas:

1. *Practicality.* A close relationship between the study and a practical problem lends support to proposed research.
2. *Generalizability.* A study that is generalizable over varied student populations would be more acceptable than one that is limited in scope.
3. *Opportuneness.* Research that relates to social problems currently under scrutiny is well received.
4. *Theorization.* A study which will analyze sets of facts and create new understanding of theory is readily justifiable.
5. *Scholarship.* A study may be justified by its contribution of new approaches to research procedures for educational problem solving.

Reasons for selecting the topic and its significance should be built into the background narrative, and the relationship of the study to current theory should be exhibited. Justification for selection can be based on the four reasons listed in Figure 8–2. For a funding agency, the case for the study's importance should be made by showing how the study fits with the criteria of the agency's guidelines, and by indicating its importance in the long-range funding policy of the agency. The significance of a student's proposal for a class or degree requirement is judged by the instructor and/or committee members. Close working relationships should be maintained between the person developing a proposal for a thesis and the thesis chairperson to make sure that the proposed study is considered significant to the field of study.

Presentation of the Problem

As the second section of the proposal, the problem presentation focuses the reader's attention on the specific area of concern for the study and develops the rationale for the study as a basis for the next section on methodology. The major emphasis should be on the problem question and the hypothesis developed for the study.

After a short introductory paragraph, the carefully prepared research question (see Chapter 5) should be presented. A lead-in sentence—such as "The study will be based on the question" or "The research study will be directed to answer the following question"—will immediately bring the reader to the problem area. An additional discussion paragraph may be needed to delimit the problem area so that there is no ambiguity about what is being covered. As this study is set off, other closely related areas not a part of the study are excluded, and the focus of the study becomes clear for the researcher and reader.

A logical next step is to present a carefully prepared statement that hypothesizes the expected answer for the proposed question. This statement is the research hypothesis (see Chapter 6) that has been developed from past personal experience and reading.

The variables under study must then be defined. A definition of any other word used in the study with other than its common meaning—either a word used in a special way or a word that has been created for the study—needs to be presented.

The researcher must also lay out the basic **assumptions** behind the study in this section. A listing of assumptions establishes the postulates on which the present investigation is based. Examples of such assumptions include (1) Multiple-choice test items can be developed to measure creativity, and (2) The physical sciences are best studied as an integrated program in the secondary school.

Any anticipated restrictions (from methodology) on generalizability of the results should be explained at this point as limitations of the study. All studies are limited in some way, since the perfectly reliable and valid study is yet to be developed. By listing **limitations,** the researcher recognizes particular places where generalization is misleading or impossible. Limitations develop where methodology is less than ideal and may be the result of the nature of the question asked, the population being studied, or inadequate procedures which cannot be made adequate.

In the final research report, the two sections of the proposal, "Background of the Problem" and "Presentation of the Problem," will (with minor changes such as order and arrangement) make up the first chapter of the research report. The following section on methodology is generally exactly the same in the proposal and the final report, except for verb tense changes from future to past.

Methodology

The proposal section on methodology, which is also the third chapter of the final report, explains the procedures to be used to answer the question and/ or test the research hypothesis. This component of the proposal should be presented in such detail that another researcher would be able to take this section and repeat the study in exactly the way that the present researcher intends to carry it out. Such detail in the methodology section is required if the study is to be replicated on another set of subjects. As much as possible, all conditions must remain the same in all replication. Varying conditions allow no comparisons of results.

Carefully detailed methodology also eliminates ambiguously stated procedures. It serves as a written record of the agreement between the researcher and the funding agency or committee for an advanced degree, and it can be an insurance policy for both the researcher and the agency or committee. This "two-way insurance policy" serves much the same purpose for research as the written contract does for the field of business.

For the historical study, the general plan for gathering data should be augmented with specific plans about where searches will be made, what information will be sought, and how conclusions will be drawn. The historical researcher has some freedom to extend the search beyond materials cited in the proposal. Since she or he may discover more sources after the plan has been implemented, it would be counterproductive to limit the search to the pre-investigation plans. Descriptive and experimental research studies do not permit this freedom and must be conducted just as the proposal states. If the researcher needs to alter any of the methodology after reaching agreement on the proposal design, he or she should consult with the other parties involved in the study before making changes in any of the planned procedures.

If a study is to be generalizable, the selection of subjects for providing the data takes special care. Random procedures should be used to select names of subjects to receive questionnaires or to supply data for descriptive studies. For experimental studies and descriptive studies involving tests of significance between groups, selection and assignment of subjects is crucial. If conditions preclude random assignment, a description of the sample may allow generalization to populations with like characteristics. In addition to describing the procedures, the proposal should include a statement about any possible effects of sampling on generalizability of the results.

The design element of the methodology section describes how to supply the most desirable data possessing a minimum of contamination from irrelevant variables and how to assure valid data for basing results and subsequent conclusions. It also supplies the methods for recording, tabulating, and organizing the data. Any statistical procedures described in this section should be defended as those most appropriate to the study.

In experimental studies, the methodology section should clearly define the treatment of the independent variable. If the investigation involves a study of teaching methods, each method must be explained at length. The difference between or among methods is the treatment for experimental studies of educational methods. Chapter 10 of the *Handbook,* "Analysis and Investigation of Teaching Methods" by Norman E. Wallen and Robert M.W. Travers, is a classic source for aid in studies of teaching methods (Gage, 1963, pp. 448–505). The bibliography lists many methodological studies conducted before 1963. Part IV of the *Second Handbook* treats methods in topics of subject matter rather than including a separate section (Travers, 1973, pp. 1072–1322).

The data section must include a time schedule for data collection and procedures for recording. Effects of data-gathering procedures on the results should be discussed—for example, how is the setting changed by introducing a test session, tape recorder, or human observer? The data analysis chosen, its name, and a description of the statistical techniques involved must be presented in this section.

Since the null hypothesis is what the test of statistical significance tests, the methodology section of the proposal should include the null hypothesis for studies which use a test of significance. If a researcher wants to show the relationship of the research hypothesis to the null hypothesis for the study, the research hypothesis can be repeated here. Such repetition of the research hypothesis should not replace its presentation in the problem presentation section.

The completeness of a methodology section should be checked by answering the question, Could someone else trained in research methods take this section of the proposal, follow the listed procedures, and complete the research in the same way that I would? When the question can be answered in the affirmative, all of the requirements for a complete plan of methodology have been attended to.

Bibliography

A necessary element for all proposals is a selected **bibliography.** The bibliography may be extensive if a review of literature is included, but in most cases it will be more limited. It should include key references which led the researcher to select the problem, those sources necessary to understand the basic problem, and other material that relates to the problem under study. Figure 8–3 is a sample outline for a proposal developed for the question, What are the effects on arithmetical computation when classtime used for drill is replaced by informal investigations of problems involving large mathematical concepts?

EFFECTS OF REPLACING ARITHMETIC DRILL TIME
WITH INFORMAL INVESTIGATION ON ARITHMETIC
COMPUTATION OF FIFTH-GRADE STUDENTS

(Untitled introductory section)

Background of the Problem

(Introductory section)

Historical Development

Significance of the Problem

Significant Related Studies

Presentation of the Problem

(Introductory Section)

The Question (Include delimitation paragraph.)

The Hypothesis

Definition of Terms

Assumptions

Limitations (These may be listed in Methodology section).

Methodology

(Introductory Section)

The Sample
  Selection
  Description

Data
  Collection
  Treatment
    Analysis of Variance
    Null Hypothesis
  Presentation of Data
Presentation of Results
Rationale

Bibliography

Appendix

Computational Test
  Table of Specifications
  Sample Items

FIGURE 8–3   Sample Outline of a Proposal for an Experiment

Preparing Materials

The proposal should include in an appendix any materials—such as questionnaires or tests—that are developed especially for the study. Since the study is still in the proposal stage, a final form of the materials is not required, but rough outlines with types of questions to be asked and general coverage should be included for questionnaires. If a test must be developed for the study, a table of specifications with sample items would be required by most proposal guidelines.

Standardized test instruments to be used only in part or adapted especially for a study should be included in the proposal along with a special description of how they are to be used in the study. Readily available standardized tests require only a reference listing, but less used or relatively unknown tests should be included in a proposal as part of an appendix.

Summary

This chapter presents the research proposal as a chain of reasoning that expands the research study from a vague idea in the researcher's mind to a set of meticulously planned procedures. These procedures are designed especially to answer the research question and to overcome some specific obstacle in the educational process. The proposal operationalizes the sections of the design as studied in Chapter 7.

The elements of the proposal are the background to the problem, presentation of the problem, methodology, and bibliography. These elements have been discussed individually. The chapter also includes a section on materials that are to be prepared specially for the study.

Figure 8–3 offers a sample outline for developing a proposal through the above elements. Other sets of guidelines generally include much the same information, but their organization may take other forms. Proposals may or may not include a complete review of related literature, depending on the set of guidelines.

The proposal serves as a communication between a researcher and a sponsor that indicates:

1. What is being sought
2. How the researcher intends to find it
3. The significance of the study
4. The researcher's qualifications to study the problem
5. How much funding will be needed to see the project to completion (only for proposals requesting a budget for funding)

Activities

1. For one of the questions on pp. 126–27 or for one of your own, write a paragraph to accompany the question in which the problem is clearly delimited for a reader of the proposal.

2. For the same question, write a set of definitions for the variables under study and any other technical words that you would envision to be needed to define or clarify terms for a reader of the proposal.
3. From a journal article or research report of your choice, reconstruct what one or more of the following sections of the proposal might have been.
   a. Background of the problem
   b. Presentation of the problem
   c. Methodology
4. Prepare an outline for a proposal using the format in Figure 8–3. Organize it for a question you would like to answer by research methodology.
5. Prepare a proposal that is ready to be submitted to a faculty committee or—if guidelines are available—to a funding agency. Follow the format and directions given by this chapter, your instructor, or the funding agency.

References

Gage, N. L. (Ed.). *Handbook of research on teaching.* Chicago, Ill.: Rand McNally, 1963.

Nowlan, S. E., Shayon, D. R., Smith, D. V. III, Wright, D. S., Allen, S. T., & Allen, P. J. (Eds.). *User's guide to funding resources.* Radnor, Pa.: Chilton, 1975.

Travers, R. M. W. (Ed.). *Second handbook of research on teaching.* Chicago: Rand McNally, 1973.

Ullman, L. L. *Preparing effective proposals* (2nd ed.). Troy, N.Y.: Technical Writers' Institute, 1971.

Bibliography: Part Two

Ary, D., Jacobs, L. C., & Razavich, A. *Introduction to research in education* (2nd ed.). New York: Holt, Rinehart, & Winston, 1978.

Bracht, G. H., & Glass, G. V., The external validity of experiments. *American Educational Research Journal,* 1968, 5 (4), 438.

Brownell, W. A. Psychological considerations in the learning and teaching of arithmetic. In W. D. Reeve, *The teaching of arithmetic* (10th yrbk.). Washington, D.C.: The National Council for Teachers of Mathematics, 1935.

Bruner, J. (Ed.). *Learning about learning.* Washington, D.C.: Government Printing Office, 1966. FS 5.212:12019.

Elkind, D. *Children and adolescents. Interpretive essays on Jean Piaget* (2nd ed.). New York: Oxford University Press, 1974.

Englehart, M. D. *Methods of educational research.* Chicago: Rand McNally, 1972.

Ferguson, G. A. *Statistical analysis in psychology and education* (4th ed.). New York: McGraw-Hill, 1976.

Gage, N. L. (Ed.). *Handbook of research on teaching.* Chicago: Rand McNally, 1963.

Gray, D. J. (Ed.). *Lewis Carroll: Alice in wonderland.* New York: W. W. Norton, 1971.

Guba, E. G. Guides for the writing of proposals. In J. A. Culbertson & S. P. Hencley (Eds.), *Educational research: New perspectives.* Danville, Ill.: The Interstate, 1963.

Hays, W. L. *Statistics for psychologists.* New York: Holt, Rinehart, & Winston, 1963.

Hodges, J. L., & Lehmann, E. L. *Basic concepts of probability and statistics.* San Francisco: Holden-Day, 1970.

Hopkins, C. D. The emerging elementary mathematics program. *The Teachers College Journal,* 1965, *36,* 151–52.

Hopkins, C. D. Mathematics in the elementary school—Why? In R. H. Jones & B. F. Walker (Eds.), *Educational perspectives of the elementary school.* Dubuque, Iowa: William C. Brown, 1969.

Hopkins, C. D. *Describing data statistically.* Columbus, Oh.: Charles E. Merrill, 1974.

Jones, R. H. (Ed.). *Methods and techniques of educational research.* Danville, Ill.: The Interstate, 1973.

Kagan, J. Motivational and attitudinal factors in receptivity to learning. In J. Bruner, *Learning about learning.* Washington, D.C.: Government Printing Office, 1966. FS5.212:12019.

Kerlinger, F. N. *Foundations of behavioral research.* New York: Holt, Rinehart, & Winston, 1973.

Krothwohl, D. R. *How to prepare a research proposal.* Syracuse, N.Y.: Syracuse Bookstore, 1965.

Kuhn, T. S. *The structure of scientific revolution* (vol. 2, no. 2) (2nd ed.). Chicago: University of Chicago Press, 1970.

Lehmann, I. J., & Mehrens, W. A. *Educational research—Readings in focus.* New York: Holt, Rinehart, & Winston, 1971.

Light, R. J. Issues in the analysis of qualitative data. In R. M. W. Travers (Ed.), *Second Handbook of Research on Teaching.* Chicago: Rand McNally, 1973.

Manheim, T. *Sources in educational research: A selected and annotated bibliography.* Detroit: Wayne State University Press, 1969.

May, C. The nature of, and a proposal for, conducting educational research studies. In R. H. Jones (Ed.), *Methods and techniques of educational research.* Danville, Ill.: The Interstate, 1973.

Nowlan, S. E., Shayon, D. R., Smith, D. V. III, Wright, D. S., Allen, S. T., and Allen, P. J. (Eds.). *User's guide to funding resources.* Radnor, Pa.: Chilton, 1975.

Rand Corporation. *A million random digits with 100,000 normal deviates.* New York: Free Press, 1955.

Resta, P. E., & Baker, R. L. *Components of the educational research proposal.* New York: American Book Co., 1972.

Runyon, R. P., & Haber, A., *Fundamentals of behavioral statistics* (2nd ed.). Reading, Mass.: Addison-Wesley, 1971.

Siegel, S. *Non-parametric statistics for the behavioral sciences.* New York: McGraw-Hill, 1956.

Smith, G. R. How to write a project proposal. *Nation's Schools,* August 1965, *76,* 33–35, 57.

Table of 105,000 random decimal digits. Washington, D.C.: Interstate Commerce Commission, May 1949. Statement No. 4914, File No. 261–A–1.

Thorndike, E. L. The effects of practice in the case of a purely intellectual function. *American Journal of Psychology,* July 1908, *19,* 374–384.

Tilden, F. *Interpreting our heritage.* Chapel Hill: University of North Carolina Press, 1957.

Travers, R. M. W. *An introduction to educational research.* New York: Macmillan, 1968.

Travers, R. M. W. *Second handbook of research on teaching.* Chicago: Rand McNally, 1973.

Tukey, J. W. The future of data analysis. *The Annals of Mathematical Statistics,* 1963, *33,* 13–14.

Ullman, L. L. *Preparing effective proposals* (2nd ed.). Troy, N.Y.: Technical Writers' Institute, 1971.

Van Dalen, D. B. *Understanding educational research* (3rd ed.). New York: McGraw-Hill, 1973.

Wiersma, W. *Research methods in education—An introduction* (2nd ed.). Itasca, Ill.: F. E. Peacock, 1975.

SAMPLE STUDIES

Professional Communication

Communication in a professional community is to a great degree carried on through journals, although personal letters, papers read at conventions, and newsletters supplement dissemination of information by scholarly writing. This section of sample studies offers five journal articles selected to show different ways to make a research report. Other chapters in this book refer to these sample studies as examples. These studies may be considered typical of articles found in education journals in their format and in their substance. They are also much like articles in journals devoted to the other social sciences. Journals of medicine, biology, and the natural sciences tend to be different in both format and substance primarily because of the nature of the questions asked in those fields. The sample studies presented here are to be read before beginning Chapter 5 in the text.

Overview

A fundamental difference between journal articles in the behavioral sciences and those in other disciplines lies in the interpretation of results. Whereas the educational researcher is expected to interpret results, that component of research is left to the discretion of the reader in the natural sciences. There are several possible reasons for including a statement of the researcher's conclusions in educational studies.

> Just why the behavioral scientist traditionally is expected to present his own interpretations and conclusions as well as the results of his investigation is not entirely clear. Perhaps it is because there are so many possible misinterpretations to avoid with behavioral data; perhaps it is because the behavioral scientist is lazy and wishes the interpretations made for him; perhaps it is because, working with people, he is more aware of the problems of communication; or perhaps it is

because he has so often been required to justify what he is doing (as contrasted with the physical, and to some extent the biological, sciences where enough concrete and immediately useful results have been produced so that the public no longer questions efforts in those areas). (Helmstadter, 1970, p. 68)

The immaturity of the sciences used by education is the most likely source of the need for interpretation of results. Other aspects of research reports in all journal articles are directed to conveying to readers enough details about a study to allow the reader to evaluate the study and its findings.

One purpose for including sample journal articles in this book is to provide a point of reference for research examples explained in the book and to allow the reader to see how the several parts of the research process integrate into the structure of inquiry. Paragraph numbers have been added in parentheses to facilitate future reference. These articles are examples of how a researcher looks beyond the self as a source of knowledge. They reveal the scientific approach to studying problems with an educational orientation. Research is conducted for different purposes and the articles reflect five ways that research procedure can be directed by a question under study and different manners of reporting.

Analysis of each study is left to the reader. Every research study is open to criticism or questioning, and these examples are not exceptions. Examination of the studies could be arranged around investigation of

1. Purpose of the study and its contribution to educational knowledge
2. Theoretical framework and assumptions
3. Methodology
4. Reporting of results and conclusions
5. Writing style for clear communication

With thorough analysis of what someone else has done, a researcher should be able to improve his or her own research. As consumers of research, all educators must become critics capable of comparing the procedures used in a study to standards set for scientific inquiry.

References

Helmstadter, G. C. *Research concepts in human behavior.* New York: Appleton-Century-Crofts, 1970.

Study Number 1

This study investigates a question comparing the present with the past. It uses historical research both to study the past and to allow study of change over time. The study further exhibits the use of the hypothesis in historical research. Sampling techniques select materials to be analyzed from a larger body of material. Finally, the methodology of analysis suggests a paradigm for studying personality traits and other media.

AN ANALYSIS OF MALE AND FEMALE ROLES IN TWO PERIODS OF CHILDREN'S LITERATURE

JUDITH STEVINSON HILLMAN
Johnson State College, Burlington, VT

(Paragraph 1)

Abstract

Overview

Conclusion

Serves as a Summary

In this study the sex role standards attributed to characters in children's books were identified and analyzed. The sample of 120 books represented two temporal periods (the 1930's and the mid-1960's to mid-1970's) equally. A comparison between these decades indicated that males were more numerous than females in both the early period and the recent period; the range of occupations for males was much broader than for females; and eight of the seventeen behavioral categories remained constant while nine changed from period to period. Specifically, males were shown to be physically aggressive and competent in both periods and females retained the characteristics of affiliation/dependence and sadness. However, aspects of masculinity and femininity that conform to stereotypic traits were more prevalent in the early period than in the recent period, thus denoting an increasing latitude of sex role standards over the three decades.

(2)

Background

Within the last decade much attention has been directed toward the characteristics of girls and boys in reading material for children. The by-product of this attention has been analyses which suggest that females are usually presented as passive, dependent, and displaying a constellation of traits not particularly valued in contemporary society (1, 4, 5, 11, 14, 16, 18). Moreover, females are not nearly as numerous as males, particularly in leading roles. Meanwhile, the abounding males are cast as powerful, achievement-oriented, independent characters.

(3)

Theoretical framework

This study is based on the premise that literature plays a meaningful role in shaping a child's cognitive and emotional growth. Because they are potential motivators of thought and action, the role models in literature should thus become

From *The Journal of Educational Research,* October 1974, *68* (2), pp. 84–88. Copyright 1974, Helen Dwight Reid Educational Foundation, 4000 Albemarle Street, N.W., Washington, D.C., 20016. Reprinted by permission.

objects of scrutiny. Obviously, a child may be learning or adding to preconceived notions about her/his gender identity while reading books. Jerome Kagan, a noted developmental psychologist, states: "By the time he is seven he is intensely committed to molding his behavior in concordance with cultural standards appropriate to his biological sex (9:162)." Cultural standards are presumably manifest in children's books; the reading process thus allows the school-age child to enter different situations vicariously, to confront diverse opinions, and to identify with models who exhibit sex role behavior. Because of this premise, a critical appraisal of authors' psycho-social themes relating to sexual role standards would seem to be in order.

(4)

Background

Within the last thirty years societal standards of appropriate "masculinity" and "femininity" have evolved, as evidenced by the increasing number of females in the labor force, legislation concerning women's rights, the growing acceptance of birth control techniques, and the wide number of books, articles, and women's groups dealing with consciousness-raising in aspects of political, economic, and social dimensions of American life (7). As attention was drawn toward a change in societal standards, the question emerged: Would children's literature reflect this scope of role diversity over a period of time?

Question

(5)

Implications from the preceding analyses suggested that characterizations in literature had not kept pace with changes in sex role standards. Indeed, authors were charged with perpetuating out-moded stereotypes of masculinity and femininity. Therefore, even though society's conception of sex roles was changing, it was suspected that significant changes would *not* be apparent in children's trade books when comparing those published thirty years ago to those published in this decade.

General Hypothesis

Problem

(6)

Rationale

The problem in this investigation was to identify changes in the sexual role standards of males and females in two periods of children's literature, the 1930's and the mid-1960's to mid-1970's. It was decided to designate the 1930's as the early period because this decade occupied a well-defined, rather homogenous space in recent history (as the era of the Great Depression) and preceded the social, political, and technological upheaval caused by World War II. The decade 1963–1973 outlined the recent period.

(7)

Rationale

To describe and quantify these changes, the following three issues were probed:

    (1) Number of females and males in each time period.
    (2) Diversity of occupational roles ascribed to females and males in each period.
    (3) Differences between the behaviors and emotions attributed to males and females in each period.

(8)

Status

Change

For all three of these issues, data were gathered to examine the differences *within* each time period. More importantly, however, the change *between* the early and recent time periods was scrutinized in order to ascertain whether any significant changes took place in children's books over the thirty-year span.

Methodology

(9)

Sampling parameter

In order to identify and analyze sex roles in children's books it was necessary to specify criteria for limitation of the sample. Criteria for book selection were established to insure a varied sample of prose fiction, of comparable quality in both periods, written for an American elementary school audience, or children aged approximately 8 through 13. Only books written by American authors and published in America were included. Eliminated were: (1) picture books, (2) fairy tales, ancient myths, and traditional fables in the style of Aesop, (3) books depicting foreign culture systems, (4) collections of stories, (5) books about religious holidays, (6) fictionalized biographies of historical characters, and (7) more than one book by a single author in the entire sample.

(10)

Sample selection

Random selection

Because a large number of books was published in each time period, the following limitations were observed: (1) Three years spanning the decade equidistantly were selected to represent the early period (1932, 1935, 1938) and the recent period (1965, 1968, 1971); (2) Three independent, reputable, and well-known publishers of children's book reviews (the American Library Association, the R.R. Bowker Company, and the Horn Book, Inc.) were selected because their periodicals furnished a substantial number of reviews in both periods from which to compile a "master list" of all those books meeting the criteria; and (3) From the master list twenty book titles were drawn randomly for each year, making a total of sixty books representing the early period and sixty books representing the recent period. The procedure to select at random those books recommended by authoritative people in children's literature rather than a random selection of all the books published in the two decades was followed simply because it was thought that the recommended books would be more apt to be purchased for libraries and schools, and therefore more accessible (and possibly influential) to the student population. A random selection was made to insure some credence to the extrapolation of results to children's literature as a whole. Sixty books representing each period was considered to be a fair sample from which to draw conclusions and a manageable number for this type of content analysis.

(11)

Selecting sources of data

In summary, the method of book selection entailed reading all the children's book reviews in each source for a specified year, then making a master list of those books which fit the criteria and finally selecting at random twenty books for each of the six years used in the analysis.

(12)

Methodology

Each book was analyzed twice. During the first reading two lists were compiled: one of the characters (male and female) and the other of occupations performed by the characters. Characters, in turn, were defined as human or human-like creatures who could speak, had proper names, and were designated as male or female by common references to "him," "her," "she," "he," and so forth. All work roles, i.e., professions, managerial positions, or labor formed the list of occupations. These endeavors had to be explicitly related to masculine or feminine performance within the literary context. For the second reading each book was divided into units for the analysis of behaviors and emotions. To find these units, a formula was used to divide the book into six parts. Then the first five pages of each part were perused carefully for the presence of the following behaviors and emotions: (1) physical aggression, (2) verbal aggression, (3) physical affection, (4) verbal affection, (5) nurturance, (6) competence, (7) independence, (8) affiliation/dependence, (9) fantasy, (10) curiosity, (11) joy (happinesss), (12) hatred, (13) sadness, (14) anxiety/fear, (15) excitement/anticipation, (16) surprise, and (17) anger. The definitions of each of these behavioral categories included behavioral referrents and examples. These categories were derived from three sources. First, the literature of developmental psychology suggested that boys and girls displayed significant differences in aggression, dependency, achievement motivation, fear, and nur-

Raltionale

turant behavior (8, 13). Therefore, it seemed appropriate to use these behaviors to differentiate sexual roles in characters created in literature for children. Second, previous studies of basal readers (1, 3, 18) indicated that behaviors such as

Rationale

imagination, autonomy, competence and affiliation were sex-linked; the first three were preponderantly ascribed to males, the last to females. Third, a survey of all the behaviors and emotions found in twenty of the children's books in the sample, picked at random from both periods, provided a list from which the most numerous (such as joy, excitement,

Rationale

surprise, etc.) were selected. The final seventeen categories represented a synthesis of the behaviors and emotions from all three sources: psychological studies of children from both periods, sex role variables in previous literary analyses, and the recorded behaviors and emotions of characters in this sample.

(13)

Explain tables

The frequencies were tabulated and placed on contingency tables. (Note the "male frequency" and "female frequency" on Tables 2 and 3.) Four comparisons were made: (1) males

Analysis

and females, early period; (2) males and females, recent period; (3) early males and recent males; and (4) early females and recent females. The data were subjected to a chi-square analysis to determine statistical levels of significance.

(14)

Analysis

The number of males and females was also analyzed by a chi-square test to determine if the ratio was statistically significant. Percentages of male-performed occupations and female-performed occupations within each time period provided the comparative data related to occupational diversity.

Hypotheses

(15)

Specifically, three major hypotheses were considered:

Hypothesis
Rationale

(1) There would be more male characters than female characters in both periods. This was based on the findings of the studies depicting male/female ratios in basal readers (5, 18) and on an earlier investigation in which it was concluded that the female was neglected in stories for children (3).

Hypothesis

Rationale

(2) The diversity of occupations performed by males would be greater than the range of occupations performed by females in both time periods. The rationale for this prediction was based on the analysis of Nilsen (14) concerning women in literature and Tangri's study of women's occupational aspirations (17).

Hypothesis

Rationale

(3) Behaviors and emotions of males and females in the early period would be similar to those in the recent period. That is, behaviors and emotions found to be more frequent in male characters (as compared to the frequency in female characters) in the early period would also be more frequent in males in the recent period. A basis for this hypothesis rested on the role theory espoused by social psychologists (15) in which the "instrumental" male role and the "expressive" female role were delineated; the pervasiveness of sex role stereotypes held by society (2, 12); and sex differences in child development. If one assumed that the characters in children's books mirrored degrees of psychological reality, developmental studies showed that specific behaviors of children in these two periods were similar. For example, developmental psychologists claimed that males were more apt to display physical aggression (6, 13) while females displayed nurturant behavior (8, 10). Therefore, it would appear that aggression would be a male characteristic in each time period and that females would be associated with nurturance when child studies were used as a basis for prediction.

Results

(16)

Results

Hypothesis

The first major hypothesis, that the number of males would exceed the number of females in both periods, was supported by the data. The average percentage of males for the early period was 64.7 percent ($p<.01$) and 61.2 percent ($p<.05$) in the recent period. Conversely, the percentage of females was 35.3 percent in the early period and 38.8 percent in the recent period. While males were more numerous, it is apparent that in the recent period the sexes were somewhat more equally distributed. (See Table 1.)

Results

Table 1—Number of Males and Females

		Early Period		
Year	Number of Males	Percent of Males	Number of Females	Percent of Females
1932	206	61.5	129	38.5
1935	191	64.7	104	35.3
1938	236	68.0	111	32.0
Total:	633		344	
Average Percent:		64.7**		35.3**
		Recent Period		
1965	153	62.2	93	37.8
1968	191	64.3	106	35.7
1971	187	57.2	140	42.8
Total:	531		339	
Average Percent:		61.2*		38.8*

** = $p < .01$.
 * = $p < .05$.

(17)

Results

Hypothesis

The second hypothesis, that the range of occupations would be greater for males than the range for females in both time periods, was confirmed by the data. In the early period 169 occupations were listed for males while thirty were listed for females. Therefore the diversity in jobs performed by males was 84.8 percent greater than the range of jobs performed by females. In the recent period approximately 150 different occupations were performed by males and 39 by females. Of the total number of occupations, then, males accounted for 79.4 percent. It is notable that there were more occupations listed for females in recent period as compared to the early period, though the difference was not significant. The discrepancy between male occupations of both periods suggested that the early books included more laborers, whereas there were more professional workers in the recent period. In addition to fulfilling a much greater variety of work roles, males were depicted in jobs associated with power and prestige, while females were cast in domestic roles almost exclusively.

(18)

Results

Hypothesis

The third hypothesis, that the statistical comparison of behaviors and emotions of the males and females in the early period would be similar to the comparison of behaviors and emotions in the recent period, was rejected. The data suggest that some significant changes have occurred in the portrayal of male and female sex role standards over the span of approximately twenty-seven years.

(19)

Results

As the results in Table 2 indicate, males were found to be more physically aggressive ($p < .001$), verbally aggressive ($p < .05$), competent ($p < .001$), and angry ($p < .001$); while females expressed physical affection ($p < .05$), nurturance ($p < .001$), affiliation/dependence ($p < .001$), fantasy ($p < .001$), and sadness ($p < .01$) to significant degrees in the early period. Other categories, i.e., verbal affection, independence, curiosity, joy, hatred, anxiety/fear, excitement/

anticipation, and surprise did not reach significance for either sex.

(20)

Results

Comparisons

Table 3 depicts the comparison between males and females in the recent period. Males continued to be physically aggressive ($p' < .001$), but females and males did not differ significantly in the frequency of verbal aggression. As in the early period, males exhibited more competence ($p < .05$) than females; however, nurturance was no longer primarily a female trait, nor was fantasy. Females continued to express affiliation/dependence ($p < .001$) and sadness ($p < .001$) to a much greater extent than males. Finally, males more frequently expressed surprise ($p < .05$) in the recent period, and anger was no longer statistically significant for males.

(21)

Results

Comparisons

In the comparison of early males and recent males, most of the categories remained relatively constant. The only significant changes were fantasy ($p < .01$), which was most prevalent in the recent period, and joy ($p < .05$), prevalent in the early period. This denoted little change in the actions of male characters.

(22)

Results

Comparisons

Comparing the behaviors of early females and recent females, six categories showed significant change. Females expressed more curiosity ($p < .05$) and anger ($p < .01$) in the recent period, and expressed less affiliation/dependence ($p < .05$), excitement/anticipation ($p < .01$), nurturance ($p < .05$), and surprise ($p < .001$). Because females displayed six categorical shifts and males only two, it would seem that the feminine role experienced a greater change than the male role from the early to the recent period.

Discussion and Conclusions

(23)

Conclusion

1.

2.

3.

Within the three specific dimensions of this study, it appears that children now are finding more females in their books, slightly more occupational diversity for females, and a greater variety of behaviors and emotions expressed by males and females. These specific findings, however, point to some general movements in children's literature over the 30-year period examined: (1) Since aspects of masculinity and femininity that conform to stereotypic traits were more prevalent in the early period than in the recent period, there seems to have been a movement toward *a broadening of sex role standards over the three decades;* (2) Females have exhibited more significant changes in their behavior profiles over the three decades, implying that *the change in the sex role stereotype is stemming from females adopting characteristics previously considered "masculine";* (3) *Differences between females and males in children's books are most apparent in the differing occupational patterns for the sexes.* Very little change has taken place in this sphere.

(24)

Relation to world conditions

Whether or not the books mirror social conditions as they actually exist is open to debate. Assuming that the actual male-female ratio is approximately 50/50, it becomes obvious that females are not characterized as frequently as males in literature, though there is a trend in this direction. Of particular interest is the data from 1971: authors seemed to be more sensitive to this issue and the percentage of female characters was noticeably higher.

(25)

Relation to world conditions

Feminine invisibility in the world of work, as depicted in children's books, does not reflect the reality of the 1970's, but perhaps mirrors present societal concerns. The paradox is that women have long held prestigious positions in industry and the professions, but this is rarely portrayed in children's literature. Societal concerns at this point in time (as demonstrated by the Equal Rights Amendment or Affirmative Action programs, for example) would emphasize the need to provide additional role models in literature and life, both for males and females. Just as the option of a career could be available to feminine characters, just so could masculine characters exercise the option of doing housework, a conception of sex role that received no support in this relatively large sample of books. (However, there are recent publications for children intent upon breaking down inhibiting sexual stereotypes. For example, see/hear the excellent book/record conceived by Marlo Thomas, *Free To Be . . . You and Me,* McGraw-Hill.)

(26)

Model for study in other areas

Broadly conceived, the methodology of this analysis suggests a paradigm pertinent to other types of analyses dealing with culture, attitudinal, or behavioral variables. If sex role behavior, as exemplified by characters in children's literature, can be analyzed and compared, then perhaps not only other dimensions of personality are open to this method, but also other media such as television and films.

Results

Table 2—Significant Male and Female Variables in the Early Period

Male Percent	Male Fre-quency	Category	Female Fre-quency	Female Percent	Chi-square value
80.8	63	Physical aggression	15	19.2	24.40***
68.0	70	Verbal aggression	33	32.0	5.56*
45.4	45	Physical affection	54	54.6	4.83*
34.5	39	Nurturance	74	65.6	19.32***
74.3	124	Competence	43	25.7	13.17***
26.0	20	Affiliation/dependence	57	74.0	37.32***
39.7	23	Fantasy	35	60.3	11.20***
42.7	35	Sadness	47	57.3	7.52**
67.8	59	Anger	28	32.2	5.38*

Total number of occurrences: 1576 (Males 887, Females 689)
Expected Male percentage of occurrence: 56.3 percent
Expected Female percentage of occurrence: 43.7 percent

*** = p<.001.
** = p<.01.
* = p<.05.

Results

Table 3—Significant Male and Female Variables in the Recent Period

Male Percent	Male Frequency	Category	Female Frequency	Female Percent	Chi-square Value
72.5	58	Physical aggression	22	27.5	11.70***
65.5	120	Competence	63	34.4	4.13*
27.1	13	Affiliation/dependence	35	72.9	32.66***
37.2	32	Sadness	54	62.8	13.56***
66.7	36	Surprise	18	33.3	5.08*

Total number of occurrences: 1538 (Males 853, Females 685)
Expected Male percentage of occurrence: 55.5 percent
Expected Female percentage of occurrence: 44.5 percent

*** = p<.001.
** = p<.01.
* = p<.05.

Background

References
(27)

1. Blom, Gaston E.; Waits, Richard R; Zimet, Sara G., "Content of First Grade Reading Books," *Reading Teacher,* 21 (no.4): 317–323, 1968.
2. Broverman, Inge K.; Vogel, Susan R.; Broverman, Donald M.; Carlson, Frank E.; Rosenkrantz, Paul S., "Sex Role Stereotypes: A Current Appraisal," *Journal of Social Issues,* 28 (no.2): 59–78, 1972.
3. Child, Irvin L.; Potter, Elmer H.; Levine, Estelle M., "Children's Textbooks and Personality Development," *Psychological Monographs,* 60 (no.3): Whole no. 279, 1946.
4. Donlan, Dan, "The Negative Image of Women in Children's Literature," *Elementary English,* 49:604–611, April 1972.
5. Frasher, Ramona; Walker, Annabelle, "Sex Roles in Early Reading Textbooks," *Reading Teacher,* 25:741–749, May 1972.
6. Goodenough, Florence L., *Anger in Young Children,* University of Minnesota Press, Minneapolis, 1931.
7. Janeway, Elizabeth, *Man's World Woman's Place,* Wm. Morrow, New York, 1971.
8. Jersild, Arthur T.; Markey, Frances V.; Jersild, Catherine L., *Children's Fears, Dreams, Wishes, Daydreams, Likes, Dislikes, Pleasant and Unpleasant Memories,* Bureau of Publications, Teachers College, Columbia University, New York, 1933.
9. Kagan, Jerome, "Acquisition and Significance of Sex Typing and Sex Role Identity," *Review of Child Development Research,* Russell Sage Foundation, New York, 1964.
10. Kagan, Jerome; Moss, Howard A., *Birth To Maturity,* John Wiley and Sons, New York, 1962.
11. Key, Mary Ritchie, "The Role of Male and Female in Children's Books—Dispelling All Doubt," *Wilson Library Bulletin,* 46:167–176, October 1971.
12. Lunneborg, Patricia, "Stereotypic Aspects of

Masculinity-Femininity Measurement," *Journal of Consulting and Clinical Psychology,* 34:113–118, February 1970.

13. Mussen, Paul Henry; Conger, John Janeway; Kagan, Jerome, *Child Development and Personality,* Harper and Row, New York, 1969.

14. Nilsen, Alleen Pace, "Women in Children's Literature," *College English,* 32:918–926, May 1971.

15. Parsons, Talcott; Bales, Robert F., *Socialization and Interaction Process,* Free Press, Glencoe, Il., 1955.

16. Stavn, Diane Gersoni, "The Skirts in Fiction About Boys: A Maxi-Mess," *School Library Journal,* 96:282–286, January 1971.

17. Tangri, Sandra Schwartz, "Determinants of Occupational Role Innovation Among College Women," *Journal of Social Issues,* 28 (no.2): 177–199, 1972.

18. Women on Words and Images, *Dick and Jane as Victims: Sex Stereotyping in Children's Readers,* Princeton, NJ, 1972.

Study Number 2

This study investigates a very specific question that arises in measurement where the element of chance is involved in selected responses which will be judged as either correct or incorrect. The very technical nature of the study is reflected in the language used. The authors seem to be speaking to an audience largely of testing experts, but implications would seem to be directed to anyone who builds tests with multiple-choice items. Those who construct their own tests as well as those who develop standardized tests might use this knowledge in their professional assignment.

THE EFFECT OF KEYED RESPONSE SEQUENCING OF MULTIPLE CHOICE ITEMS ON PERFORMANCE AND RELIABILITY*

JOHN C. JESSELL and WALTER L. SULLINS
Indiana State University

(Paragraph 1)

Most test constructors agree that proper sequencing of multiple choice test items, with respect to keyed response position, is a desirable test characteristic. Nearly every basic educational measurement textbook devotes some discussion to item sequencing, usually recommending that the correct answer appear in each position about an equal number of times and that the items be arranged randomly. The theoretical rationale underlying such procedures is that if one were to choose the same option for each item of a test, he could not obtain a score beyond that of a chance score. Other reasons are to avoid providing test-takers with systematic devices which would enable them to "beat" the test and to establish a safeguard against an unconscious bias by the test constructor to allow the correct response to occur appreciably more often in one option position than in another.

(2)

Although detailed methods for arranging items in proper sequence have been given (Anderson, 1952; Mosier and Price, 1945), there is little empirical evidence that keyed response arrangement is related to test performance. The purpose of this study was to investigate the effects on test reliability and student performance of response sequencing that would be extremely unlikely under a random model.

*The authors wish to thank Dr. Charles Gehring, Associate Professor of Life Sciences, for his cooperation in providing subjects and the test used in the study. Appreciation is also extended to Thomas Cahill, doctoral fellow, for his assistance in data collection.

From the *Journal of Educational Measurement,* Spring 1975, *12*(1), pp.45–48. Copyright 1975, National Council on Measurement in Education, Inc., East Lansing, Michigan. Reprinted by permission.

Procedure

(3)

Test Forms

The items of the test were based on two units of study in an introductory life science course and were representative of content covering the topic areas of genetics and parasitology. The test was the fourth in a series of five examinations administered over the semester. The items which were constructed by the instructor had been used in previous testings, conformed to item-construction principles, and met the criteria of acceptable difficulty and discrimination.

(4)

The original form (Form 1) of the test, which consisted of 60 multiple-choice items with four options for each item, was arranged in an ideal format with each option as the keyed response for one-fourth of the items and with the keyed response position appearing no more than twice in sequence.

(5)

Form 2 of the test was arranged so that the initial seven items of the test were keyed according to the second option (letter B) with the format of the remainder of the test identical to that of Form 1.

(6)

Form 3, seven items in the middle portion of the test (items 27 through 33) were keyed with the second option as the keyed response. All other items were keyed in accordance with Form 1.

(7)

Form 4 was arranged so that the final seven items were keyed with the second option as the keyed response and all other items as in Form 1.

Items of Form 5, 6, and 7 were arranged similarly to those of Forms 3, 4, and 5 except that 14 sequential items were identically keyed. The initial 14 items, the middle 14 items, and the final 14 items were keyed with the second option as the keyed response for Forms 5, 6, and 7 respectively. All other items of these forms were keyed in some accordance with Form 1.

(8)

The choice of the second response position (option B) as the keyed response for each of the arranged, sequential patterns was an arbitrary one. It was decided to use the same response position as the keyed response for each arranged pattern for each form, since varying the response position might introduce an uncontrolled variable.

(9)

Sample

The test forms were administered to 454 Indiana State University freshman enrolled in an introductory life science course during the Fall semester, 1973–74. A single televised lecture session with six laboratory and discussion sections was the instructional format. The test was administered to the six sections over a two-day period. The seven forms were uniformly distributed among the six sections and were distributed within sections in a random fashion.

(10)

The fact that the test was administered over a two-day period to six different sections at six different time periods, raises the possibility that information was exchanged among the students of the various sections. Since there were seven different forms of the test, the likelihood of such a development occurring so as to affect the results of the study is small.

Results

(11)

The results for the seven test forms are presented in Table 1. The numeral codes identifying the forms are the same as those used in the previous section. Although the Kuder-Richardson Formula #20 reliability estimate for Form 1 was higher than for other forms, inspection revealed no practical differences in reliability estimates; thus no tests of statistical significance were performed. Similarly, the standard errors of measurement were nearly identical.

Mean performance on the forms ranged from 35.33 to 39.00, with Form 1 yielding the highest performance. Results of a test of significance among the means of the forms are presented in Table 2. The computed value of F (1.16) indicated no statistically significant differences among the means. Since the standard deviations were similar (8.55 to 9.70), no test for homogeneity of dispersion was performed.

Discussion

(13)

The results of this study do not support the intuitively appealing notion that multiple choice test items should be keyed with the correct answer appearing in each position about the same number of times, and randomly sequenced with respect to the keyed response position. The sequential patterning of keyed responses employed for purposes of this study were of such a nature that their probability of occurring (under a random arrangement model) would be near zero, nevertheless neither test reliability nor student performance appeared to be affected.

(14)

Table 1—*Summary Statistics for the Seven Forms*

FORM	KR20	SEM	Mean	St. Dev.	N
1.	.89	3.25	39.00	9.70	67
2.	.85	3.40	35.33	8.73	66
3.	.86	3.32	38.23	8.82	64
4.	.86	3.36	37.21	9.11	63
5.	.88	3.33	37.43	9.43	67
6.	.84	3.39	37.59	8.55	64
7.	.84	3.42	36.37	8.56	63

(15)

These findings demonstrate that it is unnecessary to follow elaborate schemes to achieve a balanced distribution of keyed responses. With the exception of the occasional "pattern sleuth" or "pattern marker," it would appear that examinees pay less heed to response patternings than might be supposed. It would be presumptuous, however, to conclude that no care should be taken to avoid extreme and/or lopsided keying distributions. For a single testing and for a sequence of achievement tests in a course over a term, some attention toward achieving a nominal spread of correct response options is warranted.

(16)

Table 2—*Analysis of Variance Among the Seven Forms*

Source	SS	df	MS	F
Forms	566.47	6	94.41	1.16
Error	36226.50	447	81.04	
Total	36792.97			

(17)

The results of this study may or may not be applicable to students below or above the level of university freshmen, but this would need to be determined through further investigation.

References

(18)

Anderson, S.B. Sequence in multiple-choice item options. *Journal of Educational Psychology,* 1952, *43,* 364–368.

Mosier, C.I., & Price, H.G. The arrangement of choice in multiple-choice questions and a scheme for randomizing choices. *Educational and Psychological Measurement,* 1945, *5,* 379–382.

Authors

(19)

Jessell, John C. *Address:* Dept. of Graduate Studies in Education, Indiana State University, Terre Haute, Indiana 47809 *Title:* Professor of Education *Degrees:* B.S. Southern Connecticut State College, M.Ed. Ohio University, Ph.D. University of Wisconsin *Specialization:* Guidance and Counseling; Educational Measurement

Sullins, Walter L. *Address:* Center for Educational Research, Indiana State University. Terre Haute, Indiana 47809 *Title:* Associate Professor of Education *Degrees:* B.S., M.S. Kansas State College, Ph.D. University of Maryland *Specialization:* Statistics and Educational Measurement

Study Number 3

This study represents an investigation of a complex situation. The concern about stresses on college students is one facet of the concern about effects of stress throughout school years. Information from this study may relate to other age groups. Imaginative methods are called for in studies of this kind and these authors chose the longitudinal study with a four-year period to collect facts. Close contact with other studies being done during this time period is required to relate each study to new findings of other studies. The report reflects the attention which the authors give to previous studies and research findings.

A LONGITUDINAL STUDY OF WHO SEEKS COUNSELING WHEN[1]

W. HARRY SHARP
University of Houston

BARBARA A. KIRK[2]
University of California, Berkeley

(Paragraph 1)

This study undertook to determine when, over a four-year period, those members of the entire 1966 entering freshman class at the University of California, Berkeley, who sought counseling initiated their contacts. Generally speaking, the rate of initiation declined steeply over time, both by years and quarters within years. An occasional reversal occured for females. Also studied were characteristics of the students as related to time of initating counseling, utilizing scores on the School and College Ability Test (Form UA), Omnibus Personality Inventory (Form F), and Strong Vocational Interest Blank (Forms M and F) administered in freshman orientation. Neither male nor female clients differed significantly by test results when time of counseling initiation was considered by the four academic quarters. By year, quarter by quarter, and by parts of quarters, the Omnibus Personality Inventory yielded significant results on some scales.

(2)

Educators are concerned increasingly with the form, magnitude, and focal point of stresses affecting college students. Murray (1938) provided a productive "need-press" model for the research of Stern, Stein, and Bloom (1956). The latter conceptualized the behavior of students as an ongoing field process, "the resultant of the transaction

[1] The authors wish to thank Austin Frank for his critical reading of the manuscipt and for his suggestions.
[2] Requests for reprints should be sent to Barbara Kirk, Counseling Center, Building T-5, University of California, Berkeley, California 94720.

between the individual and other structural units in the behavioral field [p.35]." The work of Dubos (1968) has led to the conceptualization of the campus as an eco-system(s). Regardless of the conceptual framework, few would differ with the conceptualization of a transactional relationship in which different kinds of students respond to internal and external stresses differentially.

(3)

When a student comes to a college counseling center, one may assume that the student is reacting to specific stimuli. In many cases, the stimuli may be distressful. Either internal or external stimuli, or both, may influence the student's decision to seek professional counseling. Three questions related to the transactional relationship between the student and his campus can be studied in college counseling centers: (a) When do students initiate counseling? (b) Is there a relationship between whom the client is (his characteristics) and when he initiates counseling? (c) Is there a relationship between when the student initiates counseling and his expressed problem(s)? Another manner of stating the three questions is: When do students come for counseling? Who are they? Why do they come when they come? The present article, one of a series (Kirk, 1973), attempts to answer the first two questions.

(4)

Academic calendars on any campus are highly regimented. Students register at prescribed times; classes begin on a specified date; faculty give tests during the middle of the term and require completion of major papers toward the end; final examination schedules are fixed by the administration. Faculty have considerable latitude in terms of what they require of students, but they have relatively little latitude in terms of when it is required, since they are responsible for completion of grading by deadlines. Thus, the initiation of counseling may speak rather directly to the source of external stress imposed upon the student by the academic community. Snyder and Kahne (1969) concluded, "we have forceful evidence that the nature, intensity, and location of educational and other stresses strongly affect patterns of the use of psychiatrists by students (p.28)."

(5)

However, little work has been done to discover when students initiated counseling. Baker (1963) studied the pattern of incidence of appeals for services over six academic years by semesters at the Clark University Psychological Clinic. Students initiated the services at a greater rate during the first than they did during the second semester. The highest initiation rate occurred during the first half of the first semester. He suggested and later confirmed (Baker & Nidorf, 1964) that the high rate of initiation during the first half of the first semester reflected freshmen difficulties of initial adjustment to college. The similarity of initiation rate patterns for first semesters and second semesters suggested the operation of common precipitating factors. Baker reasoned that one such factor was the regularly occurring examination periods, and he speculated that students may react to examination stress by anticipating the stress and initiating assistance prior to examinations. Other students delay their reactions to stress and seek assistance following the examination period. From his results Baker hypothesized "that the effect of examination-stressers is in part a function of personality differences among students (p.363)," but this important point has yet to be explored.

(6)

Snyder and Kahne (1969) compared the term-by-term use of the psychiatric service by the class of 1965 at Massachusetts Institute of Technology, Cambridge. The class was divided into groups by academic discipline. The data were consistent with the hypothesis that departments presented their students with significantly different stresses at different times. Students enrolled in one science program made their greatest use of the psychiatric service during the first term as majors in the program. Students in another science program made the greatest use of the psychiatric service during the first term of their senior year.

(7)

Since students who use a counseling service are different from those who use a psychiatric service (Kirk, 1973) and since the matter of when students initiate counseling is related to the transactional relationship between the characteristics of the students and the campus, both students and administrators can be assisted by understanding the interaction. The present study follows an entering class over four years and addresses itself to the questions: When do students come for counseling and who comes when?

Method

(8)

New freshmen who enrolled in the fall quarter of 1966 at the University of California, Berkeley, were followed through June 1970. The later date was the time graduation might have been expected to occur. Scrupulous records of the exact date of first initiation of counseling were maintained by the Counseling Center and were analyzed for this freshman class. Enrollment data, which would reflect attrition within this class alone for each of the 15 academic quarters, were not available at the time of this study. Thus in the results reported below, the percentages of students initiating contact at any one time were based on the class entering enrollment data (1,761 men and 1,292 women) and after the first quarter were spuriously low in terms of those remaining on campus. Nevertheless, the data do reflect the pattern of use of the Counseling Center by members of the class who began college in September of 1966.

(9)

_____   The academic calendar over the four-year period was used as the baseline for the analyses. Clients were grouped in four different time periods: by year (first, second, third, and fourth), by calendar quarters combined (all fall, winter, spring, and summer quarters), by individual academic quarter (fall of 1966 to spring of 1970, 1–16), and by combined parts of quarters (registration week, first week of instructions, . . . , final examination week equal to five parts in all).

(10)

_____   The time periods were defined in the following manner. The first year included those students initiating counseling prior to their enrollment in September of 1966 through the end of the spring quarter of 1967. The second and subsequent years included students initiating counseling from the end of the previous spring quarter through the end of the appropriate spring quarter. Thus, students initiating counseling either prior to school or during the summer quarter were categorized in the following school year.

(11)

_____   The academic quarters were defined in the following manner, fall quarters, for example, extended from the end of summer quarters through the end of the fall quarters, including the short gap prior to the quarter with the succeeding quarter. The remaining quarters were defined in the same fashion. Students who sought counseling prior to their enrollment in September of 1966, were included in the fall quarter of 1966 category.

(12)

_____   The quarter was divided into the following categories: registration week, the first week of instruction, the five weeks of instruction subsequent to the first week of instruction, the last four weeks of instruction, and final examination week. The five-week period of instruction included presumably the time when instructors would have given mid-term examinations.

(13)

_____   During the week preceding registration in the fall of 1966, all incoming freshmen were asked to complete the School and College Ability Test, Form UA (SCAT), the Omnibus Personality Inventory, Form F (OPI), and the Strong Vocational Interest Blank, Forms M and F (SVIB), for each sex respectively. Of the 401 male and 319 female clients who were then seen one or more times for counseling during four years, test data were available as follows: 90.5% of the men and 95.2% of the women had taken the SCAT; 81.8% of the men and 93.6% of the women had taken the OPI; and 87.5% of the men and 92.4% of the women had taken the SVIB. The tested clients were assumed to be reasonably representative of the total client population being studied. The only SVIB scales used in the present study were the Masculinity-Femininity for both sexes and the Occupational Level for males.

(14)

Table 1—Number and Percentage of Original Class Intiating Counseling (By Academic Quarter) and Omnibus Personality Inventory (OPI) Scales, Which Show Significant Differences Between Quarters

	Counseling initiation		Differentiating OPI scales			
	Men (N = 1,761)		Theoretical Orientation		Social Extroversion	
Quarter	n	%	n	M	SD	M	SD
---	---	---	---	---	---	---	---
Prior to enrollment	29	1.6					
1. Fall 1966	86	4.9	76	20.7	5.4	19.0	8.3
2. Winter 1967	66	3.7	56	22.2	5.0	19.9	7.1
3. Spring 1967	55	3.1	42	22.4	4.9	21.3^c	7.1
First-year total	236	13.4					
4. Summer 1967	7	.4	6	22.0	3.0	13.5	5.1
5. Fall 1967	38	2.2	28	21.8	5.5	20.7	7.1
6. Winter 1968	29	1.6	26	22.3	6.0	20.4	6.4
7. Spring 1968	12	.7	10	15.9^a	5.0	26.3^d	6.3
Second-year total	86	4.9					
8. Summer 1968	1	.1	—	—	—	—	—
9. Fall 1968	20	1.1	17	22.4	5.3	17.7	8.0
10. Winter 1969	17	1.0	14	18.4^b	4.5	20.3	4.5
11. Spring 1969	12	.7	9	23.7	4.9	15.6	6.8
Third-year total	50	2.8					
12. Summer 1969	8	.5	5	21.4	3.1	21.6	6.9
13. Fall 1969	13	.7	11	23.9	5.2	18.5	7.5
14. Winter 1970	6	.3	5	22.0	6.0	15.6	4.2
15. Spring 1970	2	.1	2	19.5	2.1	24.0	9.9
Fourth-year total	29	1.6					
All fall quarters	186	10.6					
All winter quarters	118	6.7					
All spring quarters	81	4.6					
All summer quarters	16	.9					
Four-year total	401	22.8					

^{a}The mean of Quarter 7 was significantly less than the means of Quarters 1, 2, 3, 5, 6, 9, 11, and 13 ($p<.01$).
^{b}The mean of Quarter 10 was significantly less than the means of Quarters 2, 3, 11, and 13 ($p<.05$).
^{c}The mean of Quarter 3 was significantly greater than the mean of Quarter 4 ($p<.05$).
^{d}The mean of Quarter 7 was significantly greater than the means of Quarters 1, 2, 4, 9, 11, 13, and 14 ($p<.05$).

(15)

Analysis of variance was the major statistic used to test differences between groups. Kramer's (1956) extension of the Duncan multiple-range test to group means with unequal numbers was used to determine where significant differences were located. Males and females were treated separately.

Results
(16)

When Students Came for Counseling

Analysis by sequential quarters. Tables 1 and 2 present the number of students beginning college in September of 1966 who initiated counseling during the first through fourth years by quarter. An analysis of variance of 14 quarters in Table 1 showed—Theoretical Orientation:$MS_{between}$ = 53.7, MS_{within} = 26.9, F = 1.99, $p<.05$; Social Extroversion: $MS_{between}$ = 94.8, MS_{within} = 52.7, F = 1.80, $p<.05$. An analysis of variance of 15 quarters in Table 2 showed—Thinking Introversion: $MS_{between}$ = 114.5, MS_{within} = 53.9, F = 2.13, $p<.05$; Altruism: $MS_{between}$ = 528., MS_{within} = 27.7, F = 1.91, $p<.05$; Practical Orientation: $MS_{between}$ =51.8, MS_{within} = 25.6, F = 2.02, $p<.05$.

(17)

Table 2—Number and Percentage of Original Class Initiating
Counseling (By Academic Quarter) and Omnibus Personality
Inventory (OPI) Scales, Which Show Significant Differences Between
Quarters

Quarter	Counseling initiation Women (N = 1,292)		Differentiating OPI scales					
			Thinking Introversion		Altruism		Practical Orientation	
	n	%	n	M	SD	M	SD	M	SD
Prior to enrollment	19	1.5							
1. Fall 1966	67	5.2	65	26.9	6.5	21.9	5.5	11.2	4.6
2. Winter 1967	46	3.6	40	27.0	8.2	22.8	5.6	11.3	5.1
3. Spring 1967	31	2.4	28	27.0	7.3	23.7	5.2	10.4	6.2
First-year total	163	12.6							
4. Summer 1967	5	.4	5	28.4	7.9	21.8	6.7	12.2	6.7
5. Fall 1967	44	3.4	38	28.6	7.1	22.0	3.9	10.3	5.1
6. Winter 1968	22	1.7	19	25.6	7.1	20.0	5.4	11.8	4.5
7. Spring 1968	17	1.3	14	27.4	7.9	22.3	6.7	11.6	4.6
Second-year total	88	6.8							
8. Summer 1968	4	.3	2	26.0	5.7	15.5	10.6	16.0	—[j]
9. Fall 1968	12	.9	8	29.6[a]	7.1	22.1	3.4	9.3	5.7
10. Winter 1969	7	.5	3	17.0[b]	2.7	16.3	0.6	18.7[g]	5.9
11. Spring 1969	3	.2	2	10.0[c]	8.5	11.0[f]	2.8	21.0[h]	2.8
Third-year total	26	2.0							
12. Summer 1969	5	.4	5	34.2[d]	4.9	18.6	5.4	6.6[i]	1.5
13. Fall 1969	25	1.9	23	25.0	8.0	20.1	5.2	12.3	4.7
14. Winter 1970	8	.6	6	22.7	11.4	22.3	4.5	14.2	6.9
15. Spring 1970	4	.3	3	31.3	2.5	19.7	5.5	7.7	4.0
Fourth-year total	42	3.3							
All fall quarters	167	12.9							
All winter quarters	83	6.4							
All spring quarters	55	4.3							
All summer quarters	14	1.1							
Four-year total	319	24.7							

[a] The mean of Quarter 9 was significantly less than the mean of Quarter 15 at
$p<.05$.
[b] The mean of Quarter 10 was significantly less than the means of Quarters 1,
2, 5, 9, and 12 $(p<.05)$.
[c] The mean of Quarter 11 was significantly less than the means of Quarters 1
through 7 and 12 through 15 $(p<.05)$.
[d] The mean of Quarter 12 was significantly greater than the means of
Quarters 13 and 14 $(p<.05)$.
[e] The mean of Quarter 3 was significantly greater than the means of Quarters
6, 11, and 13 $(p<.05)$.
[f] The mean of Quarter 11 was significantly less than the means of Quarters 1,
2, 4 through 7, 9, 13, and 14 $(p<.05)$.
[g] The mean of Quarter 10 was significantly greater than the means of
Quarters 1, 2, 3, 5, 6, 9, 12, and 15 $(p<.05)$.
[h] The mean of Quarter 11 was significantly greater than the means of
Quarters 1, 2, 3, 5, 6, 7, 9, 12, 13, and 15 $(p<.05)$.
[i] The mean of Quarter 12 was significantly less than the mean of Quarter 14
$(p<.05)$.
[j] Data not included in analysis because of lack of variance.

Students initiated counseling at a diminishing rate over the
four-year period. Senior women, however, showed an increased rate during the fourth year when compared with the
third year. A pattern of counseling initiation was found over
each year with fall quarters representing the highest rate and
subsequent quarters decreasing.

(18)

Analysis by combined parts of quarters. Table 3 presents
data by parts of quarters. Only those students initiating
counseling during the specifically defined period of time were

(19)

Table 3—Counseling Initiation by Parts of Quarters, Four Years Combined, and Differentiating Omnibus Personality Inventory (OPI) Scores for Men

| | Counseling initiation | | | | Differentiating OPI scores for men | | | | | | | | | |
| | Men (N = 1,761) | | Women (N = 1,292) | | | Impulse Expression | | Personal Integration | | Level Anxiety | | Response Bias | |
Part of the quarter	n	%	n	%	n	M	SD	M	SD	M	SD	M	SD
1. Registration weeks	89	5.1	62	4.8	75	29.4	11.2	32.4	10.1	13.2	4.5	14.2	4.2
2. First weeks of instruction	46	2.6	30	2.3	38	31.7	9.3	30.4	9.9	12.5	4.8	13.9	4.2
3. Next five weeks	103	5.8	116	9.0	89	33.6[a]	9.6	28.1[b]	9.6	10.5[d]	4.5	12.3[f]	4.0
4. Next four weeks	103	5.8	66	5.1	84	30.3	9.6	31.0	10.4	12.4	4.4	13.6	4.5
5. Final examination weeks	14	.8	5	.4	9	36.6	5.6	20.7[c]	6.4	8.2	5.1	10.2[g]	3.2
Total	355	20.2	279	21.5	295								

[a] The mean of Part 3 was significantly greater than the means of Parts 1 and 4 ($p<.05$).
[b] The mean of Part 3 was significantly less than the mean of Part 1 ($p<.01$).
[c] The mean of Part 5 was significantly less than the means of Parts 1, 2, 3, and 4 ($p<.05$).
[d] The mean of Part 3 was significantly less than the means of Parts 1, 2, and 4 ($p<.05$).
[e] The mean of Part 5 was significantly less than the means of Parts 1, 2, and 4 ($p<.05$).
[f] The mean of Part 3 was significantly less than the means of Parts 1 and 4 ($p<.05$).
[g] The mean of Part 5 was significantly less than the means of Parts 1, 2, and 4 ($p<.05$).

included in the data presented in Table 2. An analysis of variance for male OPI score in Table 3 showed—Impulse Expression: $MS_{between} = 267.1$, $MS_{within} = 98.1$, $F = 2.72$, $p<.05$; Personal Integration: $MS_{between} = 407.5$, $MS_{within} = 98.4$, $F = 4.1$, $p<.005$; Anxiety level: $MS_{between} = 112.4$, MS_{within} 20.2, $F = 5.55$, $p<.001$; Response Bias: $MS_{between} = 60.8$, $MS_{within} = 17.8$, $F = 3.4$, $p<.01$.

(20)

The patterns of initiating counseling during an academic quarter differed somewhat on the basis of sex. Men initiated counseling with approximately equal frequency during registration week and the periods that presumably included and followed the administration of midterm examinations. Women initiated counseling at a considerably higher rate during the period following the first week of instruction and including midterm examinations than during the period following midterm examinations, not only relative to themselves but also to the men. The third highest rate for both sexes occurred during registration week. The lowest rate for both sexes took place during final examination week.

Student Characteristics in Relation to Time of Initiating Counseling

(21)

Analysis by combined quarters. Neither male nor female clients differed significantly by test results when time of counseling initiation was considered by the four academic quarters, that is, all fall quarters versus all winter quarters, etc.[3] Thus, based upon entering tests, clients who initiated counseling during the fall quarters did not differ from those initiating counseling during any of the other quarters. The same finding was true for those initiating counseling during the winter, spring and summer quarters.

(22)

Analysis by academic years. When clients were grouped by the year in which they initiated counseling, the SCAT and SVIB scales did not yield significant differences, but some OPI scales did. These are presented in Table 4. An analysis of variance of the scales in Table 4 showed—Impulse Expression: $MS_{between} = 279.4$, $MS_{within} = 93.7$, $F = 2.98$, $p<.05$; Personal Integration: $MS_{between} = 380.8$, $MS_{between} = 146.1$, $F = 2.61$, $p<.05$; Altruism: $MS_{between} = 276.9$, $MS_{within} = 56.2$, $F = 4.93$, $p<.005$; Intellectual Disposition Category: $MS_{between} = 9.6$, $MS_{within} = 3.5$, $F = 2.77$, $p<.05$.

---

[3] Where no significant differences are found among test scores for contrasted groups, the scores are not reported. Fairly complete data on the counseled group as a whole are available in Kirk (1973).

(23)

Table 4—Omnibus Personality Inventory (OPI) Scales, Which Show Significant Differences by Year of Initiating Counseling

	Men								Women	
		Impulse Expression			Personal Integration		Altruism		Intellectual Disposition Category	
Years										
	n	*M*	*SD*	*n*	*M*	*SD*	*M*	*SD*	*M*	*SD*
First	194	32.8[a]	9.6	156	28.4	12.2	21.1	7.7	4.6	1.8
Second	70	29.0	10.2	81	27.1	11.9	20.2	7.1	4.3	1.8
Third	41	30.9	9.6	23	21.2[b]	14.2	14.7[c]	9.3	3.6[d]	2.5
Fourth	23	29.9	8.8	35	25.6	10.4	19.7	6.0	4.9	1.8
Total	328			295						

[a] The mean of the first year was significantly greater than the mean of the second year (p<.05).

[b] The mean of the third year was significantly less than the means of the first and second years (p<.05).

[c] The mean of the third year was significantly less than the means of the first, second, and fourth years (p<.05).

[d] The mean of the third year was significantly less than the means of the first and fourth years (p<.05).

(24)

Male clients who initiated counseling during the first year had Impulse Expression scores significantly greater than those male clients who initiated counseling during the second year.

(25)

Female clients who initiated counseling during the third year had significantly lower Personal Integration, Altruism, and Intellectual Disposition Category scores than those initiating counseling during the first year. A significant difference in the same direction was found between females initiating counseling during the third year and the second year on the Personal Integration and Altruism scales. A similar difference was found between women initiating counseling during the third year and the fourth year on the Altruism and Intellectual Disposition Category scales.

(26)

Analysis by sequential quarters. When the temporal period was considered on a quarter-by-quarter basis, neither the SCAT nor SVIB scales differentiated male or female clients. Male clients were differentiated on the basis of the Theoretical Orientation and Social Extroversion scales of the OPI. These data are presented in Table 1.

(27)

Men who initiated counseling during the spring quarter of 1968 had significantly lower Theoretical Orientation scales than did men initiating counseling during eight other quarters. Similar differences were found for men who initiating counseling during the winter quarter of 1969 and those initiating counseling during four other quarters. The Social Extroversion scores of men initiating counseling during the spring quarter of 1967 were significantly higher than the scores of those initiating counseling during the summer quarter of 1967. Men who initiated counseling during the spring quarter of 1968 had higher Social Extroversion scores than did men initiating counseling during seven other quarters. Overall, it is interesting to note that for three of the four academic years, the spring quarter Social Extroversion scores were the highest.

(28)

———————————— Female clients were differentiated on the basis of the Thinking Introversion, Altruism, and Practical Outlook scales of the OPI. These data are presented in Table 2.

(29)

———————————— Women who initiated counseling during the fall quarter of 1968, the winter quarter of 1969, the spring quarter of 1969, and the summer quarter of 1969 (i.e., academic year 1968–69) differed significantly on the Thinking Introversion scale from women who initiated counseling during a number of other quarters. Female clients who initiated counseling during the fall quarter of 1968 and the summer quarter of 1969 had relatively high Thinking Introversion scores in comparison to other clients. Those who initiated counseling during the winter and spring quarters of 1969 had relatively low Thinking Introversion scores. Female clients initiating counseling during the spring quarter of 1967 had significantly higher Altruism scores than did those initiating counseling during the winter quarter of 1968, the spring quarter of 1969, and the fall quarter of 1969. Clients who initiated counseling in the spring quarter of 1969 had lower Altruism scores than did clients initiating counseling during nine other quarters. Only two female clients, however, initiated counseling during the spring quarter of 1969.

(30)

———————————— Females who initiated counseling during the winter, spring, and summer quarters of 1969 had Practical Outlook scores that were significantly different from those of females who initiated counseling during a number of other quarters. Again, caution must be exercised due to the small numbers in each of these three cells.

(31)

———————————— *Analysis by combined parts of quarters.* Females who initiated counseling during various parts of the quarter did not differ on the basis of SCAT, OPI, or SVIB data. Male clients did differ on four OPI scales. These data are presented in Table 3.

(32)

The mean scores for these four scales rise and fall in perfect lock-step fashion across the five segments of the quarter, the Impulse Expression scale moving in the opposite ———————————— direction from the other three scales. The scores for the few men initiating counseling during final examination weeks were most deviant, followed by the scores for those in the middle five weeks when midterm examinations were being given. The scores for those initiating counseling at the other times were essentially similar.

Discussion

(33)

Since a detailed study of the pattern of initiation of counseling by an entering class over four years has not been reported previously, one can only compare the present results with earlier inferential findings. As this study confirms, counseling starts are greatest just after the class arrives on campus and decline rather steeply over time. Every year fall quarters are heaviest and from the standpoint of overall counseling center management, provision must be made for high fall intake.

(34)

A previous study showed that women are more prone to use counseling resources than are men (Kirk, 1973). In the current study, in contrast to men, women tended to initiate contacts earlier in the quarter, which perhaps suggests greater dependence and/or concern for getting on the right path quickly. Also in contrast to men, women increased their initiation of counseling in the fourth year over that of the third year, perhaps showing greater concern over plans after graduation.

(35)

The data relating the psychological characteristics of clients to the academic calendar are impressive, particularly for men, when the corresponding parts of quarters are combined over all four years. As shown in Table 3, the differentiating scales come not from the SCAT or the two SVIB scales but from the OPI, and three of these four scales, Impulse Expression, Personal Integration, and Anxiety Level, are from the social-emotional adjustment cluster of the instrument (Heist & Yonge, 1968). The student groups are not distinguished one from the other by the clusters of OPI scales assessing intellectual orientation or authoritarianism. That the Response Bias scale is differentiating too is not surprising, since high scores on it are related to making a good impression and low scores may indicate "a low state of well-being or feeling of depression (Heist & Yonge, 1968, p.5)."

(36)

As mentioned earlier, the mean scores for these four scales move together, with the Impulse Expression scale going in the opposite direction from the other three. Clinically, as well as psychometrically within the OPI, when personal integration is low and anxiety is high (high anxiety is associated with *low* Anxiety Level scores), there tends to be less control of impulsiveness, and the picture in Table 3 is consistent; in the busy, stressful times surrounding midterms and finals, the students who initiate counseling are those who, at entrance, test as being most psychologically vulnerable. The relatively few men who started counseling at finals time were a standard deviation above the general mean on Impulse Expression and a standard deviation below the mean on Personal Integration, Anxiety Level, and Response Bias. They were also more homogeneous as a group than any other, as the standard deviations show.

(37)

Why similar results were not obtained for women is not clear. However, in year-by-year comparisons, women who came in the third year differed from women initiating counseling at other times. They appeared to be less intellectually oriented, personally integrated, and altruistically inclined. It can be hypothesized that in their junior year they may have been having particular problems of identity in reference to the institution they were attending. For men, those initiating counseling in their freshmen year had relatively higher Impulse Expression scores, which suggests recognition of difficulty in academic or general adjustment.

(38)

Remember that the contact rates are based on entering totals and do not take normal attendance attrition into account. The rates also do not take account of return contacts or amount of usage of counseling but only the frequency with which students first request service. Patterns of return usage may be quite different. The small numbers in many cells also require caution in interpreting some of the results. However, the appearance of significant differences in characteristics tested at entrance in relation to time of first seeking counseling indicates the potential for research on the transaction between specific campus environmental stress and psychological characteristics at the time of enrollment.

References

(39)

Baker, R.W. Pattern of initial contacts with a university psychological clinic and its relation to academic stressors. *Journal of Clinical Psychology*, 1963, *19*, 361–363.

Baker, R.W., & Nidorf, L.J. Pattern of occurrence of psychological disturbance in college students as a function of year level. *Journal of Clinical Psychology*, 1964, *20*, 530–531.

Dubos, R. *So human an animal.* New York: Scribners, 1968.

Heist, P., & Yonge, G. *Omnibus Personality Inventory Manual.* New York: Psychological Corporation, 1968.

Kirk, B.A. Characteristics of users of counseling centers and psychiatric services on a college campus. *Journal of Counseling Psychology*, 1973, *20*, 463–470.

Kramer, C.Y. Extension of multiple range tests to group means with unequal numbers of replications. *Biometrics*, 1965, *12*, 307–310.

Murray, H.A. *Explorations in personality.* New York: Oxford University Press, 1938.

Snyder, B.R., & Kahne, M.J. Stress in higher education and student use of university psychiatrists. *American Journal of Orthopsychiatry*, 1969, *39*, 23–35.

Stern, G.G., Stern, M.I., & Bloom, B.S. *Methods in personality assessment.* Glencoe, Ill.: The Free Press, 1956. (Received October 30, 1972)

Study Number 4

This study is an investigation of student learning organized as an experimental approach. The researcher controls the conditions by manipulating variables. The experimenter conducted the study in the classroom; however, introduction of control made this setting approach laboratory-like conditions. This study is a good illustration of the challenges that confront a researcher who attempts to devise ways to observe human behavior while checking out theory.

AN EXPERIMENTAL STUDY OF FIRST GRADE THEME WRITING*

HARRY E. ANDERSON, JR. and W.L. BASHAW
University of Georgia

(Paragraph 1)

Note: No abstract

Background

Mode of discourse is one of several variables of obvious importance in research on composition writing. Braddock, Lloyd-Jones, and Schoer (1963, pp. 8–9) list, in addition to writer variables, the important composition variables of topic, mode of discourse, time afforded for writing, and the examination situation. They specify that mode of discourse includes narration, description, exposition, argument, and criticism. They also point out that mode of discourse has been largely ignored by composition researchers, in spite of the fact that it has more effect than variations in topic on the quality of writing. Kincaid (1953), for instance, found mode of discourse, argumentative or expository, to be a significant factor in college freshman themes, particularly for the relatively inferior student. Also, Seegers (1933) had earlier shown an effect of mode of discourse on sentence structure. Seeger's study involved argument, exposition, narration, and description.

Theoretical framework

(2)

Descriptive and argumentative modes of discourse appear to be most common, but these modes have not been

*The research and development reported herein was performed pursuant to a contract with the United States Department of Health, Education, and Welfare, Office of Education, under the provisions of the Cooperative Research Program. The researchers are grateful for the assistance and cooperation of the following persons: Mr. Jasper Griffin, Superintendent of Cobb County, Georgia, Public Schools; Mrs. Gaynell Walker, co-ordinator of Elementary Education, Cobb County Public Schools; and Mr. William Leverett, Principal of Milford Elementary School, Marietta, Georgia.

Theoretical framework

studied at the first grade level. According to Piaget's (1932 and 1951) theory of child development, first grade children should do much better in the descriptive mode than in the argumentative mode. In any case, specific instruction in descriptive discourse should be more effective than instruction in the argumentative topics because, Piaget's theory states, children at this age level are *only initially* learning logical, abstract organization. But specific instruction in one mode is apt to affect the quality of writing in another mode, especially for young children.

(3)

Purpose

The purpose of the present study is to examine differences in mode of discourse for first grade themes. The general hypothesis is that stimulation in a given mode of discourse will improve the quality of compositions in that mode but decrease the quality of themes in another mode.

Hypothesis

Method

(4)

Sample

Subjects. The sample consisted of all first graders in a suburban elementary school. The results of the study are based on compositions by 92 students including 50 males and 42 females. Themes of students not present for the complete experiment were eliminated from analyses of final results.

(5)

Treatment

Themes and Treatment. Each student wrote two descriptive *(D)* themes and two argumentative *(A)* themes. For the *D* themes the students were told to write to a friend, giving a physical description of the school. The *A* themes also involved writing to a friend, but telling him why he would like to go to this school.

(6)

Treatment

The treatment consisted of 10-minute discussion periods. One discussion session (T_D) focused on the physical description of the school. Another session (T_A) centered on studies, games, and activities that would make the school attractive for a friend. A third discussion session was neutral (T_N). It was designed to avoid argumentative and descriptive discussion; the title of the T_N session was, "If I Were No Bigger Than a Peanut."

(7)

Procedure

Experimental Procedure. For the writing and discussion sessions, the students were taken out of their regular classrooms and randomly assigned to one of six groups depending on theme writing order (viz., *AD* or *DA)* and the type of treatment (viz., T_D, T_A or T_N) received in the experiment. The first two themes were written on two successive days, the treatment and third theme were handled on the third day, and the fourth theme was written on the fourth day. Groups (1) and (2) attended the same discussion session as did, respectively, groups (3) and (4), and groups (5) and (6). It may be helpful, also, to note that the themes were written in May, at the end of the first grade.

(8)

Procedure

Local teachers were trained in the conduct of the writing sessions. The teachers also collaborated with experimenters in writing materials for the discussion sessions. Three of the teachers were then trained and rehearsed for conducting the T_D, and T_A, and T_N sessions.

(9)

Rating scale (product)

Scoring

Rating scales and reliability. A seven-point D and a seven-point A rating scale was established for the rating of themes. Themes written by students absent one or more days in the experiment were used for the scale anchor points and for practice sessions. A presentation of the anchor themes will be helpful not only in understanding the rating scales but also in gaining insight into the vocabulary, grammar, and spelling extant in first grade themes. From low to high at scale points two, four and six, the argumentative anchor themes were as follows:

Criterion products (CP)

Rank 2—Low Argumentative
  I Like Miffe Scool.
  I Like The RooMs.
  I Lik The techer
  We have picher
  We bareball.
  I Like picher
  I Like Techer

(CP)

Rank 4—Medium Argumentative
  Why do my friend likes Milford
  school by kows they like school
  I like Milford school
  I like to go to school
  I like school by kowo it is fun
  I like Milford school to
  I play in school to
  I play in school

(CP)

Rank 6—High Argumentative
  my friend will like Milford skool
  be kus it is insiting and
  he will like Milford be kus
  it's Fun and he will like
  the wokr and he will like
  the nis techr's and he will
  like the prisubl and he will like
  The Cafutieu

Likewise, the descriptive anchor themes were:

(CP)

Rank 2—Low Descriptive
  Milford Has Big windows
  the CaFoteReo is Hooked
  onto the ottorem

Rank 4—Medium Descriptive
  the playground is a big
  plase. the Lunch Room
  has big Window.
  ther are 5 1st Grade.

(CP)

Rank 6—High Descriptive
there is 810 and 26
teacher. a store is down
the road. there is a
fire stashe. by the school
Is a mike Jug. and
across is two stashe.

Interpretation

For helpful "interpretation" of the descriptive themes, we should note that Milford Elementary School had 810 students, 26 teachers, five first grade classes, a "store down the road," a fire station nearby, two filling stations across the road, a Milk Jug business stand next door, a large playground, and a large window in the cafeteria which is adjacent to the auditorium. As may be noted from the anchor themes at all three points in both scales, presence of argument or description was emphasized as the criterion variable to the exclusion of other factors such as spelling, grammar, sentence structure, vocabulary and mere length.

(10)

Scoring

Ratings were made by five first grade teachers who attended training and practice sessions where the criterion (i.e., presence of argument or description) was emphasized in the use of the above anchor themes. The themes were randomly assigned to the raters within the limits of two restrictions: (1) the student was not in the rater's first grade class, and (2) the student was not in experimental sessions with the rater. A number code replaced student names which were removed from the themes so that the rater would not know the writer's identity, nor whether the theme was a D or an A type, nor even if the theme was a pre- or post-treatment theme. Each theme was rated on the D scale and on the A scale.

(11)

Coding

We will hereafter, for ease of presentation, use a capital letter to designate the theme type; a 1 or 2, respectively, for pre- and post-treatment themes; and a small letter to represent the appropriate rating scale. For example, $D1a$ designates a pre-treatment descriptive theme rated on the argumentative scale.

(12)

Establishing rater reliability

The initial ratings were made on small slips of paper attached to the themes and were used for experimental analyses. After the initial ratings, however, small samples (N's from 12 to 14) of $D1$, $A1$, $D2$, and $A2$ themes were randomly chosen for re-ratings, but no theme was re-rated by the same rater. Each theme was re-rated on both scales, but one set of the ratings, $A1d$, was eliminated for lack of variation. For the seven remaining sets of ratings, the correlations between first and second ratings ranged between .75 and .96 with a mean of .86, so it seems reasonable to assume a fair amount of reliability in the ratings of the themes.

(13)

Hypotheses

Experimental Hypotheses and Analyses. The experimental hypotheses for the study were as follows:

(1) The effects of T_D will be to raise the d quality of both D and A themes but to reduce the a quality of these themes.

(2) The effect of T_A will be to raise the a quality of both D and A themes but to reduce the d quality of both themes.

(14)

Statistics   Several alternative analyses were possible in the study. The writers chose a set of analyses that they judged would most directly test this hypotheses. It was decided to focus on pre- and post-treatment differences using analysis of variance.

(15)

Control groups   The T_N groups were used as a control in the experiment and the T_D and T_A groups were compared to the T_N groups by Dunnett's (1955) procedure. A suggested modification for unequal samples was used where necessary (Steel and Torrie,

Statistics   1960, p. 114). All tests were one-tailed and were made at the .05 level of significance. When treatment differences were not in the hypothesized direction, tests were not made.

Results

(16)

Results   For the conservation of space, complete rating means will not be presented. The pre-treatment rating means for the males ranged from 1.00 to 4.20 with an overall mean of 1.76; for the females from 1.00 to 5.20 and a grand mean of 2.29. The male post-treatment rating means again ranged from 1.00 to 4.20 and the overall mean was 1.88; for the females, from 1.00 to 5.60 and a grand mean of 2.23.

(17)

Results   The pre-treatment ratings were analyzed within treatment for sex and order effect with the following significant results (i.e., $p < .05$). For those in the description treatment,

Statistical tests   order effects were significant in the $D1d$ ratings $(F = 9.15, df = 1$ and $29)$ and in the $A1a$ ratings $(F = 5.05, df = 1$ and $29)$. Sex-by-order interaction effects were significant $(F = 6.58, df = 1$ and $24)$ for the $A1a$ ratings in groups assigned to the argumentative treatment. Finally, for the groups in the neutral treatment, the sex effects were significant in the $D1d$ ratings $(F = 9.42, df = 1$ and $27)$ and in the $A1d$ ratings $(F = 5.13, df = 1$ and $27)$.

(18)

Results   Rating differences were obtained as follows: $D2d$-$D1d$, $D2a$-$D1a$, $A2d$-$A1d$, and $A2a$-$A1a$. These four sets of data were analyzed separately for tests of hypotheses and, be-

Differences   cause of the significance of some sex and order effects in the pre-treatment analyses, sex and order as well as treatment were specified as major sources of variation in the analyses. The sample sizes are T_D, $N = 33$; T_A, $N = 28$; and T_N, $N = 31$.

(19)

Results   For the $D2d$-$D1d$ ratings, the overall treatment means were as follows: $T_D = -.12$, $T_A = -.25$, and $T_N = -.10$.

Tests of   No significant effects were found either in the analysis of

significance   variance or using Dunnett's t-test.

(20)

Results

Analysis of variance

Conclusion

The treatment means for the $D2a\text{-}D1a$ ratings were $T_D = -1.00$, $T_A = .07$, and $T_N = .39$. In the analysis of variance both treatment $(F = 5.75$ with 2 and 80 $df)$ and treatment-by-order interaction $(F = 4.26$ with 2 and 80 $df)$ are significant $(p < .05)$. The mean difference between T_A and T_N is not even in the expected direction, but the mean difference of $T_D - T_N = -1.39$ is larger than required by Dunnett's method $(D' = .957; p < .05)$ so we conclude that the a quality of the D themes was reduced under T_D and the first hypothesis is supported by the results.

(21)

Results

Analysis of variance

Interactions

The treatment means for the $A2d\text{-}A1d$ ratings were $T_D = 1.76$, $T_A = .11$, and $T_N = -.19$. In the analysis of variance, the following effects are significant (at least $p < .05$): treatment $(F = 15.43$ with 2 and 80 $df)$, order $(F = 5.10$ with 1 and 80 $df)$ sex-by-order $(F = 4.17$ with 1 and 80 $df)$, treatment-by-order $(F = 6.30$ with 2 and 80 $df)$, and sex-by-treatment-by-order $(F = 4.06$ with 2 and 80 $df)$. The significant interactions indicate that several one-way analyses might be more appropriate, but we are primarily interested in the treatment means. The mean difference $T_A - T_N$ is not in the expected direction, but $T_D - T_N = 1.95$ which is larger than the difference required by Dunnett's method $(D' = .900; p < .05)$ so we conclude that T_D had the effect of raising the d quality of the A themes.

Discussion

(22)

Limitation

There is some possibility of rater-theme interaction with respect to A themes rated for d quality and D themes rated for a quality. The possibility of a type of halo effect in which a quality affects d ratings and vice versa certainly could have a confounding effect in the $A2d\text{-}A1d$ and $D2a\text{-}D1a$ comparisons. Further study and analysis would be required to determine the likelihood and possible impact of such a rating problem. If such a phenomenon existed, it should have had no effect on the $A2a\text{-}A1a$ and $D2b\text{-}D1d$ comparisons.

(23)

Conclusion

The descriptive discussion period did not raise the d quality of the D themes but other effects of T_D on the D themes are significant and in the expected directions. The effect of T_D raised the d quality of the A themes and lowered the a quality of both the D and A themes. Indeed, the descriptive discussion had the largest effect of all three treatments and the first hypothesis regarding the effects of T_D received major support by the study.

(24)

Conclusion

The argumentative discussion appears to have had little effect on the quality of the themes with the exception of the a quality of the A theme which was raised almost significantly after the discussion. A larger sample would have provided for significant evaluation of the $A2a\text{-}A1a$ difference, but the second hypothesis is not substantiated by this set of data.

Connection to theory

(25)

Piaget (1951; particularly pp. 23–24) purports that in the 7–8-year-old child, there is a diminution of egocentrism and an increase in logical forms. Elsewhere (1932, p. 73 and pp. 125–126), he explicitly states abstract, logical thought in verbal communication for the child begins somewhere between seven and eight years of age. The data reported herein were collected at the end of the first grade, so the children are, on the average, slightly more than seven years of age and fall into the 7-8 year bracket designated by Piaget.

(26)

Connection to theory

The results of the present study would seem to support Piaget's conjecture above in some respects. The *D* themes as compared to the writing of *A* themes. The discussion required some logical organization of thought but a minimum of abstraction of physical description of the school had the expected effects in three of the four sets of ratings. The effects of the argumentative discussion, however, are not as clear. The children, according to Piaget's theory, may not be advanced enough, from a developmental standpoint, to profit from the argumentative discussion.

(27)

Speculation

Longer treatment sessions might have produced more significant effects. Experienced first grade teachers, however, opined that a longer treatment period might well dampen the treatment effects because of the children's attention. Nevertheless, the question of longer treatment periods must remain open for further study.

(28)

Effects of spelling

Finally, note must be taken of the words used in the themes. The children were encouraged to disregard spelling altogether and, as can be inferred from the scale anchor themes, the children used a great many words that they did not know how to spell. Indeed, spelling appeared to be no factor whatever in terms of the use of words in the themes.

References

(29)

Braddock, Richard, Lloyd-Jones, Richard, and Schoer, Lowell. *Research in Written Composition.* Champaign, Illinois: National Council of Teachers of English, 1963, 142 pp.

Dunnett, Charles W. A. Multiple Comparisons Procedure for Comparing Several Treatments with a Control. *Journal of the American Statistical Association,* 50: 1096–1121; December, 1955.

Hahn, Elise. "An Analysis of the Content and Form of the Speech of First Grade Children." *The Quarterly Journal of Speech,* 34: 361–366; October, 1948.

Kincaid, Gerald Lloyd. *Some Factors Affecting Variations in the Quality of Students' Writing.* Unpublished Ed.D. thesis, Michigan State University, 1953, 124 pp.

McCarthy, Dorothea Agnes. "Language Development of the Preschool Child." *Institute of Child Welfare Monograph Series* (University of Minnesota), 1930, No. 4, 174 pp.

Piaget, Jean. *The Language and Thought of the Child*. New York: Harcourt, Brace and Company, 1932, 246 pp.

Piaget, Jean. *Judgment and Reasoning in the Child*. London: Routledge and Kegan Paul Ltd., 1951, 260 pp.

Seegers, J.C. Form of Discourse and Sentence Structure. *Elementary English Review*, 10: 51–54; March 1933.

Steel, Robert George Douglas and Torrie, James H. *Principles and Procedures of Statistics*. New York: McGraw-Hill, 1960, 481 pp.

Templin, Mildred. *Certain Language Skills in Children*. Minneapolis: The University of Minnesota Press, 1957, 183 pp.

(Received February, 1967)
(Revised July, 1967)

Authors

(30)

Anderson, Harry E., Jr.   *Address:* University of Georgia, Athens, Georgia 30601   *Title:* Professor and Associate Director, R&D Center in Educational Stimulation *Age:* 38   *Degrees:* B.A., Michigan State Univ.; M.A., Memphis State Univ.; Ph.D., Univ. of Texas   *Specialization:* Statistics; research design.

Bashaw, W. Louis *Address:* University of Georgia, Athens, Georgia 30601   *Title:* Associate Professor of Ed. Psychology *Age:* 31   *Degrees:* B.S., M.S., Ph.D., Florida State University *Specialization:* Educational measurement; statistics.

STUDY NUMBER 5

This study is an investigation of a hypothesized relationship between differences in how very young children are attended and their reaction to a peer teacher. The authors place this relationship in the context of differences between cultures. Such a relationship must be studied without control, but subjects were grouped by characteristics to study the differences on an independent variable as reflected in a dependent variable. In addition, relationships among pairs of 11 different groups are reported.

THE RELATIONSHIP OF SIBLING CARETAKING AND ATTENTIVENESS TO A PEER TUTOR[1]

RONALD GALLIMORE   **ROLAND G. THARP**
University of California   *University of Hawaii*
Los Angeles   *Manoa*

GISELA E. SPEIDEL
The Kamehameha Schools
Honolulu

(Paragraph 1)
Abstract

Ethnographic measures of sibling caretaking were correlated with attentiveness to a peer tutor. Boys from families who assigned childcare tasks to male siblings were more likely to be attentive in a dyadic peer-tutoring session. General classroom attentiveness was also highly correlated with attentiveness to a peer tutor and to male sibcare. Girl tutee attentiveness and female sibcare were not correlated. Families who assign major childcare tasks to boys apparently foster behaviors that generalize to the classroom. The transfer may not be specific from sibling interaction experiences to peer tutoring situations since family reliance on sibcare also correlated with generalized classroom attentiveness and general (nonsibcare) chore demands.

[1] Appreciation is due to David Lam, Candace Fox, Steven T. Boggs and Violet L. Mays for their contributions to this research, and to Lee Sechrest, Thomas Weisner and Harold Levine for helpful comments on the manuscript. Donald Guthrie provided statistical consultation. This study was supported by The Kamehameha Early Education Program, The Kamehameha Schools, Honolulu. Additional resources were made available by the Socio-behavioral Research Group, MRRC, University of California, Los Angeles. Computing assistance was obtained from the MR/CP Computing Resources Group and the Health Sciences Computing Facility, UCLA, supported by NIH Special Research Resources Grant RR-[3].

(2)

Questions

This study was designed to examine a limited question. Will children from homes in which siblings do caretaking be more attentive to a peer tutor? Classroom peers are not older siblings; but a child from a family environment which features siblings in supervisory roles might be accustomed to learning from other children and thus be more attentive to a peer tutor.

(3)

Connection to theory

We consider this study responsive to calls for research on adapting classroom practice to cultural differences (Baratz & Baratz, 1970; Burger, 1972; Valentine, 1971). Sibling or child caretaking is a significant feature of socialization in many of the world's societies, including some U.S. minority culture groups (Weisner & Gallimore, 1977). Beginning in some cultures as early as age seven, the tasks performed range from simple childtending to important skills instruction. In a study of Hawaiian-Americans, Gallimore, Boggs, and Jordan (1974) suggested that there may be significant classroom implications for children whose families rely on sibling caretakers.

Background

Method

(4)

Background

The study was conducted at the Kamehameha Early Education Project research and demonstration school (K to third grades) located in urban Honolulu (Gallimore & Tharp, Reference Note 1). Children enrolled in the school are randomly sampled from the social and ethnic groups in a delimited low income urban area. Approximately 75% of the children are part-Hawaiian, while the remaining children are of mixed ethnic ancestry including Anglo, Filipino, and Samoan. Seventy-five percent of the children are from families receiving public assistance, while the remaining 25 percent are from lower and lower-middle class families.

Description of subjects

The 26 children in the present study were five- and six-year-olds, enrolled in kindergarten at the research and demonstration school.

Measurement of Attentiveness to Peer Tutor

(5)

Dependent variable

Attentiveness to a peer tutor was assessed in the context of the Hawaii English Program. A major program component is the "stacks," a series of progressively more difficult sets of symbols, letters, or words printed on cards. The stimuli are printed on both sides of each card so that two children can see each item as it is displayed. The program prescribes that children who have successfully finished a stack will tutor others who have not.

Explanation

(6)

Background

Prior to the present study, the stack component had not been introduced into the research school program. The material to be learned in the study was thus novel to the participating students. Peer tutoring sessions occurred each morning during (small group) learning center time. During each 60-minute learning center period, each of the tutors

Procedure

tutored three other children. A tutoring session lasted ten minutes, and was begun and ended by the teacher on a signal from the observers. There was at least a ten-minute interval between sessions for the tutors.

(7)

Data Collection

Two persons observed each tutoring session. One observer recorded the total time, and the second recorded the number of seconds the tutee attended to the tutor. The dependent variable—attending to tutor or "on-task"—was expressed as the number of seconds on-task during the ten-minute session. A specific observation code was used, for example, tutee looks at "stacks"; tutee looks at anything tutor asked tutee to look at; tutee looks away, at other children around room, etc., for three or more seconds.

(8)

Observer reliability

Two reliability checks were made for observations on the two original tutors before the study began and one on the first day of the study. Reliabilities were 98% agreement for the first two checks and 99% for the third.

Control

(9)

Each tutee was observed during the first three sessions of experience with the stacks. Tutees were randomly assigned to one of the four tutors for each of the three sessions, but in such a way that no tutee had the same tutor for two consecutive sessions.

Measurement of General Classroom Attentiveness

(10)

Measurement

Daily classroom observations were conducted. Reliability of observers was checked periodically throughout the year and averaged above 85 percent agreement. This approach is described in detail elsewhere (Tharp & Gallimore, Reference Note 2). In brief, each day each child was observed approximately nine times for on-task (doing work, attending to teacher, etc.). Each tutee's year-long average on-task rate was used as a measure of general classroom attentiveness.

Measurement of Family Sibling Caretaking Environment

(11)

Ratings

The extent to which families of tutees relied on sibling caretaking (sibcare) was based on ratings of typescript summaries of ethnographic field notes. The ethnographic material had been collected by two anthropologists over a ten-month period as part of the project's culture and family research. These summaries were in turn rated for amount of sibling caretaking in each family, or the "sibcare environment."

(12)

Scale

Two 5-point rating scales were developed to assess the degree of responsibility for child care assumed separately by female and male siblings within each family. One scale assessed the amount of sibling caretaking that occurred in the families in which the tutees lived. The other scale concerned general amount of chore demands (excluding sibcare) separately placed on male and female children in each household.

Data Collection

(13)

Two raters with no knowledge of the families and no knowledge of the research hypotheses independently rated each family using typescripts of the ethnographic summaries. There was no contact between the anthropology field workers and the raters. All identifying information was removed from the typescripts except for a description of household membership (i.e., presence/absence of parents; number, age, and sex of siblings and other residents). The reliability of rating was uniformly high; the range of agreement on the rating scales (across all families) between the two raters was from 93 to 100% using the method described by Sears, Rau, and Alpert (1965).

Reliability

Rationale for Sibling Caretaking Measure

(14)

Gallimore, et al. (1974) reported that child caretakers were likely to be available irrespective of the nuclear family birth order of the tutees. The residence and interaction patterns of many families in similar communities insures even first borns will be cared for by pre-adolescents, who are more than likely kinfolk.

(15)

Rationale

Rating family use of male and female sibcare responsibility was deliberate. While it would have been conceptually desirable to assess individual tutee experience with sibcare, earlier research suggested this to be impractical. Working with a similar population, Gallimore, et al. (1974) found that mothers did not respond well to questions about individual children. Answers were nearly always in terms of the sibling group rather than one child, though males and females were often perceived as subgroups within the family. In the presentation of results, the sibcare measures refer to families, not individuals. We assume the rating of family use of sibcare represents a general measure of individual tutee experiences of being reared in an environment characterized by sibling caretaking.

Results and Discussion

(16)

Mean

Table 1 presents mean number of seconds on-task (attentiveness to tutor) for three observation sessions for 26 student/tutees by sex. The mean number of seconds on-task decreased over the three trials, while the within group variability increased, particularly for boy tutees. Apparently, for some tutees, as the novelty of the peer tutoring situation diminished, so did attentiveness to the tutor.

Results

Table 1—Mean and Standard Deviations for Number of Seconds On Task for Three Observations of Attentiveness to a Peer Tutor

	Males N = 12 Mean	Standard Deviation	Females N = 14 Mean	Standard Deviation
Observation Trial 1	529.1	74.6	547.1	55.9
Observation Trial 2	525.5	85.9	536.1	81.6
Observation Trial 3	437.2	135.7	510.1	74.8
Overall Mean	497.3	71.8	530.4	52.9

(17)

Comparisons

Table 2 presents the intercorrelations among the peer tutoring trials for boy and girl tutees. The pattern and level of correlation among trials were essentially identical for boys and girls, with one exception. For boy tutees, trial one was not significantly related to trial two or three, nor to the overall average; for girl tutees, trial two was not related to trials one and three, and only marginally correlated with the overall average.

(18)

Correlations

Boy tutees from families in which male sibs share in childcare were more attentive to the tutor on trials two and three, and had higher three trial averages. No other significant relationships were found between sibcare and peer tutoring measures. Surprisingly, the rated contributions of female sibs to child care are not correlated with attentiveness for either girl or boy tutees. However, our confidence in these findings was increased by a study completed after the

Other research

present one was concluded. Fukuda (Reference Note 3), using similar procedures, reported that rural Hawaiian-American boy tutees from high sibcare homes were more attentive to a peer tutor; there was no difference for girl tutees.

(19)

Table 2—Product Moment Correlations of Sibcare, Number of Siblings Birth Order, and Attentiveness to Peer Tutor for Tutees: Female and Male Data Are Above and Below the Diagonal Respectively (Male N = 12, Female N = 14)

		1	2	3	4	5	6	7	8	9	10	11
1.	Female Sibcare Household Rating	—	−35	61	−21	26	15	22	−01	20	18	23
2.	Male Sibcare: Household Rating	−11	—	−05	42	−00	19	10	−02	37	21	−12
3.	Non-sibcare chore demands on females	86	02	—	43	31	25	48	06	42	41	41
4.	Non-sibcare chore demands on males	34	79	44	—	30	24	40	38	19	44	24
5.	Birth order of tutee	80	31	75	65	—	92	39	21	01	27	−17
6.	Number of sibs	67	49	67	—	95	—	44	−11	12	18	−34
7.	Tutoring Trial 1	20	10	20	−05	−04	−18	—	22	71	84	30
8.	Tutoring Trial 2	11	56	09	53	22	33	34	—	04	60	60
9.	Tutoring Trial 3	08	64	06	41	17	29	−14	57	—	77	27
10.	Tutoring: Average	16	59	14	45	18	25	40	89	81	—	54
11.	General classroom attentiveness	−14	53	−10	32	−11	05	06	59	63	65	—

(20)

Correlations

General classroom attentiveness of boy tutees was significantly related to male sibling caretaking ($r = +.53$). Also, for male tutees, general classroom attentiveness and attentiveness to a tutor were significantly correlated ($r = +.59$).

Conclusion

These data suggest that boys from homes in which male sibs do child care are more generally attentive to classroom tasks; and that the male sibcare correlation with attentiveness to a tutor reflects, for boys, a general rather than specific relationship. Male sibcare ratings may index the degree to which families train boys to be responsible and task-oriented at home—behaviors that may generalize to a variety of classroom tasks, including the peer tutoring situation. If the male sibcare ratings merely reflect general responsibility training, it also suggests a more general and parsimonious explanation of the obtained correlations between the male sibcare rating and the two measures of attentiveness—to a peer tutor, and in the classroom in general.

(21)

Conclusion

A test of the general versus specific explanation was based on partial correlation. As presented in Table 2, the ratings of families' general chore demands (nonsibcare) on male children are positively but not significantly related to boys' attentiveness during the peer tutoring sessions. But the general chore demand rating is significantly and highly correlated, for boys, with the amount of male sibcare responsibility; this suggests that the relationship of male sibling caretaking and peer tutoring attentiveness would disappear if the effects of general, nonsibcare male chore demands were statistically removed. The partial correlations are presented in Table 3. The critical correlations of male sibcare and tutee attentiveness are reduced to non-significant magnitudes, but they remain positive and relatively substantial. These results provide only slight evidence of transfer from experiences in homes with male sibcare environments specifically to the peer tutoring situation. The generalized transfer of task-oriented responsibility appears to provide the more plausible explanation of the correlation between male sibcare and attentiveness to peer tutors.

Conclusion

Table 3—Partial Correlations of Male Sibcare Ethnographic Ratings and Attentiveness to a Peer Tutor, With Non Sibcare Chore Demands as the Variable Removed

Peer Tutoring Session: 1—.09	
Peer Tutoring Session: 2—.27	
Peer Tutoring Session: 3—.56 $p < .07$	
Average: All Sessions: .43	

(22)

Limitation

Recommendation

Limitation

Because of its exploratory nature, the present study has a number of limitations that should be considered in designing future research. All the tutors were girls, a factor of potential importance given the sex-linked findings. The small sample sizes were a product of the setting; while the particular research school operation permitted maximum control of the classroom-based measurement and the opportunity to get ethnographically based sibcare measures, the population size available was a serious limitation.

Contributors
(23)

Ronald Gallimore, Professor, Department of Psychiatry, The Center for the Health Sciences, University of Califor-

nia, 760 Westwood Plaza, Los Angeles, California 90024
Roland G. Tharp, Professor, University of Hawaii, Hono-
lulu, Hawaii.
Gisela E. Speidel, Research Psychologist, Kamehameha
Early Education Projects, Honolulu, Hawaii.

Reference Notes

(24)

Background

1. Gallimore, R., & Tharp, R. G. *An overview of research strategies and findings (1971–1975) of the Kamehameha early education program* (Tech. Rep. #66). Honolulu: The Kamehameha Early Education Program, 1976.

2. Tharp, R. G., & Gallimore, R. *The uses and limits of social reinforcement and industriousness for learning to read.* (Tech. Rep. #60). Honolulu: The Kamehameha Schools, The Kamehameha Early Education Program, 1976.

3. Fukuda, Nobuko. *A study of classroom attending behavior among ethnic Hawaiian children.* Unpublished doctoral dissertation, Claremont Graduate School, Claremont, California, 1975.

References

(24)

Baratz, S. S., & Baratz, J. C. Early childhood intervention: The social science base of institutional recism. *Harvard Educational Review,* 1970, *40,* 29–50.

Burger, H. C. Behavior modification and operant psychology: An anthropological critique. *American Education Research Journal,* 1972, *9,* 343–360.

Gallimore, R., Boggs, J., & Jordan, E. *Culture, behavior, and education: A Study of Hawaiian-Americans.* Beverly Hills, Calif.: Sage Publications, 1974.

Sears, R. R., Rau, L., & Alpert, R. *Identification and child rearing.* Stanford, Calif.: Stanford University Press, 1965

Valentine, C. A. Deficit, difference and bicultural models of Afro-American behavior. *Harvard Educational Review,* 1971, *41,* 137–157.

Connection to theory

Weisner, T. S., & Gallimore, R. My brother's keeper: Child and sibling caretaking. *Current Anthropology,* 1977, *18* (2), 9–21.

PART THREE

INQUIRY METHODOLOGIES

The broad base of inquiry in education is reflected in the wide range of methods used to answer educational questions. Inquiry Methodologies, Part III, has been divided—admittedly arbitrarily and artificially—into three very general classes of research inquiry: *historical, descriptive,* and *experimental.* Questions based in the past require historiographical approaches to collecting and interpreting data. Questions that ask about current conditions require descriptive—sometimes called "correlational"—techniques. Questions involving manipulation of variables in laboratory-like conditions require experimental procedures.

In practice this division may or may not be clearly evident in the ongoing activities of the researcher. Each inquiry class is to some degree based in the past. Each inquiry class is also related in some way to a current problem.

Historical inquiry is limited to data collected from the past. Descriptive research utilizes data from the past as background for a problem based in current conditions. However, experimental research uses data from the past as background for a problem, data about the present for further guidance, and data created for the study.

Because each class of research is progressively inclusive, the order of presentation will be first, historical research; second, descriptive research; and third, experimental research. Keep in mind that events for historical and descriptive research would happen even if the research did not take place, while events for experimental studies are specially created for the studies and would not occur without the experimental situation.

CHAPTER NINE

HISTORICAL INQUIRY

*The dominant characteristics of our schools today are
the product of a long history, and those who hope to
alter those characteristics need to know their origins and
enduring functions in order to act effectively.*
—Stephen Thernstrom

What is historical research? Is there a discipline of historical research? These
are questions without generally accepted answers, and debate centers around
whether investigations based in the past can be conducted scientifically. The
discussion in this chapter assumes that educational questions can be attacked
through a scientific approach, although any structure of inquiry based on
selecting information obtained from the past is necessarily limited. The
limitations are determined by the type of question that can be asked, the
information that can be used, and the validity of the answers derived. These
limitations do not escape the eyes of historians and others who are involved
in historical analysis, as evidenced by a quotation from one who writes about
educational concerns:

> No historian can entirely divorce the categories with which he approaches the
> contemporary world from those with which he studies the past. Our concerns
> shape the questions that we ask and, as a consequence, determine what we select
> from the virtually unlimited supply of "fact." That state of affairs remains
> submerged and implicit in most historical work. (Katz, 1971, p. xxv)

Since the researcher works in the context of present knowledge, special care
must be taken in historical research to avoid **presentism,** or the imposition of
modern thought patterns on an earlier era, when making judgments about
the past.

Other matters the historical researcher must consider include collecting
needed evidence, validating it through historical **criticism,** and interpreting it

into usable conclusions. The key to valid historical research in education is the use of acceptable procedures in deducing the answers to educational questions from vast amounts of potential data for some questions and very limited information about other questions.

The body of knowledge known as "history of education" is now undergoing what Sloan refers to as "demythologizing" (Sloan, 1973, p. 246). He says that the writers of recent works on educational history have "repudiated the older tradition, exemplified by Cubberley, of writing the history of education as the progressive and triumphant evolution of public school" and replaced it with "determination to prove underlying motives and interests, to relate ideas to social and institutional structures, and to consider how theory is transformed in practice" (p. 246). Although the purpose of educational research does not include writing the history of education, the new direction for historical writing is closely related to the products of historically directed educational research.

The goal of historical research in education is to clarify present-day practices and problems by providing a historical knowledge base. The technological revolution and the resulting new social conditions have challenged established institutions and caused the reconstruction of beliefs and values. Education has been especially susceptible to widespread discussions of practices and associated problems. Knowledge gained through historical inquiry can provide the foundation for better understanding of current educational questions and can contribute to a better understanding of changing educational concerns.

This chapter studies the acceptable procedures for providing valid conclusions to historically based questions. A recently reprinted and augmented edition of the classic *Guide to Research in Educational History* (Brickman, 1973) updates a valuable aid for anyone engaged in historical research in education. The *Guide* and other references listed later should be consulted regularly by those people engaged in answering questions about the past.

Nature of Historical Research

The historical method of research (see Study Number 1 on page 205) utilizes particular procedures to verify the accuracy of statements about the past, to establish relationships, and—if possible—to determine the direction of cause and effect. Good says,

> Viewed as research, history may be defined as an integrated narrative or description of past events or facts, written in the spirit of critical inquiry, to find the whole truth and report it. (Good, 1972, p. 148)

The process of educational research about the past generates facts and draws conclusions using techniques to help interpret the remains of the past. It also evaluates and verifies statements of others, since in this case the historian cannot use direct observation or create data. For these reasons, the historical researcher works under a greater handicap than other researchers.

He or she must use existing information in its present form. Since the researcher can exert no control over what information remains for study, no valid assumptions can be made about whether something did not exist or did not take place simply because no record can be found.

Although the above limitations require the historical researcher to function differently from researchers engaged in other types of inquiry procedures, historical research techniques take an approach to inquiry similar to the steps of the scientific method, with some necessary adaptations. Historical inquiry begins when an indeterminate situation raises a question whose answer can be found in the past. It continues as a critical search for truth and ends with a defensible conclusion.

Steps in Historical Research

Historical inquiry uses a process similar to that used for other scientific inquiry. The historical researcher's activities can be identified with the following steps:

1. Identifying and isolating the problem
2. Developing a research hypothesis
3. Accumulating and classifying source materials and determining facts by criticism
4. Organizing facts into results
5. Forming conclusions
6. Synthesizing and presenting the research in organized form

There is some question about how the historian uses a research hypothesis (step 2 in the list). Some historical studies do not explicitly state research hypotheses before gathering source materials. Investigators often imply by their interests and the stated or implied questions that hypotheses underlie the investigation even though they are not stated. It seems that even narrative history designed merely to report facts is in some way based in implied hypotheses.

Hillman's study of sex roles portrayed in children's literature (Sample Study Number 1) offers examples of both implied and stated hypotheses. At the beginning (par. 5), she suggests that certain outcomes were "suspected." Although this does not constitute a clear hypothesis statement, the researcher's background knowledge is condensed here to a statement of expected findings. The three specific hypotheses considered for the study are presented later in paragraph 15 of the study.

Although studies using historical research methods do state research hypotheses, using hypotheses in this way has been attacked. Critics would claim that the test of the hypothesis in this case is different from the test used in experimental research and is therefore less acceptable within the rules of science. Whether a researcher approves of using research hypotheses in historical studies and whether or not the hypothesis statement is recognized as testable in principle are matters of individual interpretation. A question also arises whether data gathered from the past can be used as empirical data. Hempel says,

> But if a statement or set of statements is not testable at least in principle, in other words, if it has no test implications at all, thus it cannot be significantly proposed or entertained as a scientific hypothesis or theory, for no conceivable empirical finding can then accord or conflict with it. If a study is to add to the knowledge of educational concerns then the hypothesis provides a way of bridging from data gathered to theory proposed. (1973, p. 364)

There does not seem to be a clear division between statements that are not testable and hypotheses that are testable. Probing new areas, relating ideas to social and institutional structures, and considering the transformation of theory into practice causes educators to ask new questions about the past. The recent focus on investigating different kinds of questions based in the past broadens the scope and gives rise to questions about relationships among phenomena. The research hypothesis is likely to be used more and more in historical research as a result of questions about motives, interests, and relationships of institutional structures.

Identifying and Isolating the Problem

Bernard Bailyn's *Education in the Forming of American Society* "has been accorded a firm place in the historiographical canon as virtually the manifesto of a new movement" (Sloan, 1973, p. 240). Bailyn and other writers of recent articles about the impact of education on all social institutions have changed the range of historical inquiry from merely a study of formal pedagogy to the investigation of more dynamic questions about relationships among ideas and their social environment. Important educational questions stem from the study of social issues which are based in the past. Historical research is especially useful in obtaining knowledge about previously unexamined areas and in reexamining questions where the answers are not as definite as desired and present accounts are inadequate.

Historically based problems can be delimited or isolated along any of four dimensions: time, geographic area, person involved, and activities. The scope of the study may be expanded or reduced by controlling one or more of these categories. When too broad a question is asked, the researcher is likely to be forced to decrease the scope of the study. This is the most likely result of the tendency to ask questions which are too broad. Unlike other research questions, the historically based topic may also need to be widened as the data collection takes place. For example, the search may reveal a contributing factor not initially apparent when planning the scope of the study. As a consequence, the scope of the problem and the reading for it will need to be expanded.

Since the researcher begins a historical study with only a general idea as to the scope of the problem, he or she proceeds differently in this particular area of inquiry than do researchers using other approaches. When looking for data about the question, the researcher may find that the answer is actually based in an area that was not apparent before starting the search or that what appeared to relate to the problem was not relevant. Nevertheless, the project should commence only after a question has been clearly stated in a form that will give the needed direction for the research.

The identification and delimitation stage in approaching historical problems is exceedingly important in helping avoid endless collecting of data with no expressed use for the information. A vague idea about some not-too-clear task does little to provide direction for the study and procedures of inquiry. The question can clarify the problem and at the same time act as a sounding board for the activities of the researcher. If activities relate to obtaining an answer to the proposed question, then they are pertinent to the study; if they do not help answer the question, then they are not appropriate methodology for the study. When all of the accumulated information of the past is open to study, the importance of the above guidance in directing the researcher's quest for answers cannot be overestimated.

Since all research studies have a historical base and the investigator for any study must place a study in the context of the past as well as the present, every study is to some degree a historical study. The techniques of the historical researcher will serve the correlationalist who studies present conditions as well as the experimenter who studies effects of manipulation of variables. This is especially true in gathering data as background for a study and developing a research hypothesis. In this sense, both the correlationalist and the experimenter are—in part at least—practicing historians.

The Hypothesis

A certain amount of knowledge is required to develop a question specific enough for research purposes. Given more knowledge, the investigator can develop a hypothesis as a proposed answer to the question being asked. In paragraph 4 of Sample Study 1, for example, Hillman uses the direct question "Would children's literature reflect this scope [change in societal standards] of role diversity over a period of time?" This question clearly defines and clarifies the problem under study. Paragraphs 6 and 7 further clarify and delimit the investigation.

Since there is no way to test the historical hypothesis directly, the answer to the question must be based on the facts collected for the study. For these reasons, some historians prefer to work without a hypothesis. For the same reasons, what are conclusions in some historical studies take the form of hypotheses in other types of research. When the researcher has some knowledge to provide a historical context for a proposed answer to the question being studied, a hypothesis should be developed. The value of the historical hypothesis rests in its directing role, providing something to refute or support. It helps make the drawing of conclusions more objective. For these reasons, the use of the historical research hypothesis is to be encouraged, and its contribution to the research process is exemplified by the implied and stated hypotheses in paragraphs 5 and 15 of Hillman's article. For further discussion of the historical hypothesis, see Good (1972).

Accumulating and Classifying Source Materials

All of the information recorded in the past, plus any other remnants of the past, are available for historical research. The task of the historical researcher is to gather appropriate information, place it in the context of the historical period under study, and interpret its relationship to the logically conceived hypothesis, deciding whether it supports or fails to support the hypothesis. In the sample study on sex roles in children's literature, Hillman uses the stated hypothesis to organize the results in this way (see paragraphs 16, 17, 18). Knowing where to look is important in gathering appropriate information. The type of question asked should help the researcher decide where to find data that will contribute to solving the problem. For example, a question about prayer in public schools might send the researcher to consult the *Encyclopaedia of Religion and Ethics* as an overview of the problem area, while a question in a closely related area of moral education would require sources of L. Kohlberg's writings—such as *Religion and Public Education*—and their bibliographies. Another question may send the researcher to try one of the following sources:

1. Physical remains: historic sites, roads, aqueducts, pyramids, fortifications, buildings ruined or whole, furniture, human remains, clothing, food, utensils, pottery, implements, weapons, machinery, industrial processes, and fine arts and museum pieces of many kinds.
2. Orally transmitted material (sometimes in writing), such as folklore, legends, ballads, tales, anecdotes, sages, traditions, customs, manners, burials, ceremonials, social institutions, and language.
3. More elementary and durable kinds of representative or artistic materials, not written in the ordinary sense, such as inscriptions baked upon clay, chiseled stones, monuments, stamped coins, woven tapestries, vases, scenic or portrait sculptures, historical paintings, and portraits.
4. Hand-written materials (sometimes in print), including papyri, bricks bearing cuneiform writing, vellum or parchment manuscripts, and such more recent documents as chronicles, annals, biographies, memoirs, diaries, and genealogies.
5. Printed books, papers, and literature.
6. Motion-picture film, microfilm, and recordings, including radio and television.
7. Personal observation (by the writer or by people whom he interviews) (Good, 1972, p. 155)

For educational studies, school-related records, documents, buildings, furniture, equipment, textbooks, examinations, student work, and oral reports of school officials, students, and parents first come to mind as likely sources of information. Hillman, for example, went to children's books to identify and analyze sex-role standards. Historical evidence from other areas is required for studies involving social issues and institutional structures and must be considered in identifying other possible sources. Although all possible sources cannot be listed here, professional journals and newspapers should be included in most investigations of questions about education based in the past. Each study taxes the creativity of the researcher to come up with every possible source of data.

The major task of the historian is to obtain the best information available from the several sources listed earlier. A further classification of historical data sorts the sources into two major categories—**documents** and **relics**—according to whether the source was created for the expressed purpose of making a record or whether it is merely an artifact. Examples of documents of record are the *Congressional Record*, minutes of meetings, university registrar files, school attendance and grade records, diaries, memoirs, laws, charters, and maps. Relics are those physical objects which have been preserved—either by plan or by happenstance—but were not deliberately created to transmit a record for future consultation. Examples of relics are furniture, implements, utensils, art objects, portraits, literature, buildings, roads, and clothing.

FIGURE 9–1 An Example of a Historic Relic—Hieroglyphics on a Public Building

Each of these sources is valuable to the researcher in different ways: the documents for their objectivity and directness in reporting and the relics for their transmission of information in interpretation. Documents present data directly in a straightforward manner that requires no interpretation. Relics have given scientists an opportunity to reconstruct past civilizations with accuracy, although many people of the past left no documents. For example, the daily activities of inhabitants can be reconstructed through the utensils they used to obtain and prepare food. Games of skill indicate something about the amount of leisure time they may have enjoyed. Other glimpses into early cultures are provided by what they left in the way of relics.

Each of the sources is limited in some ways, however. A record may be in error because the record was deliberately falsified or because an event was incorrectly interpreted by the recorder. Documentary evidence about an event of the past may be recorded in the impressions of an eyewitness, but the recorder may knowingly or unknowingly record incorrectly. Documents are further limited by the change in word meanings over a long span of time.

Relics are also a limited source of information, since their meaning must be interpreted by the investigator. Recently created objects may be incorrectly accepted as relics of the past and erroneously used as evidence. Newly created objects of art, engravings of famous figures, and other objects have been passed off as originals and later discovered to be products of modern creation. Fraudulent data of any kind is possible.

Errors in recording, frauds, hoaxes, and forgeries have been perpetrated for many years. Motives of material gain, enhancement of the state or church, and the practical joke contribute to the problems of dealing with the past. For example, a stone figure, the "Cardiff giant," was accepted by experts in several fields and validated as a fossilized figure of an ancient giant. A reporter later uncovered that the find was a well-planned hoax to make money by displaying the relic to the public.

Carefully prepared records that have been checked—such as minutes of meetings which have been submitted by the recorder for acceptance—are in most cases easily validated for evidence. After a long time lapse, other recordings—such as memoirs of events—are often more difficult to validate.

It has been pointed out by experts in the areas of anthropology and historiography that many times people may reveal more valid evidence through physical objects than through documents. A judgment of the validity of the gathered facts serves as an evaluation of the worth of the information for forming conclusions for inquiry. The next three sections give direction to classifying and validating evidence for basing conclusions.

Determining Facts by Source and Criticism. The valid use of information as fact depends on the source of the information and how well it withstands a test of its authenticity and trustworthiness. The best evidence about the past is provided by *primary sources*—the relics that remain of the past, documents, and reports of eyewitnesses to specific events. Hillman's sex-role study reports the contents of children's books which are considered primary materials (from a primary source), since they were the books children used in different time periods. Also useful to the historian are *secondary sources*— accounts of events that were not actually experienced by the one reporting. Primary sources are considered original or underived. Such records or relics have only the observer or eyewitness coming between the information and the user of the information (the historian). A secondary source is a derived source in that the mind of a nonobserver has intervened between the information in its original form and the user of the information. If a newspaper reporter attends a city council meeting and writes a report of the meeting in an article, the article is a primary source. If she interviews those who participated in the meeting and writes an article, the article is a secondary source, since the information is interpreted and reported by the mind of a nonobserver.

The same relic may be a primary source for one investigator and a secondary source for another investigator with a different question. For example, material in students' textbooks would be classed as secondary evidence for most studies. However, for the researcher who asks the question, What topics were covered in textbooks written for the fourth-grade science classes between the years 1960 and 1965? the material in fourth-grade science texts is primary material. Books served a similar purpose for the Hillman sample study on sex-roles in children's literature. If Hillman had instead used reports from curriculum guides or writings about children's books, then she would have been utilizing secondary sources.

The classification of the data as primary or secondary depends on how the record was made and/or how the information is being used. It becomes important for the researcher to look closely at both aspects in classifying data as primary or secondary, remembering that what might be secondary for one study may be primary for another study. Sometimes there is no way to determine which parts of a source are primary and which are secondary.

Both primary and secondary sources are valuable for the historical researcher—primary sources because of their directness and underived nature, and secondary sources because of their contribution when primary sources are not available. Primary sources always carry more weight than secondary sources because of their directness and significance as authentic accounts.

A necessary part of the process of historical research is subjecting the data/information to *criticism*. Criticism is the scientific investigation of collected information focusing on matters of origin and validity. It is aimed at detecting unintentional errors or any deliberate falsification in order to establish the validity of the data. The historian must determine both the authenticity and the credibility of the information. Without criticism of the data, the hypothesis cannot be tested, and the conclusions will have no valid tie to a larger body of knowledge.

The tests of criticism use both external and internal criticism. *External criticism* examines the authenticity of the information—is it genuine? The focus of external criticism is thus not on the meaning attached to the evidence, but is rather on establishing why, where, when, how, and/or by whom the document or relic was created. In conducting her historical sex-role study, Hillman did not experience great difficulty in the process of external criticism, since the books she used could be examined objectively by date of publication and records of school use, along with other readily available information. The parameters set for this study and the criteria established for book selection are presented in paragraphs 9, 10, and 11 of the sample study.

Internal criticism investigates the meaning and trustworthiness of evidence. What meaning can be attached to the isolated facts? The focus of internal criticism is not the object or evidence itself but rather the meaning attached to it. After the process of external criticism has established the authenticity of information, the credibility of the information is checked by internal criticism of the contents. Together the two types of criticism establish the degree of validity to be attached to each bit of data used in a study. A historian remains skeptical of evidence until she or he has applied criticism to the information and is satisfied that it is usable data. Although the researcher can never have complete confidence in the data, those data deemed factual after criticism are accepted for use. Hillman explains her methods of internal criticism in paragraph 12 of Sample Study Number 1 as she explains how each book was analyzed. Some techniques used to establish validity of the data are discussed next.

Data Validation Techniques. Validation for physical characteristics of documents and relics—whether print or nonprint—is accomplished by using many tests. Very old artifacts can be tested for age by carbon dating, and physical characteristics of objects can be compared to what is known about similar objects from the same time and region. The type of ink, age, and composition of the paper, along with watermarks help establish the authenticity of documents and other printed matter. Other techniques, including photography, ultraviolet rays, and fluoroscopes, are also used in external criticism. These are employed essentially to detect fraud or to establish parameters of time and physical composition of the evidence.

In addition to physical authentication, the historian must pay attention to content and meaning, answering questions such as: Did personal gain, interest, practical joke, or pride cause the creation of the object? Did the report closely follow the event? Does the information include anything that could not have been known at that time? Has anything been lost in translation? Is this evidence typical of the author and of the time period?

After the process of external criticism has established the authenticity of the information, the researcher must analyze the documents or remains to establish their meaning, accuracy, and trustworthiness. Even genuine information from formally recorded documents must be checked for flaws, errors, and mistakes of fact, since even competent recorders are fallible. Tests of credibility are applied to determine actual meanings, losses through translation, contamination of statements by writer bias, phobias, illogical deduction, and/or innaccuracies in reporting. The question of credibility involves any aspect which would stand in the way of true reporting of an event or any involvement with outright hoax, fraud, or forgery. For example, documents must be scrutinized for any words that may have a different meaning now from the meaning attached to the word when the document was first written. A list of other "guiding principles" about historical methods gives direction for external and internal criticism used to establish authenticity and credibility:

> Since neither antiquity, nor memory, nor written characters are truly incorruptible witnesses, historians must approach all of them with critical doubt. Certain general principles, to be observed in reading and judging sources, may be briefly put: (1) do not read into earlier documents the conceptions of later times; (2) do not judge an author ignorant of certain events, necessarily, because he fails to mention them (the argument ex silentio), or that they did not occur, for the same reason; (3) underestimating a source is no less an error than overestimating it in

the same degree, and there is no more virtue in placing an event too late than in dating it too early by the same number of years or centuries; (4) a single true source may establish the existence of an idea, but other direct, competent, independent witnesses are required to prove the reality of events or objective facts; (5) identical errors prove the dependence of sources on each other, or a common source; (6) if witnesses contradict each other on a certain point, one or the other may be true, but both may be in error; (7) direct, competent, independent witnesses who report the same central fact and also many peripheral matters in a casual way may be accepted for the points of their agreement; (8) official testimony, oral or written, must be compared with unofficial testimony whenever possible, for neither one nor the other is alone sufficient; (9) a document may provide competent and dependable evidence on certain points, yet carry no weight in respect to others it mentions. (Woody, 1947, p. 190)

Van Dalen lists 17 questions which historians use to check validity externally and 14 questions to check validity internally, extending the principles listed above (1973, p. 167–170). When writing about "problems of evidence that center on the issue of validity," Beach said,

Most of them fall within one of two domains: given specified ideas or events, (1) how representative were they of larger groups of people or series of events and (2) what impact did they have, if any, upon subsequent human thought or behavior? The first is a question of correlation, the second a question of cause. (1969, p. 566)

Verification can be obtained in one of the several ways, but the researcher must still decide what is *fact*. In her sex-role study, Hillman chooses what constitutes facts as she explains tabulation procedures in paragraph 13 and establishes the categories for Tables 2 and 3. This choice also serves as validation of the facts, since the researcher decides what is valid for a study. Another equally knowledgeable person might question the data's validity for one or more reasons. A rule of thumb used to guide historical research is to accept information in documents as fact whenever there is no reason to suspect inaccuracy or fraud. Even careful verification is no guarantee of the truthfulness of the information, but the historical researcher feels more confident with using these accepted procedures of historical research than with uncritically accepting just any evidence in explaining the past.

Validating evidence through criticism becomes more and more important as historical research is increasingly asked to do more than provide a narrative of past events. Writing a narrative of history requires merely locating and verifying data. Historical research methods which primarily focus on drawing conclusions require the highest level of sophistication in techniques for validating information to assure valid conclusions. The products of validation procedures are *facts*. A fact for use in research is any bit of information that can be used in an investigation. A scientist does not claim that a fact used in one study will remain a fact to eternity; revision may be necessary given new or better information.

Organizing Facts into Results

Once facts have been validated for a study, the researcher must place them into some logical arrangement to assign or ascertain some collective meaning. This stage in the process allows the researcher to form the results of the study objectively.

The notes and established facts should already be on bibliography cards, one fact per card. These facts are now ready to be fit into some organizational framework. They could conceivably be ordered in a time sequence from an early date to the present. They could be organized by topics, geographic location, or according to some other logical classification system. The possible relationship being investigated might provide a natural division by the variables involved. If the major emphasis of the study is to identify cause and effect, the division could be made between the presumed cause (independent) variable and the criterion (dependent) variable. Sample Study Number 1 illustrates one way to organize data. Since the information for the study is easily expressed in numerical form, the results are easily organized into tables. The results of certain statistical tests are also reported in this way to complete the objective reporting of the facts as results.

Interpreting Facts

Since facts by themselves have little intrinsic meaning, after they are determined and organized, they must be interpreted. The interrelationships of all of the gathered facts must be viewed globally to determine their significance in deriving an answer to the research question. This process of interpreting the facts is called the "analysis of the data." The data for historical studies may be analyzed in one of two ways:

1. If the research hypothesis is stated, then the analysis focuses on how the facts support or refute the hypothesis. Such an interpretation tests the tenability of the research hypothesis.
2. If a research hypothesis is not used, analysis takes the form of hypothesis development. The output of the study, in this case, is a hypothesis which serves as a conclusion.

Testing the tenability of the historical research hypothesis consists of weighing the supporting evidence against the refuting evidence. The final decision is that the evidence either does or does not support the research hypothesis. If a research hypothesis is not used, the interpretation or analysis of evidence gathered about the question leads to early speculation about the overall meaning of the data first gathered. As more data are accumulated, the early speculation evolves into a tentative hypothesis. The researcher continues to form generalizations and to sophisticate these conjectures by testing the tentative hypothesis for consistency and agreement with the facts. The hypothesis ultimately developed from the investigation then serves as the conclusion for the study.

The task in either of the above approaches is taking information obtained about the past and determining its significance by interpretation. In each case, the hypothesis is intended to order the bits of information into a meaningful statement which serves as an acceptable answer to the posed question. In the sex-role sample study, for example, paragraph 23 reports the analysis as it relates to each of the three hypotheses. Stating how the evidence supports or fails to support the research hypothesis connects the findings to the original question.

Since the historian (or any researcher) works with less than all of the data, any analysis of the data can—at best—be tentative. More information may require revising the concluding hypothesis. Since the stopping point for any historical research is the researcher's decision, the conclusions for one study might provide a starting point for another study.

The interpretations drawn from the evidence are based on *what* happened in the past. More importantly, they also include *why* and *how* it happened. Hillman undertakes this aspect of research in the discussion section (pars. 24 and 25) where she speaks to the how and why of her sex-role study. The historian in general must deal with the representativeness of a study's limited data in interpreting ideas and events: Are they unique or are they representative? A popular test for representativeness of an *idea* is the measure of consumer receptivity to it. An idea is not in itself noteworthy without a test of how it was accepted and/or used by contemporaries. The importance of an idea's contribution is best tested by how much the idea influenced history over a period of time. This may be seen as a measure of its representativeness. The question of whether *events* are unique or representative is not easily resolved. An answer depends on a person's concept of the nature of historical phenomena. If each sequence of events is seen as unique, then representativeness will be difficult to claim. From this perspective, any sequence of events will be viewed as being built on a unique set of circumstances. If historical phenomena are viewed instead as being continuously correlated, establishing relationships becomes more realistic.

To show a causal relationship, the researcher must establish a direction through cause-effect, antecedent-consequence implications of evidence, in addition to showing a relationship. This is the most difficult task for the historian, and a major reason why the research hypothesis is used as a causal statement to be tested. *If-then* hypotheses are to be encouraged as a way to establish direction of cause and effect. In the *if-then* hypothesis statement, the independent variable is the presumed cause and the dependent variable the presumed effect. For example, Hillman could have written a hypothesis in this form: If the ratio between male characters and female characters portrayed in the children's literature is greater than 6 to 4 for either male domination or female domination, then the writings are considered biased. Another way of establishing whether the frequencies are biased toward males or females is a test of significance at a particular level, the method actually used in this sample study.

The task of historical inquiry is to establish cause through a direct relationship among the variables under study. The historian has the same problems as investigators in other areas—an event is usually the function of many contributing factors, making a causal study exceedingly complex. For a listing of specific procedures to assist interpretation, the researcher should consult the 16 points presented in *Understanding Educational Research* (Van Dalen, 1973, pp. 177–178).

Research Conclusions

The output or products of the analysis of the facts are the research study's conclusions. The conclusions for most historical research are presented for acceptance by the reader on the basis of faith in the researcher's knowledge. Is this different from any other type of research procedure? No, not in essence, only in degree. Even the most convincing and well-written report of an experimental study may be built on fictitious data. The type of research guarantees nothing in the way of the study's validity. Historical research is possibly more exposed to error because of the problems discussed earlier. There is no reason to believe that historians perpetrate a larger percentage of research fraud than any other group. With good procedures, historical researchers can indeed draw scientific conclusions from their data. If the historian can (1) avoid presentism, (2) make clear and plausible interpretations of appropriate evidence, (3) span the knowledge with established relationships, (4) show cause-effect, and (5) show a grasp of the field through the report of the study, then he or she is established in the scientific community and capable of conducting historical research.

Conclusions are drawn to show the reader what the study has revealed. They go beyond simple statements of support or lack of support of hypotheses. (Refer again to paragraph 23 in Sample Study Number 1 to recall how Hillman handles this section.) Since the final products of scientific inquiry are the laws and generalizations which form the framework unifying relationships established in isolation, conclusions should be generalizations tied to relevant educational theory.

Synthesizing and Presenting in Organized Form

The overall chain of reasoning of the many separate but related parts of the research process must be synthesized and presented in a logical argument supported by validated facts. Most writers find that an integrated outline fosters the needed continuity for this final stage.

The actual construction of the narrative develops the synthesis. A rough draft expands the outline, paragraph by paragraph, into the final presentation. The number of rewritings required to polish style and syntax and perfect interpretation and conclusions varies among writers. Some writers attempt a final writing the first time through, but few succeed. A more realistic view of the task is to expect several rewritings and revisions.

To achieve clarity and naturalness in the synthesis and its presentation, a good tack is to write paragraphs and/or sections after reading contributing material but not to take narrative directly from cards. After the first draft, points which have been missed can be inserted and any errors of fact can be corrected in rewritings. Do not be discouraged by the need to rewrite and revise material—all writers find this necessary as they build their narrative.

Historical Writing

The historical novel is created within the mind of someone who has excellent knowledge about a particular time period and a particular geographic location. Historical writing can, on the other hand, be merely an objective reporting of what has happened. Somewhere between these two extremes is the writing of historical research. The writer of the historical novel is expected to fill in any gaps in knowledge using imagination and historical knowledge as guides. Readers do not expect that every reported happening in a novel actually occurred nor that all the characters actually existed. Historical writing, at the other extreme, requires that the reporting be only at the highest degree of confidence. Any interpretation must be clearly set apart as such.

The writer of historical research must walk the line between writing a novel and writing a historical narrative. He or she must deal only in established facts, while at the same time building continuity through insight. Without distorting the truth, the writer must establish relationships, try to identify causes, and be able to build relationships with data that lack the conclusiveness the researcher would like. Producing a report of historical research requires the highest level of writing expertise.

The research hypothesis can give direction to what is relevant to the study. It also furnishes a basis for analysis and for conclusions, provides an agent for the synthesis that follows the criticism and validation of evidence, and serves as a vehicle to build continuity into the writing. Decisions about documentation, the arrangement of topics, the relative importance of the facts, and the interpretation can be fit into the general model for a scientific approach to inquiry presented in Chapter 1.

The organization of the material may be based on a time line (chronological), regions (geographical), or subject areas (topical). As Good states,

> A topical or thematic grouping of historical materials has been recommended as a functional organization to meet the criticism that older histories of education and courses in this field were a mass of comparatively unrelated facts, with little consideration of the pertinent social forces and the activities and problems of schools and professional workers. (1972, p. 177)

How the writer develops the logical chain of reasoning from the raw data is more of an art than a science. It is enough to say here that it should be presented in an effective style utilizing literary skills to build a report which is accurate and maintains interest without damaging the truth. The personality of the writer is reflected in his or her method of presenting a logical conclusion to the question. The narrative should include (1) a well-defined question, (2) a review of the literature as background, (3) the research hypothesis, (4) methodology for testing the hypothesis, (5) presentation of the evidence, (6) results, and (7) conclusions and implications. Further help in writing historical research will be found in *The Modern Researcher* (Barzun & Graff, 1977, pp. 209–324).

Tools for Historical Research

Since historians deal with documents and relics, it might be said that the world is their workshop. Useful historical tools include anything which will uncover evidence, ranging from shovels and bulldozers to the latest computer. Unlike other researchers, historians must be prepared to go where the evidence is rather than choose where to gather it or how to create it. With modern transportation, increased mobility provides added opportunity to gather needed evidence from both documents and relics. Historical researchers have all the tools of archaeology for physically uncovering evidence and can use them in much the same way archaeologists use them. However, most of the work of the historical researcher in education is conducted using other aids, such as libraries, bibliographies, and school-related records.

The Library

To classify a library as an aid or tool may seem strange, but the answer to many questions asked about education requires a synthesis of knowledge already recorded in bits and pieces. Unless needed information is in school records, the evidence is likely to be found in the library. Since chapter 4 discussed extensively the use of the library as an aid, this chapter need only acknowledge again the importance of development for library work in the tasks of the historical researcher.

Guides and Handbooks

The American Historical Association's *Guide to Historical Literature* is an excellent starting point for any historically based study (1961). The *Guide* gives bibliographical entries for selected historical literature to the date of its printing. Items from 1957 to 1960 are not systematically covered, but considerable coverage is given. The table of contents lists Part I, "Introduction and General History;" Part II, "Historical Beginnings;" Parts III through VIII, "Geographic Areas;" and Part IX, "The World in Recent Times." As examples of coverage, the *Guide* gives 64 entries for the topic "The Doctrine and Practice of Historiography," and the index covers 112 pages. The *Guide* does not specifically relate to education but is still a valuable tool to use early in an investigation.

Other more specific guides are available. They are listed in the index of *The Historian's Handbook—A Descriptive Guide to Reference Works* (Poulton, 1972). This is an invaluable tool for researchers of the human sciences and students who rely on their findings. The contents pages read like a list of specific tools available for the historian to use. The *Handbook* serves as a source for sources. Its main headings are

1. The Library and its Catalog
2. National Library Catalogs and National and Trade Bibliographies
3. Guides, Manuals, and Bibliographies of History
4. Encyclopedias and Dictionaries

5. Almanacs, Yearbooks, Statistical Handbooks, and Current Surveys
6. Serials and Newspapers
7. Geographical Aids
8. Biographical Materials
9. Primary Sources and Dissertations
10. Legal Sources
11. Government Publications

Census Data and Depositories

Recent census information covers wide areas and is particularly valuable when quantification can be used in data analysis. Breakdown on many factors provides data that are otherwise impossible to obtain for one study. The United States Census Bureau conducts a census on the population of the United States each decade. *The Statistical Abstract of the United States* reports a summary of statistics annually to supplement the 10-year report.

Depositories are particularly good sources of facts, because the collection is usually kept as a "collection of record" thus providing historical researchers with many documents especially prepared for future reference. *Research in Archives: The Use of Unpublished Primary Sources* (Brooks, 1969) is a reliable guide dealing with American archives and provides a way into materials available in archives and other special collections not generally catalogued. For guides to manuscripts and archives of special kinds of materials, see *The Historian's Handbook* (Poulton, 1972).

An example of special collections which are available is the extensive collection of more than 4,500 dictionaries that is a part of the Rare Books Department at the Indiana State University Library. The Cordell Collection of Dictionaries represents the entire history of Western lexicography, and continued acquisition efforts add to its numbers yearly. Other equally complete collections are available for other special areas and can be located through the above sources.

A number of libraries throughout the United States have been named as depositories for government publications. Government publications cover almost every field and are especially valuable in educational research. An aid to finding material in these publications has been prepared and is kept current by revisions (Schmeckebier & Eastin, 1969). A guide to serials and periodicals published by the federal government includes extensive listings for education (Androit, 1969–1972).

Computers

From the time that Herman Hollerith invented machine-punched cards and Frederick Jackson Turner used the data generated by their use in the 1890 census, historians have seen the need for new methods to tabulate not only quantitative data but also qualitative information—such as occupation, years of formal education, and other demographic features (Moehlman, 1969, p. 7). Each new advance in data processing gave additional encouragement to the possibility of some advanced device reducing the drudgery associated with gathering evidence for historical studies and assuming the task of interpreting data. Following World War II, the "mechanical brain" that was being developed seemed especially adaptable to the type of research done by historians. The "brain" evolved into what is now called a computer. Several generations and families of computers are now history. A study of their contribution to historical research falls mainly into the area of reducing human drudgery by doing those things that computers do best, routine menial tasks. Computers have not evolved to the level where they can take over the thought processes needed for interpretation, but that does not deny this function as a future possibility. The present status of the computer's popularity is difficult to ascertain, because the enthusiasm of historians varies. The swing is from the claim that computers will solve all (or nearly all) historical problems to the claim that they will contribute little (if anything) to solving these problems. There seem to be fewer and fewer of the latter assertions.

Computer technology has contributed a great deal to advanced indexing, checklist building, bibliographology, library cataloging, and other techniques used to organize bare facts. Such assistance has released the historian from tasks of drudgery and provided more time to think. Today, a combination of machine and human effort—each doing what it does best—seems the best way to utilize the strengths of each to answer questions based in the past.

The major contribution of the computer to historical research is the vast storage available through the **random-access disk files.** If the data are in computerized files, these files allow the researcher, who is accustomed to spending many long hours searching bibliographies and other listings of sources, rapid retrieval of information needed for an investigation. Libraries continue to capitalize on the benefits of automation by expanding their bibliographic data bases and by using the computer to process library loans. Chapter 12 will discuss further such use of computers in research. Reading in *Computers and the Humanities* (Tilly, 1973, for example) can help the person involved in historical research.

☐ CHECK YOUR UNDERSTANDING

Although the original full-length report of a historical study is needed to appreciate fully the writing of historical research, the journal article in Sample Study Number 1 (page 205) can be used to identify specific details discussed in this chapter. Read again Study Number 1 and identify the paragraph(s) that relate(s) to each of the following points:

1. That the study is historically based
2. Background information
3. Assumptions
4. Isolation of the study's problem
5. Hypothesis development
6. Sample selection

7. Criticism
8. Accumulation of source materials
9. Organization of facts into results
10. Reporting results
11. Forming conclusions

Answers

1. Title, 1, 2
2. 3
3. 3
4. 6, 7, 8
5. 3, 13
6. 9, 10, 11
7. 10, 12
8. 12, 13
9. 13, 14
10. 16 to 22, tables
11. 23, 24, 25

Summary

Historical research is that branch of the scientific method that looks to the past to answer questions. Although some would question assigning scientific status to historical inquiry, this chapter assumes that scientific approaches to historical inquiry meet the criteria of science. Scientific decisions are built from a framework of knowledge available at the time of decision making. Historical research using available data and accepted principles and practices makes decisions scientifically. All decisions, historically based or not, are open to alteration given more information. Whether the decision is being made in the physical sciences, or the human sciences, differing degrees of confidence are attached to decisions in all sciences.

Historical research has followed the general scientific approach with some differences evident in special problems dealing with collecting, criticizing, and interpreting data and forming conclusions about the past. Primary materials are important to all research. Historical criticism of evidence deals with establishing authenticity and credibility. From the validated evidence, the researcher must draw conclusions through interpretation and then write the findings in a scholarly narrative.

The major tool of historical research is the library, with other sources of public school records and relics associated with education also contributing evidence. Special tools for historical research are guides, handbooks, census data, reports, depositories, and computers. These tools all contribute to finding available evidence, with the computer supplying ways to locate and interpret data with new and creative procedures.

References

American Historical Association. *Guide to historical literature.* New York: Macmillan, 1961.

Androit, J. L. *Guide to U.S. government serials & periodicals.* McLean, Va.: Documents Index, Box 195, 1969–1972.

Barzun, J., & Graff, H. F. *The modern researcher* (3rd ed.). New York: Harcourt, Brace, & World, 1977.

Beach, M. History of education. *Review of Educational Research,* 1969, *34,* 561–576.

Brickman, W. W. *Guide to research in educational history.* Norwood, Pa.: Norwood Editions, 1973.

Brooks, P. C. *Research in archives: The use of unpublished primary sources.* Chicago: University of Chicago Press, 1969.

Good, C. V. *Essentials of educational research* (2nd ed.). New York: Appleton-Century-Crofts, 1972.

Hempel, C. The test of a hypothesis: Its logic and its force. In H. S. Broudy, R. H. Ennis, & L. I. Krimerman (Eds.), *Philosophy of educational research.* New York: John Wiley, 1973.

Katz, M. B. *Class, bureaucracy, and schools.* New York: Praeger, 1971.

Moehlman, A. H. *A guide to computer-assisted historical research in American education.* Austin: University of Texas Press, 1969.

Poulton, H. J. *The historian's handbook—A descriptive guide to reference works.* Norman: University of Oklahoma Press, 1972.

Schmeckebier, L. F., & Eastin, R. B. *Government publications and their use.* Washington: Brookings Institution, 1969.

Sloan, D. Historiography and the history of education. In F. N. Kerlinger (Ed.), *Review of research in education.* Itasca, Il.: F. E. Peacock, 1973.

Thernstrom, S. Foreword in M. B. Katz, *Class, bureaucracy, and schools.* New York: Praeger Publishers, 1971.

Tilly, C. Computers in historical analysis. *Computers and the Humanities,* September-November 1973, *7,* 323–335.

Van Dalen, D. B., Ph.D. *Understanding educational research* (3rd ed.). New York: McGraw-Hill, 1973.

Woody, T. Of history and its methods. *Journal of Experimental Education,* 1947, *15,* 175–201.

CHAPTER TEN

DESCRIPTIVE STUDIES FOR INQUIRY

A survey of present conditions is an essential guide to one's thinking, whether in evaluating the course he is now following, or in embarking on a new venture. For any purpose, the starting point is important.
—Carter V. Good and Douglas E. Scates

Historical studies are designed to answer questions based on the past. Certain procedures to aid in this historical inquiry were discussed in Chapter 9. Questions about present conditions require different techniques to arrive at answers, techniques designed to describe existing conditions (see Sample Studies 3 and 5 on pages 219 and 239). The term *descriptive research* is generally used to classify procedures used to generate knowledge by studying conditions as they currently exist.

"Descriptive research" was chosen as an appropriate label for this chapter only after much thought was given to other possible titles. The label is not wholly appropriate because this type of research does much more than just describe. It has been argued that all research is involved in describing—historical research describes the past, experimental research describes what has happened to certain variables given certain manipulation of other variables, and descriptive research explains the present through description of what now exists.

All educational questions that ask about a current state or condition require the strategy of description. Such descriptions have two basic uses: one, to assist administrators and other education personnel in making decisions within the limited scope of a politically defined school geographic area; the other, to generate generalizable knowledge and add to the body of knowledge about educational concerns. This distinction in purpose helps to clarify practices.

The study of descriptive research as a process of creating new generalizable knowledge places the study of conditions within a geographically limited region in a special category. Gathering information about school conditions for administrative uses falls in the class of a **status study.** Since status studies are important in making valid decisions, this chapter devotes a short section to the topic. An understanding of the status study should also help clarify the role of descriptive research in creating new generalizable knowledge.

The Status Study

Most researchers study existing conditions as a preliminary step to investigating questions they want to answer. Each researcher establishes the current status of the field under study to the degree that information is available. A study that *terminates* with a reporting of current conditions is called a *status study.* The status study is conducted to gather information needed to make administrative decisions for a specific school district, and there is no intention of generalizing the information gathered beyond the subjects or district where the data are collected. For example, the superintendent of Placer School District must collect data about current student enrollment and assess factors contributing to enrollment in order to project increases or decreases in enrollment for next year and the following year. Using these figures, she can then anticipate needs for buildings, faculty, and supporting facilities and make decisions accordingly.

In the sense that description is used in all branches of inquiry, each research study is in part a status study. However, to develop a research study, the investigator must go beyond mere description and utilize techniques that allow for conclusions and implications generalizable to broad areas of education. The somewhat arbitrary division between status study and research study facilitates communication about some very closely related procedures. A good grasp of the differences helps to separate for inspection many different activities that have been and—at times—still are carelessly thrown together under the loosely defined term "research." Students may wish to review the earlier discussion of the divisions among scientific strategies in Chapter 1. The basic difference between *to know* and *to choose* is again relevant to separate research activities and evaluation activities as we meet questions about *what is.*

A description of the present state of the educational institution in the Zee County School District is important to those people who are directly affected by that institution's level of functioning. It is important to society as a whole only indirectly, so a determination of its condition will not, in most cases, contribute to the body of generalizable knowledge about education. Information gathered from a school district may show that the first-grade enrollment for the next year will be about 10 percent less than this year. A closer look at the data may show that one elementary school in the district will have 15 percent more pupils next year, while another may have 20 percent less. This is important information in the district's planning for the next year, but the procedures used to gather and compile data for purposes similar to this are basically a study of status, not research procedures.

Activities to provide data for use in making administrative decisions should be associated with evaluation, not research.

Use in Evaluation and Development

Procedures designed to describe a school district's educational system for purposes of decision making fall under the inquiry strategies of evaluation and development. Although status studies do not require involvement with generalizations in the same way research studies do, careful attention must be given to sampling, questionnaire construction, and interviewing as the facts are accumulated. The important decisions based on data supplied by status studies require that the person charged with carrying out the study be informed of acceptable techniques. Separating status studies from research studies is not to be interpreted as downgrading them. The division is a pedagogical device to isolate each for discussion and to clarify the major difference. Excluding this type of activity for gathering and tabulating data from classification as a research procedure does not indicate that the activity is not important. It is an important part of educational planning, but it should not be confused with studies intended to apply to education in general.

Status studies are important in reporting existing educational practices and in gathering facts about school facilities, equipment, personnel, curricula, and so on. Such a study might be used merely to establish the ratio of teachers to pupils. It might be a broader examination of the aspects of a particular school and/or the community that the school serves. Collecting statistical data about numbers of students, teacher assignments, and other basic facts is usually carried out by someone within the school corporation itself. Very large surveys are conducted by the United States Government Bureau of Census, and also by educationally oriented organizations, which report the status of special topics in very large geographic regions. Tables of facts are available from the Bureau of Census.

Status studies are most valuable when used as vehicles to gather data for specified practical purposes. They are not intended to add to present knowledge about educational concerns in general, but they serve in a unique way to improve education in our schools. In any case, the status study merely reports conditions and refrains from any attempt at discovering relationships, making predictions, or establishing cause and effect which are generalizable beyond the district studied.

Example of a Status Study

A status study may be structured as an overview of a specific aspect or of the total scope of a local, state, regional, or national educational concern. In this case called a **school survey,** it may be conducted by a team from outside the district being studied, by personnel from within the district, or by some combination of the two. External persons usually come from a state or national educational division or from a university; however, private consultants also make school surveys.

In general, these studies focus on one or more of the following aspects:

collection of statistical information, nature of the teaching/learning process, teaching staff, student characteristics, or school facilities. The purpose of such a school survey is to make the educational process in the district more responsive to the needs of the students. It should provide information to allow strengths and weaknesses to be identified and evaluation of the information generated should give direction for administrative decision making and development.

Nature of Descriptive Research

Traditionally techniques and activities used to gather data to supply information for administrative decisions about facilities, staffing, and budgeting have fallen under the scope of descriptive research. Confusion resulted when too many different activities were included under one broad strategy. This prompted the decision to classify those procedures used to provide information for a specific decision situation under the strategies of evaluation and development. As mentioned before, the following types of inquiry have been specifically *excluded* from the scope of descriptive research:

1. Questions based in the past
2. Questions to be answered by manipulating variables in **laboratory conditions**
3. Questions about development of programs, tests, and so on
4. Questions based in the present but directed to a specific school situation for evaluation or administrative decisions about facilities, staff, and budget

What is left for descriptive research? Descriptive research seeks to answer those questions about the present state of affairs which have implications beyond the limits of the subjects or other elements studied. Questions which generate answers that contribute to principles and theory about educational concerns are many times answerable only through studying current conditions and existing relationships. Studies that use the context of ongoing phenomena to answer questions about general concerns of education make up descriptive research.

The Sharp and Kirk study (Sample Study Number 3) employs descriptive research methods to examine the use of counseling services by college students. Its purpose is to understand factors that influence student use of counseling services. In their article, Sharp and Kirk use direct questions to guide the reader to the problem under study. Likewise, Gallimore, Tharp, and Speidel use the direct question in Sample Study Number 5, another descriptive study, to present the problem for their study. Their question focuses on the effect of sibling caretaking on attentiveness in a learning situation. Answers to these questions are intended to be applied widely in the educational scene. Although data collection did take place in each case, neither study created differences in the real-world events examined and thus each is classified as a descriptive study.

Descriptive research can be viewed as having two distinct parts. First, the study by description provides the required data about present conditions, but statements of individual facts are not intended to be scientifically interesting nor are they valuable in developing new generalizable knowledge. This use of description is also a part of historical and experimental studies to provide background for interpreting facts for a present study. In research, mere description is not a goal but is rather a means to a goal. This phase of descriptive research leads to the part of description that relates to the study of research.

Second, the phase of establishing the meaning takes the data collected for the present study and by contrasting, comparing, or identifying relationships, forms conclusions about what these data mean to education in general. The first phase could be viewed as purely descriptive, while the second supplements this description by correlational techniques. The first part is much like a status study, while the second might be identified as the research aspect of the process. For example, Gallimore et al (Sample Study Number 4) set the stage for their study in paragraph 4 by giving factual data about the subjects and their backgrounds—that is, reporting on status. The rest of the article is more dynamic, tending toward the research aspect of a descriptive study, as it examines relationships and establishes possible causes for observed effects. This latter aspect of the study is intended to add to generalizable knowledge.

The Correlator

The educational inquirer who uses descriptive research as defined here would be a **correlator,** one who "studies the variation which already exists in nature (Ferguson, 1971, p. 17). In a correlational study, "the particular values of the variable, and the frequency of their occurrence are not fixed, or controlled by the investigator" (Ferguson, 1971, p. 16).

That all of the occurrences observed would have happened without the study makes the correlational study particularly valuable for the field of education, since many educational questions are either difficult to answer or unanswerable through laboratory manipulation of variables. If the effects of different treatments applied to subjects might be harmful and/or unethical, a natural setting might be used. A descriptive study also seems a logical choice when the interaction of numerous independent variables and their effects on several dependent variables are to be studied. When isolation of variables for laboratory-like studies does not provide answers that are directly generalizable to the natural setting, descriptive techniques must be used.

Since the descriptive study can be used so widely in human sciences, it is likely to remain a major strategy for answering questions about education. With the development of **multivariate** statistical techniques, educational researchers are turning to descriptive research techniques more frequently for analysis of complex situations.

For some questions, the correlational study and the experimental study can be used jointly. The correlational study can first establish a relationship that can be developed into a cause-and-effect hypothesis. The researcher then uses the carefully controlled experiment to test that hypothesis. Investigators using descriptive research, as well as investigators using experimental research, hope to establish how variables are related by using carefully executed procedures. Experimental evidence which supports the conclusions of descriptive studies adds strength to accepted theory and is encouraged when conditions permit a controlled experiment.

Steps in Descriptive Research

Well-designed studies for descriptive research follow the steps of the general scientific approach to inquiry. As in all inquiry, the problem question is the major component in making the descriptive research process function satisfactorily. On the surface, the descriptive study may appear to be simply a matter of gathering much information and interpreting it. However, the veteran researcher knows the importance of planning exactly what data are needed, how best to secure the data, and how to interpret them. The challenge to the correlator may be greater than the one before the **experimenter** because of the difficulty in controlling and interpreting the data.

Problem Clarification. After an indeterminate situation or barrier is met and the decision to attack it has been made, the researcher must phrase the problem into a clearly written question to be answered. A carefully prepared question helps direct the study. Descriptive research gives attention to those questions that can best be answered by studying present conditions through comparison, contrast, and study of relationships.

Procedures to answer the question, What is the drop-out rate at Zee High School? or a study "to explain through description the dropout problem at Zee High School" are not to be considered examples of descriptive research. The first example could not be used to generalize beyond the school studied. Conceivably the answer to the second example could be generalized beyond that school if the problem were reduced to specific aspects of the larger problem.

To say that the aim of a study is "to explain through description the dropout problem at Zee High School" is not to present a researchable problem. To qualify as a logically proposed investigation of a local problem, it would have to be either delimited to set bounds for the inquiry or divided to study the problem in parts, since the problem is too broad in this form. For example, the larger problem could be investigated by specific areas. Possible questions include: What effect does tracking of students through the high-school grades have on the dropout rate? What are the effects of an intramural program of athletics on the dropout rate? Answers to these and similar questions can be used to direct local decisions. The answers may be generalizable beyond that particular high school, but if it is studied as a local problem, the research is not specifically designed to do that.

A research question must be studied within a design that allows statements to be made that apply to more than just the subjects studied. Careful description of characteristics of subjects and the theoretical framework allow studies of existing variation to support generalization. A clearly defined problem about relationships is basic to the descriptive research study. The study of sibling caretaking effects (Study No. 5) clearly defines the scope of the problem through the question (par. 1) and connects the study to theory in paragraph 3. Description of the subjects in paragraph 3 also guides generalization to subjects with like characteristics.

Background Information. A thorough knowledge of the background of the topic for a descriptive study allows the investigator to place the conclusions of the study within the context of educational theory. Wide reading in the subject area fosters a thorough understanding of investigations and opinions about closely related aspects of a question, thus allowing conclusions to be generated that will contribute to a larger body of knowledge.

Decisions about all important aspects of the study become more valid when they are made in the context of a good understanding of closely related topics. The review of related literature in the complete report gives the reader a context within which to place the present study. Most journal articles, in contrast to the full research report (see Gallimore et al sample study, par. 3), include only the most directly related information. With the background from other research, definitions of variables under study can be carefully framed and—when possible—placed in operational terms. Techniques used in other studies may give direction to the present study.

Status reports and tables of data from the Census Bureau and other agencies are useful background information. When the overview of the research literature has been combined with all other data, the researcher has a basis for developing a hypothesis. The importance of background information for a study cannot be overemphasized, but this part of the research process is one that is often passed by too lightly.

Hypothesis. Although descriptive studies lack the control exercised by manipulating one variable while other variables are held constant, the hypothesis is still useful in descriptive research. The hypothesis gives direction for the study by providing something for the data to support or refute. A framework to gather data, analyze them, and draw conclusions uses the hypothesis as a vehicle for organizing the answer to the original question. The Gallimore et al study of sibling caretaking effects includes an implied hypothesis in paragraph 2. Although the data do not provide a direct answer to the problem question, the data collected and statistics reported in Tables 1 and 2 are tied to the implied hypothesis.

Techniques of testing hypotheses for descriptive studies tend to be more objective than those used to test the typical historical hypothesis because the information is usually reducible to numbers and statistical techniques are available to supplement the researcher's subjective judgments about what the data indicate.

Gathering and Analyzing the Data. After the hypothesis is clearly stated, the researcher must decide what information will be needed to test it and how best to obtain that information. This involves selecting and/or constructing the data-gathering instruments to provide the needed data and choosing the elements to supply the data. Finally the researcher must decide how the data will be organized, validated and/or tested for statistical significance, how they will be interpreted, and how they will be presented in the final report. As one example, a large portion of the article by Gallimore et al (pars. 5–13) is devoted to gathering and analyzing the data. Paragraphs 14 and 15 also present the rationale for measurement of sibling caretaking. This extensive presentation points up how important the authors consider the procedures and techniques of methodology.

With careful planning of data-gathering procedures, along with adequate training of the people needed to carry them out, the actual gathering of the data is routine. Pilot studies are often used to identify mechanical or procedural difficulties in gathering information from human subjects. After any alterations in methodology or changes in procedural aspects of study, the methodology of the proposal should be ready to implement.

Conclusions. After the data are in and the results organized, the researcher interprets the meaning of the data by forming conclusions. Conclusions are the output of the study and the validity of conclusions determines the worth of the study. Interpreting the results of the study is generally a sticky matter for the descriptive study because of the many contributing factors that must be taken into consideration and lack of direct control over variables. With these difficulties, the correlator meets the most intellectually demanding part of descriptive research—that of drawing conclusions from the results of the study (see Chapter 13). In the study of sibling caretaking effects, the authors chose to interweave conclusions with the results in discussing findings. Other statements of conclusions can be found in the summary abstract presented in paragraph 1.

Types of Descriptive Research

The broad base for descriptive research results in studies with widely differing characteristics. For this reason, a classification for descriptive studies varies with the writer. The following outline for this section is one way of classifying studies of the ongoing phenomena of the real world.

1. Survey studies
   a. Opinion/fact survey
   b. Documentary analysis
2. Relationship studies
   a. Case study
   b. Correlational study
   c. Causal-comparative study
3. Developmental studies
   a. Growth study
   b. Trend study

In practice a study may be difficult to assign to a single class, since the procedures may take on characteristics from more than one type. These labels should serve more as points for reference as the types of descriptive research are considered in discussion. For our purposes, the Gallimore et al sample study would be classified as a correlational study. The study by Sharp and Kirk, on the other hand, is difficult to classify but is probably best considered a causal-comparative study, because the question asks why students requested counseling services.

Survey Studies

The purpose of a **survey** study is to establish prevailing conditions at a point in time and to compare them with some established standards or with conditions in another population or time. Generalizations may also be extracted from conditions. As with all research, the survey must be directed by a clearly presented question that defines the scope and depth of the study. Careful planning is required and interpretation of facts/results into valid conclusions allows generalization beyond subjects surveyed.

Opinion/fact survey. The facts needed for many research studies concern constructs about which the personal information is difficult to obtain. A survey that collects the opinions of persons about themselves or about their relationship to someone or something else may provide the data the researcher needs for the study. School surveys, community surveys, public opinion surveys, social surveys, and achievement surveys are other over-views that fall in the class of **opinion/fact surveys** and may be used by the research worker using descriptive techniques.

The scope of the opinion/fact survey may be narrow or wide. The depth of the survey will also vary and will be directed largely by the nature of the question. Since it is generally impractical to obtain information from all subjects, surveys use sampling of a few to give information that is used to infer about the population. In all cases, the data will be used to make generalizations about groups or conditions beyond subjects studied.

Example. A study (Hales, 1975) that incorporated two types of surveys illustrates combination of the two factors of opinion and fact, although other studies may deal with only one or the other of these. This study used a Student Involvement Survey to collect facts about the student participation in school-related decision making and a Student Attitude Survey to collect personal data (facts) about students' attitudes toward school. The results were interpreted into conclusions that the data failed to support the belief that, in formal organizations, the extent of involvement in administrative decision making is directly related to development of favorable attitudes among members toward the organizational environment.

Documentary Analysis. Analysis of the content of records, documents, and other printed matter constitutes the second use of a survey to collect facts for a research study. After documents have withstood criticism for authenticity and credibility, examining the contents can reveal facts to be used in a study. Classifying the contents of documents, frequency of appearance in documents, or amount of space devoted to something can be the basis for the analysis.

Any defined set of printed matter could be used for analysis—professional journals, school records, textbooks, student schoolwork, courses of study, graphics, and newspapers are commonly used for educationally oriented questions. **Documentary analysis** can be used to examine literary style or beliefs of a writer, to ascertain bias, prejudice, or propaganda in the narrative of textbooks, to measure difficulty level of textbook content or reading level, to determine interest levels in controversial topics, and so on.

Example. A study (Johnson, 1972) that used a survey of documents to investigate relationships stated "This study relied on the body of literature generated by the guidance movement as its chief source for inference of value-orientation" (p. 5). The spirit of documentary analysis is summed up by this author's use of literature to investigate a relationship.

Relationship Studies

Nearly all descriptive studies deal with relationships. However, there are three types of studies which exhibit a particularly strong attachment to a relationship through either establishing one or investigating the direction of one. Three types of studies, ordered hierarchically according to the sophistication of the relationship under study, are **case study,** correlational, and **causal-comparative.**

Case Study. The case study gives intensive examination to many parts of some social unit—institution, community, group, or person. Since sociology and medicine use the case study widely to study individual human beings, many people fail to realize that the method is applicable in investigations beyond individuals. When an individual is the object of a case study, the focus is on solving a specific problem or set of problems for that individual. Such a case study in isolation is not research-oriented. A set of subjects with a common problem might be studied, investigating the cases for commonalities or differences. Comparisons and controls made among such subjects then form a collection of data for conclusions. Using case studies in this way could be a part of research on that problem.

In general, case studies of more than a single subject are directed toward establishing typicalness or some factor(s) common to a social class, ethnic group, or institution. The question is usually written so that the derived answer gives greater understanding of a defined social group or institution. Since human beings live in a dynamic setting, a case study becomes examination of all possible contributing relationships to establish—if possible—the direction of each relationship and to recognize cause-and-effect. The subjectivity associated with case-study methods calls for special precautions to guard against human frailties entering into the interpretation and possibly selection of data.

Example. Many case studies have been made of cultures, tribes, and other social units. One published study—Katz's (1975) study of Hamilton, Ontario—serves as an example of the case study and also represents an example of an implied question about the past. This book gives an in-depth look at the family and class during the mid-19th century (about 1854 to 1861). The presentation centers around the people, the structure of inequality, transiency, and social mobility, the class of entrepreneurs, and the experience of growing up in the 19th century.

From the vast amount of data amassed, Katz drew conclusions and made comparisons to present-day conditions. Although the separate conclusions cannot be reduced to one generalization, the author summed the finding that the study "showed an urban order fundamentally different from that of today, neither fully traditional nor modern, but poised in a moment of transition (Katz, 1975, p. 316). To understand the scope of the study fully requires reading the complete work. As is the case with most case studies, the particulars are more important than any one general finding. The case study is usually used in education to study individual students. It is generally an in-depth study that incorporates all aspects of human characteristics that bear on the case. The case study is rarely used in education in the same way that Katz studied the city of Hamilton. As will be discussed later under the heading of anthropological methods, more in-depth studies of educational institutions need to be made and the case study offers that opportunity. The school survey can readily be expanded into a case study of a school district from its primary function as a status study.

The case study is the historical antecedent of the **single-case experimental studies** which are used widely to study problems where scientifically rigorous group comparison designs have been found to be impractical. Sometimes referred to as "$N = 1$" designs, the single-case experiments attach new dimensions to the case study while retaining the advantages of case-study methodology. This close relationship is reflected in Hersen and Barlow's comments:

> The case study method, of course, is the clinical base for the experimental study of single cases and, as such, it retains an important function in present-day applied research. Unfortunately, during this period [first half of the 20th century] clinicians were unaware, for the most part, of the basic principles of applied research, such as definition of variables and manipulation of independent variables. Thus it is noteworthy from a historical point of view that several case studies reported during this period came tantalizingly close to providing the basic scientific ingredients of experimental single case research (1976, p. 9)

Single-case experiments study the behavior of one human being under changing conditions. Since behavior change takes place always within one organism, certain questions—possibly a large portion—should be answered through studying individuals separately if group averages and variances would be misleading. The important contribution of "$N = 1$" methodology is the demonstration that independent variables can be defined and systematically manipulated within single-case research. A variety of statistical procedures provide several options for studying the effects of intervention on behavior as a part of intrasubject study in the single case.

A study (Hersen, Eisler, Alford, & Agras, 1973) of work behavior change as a result of token reinforcement utilized the A-B-A design. The design was (A) **baseline data,** (B) token reinforcement, and (A) second baseline for three depressed patients in a clinic. Since each design was the same for each subject, the treatment was considered a **replication** of one study three times.

Another example, a study of Curt through differential reinforcement of incomplete behavior (DRI), is presented in Figure 10–1. Figure 4.1 in the illustration depicts graphically the effectiveness of the "sticker & TV" reinforcement intended to change behavior.

Correlational Study. A true correlational study is set up with the expressed purpose of establishing whether or not a relationship between, possibly among, variables exists. The methodology is structured to see if a relationship does exist and to assess to what degree it exists, but the study is not intended to conclude anything about the direction (cause and effect) of the relationship.

Findings about relationships produced in correlational studies may give support to a directional hypothesis which can be investigated in a new study. Discovering a relationship is also a first step toward making predictions. Classroom teachers are directly involved with many relationships as they engage in the teaching/learning process. If learning is to be the principle outcome of the process, basic questions arise about how differences on a multitude of variables are related to learning. The following example is a study of relationships that may not directly affect learning but are probably basic to understanding a student's functioning in school.

Example. A study (Crawford, Harkin, & Huenemann, 1978) was conducted to investigate relationships between environmental factors and preschool obesity. The study was directed at specific factors of nutrition and its relationship to socioeconomic levels. Interpreting the results of the several specific relationships produced the general conclusion that there is a high positive correlation between economic status and nutritional status. The implications of such a study are best found in the association (or lack of it) between the specific factors in isolation. Investigation of a wide range of student characteristics—including physical characteristics—is needed to make decisions about the teaching-learning process. Studies such as the obesity research provide good background for further research about the effects of certain influences on educational advancement.

Causal-comparative Study. Facts needed for studies of cause-effect relationships may be obtained through directly controlling circumstances of manipulation. The researcher can construct situations for fact gathering. At other times he or she may not have that option. For example, the study of the effects of smoking tobacco has for the most part been done without requiring that subjects either smoke or not smoke. Conscious manipulation in an experiment would require creating smokers out of nonsmokers. The study

CURT

A Dressing Routine[13]

This case study illustrates a simple DRI procedure proven successful in eliminating a problem common in households with exceptional children.

Curt was an 8-year-old boy who regularly took from one to two hours to get dressed each morning before school. His parents found themselves caught in a daily routine of constant reminders, occasional scoldings, pleading, and general frustration in dealing with their son's behavior. Morning often became an unpleasant scene for the entire family. Curt's parents decided to try to decrease his lengthy dressing behavior by reinforcing an incompatible behavior—dressing himself within 10 minutes each morning. Curt's parents knew he was capable of meeting the 10-minute limit because once during a week of pre-intervention, baseline measurement, Curt got dressed in a quick 4 minutes.

The program involved laying out Curt's clothes in the bathroom, waking him, and then setting a kitchen timer for 10 minutes. If Curt dressed before the timer went off, he earned a red sticker for the chart on his bedroom door, which entitled him to watch TV that evening. If he did not meet the 10-minute criterion, he had to stay in the bathroom until dressed and forfeit TV that day. Family members praised Curt when

Reported by Sibby Coxhead. graduate student. Faculty for Exceptional Children. The Ohio State University.

he met the criterion but ignored him (without getting upset) if he didn't.

Figure 4.1 shows the results of the DRI strategy. During the week of just timing Curt, he took an average of 59 minutes to get dressed. During the 17 days of the DRI procedure, Curt's average dressing time dropped to 10 minutes, and he met the limit nine times. (On three occasions, zero minutes were recorded. On these mornings, Curt woke his mother and father and was completely dressed!) The DRI intervention was then dropped—no timer, no TV chart—but Curt's clothes were still laid out for him. He was told to still get dressed as quickly as he could, but he wouldn't be timed; and he could watch TV no matter how long he took. His dressing time averaged 23 minutes over the 6 days of this phase. The DRI procedure was reinstated, and for 12 out of the next 13 days, Curt was dressed before the timer went off. His average time was 8 minutes.

Many parents would approach a problem like Curt's by threatening him with loss of privileges such as television if he failed to meet their expectations. This puts the child in a win-lose situation against his parents. But while implementing a similar contingency, Curt's parents approached it from an entirely different perspective. They chose a time limit they knew Curt could meet—he had done so during baseline—and presented the program to their son in a positive manner, as a game. Curt responded accordingly and enjoyed the program.

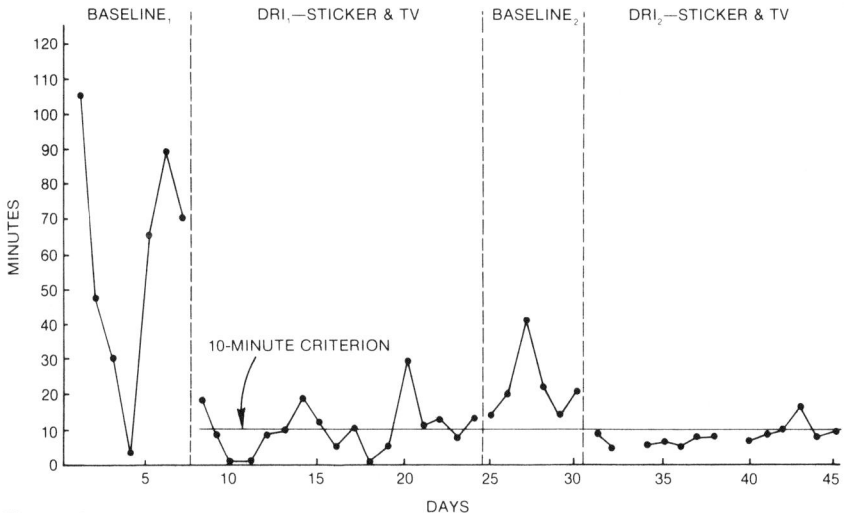

Figure 4.1
Use of differential reinforcement of incompatible behavior (DRI) to decrease morning dressing time of an 8-year-old boy.

FIGURE 10–1   Single-case Experiment *(N = 1)*

has been accomplished by associating what occurs with the aspects of why it occurs without manipulation. Whenever the situation precludes controlling conditions, the researcher must consider ways to associate causes with observed effects.

Examples. Studies of disease in medical research are made as disease occurs in the natural course of events, not as a result of causing disease in subjects at the researcher's whim. Studies of deprivation of children, studies of accidents on the highway and in school, and studies that might infringe on personal rights are largely limited to studying ongoing happenings in the world. Nature is free to make many experiments that are not ethical for researchers to perform. The study of phenomena as they occur is largely a study of nature's experiments. The best the researcher can do is to establish for the record logically conceived causes using accepted practices when possible but creating new ways to establish association between cause and effect when necessary.

Many educational studies must be conducted in the context of real-world happenings, since limiting a student's access to an effective educational experience in order to achieve experimental control is neither desirable nor ethical. Medical research and educational research have this restriction in common: in each case, the study of human beings raises questions about the validity of findings. It is thus understandable that educators question the validity of educational findings.

Developmental Studies

A study of progress over a time period (**developmental study**) is usually a study of development. **Longitudinal studies** of development are either studies of the progress of growth as it is revealed or studies of recorded data to make predictions. For education, the growth studied is primarily in human beings—not only their physical growth but also their growth in cognitive functioning and affective development. The second kind of study uses recorded data and aids administrators in projecting future requirements of the educational institution for needed facilities, staff, and so on. More importantly, these studies help institutions be responsive to social changes.

Growth Studies. The primary reason for studies of growth in educational research is to give knowledge of what to expect at different age levels and understanding of developmental sequences within patterns. Understanding growth in the cognitive, affective, and psychomotor domains also helps teachers to understand why students seem to change ("be inconsistent") in the school setting.

Growth studies are generally undertaken in response to specific questions rather than in response to growth generally. Researchers use two ways of studying growth. The first is to follow certain subjects for an extended time period. In this approach, researchers collect baseline data on designated characteristics to be studied, then collect data at a later time, and finally make comparisons. A second way to study growth is to study a cross section of a population. In this approach, researchers collect data on subjects of different ages and make comparisons. The first approach studies the same sample of subjects over an extended period of time and the second way studies an extended sample at the same point in time.

Examples. To study physical-growth patterns of development, a sample of subjects of a particular age, say 3, could be measured on specific physical characteristics. Further measurements could be made on the same subjects at predetermined time intervals, say every 6 months, until the subjects reached 20 years old. By getting mean (average) values for each 6-month period, growth patterns could be established for the sample in general. In addition, differences in the sample could be studied by investigating how subjects varied in measurements at each of the 6-month periods. Such studies of physical development have given educators highly reliable data on most physical characteristics. Of interest is a study of how these averages change over time for new sets of subjects. Over the years, children at the same age may show patterns of increases in height and other characteristics.

Another study of the same physical characteristics could be done at a single point in time by selecting samples of subjects in 6-months age increments from 3 years to 20 years and taking measures on each of these samples to reveal growth patterns. The advantage of this method—a **cross-sectional study**— is that data are available sooner than waiting for the longitudinal study to be completed. Also, with such a study the effects of time per se do not confound the data. The researcher must assume, however, that differences of age groups are due to development. Studies of growth in all areas of development can be studied in either of these two ways, but the cognitive and affective aspects of growth are more difficult to measure because these areas lack the objectivity of physical characteristics. Other human sciences employ growth studies widely to study development.

Trend Studies. One of the early uses of formal inquiry was to collect data and use the direction of movement as a part of a prediction. Today these trend studies are helpful in making statements beyond the data collected and allow a dimension not possible when the researcher merely uses past data in its narrowest sense. One advantage of trend studies is that they enable prediction to be dynamic rather than static. A drawback is that such studies must use **extrapolation** from an observed direction over a period of time. Without careful consideration of all contributing factors, the true direction may not be the interpreted direction, or changes beyond the control of the researcher may shift conditions so much that the outcome is impossible to forecast. For these reasons, trend studies are usually better at predicting general movements than specific ones. They are also better at predicting over short-range time periods than over the long range.

Since prediction of any kind is always a leap based on faith, there is no guarantee that predictions based on trends will hold. A prediction based on trend is reasonable if the predictor can expect conditions of the past to remain the same through the time of prediction. The more information the researcher has about why the trend developed, the better the predictions will be. If changes in contributing factors can be forecast, then the trend can be forecast taking expected changes into account. Although the researcher recognizes that changes occur with time, it would be misleading to think that time itself brought about these changes. Rather, processes that occur over time produce change. In addition to paying attention to these processes, the researcher must give greater weight to recent trends than to trends farther back in time.

Example. In the mid-1970s, John Hill from Indiana State University made a study of school population trends for the Vigo County, Indiana, schools. He studied data from schools which fed students into the three area high schools and the total school enrollment. Using these data, he projected future enrollments, basing the projections on birth rate estimates and history. Enrollment had peaked but started to decrease. The decrease was projected to a date when the total population was predicted to remain constant. However, the population did not appear to be the same for all school districts or for urban and suburban areas. From similar projected trends, long-range plans can be conceptualized based on expected needs for facilities and faculties.

Educators often make decisions that have a direct relationship with the future, since education is a continuing factor for all students. Teachers must also help prepare students for a social milieu that is always changing. Although specific needs for the future can not be ascertained, the curriculum must be responsive to expected changes. Administrators also use trend analysis to direct the building of facilities and hiring of staff to reflect any changes expected from trends projected into the future. The extension of trend analysis is helpful in making many school-related decisions.

□CHECK YOUR UNDERSTANDING

Classify each of the following descriptions of studies as

     S—a status study
     H—a historical study
     D—a descriptive study

1. A study to establish the relationship between students' socioeconomic backgrounds and their attitudes toward school.
2. A school survey of the community's attitude toward restructuring a school district's organization to include a middle school.
3. A study of the impact of Paul Vanriper on the school system in Lebanon, Indiana, during his tenure as school superintendent.
4. A study of the South Putnam County School District by a team of outside educators.
5. The Terman study of gifted students from the 1920s to the present.
6. A study of the effects of obesity on student school achievement.
7. Sample Study Number 1.
8. Sample Study Number 3.
9. Sample Study Number 5.

Answers

1. D
2. S
3. H
4. S
5. D
6. D
7. H
8. D
9. D

Types of Data

A major problem associated with descriptive research is interpreting the data. Since the researcher has no control over conditions beyond choosing what data to gather, interpretations are highly subjective and open to some of the criticisms attached to conclusions for historical studies. A major difference between historical and descriptive data is that a study of current conditions does have all of the data available and does not have to rely on only a portion that remains, as is true of historical research. A comprehensive study of the needed data and possible methods for obtaining them allows the researcher to give the topic total coverage by using objective methods. Conclusions to well-planned and well-executed descriptive studies seem to be more readily accepted than conclusions to historical studies, because the data are more easily validated if the proper type of data is available for interpretation.

Both qualitative and quantitative data are used in descriptive research studies. As newer and better ways of quantifying attributes are developed, however, qualitative data are coming to be used primarily to provide background for the study and to build hypotheses. Today, an attempt to study a problem by a descriptive narrative alone would be inappropriate as a technique for descriptive research.

Qualitative Data

Qualitative data can be used to give background for a problem and to derive hypotheses, but it should not be used as the primary data for a study nor as a basis for conclusions. Note, for example, the efforts expended in the Gallimore et al study of sibling caretaking effects to quantify what might have been collected as qualitative data and the relative ease with which mathematics generates the results. If a trait or characteristic is considered a variable for study, then it is quantifiable (Kerlinger, 1973, p. 40) and to do less than supply objectively obtained quantities is not acceptable research procedure. Nominal variables may be said to generate qualitative data and they can be called "qualitative variables," but this limitation seems inconsistent with the contemporary use of measurement in educational research and our earlier discussion of types of data generated by nominal variables. To consider nominal variables to be traits that can be studied only through a narrative analysis would lead the researcher away from the opportunity for much objective treatment of data by precluding quantification by counting.

Even in documentary analysis where the collected data are qualitative, quantification is used to record frequencies of occurrence, amounts of time, or degrees of emphasis given to something. This quantification permits comparison to standards or to other criteria for presenting the results. Conclusions are more likely to be made from the quantification than from the narrative statements alone. Techniques of **scaling, Q-sort,** and **semantic differential** are examples of methods of organizing what could be qualitative data into quantified form.

Quantitative Data

Variables and the data they yield can be categorized as nominal, ordinal, interval, or ratio.

Quantitative data may be:

1. Nominal (if frequencies of occurrence are counted)
2. Ordinal (if the property of order is considered in assigning the numerical description)
3. Interval (if the numbers are assigned according to a scale where intervals are constant throughout the scale)
4. Ratio (if the assignment is made so that statements of ratios can be made in the original numerical assignment)

For example, a study of race would permit data to be classified into categories which are nominal in nature. **Statistics** to be used in interpreting those data would be limited to analysis that does not require ordering or higher properties in the data. Socioeconomic classes can be ordered, but equal intervals between classes can not be established. Therefore, the collection procedures establish properties of the data, and statistical treatment is limited by the variable and the way it is collected. The type of data as established by its properties determines to a large degree the statistical procedures that can be used to interpret facts into results.

Studies that use nominal variables are limited to quantifying by counting frequencies of occurrence. Since there is no order to the set of classification categories, the only values that can be used are the counting numbers associated with the category frequencies. Meaningful mathematical treatment is limited to comparing those counting numbers directly, by figuring percentages in the several categories, ratios within the counting numbers, certain nonparametric statistical tests of significance, and appropriate correlational and regression techniques.

A rule of measurement for nominal variables is the function describing how subjects are assigned to categories of the trait being measured. A set of junior high school students might be assigned to categories using a rule of measurement based on the trait of "favorite color." The rule of measurement is: assign to the category "blue" each member who states a preference for blue; assign to category "yellow" each member who states a preference for yellow; and so on for each category. Of course, the categories must be exhaustive, which means that the variable "color" must have enough categories to accommodate all possible choices of colors. Frequencies of occurrences for the categories are the counting numbers associated with the categories after the set being studied is completely assigned. This is a method of assignment frequently used for studies that are designed to study conditions as they exist, when the variable under study cannot be classed higher than nominal or when a higher level variable is treated within categories.

Given information that permits a rule of measurement including at least ordering, the researcher has additional statistical techniques for use in interpreting data. For example, the measurement by rating scales in the sample study of sibling caretaking effects is performed so that order is built into the measures. Additional correlational techniques, other nonparametric tests, and additional statistics for describing the data can often be applied. This type of rule allows treatment in distinct categories as well. The order of finish of a race of 9 runners has the added property of order that was lacking in the nominal assignment. For analysis, the 9 runners could be categorized into 3 classes consisting of (1) the first 3 finishers, (2) the second 3 finishers, and (3) the last 3 finishers. With this assignment, the order of the 3 categories is retained, but the order within categories is lost. Since the higher the assignment of the numbers the more information the researcher has, the highest type of data should be obtained for the study. Since interval and ratio data contain more information than nominal and ordinal, other procedures are available in the form of **parametric** techniques which cannot be used on the two lower scales. Descriptive studies that include testing or measurement using equal intervals may obtain interval data, but only rarely will the data be classed as ratio. In the caretaking sample study, for example, the measurement of time that a tutee attended was made at the interval level, thus allowing means and standard deviations to be obtained. Any interval or ratio data can be ordered or categorized for data treatment when appropriate, but some of the information is lost when a lower rule of assignment is used. (See Chapter 2.)

At times researchers assign subjects to categories on the basis of the measurement of a particular attribute. When this is done, the variable is called an **assigned variable,** and it is treated as an independent variable—one that can be manipulated by an investigator. Descriptive studies use combinations of types of variables when studying relationships and cause-effect. The assigned variable may be nominal and the **criterion variable** ordinal, for example. A study could be made of comparing the running ability of philosophy majors to the running ability of anthropology majors. The two categories on the variable of college major were chosen by the researcher and the assignment made on that basis. The criterion variable, running ability, could be timed, giving the combination of an assigned variable that is nominal and a criterion variable that is interval. A study that uses an assigned variable assumes the differences to be causal, but the establishment of cause cannot go beyond the basis of assignment.

The design for the study about the running ability of philosophy and anthropology majors would be shown graphically as in Figure 10–2. The figure shows that the independent variable (assigned) is college major (two **levels**). The dependent variable (criterion) is running ability (interval). The dependent variable measure is the time needed to run a predetermined distance.

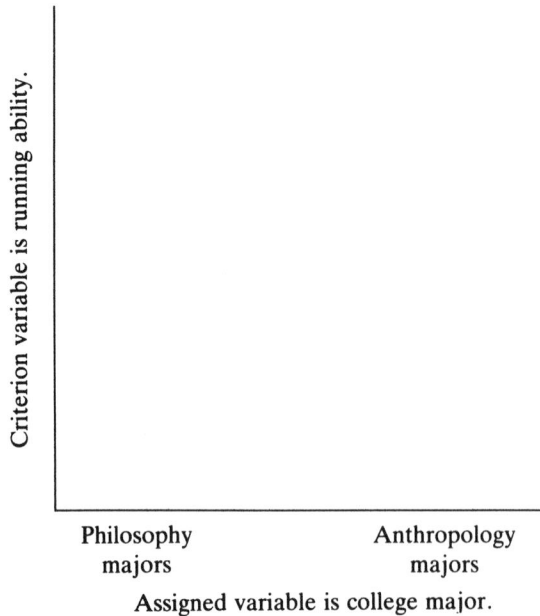

FIGURE 10–2   Running Ability of Philosophy and Anthropology Majors

The use of an assigned variable in the running study is a use of the ex post facto design where a researcher uses an experimental-like situation but rather than creating differences on an independent variable examines effects of treatment which have occurred naturally. This is a very helpful design, because the researcher can study variables that are not open to manipulation. This design is used widely in descriptive studies to take advantage of the control that assignment gives to treatment. Although the design does not give as much control as an experiment would allow, it uses the same basic structure.

Since the treatment levels of the independent variable have been made by assignment rather than by direct manipulation, the question of causation of differences on the dependent variable may not be satisfactorily resolved. If the relationship is not established, then probably no cause-effect relationship exists. However, if a relationship is identified, cause has not necessarily been established. Ex post facto designs are discussed in more depth in

Chapter 11 where they are compared to the experimental design that they resemble.

Sources of Data

The broad base for descriptive research and the all-encompassing nature of education provide almost limitless sources for data. Three ways of getting at this information are direct observation, measuring attributes of the elements of the world, or asking the elements (assuming they are human beings) for information that may be difficult to observe or measure. The sample study by Gallimore et al used direct observation (paragraph 7) by two observers to measure the dependent variable—attending to tutor or "on task." At times, combinations of the three approaches are used. To study a student's attitude toward a new method of teaching a foreign language that uses a laboratory carrel, a researcher might use direct observation to see how the student reacts and assess his willingness to use the laboratory and actions while there. The researcher might also ask the student to respond to a device designed to measure attitudes toward the laboratory or ask him directly to give his reaction in a narrative or by using a structured device.

When considering the data source, the researcher should consider what or who was the originator of the information. For example, a study may use a questionnaire to collect data. That questionnaire is not the source of the data—the people who responded constitute the source. Likewise, a set of test scores is based on the students, although the test form itself may have actually generated the facts. As another example, the source of data for the study of effects of sibling caretaking was the set of 26 children enrolled in the kindergarten.

Descriptive approaches may appear relatively simple, but many difficulties are associated with developing appropriate techniques for obtaining the needed information from subjects. Unfortunately, much of the information about human beings is personal and not readily available to the researcher. The needed information may be difficult to obtain, since the cooperation of the subjects may be difficult to acquire.

The researcher should give special attention to all available collection and interpretation tools, their use, and their possible effects on subjects to assure that the desired data are obtained. This discussion addresses four sources of data for descriptive studies, although other sources may be used from time to time. Students, the community, professional staff, and printed matter are all considered the major sources of data for education studies.

The source of information for use in educational descriptive research studies is primarily the attributes of human beings. These attributes are studied by comparing, contrasting, and investigating to establish relationships. Information for status studies is provided by a greater range of sources—such as school buildings, classroom materials, and supporting services—although such information may also be drawn from a student population. As mentioned earlier, use of printed matter as a source will be made.

Students

Many of the traits and characteristics of most concern in educational research are tied to objectives of the educational process, the instructional outcomes of the teaching-learning relation. For the educational activities of a school program to be effective, they must move students toward the desired goal or aims that form the basis for educational objectives. These traits and characteristics of students reflected in educational objectives become criterion variables in research studies. Many objectives relate to student achievement. Consequently, research studies often consider effects of variables on student achievement. However, to study the effects of variables on student achievement, the researcher must have a measure of such achievement. In general, the data for descriptive studies consist of information supplied by measuring criterion variables—for example, student achievement in biology. In the cognitive domain, student achievement in subject matter stands out as a particularly important criterion variable, thus the study of related variables makes up a large part of educational research.

The **affective domain** of personality and social development is becoming increasingly a part of the educator's concern. The **constructs** of creativity, motivation, aspiration, and so on become sources of data as they appear as criterion variables. Development of motor skills is also important, and variables that indicate skill development become criterion variables.

Since the educational process exists for students, they provide most of the data for educational research. In descriptive studies, a sample of students may be observed on the criterion variable or a correlation can be made between observations made on two variables. When neither of these can be done directly, the research worker looks for indirect effects deemed to indicate the presence of the criterion variable. For example, the impact of an intramural program on school attitudes could be studied by comparing absence rate, tardiness, and so forth as indicators of attitude toward school. School attitude, the criterion variable, is observed indirectly by investigating other characteristics; however, the source of the data is the students. For the Gallimore et al study, the effects of sibling caretaking were expected to be reflected in the degree of attending to the tutor. The correlations suggest to the researcher the degree that pairs of characteristics are related.

Community

Parents and other community people also serve as sources for data in descriptive studies. The school can not be isolated from other social groups and institutions for study because of the strong effects they have on the school. Studies of political, economic, and societal factors give direction to school decisions.

Studies of society in general have implications for education and are often utilized in the school setting. More important for educational research is an understanding of students' lives outside school and how other aspects of living are directly related to school performance. Studies relating to socioeconomic factors, parental attitudes, cultural differences, effects of early-in and early-out of the educational process are only a few examples of research where community persons serve as sources of data for educational studies.

Professional Staff

The classroom teachers and supporting administrative staff are often sources of data for descriptive studies. Although they are more directly related to research through study of their teaching methods and effects of changes in curriculum, professional educators may also be studied for the relationship of other personal characteristics to student performance in the school setting.

The professional staff is a source of data for studies which look for relationships between staff—collectively or individually—and student school performance. Case studies are likely to use data from staff members in conjunction with other data.

Printed Material

Analysis of the literature for background information and documentary analysis rely on the records and materials of the past and present. These are largely printed but may be written, oral, or graphic in form.

Since researchers ask more and more complex questions, relationships must be established within a complex frame of reference which, in turn, requires more and more information. As the questions asked become increasingly insightful, the researcher may need to look for data in new ways and in new places. Attention to equal rights has raised many questions for the educator. For example, textbook materials are subjected to examination for racial bias, sexual bias, and other forms of prejudice as social issues arise. Surveying community characteristics may involve exploring newspaper reports or other material written about the population and its activities. In these many cases, the printed material would be considered the source of the materials, since it reports about matters of concern for the study. The basic research concern is still, nevertheless, with human beings.

Tools of Descriptive Research

Descriptive research tools are needed to gather data about present conditions and to interpret those data through contrast, comparison, and relationships. These tools are of two kinds—those used to collect data and those used to interpret the data. Since the technique of descriptive research is correlational, it deals with the real-world setting without manipulation by the researcher. The researcher must take special precautions to see that neither his or her presence nor the tools used in the study itself change the existing conditions in a way that confounds the results.

Tools for gathering the data are designed to quantify or allow for quantification of the variables being studied—primarily the criterion variable. Tools for interpretation are largely the statistical procedures applied to the data. The results of such statistical interpretations aid the researcher in reaching conclusions about the study. The importance of choosing the appropriate set of tools for gathering and interpreting data cannot be overemphasized. This choice should be a major concern when planning the study.

The several aspects of the research plan must fit together, and decisions must be made in the context of what kinds of data can be obtained, what rules of measurement can be used, and which statistical techniques to employ on the results. The interdependence of these aspects precludes decisions about one area without giving due consideration to the others. For example, the nature of a question places limitations on the type of appropriate data which in turn sets limits on the proper tools to gather that data. Additional limitations on the proper statistical procedures used to interpret the data are imposed by the rules of measurement used in gathering the data.

The direction of the sample study by Gallimore et al was largely set in the question asked in paragraph 2. The study must be descriptive because it assesses the effects of something that has already happened—an ex post facto investigation. Collection of data is largely limited to direct observation, since it seems to be the only logical way to measure attending. Because time seems a logical measure of attending, the data are produced at the interval level. Assignment of subjects to groups by rating scales of characteristics was at the highest level possible, since order seems to be the highest assignment possible. Other descriptive studies are similarly directed by the question asked. Since any study must be made within existing conditions without manipulation, other circumstances of the setting may further limit the plan being developed, but the overall attack should combine the best combination of procedures for the particular situation.

Discussion in earlier chapters has brought us through the taxonomy of inquiry strategies to the fourth level (recall Figure 1–1), where specific plans are formed through a methodology designed to answer the specific question asked. A study was represented in Chapter 1 as starting in the trunk of a tree representing the scientific method used in inquiry. From here development passed through the first set of branches standing for three major strategies, and through the next set of branches representing types of research. The original question sets the direction for the study and affects decisions at all levels, especially at the fourth level where specific plans are made for the individual study. At this stage, decisions must be made with an eye to gathering appropriate data and selecting proper procedures to interpret them for the question under study.

Collecting Data

The observational tools for obtaining data about present conditions are intended to give objective information in quantitative form. Techniques must be chosen to give the best basis and input for the interpretive tools, and a close relationship should be established between collecting and interpreting procedures to be sure that a logical and functional sequence is developed. The collecting tools discussed in this chapter are those most often used in studies of present conditions—those that are most likely to provide data amenable to study for contrasts, comparisons, and relationships.

The following list presents tools which have utility in collecting data for the correlator studying existing conditions. A later section in this chapter describes each briefly and discusses some possible uses of the tool. Other, more specialized sources provide more in-depth information for a particular tool. Researchers are urged to seek these out before gathering the information needed to answer a specific research question.

Direct observation	Questionnaires
Interviews	Scales
Tests, psychological	Tests, achievement
Self-reports	Mechanical devices
Sociometry	Q methodology
Study of existing data	Anthropological field-study approach

Investigators of educational questions select from these and other tools when developing the methodology of descriptive studies. Recall that the Gallimore et al study used direct observation for data collection. The longitudinal study by Sharp and Kirk collected data over a four-year time period about frequencies of student-initiated use of counseling services by categories set up at the beginning of the study. Other less-used tools that can be used to obtain information include the semantic differential, projective methods, content analysis, and the developmental approach to collecting data for descriptive studies.

Interpreting Data

Information-gathering tools provide data. Careful planning of the study will assure that the manner of gathering information will produce data that are interpretable. For assistance in interpreting data, the researcher turns first to the broad field of statistics. Statistics can aid in interpreting information in the following ways:

1. By reducing the empirical data. Organizing the data puts it in the form for statistical treatment as well as providing tables and graphic representation for the final report.
2. By studying variation. Generalizations must take into account differences as well as typicalness. Although science is continually looking for typicalness within natural phenomena, much of science begins and ends with a study of difference.
3. By studying relationship. Statistical techniques can reveal how variations of two variables are concomitant. An identified relationship allows for hypothesis development and theorizing. Advanced techniques allow study of more than two variables.
4. By allowing a researcher to make predictions. A high relationship between two variables may provide enough information to allow for highly probable predictions. One of the functions of science is prediction.

5. By allowing the researcher to make **inferences.** A study of one part of a population allows the researcher to make statements about the population in general, through proper use of sampling procedures.
6. By testing how well obtained data fit with expectations. This provides a means of testing the agreement of the hypothesis and observation.

The interpretive tools discussed later in this chapter fall within the broad field of statistics. The scope of this book does not allow a full-blown development of each topic discussed, but the discussion does show where these tools can be used and to some extent how they can be used, particularly emphasizing those techniques most widely used. The mathematical understandings of statistics are left for the most part to books devoted to accomplishing that task. There are some computational procedures for widely used statistics in Appendix D. The coverage here should help the researcher select the proper tool for a study. If the prospective researcher does not already understand how to use the tool, she or he should turn to the appendix, to a statistics book or to someone more knowledgeable about statistics to find help in becoming proficient in its use.

Tools for Collecting Data

The list of tools that can be used to collect data for descriptive studies cannot be exhaustive because ways to observe (see Chapter 3) the real world are without limit. New questions sometimes require researchers to develop new methods of study, including new ways to observe the world and collect data about it.

Direct Observation

Direct observation is especially valuable in establishing the present condition. Since all science seeks to understand the world around us, the beginning of all scientific endeavors is direct observation. First attempts to discover regularity are nearly all based in what a person sees directly. The use of direct observation has fallen into disfavor among some researchers who claim it is unscientific and subject to distortion by the observer. Problems associated with direct observation are in most cases the result of human frailties (see Chapter 3), but when these are overcome through objective procedures—such as checklists, scorecards, scales, and extension of the senses by mechanical devices—direct observation becomes a valuable tool for descriptive research.

The use of a rating scale by an observer allows a component of judgment to be built into direct observation if the action is slow enough or takes place over a long enough period of time to allow for observer reflection on special points to be considered. A device in the form of a product scale allows judgments to be made on results of performance. Studying classroom interaction (such as Flanders' work) can be helpful in direct observation.

Classroom studies sometimes find an informal method of collecting helpful in gathering data. Behavioral diaries of students' activities may be used in a study of development or adjustment of subjects. These diaries are called **anecdotal records** (Bergstrom & Margosian, 1977, p. 9) and their use facilitates placing behavior in operational terms. (See Figure 10–3 for a sample anecdotal record.) Such records are made without judgment to allow for assessment over a period of time rather than relying on a single occurrence. Careful selection of what is reported and avoidance of certain reports could allow anecdotal records to show almost anything that the teacher wanted to show. Certainly, this tendency toward bias must be guarded against when using anecdotal records.

Anecdotal Record

Name: _Bill M._   Age: _9_

Date: _October 23_   Setting: _Playground_

Time of Day: _10:15_   Observer: _Self_

Observation:	Summary:
Bill pushes Sam on a swing. Sam says, "Too high," but Bill pushes harder and Sam asks to stop. Bill pushes higher until Sam cries. Bill stops pushing and goes to play with Marianne and Susan.	Several anecdotes about Bill show his tendency to bully his classmates to be increasing. I must make an effort to learn the causes of this behavior.

Note: Adapted from *Teaching Young Children* by Joan M. Bergstrom and Rose K. Margosian (Columbus, Oh.: Charles E. Merrill, 1977), p. 9. Copyright 1977 by Bell & Howell Company.

FIGURE 10–3   A Sample Anecdotal Record

Altering a situation by inserting an observer or observational device may affect the data collected. If the research worker feels the data would be invalidated using certain procedures, then some other collection method must be identified or invented. Unobtrusive measures (Webb, Campbell,

Schwartz, & Sechrest, 1966) may be helpful since they allow collection of data without the subject of observation knowing that she or he is being observed. If unobtrusive observation is used, a direct relationship between the measure and the characteristic being studied must be established for the study.

Questionnaire

When making a survey, the best way to collect data may be to prepare a set of questions for subjects to respond to. If the set is prepared properly, it can be distributed by mail or other means and returned by mail. The *questionnaire* is an often used (and often misused) observational device for collecting personal data and opinions.

The questionnaire provides a way to get personal information from subjects that may not be readily obtainable using other methods. In recent times, the mailed questionnaire has been heavily criticized and has consequently fallen into some disfavor as a device for gathering data. The misuse of the questionnaire, rather than its nature, has been the cause of its poor reputation. To write down a set of questions, reproduce them in sufficient numbers, and mail them to subjects who are expected to complete and return them seems an easy way to gather research data. However, without careful attention to important details, such a plan will do little to shed light on researchable problems.

Construction. Preparation of a questionnaire instrument capable of delivering the necessary data involves three aspects. First, the researcher must learn how to ask a question that is definite and clearly presented, and one that generates an answer that is also definite and quantifiable. Second, the format of the questionnaire must be structured so that the respondent will not miss any item entirely and will have no difficulty in recording a response. It must be composed of a logical sequence of questions. Third, the instructions must be precisely stated so that all ambiguity is eliminated and the final plan for reproduction completed.

Questions should be asked in a way that will allow the answers to be easily organized for reduction in data processing. **Close-ended** questions which ask that the respondent choose from a provided list will, in most cases, provide more easily processed data than **open-ended** questions that permit the responding person to create an answer. The answer to an open-ended question must be interpreted, thus reducing the reliability of the data.

After the questions have been refined, they should be presented to a few persons similar to those who will receive the questionnaire. This will check whether the questions can be read quickly, whether the implied task is clear, and whether an answer can be easily obtained. The researcher should make an overview of the questions to assure that all of the needed data will be obtained and that the respondent is not asked to take time to give information that is not relevant to the study.

Since a respondent cannot ask questions of the researcher to clear up any ambiguity, the instructions and format determine to a large degree the success of the questionnaire and the usefulness of the collected data. An instrument with inadequate instructions and a confusing format that is discarded by a large proportion of those sampled will lower the validity of the data and may cause the project to be abandoned or may require mailing a new set of questionnaires. This can happen even to a set of excellent questions.

General instructions should include how the answers are to be given for close-ended questions and whether long or short answers are to be given for open-ended questions. An excellent guide for the respondent's answers might be a box by each listing for a close-ended question and a line or lines to limit the response to an open-ended question. (See Figure 10–4.) Another useful format to use when a particular answer generates another question is shown in Figure 10–5. The format of the questionnaire should include a logical ordering of the questions according to content and the contingency of one item on other items.

---

7. Which one of the following cities would you consider to offer the best environment for a promising young violinist to advance professionally?

New York	1 ☐
Boston	2 ☐
Philadelphia	3 ☐
Chicago	4 ☐
Dallas	5 ☐
Houston	6 ☐
Los Angeles	7 ☐
San Francisco	8 ☐
Other (specify)_____	9 ☐

OR

7. Which United States city do you consider to offer the best environment for a promising young violinist to advance professionally?_____

8. Why did you choose the particular city that you listed in number 7? _____

_____

_____

FIGURE 10–4   Two Different Structures for Responses to a Questionnaire

After the questions have been refined, the directions written, and the format developed, the copies for mailing must be prepared. The method of reproducing the questionnaire is important to achieving a high rate of return for the mailing. A questionnaire will look best and be received best if it is set in type; however, this is the most expensive method and requires the most time for preparation. Copies made by multilith or photo-offset processes are a close second to typeset copy and will generally be of acceptable quality for a mailed questionnaire, require less preparation time, and be less expensive. Dittoed or mimeographed copies are to be avoided unless the costs of the others are prohibitive. Enough copies should be prepared in the first run to cover staff use and final reports as well as subject copies.

---

12. Have you attended any of the meetings of the Educational Psychology Lecture Series this school year?

     NO _____

     YES _____

     If yes, check:

          1. Professor Clouse_____

          2. Professor Jerse _____

          3. Professor Sullins _____

FIGURE 10–5   A Contingency Question Format

Demographic data for a questionnaire should be obtained in a section at the end of the instrument. Remember to ask for only that information that the study requires.

A decision about whether to make the reply anonymous will have to be made. If validation of the data calls for a follow-up interview for a portion of the responses or if efforts will be made to learn characteristics of the nonrespondents, the inclusion of a name or at least an identifying number will, in most cases, not have a major influence on returns. If the questions are of such a nature that the request to supply a name would affect the returns, the respondents should be assured of anonymity. Anonymous returns do not allow validation of data, and since low returns cannot be supplemented by a follow-up without remailing to the complete sample, returns may be confounded by duplicate returns from subjects. As with most aspects of research procedures, the most important decisions must be made in context with all other aspects.

The researcher should prepare a highly refined device to gather the data necessary to answer the research question. The above general directions should be supplemented before actually undertaking questionnaire development (see Oppenheim, 1966, and Babbie, 1973, pp. 140–156).

Distribution. Having developed an appropriate device to gather the needed data, the researcher must identify the subjects who are to receive the questionnaire. The recipients may be all of the names on a previously prepared mailing list—such as all the members of an organization, all citizens in a geographic region, or some other list that is appropriate. Many times the ones to receive the questionnaire constitute a randomly selected sample of subjects from a larger population. Generalizations are made to the population based on information obtained from the sample. The usual procedures for drawing representative samples should be made to assure randomness and independence in selection. A major consideration that is often overlooked in early planning is the need for current addresses. An outdated mailing list or a list without addresses is of little value.

Since sample data are used for generalizations, a major concern for all questionnaire studies is the response rate or percentage of return. This rate is crucial to the success of the study. Imaginative techniques have been designed to encourage questionnaire returns. A return envelope that requires no postage or addressing is essential. As further inducement to the recipient, a small monetary reward is sometimes effective. A statement that makes the recipient aware of the importance of the study for him or her could increase returns. A promise to forward a report of the study for questionnaire completion may increase the rate of returns.

Returns. If feasible, mailed questionnaires can be scheduled to be picked up by the researcher or an assistant to increase the rate of return. The questionnaire may be hand delivered, explained, and left with the understanding that the mail will be used to return it. The less effort required from the respondent, the higher the rate of return. Follow-up mailings, telephone follow-ups, and personal calls can also be scheduled to increase the number of returns.

A question often asked about a set of data gathered through a mailed questionnaire is, What is an adequate percentage of returns to allow conclusions to be drawn? Any generalization from returns to the original sample or to the larger population assumes that each element of the sample returned a questionnaire. Of course, only rarely, if ever, will the returns be close to 100 percent. More important than percentage of returns is the study of possible bias in returns when considering the larger body being generalized to. If a return of 10 percent from a large sample had no bias, then the 10 percent return would be adequate. Let us hurriedly say that any 10 percent return is very likely to be biased, and that percentage of return would generally be unacceptable. A 10 percent return probably means that the device was poorly prepared, and only the 10 percent who felt very strongly about the issue would take time to return the questionnaire. Babbie states a very conservative set of figures for rate of return: 50 percent is adequate for analysis and reporting; 60 percent is good; and 70 percent is very good (1973, p. 165). He also points out that "a demonstrated lack of response bias is far more important than a high response rate" (p. 165). However, lack of response bias is associated with a high response rate. If there is a question about response bias, the researcher can compare answers from early respondents to answers from late respondents. The assumption behind this procedure is that responses of the very late returns will, in general, be much like those of the nonrespondents. The researcher might also compare demographic data for respondents and nonrespondents (Oppenheim, 1966, p. 34).

An accepted practice when figuring the rate of return is to reduce the potential sample size by the number of undeliverables and figure the percentage by dividing the number of returns by the net sample size (number mailed less those undelivered). If a mailing of 172 had 8 that were not delivered and 128 returns, the rate of return would be:

$$\frac{128}{172 - 8} = \frac{128}{164} \qquad (78\% \text{ return})$$

This procedure of taking net sample size for the denominator assumes that the undeliverables represent a random sample of the original sample. Any independence from bias would be difficult to establish because of the characteristics of a population that is not locatable.

Opinionnaire/Attitudinal Scale

The opinionnaire or attitudinal scale (Oppenheim, 1966) can be used in conjunction with a questionnaire or as a device by itself to gather data not obtainable through a questioning process. Rather than asking the respondent a question, the researcher can ask for a response expressing the extent to which the subject holds a certain opinion or attitude. Most attempts to determine attitudes and opinions use scaling. Scaling techniques (see Chapter 3) are based on formats that give order to response classes. Sometimes referred to as the "Likert technique," since Rensis Likert (Likert, 1932) used such a scale in an early study of attitudes, scaling is used widely to measure personal characteristics. Scaling can be used with statements to which the respondent can indicate personal agreement or disagreement while weighting this reponse by marking a point on an ordered scale. The original Likert scale used five categories—strongly agree, agree, undecided, disagree, and strongly disagree. Other numbers of categories and descriptors may be used to modify the general model to a specific need. Point values can be assigned for categories with an order from low to high scoring: 1 for the least favorable response to a high of 5 for the most favorable. Favorable may be "agree" or "disagree" depending on the opinion of the researcher.

Good procedure for scale development suggests that the favorable end of the scale be varied so that the respondent must give careful attention to each item rather than merely responding without weighing the statement. If she or he is expected to agree (or disagree) with all items, the validity of the measurements may be questioned. It is not necessary to provide numbers on the scale, since this can be supplied during the scoring procedures. Without numbers, the scale gives no indication of the correct (favorable) response. The score for the scale can be a composite or total for all of the items. For a 6-point scale using 20 statements, the highest score would be 120, and the lowest score would be 20. An average derived by dividing the total by the number of statements gives a position on the ordinal scale indicating the measure of the opinion or attitude under study. A high score or high average would indicate a favorable attitude ("favorable" as judged by the constructor of the scale).

Since respondents' reactions to items on Likert-type scales are much like those for a multiple-choice examination, total scores for scales can be treated much as other test data. If needed, a cross section of the sample for each item can also be determined by averaging all responses to each item. An average response for *item 1* could be obtained from responses to the first item and so on for all the statements or for a selected sample of statements.

Careful refinement of each statement is very important to make this technique function properly. True opinions or attitudes are sometimes difficult to obtain through scaling, because the desired response (that considered desirable by the researcher or society) is usually apparent to the respondent. The subject may tend to give the "obviously correct" response rather than a true personal feeling about the statement. A backlash against an obviously correct answer may also result when a respondent gives an obviously wrong answer. This is referred to as the "boomerang effect." The subject may for personal reasons give answers other than true feelings as a way of taking revenge (Masling, 1966).

Time given to learning about how others have used scaling for measuring attitudes, to careful preparation of statements, and to attention to detail, including scoring, is well spent for enhancing the probability of getting high-quality data.

Interview

The personal interview is a face-to-face meeting between a questioner and a responder, or an oral presentation of an opinionnaire or attitude scale. In most cases, the interview is organized around a structure much like a mailed questionnaire. However, the interview has a number of advantages over a mailed questionnaire that stem from the personal contact.

Interview Questions

I. Is your reaction to the use of the language laboratory for the last six weeks generally positive or negative?

  A. If positive—Did you like for the teacher to be able to hear your interaction with the program without your knowing about it?

    1. If YES—No more questions for I.

    2. If NO—Would you rather have the teacher give a test after each session?

      a. If YES—No more questions for I.

      b. If NO—How do you think you should be evaluated? (Open-ended)

  B. If negative—Would you rather study the way the school has traditionally taught language?

    1. If YES—No more questions for I.

    2. If NO—What alternatives do you see? (Open-ended)

FIGURE 10–6 Branching Question: Assessing Student Reaction to a Language Laboratory

The response to an interview can be expected to be greater than that to a questionnaire, with returns of over 90 percent not uncommon. The interview permits an interaction not readily available within the usual structure of the questionnaire, allowing the respondent to clarify the question asked and the questioner to probe for the specific meanings of answers. A structure can be developed which allows for branching of questions based on the respondent's answers. A question that asks for a response of *agree* or *disagree* could have different follow-up questions for different responses. There might also be a follow-up question for one response but none for another. Figure 10–6 is a sample interview question sheet that shows how an interviewer could be prepared with contingency questions for differing responses.

Since quantitative data are desirable, the directness of the interview provides a way of obtaining objective data about some variables of a personal nature that may be difficult to obtain any other way. The interviewer also has the opportunity to get answers by direct observation, which is not possible for a response taken from a mailed questionnaire. A major disadvantage of the interview is the amount of time involved in gathering data. Interviews are expensive in terms of money and time expended, so the interview method should not be used if a more economical way of gathering the data will be equally effective. Most of the procedures for preparing a questionnaire apply equally to preparing the interview, and the previous discussion can be used as a guideline for structuring the order of questions and the recording of responses.

The appearance and manner of the interviewer is an added factor. As a rule, the interviewer should dress about the same way he or she expects the people to be interviewed to dress. The interviewer should assume a neutral position, so that the validity of the responses is not affected by the way the interview is conducted. To increase the reliability of the data, each question should be asked exactly the same way each time, and the responses should be recorded immediately on a previously structured recording sheet. This sheet could be in the form of a checklist. (See Chapter 3.)

Practice interviews assist in developing a thorough understanding of the total interview and its parts, as well as familiarizing the interviewer with the specific procedures of administration. If more than one person is to do the interviewing, practice sessions allow comparison of results and agreement as to what reaction should be made, given certain conditions while interviewing. The procedures should be checked to see that sufficient and accurate information is provided for interpretation. By gathering demographic data first rather than last, as is done in the questionnaire, the interviewer has an opportunity to build rapport with subjects.

As we have learned to expect from human involvement, interviewer bias may be difficult to overcome even when steps are made to objectify the interaction. Preparation for the interview and well-planned procedures for recording responses do much to keep objectivity in the process.

Tests

Testing instruments are the most widely used measuring devices for assessing the characteristics of concern to education. Well-prepared and validated tests yield descriptions of behavior that can be used to explain present status, changes over a time interval, and future expected performance. These descriptions may also be used to make comparisons between/among individuals and groups of subjects.

Scores on tests may serve as the basis for making comparisons between/ among groups being studied. If tests have norms (reported averages) for groups with certain known characteristics, then like groups or individuals can be compared to these norming groups. An appropriate test can be a powerful tool for the correlationist who studies conditions as they exist by establishing relationships and indications of cause and effect.

Proper use of the psychological test in research requires an understanding of test theory, even though a new test may not have to be developed primarily for a study. Appendix A in this book is devoted to tests. Further sources outside this text can aid the researcher in proper selection and use of existing tests and in the development of new instruments.

In selecting a test for a research study, the researcher needs a thorough understanding of a well-defined construct to fit the measuring instrument (the test) to what is being measured (the construct). Researchers have generally found contributions from achievement and aptitude testing to have more utility for educational research than work done in the area of personality testing. The study of personality and related constructs is—at least for the present—best left to clinicians who have particular expertise in this important area. Anyone planning a study in this area should at least have close touch with such a specialist.

Self Report

Inventories, blanks, and lists are useful self-reporting devices for gathering information from subjects about their likes and dislikes. This information can be compared with the known likes or dislikes of particular groups. It can also be used to compare two or more groups, an individual at different times, or a group at different times.

Any self-report device is intended to get at the wealth of information that a subject has about himself or herself, especially inner feelings that may be difficult to identify in other ways. The validity of the data rests heavily on the subject's ability and willingness to report true feelings. If the right information is requested and if the individual responds accurately, then the self report is a valuable tool in describing and studying real-world conditions.

Facts about a person's past can be very helpful in making predictions about the future. Self-report inventories that ask a series of questions—such as the following—may help to explain the expected future through prediction or may contribute to studies of relationships.

How many movies have you attended in the last 7 days?

None	1	_____
One	2	_____
Two	3	_____
Three or four	4	_____
Five or six	5	_____
Seven	6	_____
More than seven (specify _____)	7	_____

Other questions can be asked to determine interests through use of time: How would you spend a rainy afternoon if you could do anything you wanted to? A sunny afternoon? Or a cold winter afternoon?

Another technique, forced choice, is used to identify groups of interests by subjects' responses. In a forced choice, the subject being inventoried chooses, from various situations, the one that he or she would most enjoy and the one he or she would least enjoy. Choices might include fishing, wrestling, hiking, and so on. Patterns in a series of responses indicate interests.

Two standardized inventories are good examples of how self reports can be used in vocational guidance. Both *Strong's Vocational Interests Blank* (Campbell, 1927–1977) and the *Kuder Preference Record Form* (Kuder, 1934–1976) use groupings of interests, as reported by subjects, to fit with groupings of known interests of people actively engaged in particular occupations. Chemists tend to like to do the same things and used-car salesmen tend to have common interests, as do all job-alike people, but the *sets* of interests for each are different. A set of interests for an individual can be fit to a like set for a specific occupation to give guidance for selecting a vocation. Research studies find self-reporting devices a valuable help when data about inner feelings are required.

Mechanical Devices

Instruments are another consideration when a researcher is deciding how best to gather needed data. A mechanical device that introduces no new variable into a situation can be valuable in studying the world the way that it exists, because any mechanical device is designed to record ongoing events or conditions. For example, a carefully concealed thermometer to measure temperature changes within a school room is not likely to confound the usual classroom situation. Introducing a television camera with operating personnel might, on the other hand, change the setting so much that information collected would lose its validity when generalized to the usual situation.

The potential for introducing change must be a major concern when making a final decision about the use of mechanical instruments. If introducing a camera or other device would alter the data obtained from that setting, it may not be appropriate. In some cases, introducing the device for a period of time before data collection begins could overcome the impact of an abrupt change.

Sociometric Devices

Sociometry establishes the social structure of a defined group. In most cases, a situation is established, and each subject chooses one or more other subjects according to a hypothesized relationship. In a sociometric design, each subject could, for example, be asked to identify one member of the group to take him or her to the first-aid room to have a cut administered to. From the responses, a network of relationships could be exhibited on a sociogram. A *sociogram* is a figure that shows each of the choices and points up the most popular members of the group, the isolates, and other relationships of interest to the investigator. Sociometric techniques allow the researcher to ascertain the social structure of the group as determined by peers. What the sociogram or other device does is exhibit the social structure for one situation at one point in time, as illustrated in Figure 10–7. It is a way of describing present status. Social interaction is so complex that direct observation does little to detect the relationships. Of course, this structure is in constant change. A study that looks at two structures with a time interval between can be used to study effects of what happened in the interval.

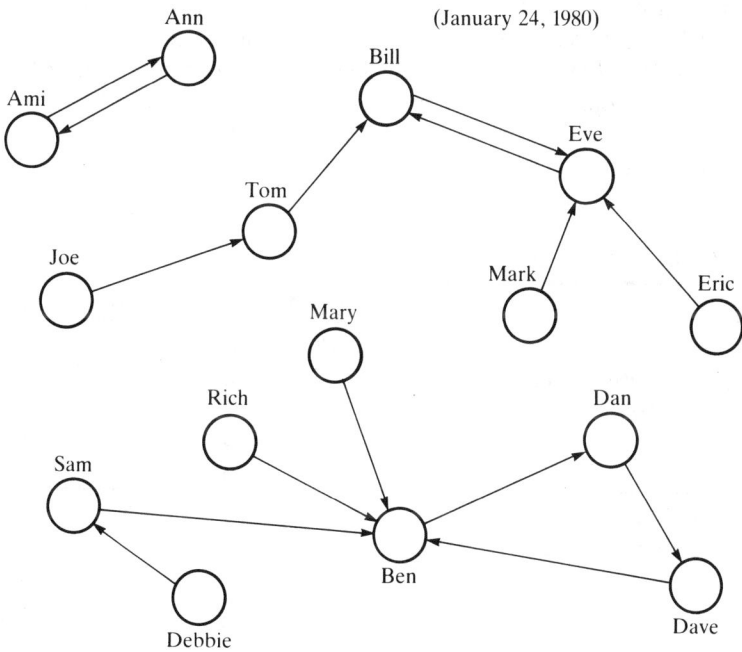

FIGURE 10–7   Sociogram for a Second-grade Class

Statistics

Q methodology is well suited to the study of one individual. In its simplest form, Q methodology uses a rank ordering of statements. After an individual ranks the statements, a correlational technique compares those rankings to rankings from one or more other individuals. A set of individuals can be grouped by finding clusters of individuals who react alike to the statements.

If three registered Republicans and three registered Democrats were asked to rank eight people seeking the office of governor, the Republicans would tend to rank Republican office seekers higher than Democratic candidates, while the Democrats would tend to rank Democrats higher than Republicans. Using a rank of one as high and eight as low, the ranking might look like the data in Table 10–1. The data show that Democrats did rank Democrats higher than Republican candidates and vice versa, as was expected. Q techniques are extended to more complex studies that are not as obvious as the well-managed example in Table 10–1. Any set of objects, statements, art objects, words, and so on can be ranked by an individual, with comparisons made individual to individual, individual to group, or group to group.

The *Q sort* is a modification of the ranking just described. The principle of ordering could be used for placing cards with statements from a large deck in a predetermined distribution according to certain criteria. For example, a large number of statements—50 to 100—about a certain topic could be placed in a scale from *agree* to *disagree*. An arrangement for 70 statement cards might ask for the distribution in Table 10–2. A study of the placement of cards in the extreme three classifications is usually used in interpretation. Q methodology is especially useful to the correlationist's study of real-world conditions. Discovery techniques often need the heuristic quality of the Q in opening up new areas.

TABLE 10–1 Rankings of Eight Candidates for Governor

		Republican Voters			Democratic Voters		
		A	B	C	D	E	F
Democratic	G	8	7	8	1	2	1
candidates	H	7	8	7	2	1	4
	I	6	2	4	3	4	6
	J	5	6	6	4	5	2
Republican	K	4	5	3	5	8	3
candidates	L	3	4	5	6	7	8
	M	2	3	1	7	6	7
	N	1	1	2	8	3	5

TABLE 10-2 Q-sort Distribution of 70 Cards

	Disagree								Agree
Value of category	8	7	6	5	4	3	2	1	0
Number of statements to be placed in each category	2	4	7	13	18	13	7	4	2

More specific uses and a more detailed discussion of Q appears in Chapter 34 of *Foundations of Behavioral Research* (Kerlinger, 1973, pp. 582–600).

Existing Information

Analysis of existing data may be a source of information for descriptive studies. Objective use of data already collected is a possibility in special cases for testing hypotheses developed from data other than those used in the study. Of course, the researcher cannot develop a hypothesis from certain data and then test the hypothesis by using the same data or even part of it.

Two major disadvantages to the use of existing data should discourage this technique if any other method is available. First, the data available are limited to those that have been collected and recorded—they may or may not represent an adequate sample of what is being studied. Second, it is difficult and dangerous in conclusin making to assume a direct relationship between variables studied in this way. However, the art of researching and use of innovative methods permit using existing data if this is the only way to attack the question under study. In this technique, the methods are more important than the data.

Techniques of Anthropology

Not only is the **anthropological approach** gaining much support in educational research, but it is also being identified as a technique which overcomes some of the limitations of coverage and accuracy of psychological data. New techniques are being created and older ones are being given new life by updating. Attention to the impact of social climate and the use of naturalistic observation to supplement tests are becoming increasingly popular in psychological research, especially in studies of infants, mentally retarded people, and brain-damaged people. Although they are not as extensive as the field-study approach of the anthropologist, the new approaches are moving toward the nature of anthropological field studies (McReynolds, 1974).

Many educators feel that the time is long overdue for another approach in educational research and that anthropological procedures should be used more in educational research. The anthropological field method is seen by some as an excellent way to develop a hypothesis, since "development of hypotheses is the special province of anthropological field method" (Lutz & Ramsey, 1974, p. 5). These proponents feel that educational researchers are "often led to a 'quick and dirty' hypothesis, at best armchaired after some library search of appropriate literature and study of theory " (Lutz & Ramsey, 1974, p. 5) and that the field methods add a new dimension to hypothesis development.

Anthropological field research studies a complete socioculture system in studying humans. In education, the system studied would be the educational system or one of its subsystems. Such a methodology amounts to more than simply writing a description of something that happens in a school setting. Field research and statistical studies must be carefully designed. Those without carefully thought-out procedures "are worth the amount of conceptual thought that has been put into them—nothing" (Lutz & Ramsey, 1974, p. 5). Educational researchers who think that **field study** could best answer their questions are encouraged to go to the original works listed in references for the Lutz and Ramsey article, to prepare and execute a valid field study using anthropological methods. Also useful is an article by Peter Snidell (1969), which has an extensive bibliography. With additional excellent studies using this method, the field study may become more accepted as a valuable tool for studying educational questions.

☐CHECK YOUR UNDERSTANDING

From the widely used data-collection tools listed below, choose the most appropriate one for each of the following situations (1–5).

Direct observation   Questionnaire
Mechanical device   Opinionnaire
Sociometric device   Attitudinal scale
Self report   Interview

1. The researcher wants to identify personal problems that junior high school students have—as individuals and as a group.
2. The researcher needs to establish the social structure of a specific classroom organization being tried experimentally in several elementary schools.
3. The researcher is concerned about the effects of certain classroom innovations on the aggressiveness of preschool children.
4. The researcher needs data about certain personal habits of a set of women students and very complex sets of questions are contingent on particular responses.
5. The American Educational Research Association would like to collect information relating to what functions members serve in their professional assignments.

Answers

1. Self report
2. Sociometric device
3. Direct observation
4. Interview
5. Questionnaire

Tools for Interpreting Data

When the data have been collected, they must be interpreted. Researchers generally use statistics to make these interpretations. Although conclusions eventually involve using judgment, standard statistical procedures lend objectivity to reporting results. The researcher must present a logically conceived statement of the data not only for use in the study but also for dissemination of conclusions to the profession. Statistical techniques help sort out the messages which the data hold.

Organizing the Facts

Data have been defined as facts where a fact is any bit of information which the researcher deems appropriate for helping decide whether the study supports or does not support the research hypothesis. The data could be a set of numbers generated by a rating scale, a set of responses to a questionnaire, a set of test scores, and so on. Each type of data must be processed keeping in mind the nature of the data— quantitative data being easier to handle than qualitative data. The phase of organizing the information collected for the study is most directly concerned with reducing the data, studying variation, and studying relationships.

Organization of the obtained information is the first task of interpretation. Descriptive studies tend to have large amounts of data that need formal processing, especially of the questionnaire, interview, or direct observation method has been used. If the planning of the study fits a logical chain of reasoning and all the steps fit together, questionnaires, checklists, and such will be organized with interpretation in mind.

For large amounts of data, the machine-readable **punchcard** reduces a very large volume of data about a subject to a series of holes that can be read by a computer or other data-processing equipment (Babbie, 1973, pp. 187–203). In fact, good data management permits a keypunch operator who codes the cards to work directly from returned questionnaires and other types of data sheets. If the type of data does not allow the necessary organization, another step must be included to get from the original form to a form that is encodable.

For smaller amounts of data, **tables** (see Appendix C) may be sufficient to present the data or allow for calculation. With hand and desk calculators able to handle **raw data** easily, calculation by hand is rarely used today. For large amounts of information, a series of tables may be needed to present the data clearly. **Graphs** (see Appendix C) may be needed to give the researcher and readers an overall picture of the data.

Tables. Tables will be needed in most studies. They are used to present data in the final report and may aid in statistical calculations. Formats for setting up tables vary from one style manual to another, but they all include basically the same components and perform the same major function: to arrange and present statistical data in a form that enables a reader to extract with little effort the meaning of the raw data. To do that, the tables should

1. Be self-explanatory. The title and contents should convey the meaning without reference to the text.
2. Be in rank order or other logical sequence. This makes comparisons easy.

3. Be broken when they contain long columns by leaving space after every 5 or 10 rows.
4. Have all necessary columns. This is especially important if the table is used for computation.
5. Be in the format of the chosen style manual.

Frequency tables (see Table 10–5 and the related graph in Figure 10–8) are used to report the frequencies of occurrence of reported values for one variable. Tables can also be used to report data and the logic of bivariate analysis (two variables) and multivariate analysis. **Contingency tables** (see Table 10–3) report for more than one variable, just as frequency tables report univariate analysis. Contingency tables for analysis divide variables into subgroups and report in cells the frequencies, proportions, or percentages of observations. Two variables, each divided into two parts, can be shown as in Table 10–3, and for more than two subgroups the contingency would look like Table 10–4. For variables that are not dichotomous more than two subgroups can be formed.

TABLE 10–3 Table of Bivariate Analysis

"Did you attend the book exhibit in the public library during the week of September 16 to 23?"

	Boys	Girls
Yes	27%	54%
No	73%	46%

TABLE 10–4 Table of Bivariate Analysis

"Did you attend the book exhibit in the public library during the week of September 16 to 23?"

	Boys			Girls		
Grades:	7th	8th	9th	7th	8th	9th
Yes	45%	15%	20%	46%	51%	64%
No	55%	85%	80%	54%	49%	36%

Well-constructed tables of data can add much to the understanding of a study by bridging the gap between sets of raw unorganized data and the manuscript text. Tables and figures including graphs, help the researcher analyze data and promote the readers' understanding of the research.

Graphs. Graphs provide a way of giving a very quick look at a set of data through pictorial representation of important characteristics. Either a table or graph, or both, can represent a frequency distribution made up of frequencies of occurrences in sets of data. Creative uses of graphs and other figures provide additional ways to present data. Figures 10–8 and 10–11 illustrate how these can be varied for different uses. Different purposes direct the construction of graphs and vary the final product. The following principles should be considered when building a graph.

1. Label both axes.
2. The sequence of data should be low values to the left and high values to the right on the horizontal axis, and low values at the bottom and high values at the top on the vertical axis.
3. The zero point for the vertical axis should be the intersection of the axes. When this guideline must be violated, the researcher should indicate it by a break in the axis line.
4. The ratio of height to width should be about 3:5 or 2:3, and the units should be chosen so that no extreme distortion takes place.

TABLE 10-5   Frequency Tables

			Interval Limits				
Interval	Tally	f	Apparent	Exact	f	cf	cpf
63–65		1	63–65	62.5–65.5	1	34	100
60–62		1	60–62	59.5–62.5	1	33	97
57–59		2	57–59	56.5–59.5	2	32	94
54–56		4	54–56	53.5–56.5	4	30	88
51–53		9	51–53	50.5–53.5	9	26	76
48–50		6	48–50	47.5–50.5	6	17	50
45–47		5	45–47	44.5–47.5	5	11	32
42–44		2	42–44	41.5–44.5	2	6	18
39–41		1	93–41	38.5–41.5	2	4	12
36–38		2	36–38	35.5–38.5	2	3	9
33–35		1	33–35	32.5–35.5	1	1	3
		34			N=34		

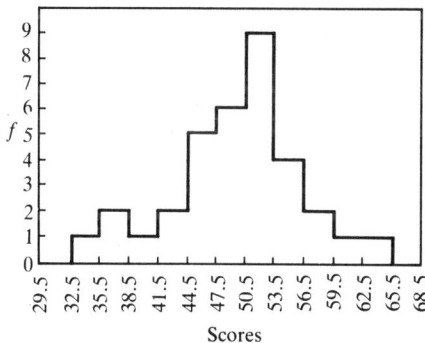

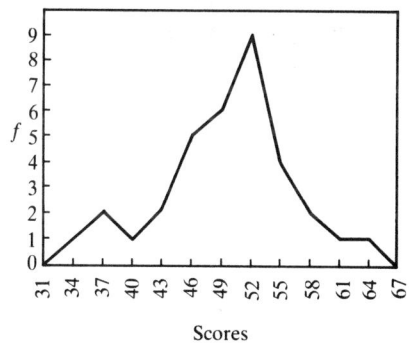

Note. From *Describing Data Statistically,* by Charles D. Hopkins. Copyright 1974 by Bell & Howell Company.

FIGURE 10–8   Sample Graphs

Tables and graphs have the advantage of presenting large quantities of data for quick overall interpretation. In addition, organization of correlation coefficients in a matrix allows the researcher and readers to see specific points of importance. In the Gallimore et al study, for example, the "general classroom attentiveness" and "male sibling caretaking" relationship can be read directly by finding the intersection of row 11 and column 2. Other relationships are equally easy to read.

Scatter Diagram. The **scattergram** is a very important interpretive tool for a correlationist. Since the scattergram gives a quick pictorial view of the relationship between two sets of data, it serves two major purposes for a researcher. It gives a quick portrayal of a relationship without deriving a correlation coefficient, and it is a vehicle for displaying relationship in graphic form.

The scattergram is constructed on a two-dimensional graph by plotting points that represent measures on two variables. In most cases, the measurements will be pairs of values for a common subject. The relationship is revealed by patterns in the scattergram. Patterns of linear relationship take shape when the data form along an imaginary line. In Figure 10–9, the pattern in (A) shows a positive or direct linear relationship, and (B) shows a negative or inverse linear relationship for the two variables that are being investigated.

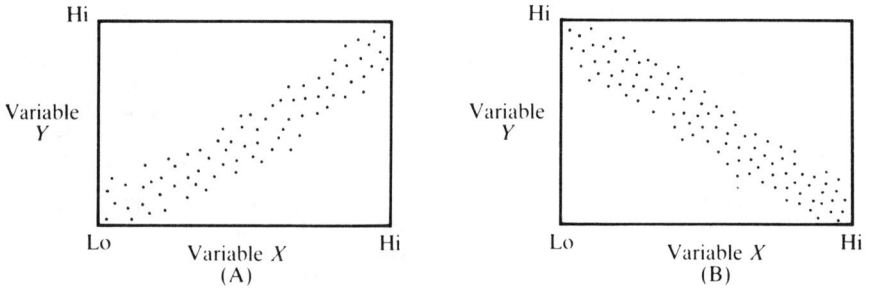

FIGURE 10–9   Positive and Negative Relationships for Variables X and Y

The scattergram in Figure 10–10 reveals no discernible relationship between two variables. The dashed lines for one point *(a)* for subject A show how the scattergram is built. Each of the other points similarly represents two measurements for one subject.

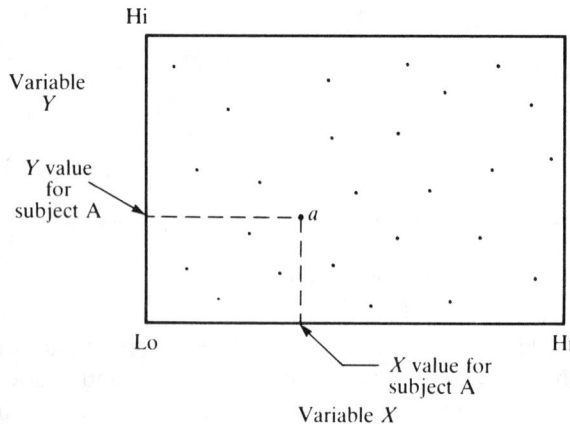

FIGURE 10–10   Scattergram Reflecting No Relationship

The closer the dots approach to forming a line, the greater the relationship. If the line moves up as the values on the X variable increase (left to right), the relationship is positive. If the line moves down as the values on the X variable increase (left to right), the relationship is negative. Correlational techniques discussed later in this chapter give an index for quantitative measure of the relationship between variables. Many lesser-used types of graphs and figures can be helpful for special needs in interpreting data.

The preliminary overview of most sets of data is facilitated through the use of diagrams—tables, graphs, or figures. Diagrams also aid the researcher and reader in bridging the gap from raw data to conclusions and provide a convenient way to shorten the narrative of research reports through data organization. Tables, graphs, figures, and diagrams are not a substitute for statistical tests, but are rather integral parts of the interpretive phase of research.

Frequency Distribution

The study of **frequency distribution** can reveal some very important facts about the data. The four characteristics of distributions—**central location, variability, skewness,** and **kurtosis**—give the correlationist an opportunity to get at information that may be hidden in sets of raw data. The frequency distribution can be presented in either tabular or graphic form (see Figure 10–8 and accompanying Table 10–5) and comparison of a number of frequency distributions indicates how they are different. Frequency is abbreviated as f.

Central Tendency. One characteristic of distributions is the grouping of scores within a limited interval on the scale. One value could be chosen as a value to indicate how the scores tend to center around a central point (see Appendix C). What one score could be chosen to represent the distribution well? Some studies use the value that appears most often (the mode), others use the arithmetical average (the mean), and still others choose a point that divides the number of values into two equal parts (the **median**). The rules used to assign the numerical descriptors determine to a large degree the indicator of central tendency that can be used to describe the frequency distribution. Central tendency for nominal data can be shown only by the mode; for ordinal data the mode or median can be used; and for interval and ratio data the mode, median, or mean may be used. The most used measure of **central tendency** (the mean) is the simple arithmetical average as determined by dividing the sum of all the values by the number of values that were summed (see Appendix C). The sample study of sibling caretaking effects reported mean values (Table 1) for the observations since the data gathered were interval by assignment of measures.

Variability. Another characteristic of distributions is variability. Although a measure of central tendency is important, it gives no information about the dispersion of scores. Widely used measures of dispersion are range, variance, and standard deviation. Lesser used measures are quartile deviation and average deviation. There are several answers to the question, How are these scores scattered or dispersed? The researcher could (1) give the difference between the highest value and the lowest value (the range), (2) find how each score differs from the mean, square that difference, and take an arithmetical average of the squared differences (the variance), or (3) find the square root of the variance (the standard deviation).

The concept of variation with *nominal data* cannot be formally summarized because the numerical descriptors were assigned without magnitude. The variation rests in the occurrence of values in the mutually exclusive categories used for assignment. A little-used measure of dispersion for ordinal data, the quartile deviation, is reported as one-half of the interval determined by the middle 50 percent of the values. A little-used measure of dispersion for interval data averages the absolute values of deviation scores (average deviation). The most mathematically useful measures (variance and standard deviation) for interval data use the mean square of the squared deviations of a set of scores from their mean. Figure 10–11 represents pictorially the idea of a mean square. Computations for Figure 10–11 would be represented in a format like the accompanying table.

Score X	Mean $\overline{X}$	$(X - \overline{X})$	$(X - \overline{X})^2$
64	60	+4	16
63	60	+3	9
62	60	+2	4
59	60	−1	1
57	60	−3	9
55	60	−5	25
		0	64

The **mean square** for the squares with areas of 25, 9, 1, 4, 9, and 16 is determined by adding the areas of the 6 squares and dividing by the number of squares, 6. (25 + 9 + 1 + 4 + 9 + 16)/6 equals 64/6, or 10.67. The *mean square* or *variance* for the 6 listed values is 10.67 units (see Appendix C). This is a two-dimensional description of the dispersion of scores. The square root of the variance, 10.67 or 3.27 (see Appendix C), is the dispersion expressed in one dimension and is called the **standard deviation.** The large part played by the study of differences or variation in research makes these two statistics very valuable to all researchers. The analysis of variance is a study of the sources of the differences and makes up a large part of statistical procedures. Properties of the standard deviation make it valuable in interpreting distributions and in tests of significance. The descriptive sample study, Gallimore et al, reported (Table 1) the variability of the groups as standard deviations.

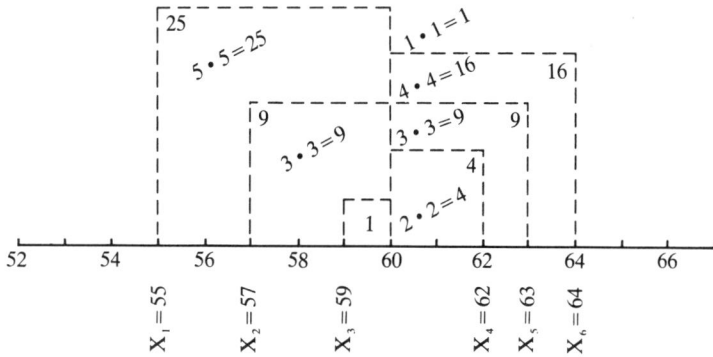

Note. From Describing Data Statistically, by Charles D. Hopkins. Copyright 1974 by Bell & Howell Company.

FIGURE 10–11   A Graph for a Computation

Skewness. A study of the symmetry of a distribution can be reported by describing any *skewness* associated with the scores. If there is no indication of highly deviate scores (scores not like the rest), the distribution will be nearly symmetrical and therefore not skewed. Deviate scores at the end with high values of the variable being measured result in a positively skewed distribution, while deviate values at the end with low variable values result in a negatively skewed distribution. The data in Figure 10–8 reveal a slight tendency toward negative skewness. Skewness is associated with only those variables measured as interval or ratio, since equal intervals are needed to develop a concept of being deviate (see Figure 10–12).

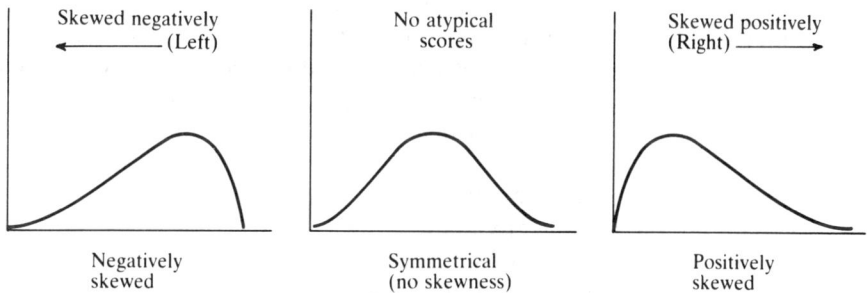

FIGURE 10–12   Three Frequency Distributions with Different Skewness

Kurtosis. A characteristic closely related to variability is *kurtosis*. A graphical representation of a frequency distribution that is peaked in the center is called *leptokurtic* and results from measurements on subjects that are homogeneous (much alike) on the variable being measured. A graph that is very flat is called *platykurtic* and results from measurements on subjects that are heterogeneous (much different) on the variable being measured. A graph that is bell-shaped (neither leptokurtic nor platykurtic) is called *Mesokurtic*. Illustrations showing the characteristics leptokurtic, platykurtic, and mesokurtic are shown in Figure 10–13. Kurtosis is associated only with data that have equal intervals in the assignment of numerical descriptors.

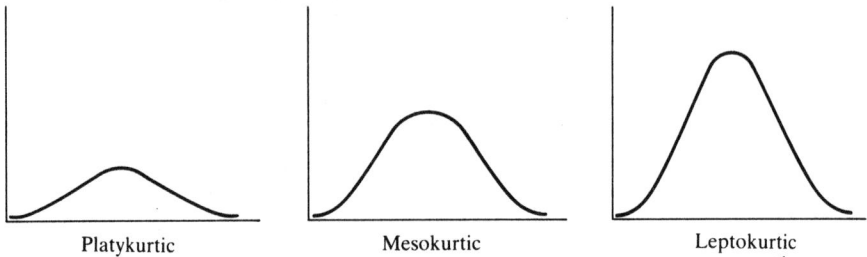

Platykurtic   Mesokurtic   Leptokurtic

FIGURE 10–13 Three Frequency Distributions with Different Kurtosis

The properties of central tendency, variation, skewness, and kurtosis, are used to describe sets of values presented as frequency distributions. A descriptive study interprets observations through studying relationships within a set of scores and, more importantly, relationships between sets of observations using these properties as a basis for comparison.

Variance

Statisticians have been criticized for treating all elements of a large population the same when representing all the values with a mean. If that were all that is done to interpret the scores in the distribution, then the criticism would be well-founded. The critics are saying, "You have forgotten to look at differences." This supposed blind spot has inspired a number of jokes about people who put too much confidence in one statistic. One is told about the nonswimming statistician who drowned in a lake that had an average depth of two feet because she put too much confidence in a mean value. There was also the statistician who had his head in the refrigerator and his feet in the oven and, on the average, felt very comfortable. Contrary to this image projected in popular culture, statisticians do spend a considerable amount of time looking at variability.

A considerable part of statistics is devoted to comparing variances—as in the F-test—and to determining scores of variance—as, for example, analysis-of-variance designs. The variance (mean square) for a set of scores is a measure of the dispersion of the scores (see Figure 10–11) and is used to explain one of the characteristics of a frequency distribution. If two or more groups are being examined and/or compared, the measure of variability gives a basis for comparing the degree of scattering of the scores between groups. If the property of the groups being examined has much the same variance in each group, they tend to be much alike on that property. If the variances are much different, then the groups are not alike on that property.

Differences in variance can be very important in research. For example, visualize two highways that have these characteristics: average (mean) speeds of the cars on highway A and highway B are very close and the variance of the speed of cars on highway A is much greater than the variance of car speeds for highway B. How will the traffic flow be different? Which highway would you predict to have fewer accidents? Probably the most important question to the traffic researcher is Why do the speeds vary so much for highway A? What is the source of the variance? The analysis of variance and related statistics give much attention to identifying sources of the differences of variation. For some reason(s), the drivers on highway B drove much the same (the variance was small), while those on highway A had large differences among the speeds, although the average speed was about the same as that on highway B. Possibly the source of variance was in the cars—maybe some were very old and could not travel very fast, while others were newer and more difficult to drive slowly. Possibly the difference was in road conditions—curves and hills on highway A might cause variation in speeds. Maybe the source of variance was in the drivers—older drivers who drove very slowly and younger drivers who drove very fast could explain a large variance for highway A. Some of the variance might be attributed to other causes, and possibly some would result from chance and remain unexplained.

Techniques of analysis of variance are used more widely in experimental research, but the study of sources of variance is still much a part of the correlational study, as evidenced by the use of analysis techniques by Sir Ronald A. Fisher (1970, pp. 213–339).

Percentage

A convenient way of presenting data (especially nominal data) for inspection is to change numbers of cases to percentages and report the percentages in tables. For example, the Sharp-Kirk study (Sample Study No. 3) uses percentages in Table 1 to report frequency of initiating counseling. These percentages may be used to compare change over time as well as differences in requests for counseling from male and female students. Further interpretation of the percentage data in a study usually includes some statistical test about differences.

The usual testing procedure for differences in nominal data is to use chi-square tests. However, percentages can be tested directly by a technique that uses a **nomograph** that interprets differences between two percentages for statistical significance. Although the nomograph lacks the precision of chi square, it is accurate enough for an initial test. Where the differences border on significance, the usual chi-square technique can be used. For tables and more information about the use of nomographs, see Oppenheim's presentation (1966, pp. 287–292).

Measures of Relationship

An extension of the concept of variation of scores on one variable is the study of simultaneous variation of two variables. Many techniques of correlation (covariation) are available to assist the researcher in identifying relationships more precisely than the scattergrams are able to do. Reflect that the Gallimore et al sample study of sibling caretaking effects used many coefficients to report relationships between pairs of groups. Measures of relationships are direct indexes* in that they reveal both the direction (nature) and the degree (magnitude) of how the two variables are related. The numerical descriptors of correlation range from -1.00 through 0 to $+1.00$, with -1.00 indicating perfect negative correlation and $+1.00$ perfect positive correlation. As a descriptor, 0.00 indicates no relationship between the two variables.

Correlation is central to research based in observation of real-world conditions and to cases where experimental studies are not feasible. In general, the calculation of the index (coefficient of correlation) by formula is straightforward. Any correlational technique produces a coefficient that stands as an estimate of the covarying of the variables. For example, the question, How do rankings of famous paintings by elementary school children compare to rankings given by college art majors? implies a study of the relationship between sets of rankings from two groups with wide differences on important characteristics. If the two groups tend to rank the art objects much the same, that relationship will be reflected in a positive coefficient: the higher the relationship, the closer to $+1.00$. If the two groups disagree in the rankings, the inverse relationship will be reflected in a negative coefficient: the higher the relationship, the closer to -1.00.

Since the preceding numerical descriptors (ranks) are ordinal in nature, an appropriate technique must be chosen. Spearman's coefficient of rank correlation is appropriate where the measurement has been made on two sets of ordinal data. The formula (see Appendix C) used is a derivation of a product-moment coefficient where the assignment of ranks assumes equal intervals. Nearly all correlation formulas—with the exception of Kendall's τ, which is a study of disarray (1962)—are based on the Pearson product-moment rationale (see Appendix C).

The choice of which correlational technique to use is based on the scales of the data for the two variables. Table 10–6 will help the student researcher identify appropriate techniques for combinations of scales of measurement of the two variables. Nominal variables suitable for correlational techniques have been further classified as dichotomous (true dichotomy) and dichotomized (forced dichotomy). An example of a dichotomous variable where the division is natural would be *male-female,* and an example of a dichotomized variable, where the division is artificial and gives up some information, would be *greater than median height* and *less than median height.*

Prediction

One aim of science is to be able to make reliable **predictions** of the future from information available in the present. Theory building deals with

---

*An index is a number that is made up of two or more numbers. The *cost of living index* is a weighted mean of typical prices of requirements of life, weighted according to the amount needed. The Dow-Jones average is an index of the price of several stocks.

TABLE 10–6 Appropriate Correlational Techniques for Combinations of Different Measurements

Measurement characteristics		Coefficient and symbol	Statistical examples
Variable X	Variable Y		
Continuous (Interval, ratio, or combination)	Continuous	Pearson Product Moment (r)	Relationship between the continuous variable height (X) and the continuous weight (Y) of a set of subjects
Continuous	True dichotomy[1]	Point Biserial (r_{pb})	Relationship between the continuous variable, history test scores (X), and the dichotomous answer (true or false) for item no. 1 (Y)
Continuous	Forced dichotomy[2]	Biserial (r_b)	Relationship between continuous mental ability test scores (X) and a dichotomy that has been forced for above or below the average score on a reading comprehension test (Y)
Forced dichotomy[2]	Forced dichotomy[2]	Tetrachoric (r_t)	Relationship of position on two tests when subjects are rated dichotomously as being above or below the median of IQ test (X) and also dichotomously on a measure of hand grip (Y)
True dichotomy[1]	True dichotomy[1]	Phi ϕ	Relationship of a true dichotomy of married/unmarried students (X) and another true dichotomy of working/nonworking students (Y)
Ranks (or capable of being ranked)	Ranks	Spearman rho ρ	Relationship of ranks for a set of paintings by art majors (X) and ranks by business majors (Y)
Nominal (or categorized)	Nominal	Contingency Coefficient (C)	Relationship of two sets of nominal data for socioeconomic status background (X or Y) and choice of favorite color (X or Y)

[1] A true dichotomy results from measurement that is made on mere presence or absence of the variable.

[2] A forced dichotomy results when an assumed normal distribution is artificially divided into two parts (test scores above 75; test scores below 75).

explaining and predicting and much of the utility of theory is being able to predict. Some scholars are ready to say that prediction is all important and that explanation is not needed if prediction gives the needed control. Explanation does become important when dealing with generalizations, however. To discover that students do less well in a testing situation when the noise level is very high will allow prediction about student performance in noisy testing environments and will in turn give direction to control of testing conditions. More important to the development of theory would be an explanation of the inner workings of all of the interrelated variables to explain why the noise affected the test scores.

Prediction and correlation are closely related topics. The level of confidence for a prediction depends on the degree of linear relationship between the predictor variable and the predicted variable. In making predictions from a scattergram where the points fall close to a line (high relationship), the confidence of prediction will be very high. As the dots spread farther from the line (less relationship), the confidence of being close in the prediction becomes less and less. The principle of prediction (**regression**) uses the shared relationship of two variables to forecast values on one variable, Y (the predicted), from the other variable, X (the predictor). The predictions are made by developing an equation for a line to fit the data. In Figure 10–12, the predictions on variable Y will be made from values on variable X. The relationship, $Y' = a + b(X)$, is used to make the predictions.

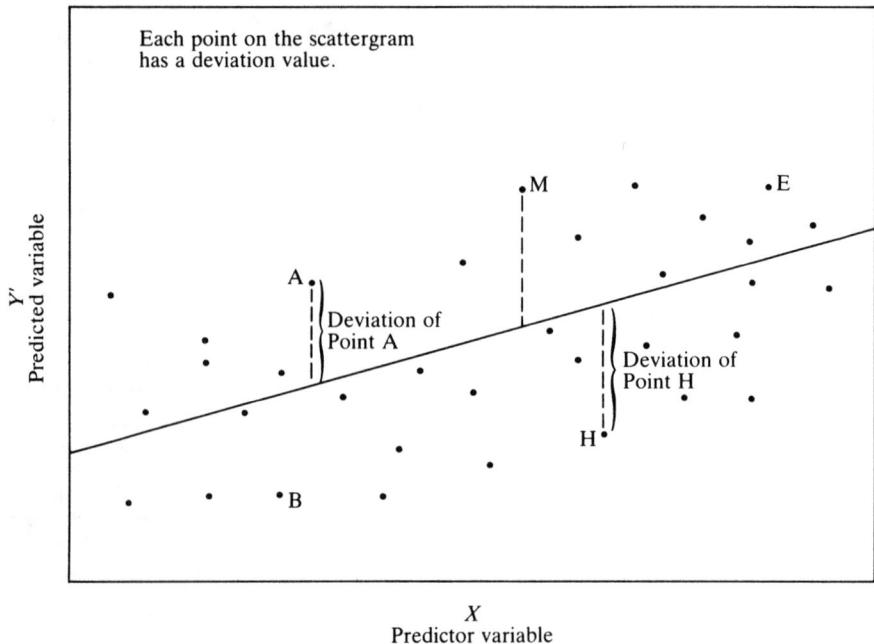

FIGURE 10–14   A Scatter Diagram Showing a Line of Best Fit

An understanding of the principle of prediction to a line is basic to understanding not only prediction from one variable, but also **multiple regression** (more than one predictor variable). As relationships are identified, prediction becomes possible, and further studies can be made to investigate for an explanation for observed phenomena. Research can use prediction in this way to further inquiry in education.

Multiple Regression

Multiple regression is an extension of correlation and prediction and is basic to the understanding of situations involving contributions of several variables. For example, rather than focusing a study on the effects of noise level on test scores in isolation from all other variables, multiple regression allows the researcher to study effects of motivation, intellect, and time of the study as well as the effect of noise level. Advanced research techniques such as this seem to be moving toward a prediction made several years ago:

> Within the decade we will probably see the virtual demise of one-variable thinking and the use of analysis of variance with data unsuited to the method. Instead, multivariate methods will be well accepted tools in the behavioral scientist's and educator's armamentarium. (Kerlinger & Pedhazur, 1973, p. v)

Multiple regression is basic to multivariate methods. Multiple regression allows the investigator to view the contribution of two or more variables to one dependent variable. Theoretically, the number of variables that can be studied is unlimited, but in practice for the researcher the number *is* limited.

Educational questions are for the most part based in complex situations where the resulting mathematical expressions to be integrated are also complex. A study of the relationship of two variables in isolation is often artificial and not particularly meaningful. Nevertheless, the techniques of multiple regression are for the most part too complex to be a part of an initial study of research methods. Since this is a textbook to introduce educational inquiry, multivariate methods and factor analysis are mentioned only to familiarize the student with the terms and what they do. A logical first step to research fundamentals is through the question suggested earlier where a relationship between two variables is investigated (bivariate rather than multivariate). With adequate groundwork in bivariate research, the extension to more complex conditions becomes a logical next step.

Multiple regression is, in principle, like predicting from one variable *(X)* to another variable *(Y')*. An added factor of more than one independent variable requires a weighting of each independent variable on a basis of its contribution to the dependent variable. The regression equation $Y' = a + b(X)$ uses a partial regression weight *(b)* which reflects the increase in Y for each unit increase in X. Multiple regression formulas are built much the same way, except the contributions of the several independent variables are weighted to explain the variability of the dependent variable.

> Multiple regression analysis is especially helpful to the correlationist attempting to establish causes but it is also used in prediction. The basic analytic techniques

of regression analysis are the same when used in studies primarily concerned with prediction or with explanation. The interpretation of the results, however, may differ depending on whether the emphasis is on one or the other. . . . Some applications of multiple regression analysis are of course appropriate in either a predictive or an explanatory framework. (Kerlinger & Pedhazur, p. 282)

Other multivariate techniques—**canonical correlation, discriminant analysis,** and **factor analysis**—extend multiple regression and allow complex situations to be studied recognizing their real-world complexity. Reading about these more advanced methods of analysis might be initiated by referring to Altman (1968) and Horst (1965), along with other advanced studies of statistics.

Goodness of Fit

A set of procedures based on a comparison of what one observes (see Appendix C) as compared to what one expects to observe given certain information and assumptions is called **goodness of fit.** These procedures are based on the chi-square (χ^2) distributions that are presented in the next chapter. These distributions are theoretical in nature and allow a researcher to compare observed frequencies in data with what might be expected to be observed given only chance factors. The common element to all tests of goodness of fit is a comparison of numbers actually observed in any number of classes (categories) with the number expected to fall in the classes. The expected number is based on what an **a priori** hypothesis says should fall in the classes. Goodness-of-fit techniques can be used to check characteristics of a sample with known values for a population. For example, an anonymous survey of a sample of university students could be checked for representativeness of class standing of those returning questionnaires, compared to proportions of students in the four undergraduate classes at the university. Let's say that the researcher finds the following numbers in the returns for questionnaire A: 73 freshmen, 18 sophomores, 10 juniors, and 9 seniors. The registrar's list reveals the following enrollment percentages for the classes: 35 percent freshmen, 25 percent sophomores, 21 percent juniors, and 19 percent seniors. Table 10–7 gives the data for the observed and expected frequencies of occurrence in the classes. For some reason, far more freshmen students returned the questionnaire than did those in the other classes. The question arises, Is there reason to believe that something other than chance factors are affecting the returns from the four class levels? What has been observed certainly does not fit with what was expected when the 110 students were distributed into proportions of enrollees, but neither would the data for Table 10–8, which are the numbers for each class returning form B of another researcher's questionnaire. Again the freshman students returned more than expected, and the observed frequencies are not the expected frequencies. Careful inspection of the expected values reveals that under no conditions could the researcher get perfect fit. Since the responding questionnaire totals will be positive whole numbers, there is no way to get a cell frequency for observed frequencies of 23.1, 32.5, and so on.

TABLE 10–7 Class Rank of Students Returning Questionnaire A

Class	Observed frequencies	Expected frequencies
Freshman	73	38.5
Sophomore	18	27.5
Junior	10	23.1
Senior	9	20.9
TOTAL	110	110.0

TABLE 10–8 Class Rank of Students Returning Questionnaire B

Class	Observed frequencies	Expected frequencies
Freshman	47	45.5
Sophomore	31	32.5
Junior	28	27.3
Senior	24	24.7
TOTAL	130	130.0

The basic question for this test of goodness of fit is, Are the returns for the questionnaires typical of class proportions except for small errors expected to be associated with any set of observed values? Some differences are not surprising, since certain deviations between expected and observed values could appear just by chance. Goodness-of-fit techniques tell the researcher when to be surprised or when to view observed differences as an event very unlikely to occur by chance. It is not likely to find returns for questionnaire A in this proportion by chance alone, while the proportions for the returns of questionnaire B would result often just by chance.

The difference between observed and expected occurrences for returns of questionnaire A is so large that the proportions of returns for the four classes are likely to be the result of something other than chance fluctuations. Possibly the basic question was of more direct importance to the first-year student, or perhaps the freshman students thought that they were required to return it, while the more sophisticated upper levels knew that return was not required.

The difference between observed and expected frequencies for returns of questionnaire B is so small that the proportions of returns for the four classes were probably not affected by anything other than chance fluctuations. The observed values fit well with what was expected. However, the test of goodness of fit showed that questionnaire A returns did not fit with what would be expected from chance differences.

The concept of goodness of fit permeates much of the statistical work done with nominal data. Other nonparametric tests can be used to test for goodness of fit for nominal data or higher ordered data that the researcher wants to treat as nominal data. Goodness-of-fit tests extend into ordinal data, where the sums of ranks for two sets of data can be tested for significance. Introductory statistics books include simple straightforward explanations of nonparametric tests (see Conover, 1971; Edgington, 1969; Siegel; 1956).

The relatively simple statistics associated with the types of tests discussed above make them particularly helpful to studies in descriptive research. They add to our knowledge rather than merely describing without generalization. There seems to be a tendency to want to apply the highest level of statistics possible to research problems. This inclination may prompt a researcher to apply a complicated model when a simpler model may be more appropriate. In some cases, the complicated model may actually inhibit logical reasoning about the problems. Inner relations among variables may be revealed by simple devices, while more complex devices could in fact conceal them. A rule of thumb for researchers is to use the simplest device available that will reveal the messages contained in the data. The problem should dictate the procedure rather than the statistical procedure dictating the problem.

□CHECK YOUR UNDERSTANDING

As an overview of Chapter 10, this Check Your Understanding section asks you to examine Sample Study Number 3 (on page 219) for important topics studied in this chapter on descriptive research. You may have noticed that descriptive labels have not been added to the Sharp-Kirk study in the left-hand column. For your review, identify the following points in the study by filling in each of the blanks to the left of the study. Remember, some points may be covered in more than one paragraph or in only a part of a paragraph, and there is always some overlapping of topics. Therefore, there will be some differences in the way individuals answer this review section.

1. Questions raised
2. The research question
3. Background
4. Abstract
5. Population
6. Subjects
7. Data collection
8. Statistics used
9. Basic methodology
10. Results (in tables)
11. Results in sequential quarters
12. Results by combined parts of quarters
13. Results of patterns
14. Results of time of initiating
15. Results by academic years
16. Results for male clients
17. Results for female clients
18. Recommendations
19. Limitation
20. General interpretation
21. Interpretation
22. Conclusions
23. Connection to theory

Inference in Descriptive Research

The idea of creating knowledge (**inference**) through descriptive research is distasteful to some people. They associate knowledge generation only with experimental procedures because of the control associated with experimentally based methodology. As a researcher loses this control, the conclusions become more subjective and some people discount the importance of such conclusions when they go beyond a mere descriptive statement. However, there seems to be more agreement now than in the recent past that descriptive studies can have a component of explanation and even include prediction in the conclusions.

If research studies were to be limited to experiments, there would be no hope of inquiry into many important areas, given today's methods. This would be true not only in education and associated social and behavioral sciences but in health sciences and other areas as well. Given properly designed research with appropriate procedures to provide results based on valid data, conclusions for descriptive studies are valuable in all areas where experimental control is difficult or impossible to obtain.

The art of the correlator may be of a higher level than that of the experimentalist if obstacles to completion are considered the criteria for evaluation. The book on statistical inference by Edgington can provide much support for the position that is taken here. He says, "Many ideas in this book will be of general interest not simply because they are new but because they are in direct opposition to commonly held beliefs about statistical inference" (1969, p. vii). Without detracting from the contribution of experimental research, researchers and professionals in education should promote more descriptive research that is generalizable.

☐CHECK YOUR UNDERSTANDING

Since the topic of descriptive research is broadly based, many new topics and terms were introduced in the chapter. A summary of the glossary words that are marked in boldface type is given below. A good understanding of these words is necessary to understanding the topics presented in Chapter 10 and utilization of these concepts in descriptive research. For each of the glossary words, write a denotation for the word in your own words and compare it with the glossary denotation.

Affective domain	Documentary analysis	Parametric
A priori	Experimenter	Punchcard
Anthropological approach	Extrapolation	Q methodology
	Factor analysis	Q sort
Assigned variable	Field study	Raw data
Baseline data	Frequency distribution	Replication
Canonical correlation	Goodness of fit	Scaling
Case study	Graph	Scattergram

Causal comparative	Inference	School survey
Central location	Kurtosis	Semantic differential
Central tendency	Laboratory conditions	Single-case
Closed-ended	Level	experimental study
Construct	Longitudinal study	Skewness
Contingency table	Mean square	Sociometry
Correlator	Median	Standard deviation
Criterion variable	Multiple regression	Statistics
Cross-sectional study	Multivariate	Survey
Demographic data	Nomograph	Table
Developmental study	Open-ended	Variability
Discriminant analysis	Opinion/fact survey	

Summary

Descriptive research studies conditions as they exist without intervention or manipulation by the investigator. In addition to studying present status, descriptive research investigates the meaning of what is being observed, interprets through detected relationships what is viewed, establishes a climate for predictions, and investigates for cause-effect direction of identified relationships.

Since it is scientific in nature, descriptive research follows the scientific approach to problem solving, utilizing information about criterion variables that represent characteristics or traits of human beings important to the teaching-learning process. Quantitative data are generated to provide information that can be treated mathematically. The tools to be used in descriptive research have been divided into those used to collect data and those used to interpret the data. Appropriate tools to gather the data are to be chosen through articulation with the problem, and tools for interpretation are to be selected keeping in mind the characteristics of the data that have been generated.

A type of study that is closely related to descriptive research—the status study—reports the present conditions without interpretation. This fact-finding and reporting study is the beginning for most research studies and also serves the question based in a practical situation where the outcome is not intended to be generalized into a theory or the body of present knowledge.

Descriptive research is used widely in education, and in the broadest sense all studies are in part descriptive, since description is involved in all research in one way or another. Although the control of those variables under study is lacking in descriptive studies, through a descriptive study many opportunities exist to study questions that are, for one reason or another, not researchable by careful manipulation of the variables involved in the question.

Reference Note

1. Hill, J. *Study of pupil population in Vigo County Schools.* Unpublished manuscript. (Available from John Hill, Assistant Dean of Education, Indiana State University, Terre Haute, Indiana)

References

Altman, E.I. Financial ratios, discriminant analysis and the prediction of corporate bankruptcy. *Journal of Finance,* 1968, *23,* 589–609.

Babbie, E.R. *Survey research methods.* Belmont, Ca.: Wadsworth, 1973.

Bergstrom, J.M., & Margosian, R.K. *Teaching young children: Basic concepts and resources.* Columbus, Oh.: Charles E. Merrill, 1977.

Campbell, D.P. (Reviser), & Strong, E.K. *Strong vocational interest blanks.* Stanford: Stanford University Press, 1927–1977.

Conover, W.J. *Practical nonparametric statistics.* New York: John Wiley & Sons, 1971.

Crawford, P.B., Hankin, J.H., & Huenemann, R.L. Environmental factors associated with preschool obesity. *Journal of the American Dietetic Association,* 1978, *72* (6), 589–596.

Edgington, E.S. *Statistical inference: The distribution-free approach.* New York: McGraw-Hill, 1969.

Ferguson, G.A. *Statistical analysis in psychology and education* (3rd ed.). New York: McGraw-Hill, 1971.

Fisher, Sir R.A. *Statistical methods for research workers* (14th ed.). New York: Hafner, 1970.

Good, C.V., & Scates, D.E. *Methods of research: Educational, psychological, sociological.* New York: Appleton-Century-Crofts, 1954.

Hales, D.M. *Student involvement in high school decision making and its relationship to student attitudes toward school.* Terre Haute: Indiana State University, 1975. (Series 3, No. 102)

Hersen, M., & Barlow, D.H. *Single case experimental designs: Strategies for studying behavior change.* New York: Pergamon Press, 1976.

Hersen, M., Eisler, R.M., Alford, G.S., & Agras, W.S. Effects of token economy on neurotic depression: An experimental analysis. *Behavior Therapy,* 1973, *4,* 392–397.

Horst, P. *Factor analysis of data matrices.* New York: Holt, Rinehart, & Winston, 1965.

Johnson, A.H. *Changing conceptions of vocational guidance and concomitant value-orientations, 1920–1930.* Terre Haute: Indiana State University, 1972. (Series 3, No. 49)

Katz, M.B. *The people of Hamilton, Canada West.* Cambridge: Harvard University Press, 1975.

Kendall, M.G. *Rank correlation methods* (3rd ed.). New York: Hafner, 1962.

Kerlinger, F.N. *Foundations of behavioral research* (2nd ed.). New York: Holt, Rinehart, & Winston, 1973.

Kerlinger, F.N., & Pedhazur, E.J. *Multiple regression in behavioral research.* New York: Holt, Rinehart & Winston, 1973.

Kuder, F. *Kuder preference record forms.* Chicago: Science Research Associates, 1934–1976.

Likert, R.A. A technique for the measurement of attitudes. *Archives of Psychology,* 1932, *140,* 1–55.

Lutz, F.W., & Ramsey, M.A. The use of anthropological field methods in education. *Educational Researcher,* November 1974, *3,* 5–8.

Masling, J. Role related behavior of the subject and psychologist and its effects upon psychological data. *Nebraska Symposium on Motivation.* Lincoln: University of Nebraska Press, 1966.

McReynolds, P. (Ed.). *Advances in psychological assessment III.* San Francisco: Jossey Bass, 1974.

Oppenheim, A.N. *Questionnaire design and attitude measurement.* New York: Basic Books, 1966.

Siegel, S. *Non-parametric statistics for the behavioral sciences.* New York: McGraw-Hill, 1956.

Snidell, P.S. Anthropological approaches to the study of education. *Review of Educational Research,* 1969, *39,* 593–605.

Webb, E.J., Campbell, D.T., Schwartz, R.D., & Sechrest, L. *Unobtrusive measures: Nonreactive research in the social sciences.* Chicago: Rand McNally, 1966.

CHAPTER ELEVEN

USING THE EXPERIMENT IN INQUIRY

Whenever a new discovery is made, crowds are ready with suggestions that this or that technique should now be used, but no one could have advised Fleming to discover penicillin or Columbus to look for America.

Still the techniques of experimental design are extremely important because few discoveries are immediately useful as such. Indeed, most of them are soon forgotten unless their ingredient elements are meticulously analyzed according to a well-conceived plan.

—Hans Selye

The goals of science to control, explain, and predict lead to theory development about natural phenomena. To use theory as a means of controlling, explaining, and predicting requires that empirical investigations be conducted to discover how well theory explains observed phenomena and to what extent it permits predictions and control. The most direct way of developing theory is through the use of empirically tested hypotheses to establish hypothesized cause-and-effect relationships. The most direct way to test hypothesized cause-and-effect relationships is by a carefully devised **experiment,** "experiment" being defined as

> The administration, under controlled conditions, of treatments to a group or groups that have been specifically constituted for the purpose, and the analysis of the effects produced or induced in the subjects or units as a result. (Good, 1973, p. 227)

The close relationship of the experiment to the goals of science explains its wide acceptance and use in research.

By experimentation, the investigator attempts to find out not only how selected variables are related, but also any cause-and-effect direction. Once this direction is established, it clarifies which variable is associated with causes. Then the effects on the dependent variable are firmly connected with differences on the independent variable. In this way, the experiment allows control not possible with correlational studies. Newly created facts about cause and effect then become part of contemporary theory that serves to explain and interrelate current knowledge. The strength of the experiment lies in the control provided by the plan through manipulation of variables. Study of a natural situation provides little if any opportunity to control the contributions of variables to the setting being studied. In a natural setting, the researcher has only limited opportunity to isolate variables for study. Investigation of ongoing events in a classroom or on a playground, for example, do not permit the control needed for an experiment. On the other hand, the experiment is quite valuable in educational research when the variables under study are amenable to **manipulation** either practically, ethically, or morally.

This chapter discusses studies using the strict control that only laboratory-like conditions provide. Most studies in education and in other human sciences must be conducted without such strict control; however, the design for experimental studies serves as the criterion (ideal) conditions. Certain questions arise in education about how already determined factors—cultural, developmental, and such—are reflected in the educational milieu. Study about the effects of deprivation during development—by limiting certain physical or environmental factors or by withholding certain educational experiences—are not ethical, nor are they desired by researchers. No researcher wants to study how a child develops with absolutely no other human contact during the first 10 years of life, even though that information would be valuable to a study of human development. Research workers should seek to build designs for studies that approximate as closely as possible ideal experimental conditions. That the ideal cannot be attained reduces the strength of the conclusions, but it also points up for the researcher the need to approach the ideal conditions as closely as possible. Studies Number 2 and 4 in the Sample Studies section (page 203) are two complete examples of experimental studies.

Nature of Experimental Research

The experimental approach requires the researcher to do something with a situation rather than merely looking at it. In the strictest sense, an experiment can take place only in a laboratory setting with the greatest possible control and study the effects of manipulation. In the broadest sense, any interjection of something different into a natural setting could be considered an experiment. In general, the setting for educational studies does not allow the researcher complete control. With appropriate statistical procedures available to aid in data interpretation, the major task before the educational experimentalist is one of collecting valid data in sufficient quantities. To do this effectively requires conducting research classed as quasi-experimental:

> There are many natural social settings in which the research person can introduce something like experimental design into his scheduling of data collection procedures (e.g., the *when* and *to whom* of measurement), even though he lacks the full control over the scheduling of experimental stimuli (the *when* and *to whom* of exposure and the ability to randomize exposures) which makes a true experiment possible. Collectively, such situations can be regarded as quasi-experimental designs. (Campbell & Stanley, 1963, p. 204 in Gage)

Although experimental in principle, most educational experiments lack the strict control provided only in a laboratory.

The study of the effects of manipulating the situation in some way involves a breakdown of differences (variability) observed in the data into controlled and uncontrolled sources of variance. The effects attributed to the uncontrolled sources are viewed as **random error** or differences that cannot be accounted for in the manipulation, while error associated with known sources is called **systematic error** or differences that can be accounted for. Random error (**chance variation**) results from factors beyond the control of the experimenter. For example, chance variation may result from subjects' physical health or mood or from environmental factors beyond the control of the experimenter. Moreover, selection of a sample from a population produces subjects which vary from the population in some way(s). That sample also varies from other samples that could have been selected at random. Systematic error, on the other hand, is introduced by experimental manipulation. For example, a leaded weight added to one side of a fair die should produce systematic error to the numbers that turn up on subsequent rolls of the die. In contrast, the differences in the rolls of a fair die occur in random fashion.

Manipulation of an independent variable is intended to produce systematic error. Obviously the experimenter loses this systematic error as he or she loses control of the contributing variables. Some researchable questions allow the researcher more control than do others. In general, researchers will use experiments where the nature of the question under investigation allows adequate control and where there are no ethical problems involved in introducing something different into the situation under study. The study of rocks permits extensive manipulation: they can be chipped, pounded, ground to a powder, treated with acids and other compounds, and studied for differences under carefully controlled conditions. Human subjects or animals are not to be manipulated in this way at the whim or decision of the researcher. "Nature" itself conducts innumerable experiments by introducing new conditions. Of course, natural changes lack the control needed for rigorous study, but they are nevertheless nature's experiments.

Our culture and researchers' inhibitions do not permit unlimited control through experiments on human beings and other animals. Thus the use of the experiment is limited in the study of educational problems. Depriving a subject of an educational benefit in order to study the effects is as unacceptable in educational research as depriving a subject of a necessity for life or introducing a disease to seek a possible cure is unacceptable in medical research. This limiting factor is not a deficiency of experimental research, but the nature of manipulation in experimental research causes the experiment to be less useful in the social sciences, behavioral sciences, and education than in the physical sciences. The biological and medical sciences also suffer from the restriction placed on them by the nature of the subjects they study.

The Experiment in Education

In spite of difficulties, opportunities to use the experiment in educational research do exist (see Sample Studies No. 2 and 4), and its use is to be encouraged where the conditions are suitable for experimental manipulation. Sample Study Number 4, for example, studied first-grade theme writing by manipulating classroom conditions to provide control for examination of differences in mode of discourse. The empirical nature of the experimental approach and its capability to control through manipulation of variables make this research method a powerful generator of new knowledge. When the strictest experimental procedures are not feasible, scientists turn to study of natural situations that are nearly comparable to desired actual experiments. Correlators using descriptive research study nature's experiments, while experimenters study the effects of variation they themselves have created. Carefully planned experimental strategies allow statements about causation resulting from the study of the effects of manipulation.

The experiment should be used for educational research when near-laboratory conditions can be created for a study. Many variables of educational concern can be studied by varying the conditions for separate groups of subjects and studying the effects that result from the different conditions. For example, different uses of classtime or different methods of presenting materials to students provide the manipulation needed for the experiment in the Anderson-Bashaw study of theme writing.

When certain characteristics cannot be arbitrarily manipulated by the experimenter—for example, the human characteristics of socioeconomic status, sex, and aptitude—the researcher may find that much the same effect can be had by assigning subjects to groups determined by differences on that particular attribute. For example, a study may involve a question of the effects of being male or female in a particular situation. Rather than changing the sex of the subjects under study, the control could come from studying the differences between a set of male subjects and a set of female subjects. Of course, the plan of the study would have to consider control of all other variables, but assuming that the control has been accomplished, the manipulation would come through assignment rather than by direct manipulation.

The above discussion implies that near-laboratory conditions can be set up for many educationally based questions. The experimental designs given later in this chapter indicate more specifically how to gain the necessary control needed to establish the antecedent-consequence relationship of variables through experimental designs to answer educational questions. A later section ("Ex Post Facto") also describes how a design using assigned variables can use the nature of the experiment for manipulation.

Steps in Experimental Research

The steps for experimental research fit the basic sequence used for the general scientific approach. The overall plan focuses on attacking questions that can best be answered by the problem-solving strategy of research. In addition, this plan is oriented toward testing hypotheses or finding solutions by developing appropriate manipulation.

Question and Hypothesis. Every experiment grows out of a doubt or indeterminate situation that provides a researchable problem. Although the Anderson-Bashaw theme-writing study does not use a direct question to state the research problem, one is implied in paragraph 3. After the problem is put into question form, the next step is to seek the answer from colleagues, experts, and the professional literature—especially from reports of research studies. If a satisfactory answer is still not found, the background knowledge produced in this search is organized to develop a research hypothesis. The research hypothesis is a researcher's best guess as to the answer that she or he expects to find from the experimentally designed investigation of the problem. The Anderson-Bashaw study provides a good example of the research hypothesis in paragraph 3.

Each research hypothesis is developed and based on all the background knowledge that has been found to bear on the question. It is usually tied in to educational theory. Research hypotheses are developed to varying degrees of confidence. Some are much like blind guesses, while others come very close to being established theory.

The research hypothesis is especially important to experimental research, since it is generally the alternate hypothesis to the statistically oriented null hypothesis used to interpret mathematical differences in the empirical data. The close relationship between the two hypotheses (research and null) is further revealed in a later section where they become a part of the researcher's experimental design.

Experimental Design. The next step is to structure an experiment through a plan to select subjects, gather empirical data, analyze them, and make an objective decision regarding whether or not the data support the hypothesis. For an example, the reader should refer again to the "Methods" section (Sample Study No. 4, pars. 4–14) of the Anderson-Bashaw study to see how a completed design integrates the several parts of methodology. Basic statistical designs must be adapted to the special problems of each study, taking into consideration the effects of each decision on other components of the study. Since different types of designs yield different kinds of information, the methodology and structure of the experiment must also be carefully constructed for the particular question under scrutiny. The structure of each study is so specialized that the developed design will be unique. Other studies may use the same statistical design, but none will be exactly the same, because the variables of the question direct each study to a unique plan. In general, the statistical design generates a result which determines whether or not the data reject a null hypothesis. The decision of whether or not to reject the null hypothesis forms the results of the study.

Conclusions. After the data have been gathered, organized, and analyzed, the conclusions are based on the experimenter's interpretation of the results. Conclusions for the Anderson-Bashaw study are presented in paragraphs 23 and 26. Other paragraphs in the discussion section imply certain conclusions, but they are not specifically stated. With a well-designed experimental study having maximum control, the rejection of or failure to reject the null hypothesis decides whether or not the research hypothesis was supported. In general, the rejection of the null hypothesis is cause to conclude that the research hypothesis has been supported. Failure to reject the null hypothesis generally indicates that the research hypothesis was not supported. Of course, the investigator is free to expand the results with a narrative discussing the relationship of the results to present educational theory and the implications of the study.

Summary. The following sentences review experimental design steps. The researcher first asks a direct question. If a suitable answer is not found in present knowledge, a research hypothesis is stated. If laboratory-like conditions can be established, an experiment is designed to collect and analyze a set of data by either rejecting or not rejecting the statistical hypothesis of no difference. Finally, the researcher interprets that decision in terms of support or nonsupport of the research hypothesis and presents the conclusions as findings for the study. The major difference between historical research or descriptive research and experimental research lies in the difference in structuring an experimental design that allows experimental manipulation of variables studied. The uniqueness of the experiment and experimental design is revealed in the rest of this chapter.

Sources and Types of Data

The source of data for most experimental studies in education is human subjects who are observed on human attributes. Measurements can be made on those characteristics where there is agreement about how a subject exhibits the degree of the characteristic that she or he has. Other characteristics will be measured where little agreement can be obtained about how a subject exhibits the characteristic. For example, a researcher would be able to obtain general agreement among educators about a student's ability to multiply by one place numbers by using a set of well-prepared examples on a test. On the other hand, another researcher would expect to have much more disagreement from educators if she attempted to measure creativity with a paper-and-pencil test. It is difficult to operationalize the construct of creativity because creativity may mean something different to each person. Creativity in one frame of reference—say art—may differ from that in another frame of reference—say expression in writing. The type of data collected from the subjects is largely dictated by the attribute studied, and the type of data in turn largely dictates the type of statistical analysis to use. See paragraph 14 in the Anderson-Bashaw study for illustration of how these influences work in an actual study.

Sources of Data

The sources of data for experimental studies are the subjects in the groups. Sample groups of human subjects who have been systematically selected and given experimental treatments involving manipulation of an independent variable are measured on a dependent variable. Measures on the dependent variable are studied for effects of treatment by analyzing the data with some statistical procedure. Sets of data from different sources or samples that have been subjected to different conditions make up the heart of an experimental study.

Types of Data

Information in the form of quantitative data is needed for experiments. The experimentalist studies human beings by assigning number values to human characteristics. Data used within experimental designs are generated by measurement techniques that quantify the variable being studied. Since categorical and continuous variables are associated with human beings, experimental data may come from one or more of the four types of scales mentioned in an earlier chapter—nominal, ordinal, interval, or ratio. A **categorical variable** generates nominal data, while a **continuous variable** will generate one of the other types of data.

Categorical or Continuous. Those variables that only allow assignment to subclasses by the possession of a characteristic that defines a subclass are measured by the simplest rule of measurement. The data are thus nominal. A subject either does or does not have the characteristic of the subclass. For example, the birthplace of a subject could be categorized and assigned to one of the 50 United States, a foreign country, or an unknown location. In all, the categories would total 52, and each subject could be assigned to one and only one category. Subclasses could be grouped by regions—New England, Midwest, and so on—or by some other grouping. Where more than two subclasses are listed, the variables are *polytomous* (divided into more than two parts). Where there are only two subclasses—male-female, above average–below average, and so on—the variables are dichotomous.

Those variables that take values from a continuous series must be labeled to indicate their relative position within the series. A system for ranking gives ordinal properties to the data. Test scores are generally considered to give not only order but also interpretation of intervals within the data. With continuous variables, each assigned value represents a range of possible values for each assignment. Thus, a weight of 137 pounds may be considered to represent a series of all possible values between 136.5 and 137.5 pounds. Similarly, measurements of other human attributes—such as scores on tests of achievement, motivation, and creativity—may represent any particular range of continuous values as measured by the experimenter.

Identification of Type. Identifying the type of data is important to choosing appropriate statistical methods. For work in education, there are three classes of measurement used with statistical methods if interval and ratio scales are combined. Table 11–1 presents this classification along with associated statistics.

TABLE 11–1 Scales, Defining Relations, and Appropriate Statistics

Scale	Defining Relations	Type of Statistical Test		Examples of Appropriate Statistics
		Parametric	Nonparametric	
Nominal	1. Equivalence		✓	Mode Frequency of occurrence Contingency coefficients
Ordinal	1. Equivalence 2. Greater than		✓	Median Percentiles Spearman rho Kendall r Friedman Anova by ranks
Interval	1. Equivalence 2. Greater than 3. Known ratio of any two intervals	✓		Mean Standard deviation Pearson r Analysis of variance t-test
Ratio	1. Equivalence 2. Greater than 3. Known ratio of any two intervals 4. Known ratio of any two scale values	✓		

Experimental designs frequently apply methods appropriate for a lower class of variables to measurements of a higher class of variables. By using less sophisticated statistical treatment, the investigator is actually discarding some information available in the data. For example, if measurements of the variable of height were determined to the nearest centimeter for a group of subjects, the groups could be studied on an interval scale or could be studied on a lower scale, such as ranks or classes. A set of 6 measurements for heights 180, 178, 176, 172, 164, and 160 in centimeters (an interval measurement) could be changed to ranks of 1, 2, 3, 4, 5, and 6 or to upper third, middle third, and lower third. Viewing the heights in ranks treats the variable as ordinal, and division into thirds coverts it to larger categories, although there is an order to the classes. Widely accepted use of nonparametric statistics in analyzing such data to study characteristics important to social sciences, behavioral science, and education makes the practice of discarding information understandable where questions arise about whether it is proper to use parametric procedures.

Experimental designs at times incorporate analyses of data by a statistical procedure that requires the investigator to assume that he or she has information which is not in the data. Data that are ordinal may, in such cases, be treated by a procedure appropriate for interval and ratio data. Scores on mental ability tests, for example, are generally treated as if they were interval data, but the assignment of numerical descriptors does not include equal intervals. Differences between intervals in a scale for mental ability tests and many other scales of measurement used in education should not be considered the same throughout the continuum. A difference between scores of 95 and 100 is not necessarily the same as a difference between 145 and 150, although each arithmetic difference is 5. The 2 intervals of 5 do not represent the same distance on the scale. Units in the center of a scale for mental abilities are usually smaller than the units at the extremes. For the same reason, a score of 150 is in no way twice a score of 75 when mental ability is being measured. However, Chapter 3 built a case (page 78) for using psychological and educational data as interval data unless it is categorical (nominal) data or data obtained by ranking.

The researcher should not discard information or assume information without considering other statistical procedures for appropriate methods. Nevertheless, if the practical situation is best served by a particular procedure it should be used. The investigator must know the information that the data contain in order to be aware of assumptions underlying all procedures. The experimenter must look carefully at the rules for assigning the numerical description, decide what type of data this study produces, and select the appropriate statistical design to interpret the information in the data into results. The investigator must know what level of information the data contain to make proper choices later in order to insure valid results and in turn valid conclusions (see paragraph 14 in the Anderson-Bashaw study).

Experimental Design

The process of planning and structuring experiments is commonly called *designing* experiments. The output of the process is an experimental design. It encompasses all of the components of methodology needed to test hypotheses, including a set of ground rules that uses empirical data as a basis for deciding whether the study shows support or nonsupport of the research hypothesis. The design allows objective interpretation of differences observed in the data.

The essence of an experiment lies in the investigator's selection of the values or categories for the treatment variable(s) and study the effects on a criterion variable. This process enables researchers to study an indefinitely large number of relations which are not amenable to study by observational or correlational methods and may not in fact have any existence in nature at all prior to the conduct of the experiment (Ferguson, 1976, pp. 211–212). For example, the researcher could study the effects of noise on test performance by controlling all extraneous variables, manipulating noise level during testing sessions, and looking at the effect of manipulation without the influence of other variables (factors).

The purpose of the design is to structure procedures so that the researcher has control within the study to allow statements about observed variance. The design plans for observation and interpretation of facts and relates the data to the hypothesis and thus to the research problem itself. The following sections discuss experimental treatment, the null hypothesis, and how decisions about support or nonsupport of the hypotheses are made.

Experimental Treatment

Basic to the understanding of experimental design is the idea of different treatment for separate groups on a chosen variable (independent) and measurement of the same groups on another variable (dependent) to determine the effects of the different kinds (levels) of treatment.

The dependent variable, sometimes called a "response" or "criterion variable," takes different values depending on the influence exerted by different levels of the independent variables, sometimes called "treatment variables." The study of experimental design in this book is limited to designs in which there is only one dependent variable. More advanced designs using a multivariate approach may be studied in a book more directed to in-depth study of designs (Hays, 1963; Marascuilo, 1971; Nie, Bert, & Hull, 1975).

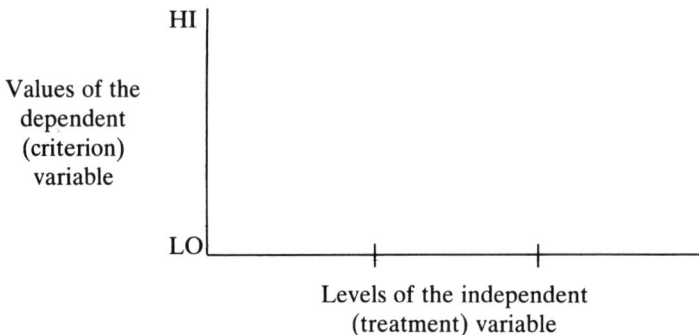

HI

Values of the
dependent
(criterion)
variable

LO

Levels of the independent
(treatment) variable

FIGURE 11–1   The Simplest Design

The simplest design (one factor, two levels) is diagrammed in Figure 11–1. In this case, there are two treatment levels on the independent variable. Other designs could have three, four, or more levels. In this type of study, the function of the design is to create conditions so that contributing factors of variables other than the independent variable will not affect the measures of the dependent variable, thus allowing a pure measure of treatment effects. The design is organized to introduce systematic variance through the different treatments of the independent variable. The statistical design studies the effects of different treatment by interpreting the values on the dependent variable.

To determine a cause-and-effect relationship, the treatment variable must be under the **control** of the experimenter. The control may be direct, as when the experimenter manipulates conditions by setting specific levels for the treatment variables. For example, an experimenter might set different temperatures in a room and ask students to study under the different physical environments. The treatment variable would be temperature of rooms, the levels would be different temperatures, and the criterion variable would be some measure of how well the subjects were able to learn in the conditions of temperature differences. In this example, we can see the importance of two aspects of control—first, the control of the treatment variable and second, the control of other contributing variables. To view different effects from one variable on the criterion variable, all contributions from extraneous variables—such as a noise level—must be held constant for the two groups.

Ex post facto designs use the same idea of treatment, except the control for the treatment variable is accomplished indirectly through the use of a priori classification of subjects to be studied. For example, the effects of socioeconomic background on the school dropout rate cannot be studied by varying, at the experimenter's will, the level of the treatment variable for each subject in the study. However, subjects from different socioeconomic backgrounds can be assigned into like groups and studied for differences. Since the experimenter is able to control conditions and assign levels on the independent variable, this design uses the characteristics of an experiment except for the lack of direct manipulation.

Independent variables whose levels are set directly are called *manipulated* variables, *active* variables, or *treatment* variables. Those independent variables with levels set indirectly through traits or properties have been called *classification* variables, *assigned* variables, *attribute* variables, or *selection* variables. In general, the statistical procedures are the same for a design using either active or assigned independent variables, but interpretation must be made in different frames of reference. The problem of interpretation in different frames of reference will be discussed in a later section.

The effects of two or more treatment variables on a single dependent variable can be studied within a single experiment, but their effects are not necessarily independent. It seems reasonable to assume that combinations of effects are not predictable from separate effects. Studies of effects of more than one independent variable must include as a part of the investigation a study of **interaction** (see Figure 11–2) among independent variables.

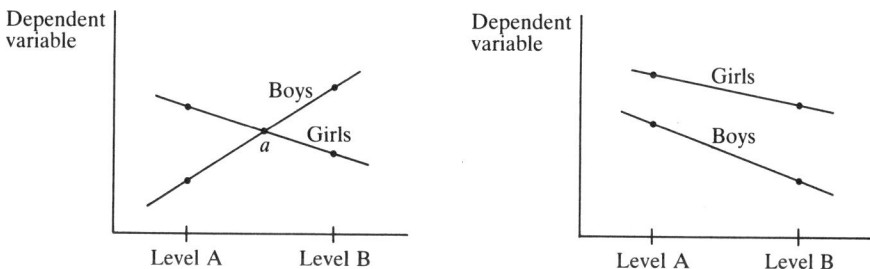

FIGURE 11–2   Interaction Effects

The design shown in Figure 11–3 (two factors, two levels on each factor) allows the study of treatment effects of each independent variable separately and of interaction of the two independent variables. For example, treatment of independent variable A (levels I and II), treatment of independent variable B (levels I and II), and interaction of the two levels of A and the two levels of B can be studied. This design can be expanded to include more levels for one or more of the independent variables.

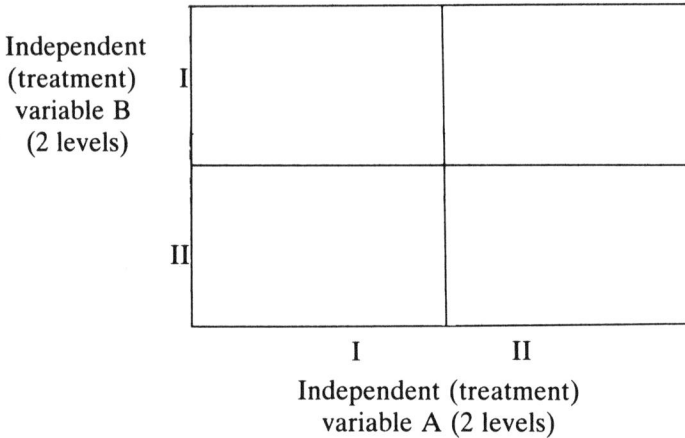

FIGURE 11–3   A More Complex Design

Experimental treatment consists of the different levels of the independent variable as manipulated by the researcher. Such treatment must be clearly understood and explained in the design. The description of such a treatment for Sample Study Number 4 is found in paragraph 6 of that study. Without a clear statement about treatment, the study lacks a vehicle for interpreting differences observed in the criterion variable.

In a well-planned design, the statistical **test of significance** tests the tenability of the null hypothesis which states that treatment has had no effect. A statistically significant difference implies a mathematical difference beyond a chance difference. The difference represents the effects of treatment that has been interjected as systematic error. If it is significant, then the treatment levels (differences) are considered the source of the difference; if statistical significance is not found, the treatment is viewed as having no effect—that is, the observed differences are there because of chance contributions. This idea is common to all tests of significance, although the principle is applied differently given different types of data and research procedures in data collection.

The Null Hypothesis

The data gathered within one experimental design allows comparison among two or more sample means (or some other statistic) where the sample groups have received different treatments. For example, an experimenter may want to determine the effects of exercise on the performance of a cognitive task, such as reading comprehension. She then selects at random (see chapter 7) two groups for study, assigning two levels of treatment for the independent variable (different treatment for each group) and measuring effects on the criterion variable. The two groups might be asked to read the passage and answer questions about the contents. The treatment levels could be quiet restful activity for 10 minutes before reading and questioning for one group, with 10 minutes of vigorous activitity before reading and questioning for the other group. A mean score for each group could be obtained on the criterion variable, and the difference could be investigated statistically.

This experiment requires a decision about the observed differences between the two means of the criterion values. Both means and the difference between the means are subject to sampling error. If the two groups were to take the test questions under exactly the same conditions (no treatment), it is not likely, because of sampling error, that they would score in such a way that the means of both groups would be exactly the same value. A study of differences in experimental studies must take into account sampling error. May the difference observed between the two means be attributed to sampling error and viewed as a difference that appears by chance or is that difference so great that it would rarely happen by chance alone? If the difference between group means is considered a rare occurrence with only sampling differences, then the observed difference may be presumed to be a result of the different treatment provided on the independent variable. In the preceding study, the treatment provided is differences in amount of exercise. A design for this study could be shown as the model in Figure 11–4.

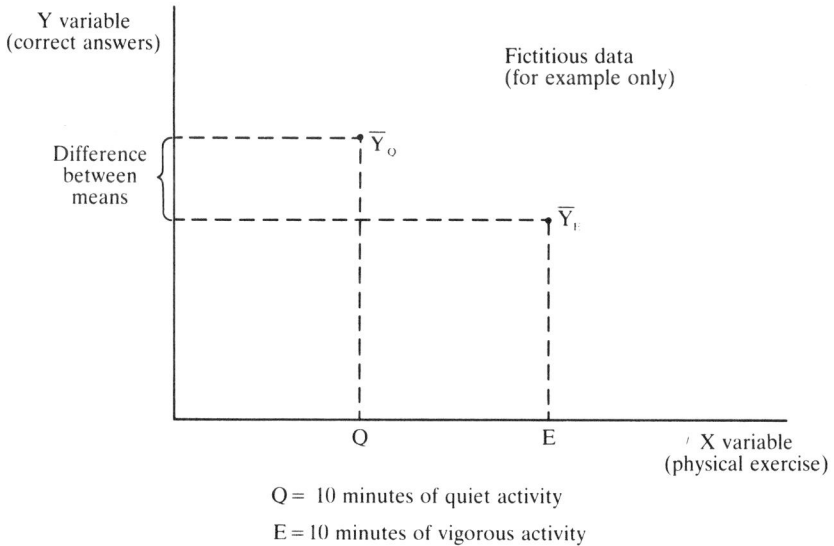

FIGURE 11–4   Effects of Exercise on Cognitive Functioning

A decision must be made about the cause of the difference in the dependent variable measures. Recall that a difference is significant if it is not attributable to chance. If the difference is sufficiently large to be considered a result of treatment, the difference is a **significant difference.** Small differences are credited to sampling error. The test of significance will make the decision about the source of differences objectively based on the data of the samples and the structure of the design.

Since the research hypothesis cannot be tested directly because statistical procedures do not exist for that test, a statistical statement—called the *null hypothesis*—provides the vehicle to be tested. Tests of significance test the tenability of the null hypothesis. Although *not* a true hypothesis in the sense of being a rational guess, the null hypothesis is a way to interpret the data and is closely related to the research hypothesis. The null hypothesis is a statement about differences on the criterion variable focusing on the source of those differences. It says, in effect, that any differences observed are there because of sampling error, not as a result of treatment. The statistical test takes into account the variances associated with the two distributions as well as the absolute differences between the means. A null hypothesis for our example study about effects of exercise might be "There is no significant difference between the group mean scores on the questions asked about the narrative read as a result of the differences in amount of exercise provided the two groups."

This null hypothesis is a trial statement that is testable statistically. One other hypothesis is implied when the null hypothesis is stated: the implied hypothesis is that there is a difference. Given strict control, two and only two possible conditions exist—either the difference is there because of sampling error or because of treatment. This discussion can be represented symbolically using symbols commonly found in statistics books and journal articles:

$$H_0:\ \mu_Q - \mu_E = 0 \text{ or } \mu_Q = \mu_E$$
$$H_1:\ \mu_Q - \mu_E \neq 0 \text{ or } \mu_Q \neq \mu_E$$

Where

H_0 is the null hypothesis.
H_1 is the alternate hypothesis.
μ_Q and μ_E are the population means for the two groups.
0 (defined as "no difference") includes any numerical value from the sample data that can be credited to sampling error.
$\neq$ means unequal.

In general, the alternate hypothesis is the experimenter's research hypothesis, and rejection of the null hypothesis as a tenable position is cause to support the research hypothesis. If the null hypothesis is rejected, the experimenter believes that the possibility of the observed difference happening by chance is remote. Nevertheless, the possibility that the difference did happen by chance exists in both theory and practice. Then how can an experiment prove that the difference came from treatment or if it came by chance? The experimenter can never be 100 percent confident that he or she has made a correct decision. In other words, the researcher cannot *prove* anything from a study, but can only state that the research hypothesis was supported at a certain level of probability or that the hypothesis was not supported at that level.

Decision Errors

The researcher hopes that any decision about whether the data support the research hypothesis or fail to support it is a correct decision. Since the researcher cannot be sure of how a decision fits with the real world, she or he must make a study of the possible **decision error** associated with the two different decisions. Rejecting the null hypothesis may mean rejecting a difference that occurred by chance. Failure to reject it may be a failure to reject a difference that did indeed come from experimental treatment. The experimenter could decide (by a statistical test) to reject a null hypothesis that should not be rejected or could be in error by not rejecting what should be rejected.

Each statement of a null hypothesis requires statement of a *significance level* for the test of significance (usually .01 or .05). The significance level for a study is the probability of rejecting a null hypothesis when it should not be rejected. This is called an *alpha error* or *type I error*. An error associated with failure to reject the null hypothesis when it should be rejected is called a *beta error* or *type II error*.

Keep in mind that in reality either the null hypothesis is true or the alternate hypothesis is true. The decision about the null hypothesis is made without knowledge about real-world conditions. The relationship of the conditions might be stated: When H_0 is rejected and H_1 is true, the correct decision has been made. When H_0 is not rejected and H_0 is true, the correct decision has been made. Rejection of H_0 when H_0 is true and failure to reject H_0 when H_1 is true are both errors (see Table 11–2).

TABLE 11–2 Two Types of Decision Error

Conditions / Decision	Real-world conditions	
	H_0 true	H_1 true
Reject H_0	Type I error Alpha (α)	OK Correct decision
Fail to reject H_0	OK Correct decision	Type II error Beta (β)

Many situations require decisions much like this one about the null hypothesis. For example, a physician must diagnose whether a patient needs medication or surgery. Each diagnosis by a physician is intended to be a correct decision, so that all patients needing medication or surgery receive it. Those patients who are diagnosed as needing medication when they do not, or who are operated on when surgery is not necessary, are victims of a type I error by the doctor. Those who do not receive medication when it is needed, or who are not operated on when they should be, are victims of a type II error. Doctors and researchers alike hope to keep both types of errors to a minimum.

The decision about whether or not to carry an umbrella when rain threatens involves possible errors in judgment. Figure 11–5 shows an analogy for experimental decisions using umbrella carrying. This is a specific case using the same principles for decision making represented in the Table 11–2 matrix. Notice that the decision to carry or not to carry an umbrella determines what kind of error a person can make. If the person carrys an umbrella, she cannot make a type II error. She makes a type I error if it does not rain when she carries it. A decision not to carry an umbrella cannot result in a type I error, but it will be the cause for a type II error if it rains. Of course, carrying an umbrella when it rains and not carrying an umbrella when it does not rain results in no error at all.

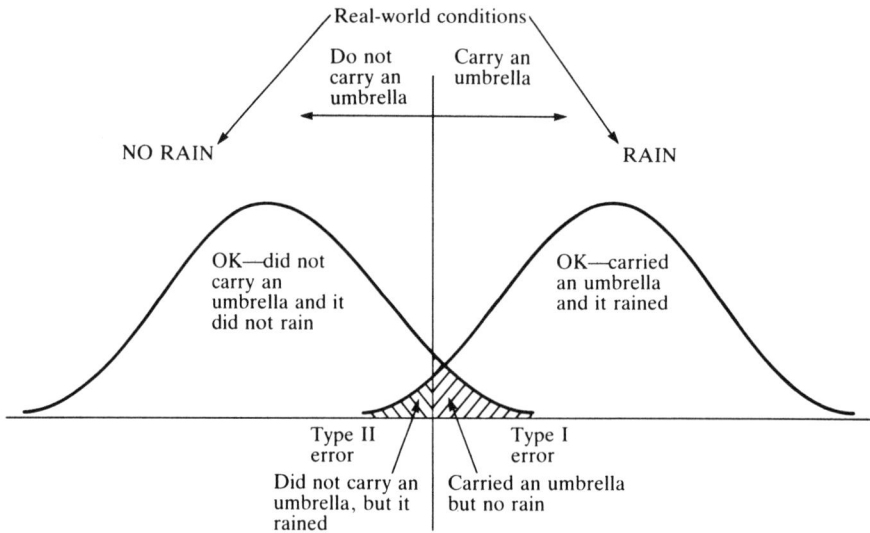

FIGURE 11–5 Study of Possible Decision Errors

Decisions about umbrella carrying are usually made without a careful structuring for each situation. Two types of people do not make individual decisions about carrying umbrellas—the person who never carries an umbrella and the person who always carries one. What possible error could each of these make? The one who never carries an umbrella will never make a type I error (α) but is subject to the type II error (β). The one who carries an umbrella at all times is subject to the type I (α) error but not the type II (β) error. The rest of the population fits at different places between these two extremes, with some more willing to carry umbrellas than others. Those who lean toward carrying an umbrella are protecting themselves from a type II error, while those who seldom carry one are more willing to risk a type II error to protect against a type I error. The relationship between the two errors is shown in figure 11–6. Part A shows the situation of the person who is protecting against the type II error, and part B shows the situation for protection against the type I error.

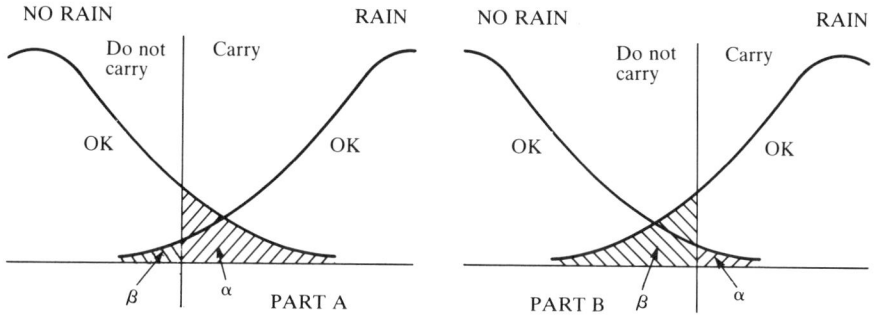

FIGURE 11–6   Relationship of Two Possible Errors

The preceding principles can be applied to the simple design in Figure 11–1. The statistical procedure should result in a correct decision about the source of the measured difference. However, if there is no real difference and the procedure indicated the null hypothesis should be rejected, an alpha error would be committed. If there was a real difference and the procedure indicated that the null hypothesis should not be rejected, then a beta error would be committed.

When testing a null hypothesis in a statistical design, the level for rejection of the null hypothesis is set using the probability of making an alpha error, the error of rejecting a null hypothesis when it should not be rejected. The researcher chooses alpha based on a review of the sampling error for the study. Figure 11–7 shows the relationship of alpha and beta errors. To reduce the probability of making an alpha error increases the probability of making a beta error. A study of the two probabilities permits a statement about the power of the test.* A relabeling of Figure11–6, as shown in Figure 11–7, shows the relationship of the two possible errors in the decision as to whether the null hypothesis is true or not true.

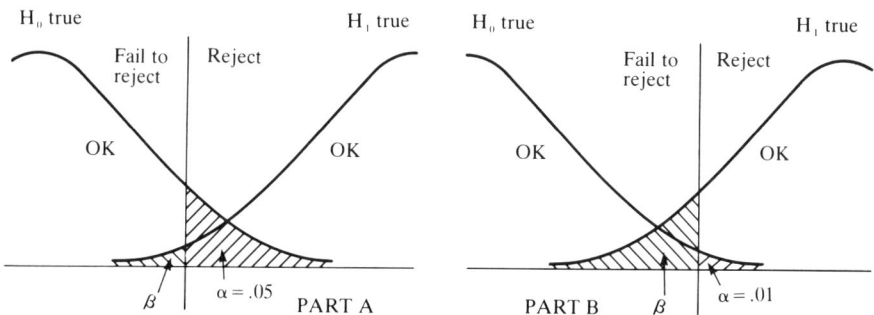

FIGURE 11–7   Relationship of Two Possible Errors

---

*The power of a statistical test is the probability that the test rejects the null hypothesis when the null is false.

The null hypothesis adds to the design a way of making an objective interpretation of whether the data support or contradict the research hypothesis being tested. The function of the experiment is to give a rigorous approach to inquiry. Within the structure of the experiment, the null hypothesis is a rigorous method for interpreting data that helps the researcher avoid subjectively determined decisions.

If the significance level is set at .05 for a test of the observed difference between means, for example, the probability of saying that there is a difference when no such difference exists is .05 or less. If the null hypothesis is rejected, the chances are five in 100, or less, that the difference could be a result of chance rather than a result of treatment applied. If the probability level is different—set at .01 or .001 for example—a declared difference is said to be significant at that chosen level. The researcher hopes to choose a significance level that minimizes the combined probabilities of α and β, but that choice is difficult to make. Most studies in education use either the .05 or .01 level for tests of significance. The relationship of the seriousness of the two errors may help in the task of setting a significance level. If the seriousness of α is great compared to the seriousness of β, then the alpha should be set lower. Conversely, α can be increased to protect the researcher from making a β error.

Can the researcher choose a significance level so that $\alpha = 0$? Yes, this is possible by stating as a decision rule "H_0 is always true." If such a decision is made β is at a maximum, and there is no reason to perform an experiment because the decision rule becomes independent of any data gathered for the study.

The null hypothesis is implied for any test of significance but should be stated in terms of specific variables under study in the experiment as a part of the description of methodology. Tests of significance are used extensively with means of sample groups, but are also used with proportions, correlation coefficients, and other statistics. For each general type of test for significance, there is often more than one specific procedure. Appropriate statistical procedures for the many tests of significance may be found in Appendix C and in particular books devoted to statistical procedures (Bruning & Kintz, 1977; Chase, 1976; Ferguson, 1976; Walker & Lev, 1953). Whatever procedure is chosen for a study, testing for significant differences is based on the principles discussed here. The experimental design of a study must include the most appropriate statistical procedure for the particular study's unique set of circumstances.

Ex Post Facto

As mentioned in Chapter 10, ex post facto statistical designs are based on the same principles as experimental designs, with one exception—the levels of treatment are created by assignment rather than by manipulation. For example, one of the independent variables for the Anderson-Bashaw sample study on theme writing was sex. They studied differences of sex by assignment, not by direct manipulation. This one difference, however, creates numerous problems of interpretation, because the control needed to make direct statements about cause is not included for assigned variables. This restriction must be taken into consideration when drawing conclusions from results generated by an ex post facto design.

Recall that ex post facto designs use assignment to levels by natural attributes rather than random assignment to groups and experimenter treatment manipulation. For example, to study differences between primary-school boys and primary-school girls, the researcher cannot assign subjects to sex groups randomly but must study a natural difference. Studies of creativity, motivation, and a multitude of other factors as independent variables causing effects in dependent variables must be conducted the same way.

Some characteristics are more difficult to deal with than others. Assignments to groups by sex is straightforward and it is probably easier to gain control when using this natural attribute than it is when making assignment on levels of creativity and other attributes. The direct relationship of differences on a variable attributed to sex is probably easier to establish than is a similar relationship using levels of creativity, but questions of control remain. How does a researcher know that observed differences on a dependent variable are the result of differences in sex rather than a result of cultural expectations that differ for girls and boys and therefore create different environments for them? The observed difference may then be differences in culture and not differences in sex. Of course, if the question's frame of reference encompasses cultural differences, then there may be no problem when drawing conclusions. Nevertheless, in a question such as this other difficulties are likely to arise.

Inferring Causal Relationship. To conclude that a variable (X) is the cause of differences in another variable (Y), three conditions must be met:

1. There must be a statistical relationship.
2. X (the independent variable) must have preceded Y (the dependent variable) in time.
3. Other variables cannot have influenced Y.

Experimental designs are structured to meet these conditions, and causal inference is direct. As an example, the study discussed earlier about the effect of exercise on reading comprehension is designed to take advantage of certain control through assignment, but certain factors are still unaccounted for, since the researcher did not have complete control. By way of contrast, in a study of temperature effects, the temperature during the study is under direct control given proper equipment to provide selected temperatures. Ex post facto research can establish statistical relationship, the first condition, in the same way experimental research does. Any unresolved question about the other two conditions may result in an invalid study.

Although ex post facto designs are subject to the same threats to validity that experimental designs are, dangers for validity of an ex post facto study generally originate from three sources: direction of the relationship, a common third variable, or contribution of other independent variables. If these three threats can be reasonably dealt with, the validity will be adequately established.

To establish the direction of the relationship, the researcher should establish that X precedes Y. If X always precedes Y, the data establish the time relationship. For example, to study the difference in running ability of philosophy majors and anthropology majors, there is no difficulty with the direction of relationship, because running ability is not an antecedent of choice of these majors. This would not hold true, however, for a comparison of physical education majors and anthropology majors on running ability. Similarly, medical research must establish direction in a large proportion of studies of health factors. If a relationship is established between a health problem and another factor, the question arises, Did the health problem create a difference in the other factor or did that factor create the health problem? A person may become nervous and develop a rash. Did the nervous condition cause the rash? Did observing the rash make the person nervous? Determining what preceded what can do much to establish cause-effect direction.

The influence of extraneous variables (any variables not under manipulation) may take two forms: first, lack of control of other independent variables may contribute differences to the dependent variable; second, influence of a third variable may affect both variables giving the illusion that the independent variable causes differences on the dependent variable. The first is relatively easy to handle if investigation of possible antecedent contributions by other independent variables is made and discounted as cause.

The influence of a third variable on both the independent and dependent variable may cause a researcher to establish a direct relationship between the two when the real situation is two indirect relationships connected by a third variable. For example, it has been noted that ice cream sales and drownings in the United States vary much the same way throughout the calendar year. Is the researcher to deduce that eating ice cream causes drownings? Or perhaps that increasing the number of drownings causes the rest of the population to eat ice cream? Without investigating for a direct relationship, most researchers would probably conclude that neither is the true state of affairs. The two separate variations are probably tied to a third factor—temperature fluctuation. As the temperature increases, the population is likely to eat more ice cream. At the same time, as the temperature increases, more people go swimming and are subject to drowning. Lack of control by direct manipulation always leaves the possibility of a third variable's influence in the ex post facto design.

Gaining Control. Some elements of control can be incorporated into ex post facto designs. Attempts by research workers to gain control vary with specific problems, so control must be dealt with after inspecting the overall research problem. Two widely used strategies are matching and **statistical control.**

Matching uses the principle of assigning like subjects to different groups to equalize the levels for studying independent variable effects. In theory, matching can be done on any number of characteristics, but in practice, the researcher is limited to matching on about two or three variables. As the number of matching variables increases, there are fewer subjects available and more interaction effects that must be considered when drawing conclusions. Such matching may be done by identifying many pairs of subjects who are equivalent (or nearly so) on the variables used to match. Then one member of each pair is randomly assigned to a group and the other member of the pair to the other group. These two groups may then be considered equivalent on the matching variables, thus giving some control. Other variations of matching are used depending on the problem under study.

Multivariate statistical analysis can also be used as a control instead of using experimental control, because multivariate techniques study effects of many variables at the same time. Quantitative methodology for social and behavioral research must include study of the interrelations of many variables and experimental research or simple correlation may not be as helpful as needed. Multivariate methods are important for organizing, analyzing, and interpreting data in large quantities.

Although the ex post facto design has some limitations, it may be the best way to deal with a difficult problem, and it is certainly better than not attacking the problem at all. It provides certain controls not possible by direct manipulation and allows study of many variables important to educators.

Validity of Experiments

An earlier section referred to the control of extraneous variables, those variables that are not a part of the treatment for a study but are contributing variables in the criterion-variable measures. A thorough study of experimental design includes analysis of weaknesses in control and evaluation of the *validity* of experimental results in terms of how well the design provides the needed control. A well-reported study points out any weakness in this area. Anderson and Bashaw, for example, raise a question about validity in paragraph 22. Validity is evaluated in terms of two possible sources of the weakness—internal-external validity and experimenter effects. Although in-depth study of validity is beyond the scope of this book, a substantial understanding can be attained from an overview of two chapters from two handbooks about educational research on teaching (Barber, 1973; Campbell & Stanley, 1963).

Internal-External

As stated earlier, the lack of laboratory conditions for experiments in the educational setting do not permit the level of control that experimentalists desire. To overcome this difficulty as much as possible, each research worker should consider how lack of control could affect the results of a study and in turn the conclusions drawn. For investigation of possible confounding effects, validity is broken down into effects from within the experimental design and effects from outside.

The two terms "internal validity" and "external validity" first appeared in an article in late 1950s (Campbell, 1957) and the topic was further developed a few years later (see Campbell & Stanley, 1963).

> *Internal validity* is concerned with the factors that contribute to making an experiment interpretable with the question, Did the treatment make a difference in this study?
>
> *External validity* is concerned with the factors that contribute to making an experiment representative. It deals with the question, To what populations and settings can this effect be generalized?

Eight different classes of **extraneous variables** that produce confounding effects on the dependent variable are relevant to a study of internal validity. When the question arises whether the treatment of the independent variable does indeed produce the effects observed on the criterion variable, the researcher should explore the following eight factors as possible competing influences. Several questions associated with these eight possible sources are listed below to help with that examination by the researcher.*

1. *History.* To what extent could outside events that occur between the start and finish of the study affect the criterion measurement?
2. *Maturation.* How did the passage of time per se function as an effect on the criterion measurement? Could differences be an effect of being older or growing more tired, less motivated, or other such natural changes?
3. *Testing.* If the same test or an equivalent test was administered two times, how did the first test experience affect the criterion measurement?
4. *Instrumentation.* Did any calibration of measuring devices change from the pretest to the posttest? Did observers or scorers change any points of reference?
5. *Statistical regression.* When subjects have been selected for study on the basis of their extreme scores, a terminal measurement on the same variable will cause the group mean scores to move toward the population mean. Could regression toward a population mean affect the criterion measure?
6. *Selection.* Did the manner of selecting subjects bias the characteristics of the groups and thus affect the criterion measure by reflecting differences in the criterion measure as a result of the assignment rather than the treatment?

---

*Discussion of these factors and those associated with external validity are based upon Campbell & Stanley, *Experimental and Quasi-Experimental Designs for Research.* Other articles on the same subject extend the presentation: Glenn H. Bracht & Gene V. Glass, "The External Validity of Experiments," *American Educational Research Journal,* 1968, *5*(3), pp. 437–474; and Richard E. Snow, "Representative and Quasi-representative Designs for Research on Teaching," *Review of Educational Research,* 1974, *44*(3), pp. 265–291.

7. *Experimental mortality.* Did the loss of some subjects chosen to be studied reflect a bias that could affect the criterion measures?
8. *Interaction.* Has interaction of any two of the factors just listed taken place to create an effect not present in either individually? Could this affect the criterion measure?

There are four additional questions that help focus on the representativeness of the study, its external validity. Inference to populations and settings beyond the study can be limited if external validity is reduced by any of these factors.

1. *Reactive effect of pretesting.* Did any pretest increase or decrease the sensitivity of subjects to experimental treatment and thus make the conclusion invalid for anyone not taking the pretest?
2. *Interaction of selection biases and treatment.* Is the sample biased in selection so that the results can be generalized to only groups with like characteristics?
3. *Reactive effects of experimental arrangements.* Have the arrangements for the study per se been such that they create a change in subjects? If so, would results then be invalid for generalizing to subjects who have not experienced the experiment?
4. *Multiple treatment interference.* Have effects of prior treatments that are not erasable limited the generalization to exclude those who have not had all treatments in sequence?

The preceding factors provide a set of guidelines for the researcher in the process of checking a design for validity. Several standard designs are given specific attention in the Campbell and Stanley materials (1963, pp. 176–239). Three tables in the Gage *Handbook* (1963, pp. 178, 210, 226) structure the strength and weaknesses of 16 different designs for experimental study. In addition, the 12 factors listed here guide the investigator as he or she checks the specific design for confounding by extraneous variables.

What should be done if the experimenter finds that the question being studied does not allow a perfectly developed plan and that there are areas where the design is deficient? Most studies are less than perfect. Rarely, if ever, will conditions in educational settings permit a design with no weaknesses, even though laboratory-like conditions have been established for the study. If, after careful investigation of all possibilities, the study has one or more weaknesses, each should be listed as a limitation and pointed up to readers of the study's conclusions. To list a weakness as a limitation implies that the researcher has confronted the problem but was unable under the conditions to overcome it. Acknowledging this may also indicate that if the problem were overcome, a greater weakness would be created elsewhere.

The researcher must select among alternatives. Many times the choice involves a sacrifice that creates a weakness because no single choice includes all of the desired characteristics. For example, a study of teaching methods may involve comparison of two groups taught by different instructional procedures. To conduct the study, first teachers must be chosen. If two different teachers are used, the effects of different methods may be confounded by differences between teachers. The researcher may attempt to overcome this problem by using the same teacher for both groups. Another source of confounding effects may be created if the teacher performs better in one condition than in the other. No matter which choice is made, some sacrifice is involved and a possible limitation created. The art of researching involves developing a study that minimizes such weaknesses. If either internal or external validity must be sacrificed, which should it be? With good reason, Campbell says "internal validity is the prior and indispensable consideration" (1957, p. 310). If external validity were protected at the expense of internal validity, the researcher would be prepared to generalize questionable results. However, the study itself would then be affected negatively, and nothing could legitimately be added to the body of knowledge about educational concerns.

Investigator and Experimenter Effects

One possible source of weakness in research techniques for experimental research is the effects contributed by those conducting an experiment. Chapter 11 in the *Second Handbook of Research on Teaching* (Barber, 1973) discusses nine possible effects caused by those conducting experiments. Barber isolates the roles of investigator and experimenter, although both roles could be played by one individual. The investigator originates the question, design, procedures, and analysis and interprets the results. The experimenter is responsible for collecting the data. This person conducts the study by administering the procedures, making the observations, and recording data.

Investigator effects—paradigm effects, loose-protocol effects, analysis effects, and fudging effects—are closely related to internal validity since the investigator selects the procedures to be used. These effects are also related to external validity in the area of sample selection and so on. Lowered validity can result from conclusions based on the investigator's design, experimental protocol, analysis of data, alteration of data, or any combination of these factors, if deficiencies are involved. Experimenter effects—attribute affects, failure-to-follow-protocol effects, misrecording effects, fudging effects, and unintentional expectancy effects—are also associated with factors that might jeopardize internal and external validity. Misleading results can be produced by the experimenter's personal attributes, by a failure to follow protocol, by errors made in recording data, by alteration of data, by personal expectations, or by any combination of these. Deficiencies in the experimenter's effects—like those in investigator effects—lower the validity of conclusions.

Each of the nine effects is discussed at length in Barber's chapter in the *Second Handbook of Research on Teaching* (1973). Researchers should become familiar with these possible sources of invalidity. The ninth effect in Barber's list (experimenter unintentional expectancy effect) is presented in greater detail than the others. This discussion uses some studies of that effect to point up where researchers have been victims of pitfalls. Twelve summary statements give direction to investigators and experimenters to help them avoid pitfalls that affect the validity of experimental studies. Most statements about experimental studies in this context are also applicable to descriptive studies and some also apply to historical studies.

Developing Experimental Designs

A true experimental design is an ideal which should be approached as nearly as possible when designing research studies. Experimental designs assure internal validity, because the real situation then meets requirements for strict control. Modifications of experimental designs retain most of the advantages of the true experiment but may be deficient in one or more ways. Reflect on the earlier discussion of the two uses of the term *design*. In Chapters 7 and 8, the overall plan was referred to as a *design* for research. At that time, *experimental design* was mentioned as a different use of the term *design*. *Experimental design* here refers to the methodology of procedures and techniques—especially the organization of subjects studied, treatment, and the statistical methods used to reduce data to results. The next several pages present models of widely used experimental designs.

The posttest-only control group design with random assignment to groups is one of the most powerful of all experimental designs, yet it has a simple structure that uses the basic design of experiments in the physical sciences. It is shown in Table 11–3 to introduce experimental design.

TABLE 11–3   Design 1—Randomized Groups, Posttest-Only Design*

	Group	Independent variable	Observation
(R)	E	X	$O_1 (Y_1)$
(R)	C		$O_2 (Y_1)$
		OR	
(R)	E_1	X_1	$O_1 (Y_1)$
(R)	E_2	X_2	$O_2 (Y_1)$

*This design can be expanded to include more than two groups.

In Table 11–3, R indicates that randomization has been used in assigning subjects to treatment groups and in assigning treatment to the groups.* This

---

*The system of symbols used here for presenting designs is a modification of symbolism from *The Handbook of Research on Teaching*, N. L. Gage (Ed.). (See Chapter 5 in the *Handbook*).

assures that initial differences between groups are attributable only to chance and that differences will follow the laws of probability. Other symbols explain other aspects of design:

> M indicates that subjects in the groups have been matched to obtain groups nearly equivalent on selected variables.
>
> A dashed line (-----) shows that intact groups are used.
>
> E stands for an experimental group.
>
> C stands for control group.
>
> X indicates when treatment is supplied to a group and a blank space is used to indicate control or absence of treatment. If treatments are compared X_1, X_2, X_3, . . . , X_n will be used.
>
> O indicates that observation (measurement) has been made. Subscripts O_1, O_2, O_3, . . . O_n indicate separate observations.
>
> Dependent measures appear as subscripted Y symbols.

The Randomized Groups, Posttest-only Design may have groups that receive different treatment either "X and control" or "X_1 and X_2." In either case, random assignment to groups and random assignment of treatment are used to equate the groups on all variables before treatment is supplied, thus controlling for all threats to internal validity.

When random assignment to conditions is possible, this design should be used. Data analysis is made by comparing measures on the dependent variable for the two groups, probably by testing a null hypothesis with a t-test (see Appendix C). If more than two groups are compared, the analysis of variance (see Appendix C) would be used to test a null hypothesis of no difference in dependent variable measures Y.

The design shown in Table 11–4 uses random assignment to groups and random assignment of treatment to equate groups for study. Each group is given a pretest on the dependent variable. This modification of Design 1 allows study of change over a time span, but using a pretest raises questions about the effects of previous testing on posttest scores and the interaction of testing and treatment.

TABLE 11–4   Design 2—Randomized Groups, Pretest-Posttest Design

	Group	Observation	Independent variable	Observation
(R)	E	O_1 (Y_1)	X	O_3 (Y_1)
(R)	C	O_2 (Y_1)	$---$	O_4 (Y_1)

The data analysis for Design 2 consists of comparing gains for the separate groups. The t-test or an analysis of covariance could be used to investigate for change.

A check on interaction effects to answer the questions raised by pretesting can be made by adding a second control group that does not receive the pretest but does receive treatment (see Design 2a in Table 11–5). If the experimental group is different from both control groups, the interaction is considered minimal.

Data analysis for Design 2a varies, depending on how the design is used. The analysis of variance using posttest measures can be used alone to test for differences. The analysis can also be done as a t-test on "gain scores" (the differences between pretest and posttest scores) with the analysis of variance on the posttest measures used to check for interaction. Variations of this design can be adapted to different situations. A fourth group might be added as a control. This group would receive neither the pretest nor the treatment. This modification is basically two studies incorporated into one study. It is rarely used because of the large number of subjects needed.

TABLE 11–5   Design 2a

	Group	Observation	Independent variable	Observation
(R)	E	O_1 (Y_1)	X	O_3 (Y_1)
(R)	C_1	O_2 (Y_1)	--.--	O_4 (Y_1)
(R)	C_2	---	X	O_5 (Y_1)

Design 3 in Table 11–6 uses matching of subjects on specified variables considered to be correlated with the dependent variable. For each matched pair, one subject is assigned at random to each group and treatment is assigned by a random procedure. The matching of subjects on attributes precludes experimenter manipulation and introduces possible threats to validity. It also limits the available subjects to those who can be matched.

TABLE 11-6 Design 3—Matched Subjects, Random Assignment Posttest Only

	Group	Independent variable	Observation
M⟨(R)	E	X	O_1 (Y_1)
(R)	C	---	O_2 (Y_1)

For Design 3, data analysis is made on the observations (O_1 and O_2) using a correlated t-test (Ferguson, 1976, pp. 166–168), since relationships have been established between the groups. Because of the established relationships larger differences between groups must be identified to indicate treatment effects to be significant.

This design can be modified as shown in Table 11–7 to resemble Design 2.

TABLE 11–7   Design 3 Modified

Group	Observation	Independent variable	Observation
M ⟨ (R) E	O_1 (Y_1)	X	O_3 (Y_1)
(R) C	O_2 (Y_1)	- - -	O_4 (Y_1)

The threats to validity for this modification incorporates those of both Design 2 and Design 3.

Factorial Designs. Factorial designs facilitating the manipulation of more than one independent variable permit the researcher to study the effects of combinations of variables. The Anderson-Bashaw study is an example of such a design. This type of design frees the experiment from the limitation of one-way designs that study only one independent variable. Factorial designs have the same strengths as respective one-way designs and the same limitations.

Factorial designs are used for one of two reasons. First, the experimenter may want to control for one or more attribute (assigned) variables while manipulating one independent variable. By investigating the effects of manipulating one variable on different levels of an attribute variable, the experimenter can determine the effects of manipulation at each of the levels. Treatment may have the same effect at all levels or differing effects at different levels. Second, the experimenter may want to manipulate two or more independent variables. The factorial design can investigate the effects of each independent variable manipulation and also the interaction of combinations of levels of the independent variables.

The design shown in Table 11–8 is the simplest factorial design—two levels on each of two independent variables. Other factorial designs combine more independent variables and/or more levels.

TABLE 11–8   Design 4—Simple Factorial Design

Experimental variable X_2 or Attribute variable	Experimental variable X_1	
	Treatment A	Treatment B
Treatment 1 or Level 1	Cell 1	Cell 3
Treatment 2 or Level 2	Cell 2	Cell 4

Graphically, the design appears in Figure 11–8.

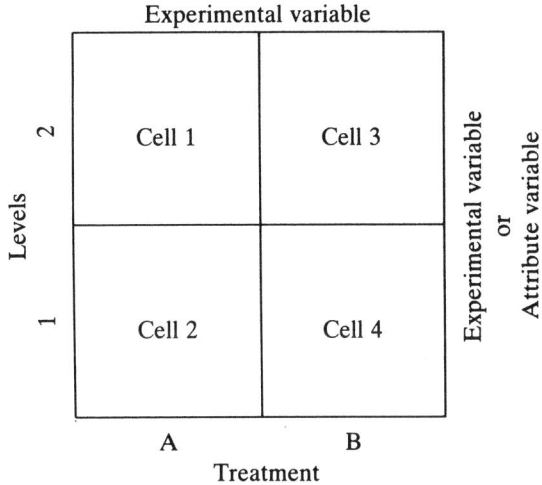

FIGURE 11–8   Graph for Factorial Design

Statistical analysis for this factorial design compares treatment A with treatment B through both levels of the second variable, compares level 1 with level 2 through both treatments, and checks the four cells for interaction of combinations of treatments and levels.

Statistical analysis could be performed on two levels of treatment of an experimental variable (see Figure 11–8) for methods of teaching reading. Treatment A could be phonics oriented instruction and Treatment B could be sight word oriented. For the attribute variable of sex, Level 1 would be boys and Level 2 would be girls. Such a design looks at differences between methods and between sex and at the interaction of the effects of methods and sex. An analysis of interaction effects could point out if boys learn better with one approach and girls with another.

Extending the principles of factorial designs allows the researcher to utilize several independent variables; however, the multiple-regression technique is being used more and more to analyze data from several variables. To allow valid conclusions from the data, the design—either factorial or regression—must incorporate safeguards of validity as much as possible.

Informal Inquiry. This section presents three situations that have been used simply to study for effects. Since they provide little or no control of extraneous variables, these situations cannot be classified as experimental designs, but the same design coding can be used to explain these forms of investigation. These situations show how lack of control renders some data invalid for scientific decisions. They are useful for informal study, however. By structuring investigation through these organizational schemes, teachers can also study changes in instruction and make preliminary studies for a full-blown research investigation. These are strategies for inquiry, but they offer little in the way of definitive terms.

TABLE 11–9   Situation 1—One-Shot Case Study

Independent variable	Observation
X	O_1 (Y_1)

The situation shown in Table 11–9 merely interjects treatment at a point in time within a series of ongoing events. Any inferences made from the resulting data must speculate about what the data from the observation would have been if treatment had not occurred. Since most of the possible sources of invalid data are not controlled for, a cause-effect relationship cannot be established, and there is no justification for establishing treatment as the cause for the observation.

TABLE 11–10   Situation 2—One-group Pretest-Posttest Study

Observation	Independent variable	Observation
O_1 (Y_1)	X	O_2 (Y_1)

The situation shown in Table 11–10 adds a pretest to the One-Shot Case Study of Situation 1. This allows the researcher to interpret the data from the final observation in comparison to an original set of data. Nevertheless, since subjects have not been compared to another group, extraneous effects of other variables could be the cause of any observed differences. Effects of the pretest on posttest scores cannot be adequately determined. Other extraneous effects can come from maturation of the subjects or intervening events (history) which may account for differences. The lack of control reduces the value of this type of study to informal investigations, not research studies.

TABLE 11–11   Situation 3—Two Intact Groups Comparison

Independent variable	Observation
X	O_1 (Y_1)
	O_2 (Y_1)

The situation shown in Table 11–11 incorporates a second group in the study, but equivalence of the groups at the start of the study must be assumed because intact groups are used. The influences of history and—to some extent—maturation are controlled for by the second group. The major limitation of this approach is that if the groups are different on relevant variables, differences in the observations may be extraneous to the treatment.

The three situations just described are appropriate for research only when conditions do not allow control by one of the better designs or when all that is desired is an informal study of problems. The researcher should make every effort to organize methodology around a design that provides adequate conditions for control by manipulation, but if this cannot be done, a less desirable set of procedures must be used including a list of inherent limitations with conclusions. Certain techniques of research can overcome some of the shortcomings of these studies, but lack of control makes establishing validity for the conclusions suspect at best. When using one of these situations or any other statistical or research design, the researcher must investigate for all possible sources of threat to internal and external validity.

☐ CHECK YOUR UNDERSTANDING

Classify each of the following descriptions of studies as

      S—a status study
      H—a historical study
      D—a descriptive study
      E—an experimental study

1. A study of how education in the United States was changed as a result of John Dewey's influence.
2. A comparison of two methods of teaching beginning typing to high school students.
3. Assessment of the attitudes of high school students to a year of compulsory military training to be completed after graduation from high school.
4. Study of the self-esteem of educationally impaired students and gifted students.
5. A report of library facilities of the Metro Library Consortium for Jefferson County, Kentucky.
6. Sample Study Number 1.
7. Sample Study Number 2.
8. Sample Study Number 3.
9. Sample Study Number 4.
10. Sample Study Number 5.

Answers

1. H	6. H
2. E	7. E
3. D	8. D
4. D	9. E
5. S	10. D

Tools of Experimental Research

Experimental research uses two types of tools—one gathers the data while the other analyzes the data. Since the success of an experiment depends on comparison between or among sets of circumstances, tools to gather data for experimental studies must be objective in all respects. The statistical procedure chosen to analyze the data must be selected for its ability to seek the specific messages contained in the data that relate to the study's question.

Collecting Data

The first criterion of any tool for collecting data in the experimental study is objectivity. Readily observable traits or characteristics can be measured with tools that produce highly objective data. Unfortunately, the traits of major concern in education, behavioral sciences, and social sciences are not readily observable. The nature of these traits makes them difficult to define and thus difficult to measure with the desired objectivity.

A second criterion for a tool used to gather data for an experiment is that it must be valid for the study. The instrument being used for a study must possess acceptable validity which is relevant to its purpose. Valid conclusions rest on valid data. Consequently, the researcher must choose an appropriate tool by considering the needs of the study and the alternatives available. Proper selection of a tool will provide valid objective data.

The tools discussed in Chapters 9 and 10 may be used to gather data for experimental studies. Anderson and Bashaw, for example, used rating scales (pars. 9–12) to collect data from their subjects. Some tools are limited to gathering data for background and to aid in developing a hypothesis. Others are appropriate for gathering data for analysis. A study based on an attitude change as a result of an intervening condition will probably use an attitudinal scale to measure the attitudes of subjects under study. Other choices of measuring instruments should be equally appropriate.

The widespread use of testing instruments to measure the criterion variable for experimental studies in education should not lead an experimenter to consider tests the only appropriate measuring devices for gathering data. A particular test should be used only if it is capable of gathering the best data for analysis. If another type of device will generate better data, it should be used. The researcher should not become locked into using tests for all situations. The nature of the dependent variable under study should be the major criterion for selecting the tool to gather data for analysis.

The process of gathering data is not a time-consuming task in most experimental studies. Generally, the gathering of data requires much less time for experiments than for historical or descriptive research. Careful planning of procedures to generate the data makes this aspect a rather insignificant part of the actual experiment. The plan should consider any possible effects on subjects produced by the procedures used to gather the data and recognize the influence of test administration on the validity of the data. For example, any testing situation is artificial in that the subjects are not in a real-world setting. Are the data collected valid for a natural situation?

Did the test make the subject anxious and thus affect the validity? When the planning incorporates special administration procedures to minimize any influence, the procedures to secure the needed data become a series of routine tasks.

Psychological and educational tests, sociometric instruments, and rating scales are often used in measuring dependent variables because of their objectivity. The procedures (rules) of measurement provide an operational definition of the variable and determine to a large extent the type of data the researcher has collected.

Analyzing the Data

The experiment provides a unique opportunity for a researcher to obtain an objective decision about what the data say about a particular research question through one or more tests of significance. (See the Anderson-Bashaw theme-writing study for an example of how this is handled—paragraphs 17 through 21.) The tools used to analyze experimental data are designed to test the tenability of a null hypothesis. In general, the research hypothesis is stated as an alternate hypothesis to the null hypothesis. Rejection of the null hypothesis means support for the research hypothesis, while failure to reject the null hypothesis represents lack of support for the research hypothesis.

The analysis of a set of data generally begins with a test of significance. This test gives the researcher direction in interpreting the source of differences that are observed in statistics of different groups of subjects. Basically a study of sampling (random) error, any test for significant difference is designed to structure within the rules of the research design an objectively made decision about the effects of different levels of independent variables as they are reflected in measurements of criterion variables.

A test of significance may involve one independent variable and one dependent variable, or it may involve more than one independent variable (see Table 11–8 and Figure 11–8). The effects of the independent variables may be viewed singly and in combination with additional information about the effects of interaction between or among independent variables. The statistical reasoning associated with tests of significance provides a unique way of making rational conclusions about the effects of experimentally applied treatment.

Statistical analysis is needed to study the variability (difference) that is imparted to those subjects studied in educational research. No two human beings are exactly alike. No one human being is the same at two different times because of intervening experiences. Statistical analysis allows examination of the effects of treatment to permit general statements about the variables, although there may be deviation from these statements in specific cases. The statistical analysis of a set of data compares what is actually observed with the probability of that occurrence by chance factors.

Statistical analysis results in a decision either to reject the null hypothesis or not to reject it, thus completing the test of significance begun earlier in the discussion about the null hypothesis. To review the total process, a test of significance consists of the following sequence of procedures. First, the researcher states a null hypothesis which assumes the applied treatment has no effect. The research hypothesis, on the other hand, most often assumes that the applied treatment has had an effect. Second, the researcher examines the data for differences for the groups studied. Third, the researcher considers the probability that a difference as large or greater than the one obtained would occur due to chance factors rather than treatment effects. Fourth, if the probability that the observed difference has occurred by chance is small, the null hypothesis is rejected. The difference is viewed as significant because it is unlikely to have occurred by chance but is instead due to the experimental treatment applied. When the differences observed between groups are small enough to have occurred as a result of chance factors, the null hypothesis is not rejected.

Testing for Significance. The tools discussed in this chapter are examples of a large class of statistical tests used to interpret sources of differences observed in sets of data. The number of tests available to the researcher seems endless. New statistical tests are constantly being created to serve unique designs, and better tests are being developed to advance the techniques of analysis. The number of tools discussed here is limited to a list of tests appropriate for the type of study that would be considered suitable for a first-time researcher. It does not exhaust even this class of tests. More advanced techniques may be found in the books listed earlier which focus on the wide range of statistical procedures appropriate for educational research studies.

A thorough study of statistics would entail understanding different types of **theoretical frequency distributions** which have been developed mathematically. These distributions are used in statistical designs as models. Theoretical frequency distributions, such as the normal distributions, compare sets of gathered data with expected outcomes assuming certain conditions. The statistical test uses a theoretical frequency distribution to indicate when a difference should be considered so great that it cannot be credited to chance happenings.

Some theoretical frequency distributions used as models include the binomial distribution, the chi-square (χ^2) distribution, the t distribution, and the F distribution. Each has unique characteristics. The choice of a model is determined by the type of data used and the question being asked.

The best known of these models is the **normal curve** which is generated from an indefinitely large $(N = \infty)$ population that has a mean equal to zero and a standard deviation equal to one. This model is chosen from a family of normal curves because of its usable characteristics. The *unit normal curve* in standard form (see Figure 11–9) is a particularly valuable research tool because the measurements of variables of most concern to educators often take the shape of a normal curve when empirical frequency distributions are built for sets of obtained data.

Because many physical traits—such as height and weight—are normally

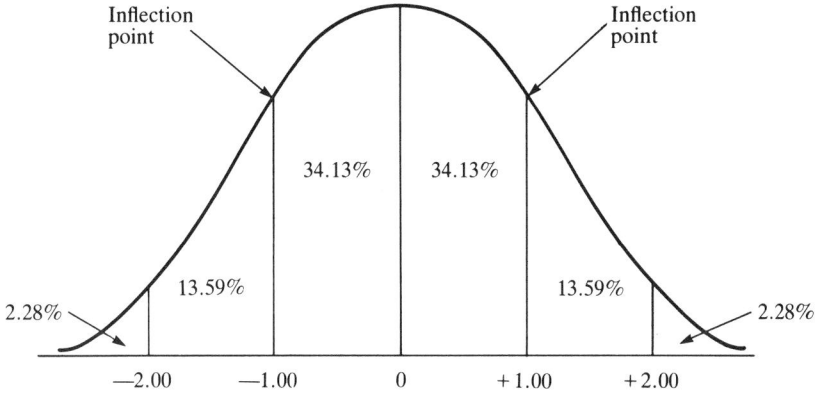

FIGURE 11–9   The Unit Normal Curve in Standard Form (percentage of area associated with base line segments)

distributed and other traits—such as intelligence and achievement—have a tendency to generate empirical frequency distributions that approach normality, it seems reasonable to assume that many other traits are so distributed. Without information to show exceptions to this tendency, it seems reasonable when confronted with a set of data to assume normal curve characteristics. Exceptions to this general rule are well-known or at least recognizable to the experienced researcher. An inappropriate measuring device could artificially create a skewed empirical frequency distribution from an attribute that is normally distributed. For example, a test developed to measure mathematical understandings of middle-school students would not give a normally distributed set of scores for second-grade students. The distribution would be skewed positively, because the difficulty level would be too high to measure second-grade pupil characteristics with high validity.

The *binomial distribution* is appropriate to use when data that fall into discontinuous categories are being compared to expected outcomes. For example, one might flip a coin 100 times and keep a record of the number of heads and the number of tails that appear. The binomial distribution assumes the equal probability of heads or tails coming up in one flip of the coin. The distribution indicates the probability of all combinations of events—for example, the probability of 50 heads–50 tails, 51 heads–49 tails, 52 heads–48 tails, . . . , 100 heads–0 tails, or 49 heads–51 tails, 48 heads–52 tails, . . . , 0 heads–100 tails. By comparing the number of times that the coin comes up heads with what the binomial distribution says should appear, the researcher can decide whether the coin should be considered biased (bent or weighted in some way to cause it to be something other than fair). The fairness of a pair of dice can be checked in the same way to see if their behavior is so unusual as to cause them to be suspect. A record of the outcomes for many tosses of the dice (observed data) can be compared with what is expected (the binomial distribution) from a pair of unbiased dice.

Research data which fall in ordered categories can be analyzed statistically by comparing what is observed with the appropriate binomial distribution. An investigation of learning, for example, might study the effects of a condition in the environment on the rate of learning a new skill. A laboratory maze for rats may have five choices, one of which—say number 2—has a pellet of food for a rat placed in the maze while the other choices have no food. A study of the rat's learning rate can be made by counting the numbers of correct food choices. As the animal learns to choose the proper way through the maze, the proportion will move away from the binomial distribution which would predict one correct choice out of five $(p = .20, q = .80)$. In this way, differences observed in the behavior of the rat are compared to chance choices as an indication of learning rate.

The *chi-square distribution* is a distribution that is skewed positively. Since it is a squared statistic, it contains only nonnegative values and is thus skewed to the right of zero. Researchers use chi-square distributions where means and variances cannot be provided for parametric tests or where the data are only categorical or ordered—that is, nominal or ordinal data. Many different types of problems can be solved using tests based on the chi-square distribution. Such tests compare the numbers observed to fall into separate categories with numbers expected to fall into the several categories. You may recall, for example, that chi-square values were reported for tests of significance in the Hillman study (see tables).

The *t distributions* are used primarily to test hypotheses about mean differences for two groups. They also test other comparisons of an observed value with a hypothesized parameter or zero. A different *t* distribution exists for each different sample size (N). Tables of values (see Appendix D) associated with degrees of freedom as determined by sample size make the *t* distribution a relatively simple analysis tool to use. It is nevertheless quite an effective tool for research studies. The *t* distribution has much the same properties as the normal curve except that it is leptokurtic. It is used in place of the normal curve when the sample size is small (less than 30 degrees of freedom). A *t*-test would be used when there are two levels of an independent variable and measures on one dependent variable.

F distributions are used to test hypotheses about differences among means much as the *t* distribution tests differences between two means. The *F* ratio used with *F* distributions is a mean square estimate and for this reason has only nonnegative values and is skewed positively from the value of 0. A different *F* distribution exists for each pair of degrees of freedom (see *F* table in Appendix D) associated with the two variance estimates—one from a within-groups measure and the other from a between-groups measure. Tables of significant criterion points for *F* tests of differences are available for comparing observed *F* values with the tabled values in the tables (see Appendix D). If an observed *F* value exceeds the value from the table (the criterion point for rejection), the null hypothesis is rejected.

F distributions are also used for testing hypotheses that involve two or more treatments as independent variables as well as studying the interaction from independent variables. The sources of differences are studied by partitioning total sums of squares into components and checking the *F* ratios against the tabled *F* distribution values. The *F* ratio is also used to test for differences in the variances of groups studied. Data interpretation can then include a discussion of how the groups differed on the characteristic of variability as well as how they differed on measures of central tendency. The *F* distribution was used in Sample Study Number 2 to report the analysis of variance in Table 2 (par. 16). Sample Study Number 4 reported results in *F* values in paragraphs 17–21.

The theoretical frequency distributions just discussed provide well-developed models for judging discrepancies between observation and hypothesis. Other theoretical distributions of frequency, bivariate distributions, and multivariate distributions are used in more sophisticated research designs. Although different theoretical distributions are used, each test for statistical significance is a study of sampling error, making a comparison between observed differences and differences possible through sampling alone. More information about all of these distributions may be obtained in books devoted to statistical procedures.

A Test for Significance

This section discusses how a test of significance can be applied to a one-factor, two-level study. Such a study (Figure 11–4) examines the mean difference between two subject groups.

A Sampling Distribution. A widely used theoretical distribution is the distribution generated by differences obtained from many pairs of samples. It is important because many research studies compare the performance of two groups considered equal in all ways except for the different treatments applied for each group on one variable.

Given a population with a standard deviation of σ, two samples could be chosen at random. Another pair with the same number in each sample group would then also be chosen. Choosing groups in this way an uncountable number of times produces an infinite number of pairs of samples with size N. Let us compute the mean for each sample in each pair, subtract the first mean from the second, and keep a record of the differences. These differences can be arranged into a frequency distribution. That theoretical (because we cannot really accumulate an infinite number of differences) frequency distribution (Figure 11–10) will have the following characteristics which are important to our study: (1) it will have a mean of zero; (2) it will be normally distributed; (3) its standard deviation can be determined; (4) proportions of areas under the curve can be determined from tables of the standard normal curve; and (5) differences can be located at points along the base line by z values $[z = (X - \overline{X})/s]$ using the **standard error** for measurement of the variation.

Since the distribution mean is zero, the points on the base line are the differences between the pairs of samples in raw score values. By putting the differences into units of the standard deviation, statements about probabilities of obtaining particular differences can be determined. Tables show that the interval between -1.96 and $+1.96$ includes 95 percent of the differences. Only 5 percent of the differences lies outside the two points

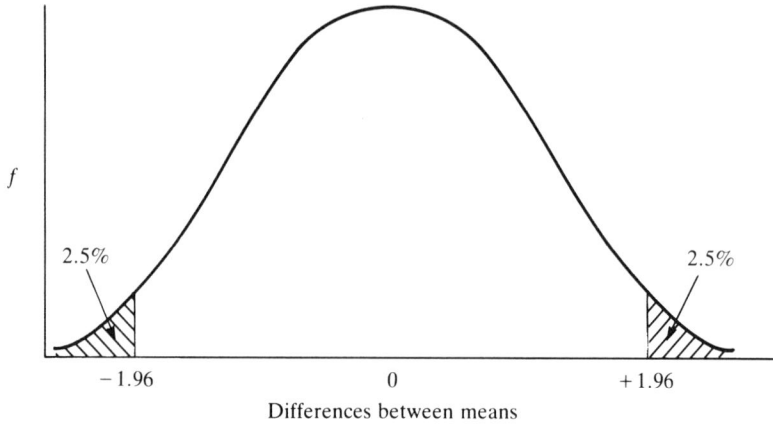

FIGURE 11–10   Differences between Pairs of Sample Means $(\bar{X}_A - \bar{X}_B)$

± 1.96. Beyond ± 2.58 lies only one percent of the differences. Using these reference points, a method to test a null hypothesis at either the .05 level or the .01 level can be established.

A Study. Let us see how a theoretical frequency distribution of differences between two means could be used in a study comparing two groups. A study of learning developed a methodology to answer the question, What effect does practice in estimating the areas of rectangles have on the ability of students to estimate the area of circles? A class of 32 fourth-grade students was given a series of lessons developing the concept of area. The lessons concluded by developing the formula for determining the area of a rectangle and included a series of problems using the formula *length times width equals area (l × w = A)*. For instruction on the final day, the class was divided randomly and assigned to 2 groups of 16 each. For 30 minutes, students in Group 2 worked individually and discussed together a set of problems involving measuring and determining the area of rectangles. Group 1 used the same set of problems, but before working each problem, each student made an estimate about the area. The students then compared that estimate with the calculated value for the area. At the end of 30 minutes, each group was presented a set of circles that varied in size. Each student guessed the area of each circle, and a score value was determined for each student paper. The original question may now be restated as, Is the mean accomplishment for one group superior to that of the other group?

    A test of significance for the difference observed in this study tests the null hypothesis: there is no significant difference in mean scores on a test of estimating areas of circles between a group that practiced estimating areas of rectangles and another group that did not (.05 level). Included in the null hypothesis are all differences from 0 to the z-value (see Appendix C on standard scores) criterion points of -1.96 and $+1.96$. Therefore, any values between -1.96 and $+1.96$ will fail to reject the null hypothesis, since they are considered small enough to have happened by chance. Differences less than -1.96 or larger than $+1.96$ are large enough to be the effect of differences in time utilization.

An appropriate test of the significance of a difference between two means is the *t-test* that utilizes a *t-ratio* to interpret the difference observed. By expressing the difference between the two means in terms of a ratio based on the standard deviation of the theoretical frequency distribution, the differences can be tested for significant effects. This test of significance transforms the observed difference between the two means into a value in a second distribution, the *t*-distribution. For the data collected for the area-estimation study (see Appendix D), the difference between the means converts to $t = +2.37$. This value would fit into a sampling distribution like that shown in Figure 11–11. For the statistical formulas and procedures, refer to Appendix C.

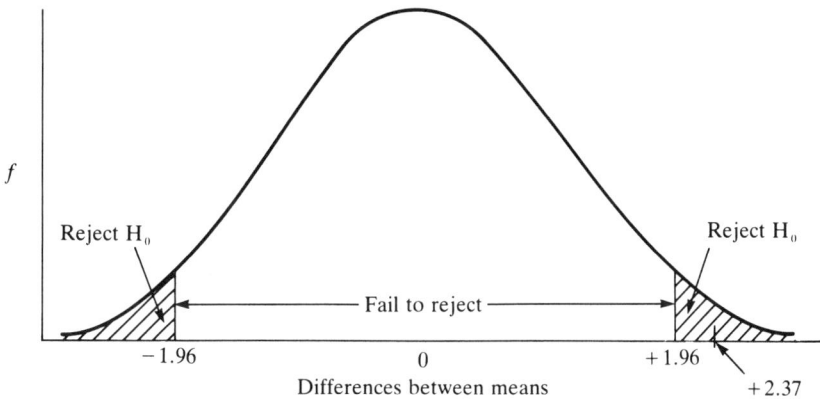

FIGURE 11–11 Comparing an Observed *t* Value with a *t* Value from a Table

Since the *t-ratio* for the area-estimation study exceeds the critical ratio of +1.96, the null hypothesis is rejected. The observed difference is great enough to consider it very unlikely that the difference occurred by chance—indicating only a sampling difference. The difference must be considered an effect of the different treatment provided. The area-estimation study thus concludes that the practice in estimating the area of rectangles was instrumental in increasing the mean criterion measurement significantly. In other words, practice in estimating the area of rectangles increased student accuracy in estimating the areas of circles.

The test administered in the area-estimation example used a *nondirectional* or *two-tailed* test (see Figure 11–11). If the null hypothesis is changed to indicate a test of superiority for one of the groups over the other, a *directional* or one-tailed test (see Figure 11–12) can be used. If the test for the above data used a .05 level of significance and a directional test, the critical ratio would change from +1.96 to +1.64. The hypothesis that Group 1, which estimated areas of rectangles, would exceed the other group would be rejected only if the critical ratio exceeded +1.64 (see Figure 11–12). For a one-tailed test at the .01 level of significance, the critical ratio becomes +2.33. The data from the study of estimation would cause rejection of the null hypothesis at the .01 level of a one-tailed test, but not at the .01 level of significance of a two-tailed test.

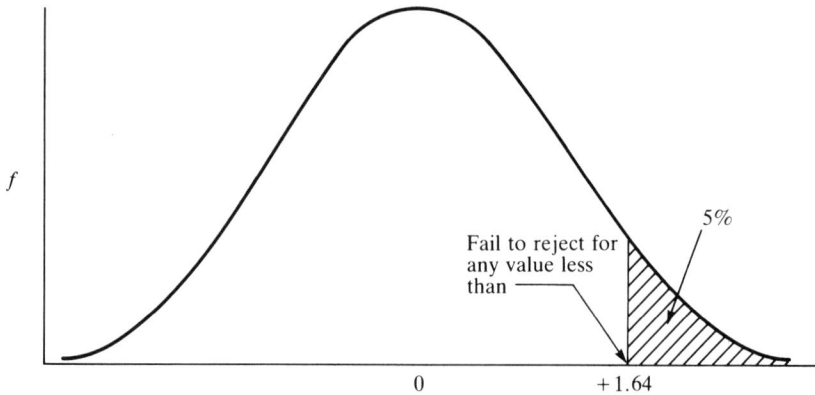

FIGURE 11–12   Rejection Area for a One-tailed Test

The *F* Test

Data from a study that involves more than two conditions on the independent variable *cannot* be analyzed with the *t* test. The *analysis of variance* allows the investigation of differences among three or more groups (See Appendix C). The basic principle underlying this procedure is a comparison of two variance estimates. The question is whether the means of the groups differ from one another (among groups variance) to a greater degree than the scores in the groups differ from their own group means (within group variance). The *F* ratio is built from the two different sources of variance as follows:

$$F = \frac{\text{among-groups variance}}{\text{within-groups variance}}$$

The null hypothesis stating no difference between these two estimates predicts an expected *F* value of one (1.00) if treatment has no effect. As the groups differ increasingly from each other and the within-groups variance remains constant or decreases, the *F* value increases. As is the case with the *t* test, small *F* values have a high probability of occurring because of sampling. *F* values in tables indicate critical points for rejecting the null hypothesis. Observed *F* values that exceed table values require rejection of the null hypothesis.

The analysis of variance allows a researcher to break down variation into component parts. It is a way to identify why a set of measures do not all have the same value. For example, the procedure for the *t* test given earlier is a special case of the analysis of variance where only two cases are studied. The principle can be used to break down the total variation (the variance) further into the separate sources of the difference. The procedures change as more variables and/or levels are included, but the rationale remains the same.

A further extension of tests of significance is to investigate the effects of two independent variables simultaneously. Since an independent variable is called a *factor,* a study of effects of two independent variables is called a *two-factor study*. If three independent variables are included, the study becomes a *three-factor study* or *three-way design*. Tests for two or more factors are discussed in the statistics books mentioned earlier in the chapter.

Parametric Techniques

The *t* test and analysis of variance procedures are used to test hypotheses by using sample values as estimates of population values. Since the population values are considered parameters, these tests are referred to as *parametric tests*. To make conclusions about population characteristics from characteristics of samples, certain assumptions are necessary:

1. Assignment to treatment groups is independent.* Selection of a subject for one group does not depend on or affect any other selection.
2. Population values are normally distributed.
3. Variances are equal.
4. Measurement assignment is in interval or ratio scale.

To the extent that the experimental design and data fail to satisfy the assumptions, the validity of inferences may be questioned. Most sets of data meet the assumptions only roughly; however, moderate departures from normality and equal variances do not seriously affect the validity of results. When the experimenter questions the tenability of the position of using a parametric test or has nominal or ranked data, she or he should use a method that does not rest on these assumptions. The next section discusses the use of **nonparametric tests.**

Nonparametric Techniques

Chapter 10 described a procedure to compare observed data with an *a priori* hypothesis. Recall the example of the two questionnaires that were mailed to the four classes. The returns were then checked for bias in the proportion of students from each class who returned the questionnaire. The data were nominal and assignment to categories did not include information that allowed a mean or variance to be calculated. The use of the chi-square distribution to interpret observed differences in Chapter 10's example constitutes a nonparametric test of significance. Observed frequencies were compared to expected frequencies in light of chance fluctuation through the theoretical sampling of chi-square values.

When measurement is in nominal or ordinal scales, means and variances cannot be determined. Distributions of some populations are not known and cannot be obtained. When distribution characteristics are unknown or unavailable and/or means and variances cannot be obtained, *nonparametric*

---

*Correlated techniques exist for studies that cannot meet this assumption. Examples: a special *t*-test technique to test differences for correlated samples and repeated measures using the analysis of variance. (See Appendix C.)

tests can be used to test differences between groups. Referred to as *distribution-free tests,* they are used with nominal and ordinal data and for data that have unknown population distributions.

The chi-square tests are used when nominal variable classes are compared and when ordinal, interval, or ratio data have been categorized into distinct classes for data treatment. Chi-square tests compare observed frequencies in discrete categories and expected frequencies in the same categories.

Example. A one-sample test can be used to analyze the number of occurrences for several categories. For example, an industrial firm might study employee absenteeism as it relates to the day of the week the absences occurred. If there is no factor of selection, then absences should occur about as often on any one day of the work week as on any other. To test whether absences are independent of the day of the week, a chart could be built from gathered data, as in Table 11–12, and a chi-square value computed for differences between observed and expected frequencies (see Appendix C).

TABLE 11–12   Absences for a Four-week Period

| Days of the week | | | | | Total absences = 985 |
Mon.	Tues.	Wed.	Thurs.	Fri.	
212	187	172	183	231	Absent from work
197	197	197	197	197	Expected absences

The expected value of 197 in the table is derived by seeding one-fifth of the total absences (985) into each of the five categories determined by the days of the work week. The number of absences associated with each day is entered above the expected number and a chi-square value is obtained using the calculation formula for chi-square.

If the actual absences had been distributed so that 197 were absent for each of the days, then χ^2 would equal 0. As the observed values depart from expected values, the chi-square value will increase. Table values for chi square indicate the value needed for null hypothesis rejection in this case. If the observed difference gives a chi-square value for the study that exceeds the table value, then the null hypothesis predicting no difference is rejected.

The observed chi-square value (11.69) is compared, at the significance level set for the test $(p < .05)$, to a table value for the appropriate degrees of freedom, 9.45. Degrees of freedom are determined by the formula $k - 1$, where k is the number of categories—in this case, the number of workdays, 5. The null hypothesis of no difference is rejected if the obtained value equals or exceeds the table value. The result of the comparison for this study indicates that absences should not be considered independent of the days of the week—that is, that the null hypothesis should be rejected. Conclusions and inferences may be made from these results.

Chi-square values are also used to test for (1) significant changes (before and after or pretest and posttest), (2) differences among independent samples, (3) the null hypothesis of no difference in breaking down frequencies in contingency tables, and (4) special aspects of other selected nonparametric techniques.

Example of a Median Test. The *median test* is used to test the hypothesis that two groups come from populations where the characteristic of order is associated with the measurement assignment. This test thus cannot be used with nominal data. A study of the effects of two different environments on children's activity rates could use the median test. By random assignment, the researcher would assign 20 children to 2 groups placing group (A) in an environment with certain characteristics and the other group (B) in an environment where one of the characteristics is changed. After a specified period of time, the researcher would take a measure of the activity of each child in both groups. Since both groups originally came from the same population, the 20 scores could then be combined and ordered, and a median could be determined for the 20 children. Next, the researcher would make a count for the children from group A who fall above the **median** and the number who fall below. Then he or she would make the same count for group B. If the environment has made no changes or caused no difference to arise in activity level, it would be expected that 50 percent of each group should appear above the median and 50 percent below (group A: 5 above, 5 below; group B: 5 above, 5 below).

The 20 children should be equally divided so that 5 children from A and 5 from B are above the median, and 5 and 5 are below. The expected frequency value for each of the 4 cells is 5. Applying the chi-square method, comparison can be made with the actual frequencies. Table 11–13 gives some possible values for activity measures for 20 subjects. Table 11–14 shows the division of the 2 groups by values that fell above and below the median in each group. Combining the actual frequencies with the expected frequencies, the data would appear as shown in Table 11–15.

TABLE 11–13 Activity Scores for 20 Children

Group A		Group B	
27	19	20	23
25	23	28	28
29	23	30	33
22	20	25	29
32	30	32	30

TABLE 11–14 Division of Children in Relation to the Median (20 children)

Group A		Group B
32		33
30	Above	32
29	the	30
	median	30
		29
		28
		28
27		25
25	Below	23
23	the	20
23	median	
22		
20		
19		

TABLE 11–15 Combined Actual and Expected Frequencies

	Group A	Group B
Above the median	3	7
(Expected)	(5)	(5)
Below the median	7	3
(Expected)	(5)	(5)

Comparing the observed and expected values and applying the chi-square test for significance, the null hypothesis of no difference is not rejected. The conclusion is warranted that the difference in environmental conditions (the independent variable) did not result in significant difference in activity rate (the dependent variable) for the two groups.

Example of a Sign Test. This final example of nonparametric techniques uses the normal distribution for the theoretical distribution. It analyzes statistically a pretest-posttest situation (or differences between matched pairs after different treatment) using a nonparametric test.

The *sign test* merely compares the increases and decreases in matched subjects' scores after the groups involved have received different treatments. If there is no difference in treatment, an increase or decrease should be a randomly determined event. Differences due to treatment are considered to have occurred when the differences are beyond a critical point determined by the significance level. The values in Table 11–16 apply to the following discussion.

Scores are arranged with matched subjects' scores side by side. If the increases (+) and decreases (−) for the two groups were randomly

TABLE 11–16 Results of Test on 50 Addition Facts by Students in 2 Treatment Groups after Matching on a Pretest

Group M	Group N	Sign M − N
43	41	+
47	40	+
19	24	−
33	33	0
38	42	−
46	42	+
32	30	+
22	23	−
47	45	+
29	27	+
39	39	0
49	46	+
44	46	−
40	38	+

determined, then the pluses should equal the minuses. Regarding the two zeroes as neither an increase nor a decrease, half of the signed numbers (12) would be the expected number of pluses and minuses.

A comparison (see Appendix C) of the observed signs with differences that could appear by chance shows that the result of 8 pluses and 4 minuses is not unlikely to have occurred by chance as a result of sampling differences. Consequently, the null hypothesis of no difference is not rejected. Within these data, no significant differences have appeared, and the conclusion is warranted that the treatment had no effect. This same procedure might be used in other designs, that compare each individual in a set before and after administration of treatment.

☐ CHECK YOUR UNDERSTANDING

For Sample Study Number 2, write a short essay that will convince another student who has not read the article that the study was experimental. Be sure to include in your essay all aspects of the study that support experimental methodology.

Answer

Your answer should include the following points.

1. Conditions were created so that they would be extremely unlikely in a real-world setting. (par. 2)
2. There was manipulation of conditions for controlled study. (pars. 4, 5, 6, 7)

3. Distribution of the test forms was made at random within sections. (par. 9)
4. A possible limitation was discussed: a result of the test being administered at different times. This indicates some lack of perfect control in the experimental situation. (par. 10)
5. The results section investigated certain possible places where control could be affected. No loss of control was found. (par. 11)
6. There was comparison of test reliability and student performance under controlled conditions to probabilities of random occurrence. (par. 13)

Multivariate Analysis

Experimental research is primarily a study of a single dependent variable. Precision within such studies is gained by controlling for extrinsic sources of variance. In education, measures on the dependent variable are, for the most part, multidimensional because of the external sources. This difficulty cannot be overcome in all cases. Newer advanced techniques of analysis substitute **statistical control** for experimental control. These multivariate methods allow understanding of relationships among several variables not possible with univariate analysis.

A relatively new approach to old problems, and a technique that holds much promise for analyzing situations involving many independent variables, is the research design that utilizes the multiple-regression approach. It is widely applicable to many different kinds of situations that arise in psychological, sociological, and educational studies. Although generally less understood than analysis of variance procedures, "multiple regression analysis can do anything the analysis of variance does—sums of squares, mean square, F ratios—and more" (Kerlinger & Pedhazur, 1973, p. 3). Although not an appropriate tool for those studying an introductory course in educational inquiry, it is a tool that behavioral scientists will be going to more and more as they become accustomed to its use. Factor analysis, canonical correlation, and discriminant analysis—and modifications of each procedure—allow researchers to study complex data, particularly situations with many interrelated variables. Such is the case with questions based in the education of human beings.

☐ CHECK YOUR UNDERSTANDING

As an overview, this Check Your Understanding section asks you to examine the experimental study, Sample Study Number 2, for some important topics studied in this chapter. You may have noticed that labels have not been given for the Jessell-Sullins study. For your review, identify the following points in the study by filling in the appropriate blanks in the column to the left of the study. Each blank should be filled in. Remember some points may be covered in more than one paragraph or in only a part of a paragraph, and there is some overlapping of topics. Therefore there will be some differences in the way individuals answer this review section.

1. Theoretical framework
2. Background
3. Test validity
4. Test reliability
5. Purpose
6. Manipulation-control-treatment
7. Data collection
8. Sample characteristics
9. Question about control
10. Limitation?
11. Statistical results
12. Conclusions
13. Limitation to generalization
14. Implications

Summary

The experiment is a direct way to test hypotheses. This chapter is an overview of the use of experiments in educational inquiry. It examines the control of variables to establish cause-and-effect relationships among variables, the essence of experimental method. This control results from doing something with a situation (manipulation) and identifying changes that take place as a result of the manipulation.

The steps of the experimental method of inquiry follow the steps usually associated with the scientific approach. The research hypothesis plays an especially important role in experimental research, since many experimental plans use a test of significance as a part of the analysis of data. Tests of significance use the null hypothesis to test for differences, and rejection of a null hypothesis is, in general, supporting evidence for a research hypothesis.

Experimental designs utilize experimental treatment where effects of different levels of an independent variable are studied in measures of the dependent variable. Through careful control within the research design, cause-and-effect relationships are identified.

Possible decision errors are associated with rejection of the null hypothesis or failure to reject it. The alpha error—rejection of the null hypothesis when it is true—is controlled by the researcher as he or she sets the significance level through an acceptable probability of making the error.

The validity of research results rests on the ability of the design to control variables not considered part of the treatment. The chapter discusses internal sources of weakness, as well as external sources, and recognizes 12 factors to provide guidelines for building validity into experimental results.

Tools used to gather data for experimental studies must be objective and must produce valid data for the study. The tools for analysis must be appropriate for the research design and type of data generated.

Theoretical frequency distributions serve as mathematical models that allow a comparison of observed values with values in the appropriate theoretical distribution. The unit normal curve values, the binomial distribution, the t distribution, F distribution and the chi-square distributions are used to judge discrepancy between observation and hypothesis.

The t-test is an example of a parametric test, while chi-square tests, the median test, and the sign test are examples of nonparametric tests. Nonparametric tests are used when the data do not have the characteristics needed for tests of means and variances; however, the basic principle of comparing obtained results with chance or theoretical frequency distributions remains the same. The technique of multiple regression is often proposed as a possible replacement for some presently used statistical techniques as it becomes better understood by researchers.

The student should now have an understanding of the principles of experimentally designed research studies and ways to check the several parts of the process for their contribution to defensible results. The design must be completed before any of the experimentation begins, and it must be applied precisely as the plan states or the results of the study will be open to question.

References

Barber, T. X. Pitfalls in research: Nine investigator and experimenter effects. In R. M. W. Travers (Ed.), *Second handbook of research on teaching.* Chicago: Rand McNally, 1973.

Bracht, G. H., & Glass, G. V. The external validity of experiments. *American Educational Research Journal,* 1968, *5* (3), 437–474.

Bruning, J. L., & Kintz, B. L. *Computational handbook of statistics* (2nd ed.). Glenview, Ill.: Scott, Foresman & Co., 1977.

Campbell, D. T. Factors relevant to the validity of experiments in social settings. *Psychological Bulletin,* July 1957, *54,* 297–312.

Campbell, D. T., & Stanley, J. C. *Experimental and quasi-experimental designs for research.* Chicago: Rand McNally, 1963. Also in N. L. Gage (Ed.), *Handbook of research on teaching.* Chicago: Rand McNally, 1963.

Chase, C. I. *Elementary statistical procedures.* New York: McGraw-Hill, 1976.

Ferguson, G. A. *Statistical analysis in psychology and education* (4th ed.). New York: McGraw-Hill, 1976.

Gage, N. L. (Ed.). *Handbook of research on teaching.* Chicago: Rand McNally, 1963.

Good, C. V. *Dictionary of education.* New York: McGraw-Hill, 1973.

Hays, W. L. *Statistics for psychologists.* New York: Holt, Rinehart, & Winston, 1963.

Kerlinger, F. N., & Pedhazur, E. J. *Multiple regression in behavioral research.* New York: Holt, Rinehart, & Winston, 1973.

Marascuilo, L. A. *Statistical methods for behavioral science research.* New York: McGraw-Hill, 1971.

Nie, N., Bent, D., & Hull, C.H. *Statistical Package for the Social Sciences* (SPSS), New York: McGraw-Hill, 1975.

Selye, H. From dream to discovery. New York: McGraw-Hill, 1964.

Snow, R. E. Representative and quasi-representative designs for research on teaching. *Review of Educational Research,* 1974, *44* (3), 265–291.

Walker, H. M., & Lev, J. *Statistical inference.* New York: Holt, Rinehart, & Winston, 1953.

CHAPTER TWELVE

AN AID TO INQUIRY:
THE COMPUTER

In the developed world of the twentieth century, man lives surrounded by a bewildering variety of machines on which his way of life and even life itself depends. . . . A computer is conceptually a machine which can receive, store, manipulate, and yield up information.

—Meek and Fairthorne

From the time that human beings first developed simple counting skills and built a structure for record keeping, they have used devices to aid in these endeavors. For example, making counting marks on the ground when sheep left for pasture gave the early shepherd a way to check on the number that returned from pasture. This counting and marking may seem far removed from modern mathematics and devices to aid in computation and record keeping, yet these are the ideas upon which present-day mathematical structures and computers are built. This chapter discusses briefly a complex machine (the computer) that records and processes data at high speed, works for long periods of time, and focuses precisely on details. The use of computers by researchers is expanding so rapidly and the field of computers itself evolves so fast that specifics written today will soon need expansion.

Although crude machines had aided in data processing as early as the late 1800s and the **abacus,** adding machines, rotary calculators, and bookkeeping machines greatly facilitated hand counting and manipulation prior to 1950, the electronic computer truly opened up new and even faster ways to handle data. Even during the 1950s, few researchers had computers available or knew how to use them in their research efforts. Since the early 1960s, technological development and computer utilization have expanded beyond what was even hoped for by researchers only a few years earlier. Not only do computers handle complex calculations, but they also are able to handle demographic and other qualitative data for quick retrieval. Further they can even analyze the content of written materials. Today, terminals may be installed miles from the central unit or may be portable enough to be carried about using telephone lines for connection with the computer. Phone-linked networks allow facilities to combine and/or expand capabilities beyond what a single central unit does. Much of the advanced technology of business, engineering, mathematics, physical and human sciences, and history would not be in existence today without computer capability.

A Description

A computer is a high-speed, general-purpose machine that receives data and a set of instructions, processes the data in accordance with the instructions, and furnishes results that are readable by a person and/or by another machine. There are basically two types of computers. The analog computer is primarily used in the technical work of engineering and laboratories and is little used presently in educational research work. The digital computer manipulates digits by working with discrete numbers. Because of the large number of applications within educational research that require counting and mathematical manipulation, the digital computer is used extensively for treating quantitative data for educational problems. Computer retrieval of stored data is also a service widely used by researchers.

The speed with which a digital computer processes data, recalls data, or analyzes content is its major asset for researchers, but accuracy, capacity for storing vast amounts of data, and analytic features are also advantages for educational research. Probably the greatest overall advantage of the computer is the access it provides to ways of dealing with complex situations which could not be adequately handled by manual techniques. The computer can routinely manipulate extremely large amounts of data and can perform computations in a few seconds that would require years by hand computation. In the past, researchers often avoided manual searches through materials because of the tedious, boring repetition, but the computer quickly and tirelessly works through retrieval without weariness or boredom.

Hardware

The physical equipment that constitutes the working parts of the computer and support devices is referred to as *hardware*. The actual set-up may be relatively simple, organized within one console, or it may be very complex, consisting of a large room containing interconnecting units. The IBM design model in Figure 12–1 is typical of the latter arrangement.

Figure 12–2 shows one portion of such a system, the control unit for a computer. In general, each unit carries out one of the four types of operation: storage, input-output, data transmission, or processing.

FIGURE 12–1   Arrangement of computer hardware in a computer facility (Photograph: Courtesy International Business Machines Corporation)

FIGURE 12–2   A computer control unit (Photograph: Courtesy International Business Machines Corporation)

For the purposes of this book, the operation of computer hardware is less important than exploring how the computer capabilities can be utilized in the research process. The details of how a system works cannot possibly be explained here, nor is it necessary to do so. In the study of computer technology, experts frequently refer to a unit within a system as a "black box." This entity is said to have certain "black-box properties," and it interacts with other black boxes with certain other black-box properties. The black-box properties of a unit are determined by its contents. For our purposes, computer hardware must largely remain an unexplained black box. However, the functions of computers (their black-box properties) are very useful for educational research.

This black box (the computer) can store information without permament alteration of the information and read back that information later in the same form. It may receive information on tape, from punchcards, or possibly by voice and then generate an output in the form of graphic symbols recognizable by a human reader. The output is usually a hard copy printed on paper, but it may also consist of a transient image, such as the display on a cathode ray tube. Computers may also transfer information from one location to another. A transmitter receives incoming information, converts it into a language suitable for transmission, adds some information for detecting errors and correction, and passes the information along a channel to a receiver which converts it to original language. Finally, computers often receive digital information in the usual number system, manipulate the data according to prescribed instructions, and produce new information asked for by the researcher. Within each of these four functions, the subtleties in use are—for practical purposes—limitless. Researchers continually find new ways to use the black box/the hardware/the computer to aid in inquiry.

Software

Before a computer can be used, instructions and supporting material must be prepared. The program that directs the computer is referred to as *software*. Software preparation includes systems flowcharting, program flowcharting, programming, writing instructions to feed into the computer, and documentation. When the programmed instructions are combined with a set of data, they constitute input for the computer. The computer will then perform one or more of four functions listed in the previous section.

Systems Flowcharting. A *systems flowchart* is a graphical representation of the interactions among equipment, people, and data needed to carry out a task on a computer. In general, this flowchart shows the relationship of data and program as input to the computer, the processing route, and the desired output. This chart tells the complete story in general terms.

Program Flowcharting. A *program flowchart* is a graphical representation of what the computer is to do. This flowchart breaks down one of the components of the systems flowchart into the operations the computer is to perform and the sequence in which they will be performed. This flowchart is the plan from which the actual program is written and should serve as a basis for writing in any one of several machine-readable languages.

Programming. A computer understands only machine language. The computer must operate from instructions written in binary form (all 0's and 1's) and performs operations using the same code. Without elaborating on intricacies, it could be said that the writing of a *program* translates instructions from the usual way of communicating into computer language, using the program flowchart as a guide. This task is not unlike translating from English to Spanish; however, the process is different.

Most programs can be written in several ways. Selecting a particular computer language should minimize the combination of time spent in writing the program and the time spent in running the program. Given the increased speed of modern "black boxes," the running time is not as crucial today as it once was. Most programs today are written in procedure-oriented languages, such as **COBOL, BASIC,** or **FORTRAN.**

Mathematical computations are likely to be written in FORTRAN, the language widely used in statistically based studies. After the initial writing of a program, the programmer must check it for errors. This process—known as **debugging**—reveals and removes two kinds of errors, clerical and logical. When the program has been debugged, it is ready to use with new data.

Documentation. Making a permanent record and reference for the completed program is the next step: it must be documented. Documentation includes recording the objectives, the software components, and samples of input data and data output. Other relevant comments are usually included in the document record.

With the recorded program and a set of appropriate data, a knowledgeable person could operate the computer to perform an assigned task. Libraries, commercial companies, businesses, educational institutions, research centers, computer centers, and many other sources have extensive files of programs which have general applicability as well as specific uses. A researcher may often be able to find a ready-made program from a program library for use in a study, or she or he may need to develop or have someone else develop a new program to deal with a particular set of data to be used with a specific computer system.

Who Uses the Computer

Computer Abstracts (1956 to the present) has over 20 divisions for categorizing "applications" of the computer including one class of "miscellaneous" which covers many other uses. Even a cursory glance through the abstracts reveals just how computer use permeates today's world. "Computer News" for one recent month included feature articles about the use of computers in widely diversified areas—air cargo inventory, a computer network for 800 retail food stores, tomography scanners, weather research, literary and linguistic computing, and patient monitoring. Other monthly issues reveal the same wide range of uses.

The personal computer market—home or individual computers—is projected to grow from 43,000 in 1977, to 1.2 million by 1982 *(Computer Abstracts,* 1978, p. 2). The personal computer is not expected to affect people's lives dramatically but is expected to be slowly integrated into the lives of about 20 million people who have special needs—either hobby or business.

Computers also serve a wide range of educational needs. Students are instructed by computer, school administrations use computers for record keeping, data processing, and check writing, and central libraries (some school libraries) are likely to have terminals connecting them with a network of other library holdings. Most important for our study is the contribution the computer makes to educational research.

All researchers are likely to use the computer for information retrieval when searching the research literature for background and other topics related to a specific problem. Other than this general use, researchers turn to the computer for one or more other reasons—the psychologist often for help in computation, the historian for help in searching printed materials, and others for processing large amounts of data that have been collected as facts for a study.

Historical Research

In addition to the traditional use of computers to locate information, there is a new way to study facts from the past using computers. Economic, societal, and political aspects of the past can now be included in computer study. It is also possible to study theoretical models of human behavior on the basis of historical data. Herliky says:

> Still, in this writer's opinion, the popularity of computation and the computer in historical research today is rooted most fundamentally in the continuing obligation of historians to experiment with their sources. If, for example, the computer allows them to discern aspects of their documents which would be otherwise hidden, then they would be professionally derelict, if they failed to seek its aid. (1978)

Study of many questions based in the past that could not be adequately handled manually are now open to investigation through the use of computer capabilities. For example, the computer could facilitate studying the impact of economic forces on politics of the American colonial period by synthesizing a total impression from particular information about individual forces.

Descriptive Research

The complexity of ongoing real-world events challenges the researcher considerably in the process of formal inquiry. Trying to understand the interrelatedness of many variables by isolating one or a few at a time for study is difficult at best. The high-speed capability of the computer and its ability to do thousands of calculations routinely without tiring is especially important in the study of multivariate relationships. Kerlinger reports:

> The responses of 296 individuals to 36 semantic differential items were analyzed on the CDC-6600. The means, standard deviations, and intercorrelations of the items (630 correlation coefficients) and a complete principal factors factor analysis with varianax rotation of two, three, four, five, six, seven, and eight factors were calculated. The factor analysis and rotations alone would take weeks

on a desk calculator. In fact, few researchers would be hardy enough to attempt such a task. The machine took 23 seconds to do the actual calculations and about 43 seconds to read in and print the data! (1973, p. 706)

Manual computation of only one correlation coefficient is tiresome, and the many separate operations make at least one error highly probable. Given a debugged program, the computer calculates with perfect accuracy.

With the aid of a computer, the correlationalist can employ a host of correlational procedures including multiple regression, canonical correlation, and other multivariate techniques. Multivariate analysis of data is perhaps the most powerful and helpful tool that a researcher has to assist in situations that are by their nature multivariate. These methods can substitute statistical control where experimental control is difficult or inadequate. To a large extent, such calculations for multivariate analysis cannot be reasonably accomplished by hand computation.

Thus, many questions based on real-world conditions that could not be adequately handled before by manual means are now open for study through computer utilization. The correlator must continue to find new ways to ask questions as newer uses of the computer are developed.

Experimental Research

Research experiments require the measurement of dependent variables. Also a part of such experiments is statistical analysis of the collected data. It may come as a surprise to many people then, that the computer has changed experimental research less than other methods of research. The major contributions computers have made to this area of research are speed and accuracy, since nearly all calculations done for analysis of variance problems connected with experimental research can be done on a good desk calculator. The computer has not expanded this area of study extensively, since the numerical analysis is, in general, within bounds of hand calculation. However, the amount of time once spent in calculation can now be spent in more profitable ways—planning and organizing new studies.

The carefully controlled factors of the experiment create an environment for mathematical analysis that is relatively simple compared to multivariate analysis. Even "relatively simple" calculation on a desk calculator is still open to human error, however, so that computers are usually employed for the accuracy they provide. Newer models of desk and **hand calculators** discussed in the last section of this chapter are capable of accepting programs. They can thus perform as routine calculation what only a few years ago would have been considered calculations requiring a computer program.

Only rarely does an experiment require a completely new program. Usually the experimentalist has only to select a program from a program library to perform the appropriate statistical calculations. Selecting the correct program is crucial, since differences among several programs may be subtle. In most cases, the researcher obtains the program in the form of a set of prepunched cards with instructions about how to organize the obtained data with the **card deck** so that the computer can read them. All information must be in the form and order called for in the program description. By establishing good communication with the staff at the computer center while preparing the input, the researcher is assured that the program will run smoothly.

The computer has made the professional life of an experimentalist easier and has released time previously used in calculation for development of more problems into researchable form. In this way, the computer has expanded the experiment. Nevertheless, its more important contributions to research as a whole have come in the other methodologies.

Using the Computer

When using the computer, a research worker must remember that the computer does only what it is told to do. Computers can be programmed to play tic-tac-toe, chess, and other games against a human opponent. It may seem in this context that the computer thinks out its moves; however, that is not the case. The computer makes choices from programmed alternatives given a certain set of circumstances. Likewise, a computer used in research gives back only what has been written into the program.

The research worker who uses a computer need not have great amounts of technical knowledge about the internal workings of the computer or even such knowledge about programming, if a good programmer is available. The researcher does need to communicate with the programmer about what is expected in the way of outcomes and what kinds of data are being collected. Decisions should actually be made before data are collected, since data collection may need to be performed in particular ways, depending on the computer capability and the programmer.

In general, programs will require all or some of the following cards,* and the researcher should become familiar with them before working out the details with the programmer: system cards, program cards, an execute card, control cards, a title card, variable format cards, data cards, a finish card, and an end-of-file card.

System cards are used to tell the computer what to expect and how to make arrangements internally to receive the instructions of the program. *Program cards* instruct the computer to perform certain procedures of search or statistical analysis. The *execute card* indicates to the computer that the instructions are completed and the data follow.

Control cards explain how the data will be transmitted and grouped. The *title card* is prepared so that the computer can print a label on the analysis report. *Variable format cards* indicate to the computer what parts of a general program to include and which to ignore.

Data cards contain the information to be analyzed. The *finish card* indicates that the data input is complete. The *end-of-file card* informs the

---

*In most cases, computers use a set of punchcards. If input is in a different form, the same instructions would be given in the other mode.

computer that all input has been delivered. When the computer reads that the input is complete, it begins a search or calculation depending on what output has been requested. As the information is retrieved or calculated, a printout is typed as the output.

Information Retrieval

As indicated earlier, the keeping of some kind of record is one of the earliest acts specific to the human race. Record keeping in science, business, government, law, and such has been increasing along with the sophistication of other human endeavors. When records are systematically ordered, a **file** is created which may serve as a reference as long as the file exists. On a national scale, a file may contain millions of entries. Organization on this scale requires efficient and accurate methods of filing information. The same efficient methods are needed for information retrieval.

These requirements for storing information extend into library holdings also. Accuracy in filing these holdings serves the researcher who needs a search of information for one of several purposes. Figure 12–3 shows a random access disk storage unit. Great amounts of information can be stored for retrieval on such a unit according to a program tailored to a researcher's need. Complete library holdings are listed in forms readable by computer,

FIGURE 12–3 Random access disk storage unit (Photograph: Courtesy International Business Machines Corporation)

and special holdings may also be found in computer files. As one of these files is built, two basic questions guide construction: What should it contain? and How should it be arranged? To facilitate use of the file, the answers should be based on the type of information to be filed and the uses to be made of the data, the operations to be performed on the file's contents, and the capability needed—or available—from the computer equipment.

The computer does not store information in original form. Letters and other symbols are represented in numeric form and filed in the computer by patterns of magnetized spots, voltage, and similar coding methods. Through this process, almost any kind of information—words, graphs, pictures, and numbers, for example—can be recorded for later retrieval. Figure 12–4 shows a flow diagram for a typical storage and retrieval system. The storage

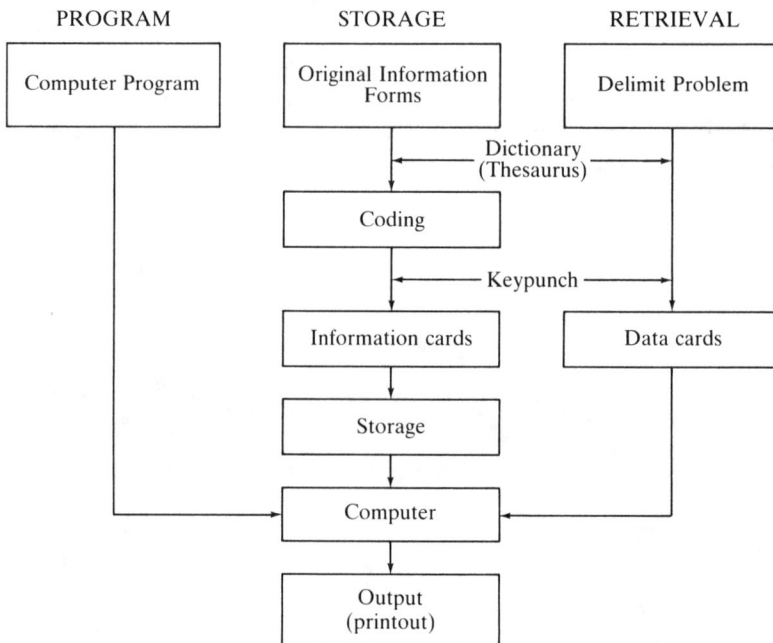

PROGRAM   STORAGE   RETRIEVAL

| Computer Program | Original Information Forms | Delimit Problem |

Dictionary (Thesaurus)

Coding

Keypunch

| Information cards | Data cards |

Storage

Computer

Output (printout)

FIGURE 12–4   Flow diagram of a storage and retrieval system

takes on different characteristics depending on the use to be made of the data and on the user—researcher, business, government, educational unit, or library. The researcher may also store data relevant to a particular study for later retrieval. Data from an extensive questionnaire or demographic data may be used for several different purposes. Efficiency may be gained by placing all of the data in storage and then placing requests for specific purposes.

The Educational Resources Information Center (ERIC) keeps a list of retrieval systems currently in use and the type of information that each storage contains. The user of a retrieval system may have a choice of the type of printout to be generated as output. Each retrieval program indicates the choices available to the user.

Several universities have developed programs to search ERIC reports in *Resources in Education* (RIE) and *Current Index to Journals in Education* (CIJE) to eliminate time-consuming manual searches. In general, these searches are made available to off-campus users for a modest fee. The following section discusses a retrieval program developed for searching ERIC materials as an example.

Example. The program combines subject headings and prints the abstracts of RIE and/or journal articles from CIJE which match a set of descriptors. Searches may be made by author, title, and by key phrases within the abstracts. The user receives a computer printout citing the relevant reports or studies and is given abstracts of the most recent.

The user should be prepared to request information through descriptors (or combinations of descriptors) as listed in the *Thesaurus of ERIC Descriptors*. The computer retrieval search is exactly the same as a manual search to locate the descriptors to define the scope of a search. After the descriptors are delivered, they are combined with the program and storage (see Figure 12-4) and the computer prints ERIC materials that relate to a study. The next step for the researcher is to go to a library that subscribes to the ERIC microfiche collection, to order microfiche or hard copy from ERIC, or to go to professional journals.

Other retrieval systems are organized much the same way, except a **dictionary** of terms specific to the program terms will be used rather than the *Thesaurus of ERIC Descriptors*. Widely used data bases for educational research which are computer readable include:

PATELL—Psychological Abstracts Tape Editions Lease License (January 1967 to present)

AIM/ARM—Abstracts of Instructional and Research Materials in Vocational and Technical Education (January 1967 to present)

ECEA—Exceptional Child Education Abstracts (January 1966 to present)

Specific information about these and hundreds of other data bases can be found in:

Martha E. Williams and Sandra H. Rouse. *Computer-Readable Bibliographic Data Bases: A Directory and Data Sourcebook*. Washington, D.C.: American Society for Information Science. (Currently updated every six months)

University libraries expand their own programs with other information services, such as Lockheed Information Systems (DIALOG), Bibliographic

Retrieval Services, Inc. (BRS), Systems Development Corporation Search Services, and *New York Times* Information Data Bank Service. These services are also available to research centers and research workers. The reference department of a library has current information about services available.

Content Analysis

The researcher uses analysis of qualitative data in two different but similar ways. First, he or she may want to analyze the contents of a set of data that have been collected for a specific study by questionnaire or interview. Second, the research worker may want to analyze the content of speech, writing, songs, or signs to reflect thoughts, opinions, or information.

The first use is a process of storage and retrieval. This process is particularly amenable to computer capabilities as presented in the previous section. The second use is somewhat different: it utilizes the computer in another capacity. **Content analysis** can be considered an observational procedure (Kerlinger, 1973, p. 525). It is also a way to "measure the unmeasurable" (Simon, 1978, p. 211). Both interpretations are correct, since content analysis looks at some communication or set of material to make a judgment about some particular aspect by comparing its content to a classification system through quantification. Such analysis consists of either counting particular words or ideas used or measuring the amount of time devoted to particular words, kinds of words, or ideas. Content analysis of mass media to determine writer biases for or against something is one example of how researchers use this method.

Content analysis has been used to investigate for specific thrusts or biases that may knowingly or unknowingly be built into textbook materials. Investigations into who actually wrote particular literary works or portions of written materials can be helped by a content analysis. For example, if another person had been selected to write this chapter on the computer, a content analysis of the words used and the ways of expressing ideas should be able to identify that someone else wrote it and perhaps even speculate about who that person was.

The choices of categories for a classification system are very important, because the classes must fit with that which is to be measured. Computers make content analysis through programs that instruct the computer to classify data according to designated key words, phrases, tense, and so on. Usage can be interpreted and certain judgments made about the characteristics of the writer and how the writing reflects the opinions and thoughts of the writer.

The computer has facilitated content analysis, because it can perform the menial tasks of scanning large amounts of material as well as the classification by categories. A researcher may find a ready-made computer program, which will reduce the workload even more. The key to the program usage is the dictionary (see Figure 12–4) and matching terms to categories of classification. The method of content analysis varies depending on how the researcher is using analysis of communications.

Statistical Analysis

The nature of the digital computer as a manipulator of numbers makes it a natural companion of the researcher. Massive calculations—burdensome, impractical, or impossible with manual techniques—are no longer a block to a researcher's search for answers. Reflect a moment on this fact:

> . . . for with addition times of much less than a microsecond they [computers] can perform as much raw arithmetic in a second as could a man in his entire 40 years of working life. To put this gee-whiz statistic another way, one such machine could outperform the population of the United Kingdom. (Laver, 1976, p. 124)

The capacity indicated in this example, along with the reliability of statistical calculations on an electronic computer based on its high accuracy, make the modern computer an irreplaceable tool for researchers.

Statistical analysis is likely to be straightforward calculation by algorithm. Numerical analysis for the computer requires that a step-by-step arithmetical method be devised for statistical methods, because the computer does not handle a formula directly. In addition, other considerations require the researchers to specify the range and precision of input data, as well as acceptable error levels. Given careful attention to these details, statistical calculations for most research data are routine for the computer.

Hand Calculators

Although the Arabic number system itself was a key to efficient calculation, the first mechanical device for computation was probably the abacus. Pascal in 1642, Leibniz in 1670, Thomas in 1820, Burroughs in 1885, Felt in 1886, and other inventors produced mechanical devices (Lynch & Rice, 1977, pp. 33–46) that aided in calculation. Other devices using vacuum tubes were the forerunners of the electronic devices used today (pp. 37–44). In the late 1960s, a device came on the market that was to revolutionize calculation that had once used slide rules and rotary or electronic desk calculators. This innovation was hand calculation by small portable electronic calculator.

It is difficult for someone who has grown up using electronic hand calculators to imagine the impact that these devices have had on scholarly work involving mathematical calculation as well as on the sciences, business, government, industry, and the home. The rotary desk calculator had been largely replaced by the electronic desk calculator in the 1960s, and the efficiency of that device speeded mechanical computation tremendously. The added features of portability and ease of use made the hand device the common calculation device that it is today. The supplementary devices of clocks, alarms, and stopwatches are more than added features to help sell the calculator—they make the instrument more functional.

The first models of the portable electronic devices were limited to performing the four basic processes of arithmetic—addition, subtraction, multiplication, and division—and were priced at over $400. Today a device that does all that those first models did and more can be purchased for less than $10. In the quantities which schools purchase, simple calculation devices cost much less than $10 each.

These **minicalculators** are made possible by large-scale integrated (LSI) circuitry, a technology first used in vehicles for the space program. A network circuitry utilizing 10,000 microscopic transistors can be placed on a silicon chip less than ¹⁄₁₆ inch square. Since there are many different models and variations of the minicalculators, this chapter will discuss them only generally. Our discussion focuses on three broad classes—basic, intermediate, and advanced.

Basic

The simplest of minicalculators is the four-function device which may include one or more of the following keys—reciprocal, square root, or percentage. These keys are added to the ten numerical keys, four process keys, a decimal key, an equal key, and a key to clear the display. The sequence for using the machine (depressing number keys, function keys, and so on) is the same logical sequence used in hand calculation, except that the basic minicalculator allows for some shortcuts. The patterns available for specific models are explained in the manuals which accompany them.

When a basic model is switched on, the display (the X-register) records a 0. To add 27 + 4, enter 2 then 7 into the X-register by depressing the keys in that order, press the addition key (+), enter 4 in the X-register (the 27 automatically goes into the Y-register), and press the equal key (=). The sum 31 will appear as the solution. Subtraction, multiplication, and division operations follow basically the same pattern. Use of the percentage key, reciprocal key, and square root key varies with the model. Experimenting with a minicalculator using the directions from the operating manual develops facility in calculating and may reveal other operations—such as the use of an automatic constant or raising a number to an integer power—which are special to a specific model.

Intermediate

In the middle 1970s, a language of computer science was adapted to the minicalculator. A new but relatively simple way of sequencing operations allowed complex algebraic equations to be solved without using parentheses or an equals key. By adding **register stacks** (more than the X- and Y-registers on the basic calculators), several important features were added to the hand-held calculator.

This intermediate model utilizes **reverse Polish notation** (RPN) to direct the operations of the device. The principle of this notation system and hence the sequencing require the entering and storing of values and intermediate answers. When these numbers are needed, they are retrieved from the stack of registers in the device. Using this system demands some new learning, but with a very short amount of time devoted to learning RPN and studying a manual explaining dual use of keys, this type of calculator expands into many uses not possible with a basic model. Given enough registers, calculation can be carried through complex formulas without writing down any intermediate answers.

Advanced

The intermediate model opened the door to calculation through complex formulas, but advanced courses in mathematics, engineering, and physical sciences require even higher levels of calculation. The advanced models of minicalculators handle scientific notation (exponential placement of a decimal point) and include functions not on either the basic or intermediate models. This type of minicalculator varies from one manufacturer to another. Operation of most models becomes routine after practice with a manual for operation.

Programmable Portable Devices

A recent addition to the range of portable calculators already available is the fully programmable personal calculators. These devices are able to handle difficult calculations that previously have been left to the computer. These models have program libraries and the facility for personal programming. Keystroke programming of the Hewlett Packard (HP) models HP-67 (see Figure 12–5) and HP-97 (see Figure 12–6) makes programming as simple as

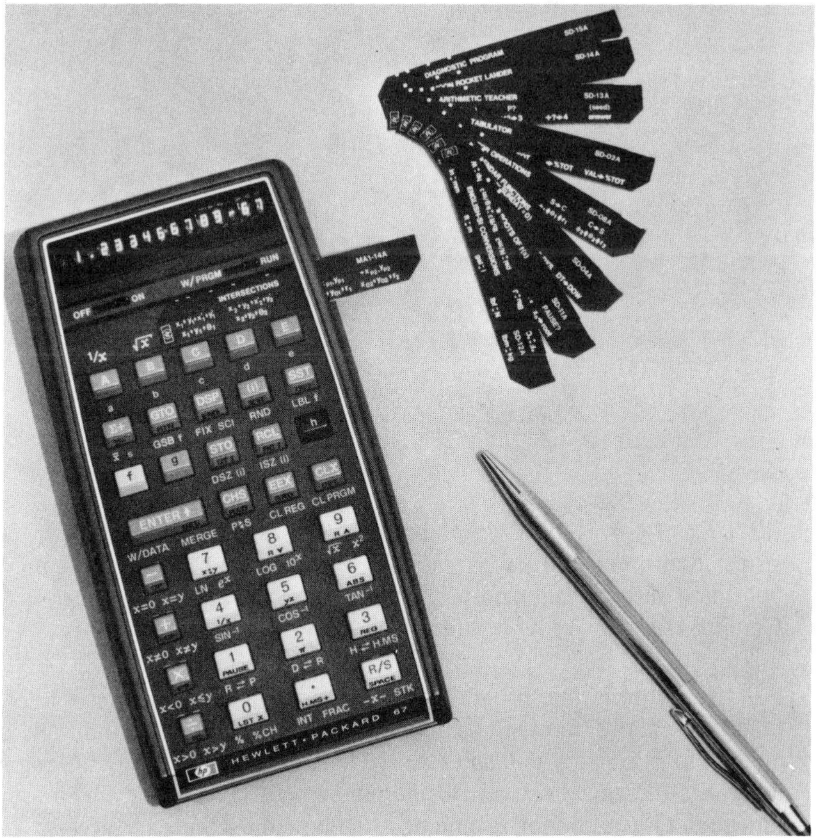

FIGURE 12–5 Fully programmable personal calculator with program strips (Photograph: Courtesy the Hewlett-Packard Company)

pressing the keys needed to calculate answers manually. Merged operations further simplify the task (and expand memory power) by letting the user see the complete operation in the display.

The exceptional capability of the programmable calculator handles lengthy, repetitive problems by letting the user write programs to 224 steps (HP-67/97 models). Every function (one, two, or three keystrokes) is merged to take only one step of program memory. With 26 data storage registers to provide memory capabilities along with the other features, these models approach computer capability for mathematical calculation. Printing capability allows some models to produce a tape to aid in editing programs and long calculations. The record allows the user to see what has been done and what remains to be done.

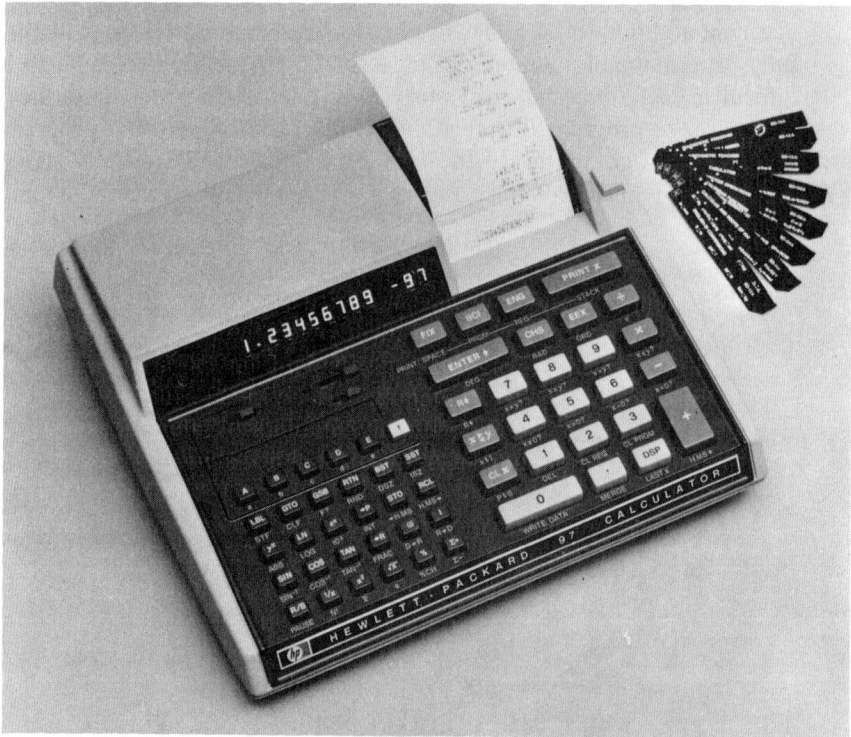

FIGURE 12–6 Fully programmable personal calculator with program strips. Same capabilities as calculator shown in Figure 12–5 plus battery operation and thermal printing. (Photograph: Courtesy the Hewlett-Packard Company)

In addition, the programmable hand calculator features a complete range of preprogrammed functions and other features that allow these models to print and/or display in fixed decimal, scientific, and engineering notation. Of special interest to the educational researcher are the statistical functions that allow for summations to be stored for easy access. With the data keyed in, a user can calculate or use summations to compute other statistical functions. Other keyboard features are angular functions, logarithmic functions, mathematical functions, number alteration functions, and display for fixed decimal, scientific, and engineering displays up to 10 significant digits plus 2-digit exponent and appropriate signs.

Undoubtedly, the pace of change in hand-held calculators and computers will soon make this chapter's presentations outmoded. However, this short overview of recent important technological advancements at least gives the reader some understanding of how electronic equipment can aid in educational research. Given merely three decades of experience with these machines behind us, it becomes difficult to project computer utilization into the future. Nevertheless, it is reasonable to expect that the exponential rate of computer utilization will probably continue.

Activities

1. Make a study of how the computer can be used to perform content analysis. The index to *Computers and the Humanities* (a periodical) contains articles that report projects utilizing the computer in differing ways to make such an analysis. You might start your reading with *Computers and the Humanities, 12* (1–2, double issue) 1978, which has reports of various ways computers are used to analyze written materials. References and notes can expand your base for reading.
2. Make a study of how the computer can be used to analyze social science data.
   Introductory study: Read Chapter 1 of *Statistical Package for the Social Sciences* (SPSS), 2nd ed. by Nie, Bent, Hull (New York: McGraw-Hill, 1975). Outline or write a review of how an integrated system of computer programs is organized. Include how you as a researcher would proceed if you have no prior computer experience.
   Intermediate study: In addition to the above, read Chapters 2, 3, and 4 of SPSS and outline or write a review of the preliminaries of organizing, coding, preparing control cards, and defining a file.
   Advanced study: In addition to the above, use a library program (SPSS or other) to analyze a set of data that you have collected.
3. Investigate how random-access disks and similar devices store data. Explain how these have revolutionized historical research study procedures.
4. Build a glossary of 25 words related to computer use. Select those terms that would be of most use to a researcher in the social sciences.
5. Choose one (or more) of the following titles and write a two-page essay on that theme.

   a. How a Computer Can Be Programmed to "Think"
   b. Why a Computer Cannot Be Programmed to "Think"
   c. The Evolution of Methods of Information Processing—Manual to Modern
   d. Transmission of Data From One Location to Another
   e. Computer-assisted Instruction
   f. Impact of Computers on Research in the Humanities

Summary

This chapter presented a brief overview of the computer to acquaint the reader with this important tool of research. A general description of computer hardware and software and the purposes of each aspect of computer operations introduced the research functions of computers. The widespread use of the computer was discussed specifically for historical, descriptive, and experimental research, clarifying how each uses the computer differently.

Description of the use of computers focused on several card decks, each of which serves a specific purpose in computer operation. Information retrieval, content analysis, and statistical analysis programs serve the researcher in different but important ways.

The relatively recent but widespread use of minicalculators has provided the researcher with convenient calculating devices and supports research quantification and statistical interpretation. This chapter offered general coverage to three classes of calculators—basic, intermediate, and advanced. The programmable portable devices expand calculation range to approach computer capability for many statistical procedures.

This chapter completes the presentation of three aids to inquiry—the library, the proposal, and the computer. These aids are not a part of the research process per se, but they are widely used to support the research process.

References

Computer Abstracts. St. Helier, Jersey; British Channel Islands: Technical Information Co., 1956 to present.

Computer news. *Computer Abstracts,* July 1978, *22* (7), 2.

Herliky, D. Computation in history: Styles and methods. *Computer,* August 1978, *11* (8), 8–17.

Kerlinger, F. N. *Foundations of behavioral research* (2nd ed.). New York: Holt, Rinehart, & Winston, 1973.

Laver, M. *An introduction to the uses of computers.* Cambridge: Cambridge University Press, 1976.

Lynch, R. E., & Rice, J. R. *Computers: Their impact and use.* New York: Holt, Rinehart, & Winston, 1977.

Meek, B., M. Sc., & Fairthorne, S., B.Sc. *Using computers.* Chichester, Eng.: Ellis Horwood, Ltd., 1977.

Nie, N., Bent, D., & Hull, C. H. *Statistical package for the Social Sciences* (SPSS). New York: McGraw-Hill, 1975.

Simon, J. L. *Basic research methods in the social sciences: The art of empirical investigation* (2nd ed.). New York: Random House, 1978.

Bibliography: Part Three

Altman, E. I. Financial ratios, discriminant analysis, and the prediction of corporate bankruptcy. *Journal of Finance,* September 1968, *23,* 589–609.

American Historical Association. *Guide to historical literature.* New York: Macmillan, 1961.

Anderson, S. B., Ball, S., & Murphy, R. T. *Encyclopedia of educational evaluation.* San Francisco: Jossey-Bass, 1975.

Andrews, F. M., & Messenger, R. C. *Multivariate nominal scale analysis.* Ann Arbor: University of Michigan—Survey Research Center, 1973.

Androit, J. L. *Guide to U.S. government guides & periodicals.* McLean, Va.: Document Index (Box 195), 1969.

Babbie, E. R. *Survey research methods.* Belmont, Cal.: Wadsworth Publishing, 1973.

Barber, T. X. Pitfalls in research: Nine investigator and experimenter effects. In R. M. W. Travers (Ed.), *Second handbook of research on teaching.* Chicago: Rand McNally, 1973.

Barzun, J., & Graff, H. F. *The modern researcher* (3rd ed.). New York: Harcourt, Brace, & World, 1977.

Beach, M. History of education. *Review of Educational Research,* December 1969, *39,* 561–576.

Bergstrom, J. M., & Margosian, R. K. *Teaching young children: Basic concepts and resources.* Columbus, Oh.: Charles E. Merrill, 1977.

Bracht, G. H., & Glass, G. V. The external validity of experiments. *American Educational Research Journal,* 1968, *5* (3), 437–474.

Brickman, W. W. *Research in educational history.* Norwood, Pa.: Norwood Editions, 1973.

Brooks, P. C. *Research in archives: The use of unpublished primary sources.* Chicago: University of Chicago Press, 1969.

Bruning, J. L., & Kintz, B. L. *Computational handbook of statistics* (2nd ed.). Glenview, Ill.: Scott, Foresman & Co., 1977.

Campbell, D. P. (Reviser), & Strong, E. K. *Strong vocational interest blanks.* Stanford: Stanford University Press, 1927–1977.

Campbell, D. T. Factors relevant to the validity of experiments in social settings. *Psychological Bulletin,* July 1957, *54,* 297–312.

Campbell, D. T., & Stanley, J. *Experimental and quasi-experimental design for research.* Chicago: Rand McNally, 1963. Also appears as chapter 5 in N. L. Gage (Ed.), *Handbook of research on teaching.* Chicago: Rand McNally, 1963.

Chase, C. I. *Elementary statistical procedures* (2nd ed.). New York: McGraw-Hill, 1976.

Computer Abstracts. St. Helier, Jersey; British Channel Islands: Technical Information Company, 1956 to present. (periodical)

Conover, W. J. *Practical nonparametric statistics.* New York: John Wiley & Sons, 1971.

Crawford, P. B., Hankin, J. H., & Huenemann, R. L. Environmental factors associated with preschool obesity. *Journal of the American Dietetic Association,* 1978, *72,* 589–596.

Edington, E. S. *Statistical inference: The distribution-free approach.* New York: McGraw-Hill, 1969.

Eisenbeis, R. A., & Avery, R. B. *Discriminant analysis and classification procedures.* Lexington, Mass.: D. C. Heath, 1972.

Ferguson, G. A. *Statistical analysis in psychology and education* (4th ed.). New York: McGraw-Hill, 1976.

Fisher, Sir R. A. *Statistical methods for research workers* (14th ed.). Darien, Conn.: Hafner Publishing, 1970.

Gage, N. L. (Ed.) *Handbook of research on teaching.* Chicago: Rand McNally, 1963.

Gardner, P. L. Scales and statistics. *Review of Educational Research,* Winter, 1975, *45,* 43–47.

Good, C. V. *Essentials of educational research.* New York: Appleton-Century-Crofts, 1966.

————. *Essentials of educational research* (2nd ed.). New York: Appleton-Century-Crofts, 1972.

————. *Dictionary of education.* New York: McGraw-Hill, 1973.

Good, C. V., & Scates, D. E. *Methods of research: Educational, psychological, sociological.* New York: Appleton-Century-Crofts, 1954.

Hales, D. M. *Student involvement in high school decision making and its relationship to student attitudes toward school.* (Doctoral dissertation, Indiana State University, 1975). Series III, No. 102. *Dissertation Abstracts International,* 1975, *36A,* 3292–A. (University Microfilms No. 75–29,877)

Hays, W. L. *Statistics for psychologists.* New York: Holt, Rinehart, & Winston, 1963.

Helmstadter, G. C. *Research concepts in human behavior.* New York: Appleton-Century-Crofts, 1970.

Hempel, C. The test of a hypothesis: Its logic and its face. In H. S. Broudy, R. H. Ennis, & L. I. Krimerman (Eds.), *Philosophy of educational research.* New York: John Wiley, 1973.

Herliky, D. Computation in history: Styles and methods. *Computer,* August 1978, *11* (8), 8–17.

Herson, M., & Barlow, D. H. *Single case experimental designs: Strategies for studying behavior change.* New York: Pergamon Press, 1976.

Herson, M., Eisler, R. M., Alford, G. S., & Agras, W. S. Effects of token economy on neurotic depression: An experimental analysis. *Behavior Therapy,* May 1973, *4,* 392–397.

Hopkins, C. D. *Describing data statistically.* Columbus, Oh.: Charles E. Merrill, 1974.

Horst, P. *Factor analysis of data matrices.* New York: Holt, Rinehart, & Winston, 1965.

Huck, S. U., Cormier, W. H., Bounds, W. G., Jr., & Sechrest, L. *Reading statistics and research.* New York: Harper & Row, 1974.

Johnson, A. H. *Changing conceptions of vocational guidance and concomitant value-orientations,* 1920–1930. (Doctoral dissertation, Indiana State University, 1972). Series III, No. 49. *Dissertation Abstracts*

International, 1972, *33A,* 3292–A. (University Microfilms No. 72–13, 933)

Johnson, H. H., & Solso, R. H. *An introduction to experimental design in psychology: A case approach.* New York: Harper & Row, 1971.

Katz, M. B. *Class, bureaucracy, and schools.* New York: Praeger, 1971.

Katz, M. B. *The people of Hamilton, Canada West.* Cambridge: Harvard University Press, 1975.

Kelly, F. J., Beggs, D. L., McNeil, K. A., Eichelberger, T., & Lyon, T. *Research design in the behavioral sciences multiple regression approach.* Carbondale: Southern Illinois University Press, 1969.

Kendall, M. G. *Rank correlation methods* (3rd ed.). New York: Hafner Publishing, 1962.

Kerlinger, F. N. *Foundations of behavioral research* (2nd ed.). New York: Holt, Rinehart, & Winston, 1973.

Kerlinger, F. N., & Pedhazur, E. J. *Multiple regression in behavioral research.* New York: Holt, Rinehart, & Winston, 1973.

Kuder, F. *Kuder preference record forms.* Chicago: Science Research Associates, 1934–1976.

Laver, M. *An introduction to the uses of computers.* Cambridge: Cambridge University Press, 1976.

Likert, R. A. A technique for the measurement of attitudes. *Archives of Psychology,* 1932, *140,* 1–55.

Lutz, F. W., & Ramsey, M. A. The use of anthropological field methods in education. *Educational Researcher,* November 1974, *3,* 5–8.

Lynch, R. E., & Rice, J. R. *Computers: Their impact and use.* New York: Holt, Rinehart, & Winston, 1977.

McReynolds, P. (Ed.). *Advances in psychological assessment III.* San Francisco: Jossey-Bass, 1974.

Madge, J. H. *The tools of social science.* New York: Doubleday, 1965.

Marascuilo, L. A. *Statistical methods for behavioral science research.* New York: McGraw-Hill, 1971.

Masling, J. Role related behavior of the subject and psychologist and its effects upon psychological data. *Nebraska Symposium on Motivation.* Lincoln: University of Nebraska Press, 1966.

Meek, B., M.Sc., & Fairthorne, S., B.Sc. *Using computers.* Chichester, Eng.: Ellis Horwood, Ltd., 1977.

Moehlman, A. H., Van Tassel, D., Goetzmann, W. H., & Everett, G. D. *A guide to computer-assisted historical research in American education.* Austin: University of Texas Press, 1969.

Mueller, J. H., & Schuessler, K. F. *Statistical reasoning in sociology.* Boston: Houghton-Mifflin, 1961.

Myers, J. *Fundamentals of experimental design.* Boston: Allyn & Bacon, 1972.

Nie, N., Bent, D., & Hull, C. H. *Statistical package for the social sciences* (SPSS). New York: McGraw-Hill, 1975.

Oppenheim, A. N. *Questionnaire design and attitude measurement.* New York: Basic Books, 1966.

Pierce, A. *Fundamentals of nonparametric statistics.* Belmont, Ca.: Dickenson Publishing, 1970.

Poulton, H. J. *The historian's handbook, a descriptive guide to reference works.* Norman: University of Oklahoma Press, 1972.

Schmeckebier, L. F., & Eastin, R. B. *Government publications and their use.* Washington: Brookings Institution, 1969.

Selye, H. *From dream to discovery.* New York: McGraw-Hill, 1964.

Siegel, S. *Nonparametrics for the behavioral sciences.* New York: McGraw-Hill, 1956.

Simon, J. L. *Basic research methods in the social sciences: The art of empirical investigation* (2nd ed.). New York: Random House, 1978.

Sloan, D. Historiography and the history of education. In F. N. Kerlinger (Ed.), *Review of research in education.* Itasca, Ill.: F. E. Peacock, 1973.

Snidell, P. S. Anthropological approaches to the study of education. *Review of Educational Research,* December 1969, *39,* 593–605.

Snow, R. E. Representative and quasi-representative designs for research on teaching. *Review of Educational Research,* 1974, *44* (3), 265–291.

Sullins, W. *Matrix algebra for statistical analysis.* Danville, Ill.: The Interstate, 1973.

Tatsuoka, M. M. *Multivariate analysis, techniques for educational and psychological research.* New York: John Wiley & Sons, 1971.

Terman, L. M., & Oden, M. H. *The gifted child grows up.* Stanford: Stanford University Press, 1947.

Thernstrom, S. Foreword in M. B. Katz, *Class, bureaucracy, and schools.* New York: Praeger Publishers, 1971.

Tilly, C. Computers in historical analysis. *Computers and the Humanities,* September–November 1973, *7,* 323–335.

Van Dalen, D. B. *Understanding educational research* (3rd ed.). New York: McGraw-Hill, 1973.

Walker, H. M., & Lev, J. *Statistical inference.* New York: Holt, Rinehart, & Winston, 1953.

Webb, E. J., Campbell, D. T., Schwartz, R. D., & Sechrest, L. *Unobtrusive measures: Nonreactive research in the social sciences.* Chicago: Rand McNally, 1966.

Whallon, R., Jr. The computer in archaeology: A critical survey. *Computers and the Humanities,* September 1972, *7,* 29–45.

Williams, M. E., & Rouse, S. H. *Computer-readable bibliographic data bases: A directory and data sourcebook.* Washington: American Society for Information Science, currently updated every six months.

Woody, T. Of history and its method. *Journal of Experimental Education,* March 1947, *15,* 175–201.

PART FOUR

COMMUNICATING ABOUT INQUIRY

Even the most carefully planned and conducted research study has no worthwhile value unless its results are translated into conclusions that can be communicated to others. The chapters in Part IV complete this book's discussion of the scientific approach to inquiry by examining ways to extend findings beyond the subjects studied and those conducting the study.

The chapter on drawing conclusions begins with the results of the study and discusses how results become valid conclusions. The implications of the conclusions for possible changes in practice and recommendations for further research then project the findings of the particular study into the future.

The next chapter discusses research reports. There are at least three types of research reports that can be considered useful to researchers. The first is a detailed report that provides complete documentation of what was done, results obtained, conclusions drawn, and implications warranted. This type of report should be written in sufficient detail to enable another person to replicate the study. A second report that does not go into detail about specifics may be prepared for dissemination through professional journals for general information. Interested individuals can then go to the detailed report or communicate with the original researcher for more details. A third type of report is the abstract which reports the variables studied, the number and type of subjects, a description of procedures, and a synopsis of the major findings in about 100 to 200 words. These abstracts appear in periodicals with the intent of communicating as quickly as possible so that others can be informed of research related to their area of interest. In many journals, an abstract precedes the report and provides the reader with enough information to decide whether or not to read the article.

The material in the final chapter has been included to give an overview of the research process and to foster a synthesis of the structure of inquiry through research. The review covers the process of inquiry as a logical chain of reasoning.

CHAPTER THIRTEEN

DRAWING CONCLUSIONS

Does my beginning begin and does my conclusion conclude? (A beginning should not go back to the flood, and a conclusion is not the same as a summing up.)

—Barzun & Graff

The major contribution of a research study to the body of educational knowledge is based on the conclusions drawn from the results. Since the generalizations are presented as the researcher's interpretation of data, they must be based on all pertinent data. This assures that the researcher makes all valid inferences, at the same time avoiding interpretations that go beyond the data.

When developing conclusions, the researcher is involved in the most intellectually demanding aspect of the total research process. She or he must call on all faculties to interpret data, generalize from it, and connect the study's findings to present knowledge. Any contribution the research study makes to the body of knowledge about the educational process rests in the researcher's ability to interpret the results into valid conclusions. Valid conclusions are those which agree with real-world conditions.

Each of the five Sample Studies presented earlier in this book has as a last section a discussion of the results of the study and the conclusions which the researcher has reached. The varied approaches taken by the several writers in these sections reflect how different studies and different authors generate alternate ways of handling this aspect of the research process. The reader may wish to refer to the "Discussion" sections of these studies before continuing in this chapter.

Nature of Conclusions

The conclusions of research studies are used to derive implications for educational practices in the school and other learning settings. When drawing conclusions, the researcher is not implying anything about practice, but may later give views on how practice might be changed in light of the conclusions. Since conclusions for one research study must be viewed in light of other factors, a conclusion for one study will in itself most likely not warrant a direct implication for educational change. For example, if a study of spelling achievement showed that students who drink a glass of "Mrs. Clyde's Mineral Springs Water" learn more words while studying than students who use a traditional study method, it does not mean that *all* students who study a list of spelling words should drink from the same well. Other factors must be considered and practical applications recommended in light of all known contributing factors. If the mineral springs water caused students' fingernails to turn a bright orange, one would have to consider both results and any other knowledge about how students learn to spell before making final decisions about how to structure activities for spelling classes.

Since most researchers work in an area of education that they know well, implications for practice may be suggested as a final part of many research reports, but these implications should be separated from the conclusions. In essence, the research process is completed with the presentation of the conclusions drawn for the study. Curriculum development takes over after the conclusions of research are made public through the research report, journal articles, presentations before professional organizations, and personal contact with colleagues.

Conclusions are generally derived to give an answer to the researcher's question by referring to whether the research hypothesis was or was not supported by valid evidence obtained in the study. A carefully planned study provides valid conclusions. These conclusions are justified and valid to the degree that they are based on facts and hard data. The interpreter must look at the facts and base the conclusions precisely on what the facts imply.

When planning the study, the researcher should anticipate potential outcomes and decide on the conclusions to be drawn in each case. In this way, procedures can be included in the study to allow for any possible outcome. Since conclusions can be made only on the basis of available data, they cannot be left for consideration only after the data are gathered. The researcher must make them part of planning from the very start. The results of the study should be well organized to allow the researcher to interpret their meaning clearly and make a clear separation between results and conclusions. When drawing conclusions, the researcher should also establish clearly relationships among the question, hypothesis, results, and the conclusions, the relationship represented in Figure 13–1.

Interpretation

The major purpose of the conclusions is to interpret the results and make meaningful statements about whether or not the research hypothesis was supported. If the study supports the research hypothesis, the conclusions should include a section that connects this contribution to related literature

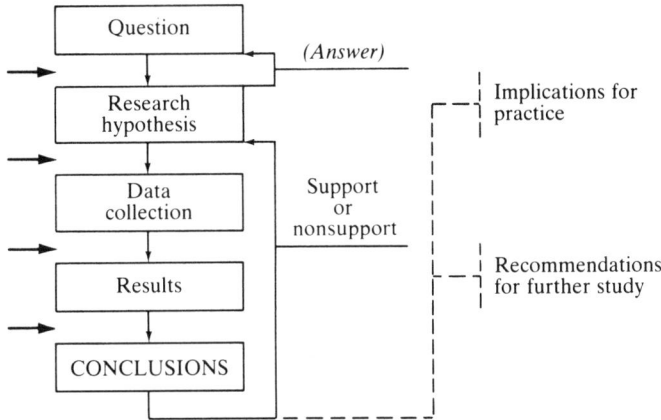

FIGURE 13-1 Study of Educational Questions

and research. A full-blown discussion of how the newly created knowledge will affect theory or cause other educators to alter their thinking is an important part of the section devoted to conclusions. If the study does not support the research hypothesis, an equally detailed discussion should be made of the results' relationship to theory.

Supporting Results. Interpretation of results that agree with the hypothesis is easy to make, since there is agreement between the study's rationale and the results. The conclusions are for the most part ready-made in this situation, and a logical argument about the results' connection with theory is already spelled out. Confirmation adds support to a logically developed conjecture made within a theoretical framework.

Limitations identified earlier in the proposal and those which appeared during implementation must be reevaluated at this stage to assess the extent of their influence on results. What appeared to be a major limitation might be less important than previously supposed. On the other hand, an unanticipated limitation might become a major limitation by the end of data-gathering procedures. For example, an anticipated high percentage of returned questionnaires may become a marginal percentage and emerge as a major limitation. On the other hand, an anticipated limitation from a low percentage of returns might be overcome by an effective incentive to return the form.

If statistical tests are used to assist in interpretation, the researcher must clarify their importance to the overall conclusions. If results are said to be statistically significant, this means that the results are unlikely to be found from chance happenings at a specified significance level with particular degrees of freedom. Beyond evaluating the data statistically, the researcher must consider the meaningfulness and importance of the study. Small differences that are statistically significant may or may not be meaningful in practical terms. For example, significance for a correlation coefficient merely indicates that the derived coefficient is statistically different from zero. Each of the coefficients in Table 2 of Sample Study Number 5 could have been tested to see if each coefficient was mathematically significant from no correlation of 0. In addition to assessing that significance, the researcher must make judgments about whether or not the measured relationship is meaningful within the framework of the study. When a large number of cases has contributed to a measured relationship, very small coefficients may test as statistically significant when the relationship itself has little meaning to the study. Similarly, the results of all other tests of significance need this same type of interpretation to produce meaningful conclusions. The investigator must go beyond the statistical test when drawing conclusions.

Nonsupporting results. Interpreting **negative results** is not as eagerly approached as interpreting supporting results. Too often negative results are not used to create new knowledge. Results of nonsupport, as well as support, certainly can make a contribution to what is known about the educational process. Gilman observes how another field—industrial research—uses both positive and negative results:

> It comes as quite a shock to most laymen to find that the results of more than 90 percent of the experimental research studies conducted by industry are inconclusive. Such costly research is maintained because of the small gains a company can make as a result of the few conclusive studies, and because of a research philosophy that even inconclusive tests are valuable in providing information that the corporation needs to know. (1971, pp. 155–156)

A frame of mind more open to the negative results from educational studies could foster dissemination of information from these studies and give direction to future studies as well as making a contribution to present knowledge. For example, the fact that Jessell and Sullins (Sample Study No. 2) did not support with their data the intuitive notion about arrangement of test items is very positive information for teachers and other test constructors. The theory is clarified with this finding.

Knowledge about what is not supported may give the exact information needed to prompt the researcher or colleagues to develop a new hypothesis to be tested in another study, since failure to support a hypothesis is not a reflection on the researcher. The ego involvement of being wrong should not influence the researcher negatively. Likewise, the profession should welcome reports of studies which conclude that the collected information does not give support to the hypothesis. At present, this is rarely the case, and few reports of studies of this kind are found in professional journals.

Reports of studies that have results opposing the research hypothesis are usually written defensively, with careful explanation about the shortcomings of the study and the unexpected magnitude of the limitations. Any carefully planned study hypothesizes results based on a wide background of information about theory and results of other studies. If the prediction were made with perfect confidence about the outcome, there would be no need to conduct the study. The scientist is committed to establishing the true state of affairs, and a researcher must push into the unknown to add to our knowledge. Negative results provide an opportunity to reflect on theory and to reconsider it in light of the newly obtained information. The well-formulated research study will create useful new knowledge with either positive or negative results.

Bases for Research Conclusions

A researcher's skill in making careful extrapolation of conclusions from the facts will vitally influence the study's contribution to the educational scene. Since a researcher is free to conclude anything from a study, self-discipline is required to avoid the pitfall of seeing only what he or she wants to see in the data. For example, if another person had written paragraph 26 in the Anderson-Bashaw sample study on theme writing, other conclusions might have been drawn from the same set of results.

Self-imposed discipline also helps the researcher avoid making extravagant claims that are only suggested by the information and not truly warranted by fact. Research conclusions must be based on validated data. If extrapolation is desirable in a study, the researcher must clearly indicate where stated conclusions go beyond the facts of the study.

Historical Research

Since the purpose of historical research in education is utilitarian, any conclusions should be based on data that have withstood the most rigorous criticism by the researcher. The greatest pitfall of historical research is drawing conclusions from limited amounts of data. Like the paleontologist who constructs a complete skeleton from a few bones, the researcher using historical approaches to inquiry must recreate much of the past from a relatively small number of carefully documented clues. Objectivity and breadth of vision become essential tools for providing valid conclusions to historically based studies.

After the choice of an integrating question, a hypothesis is developed, and evidence is gathered from relics and documents. At this stage in historical research, the carefully prepared bibliography cards hold the needed information that has been subjected to formal criticism. The researcher is ready at this point to fit together a logically constructed pattern of truth as the answer to the original question. A general structure for the report of historical research uses a broad base of previous knowledge as a foundation, followed by the presentation of evidence central to the question in as direct and narrow a way as possible. This leads to the conclusion that broadens again to encompass, through generalizations, the findings of the study.

Conclusions in such a study must be written with the awareness that a reader will be directed only through the words and associated meaning.

Although the writer knows what he or she wants the words to convey, the intended meaning may be lost by letting the actual written words express something different to the reader. The researcher must make sure that the meaning expressed is the meaning *intended* by scrutinizing each word until every word conveys exactly what it is meant to say.

Bad reasoning is a primary pitfall for historical studies. A study of logic often helps in interpreting the data into conclusions. Such study could help to overcome some tendencies to beg the question, deny the antecedent, create a **non sequitur,** and so on. Rhetoric books offer extensive coverage to help writers avoid possible pitfalls to logically conceived conclusions. Bad generalizations, the result of using words like "all," "every," and "never" when the data only cover a small area, could be improved by using qualifiers, such as "nearly," "almost," and "perhaps." However, too generous use of qualifiers results in an uninteresting and useless piece of material. Conclusions must be based on available data, but the research writer should not avoid a commitment simply because data are incomplete.

Overgeneralization can result from a failure to consider the negative instances. To form the conclusion, "It rains every time an outdoor cookout is planned, since it happened on two occasions" without considering the several times that it did not rain, is an example of a failure to consider the negative instances. To avoid this danger, consider all data and include in the plan procedures that assure that all possible outcomes are open to support.

Another fallacy that awaits the unwary is condensing diversity into unity. This is the opposite of overgeneralizing and may come about when a researcher groups a number of factors into one category. To say that the bombing of Pearl Harbor on December 7, 1941, was the reason that the United States entered World War II is an example of a complex system being reduced to one event. Similarly, a senior who approaches a teacher near the end of the semester saying, "If I don't get at least a B in the course, I won't be able to graduate," is reducing all of the college hours and their contributions to the present course. When teachers meet a newly devised curriculum, they may be inclined to view it as nothing but the same old thing in a new dress, but here again the reduction fallacy has been put into play.

In sum, drawing conclusions—especially those for a historically-based question—requires both imaginative insight and scholarly objectivity to produce a logically conceived set of valid concluding statements. Careful attention to detail and use of appropriate language are important contributors in shaping a historical study into a valuable contribution to educational knowledge. Hillman, for example, in her sample study on sex roles portrayed in children's literature, exhibits skill in writing that balances the two extremes (see especially pars. 23, 24, 25). Conclusions from historical research studies are generalizations that should be based in principles of probability similar to those used by more formally designed studies. By developing a hypothesis, gathering sufficient data, and verifying it for the study, the researcher can reach valid conclusions. Implications about the validity of the conclusions in different times and places must be made in much the same way that other conclusions are verbalized or left to the reader for decision.

Descriptive Research

Many of the difficulties in drawing conclusions from historical studies hold also for descriptive research studies, because subjectivity is always involved. The major advantage descriptive studies have in enhancing the validity of conclusions is their opportunity to choose data from a complete setting rather than being forced to study only that information which remains from the past as historical studies must do. Assuming that the tools are available to collect facts needed for the study, all data about the present are available to the researcher.

Methods of observation used in descriptive studies generally provide more reliable data and results to be used as bases for conclusions than do the methods used in historical research. Although direct manipulation of variables is not possible, manipulation by selecting what to observe from present data gives the researcher and readers of the research increased confidence in conclusions. In turn, users of the conclusions tend to have more confidence in implications that are drawn from validly based conclusions.

Since the *case study* is an intensive investigation centered on a particular subject, the data in this situation are limited in generalizability. The researcher who uses the case study to probe deeply into a particular subject or unit is usually concerned more with that one particular case than with the development of far-reaching generalizations. A case study may, however, provide the opportunity to uncover previously unsuspected relationships. The scientific approach does not allow a hypothesis developed from a set of data to be tested using the same data. A hypothesis developed in a case study cannot be tested within itself, but can be tested in another study.

A part of the conclusions from a case study should include any observed relationships as hypotheses. The empirical data used to develop the hypothesis should be presented and used to establish a rationale for the hypothesis. Further investigation of a hypothesis' tenability requires further testing using newly gathered data. The strength of the hypothesis and its acceptability is a function of the extent to which it has withstood such tests. For research, the case study is more likely to be a producer of hypotheses than a tool for testing a hypothesis. In a clinical setting, for example, a number of case studies collected individually could provide the basis for a hypothesis to be tested. The major concern for each case study is the one individual being studied, and the results of that one study are not general enough to form widely applicable findings.

Researchers concerned with studying particular effects may use a series of case studies where a change is introduced in a number of subjects and a study is made of the effects. Generally this use of the case study as a tool for gathering data for an experimental study is not a true case study where an in-depth investigation is made for the purpose of bettering the subject being studied. It is used more as a data-collecting device than as a device to test a hypothesis.

A *survey* of present conditions is intended to culminate in statements about the present state of affairs and generalizations that interpret the data.

In general, the data for studies in a survey are collected using direct observation or some supplement to this method, such as a questionnaire, opinionnaire, interview, or mechanical device. After organizing the data by tabulation and graphing, the researcher can make statements about conditions referring directly to the tables and graphs. Then the generalizations as conclusions can be derived from causal and meaningful aspects interpreted from the data.

To interpret the data, the researcher must become familiar with it. Often expressing the data in different formats helps. A graph may reveal a characteristic that is hidden in a table. Meaningful patterns may be revealed by organizing data into ascending order, descending order, or alphabetical order. The researcher should try as many arrangements as possible to gain insight beyond that revealed through interpretation by computational outcomes. Since the manner in which the data are prepared for further interpretation is critical, the researcher must be prepared to defend any procedure, keeping in mind the question that has been asked.

Any conclusions from a survey are made in the context of a complex situation. The interaction of many factors makes hasty conclusions tenuous at best. The choice of what data to gather should contribute toward drawing valid conclusions in a complex situation, if the researcher has considered all possible conclusions during the planning stage. The plan of the study should assure that the data needed for valid conclusions are available in the results of the study. A good design is a prerequisite for valid conclusions.

The researcher using a survey has many tools and procedures for data collection to choose from and thus should not be guilty of relying on one tool—such as the questionnaire—for all surveys. A researcher who falls into the pattern of using one tool would be guilty of committing a Type V error, defined as "the error committed by a researcher by rigidly adhering to one investigative design without a systematic approach (see Huck, Cormier, Bounds, & Sechrest, 1974, pp. 375–376). By using the most appropriate tool or tools to collect the data and considering the total situation, the researcher can present generalizations as conclusions for research surveys that will score high in validity.

Developmental studies are important to education because of the need to know how human beings grow and develop and how they differ at various ages. Generally, a specific trait or set of traits is studied for one selected group over a time period of several years. Terman used this longitudinal method to study over 1,500 subjects who were classed as gifted in 1921. A series of publications has reported results of the study. The reportings included conclusions based on data collected and related to present theory. In 1946, for example, 25 years after the study commenced, Terman concluded:

> Contrary to the theory of Lange-Eichbaum that great achievement is usually associated with emotional tensions which border on the abnormal, in our gifted group success is associated with stability rather than instability, with absence rather than presence of disturbing conflicts—in short, with well-balanced temperament and with freedom from excessive frustration.

. . . At any rate, we have seen that intellect and achievement are far from perfectly correlated. Why this is so, what circumstances affect the fruition of human talent, are questions of such transcendent importance that they should be investigated by every method that promises the slightest reduction of our present ignorance. (1947, p. 352)

Terman offered other conclusions he felt had been established in the final chapter (pp. 377–379) of *The Gifted Child Grows Up*. The major thrust of the study in recent years has been to "increase our knowledge of the dynamics of human behavior, with special reference to the factors that determine degree and direction of creative achievement (Terman & Oden, 1947, p. 381).

Longitudinal/developmental studies require that someone or some group devote considerable amounts of time and money over the several years that the study continues. Problems also arise as the subjects under study move and/or become disinterested in the project. Study of a variable for change over a time span requires baseline data for conclusions about change. Important variables may be difficult to identify early in the project, therefore reducing the information needed to draw valid conclusions.

An alternative to studying change for one group over a time period makes use of what is called the *cross-sectional survey*. Changes due to development are studied by looking at various age levels at one point in time. Height and weight charts, for instance, can be constructed by measuring children of different ages at one point in time rather than following a set of children from birth to adulthood. Likewise, educational development can be ascertained in cross section using students of different ages to supply needed data. Data are gathered on variables being studied and conclusions about development are made with regard to differences in the sample studied. The assumption behind this method is that if groups were studied over a period of time, the data would look like that in a cross-sectional study. Conclusions drawn from cross-sectional studies are not affected by extraneous variables that change over time and affect data collected longitudinally. Part of observed changes over time is attributable to change in general. A study of change per se, with all contributing factors taken into account, is best conducted by the longitudinal method. The researcher must draw conclusions in the light of the total change. A study of typicalness, on the other hand, might best be studied by a cross-sectional design. The researcher assumes in this case that differences are a result of development.

A *correlational study* identifies what the researcher hopes are meaningful and direct relationships between pairs of variables. Correlational techniques alone cannot ascertain which variable is the cause and which variable is affected. Conclusions for studies using correlational techniques are generally hypotheses about relationships among variables. A correlational study may be conducted to establish a relationship (the conclusions) and generate a hypothesis about cause which will then be tested by an experimental study. The correlational study may also be used to establish the magnitude or strength after causal factors have been previously identified.

Conclusions for studies using correlation in this way appear to be more like conclusions written for experimental studies.

Conclusions may be presented in different ways. The authors of Sample Studies 3 and 5 have used different ways to present conclusions. Sharp and Kirk separated the discussion and presentation of conclusions into separate sections (pars. 33–38). Gallimore, Tharp, and Speidel, on the other hand, combined presentation of results and conclusions as an integrated section (pars. 16–22).

Experimental Research

The experimental design and the data generated by a design with high internal and external validity provide an opportunity for the researcher to draw highly valid conclusions. Without high internal validity, data cannot be interpreted into conclusions; without high external validity, the results cannot be widely generalized.

Conclusions for experimental studies are generally intended to be tied directly to educational theory, because the control of the experiment gives the researcher a solid base for theory development. Levels of probability set for statistical tests allow statements about how likely it is that the result is a chance occurrence rather than a product of experimenter manipulation. Thus, if a statistical test is significant, a statement that the outcome of the study did not happen by chance can be made with confidence. These are the results of the study which must be interpreted further into conclusions by the researcher.

Results of tests of significance have too often been used as conclusions for studies. Since significance tests are interpretative tools, researchers have been comfortable in letting these tests of significance provide the whole interpretation. What is sorely needed in such cases is interpretation by the researcher who views all of the information in a total context. The importance of objectivity must not be allowed to overshadow other important aspects of interpretation and integration.

The present stage in the development of educational research—as is true in all human sciences—does not allow the highest level of objectivity. As in all research of complex systems, there seems to be a conflict between objectivity and import. What researchers must seek in drawing conclusions for experimental research problems is a compromise point at which both objectivity and import are maximal. This is the best that can be accomplished until problems of inexactness are overcome.

Since the empirical distribution of data determines the proper parametric or nonparametric comparative method to be used in analyzing data statistically, appropriate methods must be chosen to interpret the data. Alternative forms of analysis can be proposed in the overall plan and a decision made concerning which assumptions are appropriate for parametric techniques. If the assumptions for a parametric test have not been met, then an appropriate nonparametric test can be employed. Recently researchers have been discussing the assumptions needed for use of parametric tests. An overview of current and historical thought on this topic appears in the *Review of Educational Research* (Gardner, 1975).

Following the statistical interpretation, with the results in hand, the researcher determines the inferences which can be made from the information. A well-developed research hypothesis provides a firm base for conclusions in experimental studies, since rejection of the null hypothesis will, in general, be cause to support the alternate—the research hypothesis.

In general, conclusions for experimental research are more direct than those for historical and descriptive studies, because results of the statistical procedures used allow direct bridging from results to hypothesis via conclusions. Sample Studies 2 and 4 represent the directness that experimental research gives the research process. The use of statistics in the other sample studies helps build in objectivity, thus showing that statistics can serve the same purpose for historical and descriptive studies in certain cases.

Generalization

The reader of a research report uses the researcher's conclusions to achieve better understanding of educational concerns. Much of the generalizing done by the researcher must be put into the context of conditions that vary given different settings. Complete descriptions of subjects, conditions, treatments, and all contributing factors allow the reader to generalize from a study to similar real-world situations. A study conducted on subjects in a rural midwestern community may have conclusions that are generalizable to similar subjects in other rural midwestern towns, but not to those in mountain communities of Appalachia or urban areas of mid-city Miami, where the citizens are largely of Latin descent.

Some conclusions are widely generalizable while others are not. The less the studied trait is affected by environment, the greater the possibility of generalization. Study of a factor that is basic to the nature of human beings— such as the effects of temperature on bodily functions—would be more widely generalizable than conclusions from a study of a factor based more in a culture—such as the effects of a counseling technique.

The section reporting the conclusions should also acknowledge any limitations or weaknesses of the study. Since all research studies have inadequacies, limitations are associated with all stated conclusions. Any weakness that is relevant to the outcome of the study should be mentioned, and the magnitude of its contribution should be estimated.

Limitations listed in this way are those factors that might have affected the results and, in turn, the conclusions. These usually come from less-than-ideal sampling techniques, limitations placed on methodology, and statistical design. In your reading of the sample studies, you found limitations or possible limitations listed for Sample Study Number 2 (pars. 10, 17), Study Number 3 (pars. 8, 38), Study 4 (pars. 22, 24, 27), and Study 5 (par. 22). Limitations are listed not only to fulfill the responsibility the researcher has to the reader, but also to instill confidence in the reader about the researcher's skill in researching. If obvious weaknesses are not listed, the astute reader will question whether the investigator was knowledgeable enough to recognize the limitation. Listing a limitation usually indicates that the researcher was limited by a particular condition. Limitations appear as the researcher makes choices among alternatives, where each alternative has desired characteristics but no one of them has all the desired traits. It is not likely, for instance, that any one automobile has all the features a buyer may desire (especially price), but purchasing one says that, of all possible combinations, this is the one that is an optimum choice. Selections in a research plan follow much the same logic, with weaknesses becoming limitations.

Limitations also come about through unpredictable events. Subjects may move or become ill, thus injecting sampling limitations outside the control of the researcher. Any limitations which have occurred during the study but which were not foreseen should be presented with the conclusions with a list of their possible effects on outcomes.

After the conclusions are presented and defended, the researcher may choose to speculate about how the results might have been different given different conditions. She or he may also make interpretations that go beyond the data for the study at this point. Such speculation and interpretation beyond the data must always be accompanied by a clear statement that the particular section is speculation.

Implications and Recommendations

Conclusions from research studies often carry some implications for practical application. A researcher may choose to present any practical application that appears to be recommended by a discovered principle. In general, curriculum specialists and other developmental people take over at this point and place the results in context with other factors for direct application.

While studying a specific question, a researcher is actually considering a wider scope than just the area defined by the problem. The review of literature and in-depth understanding of the problem question should generate other possible questions. The investigator may have identified some closely related questions that need to be investigated or may have generated more questions through results of the study. Familiarity with the question under study allows and demands a good understanding of a wider scope about closely related questions. As an authority in this general area, the researcher is obligated to project into the future by giving personal ideas for recommended research. **Recommendations** complete the task that commenced when the indeterminate situation was met and a study was developed to overcome the obstacle.

All that remains at this point is to write up the study in detail and disseminate the conclusions (findings) to other professional educators. The next two chapters examine these steps in communicating the conclusions of a study. However, the process of inquiry does not stop here. Rather, further study of the question requires replication of this study or investigation of other closely related problem questions.

☐ CHECK YOUR UNDERSTANDING

As a review for this chapter and as a reflection on the integration of the research process as diagrammed in Figure 13–1, locate a recent study done in your field. See if you can follow the research process through the question, hypothesis, data collection, results, and conclusions. Then observe the bridging back to the research hypothesis and the original question. Did the author give implications for practice? Recommendations for further research? Connections to theory?

Summary

This chapter views the process of drawing conclusions as the most intellectually demanding aspect of the total research process. These statements will ultimately be used to derive educational practices for the school and other learning settings, so they are important to determining the study's contribution to the field.

The process of drawing conclusions requires careful interpretation of the study's results, recognizing the implications of statistical procedures and acknowledging limitations on the entire research process, regardless of whether the study produces positive or negative results. In making these interpretations, the researcher must be aware of a variety of fallacies in logic and the dangers of overgeneralization as well as overqualification. This discipline on the researcher's subjective input applies to every stage of interpretation as well as to the researcher's ego involvement in interpreting negative results. Great care must also be taken to be sure the words chosen to convey conclusions and interpretations do indeed convey what the researcher wants them to convey.

In addition to discussing the general role of the researcher in drawing conclusions, this chapter covers the differing nature of conclusions in the various specific areas of research—historical research, descriptive research (case studies, surveys, developmental studies, correlational studies), and experimental research.

Along with the task of drawing conclusions comes the opportunity for pointing out implications of the study for practice. To complete reporting of the study, the researcher is obligated to make recommendations for further research into related questions.

References

Barzun, J., & Graff, H. F. *The modern researcher* (3rd ed.). New York: Harcourt, Brace, & World, 1977.

Gardner, P. L. Scales and statistics. *Review of Educational Research,* Winter 1975, *45,* 43–57.

Gilman, D. A. Why don't you publish it in the journal of nonsignificant differences? *Contemporary Education,* January 1971, *43,* 155–156.

Huck, S. U., Cormier, W. H., Bounds, W. G., Jr., & Sechrest, L. *Reading statistics and research.* New York: Harper & Row, 1974.

Terman, L. M., & Oden, M. H. *The gifted child grows up.* Stanford: Stanford University Press, 1947.

CHAPTER FOURTEEN

WRITING RESEARCH REPORTS

All over the globe, every moment of the day, someone is being asked to make a search and write a report on some state of fact, or else to read and analyze one, so that action may be taken. Reports are the means by which we try to substitute intelligence for routine and knowledge for guesswork.

—Barzun and Graff

A necessary part of any research study is the writing of a report describing the study's design in detail and conveying the results and conclusions to the professional community. The two major tasks of research—*conducting* and *writing*—require different talents from the researcher. A researcher should be able to function well at both tasks and be able to bridge the gap between them. Most people, however, find that they work better at one of the levels than the other. Most researchers would choose conducting as their stronger area. This attitude explains why research teams usually include one person who is charged with the major part of the writing. Since operating funds are so important to research studies, specialists in writing proposals have also emerged on the educational scene. Such researchers seem to be stronger through interest and/or skill in writing the final report.

In general, what will be said about writing reports in this chapter applies equally well to writing proposals. Since what is known about a study must be relayed in proposals and final reports, what is written and how it is written determines the readers' impressions, their confidence in the conclusions, and ultimately the contribution of the study to the body of knowledge about educational concerns.

Research reports take different forms and have different emphases depending primarily on the audience for which they are intended. Many times a research report is condensed into a very limited (100–200 words) coverage of the study. This report is usually in the form of an abstract that focuses on the conclusions, revealing only the barest skeleton of other factors. The purpose of such a report is to give the reader enough information to decide whether the study might be of personal interest professionally and whether or not to look into a more detailed account of the study. Several examples of abstracts have been offered earlier in this book and other examples are found in the Hillman sample study (par. 1), Sharp-Kirk (par. 1), and Gallimore et al (par. 1).

A detailed report containing a complete description of what has been done is written as documentation and as a record for reference. Since a copy of a detailed research report would be inappropriate for this book, Chapter 15—the next chapter—will only discuss examples of the condensed report as published in professional journals. A student thesis or dissertation is an example of a complete research report. The components of the dissertation provide a model for other detailed reports. Writing the substance of this report is discussed later in this chapter.

The researcher may prepare a condensed report of the study for publication in a professional journal. The purpose of this type of report is to provide enough information about the problem, methodology, results, and conclusions to allow a reader to evaluate the study. In general, each journal has a form for all studies it accepts for publication. Your reading of the sample journal articles has given you a good overview of how these elements are incorporated into reports, but you may want to review them again and compare their formats. In the absence of guidelines for a specific journal, the style manual of the APA (American Psychological Association, 1974) serves well as a format for most scholarly writing of research reports.

The form and style of scholarly writing in research involves basically two components: (1) the substance of the report, or the information conveyed and its logical arrangement, and (2) the technical format and aspects of the **mechanics of writing,** or the way in which something is written down (Angell, 1973).

The nature of the research determines the specific content of the report, and the requirements of the audience to which the report is submitted determines its emphasis and format. Various combinations of the following components are incorporated in reports: title, background, problem, method, results, discussion, conclusion, summary, abstract, references, and bibliography. Elements of the problem question, hypothesis, definitions, assumptions, and so on also are included as needed, depending on the type of presentation being made.

Technical Style

The *mechanics* of style include the format and arrangement for headings, tables, figures, footnotes, bibliography, and so on. They also include spelling, punctuation, capitalization, use of italic, quotations, and abbreviations. Most departments of universities, schools within universities, or universities as a whole have adopted what they call an acceptable style for papers, essays, theses, and dissertations.

A maxim for the research writer is "Use a style manual." The style that has been adopted for use—either by the school or the funding agency—should be adhered to precisely. References to styles established by APA, Campbell and Ballou, Dugdale, and Turabian are listed in the bibliography following Chapter 15. Some other style manual may be prescribed in certain cases or supplements to a generally used style may be added for a specific use. Where no particular style is mandated for a study, the writer should choose one for his or her writing and follow it exactly.

The most important characteristic of writing style is consistency throughout the writing. Most technical decisions are arbitrary in isolation, but the plan of a particular style fits all of the decisions into a scholarly form for reporting scholarly work. For example, Campbell's style book says to indent each paragraph eight typewriter spaces, while other style manuals specify other indentions. A writer might arbitrarily choose nine spaces. Which is the right number of spaces to ident for paragraphs? To my knowledge, that question has not been answered. Instead, each style develops its own unique format. The important question is not, What is the correct number of spaces? but rather, What does my style manual say is correct? At best, many isolated decisions are arbitrary ones made by the author of the style manual, but the format results in a consistent presentation that is aesthetically pleasing, orderly, and easy-to-read.

Since a style manual can be used to specify the mechanics of a report, the rest of this chapter is devoted to the aspect of substance and its arrangement in the research report. Style manuals give varying amounts of treatment to this topic but each will include some important suggestions about what to include and how to arrange it.

Substance of the Report

Most research reports are organized around five or six components presented within the framework of the three major areas of *planning, investigation,* and *generalization* (see Chapter 7). In general, the first three chapters of a report are devoted to the planning activities. The third chapter, which explains the methodology, belongs in part to planning and in part to investigation. The fourth chapter reports the results, and the fifth (sometimes a sixth) reports conclusions and generalizations drawn from the study. Not all reports are divided into chapters, but the basic divisions are the same components found in these chapters. Ballou's book, *A Model for Theses and Research Papers* (1970), is in the form of a six-chapter report, although it is not a report of a research study. Each section of the research report is discussed where it would appear in such a report. The substance of the *Model* provides helpful suggestions concerning content and style and is a valuable aid to anyone writing a research report. It is presented in a way that permits the flexibility needed when writing about a study based in a specific type of educational research. It also includes some rationale for the choices made about acceptable format and prepares the researcher to write about historical, descriptive, or experimental research.

Each report should have a title. If the researcher worked from a proposal, a title has probably already been developed. If it has not been developed, a good report title should be written to include the variables studied, the relationship investigated, and the population for generalization. The writer should avoid using unnecessary terms and keep the number of words in the title to no more than 15.

Planning

The first two parts of the research report usually explain the groundwork for the development of the problem into researchable form and report a review of related knowledge about the study. The first chapter deals basically with the material used in the first two sections of the proposal, titled "Background of the Problem" and "Presentation of the Problem." It includes a brief background to the problem, statement of the problem question, delimitation of the study, hypotheses, definitions, assumptions, limitations, and any other information considered important to readers of the study. This section should provide an analysis of the problem and describe the problem's relationship to the theoretical framework. The entire chapter should be quite detailed in its presentation. Material on proposal preparation in Chapter 8 will be helpful in developing this part of the final report.

The second chapter of the report should include a reporting of all related literature, including research that deals directly with the study. Generally this will be new writing. If the proposal included an extensive review of literature, this section would be much the same as the proposal's section on related literature. This chapter serves two purposes. First, it shows the reader that the researcher is knowledgeable about the field. Second, it brings the reader up to date on the topics under study. Although there are differences of opinion about how to structure this review, organization by topics of variables under study seems to be the most common. For example, if the study is about the relationship of intentional and incidental learning for retarded children, a logical division of the review might be "Teaching the Retarded Child," "Incidental Learning," and "Intentional Learning." Within each topic, chronological organization, commencing with the earliest writing and finishing at the present, yields a logical and meaningful format which may contain some subdivisions if needed. The special nature of historical research may permit this section to be omitted or require only a brief treatment.*

A good practice to use in introducing Chapter 2 is to repeat the problem question in an introductory paragraph. Such repetition of parts of the report may seem contrary to good writing style, but writing the research report is different from other types of writing. Different people read the report for different reasons and generally do not read it from cover to cover. Some may

---

*The rest of this chapter on writing the research report primarily applies to the quantitative methods of descriptive and experimental research. The reader is directed to Chapter 9 for guidance in writing historically based studies. Jacques Barzun and Henry F. Graff's *The Modern Researcher* is also an excellent reference for writing about integrative studies (Barzun & Graff, 1977).

be interested only in results and conclusions, others in methodology, and still others may only have an interest in a review of the literature. The person reading only Chapter 2 will be saved the time it takes to look through the first chapter to find the question if it is included as an introduction to the review of literature.

The researcher must decide what material is related to the problem before writing the review of related knowledge. For example, a study of the effectiveness of phonics instruction as an aid to spelling achievement is based in language arts. Does this mean that every study in language arts should be reported as "related knowledge," since all language arts studies are related? Of course not. At the same time, to limit the report to studies conducted on only the same question may severely limit the chapter. The decision about what literature to include is best made on the criterion of what the writer sees as relevant. All relevant literature should be included in the review.

The substance of this chapter comes from the carefully prepared note cards written in the library before the study was finalized. Some selection and screening of material will already have been made, but this is the stage for the final selection and organization of the review of related information. The writer most often conveys primarily the conclusions of studies but may, in some instances, find the need to report the design of a study, its data-collection techniques, and population-sample characteristics in addition to establishing clearly the identity of the variables studied and the investigated relationships. Ballou says, "As a general guide, sufficient sources should be cited to establish the theoretical framework within which the immediate study finds its setting" (1970, p. 23).

After deciding what citations to use, the writer must decide how to arrange the material and the manner in which it will appear. Most writers find the review a difficult writing task. Since this is a report of someone else's work, the writer is restricted in providing personal feelings. The objective report precludes subjective additions, but at the same time, the narrative must have continuity and be written so that it is interesting—not an easy task.

A series of paragraphs consisting of direct quotations or a series of paragraphs each reporting a separate study will be of little use to the report. Direct quotations are to be avoided except in the rare cases where the meaning would be lost in a paraphrase or where the original writer has expressed an idea so well that it is best to keep it in that form for emphasis. In any case, a footnote or citation of a reference—whether a paraphrase or quotation—must be made for each idea included in the chapter.

Good and poor examples of organization of the review of literature can be found in copies of theses and dissertations in any university library. The student should read some of the reviews, pick out examples of good techniques, and note poor practices in order to direct his or her own writing to proper organization. Further sources of ideas for organization are those selections in the *Encyclopedia of Educational Research* where the writers are reviewing literature about research in particular areas (Ebel, 1969; see also 1940, 1950, 1960). To avoid repeating each one separately, the author of the *Encyclopedia* groups studies that have much the same outcome. Other examples of writing in this difficult area can be found in the *Review of Educational Research* (all issues) and *Second Handbook of Research on Teaching* (Travers, 1973, pp. 530–1322), where the writers give reviews of research on specialized topics.

A complete review of the research literature will include results of research studies and articles of opinion by experts knowledgeable about the topics of concern. The concluding section of the chapter should tie together the relationships that were separated by the topical divisions of the chapter. A summary at this point can serve two major functions. First, it should strengthen the presentation of the review as a background for the study. Second, it should provide the researcher with a starting point for comparing results with other opinions and for connecting the current study's conclusions with theory. It should not present any conclusions or include any reactions of the writer.

☐ CHECK YOUR UNDERSTANDING

1. Locate a review of literature in the *Encyclopedia of Educational Research* or a dissertation that you find to be well-presented for you, the reader. List the factors that contribute to your understanding.
2. Locate a review of literature that is difficult for you, the reader, to understand. List the deficiencies of that review that you think contribute to your difficulty in understanding.
3. Prepare a list of "do's and don'ts" for writing such a section to guide your future writing. Leave this list open-ended and add to it as you continue your reading.

Investigation

The investigation part of the study is reported in the chapters dealing with design and results. The design is usually reported in Chapter 3 and the results in Chapter 4. Even though the section on design is created during the planning stage, it is usually best to consider it part of the investigation stage of research, since it is a report of investigation activities.

Since the proposal spells out specifically what procedures and materials will be used, writing Chapter 3 for the report involves only changing the tense from future (proposal) to past (final paper). Of course, any changes in the procedures from what was proposed should be reported in the final report, along with the reasons why the original plan had to be abandoned. Chapter 8 in this book on the research proposal describes the basic components for this section of the research report. This section deals with:

1. Target population and method of sampling
2. Materials and instrumentation
3. Statistical design and rationale for selection
4. Type(s) of data and collection method

5. Data analysis methods
6. Pilot study information

A part of the final report (usually Chapter 4) is devoted to reporting the facts of the study. This reporting should be an objective presentation of results, including tables that organize the data collected, statistical analysis, and/or descriptive analysis. A well-organized report of results should be sequenced and presented in such a way that it will be clear to the reader whether the data support or fail to support the research hypothesis.

All of the data presented in this section should be relevant and essential to the question and the conclusions. Sets of original scores and other data that may only be important to a few readers can be placed in an appendix of the report. Original scoresheets, questionnaires, and other gathered information should be kept on file but are not, in general, a part of the research report. If it is necessary that some be included, they should also be placed in an appendix.

The research report writer must keep in mind that writing results is expository rather than interpretive writing. The results section must follow guidelines that insure inclusion of any data that fail to support the research hypothesis as well as data that support it.

Finally, the results need to be synthesized and reported by identifying relationships among findings that reinforce or contradict each other. The summary of this results section and the summary of the chapter on related literature provide the basic input for the final section of generalization where conclusions will be drawn. A careful fitting of the results into present theory can be made from this base.

Generalization

The last major part of the research report synthesizes an answer to the research question and discusses the implications of the study. This is the section where the investigator draws conclusions in light of the results (see Chapter 13) and projects the study of the problem into future research studies.

The generalizations may be presented in one or two chapters, starting with the results and carrying through to the solution of the problem, finally connecting the study's results to present theory. A section on implications should indicate suggested changes in practice. Recommendations should project subsequent research on this topic into possible future studies.

The chapter that interprets the results by drawing the conclusions (usually Chapter 5) may also include the sections on implications and recommendations. If they are a part of Chapter 5, then the last chapter presents a summary of the complete study. If the fifth chapter is reserved for drawing conclusions and connecting them to theory, then the sixth chapter may include implications, recommendations, and summary. If the report requires a very long summary, it should be placed in a separate and concluding chapter.

The limitations of the study should be included in the discussion of the research conclusions, since they are restrictions placed on the generalizations. The investigator should point up for the reader any aspect of the design that might reduce the validity of the conclusions and the generalizations subsequently derived from them. A listing of the limitations is made to inform the reader that the investigator is aware of certain weaknesses that resulted because of the nature of the problem and the restrictions on developing an ideal set of procedures. The researcher's awareness of the limitations should strengthen the reader's confidence in the researcher. For example, failure to list the fact that all tests are unreliable to a degree might cause the reader to question whether the researcher was aware of this when drawing conclusions. Limitations caused by lack of control over certain variables might exist, not because of poor researching procedures, but as a result of something beyond the control of the investigator.

The following are some cautions to be observed in interpreting results into conclusions and in accompanying discussion:

1. Guard against erroneous interpretations due to preconceived ideas, biases, and prejudices.
2. Be careful not to omit evidence or inferences that are contrary to the hypothesis or to your opinion.
3. Scrupulously avoid statements that are dependent upon subjective judgment.
4. Do not try to draw conclusions from results provided by inaccurate instruments of measurement (or instruments the accuracy of which is not known.)
5. Do not generalize from insufficient data. Be careful not to generalize from a single or limited number of cases.
6. In associational studies, be certain you do not mistake correlation for causation. A common causal factor may be accounting for the correlation.

The summary of the study should present the problem being studied, a statement about the procedures, findings, implications for theory and practice, and recommendations. This final summary should give the reader a good overview of the study and should transmit the real message of the study to education.

Reference Materials

Each report is expected to include a bibliography and may include one or more appendixes. Together they form an addendum to the report narrative that gives the reader an opportunity to go beyond the bare essentials that were included in the study.

The appendix (or appendices) consist(s) of the supplementary material which may be of interest to some or all of the readers, but whose inclusion in the basic narrative would be awkward and/or cause the continuity to be broken. Material for the appendix might consist of original data, tables that contain data not directly related to the major question, lengthy quotations, copies of standardized tests not readily available to all readers, instruments constructed for the study (questionnaires, tests, opinionnaires, and the like), and documents, letters, and any supportive evidence for significance. Either preceding or following the appendix is a bibliography consisting of an entry for every piece of material cited in footnotes, plus other entries which the writer considers important to the study and its theoretical framework.

The bibliography gives the reader the advantage of the writer's knowledge about relevant materials and also serves as a step into the vast amount of knowledge about educational concerns closely related to the study. The decision about what to include must be made by the writer, keeping in mind that including materials which are not relevant does little to help the reader. If a very long bibliography is necessary, it may be divided into parts by type of publication. Books may be catalogued together in one group, periodicals in another, and so on. For historical studies, the division may be primary sources and secondary sources.

Some bibliographies include an annotation consisting of a sentence or short paragraph about each item as a convenience to the reader. The *annotated bibliography* entry should describe the content of the material cited and its relationship to the study.

Abstract

The investigator may need to write an abstract of the study in the form of a condensed report of about 100 to 200 words. An abstract focuses on the methods, results, and conclusions of the study. It is intended to give just enough information for the reader to decide whether the study will be of personal interest.

The abstract should include the research question, a description of the subjects, a brief accounting of methodology, the results, and derived conclusions. The conclusions, being the most important part of the study, receive major emphasis in an abstract.

Careful use of words for this very condensed version is necessary to convey the real meaning of the study to the reader. The writer must make every word count and check carefully the logic of the abstract so that the continuity from conception to completion is not lost in the reduction.

Writing Journal Articles

Articles within a journal should be as much alike as possible to avoid distracting the reader with varying formats. To achieve this necessary consistency throughout the journal, manuscripts need to be much alike in form to promote consistency in the printed page. This goal of consistency is best attained by following a set of rules and/or guidelines in the form of a manual prescribing the style to be used for manuscripts. Before writing for a particular journal, the report writer should find out the proper form to use. When writing a report without some specific directions, the writer should use the guidelines of the APA *Publication Manual* (1974) as this format is widely accepted.

The body of a journal article consists of five components: Introduction, Methodology, Results, Discussion, and References. A title page that gives the title, author's name and institutional affiliation, an abstract (100–200 words), and possibly an appendix all support the main body of the article. (Figure 14-1 presents a schema of this format.)

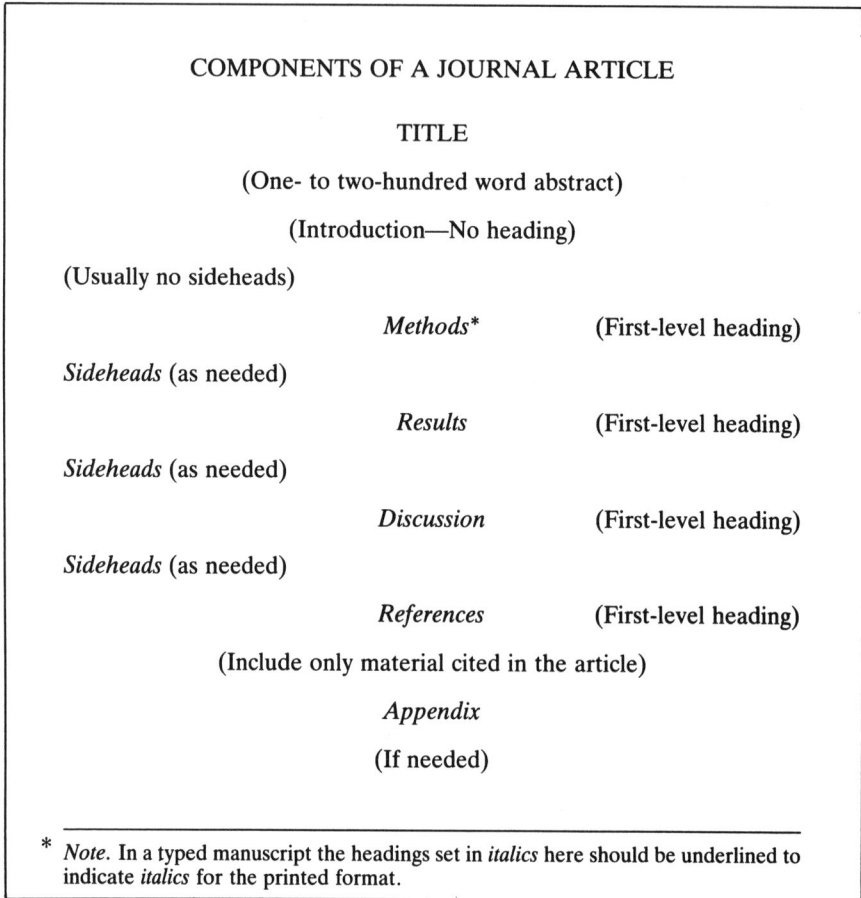

COMPONENTS OF A JOURNAL ARTICLE

TITLE

(One- to two-hundred word abstract)

(Introduction—No heading)

(Usually no sideheads)

	*Methods**	(First-level heading)

Sideheads (as needed)

	Results	(First-level heading)

Sideheads (as needed)

	Discussion	(First-level heading)

Sideheads (as needed)

	References	(First-level heading)

(Include only material cited in the article)

Appendix

(If needed)

---

* *Note.* In a typed manuscript the headings set in *italics* here should be underlined to indicate *italics* for the printed format.

FIGURE 14–1   Schema for a Journal Article Using APA Style

The *title* of the article should inform the reader of the variables under study and summarize the principal idea of the report (note the titles for Sample Studies 1, 2, 3, 4, and 5). The title of the proposal, if well-written, can serve as a title for the journal report (see Chapter 8, the section called "The Proposal Title"). To assure proper indexing for retrieval systems, avoid misleading words and words that serve no purpose. For example, shorten titles by omitting any reference to methods, results, and beginning phrases such as "an experiment of" or "a study designed to." A title should not exceed 15 words.

The *abstract* of the study usually appears under the author's name and affiliation (see par. 1 of Sample Studies 1, 3, and 5) and allows the reader to review the study quickly. The abstract for a journal article contains the same information as the abstract for a detailed research report.

The *introduction* of the article provides the background and presents the problem studied, much as the proposal did. Note that no heading is used. This section includes the problem question, definitions of the variables, and the research hypothesis, as well as an adequate background section.

The *method* section (see Sample Studies) should describe procedures in detail to allow the reader to evaluate research methods and establish the degree of validity of the results and conclusions. Attention should be given to characteristics of subjects, how they were selected and assigned, and any other information that will help the reader understand the study. A detailed accounting of all procedures and treatment, including statistical analysis, allows the reader to judge the validity of results. Measuring instruments and special apparatus should also be described.

To this point the article is very much like the research proposal, except that the verb tense for methods has changed from future to past. Because the beginning sections always seek to inform, these two forms of reporting cover approximately the same topics to the same degree. The remaining sections—results and discussion—are new to the final journal article.

The *results* section (note that Sample Study No. 4 combines results and discussion) organizes, tabulates, and summarizes the collected data and reports the results of the statistical treatment. Included are results that support the hypothesis and any results that fail to support it, but no conclusions are drawn.

The *discussion* section (see Sample Studies) reports conclusions and interpretations of the results including implications and recommendations. The reader should also be made aware of any limitations at this point. This section should also state whether or not the research hypothesis is supported and how this result fits with theory. Any speculation on the part of the writer should be clearly presented as what it is—speculation. Implications for educational practice can be presented here along with recommendations for further research.

The *references* section (see Sample Studies) includes an entry for each citation in the article. A bibliography is not included for a journal article except when it serves a special purpose or when one is requested by the journal staff. An appendix is not generally required but may be included if it is necessary to present material that would otherwise break the continuity of the article.

Writing Style

Each writer develops a unique style of writing about research and uses guidelines to the advantage of that style. He or she should keep in mind the process being written about is *inquiry,* and that objectivity in reporting about a question and its answer is the key criterion.

The writing should be concise and straightforward, to inform rather than impress the reader. For a report to be accurate, the language must be precise. To make the report meaningful, the important points must be emphasized. A combination of accuracy and emphasis of important points, along with careful attention to detail in giving a logically organized presentation, will result in a report which is capable of disseminating the information from the study to other professionals in the field of education.

It is often useful to think about the reporting of the research while it is still in the planning stage. Preplanning a report through an outline begun early in the process contributes much to a meaningful final report of the study because it forces the writer to present the material in a logically organized arrangement. With preplanning, the actual writing will fall into about six steps:

1. Writing the first draft. The first draft is best written without too much concern about choice of words or grammar, paying more attention to thoughts, ideas, and facts that need to be included in the report.
2. Revision of the first draft. Attention at this stage is given to rewriting unclear sentences and paragraphs, filling gaps, correcting sentence structure, spelling, grammar, and punctuation, along with choosing exact words to convey precise meanings. (Check the style manual.)
3. Additions of footnotes, tables, figures, and appendices. A table of contents, if needed, can now be made. (Check the style manual.)
4. A final editing. This task should focus on the consistency of statements throughout the paper and the readability of the material, emphasizing smooth transitions between ideas. This step should polish the paper into a logical presentation of the chain of reasoning set as a goal for the research.
5. Read the paper thoroughly. Read it word for word, comma for comma, checking for every detail of format to see that style guidelines are followed. After this step, the only remaining corrections are typing errors.
6. Final typing and correction of typing errors.

If the research writer has used clear and concise language, presented the case in a logically organized manner, and given the needed attention to detail by rereading and proofreading, the product will be the scholarly reporting needed as an integral part of the research process.

Without this reporting of research to colleagues and to other interested professional people, the time spent in research is largely wasted, except for the aesthetic rewards earned by the researcher. The difference between a major contribution and a lesser contribution from the same study is being able to write a scholarly report of the research. It should be every researcher's goal to create reports of research efforts which reflect the same high level of accomplishment as those research efforts.

☐ CHECK YOUR UNDERSTANDING

For Sample Study Number 4 write an abstract (150 to 175 words) that explains the study and clearly defines it as an experimental study.

Answer

The writing style will vary, of course, but your abstract should include statements of the problem, method, results, and conclusions—specifically:

1. Describe the subjects studied—age, sex, number, and so on.
2. Describe the design—treatment, data-collection procedures, and so on.
3. Summarize the data including results of tests of significance.
4. Report findings from inferences drawn from the data.

From your short abstract, the reader should have a good overview of the study and know that the study was conducted within the design of experimental methodology.

Summary

Writing the research report is the second major task of the researcher. After the researcher has conducted a study, he or she must then present that study and its findings to the professional community at large. The form this reporting takes varies with the agency or journal for which it is intended, but the elements of consistency and clarity are of paramount importance regardless of the format chosen.

The substance of the report is contained in five or six major sections, the first three of which are devoted to planning while the last two or three are spent reporting results, drawing conclusions and generalizations, and making recommendations. This chapter presents certain criteria as guidelines for writing each of these sections of the report. Additional sections of the research report—the abstract, title, bibliography, and appendices—also receive attention. Finally, the writing style of the research report and some guidelines for good writing and revision complete the chapter.

References

American Psychological Association, Council of Editors. *Publication manual of the American psychological association* (2nd ed.). Washington, D.C.: American Psychological Association, 1974.

Angell, J. Technical aspects of form and style. In R. H. Jones (Ed.), *Methods and techniques of educational research*. Danville, Ill.: The Interstate, 1973.

Ballou, S. V. *A model for theses and research papers.* Boston: Houghton Mifflin, 1970.

Barzun, J., & Graff, H. F. *The modern researcher* (3rd ed.). New York: Harcourt, Brace, & World, 1977.

Ebel, R. L. *Encyclopedia of educational research.* Washington, D.C.: American Educational Research Association, 1969.

Review of Educational Research. Washington: American Educational Research Association, all issues.

Travers, R. M. W. (Ed.). *Second handbook of research on teaching.* Chicago: Rand McNally, 1973.

CHAPTER FIFTEEN

LOOKING AT THE COMPLETE STUDY

> *Moreover, in topics such as these [problematical top-
> ics], there are always legitimate grounds for differences
> of opinion as to* what *they are,* how *they should be
> spoken about, and the kinds of knowledge we can have
> of them.*
>
> —Hayden White

The dissemination of information from research studies is done largely through the pages of professional journals. A monthly scan through *Education Index* and *Current Index to Journals in Education* should reveal to the educator what research has been reported about topics of personal interest. Reading the contents lists of selected journals is likely to be rewarding, since some articles may not be categorized and cataloged in the two indexes under terms that were used in your search of the two indexes.

Since the amount of time a person has for reading is usually limited, each person should be skilled not only in locating articles (see Chapter 4) but also in reading the contents of the articles. The writer of a journal article is limited by space allotment and must be selective in presenting the study. For this reason, the reader may not find exactly what she or he might want. Correspondence with the researcher(s) allows the reader to pursue those points or to obtain a copy of the complete report.

In general, the writer of a journal article will attempt to establish in the report what was done and what was observed. The following elements (not necessarily in this order) should be incorporated within each article:

1. A historical base
2. Clear presentation of the problem and hypotheses

3. Theoretical framework
4. Data collection and treatment
5. Results and conclusions drawn
6. Adequacy of the design within practical limitations
7. Awareness of basic assumptions
8. Other information specific to the study

The following report is a typical journal article about research on an educationally-based question. The authors have established some aspects of the laboratory experiment, but as is the case with most studies in education, they were limited by the type of question asked and the incomplete control of extraneous variables. A discussion of the article ends this chapter. Paragraph numbers are indicated in boldface type.

The Study

HUMOROUS LECTURES AND HUMOROUS EXAMPLES: SOME
EFFECTS UPON COMPREHENSION AND RETENTION

ROBERT M. KAPLAN and GREGORY C. PASCOE
San Diego State University

(Abstract)

This experiment studied the effect of humor and humorous examples upon the comprehension and retention of lecture material. Intact classes of university students $(N = 508)$ viewed either a serious lecture or one of three versions of a humorous lecture. The three versions of the humorous lecture included humorous examples related to the concepts in the lecture (concept humor), unrelated to the concepts (nonconcept humor), or a combination of concept and nonconcept examples (mixed humor). A test of comprehension and retention was given twice: immediately after the lecture and six weeks later. Results indicated that immediate comprehension was not facilitated by the use of humorous examples. Upon retesting, however, retention of concept humor material was significantly improved by viewing a lecture with humorous examples illustrating concepts. Earlier research findings are accounted for in terms of these results.

(Paragraph 1)

The advice to use humor for communication enhancement has been considered in several empirical studies (Berlo & Kumata, 1956; Gruner, 1965, 1966). Only a handful of studies, however, have focused upon the efficacy of humor for lectures in a teaching situation. Although several studies have shown that humor can increase attention and interest in a topic (Gruner, 1970; Markiewicz, 1974), comprehension and acceptance of a message have not been demonstrated to improve when the message includes

From the *Journal of Educational Psychology*, 1977, *69* (1), pp. 61–65. Copyright 1977 by the American Psychological Association. Reprinted by permission.

humor (Gruner, 1967, 1970; Kennedy, 1972; Markiewicz, 1974; Taylor, 1964).

(2)

One problem with humor studies that focus on learning is determining the nature of the humor the investigators used. Subjects' ratings of the perceived humorousness of a message were taken in only a minority of studies (Gruner, 1967, 1970; Kennedy, 1972; Lull, 1940). Most reports omit discussions of fundamental questions, such as how the humor was chosen in the first place and how the humor related to the persuasive or educational message.

(3)

Another difficulty with the research on humor and learning has been the method of evaluating learning. No experimenter stated exactly from where in the message that test items were taken. Because of this, two important questions become obvious: Did any test questions assess recall of material presented immediately before or after a humor item? Was humor associated in some way with the major points on which a listener was to be tested? Knowing how the humorous items in a message corresponded to subsequent test questions would allow a more accurate appraisal of humor's effect on learning.

(4)

The purpose of the present study was to explore the effect of two types of humor upon learning in a lecture situation. The two types of humor are humor related to the concepts presented in the lecture (or humorous examples) and humor unrelated to the lecture's content. The primary concern is to determine how varying correspondence of humor with the topics of a classroom lecture moderates the comprehension and retention of lecture material.

(5)

It is our hypothesis that people have good recall for specific humorous examples. A concept which is illustrated in a humorous manner might be learned more easily than a concept presented in a dull style. Humor unrelated to concepts, however, should not enhance learning. Previous research has not addressed this hypothesis because no study has investigated the effectiveness of humor for the presentation of substantive points.

Method

Subjects and Setting

(6)

The subjects were 508 undergraduate students at a large public university. These participants were enrolled in 16 sections of introductory psychology and the experiment was part of their regular instruction. Thus, subjects were run in large groups ranging from 23 to 45 students. Closed-circuit videotapes were customarily shown to all sections as part of the course instruction.

Lecture

(7)

Subjects saw one of four versions of a 20-min. black and white videotaped lecture about Freudian personality theory. Factual material in the lecture came from the chapter on Freud presented in Hall and Lindzey (1970). Points covered in the lecture included a biographical sketch of Freud; the concepts of id, ego, and superego; anxiety and defenses; stages of psychosexual development; neo-Freudians; and projective techniques of personality assessment.

Style Manipulation

(8)

One serious version and three humorous versions of the lecture were recorded on videotape. The humorous versions included humor directly related to some concepts in the lecture (concept humor), humor unrelated to any of the concepts (nonconcept humor), and a combination of some nonconcept and concept humor (mixed humor). Six main concepts were presented in each version and they were spaced evenly throughout the lecture. In the concept humor version, all of the concepts were illustrated by way of humorous example. For the mixed humor version, three of the six concepts were presented in the form of a humorous example. An Assistant Professor of Psychology delivered all four versions of the lecture.

(9)

All humorous lines were practiced with a pilot audience and delivered on videotape with appropriate inflection to maximize their impact. An example of concept humor centered on the difficulty in interpreting sentence completion assessments of personality. After explaining the typical clinical procedure, the lecturer offered a variety of straight and humorous sentence completions. To the sentence root "Animals . . ." the speaker responded with "scare me" for the nonhumorous version and used "often try to fool me" as the humorous punch line. Similarly, the stem "I would like . . ." met with "to be a doctor" for the serious condition and "to drink blood" for the humorous condition. An example of nonconcept humor regarding psycho-sexual stages of development was the lecturer's comment that "Freudians would probably have a good time deciding what stage Linda Lovelace was fixated at."

(10)

Since earlier studies demonstrated that humorous comments enhance interest (Gruner, 1970; Markiewicz, 1974), it was anticipated that using either concept or nonconcept humor would heighten interest in our lecture. Greater interest due to humorous remarks could produce better attention to material after interest had been aroused. If so, students would perform better on items testing concepts presented after a humorous instance than on material covered prior to the use of humor.

(11)

Cover story. Immediately before viewing the lecture, the following cover story, which was signed by a member of the faculty, was read to all participants:

(12)

The lecture today will be a videotape on personality theories. Sometimes we present new lectures on an experimental basis. We are interested in finding out whether or not this tape provides a useful learning experience for students. To decide how well the tape presents the material, we will need your reactions immediately after the tape is shown.

(13)

One set of information we would like to get from each of you is your impression of the videotape. To do this, you will each fill out a checklist to describe the speaker and the content of his lecture. The other measure we would like from you is your answers to a brief quiz on the lecture's content. This quiz will not count towards your class grade; we simply want an indication of how effectively this tape conveyed the information. You may, however, be held responsible for some of this information on your next regular quiz.

(14)

Although the quiz and descriptions won't figure into your grade, please fill out your responses carefully and do the best you can on the quiz. This will help us make an accurate evaluation of the tape.

(15)

Manipulation check. After the videotape was played, a two-part questionnaire and an answer sheet were distributed to each student. The first section consisted of semantic differential scales describing separately the speaker and the lecture. Six word pairs taken from Smith (1959) were used to rate the speaker and the lecture. These word pairs were as follows: valuable-worthless, interesting-boring, serious-humorous, cold-hot, optimistic-pessimistic, and light-heavy. A numbered, five-choice response space separated each word pair. Subjects were instructed to mark on their answer sheet the number of the choice in each word pair that best described the lecture they had seen.

(16)

Comprehension check. The second part of the questionnaire was comprised of 11 multiple-choice questions on the content of the lecture. Of these items, 6 focused on the 6 critical examples used in the concept humor version. These items were dubbed humor items. The other 5 items were based upon other information in the lecture and are defined here as nonhumor items. Subjects were instructed to record on their answer sheet which of the 4 alternatives was the best response for each. Two additional items on the questionnaire included to code each subject's class section and grade on the previous unit exam.

(17)

Retention check. The same 11-item quiz was administered to the subjects 6 weeks after the initial tape viewing and testing. This retesting was conducted by the instructor of each section.

Results

Manipulation Checks

(18)

To assess the effectiveness of the humor manipulations, mean ratings were examined for items asking where the speaker and the lecture stood on the continua serious-humorous and light-heavy. These two continua were selected because Smith (1959) found these variables to be reliable indicators of the humorousness of a message. Table 1 displays the results of this analysis.

Table 1 *Means, Standard Deviations, and Analysis of Variance Results for Manipulation Check Scale Ratings*

	Speaker				Lecture			
Group	Serious-humorous		Light-heavy		Serious-humorous		Light-heavy	
	M	SD	M	SD	M	SD	M	SD
Serious	1.69	.79	3.08	.85	1.75	.85	3.25	.92
Nonconcept	2.94_{ab}	.89	2.63	.84	2.87_{ab}	.91	2.90	.91
Mixed	3.07_{ab}	.97	2.59	1.04	2.75_{ab}	.98	2.90	.97
Concept	2.69_{a}	1.10	2.74	.95	2.59_{a}	1.07	2.99	.91
F(3.461)	53.75**		6.85**		33.33**		3.63*	

Note. Groups within columns marked by a common subscript do not differ at the .01 level. Anchors for the scales were serious (1)–humorous (5) and light (1)–heavy (5).
*$p < .05$.
**$p < .001$.

(19)

Inspection of Table 1 suggests that all of the humorous lectures were perceived as significantly more humorous and light than the serious presentation. Although there were some differences between humorous lecture groups (e.g., the concept humor lecture was slightly less effective than the other humorous presentations), differences between the humorous groups were trivial in comparison to the strong difference between each humor group and the group hearing the serious presentation. These distinctions were noticeable when audiotapes, which were recorded while subjects viewed the lectures, were compared for volume of laughter. Unlike students viewing the serious version, those viewing humorous versions laughed during the lecture, especially in response to humorous punch lines. Thus there is compelling evidence that the manipulation was effective.

Group Equivalence

(20)

The present study was a quasi experiment in which treatments were allocated to intact classes of students. To determine whether there were preexisting differences between classes, scores on tests given prior to the experiment were compared. It was observed that any preexisting differences were statistically nonsignificant. To assure that the minor preexisting differences did not influence the interpretation of other data, prior test scores were used as a covariate and partialed out of all other analysis.

(21)

Results of test performance are presented in Table 2. Examination of Table 2 suggests that the groups differed on performance for nonhumor items, but did not differ for humor items. Results of a Scheffé test revealed that those witnessing the lecture containing the humorous examples (concept humor) performed least well on items based on seriously presented concepts in the lecture. It should be noted that these students performed nonsignificantly better on the items based on the humorous examples.

Table 2 *Summary of Test Performance Comparison*

| Group | Item | | | | Total | |
| | Humor | | Nonhumor | | | |
	M	SD	M	SD	M	SD
Serious	4.24	1.26	3.00	.94	7.24	1.76
Nonconcept	4.37	1.55	2.97	.83	7.34	1.98
Mixed	4.09	1.22	2.83	1.04	6.92	1.82
Concept	4.53	1.22	2.68	.88	7.21	1.59
$F(3, 473)$	2.42		2.96*		1.38	

Note. (Data are based on 477 completed tests. Tests with missing responses were not processed.
*$p < .05$.

(22)

One test item was based upon a concept presented immediately after a joke in the nonconcept version of the lecture. A comparison of the serious and nonconcept humor groups for performance on this item and another item, taken from a concept presented immediately before the joke, allowed for a test of the hypothesis that humor-induced arousal facilitates learning. Analysis revealed no significant difference between the two groups on either of these test questions. However, performance on the postjoke item for the nonconcept humor group was slightly better and in the direction predicted by the arousal hypothesis *($p< .1$)*.

Posttest Performance

(23)

Table 3 summarizes the posttest performance results. Inspection of Table 3 indicates that the groups differed on performance for humor items, but not for nonhumor items. The analysis of variance results were as predicted—groups viewing lectures with more concept-related humor did significantly better on items testing recall of the humorous examples than did the serious lecture group. Although total test scores were not significantly different, results were in the predicted direction.

Table 3 *Summary of Posttest Performance Comparison*

Group	Item Humor M	Item Humor SD	Item Nonhumor M	Item Nonhumor SD	Total M	Total SD
Serious	3.69	1.05	3.00	.88	6.69	1.54
Nonconcept	3.74	1.52	3.07	.96	6.81	1.72
Mixed	3.91	1.18	2.79	.91	6.70	1.66
Concept	4.23	1.49	2.92	.78	7.15	1.70
$F(3, 295)$	2.83*		1.54		1.19	

Note. Data are based on 299 completed tests.
*$p < .05$.

Discussion

(24)

The results of this study suggest that recall for humorous examples is good. As suggested by the first test, concepts presented in humorous examples were comprehended slightly, but not significantly, more by groups who had been exposed to humorous lectures. The posttest showed significantly greater retention of concept humor information among subjects who had been exposed to more humorous examples. Humorous examples may have served as cues for recalling information. In this case, the speaker's use of humor could have prevented the significant loss of communication effectiveness observed previously with high-credibility sources (Gillig & Greenwald, 1974).

(25)

Total test performance was not significantly improved by using humor in the lecture. Total test results for the initial quiz demonstrated that those exposed to humor performed equivalently to those viewing the serious presentation. Although their performance improved upon retesting, students viewing humorous lecture versions still did not perform significantly better than students viewing the serious lecture version. These overall test findings are consistent with the majority of research studies on the relationship between humorous lectures and learning (Markiewicz, 1974).

(26)

The present study indicates that the benefits of humor in the classroom are most clearly demonstratable for recall of humorous examples. Attention is probably focused on these humorous examples, which may distract listeners from information presented in a straightforward manner. Therefore, general comprehension and retention of a classroom message is not significantly improved by the use of humor.

(27)

The outcome of the present study can account for the inability of earlier research to demonstrate an effect of humor upon learning. The use of humor significantly increased recall for only those test items based on humorous examples. Other studies on the relationship between humor and learning have rarely stated how their test questions corresponded to the concepts in the lecture. It is probable that the test items in previous studies were not all based on humorously illustrated material. In other words, earlier studies may not have been asking the appropriate test questions for determining the effect of humorous examples upon learning. The present study indicates that a positive effect of humorous examples only results when test items are based on those particular examples.

(**28**)

Our results concerning retention of humorously illustrated concepts provide an additional explanation for the lack of treatment differences reported in earlier humor and learning studies. Initial testing of subjects in the present study produced the expected, but nonsignificant, effect of humor examples on the comprehension of humor-related material. This trend gained statistical significance upon retesting. Some of the earlier research (Gruner, 1967, 1970) did not include any posttest of message content. Such retesting might have demonstrated a significant difference if the test questions related to the humor had been used. Studies which did retest subjects used quiz items which were apparently not based on humorous examples. As shown by the present results, only posttest questions based on humorous material indicate a significant improvement in learning.

A similar version of this article was presented at the meeting of the Western Psychological Association, Los Angeles, April 1976. Requests for reprints should be sent to Robert M. Kaplan, Psychological Clinic, San Diego State University, San Diego, California 92182.

References

(**29**)

Berlo, D. K., & Kumata, H. The investigator: The impact of a satirical radio drama. *Journalism Quarterly*, 1956, *33*, 287–298.

Gillig, P. M., & Greenwald, A. G. Is it time to lay the sleeper effect to rest? *Journal of Personality and Social Psychology*, 1974, *29*, 132–139.

Gruner, C. R. An experimental study of satire as persuasion. *Speech Monographs*, 1965, *32*, 149–154.

Gruner, C. R. A further experimental study of satire as persuasion. *Speech Monographs*, 1966, *33*, 184–185.

Gruner, C. R. The effect of humor on speaker ethos and audience information gain. *Journal of Communication*, 1967, *17*, 228–233.

Gruner, C. R. The effect of humor in dull and interesting informative speeches. *Central States Speech Journal*, 1970, *21*, 160–166.

Hall, C. S., & Lindzey, G. Theories of personality (2nd ed.). New York: Wiley, 1970.

Kennedy, A. J. *An experimental study of the effect of humorous message content upon ethos and persuasiveness.* Unpublished doctoral dissertation, University of Michigan, 1972.

Lull, P. E. The effectiveness of humor in persuasive speech. *Speech Monographs*, 1940, *1*, 26–40.

Markiewicz, D. Effects of humor on persuasion. *Sociometry*, 1974, *37*, 407–422.

Smith, R. G. Development of a semantic differential for use with speech related concepts. *Speech Monographs*, 1959, *26*, 263–272.

Taylor, P. M. The effectiveness of humor in informative speeches. *Central States Speech Journal*, 1964, *14*, 295–296.

Discussion

This article by Kaplan and Pascoe follows the APA format and conforms to the five-section schema detailed in the last chapter. Since the conclusions of a research study are its product, a reader may be satisfied to read only the section on discussion. A deeper interest would suggest further reading. Critical reading of research studies requires judgments about procedures and threats to the validity of conclusions. Each reader must decide the level of reading appropriate in a particular instance. The standard format guides the reader to selected parts for each study. After reading several journal articles which follow the standardized sequence of presentation, the reader should be able to locate any desired information efficiently when reading further in the journals. The separate sections of the article just presented are described below in the order they appeared.

Abstract

Section one of the article gives the title, authors' names, their institutional affiliation, and an overview of what follows as an abstract of the article. The purpose of the abstract is to help the reader decide whether or not to read the complete article. It also serves as a very brief summary of the article.

The first sentence of the abstract may include enough information to allow the reader to decide whether or not the article is related to personal interests. A brief outline of procedures follows the description. Then results are presented and connected to other findings. The contents and length of the abstract for this study are typical of journal article abstracts.

Introduction

Though not titled, Paragraphs 1 through 5 synthesize an introduction to the study. They include the historical base in the form of a brief review of literature, the purpose of the study, and the statement hypotheses.

Paragraphs 1 and 2 cover relevant research studies and combined with paragraph 3 establish the framework for the study. Paragraph 3 bridges past research into questions that are dealt with here.

Paragraph 4 uses the previously established framework to present the purpose. This paragraph identifies the variables "humor" and "learning" and raises the question about how they are related. (The approach described in this book would have asked a direct question at this point to focus directly on the point of the research endeavor.) By this stage, the scope of the study has been established, and the reader is informed that learning will encompass comprehension and retention.

Paragraph 5 presents the hypotheses to be tested in the study. A more direct statement for each hypothesis might have made it easier for the reader to establish how the researcher predicted the outcomes. A direct question in paragraph 4 followed by the appropriate hypotheses would aid a reader in establishing the purpose of the study.

Method

The section on method is used to explain how the study was conducted. In general, this section is directed to discussing the source of the data (subjects), what subjects were required to do, the setting and materials, and the statistical design. Frequently used subheadings for this section are "subjects," "design," "materials used," "procedure," "treatment," "measurements," "data analysis," and "training of observers." However, these authors used subheadings which more directly describe this study. In paragraph 6, the authors describe the subjects, tell how many were used, and detail the circumstances associated with data collection. Paragraph 7 explains the material covered in a lecture and reveals that it was presented as one of 4 versions of a 20-minute videotape.

Paragraphs 8 through 14 explain treatment (4 versions of the lecture), the setting for data collection, and the instructions given to the subjects. The data collection devices (materials) are described in paragraphs 15, 16, and 17. Notice that 5-choice responses for semantic differential scales were used to rate the speaker and the lecture. Comprehension was measured by an 11-item multiple-choice test. Retention after 6 weeks was checked by administering the same 11-item quiz again.

The section on method does not include the statistical design used to reduce the data into results. This absence of detail must be considered a major deficiency of the article. The analysis is implied in the reporting of results and in Tables 1, 2, and 3 which refer to comparisons obtained by the analysis of variance. In most studies, the section on method includes the researcher's description of the design and some graphic representation which constructs for the reader a clear picture of how the relationships of the variables were investigated and how the comparison groups were arranged.

Results

The section on results is intended to condense the data into a format that reports objectively not only the data but also the results of statistical analysis. There are three ways of reporting results. First, tables can summarize results of statistical analysis. Second, graphics (figures) can show trends and relationships in the data. Third, a narrative description within the text of the article can further analyze the numbers by relating them textually to the variables under study.

Paragraphs 18 and 19 present the information from Table 1 in a narrative written as results. The results from the semantic differential scales are presented and discussed. Paragraph 21 expands into a narrative discussion the data from the first test for comprehension summarized in

Table 2. Paragraph 23 expands the summary of the test for retention presented in Table 3.

This results section also includes two paragraphs devoted to other statistical analysis. Paragraph 20 reports the results of an investigation made about characteristics of the subjects. Since intact groups were used, the researchers wanted to determine how the groups compared on scores on tests given prior to the experiment. Differences on the earlier tests showed preexisting differences to be statistically nonsignificant; however, data treatment of test scores used prior test scores to partial out differences in analysis of test scores. Paragraph 22 reports results of a separate investigation based on two selected test items. Careful reporting of results serves as a bridge from the raw data into conclusions and also allows the reader to judge critically the methods used and the conclusions drawn by the researchers.

Discussion

The final section of a journal article is used to explain what the results mean to the particular study. This discussion should be directed to whether the data support or do not support the research hypotheses and should give a direct answer to the question under study. The researcher draws conclusions here on the basis of how the original question was answered. This section should also be used to relate the study's findings with theory and outcomes of other research studies. Paragraphs 24 through 28 in the Kaplan and Pascoe article exhibit how writers discuss the results and draw conclusions for a study.

The research writer may also use the discussion section to make recommendations for further research on the current question and related questions. Kaplan and Pascoe did not include such recommendations. The detailed report would probably include that information and a section about implications for change as a result of findings for this study.

References

The article is presented here complete with the listing of sources that have been cited in the text material. The APA format lists sources alphabetically and makes citations in the text by authors' names and dates. Notice that footnotes are not used for citations in APA form. Also note that most references are to articles in professional journals—the exceptions being one dissertation and one book.

Analysis

Basic to the teaching-learning process are two questions teachers ask of themselves. First, how can I become a more effective teacher? Second, how well are my students learning? The Kaplan and Pascoe study seeks answers to these two questions. Kaplan and Pascoe have built a theoretical framework around these questions for their study by citing results of other related studies and pointing up gaps in knowledge that their study seeks to fill. They decided to plan their study to deal with two specific questions about the effect of humor on learning: How does the use of humor in presenting material affect recall and retention? How does the use of humor during presentation of a major point affect recall and retention?

From the reading of previous studies and their own knowledge, the authors developed a hypothesis for each question; however, they point out that no specific investigation had been made on the effectiveness of humor for presenting substantive points. Their investigation was designed to do this by keying test items to different modes of presenting humor.

The first part of the article is a logical progress through the historical base into the theoretical framework, presentation of the questions to be answered, and statements of their hypotheses:

1. A concept illustrated with humor was expected to be learned more easily than one presented in a dull style.
2. Humor unrelated to concepts was not expected to enhance learning.

Although it seems clear that these sentences are conjectural, there is no statement for the data to support or not to support. One term that seems ambiguous is "easily." Do the authors really mean "easily?" From the context of the material, it appears that they mean to ask, How well do the students learn? rather than, How easily do the students learn? With this in mind, two hypothesis statements more appropriate by our criteria would be:

1. Learning of a concept will be enhanced when it is illustrated in a humorous manner rather than being presented in a dull style.
2. Humor unrelated to a concept will not enhance learning of that concept.

If methodology is directed to collecting data relating to these hypotheses, then the data will have something to either support or not support. Without direct statements, ambiguity may cause confusion about what the data are to relate to.

In the method section, subtopics "Subjects and Setting," "Lecture," and "Style Manipulation" explain very well how the study was conducted. This allows the reader to evaluate the results and conclusions for validity. There is some question about whether or not the lines intended to be humorous were indeed humorous. No humorous line is humorous for every person who hears it, and what is humorous to one person may not be humorous to another person. This is especially important because humor is the treatment and the outcome of the study depends on whether or not the humor was effective. The authors do have some evidence that the humorous lectures were indeed *more* humorous than nonhumorous lectures. Procedures listed in the "manipulation check" section support this. The "results" section also speaks to this point when audiotapes made during the lectures revealed more laughter for the humorous lectures.

Paragraph 10 about interest appears to be oblique to the study, however this characteristic may have been implied in earlier paragraphs. It is in paragraph 10 that the term "interest" is first introduced, however, and a study cited. This concept assumes relevance only in the section on results. Paragraph 22 again refers to "interest" in discussing test performance and introduces another hypothesis. The reader should have been made aware of this concept and the corresponding hypothesis in the introductory section of the article.

The cover story was well-written. It explains why the subjects are asked to perform differently from other class sessions, builds a foundation for the student's personal interest, and relieves any possible pressure from a test that will count as a part of the grade. It should increase the validity of the study.

The manipulation check (paragraph 15) may seem to be extraneous to the study, since it does not relate directly to answering the proposed questions. Further reading (paragraphs 18 and 19) reveals how these data were used.

The comprehensive check seems to be in reasonable order. A question might be created about how the 6 humorous items and the 5 nonhumorous items could be combined as a measure of the effect of humor. Tables 2 and 3 and accompanying test explain how they were used. The small number of items may restrict the reliability of the test scores and hence their validity. Since no reliability values are reported, test reliability remains suspect. The use of the same test as a posttest raises the question of how the taking of the test a second time was affected by the first administration. Questions about the effect of history and maturation also arise when time lapses. In this case, the authors can assume that if there was any effect it would be constant across treatment conditions. The authors should deal with those questions in the article by making clear their opinions about possible effect.

The results of the manipulation check and tabled data support the authors' contention that evidence suggests that the manipulation was effective. The audiotapes also support that opinion.

The use of intact groups always raises questions about the equivalence of groups who are compared. In paragraph 20, data establish that posttest performance differences are not large enough to result in any significant differences. This does not establish equivalence. It only shows that the groups are not statistically different. For this reason, a statistical procedure of partialling out differences by covarying on past test scores allows statistical control for the test performance scores in this study.

The results of test performance are well-presented and the tables imply the statistical treatment of groups by analysis of variance. In paragraph 21, the reader is informed that the significant F value for differences among means for the nonhumor items was further investigated by a Scheffé test. This is a post hoc test that identifies sources of significant differences between pairs of means. This test identified a significant difference between the serious lecture group and the concept humor group on the five nonhumor items. The concept humor group did less well than the serious group. The concept group scored higher than other groups on the humorous items, but the difference was nonsignificant. The authors note that the concept humor group performed higher on the humor items than did the other three groups, but that the difference was not significant.

Paragraph 22 gives the results of the oblique move taken in paragraph 10. The results for the test of that hypothesis—humor-induced arousal (interest) facilitates learning—show no difference in performance for an item presented after a joke or another item presented before a joke, when the serious and nonconcept versions of the lecture were compared. The nonconcept group was chosen because that group did not have concepts presented with humor. They had humor interspersed throughout the lecture but not during presentation of material on concepts to be learned. Although this question was raised in the introduction (paragraph 3), the authors did not present a hypothesis for this part of the study. The lack of this bridge to results limits reader understanding.

Results of the posttest scores reveal only one difference that is statistically significant. The concept humor group is significantly different from the serious group for recall of humorous items.

The study interprets results by discussion and presents implied conclusions according to the authors' interpretations. In general, the discussion implies conclusions that are supported by the results of data treatment, and the authors have made it clear when they have gone beyond the data. For example, "Humorous examples may have served as cues for recalling information. In this case, the speaker's use of humor could have prevented the significant loss of communication effectiveness observed previously with high-credibility sources" (paragraph 24).

The authors also related the findings of this study to other research findings. For example, "These overall test findings are consistent with the majority of research studies on the relationship between humorous lectures and learning" (paragraph 25).

Paragraph 27 speculates (extrapolates beyond the data) a proposed answer to why other studies might have failed to pick up effects of humor. This is proper procedure as long as the reader is clearly informed that the writer is beyond the conclusions drawn from the results of this study. Paragraph 28 completes the speculation by explaining why other studies might have had other outcomes if the quiz items had been on concepts presented in a humorous context.

The following list refers to specific points that raise questions about what was done and what was observed. These could be considered shortcomings of the article. It should be remembered that the authors and all writers for journals are limited by space and must consequently limit their coverage. A more detailed report of the study may cover the following criticisms of this article.

1. The study lacked the unifying question-hypothesis-results relationship needed for a clear understanding of the conclusions.
2. The use of only six example items in the comprehension check presents two difficulties. The first involves sampling error. With small numbers, the selection of a specific six items possibly allows a large

sampling error. Second, the reliability is likely to be very low with only six items. In each case, the authors should have considered these important enough considerations to discuss for the readers.

3. The authors did not deal with the problems of history and maturation, nor the testing effects of using the same test twice. In this case, since pretest and posttest scores are not compared, history and maturation probably did not affect the outcomes. Nevertheless, they should have been considered in the article. Use of the same test—especially one with only six items—is questionable procedure. On the other hand, problems might arise if new items were written. The authors should defend their use of the same test.

4. Experimental mortality was not dealt with in the article. Table 2 reports data on 477 subjects; Table 3 reports data on 299 subjects. The possible effects of selection for those who appeared six weeks later and those who did not should be discussed and related to the validity of the data.

5. There is a lack of discussion about the statistical procedures used to treat the data.

Despite these drawbacks, the overall impression gathered from the article's contents is one of confidence. Even the listed shortcomings do not negate the conclusions drawn. They do raise questions, however. The perfect educational research study—one above question—has yet to be developed. As the methodology for a study develops, choices among alternatives create less-than-ideal situations. These writers have dealt very well with a difficult question. A direct conversation with them would reveal why they proceeded as they did and would also reveal some information that could not be included in the abbreviated report of a journal article.

Summary

Readers of research reports can interact with the information on a variety of levels—from just noting the title or reading the abstract to writing directly to the authors or acquiring a copy of the complete research account. The writer of a research report must make these levels of interaction possible through maintaining a logical organization and by presenting adequate information for readers with further interest in the topic.

This chapter presents such a research report, describes it, and analyzes it as would a person with a sincere interest in the entire report from conception and methodology through recommendations. I hope this chapter will complete the preparation of students to be good consumers of research. This presentation will also direct the writings of those who have conducted a study and are preparing to report their findings to professional educators.

References

Current index to journals in education. New York: Macmillan, 1969 to date.
Education index. New York: H. W. Wilson, 1928 to date.

White, H. *Tropics of discourse: Essays in cultural criticism.* Baltimore: Johns Hopkins University Press, 1978.

Bibliography: Part Four

American Psychological Association, Council of Editors. *Publication Manual of the American Psychological Association* (2nd ed.). Washington, D.C.: American Psychological Association, 1974.

Anderson, H. E., & Bashaw, W. L. An experimental study of first grade theme writing. *American Educational Research Journal,* March 1968, *5,* 239–247.

Angell, J. Technical aspects of writing form and style. In R. H. Jones, *Methods and Techniques of Educational Research.* Danville, Ill.: The Interstate, 1973.

Ballou, S. V. *A model for theses and research papers.* Boston: Houghton-Mifflin, 1970.

Barzun, J., & Graff, H. F. *The modern researcher* (3rd ed.). New York: Harcourt Brace Jovanovich, 1977.

Bloom, B. S. (Ed.) *Taxonomy of educational objectives: The cognitive domain.* New York: David McKay, 1956.

Bruning, J. L., & Kintz, B. L. *Computational handbook of statistics* (2nd ed.). Glenview, Ill.: Scott, Foresman, 1977.

Campbell, W. G., & Ballou, S. V. *Form and style: Theses, reports, term papers* (5th ed.). Boston: Houghton-Mifflin, 1977.

Chase, C. I. *Elementary statistical procedures* (2nd ed.). New York: McGraw-Hill, 1976.

Cook, D. R., & LaFleur, N. K. *A guide to educational research* (2nd ed.). Boston: Allyn and Bacon, 1975.

Current index to journals in education. New York: Macmillan, 1969 to date.

Dugdale, K. *A manual of form for theses and term reports* (4th rev.). Bloomington: Indiana University Press, 1972.

Ebel, R. L. *Encyclopedia of educational research.* Washington, D.C.: American Educational Research Association, 1969.

Education index. New York: H. W. Wilson, 1928 to date.

Gallimore, R., Tharp, R. G., & Speidel, G. E. The relationship of sibling caretaking and attentiveness to a peer tutor. *American Educational Research Journal,* Spring 1978, *15,* 267–273.

Gardener, P. L. Scales and statistics. *Review of Educational Research,* Winter 1975, *45,* 43–57.

Gilman, D. A. Why don't you publish it in the journal of nonsignificant differences? *Contemporary Education,* January 1971, *43,* 155–156.

Guion, R. M. *Standards for educational and psychological tests.* Washington, D.C.: American Psychological Association, 1974.

Helmstadler, G. C. *Research concepts in human behavior.* New York: Appleton-Century-Crofts, 1970.

Hopkins, C. D., *Describing data statistically.* Columbus, Oh.: Charles E. Merrill, 1974.

Hopkins, C. D., & Antes, R. L. *Classroom measurement and evaluation.* Itasca, Ill.: F. E. Peacock, 1978.

Hopkins, C. D., & Antes, R. L. *Classroom testing: Administration, Scoring, and Score Interpretation.* Itasca, Ill.: F. E. Peacock, 1979.

Hopkins, C. D., & Antes, R. L. *Classroom testing: Construction.* Itasca, Ill.: F. E. Peacock, 1979.

Huck, S. V., Cormier, W. H., Bounds, W. G., Jr., & Sechrest, L. *Reading statistics and research.* New York: Harper and Row, 1974.

Jessell, J. C., & Sullins, W. L. The effect of keyed response sequencing of multiple choice items on performance and reliability. *Journal of Educational Measurement,* Spring 1975, *12,* 45–48.

Kaplan, R.M., & Pascoe, G. Humorous lectures and humorous examples: Some effects upon comprehension and retention. *Journal of Educational Psychology,* 1977, *69* (1), 61–65.

Krathwohl, D. R., Bloom, B. S., & Masia, B. B. *Taxonomy of educational objectives: The affective domain.* New York: David McKay, 1964.

Perrin, P. G. *Writer's guide and index to English* (4th ed.). Chicago: Scott, Foresman, 1968.

Review of Educational Research. Washington, D.C.: American Educational Research Association, 1931 to date.

Sharp, W. H., & Kirk, B. A. A longitudinal study of who seeks counseling when. *Journal for Counseling Psychology,* 1974, *21,* 43–50.

Terman, L. M., & Oden, M. H. *The gifted child grows up.* Stanford: Stanford University Press, 1947.

Thorndike, R. L. (Ed.). *Educational measurement.* Washington, D.C.: American Council on Education, 1971.

Travers, R. M. W. (Ed.). *Second handbook of research on teaching.* Chicago: Rand McNally, 1973.

Turabian, K. U. *A manual for writers of term papers, theses and dissertations* (4th ed.). Chicago: University of Chicago Press, 1973.

White, H. *Tropics of discourse: Essays in cultural criticism.* Baltimore: Johns Hopkins University Press, 1978.

EPILOGUE

UNDERSTANDING EDUCATIONAL RESEARCH

This book has structured the inquiry process of educational research to prepare you for two major aspects of research. The conceptualization of the research process has been accompanied by knowledge about procedures to allow you to *conduct* research studies. Maybe even more importantly, this study of educational research should allow you to utilize conclusions from research studies, to help you become a knowledgeable *consumer* of research.

The focus of the book upon structure is justified by past evidence supporting the hypothesis that studying a new topic through structure stimulates interest for the topic and promotes efficient learning. It is possible that your study has also fostered a third benefit: the aesthetic rewards of an interesting and fascinating study.

Any study of research ideally should bring these three aspects in balance. I hope that this book has given you a better understanding of the formal approach to inquiry about educational concerns, and that you are prepared to conduct research and to interpret results of studies to allow you to function better as a professional educator. Most of all, I hope that the study will be reflected in your role as a professional educator, that as you go about doing whatever you do in education you do it better because of your interest in research, because you have a better understanding of how to attack new problems and create new knowledge, and because you can incorporate in your practice the results of others' studies.

GLOSSARY

The text of a book on research is somewhat technical in nature and some words may be used in a way new to the reader. Some words also have uses special to the field and related studies. For these reasons, certain words have been selected and explained for the reader in the following glossary. Usage here is intended to conform to general use in research, but since precise definitions are not universal for all books, this glossary serves more to clarify usage in this book rather than attempting to provide universal definitions.

The first time a glossary word appears in the text of the book, it is in **boldface**. At that time, the reader should refer to the denotation in the glossary to understand the way the term will be used in the book. Educational dictionaries and general dictionaries can further clarify terms that have not been selected for this limited glossary.

Abacus. a manual computing device built with a frame and wires with movable counters; probably the oldest computing device.

Absolute zero. a point on a scale that indicates total absence of the property being measured (in contrast to a zero used as a reference point or placeholder).

Abstract. a brief summary of a study's formal and lengthy report; also, a formal summary of a journal article used by APA and other journals to replace a concluding statement or summary.

Action research. a tool of curriculum development used for the study of local problems to guide, correct, and evaluate educational decisions and actions. It may include research procedures as defined for our study.

Affective domain. the area of human action that deals with the internalized processes. (Examples: attitude, opinion, interest)

Anecdotal record. a factual statement that describes a student's behavior in a specific situation recorded as being either typical or unusual behavior.

Anthropological approach.   ethnographic fieldwork that attempts to see how each discrete fact relates to the total of facts collected on the sociocultural situation; uses direct observation and participation of the researcher in the flow of living; can be applied to studying the educational scene.

A posteriori.   related to reasoning from observed facts (inductive).

A priori.   related to reasoning from experience or propositions (deductive).

Assigned variable.   a kind of independent variable where treatment consists of assignment to groups by some characteristic either inherent or learned.

Assumption.   an aspect of a research study that is presumed to be true with or without general agreement in the discipline at large, taken as self-evident to start a train of reasoning for the study.

Attitudinal scale.   a data-collecting device intended to measure personal attitude toward a specific thing or concept. It usually records reactions on a rating scale.

Baseline data.   information collected to comprise a reference set for comparison of a second set of data collected at a later time; used to interpret changes over time usually after some condition has been changed.

BASIC.   a simple, but limited, programming language used with computer terminals and as an introductory language to facilitate student use.

Behavioral objective.   a statement that describes what a student should be able to do after completing prescribed instruction or another learning task. The statement spells out the aim of instruction stated as observable description of measurable behavior.

Bias.   not neutral; an inclination to some form of prejudice. (Examples: sampling bias, statistical bias).

Bibliography.   a list of sources on a particular subject; used in a proposal or report to cite references and list materials related to the research study.

Canonical correlation.   a multiple-correlation technique that adds more than one dependent variable to the regular multiple-regression model.

Card deck.   a set of punch cards that supplies the data and informs the computer what to do.

Case study.   an encompassing study of some entity using all available evidence. The object of a study may be a person, defined group of persons, event, institution, or community.

Categorical variable.   a property that allows assignment to subclasses on an all-or-none basis. The classes used for assignment must be exhaustive. Nominal measurement is associated with categorical variables.

Causal-comparative.   a type of descriptive research that studies a complex set of circumstances without direct manipulation but attempts to establish causes of observed effects.

Central location.   (See *Central tendency*).

Central tendency.   a value used to represent a set of scores in a frequency distribution. Examples: mean (arithmetical average), median, mode.

Chance variation.   a difference between two values that appears without bias, such that the sum of error approaches zero as a limit.

Checklist. an aid to direct observation which lists items to be given attention. Checkmarks indicate presence, absence, or frequency of occurrence for each item.

Close-ended. a structure that does not allow for contingency beyond the frame of reference. Example: a close-ended question which allows for only specified responses.

COBOL. common business oriented language. A computer language designed for business uses of inventory record and control, payrolls, and so on.

Cognitive domain. the area of human action that pertains to mental processes. Example: learning, problem solving, intellect.

Conclusion. the end product of a process of reasoning. The researcher's interpretation of the study's results stated as a generalization.

Confounding effects. influence of contributing variables that reduces the clarity of the results of a research study. Differences contributed by variables other than treatment variables make interpretation of treatment effects difficult.

Construct. a concept invented to explain some aspect of human behavior. It is created to name a certain nonphysical trait. Examples: creativity, hostility.

Content analysis. the separation of communications into its constituent parts with a view to examination and interpretation.

Contingency table. the frequency distribution presented as a two-way statistical classification.

Continuous variable. a characteristic that can take on ordered values within a certain range. A continuous variable must be amenable to ordering, interval, or ratio assignment of values.

Control. a systematic ruling out of contributions by confounding variables. Possible causes are held in check to permit study of manipulation effects.

Correlation. the tendency for one set of values to vary concomitantly with another set. Used to study relationships among variables under study.

Correlation coefficient. a pure number that expresses the degree of relationship between two sets of values considered to be directly connected. Correlation coefficients range from .00, denoting complete absence of relationship, to +1.00, indicating perfect positive relationship, and from .00 to −1.00, which indicates perfect negative relationship.

Correlational study. a research endeavor that is conducted without manipulation of variables by treatment.

Correlator. one who studies ongoing events of the real world without conscious manipulation of conditions. (Syn.: *correlationalist*)

Criterion variable. the dependent variable. The measured variable in an experimental study which is used to judge the effects of experimental manipulation.

Criticism. study of documents and relics for the purpose of evaluating their authenticity and credibility; methods of establishing trustworthiness based on genuineness and meaningfulness; used in historical research to establish facts

Cross-sectional study. investigation of development by considering different age groups at one point in time rather than following one group through an extended time period.

Data. information. Factual information used as a basis for reasoning or calculation, especially for testing a research hypothesis.

Debugging. detecting, locating, and removing mistakes from a program routine or computer malfunction. (Syn.: *troubleshoot)*

Decision error. a mistake in tests of statistical significance when a null hypothesis is rejected and it should not be (type I error) or when a null hypothesis is not rejected and it should be (Type II error). The probability of making a Type I error is the significance level for the test of significance.

Deduction. a process of reasoning that starts with a generalization and infers a conclusion in the context of that premise.

Delimit. setting the scope of a research study by establishing clearly defined boundaries about what is being studied.

Delimitation. a fixation of the limit for some aspect of the research study. A series of delimitations explains the scope of the study. It is used to clarify the area of concern for the study.

Demographic data. vital information about subjects under study. Usually not a part of the data used to reason about the study's hypothesis, it is instead used to explain characteristics of studied subjects.

Dependent variable. the measured variable in an experimental study. (Syn.: *criterion variable)*

Depository. a place where anything is placed for storage and safekeeping.

Descriptive research. inquiry into questions by studying conditions as they currently exist. Present conditions are not altered for study by direct manipulation.

Design. an overall plan of a research study. Also used to prescribe statistical treatment of data. The statistical design is a part of methodology which is, in turn, a part of the general design of the study.

Development. procedures used to produce tools, curriculum, and techniques for instruction. Acts associated with the inquiry strategy associated with a need to do something.

Developmental study. a research endeavor that studies change—such as the growth, function, or organization of something—or some concept over a long time span.

Dictionary. a reference book that keys material in a data base to research topics.

Direct observation. taking note of phenomena under circumstances that allow no intervention between the one observing and that which is being observed.

Discriminant analysis. a technique for discriminating to which group an individual belongs. It is based on a prediction using a dependent variable that represents membership in a group.

Discrimination power. the capacity of a test item to distinguish levels of achievement for students who are being tested.

Document. any written item of a factual or informative nature; used to obtain facts for historical studies.

Documentary analysis. study of documents to separate the constituent elements; a process which is intended to generate facts for a research study.

Educational research. structured scientific inquiry into educational questions that provides answers which contribute to the generalizable knowledge about educational concerns.

Empirical testing. a manner of assessing the tenability of a belief by checking it against objective reality. This involves objective collection of data to test a subjective notion.

Error. variation. Differences may be introduced by inaccuracies of measurement, probabilities associated with sampling, or other random events. This is not to be confused with a mistake. (Decision to reject or not to reject a null hypothesis may be a mistake. This involves Type I and Type II errors which are possible erroneous decisions.)

Evaluation. the inspection of information concerning something to form valid judgments about it; deals with appraisal and assessment; acts associated with the inquiry strategy associated with a need to choose or select.

Exhaustive. all inclusive. Description of a property which provides a subcategory for each element being classified is said to be exhaustive.

Experiment. administration of treatment to a set of elements by manipulation in controlled conditions to allow for analysis of the observed effects as to causes.

Experimental research. a study made under laboratory-like conditions to allow for control of variables and manipulation to study cause-effect relationships. Most studies in education are considered experimental if the conditions approach those in a laboratory setting.

Experimental treatment. assignment of conditions on the independent variable. The different conditions allow for establishment of causes for observed effects.

Experimenter. A researcher who uses the manipulation of a research experiment to study a problem. (Syn.: *experimentalist*)

External validity. The degree to which results of a study can be generalized to other populations and settings. This concept deals with representativeness of an experimental design.

Extraneous variable. a variable—other than the independent variable—that contributes to dependent variable measures.

Extrapolation. estimation of variate values outside the observed range.

Fact. any bit of information that has validity for use as data in a research study. Facts are used to test the tenability of research hypotheses. (See *Observation*)

Factor analysis. a method for analyzing relationships among a set of values in a matrix; used to determine what is unique to one variable or common to several variables.

Field study. a research project conducted without the manipulation of treatment under laboratory conditions.

Field test. a trial administration of a preliminary form of a standardized test. Test directions, time limits, format, and item performance are evaluated in terms of the trial run and student reactions.

File. an organization of papers, cards, or information into some useful order.

Formative evaluation. an ongoing evaluation conducted to provide information for a feedback loop into a continuing program.

FORTRAN. FORmula TRANslating system. A compiler type computer language designed to solve mathematical problems.

Frequency distribution. an arrangement of data according to the frequency of occurrence for each possible value in the range of score values. It may be presented in tabular or graphic form. A *theoretical* frequency distribution is a frequency distribution built on a mathematical structure for all possible values. Usually a sampling distribution is obtained by direct reference to probability considerations.

Generalization. a conclusion drawn from relevant data. Also, the process of inferring beyond the sample studied to a greater population using sample information.

Goodness of fit. the extent to which a set of obtained frequencies agrees with frequencies based on a set of theoretically or empirically generated expected values.

Graph. a diagram depicting a system of interrelationships among two or more things by physical representation using dots, lines, and so on.

Hand calculator. See *Minicalculator*.

Historical research. study of a question based in the past that requires collection of data from the past to serve as facts for the study.

Hypothesis. a proposition presented as a premise for argument or as a basis for testing the tenability of a position.

Hypothesis, null. a statement that there is no difference in measures of the criterion variable except what would be expected from sampling; requires that a significance level be stated (.05, .01, . . .). The null (statistical) hypothesis is what the test of significance tests. (See *Unhypothesis.*)

Hypothesis, research. the statement of what the researcher deems to be the most probable answer to the study's problem question; a tentative statement subject to verification through subsequent investigation.

Implication. a close connection of a study's conclusion to suggested changes in the educational scene; a suggested change in the educational setting as a result of a study's conclusions.

Independent variable. a variable to which levels can be assigned at will; the variable that the researcher manipulates in an experimental study.

Induction. a process of reasoning that starts with specifics and moves to a generalization.

Inference. the act of generalizing from sample to values of population parameters; also the making of general statements from the study of particular cases.

Information. anything the investigator uses to make a decision about the research hypothesis. It includes facts from documents, relics, direct observation, measurement, and so on. (Syn.: *data.*)

Inquiry. a systematic investigation of some question, stated or implied. A search for knowledge based on a problem-solving procedure organized to seek an answer to a clearly presented question.

Interaction. a combined action of two independent variables. In a study, part of the difference effects will be from one variable under study, part will be from a second variable, and some differences will occur because of the joint action of the two variables. This also applies to three or more independent variables.

Internal consistency. analysis of the interrelatedness of responses to items on a test that gives an estimate of consistency at a point in time. A single test is usually divided into odd and even items and a correlation coefficient derived as a measure of reliability.

Internal validity. the degree to which the effect of the experimental stimulus is *not* confounded by extraneous variables. This concept deals with interpretation of the question, Did treatment make a difference?

Interview. a formal meeting in which a research worker asks questions of a person from whom material is sought as facts for a research study.

Isomorphic. something similar or identical in structure or appearance to something else.

Kurtosis. the relative degree of flatness or peakedness of a frequency distribution.

Laboratory conditions. an environment which allows the same degree of control as a laboratory where strict control of all variables is possible; constitutes ideal conditions for experimental studies of educational concerns.

Level. one of the treatments on the independent variable. If two groups are studied, where different temperatures are provided for each group, the factor of temperature has two different levels—one for each group.

Limitation, research. any restriction on the study with respect to inferring or generalizing beyond the subjects studied. Limitations should be kept at a minimum; however, the art of researching lies in being able to deal with each study and its limitations.

Longitudinal study. a research study that is conducted over a long period of time to study development or factors which change over time.

Manipulation. assignment of treatment to the independent variable. Other variables are controlled or held constant for groups being studied.

Mean square. the variance (σ^2); the average (mean) value of all the squared deviations of each score from the mean.

Measure. (*noun*) the value, extent, dimensions, capacity of something as reported in terms of some unit. A number value obtained by the measurement process; (*verb*) process of measurement.

Measurement. a process of assigning by rule a numerical description to some attribute of an object, person, or event.

Mechanical device. a physical apparatus used to collect data.

Mechanics of writing. the functional details of format for written scholarly works. (See *Style Manual.*)

Median. the midpoint (sometimes the middle score) of a score distribution.

It divides the distribution so that 50% of the scores fall above it and 50% fall below it.

Metaphysical.   concerned with abstract thought about subjects such as causality, existence, or truth.

Microfiche (MF).   a four-by-six film on which material may be reduced by 24 times (to $\frac{1}{24}$ of the original); used to reproduce written material for convenient and inexpensive storage. One sheet can hold over 75 pages of material. ERIC uses microfiche for storage.

Minicalculator.   a portable electronic calculating device; may be electric or battery powered. Very advanced models may be programmable.

Model.   something that serves as a pattern or representation for something else. (See *Paradigm.*)

Multiple regression.   a prediction method that uses more than one predictor (independent) variable to predict values on a predicted (dependent) variable.

Multivariate.   more than one variable on either the independent or dependent dimension, or both. Any technique that is a simultaneous analysis of k independent variables and m dependent variables (either both k or m greater than one) is considered multivariate.

Mutually exclusive.   happenings or events are said to be "mutually exclusive" if when one event occurs, the other cannot occur.

Negative results.   outcome of a study that does not support the research hypothesis. The collected facts fail to give strength to the proposed conjecture.

Nomograph.   a procedure for testing the significance of difference between two percentages; only a rough estimate. For cases that border on significance, a chi-square technique should be used.

Nonparametric test.   a test of significance that may be applied to analyze data without any assumption as to the shape of the distributions involved; used for nominal and ordinal data and for special cases of interval and ratio data where certain assumptions cannot be met.

Non sequitur.   something that does not logically follow from premises or previous statements.

Normal curve.   an approximate graphical representation of the normal distribution.

Null hypothesis.   See *Hypothesis, null.*

Observation.   the act of gathering data on which to base research conclusions. Also any fact that is the result of the process of observing is called an "observation." Thus, observation (the act) generates the basic elements of science—facts that are called observations (results of the act).

Open-ended.   a structure that allows for contingencies beyond the frame of reference. (Example: an open-ended question that allows the respondee to create any response)

Operational definition.   a statement that describes something in terms of observable properties or behavior. This description by operations avoids lengthy word definitions for constructs that may be ambiguous in such a definition.

Opinion/fact survey.   any formal collection of particulars made to ascertain opinion or the conditions within a specified set of subjects. Sampling may be used for large populations.

Opinionnaire.   a self-reporting device intended to obtain a subject's opinions on some specified subject.

Optical illusion.   a false mental image that is a misrepresentation of the real appearance, or something that could be interpreted in more than one way without change in the appearance.

Paradigm.   a model, pattern, or example. "A paradigm is what the members of a scientific community share, *and,* conversely, a scientific community consists of men who share a paradigm."*

Parametric.   a test of significance that uses values computed on samples in order to make conclusions about characteristics of populations. Sample statistics are used as estimates of population parameters.

Periodical.   a publication issued at intervals as part of a continuing series with no predetermined date for termination; usually referred to as a "magazine" or a "journal."

Pilot study.   a miniature study conducted on a group of subjects that is not to be used as a part of the major study. It is used to try out the mechanics of procedures and/or instruments.

Population.   any defined aggregate of persons, objects, or events. A population may be described by a statement, such as "all students enrolled in Education 393 for the fall semester, 19____," or—if it is practical—the elements of the population may be listed.

Prediction.   in general, a forecast. Statistically, prediction is made by use of regression equations that utilize knowledge about relationships and values on one or more variables to forecast on a criterion (dependent) variable.

Presentism.   to invoke the present on the past. The one who studies the past must not interpret the past with a frame of reference based in the present.

Primary source.   the originator of information who or which supplies firsthand evidence with no intervention necessary between the researcher and the object or account. The source must be original or firsthand to be classed as primary.

Problem question.   the indeterminate situation being studied that is presented as a question. The answer to the problem question is the object and output of the research study.

Problem solving.   a process of inquiry that combines inductive methods and deductive methods with the use of a research hypothesis. In general, any process used to overcome a felt difficulty.

Product scale.   a measurement device consisting of graded samples of performance against which some things can be compared as a standard.

Proposal.   a document that pulls together all of the aspects of an intended

---

*Kuhn, Thomas S. *The structure of scientific revolutions* (2nd ed.), Vol. 2 (2). Chicago: University of Chicago Press, 1970 (p. 176).

study. A logical chain of reasoning translates an indeterminate situation into a step-by-step plan for creating new knowledge.

Punch card.   a device used both to instruct a computer and to feed data for computer operations.

Q methodology.   procedure used to gather and interpret data to research workers on psychological traits. It usually studies the way an individual sorts a deck of cards that have been prepared for the study. Correlations among responses from different individuals allow study between persons.

Q sort.   a method of rank ordering into categories. Clusters of individuals are identified as being alike according to how cards are sorted into piles.

Qualitative data.   information in the form of statements or narrative as opposed to quantitative data that have been expressed numerically.

Quantify.   to assign meaningful numbers to observations for the purpose of mathematical interpretation.

Quantitative data.   information that has been expressed in terms of mathematically manipulable numbers. (Assignment of numbers merely for identification is not a procedure for quantification.)

Questionnaire.   a list of questions about a specific topic organized so that it can be reacted to by subjects under study. Includes directions for the respondee so that it can be self-administered.

Random-access disk files.   a system of storing qualitative data within a computer system for quick retrieval. The files allow retrieval according to instructions given the computer.

Random assignment.   assignment procedures designed so that selection into groups for study has the qualities of equiprobability and independence. The two groups are equated for study by statistical tests of significance.

Random error.   differences ascribable to chance. There is no bias or system to chance error. When variation involves system or bias, a constant error is involved. In the first instance, differences cancel out, but in the second instance they do not.

Random sample.   a subaggregate of a population chosen so that each element of the population has equal probability of appearing in the sample and each sample element is chosen independently of all other sample element selection.

Random selection.   procedures to study material, sources, or subjects such that each element chosen for study is selected with equal probability and independence. Random selection may include stratification and proportional stratification to control for important contributing variables. Samples chosen at random allow generalization back to the parent population.

Range.   the difference between the lowest and highest score in a distribution. $(X_h - X_l)$ or sometimes $(X_h - X_l) + 1$.

Ranking.   an arrangement of a set of values in sequential order of magnitude (size) and assignment of a rank number to each one.

Rating scale.   a device used to score some particular attribute. Usually a chart for an observer to use, but may also be used by a human subject to rate herself/himself. Fine discriminations are not intended, but equal intervals between points on the scale are assumed to allow mathematical manipulation of the values.

Raw data. information that is in the same form as when it was collected.

Raw score. the first value assigned to a test paper. It may include a weighting technique and correction for guessing but no other transformation. *(NOT* a standard score).

Recommendation. a statement made at the end of a research report to indicate what additional studies should be made or how other techniques could be employed for study of the same question.

Reference material. published works designed to direct the reader or consulter to other sources of information; in general, not a source of data for research studies, but widely used by researchers who are searching the literature for information about their studies.

Register stack. a series of devices capable of storing a specified piece of data such as a word or answer to a mathematical operation.

Regression. prediction of values of one variable when given values on another and a measure of the relationship between the two variables. (See *Multiple regression.)*

Reliability. consistency of observation. The consistency with which a data collection device measures whatever it is that the device measures.

Relic. a physical object that has been preserved—either by plan or happenstance—but was not deliberately created to transmit a record for future consultation.

Replication. a reproduction of a research study using the same design on a new set of subjects. No deviation of procedures is allowed in a replication study.

Representative sample. a sample of subjects who take the same characteristics as the parent population.

Research. structured inquiry that (1) utilizes acceptable scientific methodology to solve problems and (2) creates new generally applicable knowledge.

Research report. a writing that covers all aspects of a research study— planning, investigation, and generalization. All receive equal emphasis. An extensive review of literature is usually included except for a journal manuscript.

Results. the presentation of the data for the study. Results include the outcomes of statistical tests and graphs or tables to organize the data for interpretation.

Reverse Polish notation (RPN). a form of logic and arrangement of steps in calculation used in advanced and programmable personal minicalculators.

Sample. any subaggregate of a larger population; a small part of something or a few of many to serve as an example.

Sampling error. the difference between a particular sample value and its corresponding population value. A test of significance is a study of sampling error estimated to be a part of the study.

Scaling. a succession of marks or objects laid down at specific distances, as along a line, to serve as a measurement device.

Scattergram. a visual representation of the relationship between sets of values on two variables, constructed by plotting a point for each pair of values obtained from a common subject.

School survey. a collected description of the education in a school building, district, state, or nation to allow for evaluation of the several parts of the educational process.

Scientific approach. the common strand that is a part of any systematic inquiry that uses accepted procedures to answer questions.

Scorecard. a device that extends the concept of a checklist to include weighting of contributing parts of a whole, rather than simply noticing either presence or absence of a contributing part.

Secondary source. the supplier of information which is an intermediary between the researcher and the original source. Something intervenes between the original and the person who is using the data.

Self report. any data that have been collected from a subject to record her or his inner thoughts about something.

Semantic differential. a method of interpreting the psychological meaning of a concept by use of what words mean to individuals or how they are used by individuals. The idea of semantic space in two and three dimensions is used to explain how a word has different meaning for different persons or different groups.

Significant difference. an observed difference in a study that is so great that the statistical test rejects the hypothesis that the difference appeared by sampling alone. A difference becomes statistically significant when the observed difference exceeds the criterion point for rejecting the null hypothesis. The significance level is set as the probability of making a Type I error—usually .05 or .01 for most educational studies.

Single-case experimental study. sometimes called "*N* of 1 study"; the extension of a case study to include the aspect of manipulation through an experimental structuring of a situation.

Skewness. a distortion or unbalancing effect within a set of data, caused by deviant or atypical scores.

Sociogram. a device used to assess preferences within a group to determine the social structure of that group. Usually a map of names connected by lines and arrows showing the choices of the individuals.

Sociometry. methods of collecting and analyzing data about choice and interaction of individuals within a social group. It studies attraction and repulsion within a set of human beings.

Standard deviation. a measure of the variation of a set of scores obtained by taking the square root of the variance. (See *Variance.*)

Standard error. the standard deviation of some sampling distribution. It is a measure of the variability of a statistic over repeated sampling. A standard error of difference between means is the standard deviation of the sampling distribution built from differences between means of pairs of samples.

Standard score. a score that expresses each individual raw score in terms of standard deviation units from the mean or in terms of other further transformations, such as T-score, CEEB score.

Standardized test. a commercially prepared test for which content has been selected and checked empirically. Administration and scoring procedures are the same for all test takers.

Statistical control. use of statistical analysis rather than experimental control to interpret effects of contributing variables.

Statistical design. the structure of the scheme of the operation for the variables; the outline presented as a diagram or written as a narration to show the variables and their relationship.

Statistical inference. See *Inference.*

Statistics. *(plural)* the variate values which make up a set of data. A group of 36 weights of students is represented as 36 statistics; *(singular)* what statisticians do. The treatment of data by mathematical manipulation is referred to as statistics.

Status study. gathering of information about school conditions for making administrative decisions. To a large extent, demographic data are used to make decisions other than instructional.

Stratified random sample. a modification applied to random sampling, whereby subjects for study are selected randomly from subgroups of the population. A sample of university students could be selected from the four strata of class rank—freshman, sophomore, junior, and senior.

Structure. a framework of a subject topic such that its understanding permits many other things to be related to it. The interrelatedness of many elements is explained and/or revealed by a structure.

Style manual. a set of rules concerning format for scholarly writing; covers all aspects of the mechanics of preparing a document for submission and/ or publication. (Example: *Publication Manual of the American Psychological Association)*

Summative evaluation. a terminal assessment used to judge the cumulative outcomes over a considerable term of instruction or treatment.

Survey. a field study that deals in cross section with a large number of cases at a particular time. The purpose is to determine characteristics of a definite population or to generalize from subjects of a sample to a parent population.

Syllogism. a form of deductive reasoning that utilizes a major premise, a minor premise, and a logically deduced conclusion.

Systematic error. observations which consistently overestimate or underestimate a true value.

Systematic sampling. a process of choosing elements for a sample by selecting every so many from a list of a population. To select 20 subjects for study from a total aggregate of 200, every 10th name could be selected from an alphabetical listing.

Table. an orderly display of data usually presented in rows and columns.

Table of random numbers. a set of digits which is presented with no pattern. Each digit is chosen for its place independently and with equal probability of selection with all other single digits. A sample selected by use of a table of random numbers is a "random sample."

Table of specifications. a two-way table that organizes specific objectives according to behaviors and subject-matter topics. It serves as a blueprint for a test to help build relevance and balance into the test instrument.

Taxonomy. a classification system according to general principles or relationships. Used to organize problem-solving strategies (Chapter 1) and educational objectives (Appendix A).

Test instrument. a measuring device built as a series of tasks to which a person is to respond. When scored, the test gives a quantification of the characteristic that the test is designed to measure. It serves the same purpose for educational and psychological measurement.

Test of significance. a set of statistical procedures designed to make decisions about the tenability of the null hypothesis.

Test-wiseness. knowledge that allows selection of a correct response to a test item without understanding the principle being tested. The respondent uses clues, not understanding, to select correct responses.

Theoretical frequency distribution. a mathematically developed distribution used as a model for comparison of observed data to the mathematical model. (Examples: normal, chi square, binomial, *t-* and *F-* distributions)

Theory. "a set of interrelated constructs (concepts), definitions, and propositions that presents a systematic view of phenomena by specifying relations among variables, with the purpose of explaining and predicting the phenomena." *

Unhypothesis. a nickname for the null hypothesis. Since the null hypothesis does not involve conjecture, it does not have that property usually associated with hypothesis development. (See *Hypothesis, null*)

Unobtrusive. inconspicuous. Instances of observation may be made in such a way that the person being observed does not know that she or he is being observed. When data are collected in that way, it is said that the research worker uses unobtrusive observation.

Usability. as a test characteristic, usability refers to the ease with which the test can be administered, scored, and interpreted.

Validity. the degree to which an observation describes consistently what is being observed. Test validity is concerned with how well the test measures what it is used to measure. It is the most important single characteristic associated with test instruments.

Variability. differences associated with phenomena. Variation within nature and within measurement is a concern for the researcher as well as the statistician.

Variable. a trait, characteristic, or property of something. A variable is capable of taking on many variate values for elements being studied. A property that varies over elements of a sample or population.

Variance (σ^2). the mean square; the mean of a set of squared deviation scores. Defined as: $\Sigma (X - \bar{X})^2 / N$. It is used to study differences and relations among variables.

---

* Kerlinger, F. N. *Foundations of behavioral research* (2nd ed.). New York: Holt, Rinehart, & Winston, 1973 (p. 9).

APPENDIX A

DEVELOPING A TEST

Test development falls outside the scope of research, belonging to the "need to do" strategy mentioned in the first chapter. Then why discuss it in a book on research? A researcher needs to know how a test is developed to be able to use the test properly, and the researcher may, at some point, have to assume the role of test developer and create his or her own test instrument. This appendix is not intended to teach how to develop a test, but rather it is included to indicate those aspects that need to be considered when building a test and characteristics to consider when selecting a test. A document published by the American Psychological Association proposes standards for standardized tests, gives guidance to selection of tests for research, and aids in test development (Guion, 1974). *Classroom Testing: Construction* (Hopkins & Antes, 1979) and *Educational Measurement* (Thorndike, 1971) provide specific and detailed aids for test development. Some general considerations are presented in the next few pages.

When building a test, the test maker must keep in mind that he or she is developing a measuring device. A test instrument is as much a measuring device as a ruler, yardstick, or weighing scales. The tester must decide what is to be measured, how *best* to measure it, and how to validate the measuring device to assure valid observations. A test is

> An instrument, device, or procedure which proposes a sequence of tasks to which a student is to respond. The results are then used as measures to define relative value of the trait to which the test relates (Hopkins & Antes, 1978, p. 432)

The purpose of a test is to quantify the trait being measured by assigning a numerical descriptor to each individual being considered. The test maker must decide what tasks are best for measuring the characteristic. Tests utilize many different types of tasks for subjects being measured. Essay, short-answer, and completion test items place different demands on the student than do true-false, multiple-choice, classification, and matching items. The first set requires the test taker to supply the response, while the second set asks the test taker to select a response from possible responses that are provided by the instrument. Each type of approach has advantages and disadvantages that must be considered. The major consideration, however, must be the reliability of responses and interpretations made from the scores.

Construction of a high-quality test for research purposes will include these steps:

1. Plan specifications of the test, including item type, number of items, specific items, and format.
2. Write items of appropriate difficulty to allow the device to distribute the quantification along the measuring scale (discrimination).
3. **Field test** the items and analyze the data.
4. Rewrite the items according to indications provided by the item analysis.
5. Prepare a preliminary form of the test.
6. Administer the preliminary test to a second group as a pilot to (a) check the mechanics of administration, (b) see if time limits are appropriate, and (c) provide more data to analyze about the items themselves.
7. Make changes to put the test in final form.

After the general purposes of the observation have been established and the specific areas to be measured by the test has been clearly delimited, decisions about specifications must be made. Within any specific area, there are a large number of tasks which could be used to quantify a trait. In most cases, the test maker has innumerable individual tasks available that could be used in the test instrument. Nevertheless, test time is limited. Which ones should be used, and how should they be chosen? Most test makers find that a blueprint in the form of a **table of specifications** is helpful (most consider it necessary) in building a valid test. The next section is devoted to such a technique for defining the scope and emphasis of a test. In addition to helping in test building, the table of specifications can help guide test selection. Working backward from the test itself, the researcher can reconstruct the table by identifying topics covered in the items and noticing the emphasis given each topic. In choosing a test for a particular use, it helps to relate test emphasis to needs.

Table of Specifications

One of the most important aspects of establishing validity is to define what is being measured. Since what is being measured is defined operationally through the tasks provided, selecting appropriate tasks in proper relationship to the total test is extremely important. The content of the test must be a reflection of subtopics, given their respective importance, and must elicit the desired behavior. The *table of specifications* is built in two dimensions to coordinate in one matrix the topics covered in the test and the behavior needed to react to test tasks. A table of specifications may take many different forms, but the skeleton in Table 1 shows the basic components needed to build one for a specific test.

TABLE 1 Basic Components for a Table of Specifications

Topics \ Behaviors	1.	2.	...N	% of test	No. of items
1.	?% / ?			?%	/ ?
2.	?%			?%	/ ?
3.					
N				Total ↓	Total ↓
Totals / Totals	?% / ?	?% / ?	→	100%	/ →100%

The descriptors for the behaviors (across the top of Table 1) are usually taken from taxonomies of educational objectives, which have been written by Bloom and Krathwohl. Some possible divisions are knowledge, comprehension, application, analysis, synthesis, and evaluation for the cognitive domain; receiving, responding, valuing, organization, and characterization by a value or value complex for the affective domain. Examples of both are in the accompanying outlines.

Cognitive Domain (Bloom, 1956, pp. 201–207)

    I. Knowledge
       A. Specifics
          1. Terminology
          2. Facts
       B. Ways and means of dealing with specifics
          1. Conventions
          2. Trends and sequences
          3. Classifications and categories
          4. Criteria
          5. Methodology
       C. Universals and abstractions
          1. Principles and generalizations
          2. Theories and structures
   II. Intellectual abilities and skills
       A. Comprehension
          1. Translation
          2. Interpretation
          3. Extrapolation

B. Application—use of abstractions in particular situations
C. Analysis
    1. Elements
    2. Relationships
    3. Organizational principles
D. Synthesis
    1. Production of a unique communication
    2. Production of a plan or proposed set of operations
    3. Derivation of a set of abstract relations
E. Evaluation
    1. From internal evidence
    2. From external criteria

Affective Domain (Krathwohl, Bloom, & Masia, 1964, pp. 174–193)

1.0 Receiving (attending)
    1.1 Awareness
    1.2 Willingness to receive
    1.3 Controlled or selected attention
2.0 Responding
    2.1 Acquiescence in responding
    2.2 Willingness to respond
    2.3 Satisfaction in response
3.0 Valuing
    3.1 Acceptance of a value
    3.2 Preference for a value
    3.3 Commitment (conviction)
4.0 Organization
    4.1 Conceptualization of a value
    4.2 Organization of a value system
5.0 Characterization by a value or value complex
    5.1 Generalized set
    5.2 Characterization

The descriptors used are largely determined by the characteristic being measured. The use of specific behaviors depends largely on how the test maker feels about using specific **behavioral objectives.** Regardless of bias (either for or against) about how valuable specifics are, some sort of classification should be built along the dimension of behavior—the behaviors being expected on the test.

For an achievement test, topics are based on some kind of content. The dimension of topics is listed in content to be covered, but the amount of detail to be employed must remain a decision for the test maker as she or he considers the material to be covered. Topics for psychological tests are specific to the particular behavior being considered or they may not be used in tables for psychological tests. The following discussion pertains primarily to achievement tests, but principles generalize to other kinds of tests.

In general, the number of behaviors to be elicited should not exceed three, and topics should be limited to not more than five. With too many cells, the distribution of items becomes difficult. After deciding what behaviors to include and the topics to cover, the test maker can distribute topics according to their relative importance through the cells, providing an effective method of balancing a test.

To illustrate the process, consider the home economics teacher who wants to measure achievement in a unit on textiles. He may have the following general objectives:

1. The student can name and describe the natural and synthetic fibers used in clothing construction.
2. The student understands the properties of pilling and shrinking of textiles.
3. The student can apply knowledge and understanding of textiles and their properties to clothing selection.

Using these broad objectives, the test maker should decide the relative importance of behaviors and topics. The decisions might look like this:

A. Behaviors
    1. Recall of information (knowledge)   20%
    2. Understanding (comprehension)   50%
    3. Ability to apply knowledge and understanding (application) 30%
B. Topics
    1. Natural fibers   15%
    2. Synthetic fibers   20%
    3. Pilling   10%
    4. Shrinkage   10%
    5. Choosing casual clothes   45%

The decisions on behaviors and topics, with associated percentages, are next incorporated into the table of specifications, and the cells are filled in based on the best judgment of the test maker, as indicated in Table 2.

TABLE 2 Table of Specifications for a Test on Textiles

Topic \ Behavior	Recall (knowledge)		Understanding (comprehension)		Apply (application)		%		No. of items
1. Natural fibers	6	3.6	9	5.4	0	0.0	15		9
2. Synthetic fibers	4	2.4	16	9.6	0	0.0	20		12
3. Pilling	0	0.0	5	3.0	5	3.0	10		6
4. Shrinkage	0	0.0	5	3.0	5	3.0	10		6
5. Choosing textiles for casual clothes	10	6.0	15	9.0	20	12.0	45		27
Totals % / items	20	12	50	30	30	18	100		60

Obviously the test maker cannot write fractions of test items, such as 3.6 or 2.4. Some adjustment must be made as the test is finally formed, but the table of specifications—in spite of its roughness—is necessary to direct the construction of a test instrument that provides valid data. The next step in test preparation provides an opportunity to clarify further some of the objectives and utilize specific educational objectives.

Writing Test Items

A full-blown discussion of the task of writing items for a test is beyond the scope of this book, but a few suggestions as to what is involved may help provide direction in choosing tests. Basically, item writing consists of these steps:

1. Choose the appropriate type of item.
2. Write items that relate to the objectives.
3. Plan the difficulty level of each item and the test instrument as a whole.
4. Write items that discriminate levels of differences.

Choosing a task that is relevant to measurement of the trait being considered is especially important in testing. Different types of items are available to the test maker, and he or she should choose carefully the task that best fits the topic and behavior being measured. At times, either of the two types will do equally well and then the decision is rather arbitrary. At other times, the decision is crucial.

Relating items to general objectives is handled adequately with a well-developed table of specifications. The more specific objectives must be reflected in specific items and then fit to the appropriate cell of the table.

Decisions about item difficulty require more knowledge about test theory than can be presented here, but they can be made only after considering whether the testing is for mastery or for distributing sample scores along a scale. For research purposes, measurement is needed to show differences of characteristics. Two ways are employed to do this. The first uses what is called a *power test,* where the test provides tasks of varying difficulty from very easy to very difficult. The assumption is that if the test starts with easy items and the tasks become progressively more difficult, each student will drop off at his or her level. The second approach uses only those items that fall in the middle of the scale and omits very easy items and very difficult items, including only what are referred to as *medium difficulty* items. The medium difficulty item is one for which the proportion of test takers getting the item correct is approximately halfway between that proportion associated with chance and the proportion where all get the item right.

Formula A.	Formula B.
$P_E = \dfrac{N_R}{N_T}$ (100)	$P_D = \dfrac{N_W}{N_T}$ (100)
P_E = difficulty level	P_D = difficulty level
N_R = no. getting item right	N_W = no. getting item wrong
N_T = no. who tried the item	N_T = no. who tried the item
(An easiness index)	(A difficulty index)

For an easiness index, a true-false item would have a medium difficulty level of 75 (halfway between 50 and 100), while for a difficulty index a true-false item would have a medium difficulty level of 25 (halfway between 0 and 50).*

For most tests used in research, Formula B listed in the footnote on page 470, with its direct measurement of difficulty, is better. Although it may seem plausible that varying levels of difficulty for the items would be best, research shows that the desirable characteristics to allow for discrimination are best met by providing tasks of medium-difficulty level. Very difficult items that are missed by nearly all test takers contribute little to the **variance** or scattering of the scores along the measurement scale. Very easy items that are answered correctly by nearly all test takers also contribute little to increase the variance and scattering of scores along the scale. To show differences among subjects, the scores should be distributed along the scale, not grouped together at one point.

Tests used for such purposes as diagnosing, screening, and ascertaining characteristics—such as interests—are not intended to be used for comparison purposes. Thus different approaches to item difficulty will be used. Be aware of the importance of giving attention to item difficulty when building tests for research. Look to educational measurement books for specific types of tests.

The **discrimination power** of test items is especially important for tests used in research. If the instrument is to provide valid measurement and to identify differences, the test must accurately measure the trait being measured. Highly discriminating items provide test scores that vary according to the true differences among the subjects tested and provide more valid measurement.

Preparing the Final Test Form

After the items have been written, they must be pretested, analyzed, and rewritten for the final form of the test. Careful administration is important for pretesting, since the final form of the item rests on decisions made from the pretest data. The last step is to develop the final test instrument that will be administered to the subjects. Decisions must be made about the kind of reproduction, directions, page format, item format, and art work.

Chapter 5, "Gathering, Analyzing and Using Data on Test Items," in *Educational Measurement* (Thorndike, 1971, pp. 130–159), is an excellent source of information about how to pretest and how to use the data for rewriting items. Chapter 6, "Reproducing the Test," is an excellent source for the final decisions about developing the final form. Other books on educational measurement expand on these and other tasks associated with test development to help in making the final decisions about developing the final form.

---

*The two formulas in the footnote on p. 470 are currently used to indicate how easy or difficult an item is. Formula A gives a percentage of those responding who answered correctly, thus an "easiness index." Formula B gives a percentage of those responding who answered incorrectly, thus a "difficulty index."

References

Bloom, B. S. (Ed.). *Taxonomy of educational objectives: The cognitive domain.* New York: David McKay, 1956.

Guion, R. M. *Standards for educational and psychological tests.* Washington, D.C.: American Psychological Association, 1974.

Hopkins, C. D., & Antes, R. L. *Classroom measurement and evaluation.* Itasca, Ill.: F. E. Peacock, 1978.

Hopkins, C. D., & Antes, R. L. *Classroom testing: Construction.* Itasca, Ill.: F. E. Peacock, 1979.

Krathwohl, D. R., Bloom, B. S., & Masia, B. B. *Taxonomy of educational objectives: The affective domain.* New York: David McKay, 1964.

Thorndike, R. L. (Ed.). *Educational measurement.* Washington, D.C.: American Council on Education, 1971.

APPENDIX B

PROPOSAL AND REPORT CHECKLISTS

Research Proposal Checklist

Uses:

1. To direct student proposal preparation.
2. To structure evaluation of students' proposals. (A point system can be added if analytical scoring is desired.)

This list can be supplemented by adding more topics or subtopics to be considered by the person preparing or evaluating the proposal. Care must be taken to see that the objectives are clearly defined and that evaluation is performed with these objectives in mind.

Proposal Checklist

Title

1. Length is less than 16 words.
2. Variables to be studied are included.
3. Relationship of variables to be studied is clearly established.
4. Population to be studied is named.

Cover Sheet

1. Correct format
2. Title
3. Author
4. Other information as required by instructor, school, agency

Background of the Problem

1. Correct format (APA or other)
   a. Subheadings at the second level
   b. Citations for references
2. Personal interest in the problem
3. Brief historical development
4. Significance
   a. Importance to educators
   b. Contribution to education
5. Relation of study to present theory
6. Important related studies cited
7. Establishment of firm basis for problem presentation

Presentation of the Problem

1. Correct format
   a. Subheadings at second level
   b. Correct form for lists of terms, assumptions, limitations
2. Direct question to be studied
3. Scope of the study is clearly delimited
4. Hypothesis or hypotheses to be tested
5. Definition of terms
6. List of assumptions
7. List of limitations
8. Firm basis for understanding the methodology

Methodology

1. Correct format
2. Sample
   a. Selection
   b. Characteristics
   c. Adequate size
   d. Safeguards subject with adherence to ethical standards
3. Detailed descriptions of:
   a. Instruments used to collect data
   b. Techniques of data collection
   c. Treatment (if experimental)
   d. Criticism (if historical)
4. Statistical procedures
   a. Procedures for recording data
   b. Kind of data

    c. Organization into tables
      (1) For computation
      (2) For presentation to readers
    d. Analysis
      (1) Appropriate for kind of data
      (2) Tests of significance (if used)
5. Will methodology withstand internal and external validity checks?
6. Presentation of results outlined

Bibliography

1. Correct format for entries
    a. Includes all information
    b. Correct order and punctuation
    c. Italics (underlined) added
2. Includes all referenced material
3. Includes other pertinent material
4. Reference notes (if needed)

Appendix

1. Letters of inquiry
2. Letters to parents
3. Permission blanks
4. Copies of tests developed for the study
5. Copies of questionnaires developed for the study
6. Other supplementary material

General Considerations

1. Technical style
    a. Spacing
    b. Margins
    c. Headings
    d. Citations
    e. Lists
2. Completeness
3. Conciseness
4. Grammatically correct
5. Good expression
6. Does it hang together?
    a. Logical sequence
    b. Chain of reasoning
7. Can it be carried to completion?
8. Is a pilot study needed?

Research Report Checklist

Uses:

1. To direct student preparation of research reports
2. To direct evaluation of research reports

With modification this checklist can also be used to evaluate research articles in professional journals, thus preparing the students to be critical readers of reported research.

Report Checklist

Title

1. Less than 16 words in length
2. Includes variables studied
3. Relationship of variables clearly defined
4. Names the population studied
5. Avoids redundancies, e.g., "An Experiment to," "A Study of"

Front Matter

1. Title page
2. Approval sheet (if needed)
3. Table of Contents
4. List of Tables
5. List of Figures
6. Correct technical style

Organization of Chapters

1. Chapter 1
   a. Introductory in nature
   b. Includes "Background of the Problem" and "Presentation of the Problem" information from the proposal
2. Chapter 2
   a. Reviews related literature and reports of previous studies
   b. Completes the basis for presentation of the methodology
3. Chapter 3
   a. Explains procedures
   b. Explains techniques
   c. Includes information from proposal section "Methodology"
4. Chapter 4
   a. Organizes the presentation of results
   b. Avoids drawing conclusions

5. Chapter 5
   a. Reports findings
   b. Conclusions drawn
6. Chapter 6
   a. Summarizes study
   b. Presents implications
   c. Lists recommendations
   d. May include summary, implications and recommendations in Chapter 5

End Matter

1. Reference notes (if needed)
   a. List material not widely or easily available
   b. Give as much information about source as possible
   c. Use only if cited in the research report
2. Bibliography
   a. Check format carefully
   b. Include all cited material
   c. Include other pertinent material
3. Appendix
   a. Copies of tests
   b. Copies of questionnaires
   c. Other material

General Considerations

1. Technical style
   a. Spacing
   b. Margins
   c. Headings
   d. Citations
   e. Lists
   f. Tables
   g. Figures
   h. Other special points
2. Does it hang together?
   a. Logical sequence
   b. Articulation of parts
   c. Is the derived answer related to presently accepted theory?
   d. Is the derived answer to the question clear?
3. Good expression
4. Complete

Special Considerations

1. The Problem
   a. Background thoroughly developed
   b. Theoretical framework established
   c. Question presented
   d. Problem clearly delimited in scope
   e. Significance established
   f. Consideration of risk to subjects in regard to the importance of needed knowledge
2. Hypothesis
   a. A logical answer to the question asked
   b. Logically derived from present knowledge
   c. Expresses a relationship between two variables
   d. Testable
3. Definition of terms
   a. All variables defined
   b. Important terms defined
   c. Dependent variable defined operationally
   d. Assigned variable(s) defined operationally
4. Assumptions
   a. Listed in separate section
   b. Tied to theoretical framework
5. Limitations
   a. Do limitations predicted in the proposal remain?
   b. Any limitations not anticipated?
   c. Effect on conclusions
   d. Major or minor restriction on generalization
6. Methodology
   a. Explained specifically so that someone else could conduct the same study from this information
   b. Sampling techniques
      (1) As close as possible to ideal conditions
      (2) Sample characteristics given
      (3) Adequate size
      (4) Statement about meeting ethical standards
   c. Detailed description of:
      (1) Instruments used to collect the data
      (2) Techniques of data collection
      (3) Treatment (if experimental)
      (4) Criticism (if historical)
   d. Statistical procedures
      (1) Method to record data
      (2) Tables of data
      (3) Kind of data
      (4) Analysis of data
      (5) Tests of significance (if used)

        (6) External and internal validity of statistical design (If experimental)
7. Results
    a. Organization of facts
        (1) Tabular
        (2) Results of statistical tests
    b. Articulation between hypothesis and conclusions
    c. Report of disconfirming results as well as results that support
8. Conclusions
    a. Based on facts collected in the study
    b. Research hypothesis supported?
    c. Bridges from results to hypothesis to original question
    d. Use extrapolation beyond the data only if:
        (1) it is identified as speculation.
        (2) it is related closely to the data.
        (3) it is presented concisely as a supplement to your conclusions.
9. Implications
    a. Clearly implied from findings
    b. Consistent with other theory
10. Recommendations
    a. Extension of this study
    b. Broadened to encompass related questions

Overview

The report should be clear in regard to its contribution and how the answer related to the research question. Implications and recommendations are also expected by the readers.

The Abstract

1. Brief summary of the content of the report
2. Self-contained
3. Suitable for publication by abstracting services
4. Write it after completing the full report
5. Contents
    a. Problem question and hypothesis
    b. Brief report of methodology
        (1) Subject population
        (2) Design
        (3) Data collection procedures (e.g. test, self-report)
        (4) Statistical procedures
        (5) Results
    c. Findings as conclusions
    d. Implications
6. Number of words
    a. APA: 100-175 words
    b. Other journals or services: up to 250 words

APPENDIX C

STATISTICS

The text of *Understanding Educational Research: An Inquiry Approach* is directed primarily to understanding the processes of research. Closely associated with research is a working knowledge of statistics, the tools of research. Certain basic principles of statistics are presented in this appendix for those readers who need a review of or introduction to some commonly used statistics. While discussion in earlier sections dealt with theoretical aspects of statistics topics and ways to use particular tools in research, the following pages deal with computation and examples applying statistical concepts to treatment of data collected for a research study.

The topics in this appendix have been selected from a wide range (population) of possible coverage. They are considered the topics most likely to be used by students beginning a study of research. No attempt has been made to anticipate what statistics would be encountered in journal articles or in other reports of research. Statistics textbooks and self-study materials extend the presentation made in this appendix (Bruning & Kintz, 1977; Chase, 1976; Hopkins, 1974). As a worker develops the art of researching, knowledge of statistics or a statistician's help will be required to complete the research process. Many researchers function very well with only limited knowledge of statistics by using a statistician to guide data treatment, but each research worker must be able to communicate about the study's overall design and the nature of the data to be collected. In this day of specialization, it is not uncommon to find research being conducted by teams which distribute assignments to special areas like writing, research, statistics, and so on.

The data used in the following examples are fictitious and relatively few values are included to facilitate the computation and conceptualization. The principles remain the same with data collected in greater quantity for research studies.

Frequency Distribution

The most convenient way to report data or to organize them for computation is to use a frequency distribution. The distribution may be arranged either as a table or as a graph, depending on what is to be presented or how computation is to be carried out.

Tables

Tables within a report of a research study condense data into a readable form and most likely present information as grouped data. The accompanying table shows how 34 scores appear after a wide interval, 33 to 65, was collapsed into 11 intervals of 3 units each. Scores are reported by listing the frequency (*f*) of occurrence beside the interval.

Interval	*f*
63–65	1
60–62	1
57–59	2
54–56	4
51–53	9
48–50	6
45–47	5
42–44	2
39–41	1
36–38	2
33–35	1
	$N = 34$

Tables 10–7 and 10–8 in the text (page 323) also show how frequencies can be shown in tabular form. Other variations can be used to accommodate special needs.

Tables for computation are likely to present the data as originally collected with a frequency for each value that appears in the raw score distribution as shown in Table 1.

Early researchers computed from grouped distributions to reduce calculation time and work load, because the computation was done largely by hand. Today, pocket or desk calculators and computer utilization reduce the computation load, and the use of ungrouped scores provides more precision in the statistics. Other columns for calculations may be entered in the table as needed (see tables and figures throughout Appendix C).

Graphs

Graphical representation of a frequency distribution can give a quick visual picture of the characteristics of a distribution. Although many variations are

TABLE 1 Two Tabular Frequency Distributions

Score value	f	Score value	f
65	1	65	1
64	0	61	1
63	0	59	1
62	0	58	1
61	1	56	1
60	0	55	2
59	1	54	1
58	1	53	3
57	0	52	2
56	1	51	4
55	2	50	1
54	1	49	3
53	3	48	2
52	2	47	2
51	4	46	1
50	1	45	2
49	3	44	1
48	2	43	1
47	2	41	1
46	1	38	1
45	2	37	1
44	1	33	1
43	1		34
42	0		
41	1		
40	0		
39	0		
38	1		
37	1		
36	0		
35	0		
34	0		
33	1		
	34		

utilized by research workers, two graphs—the histogram and the frequency polygon—are the most common.

Histogram. The histogram is a two-dimensional diagram that associates the frequency of occurrence vertically with score value horizontally. The table and associated histogram for 34 scores appear in Figure 1.

Notice that apparent interval limits have been extended to include all points on the baseline. The interval 47.5–50.5 is divided into blocks for each frequency, to represent the concept of the area reflecting frequency. If each

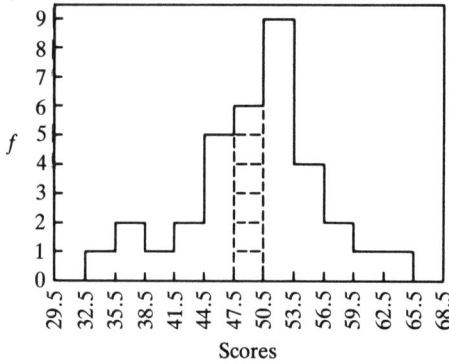

Interval limits		f
Apparent	Exact	
63–65	62.5–65.5	1
60–62	59.5–62.5	1
57–59	56.5–59.5	2
54–56	53.5–56.5	4
51–53	50.5–53.5	9
48–50	47.5–50.5	6
45–47	44.5–47.5	5
42–44	41.5–44.5	2
39–41	38.5–41.5	1
36–38	35.5–38.5	2
33–35	32.5–35.5	1
		$N = 34$

FIGURE 1   Histogram and Associated Table

interval were divided into blocks, then the total number of blocks would equal 34, the N for this set of data.

Frequency Polygon. The frequency polygon is a two-dimensional diagram that associates the frequency of occurrence (on the vertical axis) with midpoint interval values (on the horizontal axis). The grouped table and associated frequency polygon for the 34 scores are shown in Figure 2.

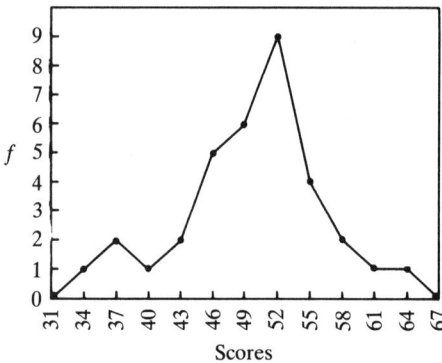

Interval	Midpoint	f
63–65	64	1
60–62	61	1
57–59	58	2
54–56	55	4
51–53	52	9
48–50	49	6
45–47	46	5
42–44	43	2
39–41	40	1
36–38	37	2
33–35	34	1
		$N = 34$

FIGURE 2   Frequency Polygon and Associated Table

Notice that an interval midpoint with a frequency of zero has been added at each end to bring the polygon back to the baseline. The total area under the frequency polygon also represents the frequency of 34, but it is more difficult to identify in this graph than it is in the histogram.

Central Tendency

When describing a set of data, the most representative score could be computed or selected. The measures of this central tendency are used to report a score value that seems to represent the values best collectively. With ordinal data, the middle score value (the *median*) is used. With interval and ratio data, the *mean* (arithmetical average) is used.

The most-used measure of central tendency is the mean. It is computed in this manner:

Formula (mean):

$$\overline{X} = \frac{\Sigma X}{N}$$

Where

$\overline{X}$ = the mean
Σ = to add; summation
X = a value on the X variable
ΣX = sum of X values ($X_1 + X_2 + \ldots + X_N$)
N = the number of scores

Problem: A laboratory animal ran a maze with the following recorded times in seconds: 19, 20, 16, 9, 10 (seconds). What was the average (mean) time for the 5 trials?

Computation:
Step 1: Table the data (any order).
Step 2: Add to get the sum.
Step 3: Compute the mean by dividing the total number of seconds by the number of trials.

(1)* Trial	Seconds
1	19
2	20
3	16
4	9
5	10
(2)	74

(3) $\overline{X} = \dfrac{\Sigma X}{N} = 74 \div 5 = 14.80$

$\overline{X} = 14.80$

---

*Throughout this appendix, the steps will be keyed to the computation in this way: (1) represents *Step 1*, (2) is *Step 2*, (3) is *Step 3*, and so on.

The arithmetical average, the mean, is like a balance point in the distribution, since each value contributes to the mean according to its distance from the point of balance. If the mean value is subtracted from each trial value and the differences are summed, the values cancel out to 0: $[(19 - 14.80) + (20 - 14.80) + (16 - 14.80) + (9 - 14.80) + (10 - 14.80) = 4.2 + 5.2 + 1.2 + (-5.8) + (-4.8) = 0]$, that is, $[\Sigma(X - \overline{X}) = 0]$.

Variability

Although a single value can give a location on the number line as a representative value for a set of data, it gives no indication of how the scores are dispersed or scattered one from another. The **range** (high score minus low score) of the scores gives some indication of dispersion, but since it takes into account the position of only two extreme values, it is rarely used in statistical treatment of data.

For statistical purposes, the variance and the standard deviation (square root of the variance) are used. Each of these measures of variability is computed from data for all subjects. As the formula reveals, it is based on differences from the mean, making it convenient in further statistical work.

Formulas (variance):

$$\sigma^2 = \frac{\Sigma x^2}{N} \quad \text{or} \quad s^2 = \frac{\Sigma x^2}{N - 1}$$

Where
    σ^2 = variance for a total population of values
    s^2 = variance for a sample used to estimate a population variance
    Σ = to add; summation
    x = $X - \overline{X}$; the deviation of a value from the mean
    N = number of values

Computational formulas:

$$\sigma^2 = \frac{\Sigma X^2 - \frac{(\Sigma X)^2}{N}}{N} \qquad s^2 = \frac{\Sigma X^2 - \frac{(\Sigma X)^2}{N}}{N - 1}$$

Where
    ΣX^2 = sum of squared values
    $(\Sigma X)^2$ = sum of values squared

Problem: Find the variance for the 5 trials of the laboratory animals.

Computation:

Step 1: Table the data.
Step 2: Add the values.
Step 3: Square each value and add the squared values.
(*Note:* If a calculator has memory capacity, *Steps 2* and *3* can be transacted at the same time.)

Step 4: Square the sum from *Step 2* and divide by the number of values (*N*).

Step 5: Subtract the value in *Step 4* from the value in *Step 3*.

Step 6a: Divide the value from *Step 5* by *N*. (σ^2)

Step 6b: Divide the value from *Step 5* by ($N - 1$). (s^2)

(1) Trial	X	X^2
X_1	19	361
X_2	20	400
X_3	16	256
X_4	9	81
X_5	10	100
	$\Sigma X = 74$	$1198 = \Sigma X^2$
	(2)	(3)

(4) $74^2 \div 5 = 5476 \div 5 = 1095.20$
(5) $1198 - 1095.20 = 102.8$
(6a) $102.8 \div 5 = 20.56 = \sigma^2$
(6b) $102.8 \div 4 = 25.70 = s^2$

(Since it is not known how the variance will be used, both solutions are given in steps 6a and 6b. In practice, it would be clear to the researcher which solution procedure should be used.)

$$\sigma^2 = \frac{1198 - \dfrac{74^2}{5}}{5} \qquad\qquad s^2 = \frac{1198 - \dfrac{74^2}{5}}{4}$$

$$= \frac{1198 - 1095.20}{5} \quad \text{or} \quad = \frac{1198 - 1095.20}{4}$$

$$= \frac{102.80}{5} \qquad\qquad = \frac{102.8}{4}$$

$$\sigma^2 = 20.56 \qquad\qquad s^2 = 25.70$$

Formulas (standard deviation):

$$\sigma = \sqrt{\frac{\Sigma x^2}{N}} \quad \text{or} \quad s = \sqrt{\frac{\Sigma x^2}{N - 1}}$$

Refer now to the formulas for σ^2 and s^2. The standard deviation is the square root of those formulas.

Computational formulas:

$$\sigma = \sqrt{\frac{\Sigma X^2 - \dfrac{(\Sigma X)^2}{N}}{N}} \quad \text{or} \quad s = \sqrt{\frac{\Sigma X^2 - \dfrac{(\Sigma X)^2}{N}}{N - 1}}$$

These formulas are the same as the computational formulas for the variance except the square root is extracted. Refer to computational formulas for σ^2 and s^2.

Problem: Calculate the standard deviation for the 5 trials of the laboratory animals.

Computation:
  Steps 1 through *6* are exactly the same as those for the variance.
  Step 7: Take the square root of the value from *6a* or *6b*.

$$(7)\ \sigma = \sqrt{20.56} = 4.53 \qquad s = \sqrt{25.70} = 5.07\ (7)$$

The variance is a mean square (two-dimensional) statistic that reflects the variability of a set of scores by using differences between all values in a distribution from the mean value $(\overline{X})$. The term "mean square" is used extensively in inferential statistics. The standard deviation is a measure of variability in one dimension and uses the same basic principle of differences associated with computation of the variance. The next section uses a measure of central tendency (the mean) with a measure of variability (the standard deviation) to develop a standard unit that is widely used in both descriptive and inferential statistics.

Standard Scores

Scores in their original form are called "raw scores." The deviation, x or $(X - \overline{X})$, is called a "deviation score." A set of deviation scores has a mean of zero and the original distribution's standard deviation. If a deviation score is divided by the distribution's standard deviation, then a standard score is obtained. When a raw score distribution has been transformed into a set of standard scores, the set of standard scores has a mean of zero and a standard deviation of one. The use of this new score permeates descriptive and inferential statistics.

The standard score, z, is computed in the following sections.

Formula (z):

$$z = \frac{x}{s} = \frac{X - \overline{X}}{s}$$

Where
  $z = $ standard score
  $x = X - \overline{X}$
  $s = $ standard deviation

Problem: Express the 5 trial values in standard score form.

Computation:

  Step 1: Table the data.
  Step 2: Subtract the mean value from each score.

Step 3: Divide the deviation scores from Step 2 by the standard deviation.

Step 4: Record the z-score in the last column of the table.

(1) Trial	X	(2) $X - \overline{X}$ (x)	(3) $\dfrac{X - \overline{X}}{s}$	(4) z
X_1	19	4.2	4.2/5.07	.828
X_2	20	5.2	5.2/5.07	1.026
X_3	16	1.2	1.2/5.07	.237
X_4	9	-5.8	-5.8/5.07	-1.144
X_5	10	-4.8	-4.8/5.07	-.947

The sums, means, and standard deviations are as follows:

Sum	74	0.0	—	0.000
$\overline{X}$	14.8	0.0	—	0.000
s	5.07	5.07	—	1.000

The z-scores have algebraic properties which allow algebraic manipulation, and the mean of 0 and standard deviation of 1.00 are values for the unit normal distribution which is widely used in statistics. Other transformations are in the form of: standard score $= (s)z + \overline{X}$, where any value can be substituted for s, and it becomes the standard deviation of a new distribution. Also, any value can be substituted for $\overline{X}$ and it becomes the new mean. For example, the values 10 and 50 can be substituted for s and $\overline{X}$.

Extending the preceding problem, the second set of standard scores is obtained like this:

Step 1: Substitute a new standard deviation value for the formula.
Step 2: Substitute a new mean value for the formula.
Step 3: Compute Z.

$$Z = \underset{(1)}{10(z)} + \underset{(2)}{50}$$

Trial	z	(3) Compute	Z
1	.828	10(.828) + 50	≈ 58
2	1.026	10(1.026) + 50	≈ 60
3	.237	10(.237) + 50	≈ 52
4	-1.144	10(-1.144) + 50	≈ 39
5	-.947	10(-.947) + 50	≈ 41

The means and standard deviations are as follows:

$\overline{X}$	0.000	—	50
s	1.000	—	≈ 10

Other popular transformations are:

$$\text{standard score} = 100(z) + 500$$
$$\text{standard score} = 20(z) + 100$$
$$\text{standard score} = 15(z) + 100$$

These give convenient mean and standard deviation values for interpretation of test scores.

Correlation

Questions of research which involve the relationship of two variables may require a correlational statistical procedure. Correlation is a study of the associated variability of measures on two variables. This appendix discusses only a coefficient derived from two rankings and a coefficient to use with two sets of interval or ratio data. Many other correlation procedures are available for other combinations of types of data. (See p. 319.)

Spearman Rho

The Spearman *rho* (ρ) procedure is to be used when two sets of paired ranks are investigated for relationship. There must be two sets of ranks on a common set of elements.

Formula (rho):

$$\text{rho } (\rho) = 1 - \frac{6\Sigma D^2}{N(N^2 - 1)}$$

Where

$$\rho = \text{correlation coefficient}$$
$$D = \text{difference in ranks}$$
$$N = \text{number of paired ranks}$$
$$\Sigma = \text{summation}$$
$$6 = \text{a constant}$$

Problem: Determine the degree and direction of the relationship of ranks for a set of student papers assigned separately by Professor Mean and Professor Median.

Computation:
   Step 1: Enter the two sets of ranks in a table.
   Step 2: Compute the difference (D) between the paired ranks for each paper.
   Step 3: Square all D values and sum.
   Step 4: Multiply the value from *Step 3* by the constant 6.
   Step 5: Square N, subtract 1, then multiply by N.
   Step 6: Divide the value from *Step 4* by the value from *Step 5*.

Step 7: Subtract the value from *Step 6* from 1. Record the sign of this number to indicate direction of the relationship.

		(2) Ranks by Professor		D	D²
(1)	Student	Mean	Median		
	Ann	1	2	−1	1
	Ben	2	3	−1	1
	Carl	3	1	2	4
	Dan	4	6	−2	4
	Eileen	5	5	0	0
	Fred	6	8	−2	4
	Gayla	7	4	3	9
	Howard	8	7	1	1
					24 (3)

$$\text{(4)} \quad \rho = 1 - \frac{(6)(24)}{(8)(63)}$$
(5)

$$\text{(6)} \quad = 1 - \frac{144}{504}$$

$$\text{(7)} \quad = 1 - .29$$

$$\rho = +.71$$

This coefficient has two important parts: + and .71. The .71 is a measure of the concomitant variation (relationship) of the two sets of ranks. This can be considered a measure of the agreement between the two readings. The sign gives the direction of this variation. Notice that if each had exactly the same rank for each student, ρ would equal $+1.00$, the highest possible value for the coefficient. If the most extreme differences (1 and 8, 2 and 7, 3 and 6, 4 and 5, 5 and 4, 6 and 3, 7 and 2, and 8 and 1) had occurred, ρ would equal -1.00, the lowest possible value for the coefficient.

Pearson *r*

A correlation procedure that uses interval or ratio data reflects the more precise measure of relationship because of the nature of the data. There must be two sets of interval or ratio data on a common set of elements.

Formula (*r*):

$$r = \frac{\Sigma z_x z_y}{N - 1}$$

Where

r = correlation coefficient

Σ = summation

N = number of pairs
z_x = standard score on X
z_y = standard score on Y

Computational formula:

$$r = \frac{N\Sigma XY - (\Sigma X)(\Sigma Y)}{\sqrt{[N(\Sigma X^2) - (\Sigma X)^2][N(\Sigma Y^2) - (\Sigma Y)^2]}}$$

Where

r	=	correlation coefficient
(ΣX)	=	summation of X variable scores
(ΣY)	=	summation of Y variable scores
ΣX^2	=	sum of squared X scores
ΣY^2	=	sum of squared Y scores
ΣXY	=	sum of products of paired X and Y scores
N	=	number of pairs; number of elements

Problem: Eight students had paired raw scores on 2 tests. Determine the relationship between the 2 sets of scores.

Computation:

Step 1: Enter the data in a table, keeping the pairs for each student.
*Step 2: Sum the X column.
*Step 3: Sum the Y column.
Step 4: Multiply the 2 numbers in each pair and record in column XY.
*Step 5: Sum the XY column.
Step 6: Multiply the value from *Step 5* by N.
Step 7: Square each X value.
*Step 8: Sum the squared X's.
Step 9: Multiply the value from *Step 8* by N.
Step 10: Square each Y value.
*Step 11: Sum the squared Y's.
Step 12: Multiply the value from *Step 11* by N.
Step 13: Multiply the sum of the X's by the sum of the Y's.
Step 14. Subtract the value from *Step 13* from the value from *Step 6*.
*Step 15: Square the sum of X scores from *Step 2*.
*Step 16: Square the sum of Y scores from *Step 3*.
Step 17: Subtract the value in *Step 15* from the value in *Step 9*.
Step 18: Subtract the value in *Step 16* from the value in *Step 12*.
Step 19: Multiply the value from *Step 18* by the value from *Step 17*.
Step 20: Extract the square root of the value from *Step 19*.
Step 21: Divide the value from *Step 14* by the value from *Step 20*.

---

*These values appear in the computational formula.

| | | Raw scores | | (4) | (7) | (10) |
(1)	Student	X	Y	XY	X^2	Y^2
	Ian	14	7	98	196	49
	John	15	5	75	225	25
	Kim	11	6	66	121	36
	Les	10	7	70	100	49
	Mae	10	4	40	100	16
	Nan	9	7	63	81	49
	Opal	5	2	10	25	4
	Pete	6	2	12	36	4
	Sums	80	40	434	884	232
		(2)	(3)	(5)	(8)	(11)

(6) (8)(434) = 3472
(9) (8)(884) = 7072
(12) (8)(232) = 1856
(13) (80)(40) = 3200
(14) 3472 − 3200 = 272
(15) (80)(80) = 6400

(16) (40)(40) = 1600
(17) 7072 − 6400 = 672
(18) 1856 − 1600 = 256
(19) (672)(256) = 172,032
(20) $\sqrt{172,032}$ = 414.77
(21) 272 ÷ 414.77 =
        +.656 = ≈ +.66

$$r = \frac{(8)(434) - (80)(40)}{\sqrt{[(8)(884) - (80)^2][(8)(232) - (40)^2]}}$$

$$= \frac{3472 - 3200}{\sqrt{(7072 - 6400)(1856 - 1600)}}$$

$$= \frac{272}{\sqrt{(672)(256)}} = \frac{272}{\sqrt{172,032}} = \frac{272}{414.77}$$

$$r = \quad +.656 = ≈ +.66$$

Goodness of Fit

Situations arise in research when a comparison of observed frequencies of occurrence must be made with frequencies of expectation. Observed frequencies are facts collected for a study by observation or experiment. Theoretical frequencies are generated through probability, hypothesis, theoretical speculation, or past information. Questions arise about the degree that observation fits with expectation—hence the term "goodness of fit."

Formula (Chi square):

$$\chi^2 = \sum \left(\frac{(O - E)^2}{E} \right)$$

Where
χ^2 = chi square; squared measure of differences
Σ = summation
O = observed frequencies
E = expected frequencies

Problem: Test to see if an American quarter is constructed in such a way that it would be considered unbiased—unbiased, meaning that if the coin is flipped, there is no reason to believe that it is other than a regularly minted coin. Make the decision with alpha equal to or less than .05.

Computation

Step 1: Determine probabilities for a regularly minted coin for heads and tails.

Step 2: Collect a large quantity of data for the coin by flipping it and recording the results.

Step 3: Enter the data in a table.

Step 4: Subtract the expected frequency for each event from the observed frequency.

Step 5: Square the differences in *Step 4*.

Step 6: Divide each value from *Step 5* by the expected frequency for that event.

Step 7: Sum the values from *Step 6*. (This gives a chi square value.)

Step 8: Determine the degrees of freedom for the test of significance.

Step 9: Look up the .05 level for appropriate degrees of freedom in table "Critical values of chi square."

Step 10: Compare the observed chi-square value with the table value at .05 level.

Step 11: Reject null hypothesis of no difference if the observed value exceeds the table value. Do not reject the null hypothesis if the observed value does not exceed the table value.

(1) Probability for heads equals .50.
    Probability for tails equals .50.
(2) Flip the quarter 200 times and record the number of heads and tails.

		(3) Outcomes	O	E	(4) $O - E$	(5) $(O - E)^2$	(6) $\dfrac{(O - E)^2}{E}$	
		Heads	80	100	-20	400	4.00	
		Tails	120	100	20	400	4.00	
						$\chi^2 =$	8.00	(7)

Table value for chi square $(\chi^2) = 3.84$ (9)

(8) Two possible events minus one equals 1 *df*.
(10) Table   3.84
     Observed   8.00
(11) Reject the null hypothesis of no difference (unbiased). The coin does not have the properties of a normal coin. It may be bent or weighted to cause a systematic departure from expectation.

Problem: Test to see if absences over a 4-week period are independent of the day of the week.

For one 4-week period, the following absences were recorded from a factory:

Day of week	Number of absences
Monday	212
Tuesday	187
Wednesday	172
Thursday	183
Friday	231

Computation:

	Days of the week				Total
Mon.	Tues.	Wed.	Thurs.	Fri.	absences = 985
212	187	172	183	231	Absent from work
197	197	197	197	197	Expected absences

$$\chi^2 = \frac{(212-197)^2}{197} + \frac{(187-197)^2}{197} + \frac{(172-197)^2}{197} + \frac{(183-197)^2}{197} + \frac{(231-197)^2}{197}$$

$$= \frac{15^2}{197} + \frac{-10^2}{197} + \frac{-25^2}{197} + \frac{-14^2}{197} + \frac{34^2}{197}$$

$$= 1.14 + .51 + 3.17 + 1.00 + 5.87$$

$$\chi^2 = 11.69$$

$df = 4$

Table chi square (.05 and 4 df) = 9.48

Observed chi square = 11.69

Reject the null hypothesis of no difference. These data indicate that absences are not independent of the day of the week.

Median Test

The median test can be applied to test to see if two groups come from a population having the same median value. The chi-square distribution is used to test the null hypothesis that the groups are of the same population. As with all tests of significance, if large differences are observed, the null hypothesis is not tenable and the alternate hypothesis of difference is supported.

Problem: Twenty children have been assigned at random to 2 groups. A coin was flipped and Group A was placed in an environment with certain characteristics, and Group B was placed in an environment with exactly the same conditions except for one change. After a specified length of time, the activity level of each child in each group was measured. Test to see if the 2 groups are from the same population in regard to the level of activity.

Computation:

Step 1: Enter the data from the 2 groups in a table.

Step 2: Combine the data from the 2 groups and establish the median.

Step 3: Build another table dividing each group into scores above and below the median.

Step 4: Count the number of scores above and below the median for each group.

Step 5: Build a table with the observed frequencies.

Step 6: Enter the expected values in the table.

Step 7: Calculate chi square.

Note: See p. 494 for Steps 8 through 11.

Step 8: Determine the degrees of freedom.

Step 9: Look up the .05 level for the appropriate df in table.

Step 10: Compare observed and expected values for chi square.

Step 11: Reject or not reject.

(1)

Group A		Group B	
27	19	20	23
25	23	28	28
29	23	30	33
22	20	25	29
32	30	32	30

(2) 19 20 20 22 23 23 23 25 25 27
28 28 29 29 30 30 30 32 32 33
Median = 27.5

(3)

Group A		Group B
32		33
30		32
29	Above	30
	the	30
	median	30
		28
		28
	——— Median———	
27		25
25		23
23	Below	20
23	the	
22	median	
20		
19		

(4) Group A: 3 above, 7 below; Group B: 7 above, 3 below

	Group A		Group B
(5)	3	Above the median	7
(6)	5	Expected	5
		Median	
(5)	7	Below the median	3
(6)	5	Expected	5

(7) $\chi^2 = \dfrac{(3 - 5)^2}{5} + \dfrac{(7 - 5)^2}{5} + \dfrac{(7 - 5)^2}{5} + \dfrac{(3 - 5)^2}{5}$

$ = \quad .8 \quad + \quad .8 \quad + \quad .8 \quad + \quad .8$

$\chi^2 = \quad 3.20$

(8) $df = (r - 1)(c - 1) = (1)(1) = 1$
(9) 3.84
(10) Observed chi square = 3.20
Table (.05) $(df = 1) = 3.84$
(11) Do not reject the hypothesis that both groups are still from the same population (no difference).

Sign Test

The sign test is used to study increases or decreases for subjects under study. If there is no effect of treatment, then decreases and increases will be determined randomly. Differences due to treatment are considered significant if differences are beyond a critical point in the normal distribution.

Problem: Each of 14 subjects was matched with another subject using scores on a pretest. Two different treatments were used for instruction. Test to see if the treatment was effective.

Computation:
Step 1: Enter the data in a table keeping each matched pair in a row.
Step 2: Compare each subject of one group with the matched subject in the other group. Assign +, −, or 0.
Step 3: Count the number of signs, either plus or minus. This becomes N.
Step 4: Count the number of pluses. This becomes X.
Step 5: Calculate z using formula below.
Step 6: Compare z to values for a normal curve. Less than 1.96 or greater than +1.96 rejects null hypothesis of no difference at .05 level. Less than −2.58 or greater than +2.58 rejects the test at the .01 level. For directional tests, the difference must exceed +1.64 for the .05 level and +2.33 for the .01 level.

			Sign	
(1)	Group M	Group N	(M − N)	
	43	41	+	(2)
	47	40	+	
	19	24	−	
	33	33	0	
	38	42	−	
	46	42	+	
	32	30	+	
	22	23	−	
	47	45	+	
	29	27	+	
	39	39	0	
	49	46	+	
	44	46	−	
	40	38	+	

(3) $8 + 4 = 12 = N$

(4) $8 = X$

(5) $z = \dfrac{(X + .5) - .5N}{.5\sqrt{N}}$ (If the number of pluses is less than $.5N$)

$z = \dfrac{(X - .5) - .5N}{.5\sqrt{N}}$ (If the number of pluses is greater than $.5N$)

Since 8 is greater than $(.5)(12)$ or 6, the following formula is used in computing this example:

$$z = \frac{(X - .5) - .5N}{.5\sqrt{N}}$$

$$z = \frac{(8 - .5) - 6}{.5\sqrt{12}} = \frac{7.5 - 6}{(.5)(3.46)} = \frac{1.5}{1.73}$$

$$z = +.87$$

(6) The null hypothesis of no difference in the two groups is not rejected. Treatment effects were not significant at the .05 level (±1.96).

t-Test

The t-test is a commonly used test of significance. The comparison cannot be made for more than two values, but it is appropriate for many statistics where comparison of a sample value is made to a known population value. It is also used when two sample values are to be compared.

The *t*-test determines differences between two groups on a specific characteristic. Computation examples follow for testing the differences between mean values: first, the test for differences between means of two groups that have been selected at random; and second, for two groups that have means that are correlated.

t-Test for Independent Means

The *t*-test for independent mean is used when groups have been selected with random procedures and also when assignment to groups is made by a known characteristic to investigate for differences with respect to another variable. The computation example that follows uses random assignment. The same *t*-test procedure would be used with differences on an assigned variable. For example, the two levels of sex (male and female) could be used to select two unrelated groups. Then measures on a second variable—say memory of nonsense words—could be obtained. The *t*-test for independent means could then be computed. That procedure would be like the one that follows, although the example uses random assignment.

Formulas (*t*-test):

$$s^2 = \frac{\Sigma x^2_1 + \Sigma x^2_2}{N_1 + N_2 - 2}$$

Where

s^2 = pooled variance estimate
Σx^2 = sum of the squared deviations for one group
N_1 = number in the first group
N_2 = number in the second group

$$s_{\text{diff}} = \sqrt{\frac{s^2}{N_1} + \frac{s^2}{N_2}}$$

Where

s_{diff} = standard error of difference between two means
s^2 = pooled variance estimate
N_1 = number in group 1
N_2 = number in group 2

$$t = \frac{\overline{X}_1 - \overline{X}_2}{s_{\text{diff}}}$$

Where

t = obtained *t*-ratio
$\overline{X}_1$ = mean of the first group
$\overline{X}_2$ = mean of the second group
s_{diff} = standard error of difference between two means

Problem: A class of students studied measuring the area of two-dimensional figures. Instruction was given throughout the study to the class as a whole, except that presented on the last day. At that time, a table of random numbers was used to assign the students to two independent groups. For the first part of the final day, one group studied individually and discussed together problems of measuring the area of rectangles. In another room, the other group studied the same set of problems individually and discussed them as a group, but before working each problem, each student made an estimation of the area before calculation. After the same amount of time in study, each class member was given a set of circles and asked to guess the area of each circle. A score value was determined by a formula that took into consideration how close the estimate was to the computed area. Test the significance of the difference between the two means.

Computation:

Step 1: Table the data.

Step 2: Add the scores in Group 1.

Step 3: Square each score in Group 1 and sum.

Step 4: Square the value from *Step 2* and divide by N.

Step 5: Subtract the value *Step 4* from the value *Step 3*.

Step 6: Add the scores in Group 2.

Step 7: Square each score in Group 2 and sum.

Step 8: Square the value from *Step 6* and divide by N_2.

Step 9: Subtract the value in *Step 8* from the value in *Step 7*.

Step 10: Add the values from *Step 5* and *Step 9*.

Step 11: Add the number in Group 1 to the number in Group 2. Now subtract 2.

Step 12: Divide the value from *Step 10* by the value from *Step 11*.
$(N_1 + N_2 - 2)$
Note: (This gives the s^2 value.)

Step 13: Divide the value from *Step 12* by the number in Group 1.

Step 14: Divide the value from *Step 12* by the number in Group 2.

Step 15: Add the value from *Step 14* to the value in *Step 13*.

Step 16: Extract the square root of the value from *Step 15*.

Note: This gives the s_{diff} value. (Standard error of difference)

Step 17: Divide the value from *Step 2* by N_1. (Gives the $\overline{X}_1$)

Step 18: Divide the value from *Step 6* by N_2. (Gives the $\overline{X}_2$)

Step 19: Subtract the mean of Group 2 from the mean of Group 1.

Step 20: Divide the value from *Step 19* by the value from *Step 16*.

Step 21: $df = (N_1 + N_2 - 2)$

Step 22: Compare the value from *Step 20* (obtained t-ratio value) with the tabled value using the established significance level and *df*. If the obtained t value is less than the lower criterion value or greater than the upper criterion value, reject the null hypothesis of no difference. If the obtained t is between the two criterion points, do not reject the null hypothesis.

(1)	Scores for Group 1 (Practice)		Scores for Group 2 (No practice)	
	19	14	9	10
	11	17	14	14
	20	9	11	13
	13	15	12	14
	14	16	12	13
	14	15	11	10
	13	16	18	17
	16	12	8	11

(2) $\Sigma X_1 = 234$
(3) $\Sigma X_1^2 = 3540$
(4) $(234)^2/16 = 3422.25$
(5) $3540 - 3422.25 = 117.75$
(6) $\Sigma X_2 = 197$
(7) $\Sigma X_2^2 = 2535$
(8) $(197)^2/16 = 2425.56$
(9) $2535 - 2425.56 - 109.44$
(10) $117.75 + 109.44 = 227.19$
(11 $N_1 + N_2 - 2 = 16 + 16 - 2 = 30$
(12) $227.19/30 = 7.573$

$$s^2 = \frac{\Sigma X_1^2 - \dfrac{(\Sigma X_1)^2}{N_1} + \Sigma X_2^2 - \dfrac{(\Sigma X_2)^2}{N_2}}{N_1 + N_2 - 2}$$

$$s^2 = \frac{3540 - \dfrac{(234)^2}{16} + 2535 - \dfrac{(197)^2}{16}}{16 + 16 - 2}$$

$$= \frac{3540 - 3422.25 + 2535 - 2425.56}{30}$$

$$\frac{117.75 + 109.44}{30} = \frac{227.19}{30}$$

$$s^2 = 7.573$$

(13) $7.573 \div 16 = .4733$
(14) $7.573 \div 16 = .4733$
(15) $.4733 + .4733 = .9466$
(16) $\sqrt{.9466} = .973$

$$s_{diff} = \sqrt{\frac{7.573}{16} + \frac{7.573}{16}} = \sqrt{.4733 + .4733}$$

$$s_{diff} = \sqrt{.9466} = .973$$

(**17**) $234 \div 16 = 14.62$
(**18**) $197 \div 16 = 12.31$
(**19**) $14.62 - 12.31 = 2.31$
(**20**) $2.31 \div .973 = 2.37$

$$t = \frac{\overline{X}_1 - \overline{X}_2}{S_{\text{diff}}} = \frac{14.62 - 12.31}{.973} = \frac{2.31}{.973}$$

$t = +2.37$
(**21**) $16 + 16 - 2 = 30$
(**22**) obtained $t = 2.37$
    Table t at .05 with 30 $df = 2.042$

Reject the null hypothesis. With these data, it appears that the practice was effective in helping students to estimate areas of circles. General practice allows this test to be made with ± 1.96 for the .05 level and ± 2.58 for the .01 level, if the df is greater than 29. However, this test was made at the table value for 30 df. The same decision results in each case.

t-Test for Correlated Data

If the same group is studied at two different points in time with intervening treatment or if pairs of subjects are matched on one or more variables, a different t-test must be used to take into consideration the relationship of subjects.

Formula (t-test):

$$t = \frac{\Sigma D}{\sqrt{\dfrac{N\Sigma D^2 - (\Sigma D)^2}{N - 1}}}$$

$t =$ obtained t value
$D =$ difference value for two measures
$N =$ number of pairs

Problem: A political candidate is planning a spot commercial and wants to see if a particular presentation is favorable to her election. The local television station taped a 2-minute spot which was prepared for the candidate. To test the commercial's effectiveness, measures of 20 voters' opinions were made before and after viewing the commercial. Was the commercial effective with this sample of voters?

Computation:
    Step 1: Table the data.
    Step 2: Subtract the difference for each pair. Subtract the score of the premeasure from the postmeasure.
    Step 3: Sum the differences obtained in Step 2. (Watch the sign.)
    Step 4: Square the differences (D^2) and sum.

Step 5: Square the value from *Step 3*.
Step 6: Multiply the value from *Step 4* by N.
Step 7: Subtract the value *Step 5* from the value *Step 6*.
Step 8: Divide the value from *Step 7* by $(N - 1)$.
Step 9: Extract the square root of the value from *Step 8*.
Step 10: Divide the value from *Step 3* by the value from *Step 9*.
Step 11: df = number of pairs minus one = $N - 1$.
Step 12: Compare the value from *Step 10* (obtained t value) with the table value using the established significance level and df. If the obtained t value is less than the lower criterion value or greater than the upper criterion value, reject the null hypothesis of no difference. If the obtained t is between the two criterion points, do not reject the null hypothesis.

(1)	Postmeasures	Premeasures	(2) D	D²
	5	7	-2	4
	8	7	1	1
	15	9	6	36
	18	16	2	4
	7	4	3	9
	8	5	3	9
	13	14	-1	1
	16	12	4	16
	5	6	-1	1
	4	5	-1	1
	7	3	4	16
	8	4	4	16
	10	8	2	4
	9	9	0	0
	10	5	5	25
	10	6	4	16
	6	6	0	0
	5	4	1	1
	16	12	4	16
	2	4	-2	4
			+36	180
			(3)	(4)

(5) $36^2 = 36 \times 36 = 1296$
(6) $180 \times 20 = 3600$
(7) $3600 - 1296 = 2304$
(8) $2304 \div 19 = 121.26$
(9) $\sqrt{121.26} = 11.01$
(10) $36 \div 11.01 = +3.27$
(11) $df = N - 1 = 20 - 1 = 19$
(12) obtained $t = 3.27$
    table t at .05 with 19 df = 2.093

Reject the null hypothesis. With these data, it appears that the 2-minute spot commercial is effectively presenting the candidate to the voters.

Analysis of Variance

The analysis of variance is a way of partitioning sums of squares by their source. The many procedures for analysis of variance allow a wide range of research designs involving one, two, or more independent variables to be studied simultaneously. These procedures extend beyond the study of two groups to three or more groups. Analysis of repeated measures is also extended by analysis of variance computation. The following discussion gives an example of the simplest analysis of variance procedure that studies differences of three groups (three levels) on one independent variable (one factor). This design is identified as a one factor–three levels study. Other procedures extend into two or more factors with two or more levels.

Formulas (analysis of variance): The formulas for this procedure are presented for a study which has only 3 levels. If a 4th (or more) level is (are) added, the formulas extend to include those values. These formulas were chosen to avoid double summation which may be somewhat confusing for those with little statistical background.

$$SS_{bg} = \frac{(\Sigma X_1)^2}{n_1} + \frac{(\Sigma X_2)^2}{n_2} + \frac{(\Sigma X_3)^2}{n_3} - \left[\frac{(\Sigma X_1 + \Sigma X_2 + \Sigma X_3)^2}{N} \right]$$

$$SS_{wg} = \Sigma X_1^2 + \Sigma X_2^2 + \Sigma X_3^2 - \left[\frac{(\Sigma X_1)^2}{n_1} + \frac{(\Sigma X_2)^2}{n_2} + \frac{(\Sigma X_3)^2}{n_3} \right]$$

$$SS_t = \Sigma X_1^2 + \Sigma X_2^2 + \Sigma X_3^2 - \left[\frac{(\Sigma X_1 + \Sigma X_2 + \Sigma X_3)^2}{N} \right]$$

Where
SS_{bg} = sum of squares between groups
SS_{wg} = sum of squares within groups
SS_t = sum of squares total $(SS_{bg} + SS_{wg} = SS_t)$
n_1 = number in group 1
n_2 = number in group 2
n_3 = number in group 3
$N = n_1 + n_2 + n_3$
X = a measure on the dependent variable
ΣX = sum of X values
ΣX^2 = sum of squared X values

Problem: In a study of the effect of environmental conditions on test scores, a 50-minute lecture was videotaped and shown to 3 random groups of students with like backgrounds. All conditions were the same, except the temperature of the lecture room was varied for each group. Study the differences of mean test scores for significance.

Computation:

Step 1: Table the data.

Step 2: Sum the scores for each group separately.

Step 3: Square the scores for each group and sum.

Step 4: Compute the sum of squares between groups using the computational formula. (ss_{bg})

Step 5: Compute the sum of squares within groups using the computational formula. (ss_{wg})

Step 6: Compute the sum of squares total using the computational formula. (ss_t)

Step 7: Check to see that ss_{bg} from *Step 4* and ss_{wg} from *Step 5* equal ss_t from group 6.

Step 8: Compute *df* for between groups variance estimate using formula—$k - 1$—where $k = $ the number of groups.

Step 9: Compute *df* for within groups estimate using formula—$N - k$.

Step 10: Compute *df* for total sum of squares using formula—$N - 1$. The value from *Step 8* plus the value from *Step 9* should equal the value for *Step 10*.

Step 11: Enter the values from *Steps 4, 5, 8,* and *9* in the following table.

Source	SS	df	Mean square	F-ratio
between	ss_{bg}	$k - 1$	$ss_{bg}/k - 1$	$\dfrac{MS_{bg}}{MS_{wg}}$
within	ss_{wg}	$N - k$	$ss_{wg}/N - k$	
total	ss_t	$N - 1$	—	$F =$

Step 12: Divide value from *Step 4* (ss_{bg}) by *df* from *Step 8*.

Step 13: Divide value from *Step 5* (ss_{wg}) by *df* from *Step 9*.

Step 14: Divide the mean square estimate between from *Step 12* by the mean square estimate within from *Step 13* and enter in the lowest cell in the right-hand column. This is the obtained *F*-ratio.

(1) Group 1	X_1^2	Group 2	X_2^2	Group 3	X_3^2
12	144	12	144	11	121
10	100	14	196	13	169
11	121	9	81	8	64
11	121	8	64	9	81
8	64	12	144	5	25
10	100	19	361	7	49
7	49	13	169	8	64
6	36	15	225	6	36
9	81	11	121	10	100
10	100	10	100	7	49
94	916	123	1605	84	758
(2)	(3)	(2)	(3)	(2)	(3)

(4) $SS_{bg} = \dfrac{94^2}{10} + \dfrac{123^2}{10} + \dfrac{84^2}{10} - \dfrac{(94 + 123 + 84)^2}{30}$

$= \dfrac{8836}{10} + \dfrac{15129}{10} + \dfrac{7056}{10} - \dfrac{301^2}{30}$

$= 883.6 + 1512.9 + 705.6 - 90601/30$

$= 30102.1 - 3020.03$

$SS_{bg} = 82.07$

(5) $SS_{wg} = 916 + 1605 + 758 - \left[\dfrac{94^2}{10} + \dfrac{123^2}{10} + \dfrac{84^2}{10} \right]$

$= 3279 - (883.6 + 1512.9 + 705.6)$

$= 3279 - 3102.1$

$SS_{wg} = 176.9$

(6) $SS_t = 916 + 1605 + 758 - \dfrac{(94 + 123 + 84)^2}{30}$

$= 3279 - \dfrac{301^2}{30}$

$= 3279 - 3020.03$

$SS_t = 258.97$

(7) $82.07 + 176.9 = 258.97$

(8) $k - 1 = 3 - 1 = 2 \ (df \text{ for } SS_{bg})$

(9) $N - k = 30 - 3 = 27 \ (df \text{ for } SS_{wg})$

(10) $N - 1 = 30 - 1 = 29 \ (df \text{ for } SS_t)$

$2 + 27 = 29$

(11)

Source	SS	df	Mean square	F-ratio
between	82.07	2	82.07/2	41.04
within	176.9	27	176.9/27	6.55
total	258.97	29	—	$F = 6.27$
			(12) **(13)**	**(14)**

(12) $82.07 \div 2 = 41.04$

(13) $176.9 \div 27 = 6.55$

(14) $41.04 \div 6.55 = 6.27$

Step 15: Look in a table of F-ratios for the critical value for rejection of the null hypothesis of no difference. For this problem, read across the top of the table for column 2 for df for between ($k - 1$), and down the table to row 27 for df for within ($N - k$). See an excerpt from the table in Table 2.

TABLE 2 Excerpt From Table of Critical F Values (.05 level)

between ss / within ss		df for the numerator of F-ratio							
		1	2	3	4	5	6	7	— — — — — — — —
df demoninator	25								
	26								
	27	3.35 5.49							
	28								
	29								
	30								

Step 16: Compare the obtained F-ratio from Step 14 with the table F-ratio. If the obtained F exceeds the table value, reject the null hypothesis of no difference. If the obtained F does not exceed the table value, do not reject the null hypothesis. For this problem, the obtained F value exceeds the .05 probability (3.35) and the .01 probability (5.49). The null hypothesis is rejected at either level of probability.

References

Bruning, J.L., & Kintz, B.L. *Computational handbook of statistics* (2nd ed.). Glenview, Ill.: Scott, Foresman & Co., 1977.

Chase, C.I. *Elementary statistical procedures* (2nd ed.). New York: McGraw-Hill, 1976.

Hopkins, C.D. *Describing data statistically*. Columbus, Oh.: Charles E. Merrill, 1974.

APPENDIX D

STATISTICAL TABLES

TABLE 1 Areas of the Normal Curve in Terms of x/σ.

Standard score z $\dfrac{x}{\sigma}$	.00	.01	.02	.03	.04	.05	.06	.07	.08	.09
0.0	.0000	.0040	.0080	.0120	.0160	.0199	.0239	.0279	.0319	.0359
0.1	.0398	.0438	.0478	.0517	.0557	.0596	.0636	.0675	.0714	.0753
0.2	.0793	.0832	.0871	.0910	.0948	.0987	.1026	.1064	.1103	.1141
0.3	.1179	.1217	.1255	.1293	.1331	.1368	.1406	.1443	.1480	.1517
0.4	.1554	.1591	.1628	.1664	.1700	.1736	.1772	.1808	.1844	.1879
0.5	.1915	.1950	.1985	.2019	.2054	.2088	.2123	.2157	.2190	.2224
0.6	.2257	.2291	.2324	.2357	.2389	.2422	.2454	.2486	.2517	.2549
0.7	.2580	.2611	.2642	.2673	.2704	.2734	.2764	.2794	.2823	.2852
0.8	.2881	.2910	.2939	.2967	.2995	.3023	.3051	.3078	.3106	.3133
0.9	.3159	.3186	.3212	.3238	.3264	.3289	.3315	.3340	.3365	.3389
1.0	.3413	.3438	.3461	.3485	.3508	.3531	.3554	.3577	.3599	.3621
1.1	.3643	.3665	.3686	.3708	.3729	.3749	.3770	.3790	.3810	.3830
1.2	.3849	.3869	.3888	.3907	.3925	.3944	.3962	.3980	.3997	.4015
1.3	.4032	.4049	.4066	.4082	.4099	.4115	.4131	.4147	.4162	.4177
1.4	.4192	.4207	.4222	.4236	.4251	.4265	.4279	.4292	.4306	.4319
1.5	.4332	.4345	.4357	.4370	.4382	.4394	.4406	.4418	.4429	.4441
1.6	.4452	.4463	.4474	.4484	.4495	.4505	.4515	.4525	.4535	.4545
1.7	.4554	.4564	.4573	.4582	.4591	.4599	.4608	.4616	.4625	.4633
1.8	.4641	.4649	.4656	.4664	.4671	.4678	.4686	.4693	.4699	.4706
1.9	.4713	.4719	.4726	.4732	.4738	.4744	.4750	.4756	.4761	.4767
2.0	.4772	.4778	.4783	.4788	.4793	.4798	.4803	.4808	.4812	.4817
2.1	.4821	.4826	.4830	.4834	.4838	.4842	.4846	.4850	.4854	.4857
2.2	.4861	.4864	.4868	.4871	.4875	.4878	.4881	.4884	.4887	.4890
2.3	.4893	.4896	.4898	.4901	.4904	.4906	.4909	.4911	.4913	.4916
2.4	.4918	.4920	.4922	.4925	.4927	.4929	.4931	.4932	.4934	.4936
2.5	.4938	.4940	.4941	.4943	.4945	.4946	.4948	.4949	.4951	.4952
2.6	.4953	.4955	.4956	.4957	.4959	.4960	.4961	.4962	.4963	.4964
2.7	.4965	.4966	.4967	.4968	.4969	.4970	.4971	.4972	.4973	.4974
2.8	.4974	.4975	.4976	.4977	.4977	.4978	.4979	.4979	.4980	.4981
2.9	.4981	.4982	.4982	.4983	.4984	.4984	.4985	.4985	.4986	.4986
3.0	.4987	.4987	.4987	.4988	.4988	.4989	.4989	.4989	.4990	.4990
3.1	.49903									
3.2	.49931									
3.3	.49952									
3.4	.49966									
3.5	.49977									
3.6	.49984									
3.7	.49989									
3.8	.49993									
3.9	.49995									
4.0	.50000									

(Table values show the proportion of the area between the mean of the unit normal curve and ordinates at listed z-scores.)

TABLE 2 Critical Values of *t*

df	Level of significance for two-tailed test					
	.20	.10	.05	.02	.01	.001
1	3.078	6.314	12.706	31.821	63.657	636.619
2	1.886	2.920	4.303	6.965	9.925	31.598
3	1.638	2.353	3.182	4.541	5.841	12.924
4	1.533	2.132	2.776	3.747	4.604	8.610
5	1.476	2.015	2.571	3.365	4.032	6.869
6	1.440	1.943	2.447	3.143	3.707	5.959
7	1.415	1.895	2.365	2.998	3.499	5.408
8	1.397	1.860	2.306	2.896	3.355	5.041
9	1.383	1.833	2.262	2.821	3.250	4.781
10	1.372	1.812	2.228	2.764	3.169	4.587
11	1.363	1.796	2.201	2.718	3.106	4.437
12	1.356	1.782	2.179	2.681	3.055	4.318
13	1.350	1.771	2.160	2.650	3.012	4.221
14	1.345	1.761	2.145	2.624	2.977	4.140
15	1.341	1.753	2.131	2.602	2.947	4.073
16	1.337	1.746	2.120	2.583	2.921	4.015
17	1.333	1.740	2.110	2.567	2.898	3.965
18	1.330	1.734	2.101	2.552	2.878	3.922
19	1.328	1.729	2.093	2.539	2.861	3.883
20	1.325	1.725	2.086	2.528	2.845	3.850
21	1.323	1.721	2.080	2.518	2.831	3.819
22	1.321	1.717	2.074	2.508	2.819	3.792
23	1.319	1.714	2.069	2.500	2.807	3.767
24	1.318	1.711	2.064	2.492	2.797	3.745
25	1.316	1.708	2.060	2.485	2.787	3.725
26	1.315	1.706	2.056	2.479	2.779	3.707
27	1.314	1.703	2.052	2.473	2.771	3.690
28	1.313	1.701	2.048	2.467	2.763	3.674
29	1.311	1.699	2.045	2.462	2.756	3.659
30	1.310	1.697	2.042	2.457	2.750	3.646
40	1.303	1.684	2.021	2.423	2.704	3.551
60	1.296	1.671	2.000	2.390	2.660	3.460
120	1.289	1.658	1.980	2.358	2.617	3.373
∞	1.282	1.645	1.960	2.326	2.576	3.291

Note: Table 2 is taken from Table III (p. 46) of Fisher and Yates: *Statistical Tables for Biological, Agricultural and Medical Research*, 6th ed. New York: Hafner Publishing Co., 1963. Published by Longman Group Ltd., London. (Previously published by Oliver and Boyd, Edinburgh). Abridgement by permission of the authors and publishers.

TABLE 3 Critical Values of Chi Square

			Probability under H_0 that $x^2 \geq$ Chi square				
p / *df*	.990	.950	.500	0.100	0.050	0.010	0.001
1	—	—	0.45493	2.70554	3.84146	6.63490	10.828
2	0.0201007	0.10258	1.38629	4.60517	5.99147	9.21034	13.816
3	0.114832	0.35184	2.36597	6.25139	7.81473	11.3449	16.266
4	0.297110	0.71072	3.35670	7.77944	9.48773	13.2767	18.467
5	0.554300	1.14547	4.35146	9.23635	11.0705	15.0863	20.515
6	0.872085	1.63539	5.34812	10.6446	12.5916	16.8119	22.458
7	1.239043	2.16735	6.34581	12.0170	14.0671	18.4753	24.322
8	1.646482	2.73264	7.34412	13.3616	15.5073	20.0902	26.125
9	2.087912	3.32511	8.34283	14.6837	16.9190	21.6660	27.877
10	2.55821	3.94030	9.34182	15.9871	18.3070	23.2093	29.588
11	3.05347	4.57481	10.3410	17.2750	19.6751	24.7250	31.264
12	3.57056	5.22603	11.3403	18.5494	21.0261	26.2170	32.909
13	4.10691	5.89186	12.3398	19.8119	22.3621	27.6883	34.528
14	4.66043	6.57063	13.3393	21.0642	23.6848	29.1413	36.123
15	5.22935	7.26094	14.3389	22.3072	24.9958	30.5779	37.697
16	5.81221	7.96164	15.3385	23.5418	26.2962	31.9999	39.252
17	6.40776	8.67176	16.3381	24.7690	27.5871	33.4087	40.790
18	7.01491	9.39046	17.3379	25.9894	28.8693	34.8053	42.312
19	7.63273	10.1170	18.3376	27.2036	30.1435	36.1908	43.820
20	8.26040	10.8508	19.3374	28.4120	31.4104	37.5662	45.315
21	8.89720	11.5913	20.3372	29.6151	32.6705	38.9321	46.797
22	9.54249	12.3380	21.3370	30.8133	33.9244	40.2894	48.268
23	10.19567	13.0905	22.3369	32.0069	35.1725	41.6384	49.728
24	10.8564	13.8484	23.3367	33.1963	36.4151	42.9798	51.179
25	11.5240	14.6114	24.3366	34.3816	37.6525	44.3141	52.620
26	12.1981	15.3791	25.3364	35.5631	38.8852	45.6417	54.052
27	12.8786	16.1513	26.3363	36.7412	40.1133	46.9630	55.476
28	13.5648	16.9279	27.3363	37.9159	41.3372	48.2782	56.892
29	14.2565	17.7083	28.3362	39.0875	42.5569	49.5879	58.302
30	14.9535	18.4926	29.3360	40.2560	43.7729	50.8922	59.703
40	22.1643	26.5093	39.3354	51.8050	55.7585	63.6907	73.402
50	29.7067	34.7642	49.3349	63.1671	67.5048	76.1539	86.661

Note: From Table 8 (pp. 130–131) by R.S. Pearson and H.O. Hartley (Eds.), *Biometrika tables for statisticians,* Vol. I (2nd ed.). London: Cambridge University Press, 1954, © 1972 by Biometrika Trustees. Abridgement by permission.

TABLE 4 Critical values of F (.01 level)

Degrees of freedom for denominator	Degrees of freedom for numerator																		
	1	2	3	4	5	6	7	8	9	10	12	15	20	24	30	40	60	120	∞
1	4052	4999.5	5403	5625	5764	5859	5928	5982	6022	6056	6106	6157	6209	6235	6261	6287	6313	6339	6366
2	98.50	99.00	99.17	99.25	99.30	99.33	99.36	99.37	99.39	99.40	99.42	99.43	99.45	99.46	99.47	99.47	99.48	99.49	99.50
3	34.12	30.82	29.46	28.71	28.24	27.91	27.67	27.49	27.35	27.23	27.05	26.87	26.69	26.60	26.50	26.41	26.32	26.22	26.13
4	21.20	18.00	16.69	15.98	15.52	15.21	14.98	14.80	14.66	14.55	14.37	14.20	14.02	13.93	13.84	13.75	13.65	13.56	13.46
5	16.26	13.27	12.06	11.39	10.97	10.67	10.46	10.29	10.16	10.05	9.89	9.72	9.55	9.47	9.38	9.29	9.20	9.11	9.02
6	13.75	10.92	9.78	9.15	8.75	8.47	8.26	8.10	7.98	7.87	7.72	7.56	7.40	7.31	7.23	7.14	7.06	6.97	6.88
7	12.25	9.55	8.45	7.85	7.46	7.19	6.99	6.84	6.72	6.62	6.47	6.31	6.16	6.07	5.99	5.91	5.82	5.74	5.65
8	11.26	8.65	7.59	7.01	6.63	6.37	6.18	6.03	5.91	5.81	5.67	5.52	5.36	5.28	5.20	5.12	5.03	4.95	4.86
9	10.56	8.02	6.99	6.42	6.06	5.80	5.61	5.47	5.35	5.26	5.11	4.96	4.81	4.73	4.65	4.57	4.48	4.40	4.31
10	10.04	7.56	6.55	5.99	5.64	5.39	5.20	5.06	4.94	4.85	4.71	4.56	4.41	4.33	4.25	4.17	4.08	4.00	3.91
11	9.65	7.21	6.22	5.67	5.32	5.07	4.89	4.74	4.63	4.54	4.40	4.25	4.10	4.02	3.94	3.86	3.78	3.69	3.60
12	9.33	6.93	5.95	5.41	5.06	4.82	4.64	4.50	4.39	4.30	4.16	4.01	3.86	3.78	3.70	3.62	3.54	3.45	3.36
13	9.07	6.70	5.74	5.21	4.86	4.62	4.44	4.30	4.19	4.10	3.96	3.82	3.66	3.59	3.51	3.43	3.34	3.25	3.17
14	8.86	6.51	5.56	5.04	4.69	4.46	4.28	4.14	4.03	3.94	3.80	3.66	3.51	3.43	3.35	3.27	3.18	3.09	3.00
15	8.68	6.36	5.42	4.89	4.56	4.32	4.14	4.00	3.89	3.80	3.67	3.52	3.37	3.29	3.21	3.13	3.05	2.96	2.87
16	8.53	6.23	5.29	4.77	4.44	4.20	4.03	3.89	3.78	3.69	3.55	3.41	3.26	3.18	3.10	3.02	2.93	2.84	2.75
17	8.40	6.11	5.18	4.67	4.34	4.10	3.93	3.79	3.68	3.59	3.46	3.31	3.16	3.08	3.00	2.92	2.83	2.75	2.65
18	8.29	6.01	5.09	4.58	4.25	4.01	3.84	3.71	3.60	3.51	3.37	3.23	3.08	3.00	2.92	2.84	2.75	2.66	2.57
19	8.18	5.93	5.01	4.50	4.17	3.94	3.77	3.63	3.52	3.43	3.30	3.15	3.00	2.92	2.84	2.76	2.67	2.58	2.49
20	8.10	5.85	4.94	4.43	4.10	3.87	3.70	3.56	3.46	3.37	3.23	3.09	2.94	2.86	2.78	2.69	2.61	2.52	2.42
21	8.02	5.78	4.87	4.37	4.04	3.81	3.64	3.51	3.40	3.31	3.17	3.03	2.88	2.80	2.72	2.64	2.55	2.46	2.36
22	7.95	5.72	4.82	4.31	3.99	3.76	3.59	3.45	3.35	3.26	3.12	2.98	2.83	2.75	2.67	2.58	2.50	2.40	2.31
23	7.88	5.66	4.76	4.26	3.94	3.71	3.54	3.41	3.30	3.21	3.07	2.93	2.78	2.70	2.62	2.54	2.45	2.35	2.26
24	7.82	5.61	4.72	4.22	3.90	3.67	3.50	3.36	3.26	3.17	3.03	2.89	2.74	2.66	2.58	2.49	2.40	2.31	2.21
25	7.77	5.57	4.68	4.18	3.85	3.63	3.46	3.32	3.22	3.13	2.99	2.85	2.70	2.62	2.54	2.45	2.36	2.27	2.17
26	7.72	5.53	4.64	4.14	3.82	3.59	3.42	3.29	3.18	3.09	2.96	2.81	2.66	2.58	2.50	2.42	2.33	2.23	2.13
27	7.68	5.49	4.60	4.11	3.78	3.56	3.39	3.26	3.15	3.06	2.93	2.78	2.63	2.55	2.47	2.38	2.29	2.20	2.10
28	7.64	5.45	4.57	4.07	3.75	3.53	3.36	3.23	3.12	3.03	2.90	2.75	2.60	2.52	2.44	2.35	2.26	2.17	2.06
29	7.60	5.42	4.54	4.04	3.73	3.50	3.33	3.20	3.09	3.00	2.87	2.73	2.57	2.49	2.41	2.33	2.23	2.14	2.03
30	7.56	5.39	4.51	4.02	3.70	3.47	3.30	3.17	3.07	2.98	2.84	2.70	2.55	2.47	2.39	2.30	2.21	2.11	2.01
40	7.31	5.18	4.31	3.83	3.51	3.29	3.12	2.99	2.89	2.80	2.66	2.52	2.37	2.29	2.20	2.11	2.02	1.92	1.80
60	7.08	4.98	4.13	3.65	3.34	3.12	2.95	2.82	2.72	2.63	2.50	2.35	2.20	2.12	2.03	1.94	1.84	1.73	1.60
120	6.85	4.79	3.95	3.48	3.17	2.96	2.79	2.66	2.56	2.47	2.34	2.19	2.03	1.95	1.86	1.76	1.66	1.53	1.38
∞	6.63	4.61	3.78	3.32	3.02	2.80	2.64	2.51	2.41	2.32	2.18	2.04	1.88	1.79	1.70	1.59	1.47	1.32	1.00

Note: From Table 18 (pp. 159, 161) by R. S. Pearson and H.O. Hartley (eds.), *Biometrika tables for statisticians*, Vol. I (2nd ed.). London: Cambridge University Press, 1954, © 1972 by Biometrika Trustees. Abridgement by permission.

TABLE 5 Critical Values of F (.05 level)

Degrees of freedom for denominator	Degrees of freedom for numerator																		
	1	2	3	4	5	6	7	8	9	10	12	15	20	24	30	40	60	120	∞
1	161.4	199.5	215.7	224.6	230.2	234.0	236.8	238.9	240.5	241.9	243.9	245.9	248.0	249.1	250.1	251.1	252.2	253.3	254.3
2	18.51	19.00	19.16	19.25	19.30	19.33	19.35	19.37	19.38	19.40	19.41	19.43	19.45	19.45	19.46	19.47	19.48	19.49	19.50
3	10.13	9.55	9.28	9.12	9.01	8.94	8.89	8.85	8.81	8.79	8.74	8.70	8.66	8.64	8.62	8.59	8.57	8.55	8.53
4	7.71	6.94	6.59	6.39	6.26	6.16	6.09	6.04	6.00	5.96	5.91	5.86	5.80	5.77	5.75	5.72	5.69	5.66	5.63
5	6.61	5.79	5.41	5.19	5.05	4.95	4.88	4.82	4.77	4.74	4.68	4.62	4.56	4.53	4.50	4.46	4.43	4.40	4.36
6	5.99	5.14	4.76	4.53	4.39	4.28	4.21	4.15	4.10	4.06	4.00	3.94	3.87	3.84	3.81	3.77	3.74	3.70	3.67
7	5.59	4.74	4.35	4.12	3.97	3.87	3.79	3.73	3.68	3.64	3.57	3.51	3.44	3.41	3.38	3.34	3.30	3.27	3.23
8	5.32	4.46	4.07	3.84	3.69	3.58	3.50	3.44	3.39	3.35	3.28	3.22	3.15	3.12	3.08	3.04	3.01	2.97	2.93
9	5.12	4.26	3.86	3.63	3.48	3.37	3.29	3.23	3.18	3.14	3.07	3.01	2.94	2.90	2.86	2.83	2.79	2.75	2.71
10	4.96	4.10	3.71	3.48	3.33	3.22	3.14	3.07	3.02	2.98	2.91	2.85	2.77	2.74	2.70	2.66	2.62	2.58	2.54
11	4.84	3.98	3.59	3.36	3.20	3.09	3.01	2.95	2.90	2.85	2.79	2.72	2.65	2.61	2.57	2.53	2.49	2.45	2.40
12	4.75	3.89	3.49	3.26	3.11	3.00	2.91	2.85	2.80	2.75	2.69	2.62	2.54	2.51	2.47	2.43	2.38	2.34	2.30
13	4.67	3.81	3.41	3.18	3.03	2.92	2.83	2.77	2.71	2.67	2.60	2.53	2.46	2.42	2.38	2.34	2.30	2.25	2.21
14	4.60	3.74	3.34	3.11	2.96	2.85	2.76	2.70	2.65	2.60	2.53	2.46	2.39	2.35	2.31	2.27	2.22	2.18	2.13
15	4.54	3.68	3.29	3.06	2.90	2.79	2.71	2.64	2.59	2.54	2.48	2.40	2.33	2.29	2.25	2.20	2.16	2.11	2.07
16	4.49	3.63	3.24	3.01	2.85	2.74	2.66	2.59	2.54	2.49	2.42	2.35	2.28	2.24	2.19	2.15	2.11	2.06	2.01
17	4.45	3.59	3.20	2.96	2.81	2.70	2.61	2.55	2.49	2.45	2.38	2.31	2.23	2.19	2.15	2.10	2.06	2.01	1.96
18	4.41	3.55	3.16	2.93	2.77	2.66	2.58	2.51	2.46	2.41	2.34	2.27	2.19	2.15	2.11	2.06	2.02	1.97	1.92
19	4.38	3.52	3.13	2.90	2.74	2.63	2.54	2.48	2.42	2.38	2.31	2.23	2.16	2.11	2.07	2.03	1.98	1.93	1.88
20	4.35	3.49	3.10	2.87	2.71	2.60	2.51	2.45	2.39	2.35	2.28	2.20	2.12	2.08	2.04	1.99	1.95	1.90	1.84
21	4.32	3.47	3.07	2.84	2.68	2.57	2.49	2.42	2.37	2.32	2.25	2.18	2.10	2.05	2.01	1.96	1.92	1.87	1.81
22	4.30	3.44	3.05	2.82	2.66	2.55	2.46	2.40	2.34	2.30	2.23	2.15	2.07	2.03	1.98	1.94	1.89	1.84	1.78
23	4.28	3.42	3.03	2.80	2.64	2.53	2.44	2.37	2.32	2.27	2.20	2.13	2.05	2.01	1.96	1.91	1.86	1.81	1.76
24	4.26	3.40	3.01	2.78	2.62	2.51	2.42	2.36	2.30	2.25	2.18	2.11	2.03	1.98	1.94	1.89	1.84	1.79	1.73
25	4.24	3.39	2.99	2.76	2.60	2.49	2.40	2.34	2.28	2.24	2.16	2.09	2.01	1.96	1.92	1.87	1.82	1.77	1.71
26	4.23	3.37	2.98	2.74	2.59	2.47	2.39	2.32	2.27	2.22	2.15	2.07	1.99	1.95	1.90	1.85	1.80	1.75	1.69
27	4.21	3.35	2.96	2.73	2.57	2.46	2.37	2.31	2.25	2.20	2.13	2.06	1.97	1.93	1.88	1.84	1.79	1.73	1.67
28	4.20	3.34	2.95	2.71	2.56	2.45	2.36	2.29	2.24	2.19	2.12	2.04	1.96	1.91	1.87	1.82	1.77	1.71	1.65
29	4.18	3.33	2.93	2.70	2.55	2.43	2.35	2.28	2.22	2.18	2.10	2.03	1.94	1.90	1.85	1.81	1.75	1.70	1.64
30	4.17	3.32	2.92	2.69	2.53	2.42	2.33	2.27	2.21	2.16	2.09	2.01	1.93	1.89	1.84	1.79	1.74	1.68	1.62
40	4.08	3.23	2.84	2.61	2.45	2.34	2.25	2.18	2.12	2.08	2.00	1.92	1.84	1.79	1.74	1.69	1.64	1.58	1.51
60	4.00	3.15	2.76	2.53	2.37	2.25	2.17	2.10	2.04	1.99	1.92	1.84	1.75	1.70	1.65	1.59	1.53	1.47	1.39
120	3.92	3.07	2.68	2.45	2.29	2.17	2.09	2.02	1.96	1.91	1.83	1.75	1.66	1.61	1.55	1.50	1.43	1.35	1.25
∞	3.84	3.00	2.60	2.37	2.21	2.10	2.01	1.94	1.88	1.83	1.75	1.67	1.57	1.52	1.46	1.39	1.32	1.22	1.00

Note: From Table 18 (pp. 159, 161) by R. S. Pearson and H.O. Hartley (eds.), *Biometrika tables for statisticians,* Vol. I (2nd ed.). London: Cambridge University Press, 1954. © 1972 by Biometrika Trustees. Abridgement by permission.

INDEX OF NAMES

INDEX OF SUBJECTS